# Annual World Bank Conference on Development Economics 1999

Edited by **Boris Pleskovic and Joseph E. Stiglitz**

The World Bank   Washington, D.C.

© 2000 The International Bank for Reconstruction and Development / THE WORLD BANK
1818 H Street NW, Washington, DC 20433, U.S.A.
All rights reserved. Manufactured in the United States of America.

First printing December 2000
1 2 3 4 03 02 01 00

The Annual World Bank Conference on Development Economics is a forum for discussion and debate of important policy issues facing developing countries. The conferences emphasize the contribution that empirical and basic economic research can make to understanding development processes and to formulating sound development policies. Conference papers are written by researchers in and outside the World Bank. The conference series was started in 1989.

Conference papers are reviewed by the editors and are also subject to internal and external peer review. Some papers were revised after the conference, sometimes to reflect the comments by discussants or from the floor. Discussants' comments were not revised. As a result, discussants' comments may refer to elements of the paper that no longer exist in their original form. Participants' affiliations identified in this volume are as of the time of the conference, April 28–30, 1999.

The findings, interpretations, and conclusions expressed in this paper are entirely those of the authors and should not be attributed in any manner to the World Bank, to its affiliated organizations, or to members of its Board of Executive Directors or the countries they represent. The World Bank does not guarantee the accuracy of the data included in this publication and accepts no responsibility for any consequence of their use. The boundaries, colors, denominations, and other information shown on any map in this volume do not imply on the part of the World Bank Group any judgment on the legal status of any territory or the endorsement or acceptance of such boundaries.

The material in this publication is copyrighted. The World Bank encourages dissemination of its work and will normally grant permission promptly. Permission to photocopy items for internal or personal use, for the internal or personal use of specific clients, or for educational classroom use is granted by the World Bank, provided that the appropriate fee is paid directly to Copyright Clearance Center, Inc., 222 Rosewood Drive, Danvers, MA 01923, U.S.A., telephone 978-750-8400, fax 978-750-4470. Please contact the Copyright Clearance Center before photocopying items.

For permission to reprint individual articles or chapters, please fax your request with complete information to the Republication Department, Copyright Clearance Center, fax 978-750-4470.

All other queries on rights and licenses should be addressed to the World Bank at the address above or faxed to 202-522-2422.

Meta de Coquereaumont, Paul Holtz, and Barbara Karni edited this volume. Wendy Guyette prepared the cover and layout, and Daphne Levitas proofread the book. All are with Communications Development.

*Annual World Bank Conference on Development Economics* is indexed in *Human Resources Abstracts,* the *Index of Economic Articles,* the *Index of Social Science and Humanities Proceedings,* the *Index to International Statistics,* the *Public Affairs Information Service, Sage Public Administration Abstracts,* the *Standard Periodical Directory,* and *Ulrich's International Periodicals Directory* and online by ABI/INFORM and DIALOG.

ISSN 1020-4407
ISBN 0-8213-4905-8

# Contents

Introduction ............................................................................................. 1
Boris Pleskovic and Joseph E. Stiglitz

KEYNOTE ADDRESSES
Knowledge as a Factor of Production ............................................... 15
Kenneth J. Arrow

Six Questions for Development Researchers and Policymakers ...... 21
Lawrence H. Summers

Whither Reform? Ten Years of the Transition ................................. 27
Joseph E. Stiglitz

## Economic Architecture ........................................................... 57

Short-Term Capital Flows ................................................................. 59
Dani Rodrik and Andrés Velasco

The Underpinnings of a Stable and Equitable Global Financial System:
From Old Debates to a New Paradigm .......................................... 91
Joseph E. Stiglitz and Amar Bhattacharya

    Comment ...................................................................................... 131
    Kenneth A. Froot

The Changing Corporate Governance Paradigm:
Implications for Developing and Transition Economies ............... 135
Erik Berglöf and Ernst-Ludwig von Thadden

Does the Invisible Hand Need a Transparent Glove?
The Politics of Transparency ............................................................. 163
Ann M. Florini

    Comment ...................................................................................... 185
    Florencio Lopez-de-Silanes

Annual World Bank Conference on Development Economics 1999
© 2000 The International Bank for Reconstruction and Development / THE WORLD BANK

## Social Issues — 197

Crime, Violence, and Inequitable Development — 199
*François Bourguignon*

    Comment — 221
    *Mauricio Rubio*

Social Exclusion and Ethnic Groups: The Challenge to Economics — 225
*Glenn C. Loury*

Prospects and Strategies for Land Reform — 253
*Abhijit V. Banerjee*

    Comment — 275
    *Karla Hoff*

Why Is Inequality Back on the Agenda? — 285
*Ravi Kanbur and Nora Lustig*

    Comment — 307
    *Karla Hoff*

## Economics of Transition — 315

Macroeconomic Lessons from Ten Years of Transition — 317
*Charles Wyplosz*

Restructuring in Transition Economies: Ownership, Competition, and Regulation — 345
*Simon Commander, Mark Dutz, and Nicholas Stern*

    Comment — 374
    *Philippe Aghion*

The Institutional Foundations of China's Market Transition — 377
*Yingyi Qian*

Why Has Russia's Economic Transition Been So Arduous? — 399
*Anders Åslund*

    Comment — 425
    *Leonid Grigoriev*

    Comment — 430
    *Jan Svejnar*

# Introduction

*Boris Pleskovic and Joseph E. Stiglitz*

The Annual World Bank Conference on Development Economics brings together eminent development policy scholars and practitioners from around the world. Experts from international financial institutions, government agencies, universities and policy think tanks gather to exchange ideas on cutting-edge research, challenge and contribute to each other's research, and reexamine current development theories and practices. They revisit issues of long-standing concern and explore emerging issues that promise to be central to future development discourse. By enhancing the understanding of development processes, the conference ultimately contributes to a more informed policymaking process within the World Bank and its member countries, helping to narrow the gap between policy and economic science. The conference reflects the World Bank's commitment to intellectual openness and its embrace of challenges—from academics as well as from policymakers.

The 11th annual conference, held in Washington D.C. on April 28–30, 1999, focused on three trends in development: the emerging international financial architecture, challenges to social development, and lessons from a decade of transition. Twelve papers were presented on a variety of topics including corporate governance, short-term capital flows, and the relationships between crime, violence, and inequitable development.

## New Directions and Course Corrections

The keynote addresses by Nobel Laureate Kenneth Arrow of Stanford University; Secretary of the U.S. Treasury Lawrence Summers, a former vice president, Development Economics, and chief economist at the World Bank; and Joseph E. Stiglitz, senior vice president, Development Economics, and chief economist at the World Bank and former chair of the United States Council of Economic Advisors, broach many of the topics that are central to this year's conference. They examine

---

Boris Pleskovic is administrator, Research Advisory Staff at the World Bank. Joseph E. Stiglitz is senior vice president, Development Economics, and chief economist at the World Bank.

*Annual World Bank Conference on Development Economics 1999*
©2000 The International Bank for Reconstruction and Development / THE WORLD BANK

technological knowledge and innovation and global integration and look back at the arduous process of transition in the former Soviet Union.

**Kenneth Arrow,** in his keynote address, traces the efforts of economic theory to incorporate technological knowledge as an input to and output of the production process. Its unique economic characteristics—it moves through channels not easily thought of as markets, and it is costly to develop, but once developed, can be used costlessly again and again—raises a different set of issues than other productive factors.

Classical and neoclassical theory successively refined theories of value, but these did not accommodate the process of innovation or increasing returns. Adam Smith developed the beginnings of a theory of technological progress, engendered by the division of labor, but only hinted that innovation was affected by endogenous economic factors. Ricardo, too, recognized the importance of technological progress, but failed to explain it or its influence on entrepreneurs or other economic agents. Schumpeter is acknowledged as the first to explicitly introduce innovation into economic theory, but his model did not explain in any real detail the economic motive for innovation. Even today, Arrow claims, no general theory of value explains this motive. There are two issues for value theory. How are prices determined and, in particular, how do they create incentives for innovation? To what extent do individuals about to invest take account of the possibility of future innovations that may affect the returns on their investment?

Solow initiated the literature on economic growth with two classic papers published in the mid-1950s. His model is a starting point for an economic analysis. Other approaches to examining innovation include historical studies of the social and economic conditions surrounding innovations, statistical studies based on data on innovations, and engineering studies on the conditions for successful innovation.

Arrow holds that efforts to model the process of innovation must take into account two main issues. First, the production of knowledge requires not only knowledge but also capital, labor, and marketed resources. Second, aggregate models seriously misrepresent the nature of knowledge: knowledge is not knowledge in general, but highly specific in nature, yet knowledge acquired by one firm or by one sector can yield benefits to others. These two points have opposite implications for policy on the diffusion of technological knowledge. The first states that marketable resources have to be invested, and this will not happen unless there is some protection for investors' rights to some monopoly use of the knowledge. But the second point indicates that it is better to have the free flow of ideas, because everyone will benefit from the ideas of others.

The diffusion of knowledge can be accomplished through several routes: imitation (seeing the success of others), public agencies (particularly important in agriculture), and search (conventions, trade meetings, discussions with customers). Geographic proximity, informal communication, and the mobility of workers across firms all speed diffusion. Arrow stresses that those to whom knowledge is diffused must be able to understand and adapt it—a particular challenge for developing countries. Thus he concludes that every country and firm must have education and training in technology and science, even if the research is not on a par with that being conducted elsewhere: knowledge cannot be absorbed unless some knowledge is already possessed. Further, countries and firms must be open to new ideas, have multiple sources of new ideas, and see that ideas are diffused.

In his keynote address, **Lawrence H. Summers** poses "Six Questions for Development Researchers and Policymakers." Along with many others he asks how we can reconcile global economic integration with two other crucial imperatives: national sovereignty and the pursuit of public purposes that markets alone cannot guarantee (creating opportunities for the poor, developing the right environmental policies). While it is relatively easy to take only two under consideration and to neglect the third, ignoring one or imbuing another with too much importance leads to unsatisfactory outcomes. The challenge for researchers and policymakers is to find a way to reconcile all three, though they can never be perfectly reconciled.

As countries integrate further into the global economy, what stance should they take on capital flows? Policies need simultaneously to avoid inappropriate encouragement of short-term capital flows of the magnitude that led to the recent crises while recognizing the cost savings and liquidity role of short-term capital. Summers predicts that exchange rate regimes will be important, with optimum policies lying more toward flexible regimes or heavily institutionalized pegged arrangements. A related question is how to resolve financial crises. Here, Summers stresses, policy issues involve very difficult questions of the proper balance between public sector liquidity and private sector involvement. Crises need to be solved on a case by case basis. Appropriately conditioned international development finance will continue to play a prominent role in crisis resolution.

Attention to the vulnerable is morally right, politically necessary, and internationally prudent in time of crisis. To move from recognition of that sentiment to action, Summers asks the international community to reflect on an array of issues that need to be reconciled: calls for action, and the realities of budget deficits and priorities; calls for more focused conditionality, and far-reaching investigation of a country's spending priorities; and the imperatives of crisis resolution, and longstanding social imperatives. Are crises times when assistance should go to the poorest, because they are most vulnerable, or to those whose lives have been most disturbed by the crisis (regardless of whether they are the poorest) and who have the greatest potential to incite political or social instability?

Summers concludes by calling on policymakers and researchers to examine the development doctrine that is part of today's conventional wisdom with an eye to its future relevance. During the past 30 years, theories once widely accepted have been discarded as circumstances changed. As policymakers we can only operate within our best judgments about how the world works today, Summers notes. But researchers can try to anticipate what changes in doctrine may be needed. If we reflect on past changes and adaptations, Summers suggests, most of us would agree that the world might be a better place today had the changes come somewhat sooner.

The 20$^{th}$ century was marked by two great economic experiments: the communist experiment and the transition from a communist economy to a market economy. The first, which dominated much of the century, is nearly over, and we are 10 years into the second. **Joseph E. Stiglitz**, in his keynote address, reviews some of the lessons we have learned since the beginning of the transition.

China, whose transition is considered a success by most observers, doubled its GDP in the past decade, whereas GDP in Russia fell by more than half and inequality doubled. China succeeded in creating a vibrant non–state-owned collective enterprise sector; investment in manufacturing grew dramatically. It stagnated in Russia. Stiglitz claims that the failure of reforms in Russia and other countries of the former Soviet Union was not just the result of poor implementation of sound policies, but also of a failure to understand the foundations of a market economy and the basics of institutional reform. Part of the problem was reliance on textbook neoclassical models of economics, and part was confusing means with ends—taking privatization, for example, as an end rather than as a means to achieve more fundamental ends.

Privatization did not provide the basis of a market economy in Russia because it was conducted in a way that was widely viewed as illegitimate and in an environment that lacked the necessary institutional infrastructure. Few people had the skills or capital to become entrepreneurs, there were significant barriers to entry and exit, the institution of bankruptcy did not exist, little attention was paid to the separation of ownership and control. Privatization according to standard Western advice did not lead to the establishment of controlling owners who were motivated to restructure firms for long-run success.

Neoclassical theory also had little to say about the pacing and sequencing of reforms. Many countries adopted a "privatize now, regulate later" policy, proceeding even though an appropriate legal framework was not in place. Underlying this strategy was the Coasian idea that initial private owners did not matter too much, since the market would reallocate assets to efficient owners. But this outcome did not materialize, in part because there were no real primary or secondary markets; assets were looted more than resold.

In retrospect, it seems clear that China's policy of incrementalism proved a better path to a market economy than Russia's shock therapy. Whereas the Chinese policymakers had the wisdom to know that they did not know what they were doing, and so proceeded gradually, the Russians let themselves be guided by prophets bearing clean textbook models. Stiglitz supports the Comprehensive Development Framework, which favors inclusion and popular participation. Given a choice between bottom-up involvement in "imperfect" reforms and top-down imposition of "model" institutions, the Comprehensive Development Framework calls for working to improve the bottom-up approach, rather than tossing it aside in favor of ideal models.

## An Emerging International Financial Architecture

**Dani Rodrik and Andrés Velasco** begin their study of short-term capital flows with the observation that the countries that suffered financial crises in the past five years—countries in Latin America, the former Soviet Union, and especially East Asia—had one thing in common: high ratios of short-term foreign debt to international reserves.

Few researchers doubt that exposure to short-term debt left countries, particularly in East Asia, vulnerable to sudden changes in market sentiment and financial panic.

Rodrik and Velasco formalize this conjecture with a simple model of the simultaneous determination of debt maturity and the term structure of interest rates, showing how excessive short-term debt can leave borrowing countries vulnerable to shifts in lender expectations—shifts that can become self-fulfilling. The model reveals that runs can occur only when investors take on sufficiently large amounts of short-term debt; that the larger is the amount of short-term debt, the greater are the real consequences of a run; and that distorted incentives can lead investors to take on short-term debt, even when doing so is socially costly. The optimal amount of short-term debt will depend on the cost of early investment liquidation, the possibility that a run will occur, and the likelihood and cost of default.

Rodrik and Velasco then turn to an empirical evaluation. Using data from 32 developing countries, they show that the ratio of short-term foreign debt to international reserves is a robust predictor of financial crises. Countries whose short-term liabilities to foreign banks exceed reserves are three times more likely to experience a sudden reversal in capital flows and are more likely to suffer a severe crisis. The authors also find that shorter-term maturities of external debt are associated with higher per capita income and higher ratios of broad money (M2) to GDP. They do not, however, find a relationship between the volume of international trade and the level of short-term debt, implying that trade credit played little or no role in driving short-term capital flows in the 1990s.

Rodrik and Velasco warn policymakers to pay attention to the composition of debt and the ratio of short-term liabilities to liquid assets and to discourage short-term inflows during upswings in the lending cycle. By lengthening average maturities, countries can reduce their vulnerability to crises, although restraining short-term borrowing has costs as well. If a crisis does arise, how should policymakers manage it? Current account–driven crises typically require a real depreciation and contraction of demand, whereas illiquidity-driven crises may require, for example, negotiated debt rollovers and temporary suspensions of payments.

**Joseph Stiglitz and Amar Bhattacharya** begin their study of the global financial system with observations on how far policy discussions of the global economic architecture have traveled in the past two years: from a focus on advancing capital market liberalization to restraining the flow of short-term capital. The recent financial crises—the most cataclysmic set of events to face the world economy since the Great Depression—forced this pace. Stiglitz and Bhattacharya broaden the debate, focusing on five key issues: improving transparency and disclosure, discouraging excessive unhedged borrowing, addressing problems of illiquidity, managing systemic distress, and strengthening social safety nets.

Stiglitz and Bhattacharya stress that recent financial crises must be understood within the framework of the modern theory of market failures and the informational role financial markets play in allocating capital and monitoring its use. The appropriate way to approach these issues is to ask, given market failures and the limitations of government, which interventions are best, taking into account their distributional consequences? Well-formulated policies can reduce the likelihood of adverse shocks, ensure that small shocks do not turn into systemic crises, and create mechanisms to cope with systemic problems. For example, Stiglitz and Bhattacharya claim that governments can respond to calls for greater transparency by establishing auditing standards, imposing disclosure requirements, enacting and enforcing fraud laws, and promoting transparency in their own operations. They also draw attention to the importance of resolving bankruptcies in East Asia and ensuring the resumption of credit flows. We can no longer question the need for bankruptcy laws or financial market regulations, but instead must concentrate on how governments can design such regulations to best serve their countries' specific needs. Regarding safety nets, they write that minimizing the risks and severity of economic downturns is probably the most important step that developing countries and the international community can take to contain the social costs of the crises. There is a high premium to avoiding vulnerability, including through managing capital flows, and policy responses must not lead to large declines in aggregate demand and unemployment.

Corporate governance has dominated policy agendas in industrial countries for more than a decade. More recently, it has become an important issue for developing and transition economies. **Erik Berglöf and Ernst-Ludwig von Thadden** interpret the recent literature that addresses the issue of corporate governance from a comparative economic perspective. The authors of this literature examine the interaction between law and finance, and the role of institutions in economic development. They study how the concentration of ownership and financing arrangements vary across countries. The premise of this research is that the main corporate governance problem is self-interested management and weak, dispersed shareholders. However, Berglöf and von Thadden point out that outside of the United States and the United Kingdom, widely held firms are rare. Most have a dominant owner. This changes how we view the corporate governance problem, shifting the focus from the conflict between management and shareholders to the conflict among management, minority investors, and large block holders. This literature is thus incomplete, and normative implications are premature.

Berglöf and von Thadden argue that the analysis should be broadened to include not only small outside investors, but other actors inside and outside the firm. In both developing and transition economies small investors do not play an important role, and external investors are more likely to assume the role of strategic investors or creditors, particularly in transition economies. To understand the problems facing developing and transition economies, the authors present a broad paradigm that includes many different stakeholders (employees, customers, suppliers) and several mechanisms of corporate governance. The corporate governance problem in developing countries is essentially an equilibrium problem: the absence of organized markets and small investors gives rise to substitute contracts, which prevent capital markets and market-based shareholdings from emerging. The overriding issues in transition economies are law enforcement and government commitment to economic reform. Berglöf and von Thadden conclude with several policy recommendations, including the protection of external investors, creditors, and other stakeholders, and the enforcement of conditionality by external bodies, such as the European Union and the international financial institutions.

**Ann M. Florini** writes that the "invisible hand" of the market relies on a "glove" of rules, norms, and institutions—and that demands that this glove be made transparent have reached a fevered pitch. The clamor can be heard in many areas: banking standards, drug trafficking, pollution control, multilateral development assistance. What are people asking for? Florini defines transparency as the release by institutions of information relevant to evaluating those institutions. Thus the key to increasing transparency is to create incentives for government and corporations to provide information.

Florini claims that the call for transparency is loudest in the debate over the new financial architecture. Many people believe that transparency can ease the problems of globalization, such as the increase in volatility and money laundering. But Florini argues that substantial increases in transparency alone could not prevent or ameliorate the types of financial crises seen in the past few years; transparency is never absolute and lack of information was not the only cause of these crises. There are still many reasons why greater transparency is beneficial, even indispensable. It can smooth the operation of financial markets, attract investment, provide a means of detecting errors in the policies of governments and international institutions, and make it easier to achieve social consensus. Transparency is necessary for accountability in governance—it is the political equivalent of the efficiency generated by competition between firms.

Achieving transparency may be difficult, however. Doing so requires the power to induce disclosure, particularly since those under scrutiny have obvious incentives to conceal their actions. Florini calls for the creation of a culture of transparency. In this the World Bank and International Monetary Fund can play a leading role, starting by ensuring that they themselves operate in a transparent manner. Then, to promote transparency in client countries, the two institutions could prepare country-specific reports on compliance with internationally recognized disclosure standards, making loans conditional on such compliance, and provide information about their projects to the people most affected.

## Challenges to Social Development: Inequality, Poverty, and Social Exclusion

Excessive inequality may slow a country's economic development. **François Bourguignon** asks whether some of this effect works through the influence of inequality on crime and violence. Does inequality exacerbate collective and private violence? What are the social costs of these ills? His analysis is inspired by the high rates of crime and violence in developing countries—particularly Latin American countries—that also have high levels of inequality and low growth. United Nations figures show a clear upward trend in crime since the early 1980s, most notably in Latin America, Eastern Europe, and Central Asia, where rates doubled between the early 1980s and early 1990s.

What is behind this evolution? The distribution of income may affect a country's crime rate in complex and subtle ways. To capture these, Bourguignon develops a theoretical model in which crime is a function of five arguments: the proportion of poor people, the potential relative gain from engaging in crime, the severity of sanctions, the probability of detection, and an "honesty" parameter. In the short term an increase in relative poverty, captured by changes in the first two variables, should raise the crime rate. Thus the model predicts that severe economic recessions may be accompanied by an increase in crime. Further, if hysteresis is part of this process, the volatility of economic activity could magnify this effect. Volatility may also affect crime through the honesty variable: economic cycles or the bumpy process of economic development may exacerbate some of the sociological factors that raise people's propensity to commit crime.

The main conclusion of this model is that inequality and poverty may be the primary economic determinants of crime and violence. But is there evidence of such a relationship? Using both cross-sectional and panel data, Bourguignon shows that the distribution of income appears to be a significant determinant of international and intertemporal differences in crime rates. These trends are more pronounced for robberies than for homicides, which fits with the intuition that the economic determinants of crime are likely to be stronger for property crimes than for other crimes.

Through its effect on crime and violence, inequality may have a high social cost. Summing the monetary and nonmonetary costs of crime leads to rough estimates of the social cost of 3.8 percent of GDP in the United States and 7.5 percent in Latin America. In countries where crime is already high, such as Latin American countries, a 5 point increase in the Gini coefficient or a 5 percent drop in GDP could generate social losses as high as 2 percent of GDP.

To understand social exclusion one needs to bring to bear a composite of theories on poverty, inequality, and disadvantage. **Glenn C. Loury** assesses the utility of the concept of social exclusion for studying ethnic and racial inequality in the modern nation state. Social exclusion theorists are concerned with the dissolution of social bonds, the incomplete extension of social rights and protection to all groups, and the links between the idea of exclusion and more conventional understandings of inequality. Although developed in industrial countries, it is being applied to study such issues in developing countries. Its use in development work helps to highlight the economic, political, and social components of poverty, and forces researchers and policymakers to examine the mechanisms and institutions that work to exclude certain groups of people.

According to Loury, economists cannot explain intergroup ethnic or racial conflict by focusing on market discrimination alone. They must look beyond distortions in labor, capital, and credit markets. Focusing on racial inequality in the United States, Loury cites evidence supporting the view that the skill gap between blacks and whites accounts for much of the racial inequality in the labor market. Yet the skill gap is itself the result of processes of social exclusion—geographic segregation, destructive social norms and peer influences, poor education—which independently warrant study and remediation. Loury stresses the importance of social networks in shaping a person's outlook on life; family and communal resources—social and cultural capital—influence the acquisition of human capital. An important part of racial inequality arises from the way that geographic and social segregation along racial lines makes an individual's opportunities to acquire skills dependent on skill attainment by others in the same social group. Limited access to social and cultural resources contributes to a legacy of economic inequality from one generation to the next. Loury speaks out in favor of "developmental" affirmative action, in which efforts are made to raise the performance of socially excluded groups, rather than simply lowering standards for hiring or admission.

Making the case for land reform (used here in its standard sense of redistributing land to the rural poor) means demonstrating first that land reform is desirable and second that, given the costs involved and alternative uses of the same resources, it is still worthwhile to work toward a more equitable land distribution. **Abhijit Banerjee** argues that land redistribution may promote equity and efficiency, but that it may not be the best way to help the poor given the monetary, bureaucratic, political, and opportunity costs of land reform. Banerjee asks, "would it be better to expropriate land from the very rich, sell it, and invest in education and health?" His tentative conclusions on land reform are not meant to be an argument against them, but rather a way of emphasizing the need to consider alternative approaches and to conduct more empirical studies on traditional (coercive) forms of redistribution.

If implementation were not a constraint, coercive land reform would likely be more extensive, less costly, and have a greater effect on production than market-assisted (noncoercive) land reform or tenancy reform. But since implementation problems may be a serious constraint, the other forms may have better outcomes. In general, Banerjee claims that land reform should discriminate between different types of landlords and should be based on a uniform limit on the amount of land owned by an individual, with the limit allowed to be exceeded only if the buyer pays a high enough price. Although Banerjee argues for restrictions on reselling (but not renting out) redistributed land, he recognizes that this may prevent the poor from coping in emergency situations. For this and other reasons Banerjee suggests incorporating emergency income support programs and agricultural extension programs in any land reform scheme.

Although relatively neglected in the 1980s, inequality and distribution have resurfaced as central issues in economic development. **Ravi Kanbur and Nora Lustig** argue that this resurgence is the culmination of several trends in the theoretical, empirical, and policy literature.

One reason that inequality is back on the agenda is that, in the past two decades, it has remained stable (or declined) in some countries and risen dramatically in others. Researchers have begun to ask how these different experiences can be explained, given that countries face the same global conditions. Overall, there has been an increase in inequality between countries since 1980. This increase has led to a rich literature on what determines relative growth rates and whether growing inequality between nations is inevitable. Microeconometric analysis of inequality has also reemerged, aided by the recent availability of times series data from household surveys of developing countries. These data have enabled researchers to take a deeper look at inequality than Gini coefficients would allow. Kanbur and Lustig present case studies of Brazil, Mexico, and Taiwan (China), which reveal that structural forces, such as the evolution of markets, and institutions, are at work, on top of straightforward demographic shifts.

Theoretical developments have also reinvigorated discussions of inequality. Kanbur and Lustig point to the ascendance of the perspective of imperfect markets and imperfect information in mainstream economics during the 1980s and 1990s. The two fundamental theorems of welfare economics establish that, under a set of rigid assumptions, equity and efficiency are separable. But researchers in the 1970s and 1980s discovered that when they relaxed these assumptions—perfect information, complete markets, the availability of lump-sum transfer instruments—equity and efficiency were no longer separable. The two may be complements or substitutes, and a detailed, case-by-case approach was needed to specify their relationship. Distribution has thus become an integral part of the analysis of economic performance.

Opinion on the nature of the relationship between equity and growth has also shifted since Kuznets introduced his inverted U hypothesis: inequality first increases and then decreases as per capita income rises. The conventional wisdom today is that there is no systematic relationship between growth and income inequality. Kanbur and Lustig write that this conclusion has policy implications only if it is assumed that there are separable instruments for growth and income redistribution—an assumption with no basis in economic theory. Identifying the right combination of instruments requires that each be evaluated for its effect on income distribution.

## Economic Transition—Ten Years Later, What Have We Learned?

**Charles Wyplosz** looks retrospectively at the economic transition in Central and Eastern Europe and the countries of the former Soviet Union. With some exceptions, he claims, most transition economies are on the right track, although the transition hasn't been easy. Wyplosz draws five useful lessons from the experience. First, it paid to start early and move fast. Although the big bang approach is highly desirable, but impractical, gradualism should be compressed as much as possible. Second, macroeconomic stabilization is a prerequisite for growth, although it should not continue to overshadow and supercede structural reform. Third, the exchange rate regime is irrelevant. Countries that floated their exchange rates have tightly managed them, whereas countries with fixed regimes repeatedly devalued and often ended up floating. Fourth, structural reform is crucial, including establishing property rights, hardening budget constraints, building a healthy banking system, and ensuring competition in domestic markets. And fifth, implementing policies that cannot be reversed early on allows governments to pursue change without fear that a shaky economic base will give rise to policy reversals that can set back the clock for several years.

Which issues are still pending? Wyplosz holds that countries will probably have to tolerate moderate inflation to further growth. A priority for transition countries at this time is to liberalize exchange rates and capital markets, establish sound banking systems, and control unemployment. Still, further research into these issues is needed, particularly research on the long-term growth effects of contractionary stabilization and the desirable level of inflation. From a political economy perspective, the impact of electoral changes and interest groups on the transition should be explored.

Transition requires that resources be reallocated across activities and that activities be restructured. Reallocation involves closing inefficient firms and creating new ones, and restructuring involves reorganizing existing firms that seem capable of long-run viability. Both lead to productivity growth. **Simon Commander, Mark Dutz, and Nicholas Stern** examine how countries of the former Soviet Union and Central and Eastern Europe have fared with these two processes. They find that countries have generally succeeded with both or failed with both.

In some countries, particularly those in Central Europe, policymakers have considerably reduced state interference in privatized firms and provided incentives for private agents to establish or restructure businesses and to invest. As a consequence, growth has accelerated and structural transformation has taken place. In other countries, particularly those of the former Soviet Union and Eastern Europe, reallocation and restructuring have been highly limited, despite seemingly radical changes in ownership regime. Excess government intervention and insider privatization have been common, banking sectors are fragile and bank credit to the private sector has declined, and foreign investment has been weak and unstable. The result is excessive rent seeking and few incentives for entry or restructuring. Another consequence, the widespread use of barter and nonmonetary transactions, has impeded any disciplining effects of trade liberalization. The failure to break the financial and other links between government, firms, and banks, has severely undermined the credibility of government policies.

Regulatory institutions remain weak in all of the transition economies, not just those of the former Soviet Union. The authors recommend that policymakers give external investors greater protection, remove barriers to entry, and eliminate continuing distortions for both firms and banks. In the countries of the former Soviet Union regulation and barriers to entry stifle innovation and growth of new firms; the continued propping up of failing firms limits the potential for restructuring and contributes to the persistence of soft budget constraints. These countries are caught in a "low restructuring trap" and will need better targeted programs and instruments to break out.

Between 1978 and 1998 China transformed itself from a centrally planned economy into an emerging market economy—following a transition path so unusual that, according to **Yingyi Qian,** it casts doubt on some of the conventional thinking on reform and system changes. Mainstream economics has not properly accounted for China's experience. Reform in China proceeded, despite the lack of complete market liberalization, privatization, secure property rights, and democracy— conditions that conventional wisdom deems necessary for a successful transition. Over the two decades growth averaged more than 10 percent a year and per capita GDP more than quadrupled.

Qian describes China's transition as a two-stage process; success in the first stage (1979–93) built momentum for the second stage (1994–present). Four institutional changes were critical to the success of the early stage. The government began to decentralize; encouraged the entry and expansion of nonstate enterprises, rather than privatize state-owned enterprises; maintained financial stability in the face of sharp reductions in fiscal revenue by relying on quasi-fiscal revenues from the banking system; and liberalized prices according to a "dual-track" approach, in which planned prices and quotas were phased out gradually, minimizing the number of losers from reform. In the second stage China unified its foreign exchange market and made its current account convertible, overhauled its tax and fiscal systems, centralized the central bank, downsized the government bureaucracy, forced the military to give up its commercial operations, and began privatizing state-owned enterprises.

China's reform has shown that considerable growth is possible with sensible but imperfect institutions—some transitional institutions can be more effective than best-practice institutions for a period of time. Institutional innovations like fiscal contracting, township and village enterprises, and anonymous banking worked well for a while in China. Qian draws three basic lessons. First, changes that create incentives, impose hard budget constraints, and introduce competition should apply to governments as well as to firms. Second, successful reform requires political support, which in turn depends on delivering tangible benefits to a majority of the population. And third, successful institutional change requires appropriate, although not necessarily optimal, sequencing. Whenever politically feasible, an institutional vacuum should be avoided: existing institutions should be dismantled only after new institutions are in place. Thus China's failure to reform its financial system, privatize large state-owned enterprises, and establish the rule of law—its three most serious challenges today—early on did not derail the transition.

Since 1989 Russia's GDP has fallen more than 40 percent, and income inequality, poverty, and unemployment have increased dramatically. Why has radical economic reform largely failed? **Anders Åslund** explains that it was because of extraordinary rent seeking in the early years of the transition. Whereas some analysts have argued that Russia's reforms have been too radical and too fast, Åslund argues just the opposite: reforms have been too slow and incomplete.

Russia's main problem is that a few people—members of the old Soviet *nomenklatura*—got rich by taking advantage of institutional and economic anomolies—monetary emission, low interest rates, distorted relative prices—and have bought off many of the politicians and officials. Using their privileged positions, they collected rents—free money made directly through government subsidies or indirectly through government regulation—and to protect those rents, wielded their new economic power to block liberal reforms that could boost growth and welfare. Åslund claims that Russia's postcommunist period has been a struggle between reformers and rent seekers. For the most part the reformers have lost.

Given that, from the start, Russia's market reforms were not perceived as credible, what could have been done to enhance credibility? Åslund argues that the shift from the old system could have been swifter, and the Russian government could have done more to support democratic and market-oriented institutions early on in the transition. He also faults the West for not seizing the opportunity to make a difference in the first quarter of 1992, when Yeltsin asked for help in financing needed liberalization measures.

To reinvigorate Russia's stalled transition, Åslund advises curtailing rent seeking by creating competition over rents, reducing the tax rate, decreasing public expenditures, and introducing a lump sum tax to protect small entrepreneurs. International financial institutions could play a crucial role by adopting an anti–rent seeking and anti-corruption stance and helping to strengthen Russia's weak civil society.

***

As in previous years, many individuals were involved in the planning and organization of the 1999 conference. We would like to extend a special thanks to staff members, especially several anonymous reviewers for their assistance, and conference coordinators, Mantejwinder Jandu and Jean Gray Ponchamni, whose outstanding organizational skills helped ensure a successful conference. Finally, we thank the editorial staff, especially Meta de Coquereaumont, Paul Holtz, Barbara Karni, and Daphne Levitas, and production artist, Wendy Guyette, all of Communications Development Inc.

# KEYNOTE ADDRESS
# Knowledge as a Factor of Production

*Kenneth J. Arrow*

What issues must be addressed in seeking to incorporate technological knowledge as an input to and output of the economy? First, new technological knowledge has interesting economic properties. It is costly to develop. But once developed, it can be used repeatedly with no additional cost. Thus it is fixed cost, a source of increasing returns. As will be seen below, this creates a problem for value theory. Second, new technological knowledge diffuses through channels that cannot easily be thought of as markets. The issues raised by this observation are also discussed below.

## Technological Knowledge in Economic Theory before 1950

Mainstream economic theory—which stems in style and formulation from David Ricardo's (1817) *Principles of Political Economy and Taxation*—has as one of its key bases a theory of production. In one form or another the technological foundation of the economic theory of production is the proposition that output is determined (or at least limited) by inputs. This is clear in Ricardo's analysis of the farm, where the output of corn depends on inputs of capital, labor, and land. The corresponding analysis for nonagricultural output was more primitive and went through phases of fixed-coefficient models that placed some emphasis on lags between inputs and outputs. This analysis was ultimately crystallized in the production function formulations of John Bates Clark (1890), Stuart Wood (1888), and the later editions of Walras's *Éléments d'économie politique pure* (1900).

For the complete theory of production, an economic relation has to be added to the technological relation. This economic relation has traditionally been some sort of profit maximization condition, with or without an assumption of market power. In any case the economic relation has usually implied cost minimization. Although modern analysis has suggested an internal structure for the firm—with regard both to a multiplicity of owners (stockholders) and to the incompletely controllable work-

Kenneth J. Arrow is Joan Kenney Professor of Economics, emeritus, and professor of operations research, emeritus, in the Department of Economics at Stanford University.

force—that seems to lead to conditions different from cost minimization, I will not dwell on that aspect here.

That a technological relation between inputs and outputs is an embodiment of knowledge may seem obvious. But the point has more force when productive knowledge changes—that is, when it becomes a variable. Ricardo hardly denied that technological progress occurs. Indeed, he refers to it, for example, as postponing the arrival of the stationary state in which labor gets no more than its subsistence while landlords engross the net social product. But his theory does not in any way explain technological progress, nor does the expectation of such progress play any role in the decisionmaking of his entrepreneurs or other economic agents.

Adam Smith (1776, book 1, ch. 1) developed the beginnings of a theory of technological progress or, at any rate, of increasing productivity; it was due to the division of labor. Implicitly, Smith had the sketch of a theory of growth in which an increased division of labor improved productivity, which increased demand, which permitted an increase in the division of labor—that is, there were scale economies. Of course, it was only a sketch. One must ask under what conditions the process will continue indefinitely rather than converge to a limit.

In this form it would appear that knowledge is constant, that growth is simply a matter of increasing returns to scale. But when Smith explained why the division of labor increased productivity, one of the reasons was the increased skill of an operator after performing a task repeatedly (what is now called learning by doing). Another was the increased ability to innovate. There was at least a hint, then, that innovation was affected by endogenous economic factors.

Schumpeter (1939, pp. 84–109) is the name most closely associated with the explicit introduction of innovations into economics. The details are not very rich. He distinguishes between inventions and innovations. Inventions are ideas or concepts; they are conceived as floating about and freely available. Inventions have to be translated into usable products or processes, a costly step that constitutes innovation. The costs are recouped by short-term monopoly profits.

Classical and neoclassical theory had successively refined theories of value, but these did not accommodate the process of innovation or, indeed, increasing returns. Even today no general theory of value explains in any real detail the economic motivation for innovation. There are two issues for value theory. First, how are prices determined and, in particular, how do they create incentives for innovation? Second, to what extent do individuals about to invest take account of the possibility of future innovations that may affect the returns on their investment?

## Economic Analysis of Growth since 1950

The literature on economic growth began with two classic papers by Robert Solow (1956, 1957). The basic concept of intensive growth—that increasingly more can be produced from a given amount of labor and capital—had been documented earlier by Tinbergen (1942) and Abramovitz (1956). But Solow's model gave a starting point for systematic analysis, both theoretical and empirical. In the model technological progress is simply exogenous; it is not determined by economic considerations such as profitability.

In Solow's model technological progress can be slightly restated in a way that permits the beginning of an economic analysis. There are four variables: output, capital, labor, and knowledge. Output is produced from capital, labor, and knowledge. Knowledge is produced from knowledge alone. (There are no other inputs.) Knowledge is a public good. With a given input of knowledge, there are constant returns to the other two inputs, capital and labor, which are private goods. There are really no decisions in Solow's model because savings is determined as a fixed portion of income. Hence anticipations do not matter.

Because knowledge is a public good and is the sole input into the production of knowledge, the knowledge-producing industry has zero costs and zero revenues. The prices of goods are determined by standard neoclassical principles. (The trick of assuming constant returns to private factors, with all other inputs being externalities, is already found in Marshall (1920, book 5, ch. 12, and appendix H; the concept already appeared in the first edition in 1890.)

Subsequent literature along Solow lines has largely used control theory. The economy maximizes some sum of discounted utilities of consumption, so that savings (and investment) are determined within the system. In these models anticipations play a role; they are assumed to be perfect.

There are different approaches to the study of innovation and growth. One has been the historical study of the development of innovations and the social and economic conditions surrounding them, as in Landes (1998) and Rosenberg (1982). There have been statistical studies based on data about innovations (such as patent data); an early example is Schmookler (1966), who sought to show the extent to which innovation is driven by demand. There is also an extensive literature among engineers in the field of technological management devoted to conditions for successful innovation.

An important part of the literature has emphasized the diffusion of knowledge. In a decentralized economic system it is essential that knowledge be, at any one moment, localized. One entrepreneur does not necessarily know what another knows. That is why the price system is considered remarkable, because it arranges for allocative efficiency in the absence of widespread knowledge of the production capabilities and tastes of others. Still, we know from historical experience that new technological ideas diffuse and are gradually absorbed by others, including people in other countries. Diffusion is far from instantaneous, however. Among the pioneering studies were those of Griliches (1957) on the spread of hybrid corn and David (1974) on the diffusion of the reaper. The spread of these technologies was demand-oriented—that is, the innovation existed and was adopted, not instantaneously, but at a rate that depended on its profitability.

Other studies have emphasized sheer imitation, though we do not expect imitation unless there is profitability. Rashevsky (1947) offered simple models that analogized the diffusion of an innovation to that of an epidemic. At any one time there were two populations, those who knew about the innovation and those who did not.

Members of the two populations met at random, and each time a knower met a nonknower, there was a probability that the nonknower would learn about the innovation. This simple reasoning gives rise to a logistic curve for the diffusion of the innovation. Much more specific models were studied by Coleman and Katz (1966) and, with more concern for economic considerations like profitability, by Mansfield (1961). Studies on the diffusion of agricultural innovations, on which data are unusually good, have been surveyed by Rogers (1962).

## Creation of Technological Knowledge

Efforts to model the production process for innovation must take into account two main issues. First, the production of knowledge requires not only knowledge but also marketed resources, capital, and labor. Second, aggregate models seriously misrepresent the nature of knowledge. Knowledge is not knowledge in general but highly specific in nature; this is true for knowledge both as an input and as an output. Ideas can be put together to create new ideas (Weitzman 1998).

The two points merge to some extent when one considers where knowledge is located. Some knowledge is embodied in individuals, in a tacit and implicit form, in which case it becomes part of human capital. Other knowledge is available in codified form, such as books, patents, and databases, and can be transmitted and received with low resource cost. The second kind of knowledge gives rise to problems of intellectual property. Tacit knowledge joins in the general market for resource use.

The supply of knowledge includes general education. It also includes the habits needed for research and development; it is for this reason that countries find it useful to have graduate education even though they could import ideas developed elsewhere. The ability to understand is a scarce good and can be expanded by suitable training.

The two points have opposite implications for policy on the diffusion of technological knowledge. The first states that marketable resources have to be invested; this will not happen unless there is some protection for investors' rights to some monopoly use of the knowledge. The second point, by contrast, indicates that it is better to have a free flow of ideas, because everyone will benefit from the ideas of others in arriving at new ideas.

Several additional points seem to be important in the creation of knowledge. One is the value of independent approaches to research—what has been called parallel development (for an early but worthwhile examination of parallel development, see Klein and Meckling 1958). This is simply an application of the principle of diversification in decisions made under uncertainty. In theory a large firm should be able to take independent approaches to developing some new technology and internalize the benefits, but in practice this seems difficult to achieve. Hence there is an argument for relying on competition to achieve independence of thought.

Let me say a few words about incentives to innovate. One reward, as Schumpeter noted, is the creation of a niche in the product market—that is, the ability to exercise monopolistic power by having a suitably differentiated product. This point was central to Chamberlin's (1933) theory of monopolistic competition. In addition, there is what has been called a first-mover advantage. In many cases a new product needs highly specific complementary goods, and innovators can use their temporary advantage to design the complementary goods in a way that makes entry by others much more difficult. Since innovation leads to fixed costs, the innovation in complementary goods will be directed to the largest market, which will complement the current leader.

Even though niches and first-mover advantages are subject to erosion by diffusion of knowledge, the temporary lead can be self-reinforcing and lead to a long-term monopoly. But by its nature a monopoly dampens incentives to innovate. A monopolist is realizing a surplus from current outputs. Thus an innovation by the monopolist that competes with those outputs will destroy an existing profit, at least partly offsetting any gain in new markets.

## Diffusion of Products and Ideas

Once a product is on the market, its method of production can spread. There are several routes to diffusion: imitation (seeing the success of others), public agencies (particularly important in agriculture), and search by firms (conventions, trade meetings, discussions with customers).

Licensing is the diffusion channel that is closest to a market. But is an idea the commodity being priced—that is, through a lump-sum fee for the license—or is it the use per unit activity of the licensee? Informal communication among engineers from different firms is a well-known and powerful instrument for diffusion. This communication is sometimes even encouraged by firms, who see themselves as trading ideas (von Hippel 1988). The success of Silicon Valley (California) relative to other technology centers has been partly attributed to the area's high propensity for informal communication (Saxenian 1996). In the same vein geographic proximity greatly speeds up diffusion of knowledge. Finally, the mobility of workers across firms is another important source of knowledge diffusion.

Those to whom knowledge is diffused must be able to understand and adapt. The problem is particularly challenging for developing countries with very different amounts of accumulated knowledge. To use the standard phrase, these countries require absorptive capacity.

## Conclusion

There are many unknowns in the creation and use of knowledge as a factor of production. Still, two main lessons stand out:
- Every country or firm must have education and training in technology and science, even if the research is not on par with that being conducted elsewhere. Knowledge cannot be absorbed unless some knowledge is already possessed.
- Countries and firms must be open to new ideas, have multiple sources of new ideas, and see that ideas are diffused. This point strongly argues for freedom of entry, even when it seems to forgo economies of scale.

## References

Abramovitz, Moses. 1956. "Resource and Output Trends in the United States since 1870." *American Economic Review Papers and Proceeding* 46 (May): 5–23.

Chamberlin, Edward H. 1933. *Theory of Monopolistic Competition.* Cambridge, Mass.: Harvard University Press.

Clark, John Bates. 1890. "The Law of Wages and Interest." *Annals of the American Academy of Political and Social Science* 5: 289–318.

Coleman, J., and E. Katz. 1966. *Medical Innovation: A Diffusion Study.* Indianapolis, Ind.: Bobbs-Merrill.

David, P. A. 1974. "The Mechanization of Reaping in the Ante-Bellum Midwest." In P. A. David, ed., *Technical Choice, Innovation and Economic Growth.* New York: Cambridge University Press.

Griliches, Zvi. 1957. "Hybrid Corn: An Exploration in the Economics of Technological Change." *Econometrica* 25: 501–22.

Klein, B. H., and W. H. Meckling. 1958. "Applications of Operations Research to Development Decisions." *Operations Research* 5: 352–63.

Landes, David. 1998. *The Wealth and Poverty of Nations.* New York: Norton.

Mansfield, Edwin. 1961. "Technical Change and the Rate of Imitation." *Econometrica* 29: 741–66.

Marshall, Alfred. 1920. *Principles of Economics,* 8th ed. London: L Macmillan.

Rashevsky, Nicolas. 1947. *Mathematical Biophysics.* Chicago, Ill.: University of Chicago Press.

Ricardo, David. 1817. *Principles of Political Economy and Taxation.* London: Murray.

Rogers, Everett. 1962. *Diffusion of Innovations.* Glencoe, Ill.: Free Press.

Rosenberg, Nathan. 1982. *Inside the Black Box.* New York: Cambridge University Press.

Saxenian, AnnaLee. 1996. *Regional Advantage: Culture and Competition in Silicon Valley and Route 128.* Cambridge, Mass.: Harvard University Press.

Schmookler, Jacob. 1966 *Invention and Economic Growth.* Cambridge, Mass.: Harvard University Press.

Schumpeter, Joseph. 1939. *Business Cycles.* New York: McGraw-Hill.

Smith, Adam. 1776. *An Inquiry into the Nature and Causes of the Wealth of Nations.* London: Strahan and Cadell.

Solow, Robert M. 1956. "A Contribution to the Theory of Economic Growth." *Quarterly Journal of Economics* 65: 65–94.

———. 1957. "Technical Change and the Aggregate Production Function." *Review of Economic Statistics* 39: 312–20.

Tinbergen, Jan. 1942. "Zur Theorie Der Langfristigen Wirtschaftsentwicklung." *Weltwirtschaftliches Archiv* 55: 511–49.

von Hippel, Eric. 1988. *The Sources of Innovation.* New York: Oxford University Press.

Walras, Léon. 1900. *Éléments d'économie pure,* 4ième éd. Lausanne: Rouge.

Weitzman, Martin. 1998. "Recombinant Growth." *Quarterly Journal of Economics* 113: 331–60.

Wood, Stuart. 1888. "A New View of the Theory of Wages." *Quarterly Journal of Economics* 3: 60–86, 462–80.

KEYNOTE ADDRESS
# Six Questions for Development Researchers and Policymakers

*Lawrence H. Summers*

What should development policy researchers and policymakers be thinking about today, and what should they be thinking about over the next few decades?

When I try to reflect on what the world doesn't understand as well as it would like to, I am left with the feeling that we have a lot more thinking and institutional development to do. So, I would like to share six questions with you. I'll reflect a little bit on the answers, but much of my motivation is to stimulate thought.

1. HOW DO WE RECONCILE GLOBAL INTEGRATION WITH OTHER CRUCIAL OBJECTIVES?
As we look at the global economy and at national policy toward international economic issues, three imperatives seem clear.

We are for integration because of the benefits of freer trade, because of the benefits of fair investment, because of what integration means for links between states and reductions in the risks of conflict.

We are, in addition, for national sovereignty, the idea that we as Americans choose our taxes, choose our redistributive policies, choose our environmental standards—and similarly for the people of other nations. So the second imperative is sovereignty.

And a third imperative for most of us is the pursuit of public purposes that markets, left to their own devices, may not produce—the right opportunities for the poor, the right environmental policies, the kind of outcomes we want.

As we think about the development of our global economic institutions, it is these three things that need to be reconciled. For many people this is easy. For Milton Friedman, public purpose is a minimal objective. If we have integration and if we have sovereignty, then—because of the tremendous mobility of capital and businesses—it will prove difficult to impose redistributive tax rates and difficult to regulate in an effective way. And he sees that as an advantage rather than a disadvantage.

---

Lawrence H. Summers is the secretary of the U.S. Department of the Treasury and a former chief economist of the World Bank.

*Annual World Bank Conference on Development Economics 1999*
©2000 The International Bank for Reconstruction and Development / THE WORLD BANK

For Pat Buchanan and other isolationists, this is not a difficult problem. It is imperative to maintain national sovereignty. Public purpose in the form of appropriate regulation and taxation is essential. So, integration has to be sacrificed.

For global visionaries, this is not a hard problem. They suggest that just as federal regulation in the United States entered a whole set of areas that had traditionally been reserved to the states as interstate commerce increased, so too we need more regulation of questions about the flow of capital, questions about the level of taxes, questions about standards set at the international level. They rarely, as global visionaries, have to run for office in any of our countries.

And so if one adopts any two of these goals, solving the problem is quite easy. But it seems to me that for those who are thoughtful, the challenge really is to reconcile all three, and they can never be perfectly reconciled. Our challenge is to find the right ways to reconcile them. But if we try in our policy approaches, as we sometimes do, to elevate any one or even any two, we will go very much astray. And as we think about the development of the global trading system in particular, this is a special imperative.

## 2. What posture should countries take on global capital flows?

It is tempting to see the global capital market as imposing large costs on nations as capital moves in and out too quickly. Certainly, events give cause for concern in that direction.

I have been struck, though, as we have looked at the various crises, that in almost every case where those problems appear most central, policy created a substantial bias in favor of short-term capital flows, whether through the issuance of short-maturity debt with Mexican Tesobonos, through tax breaks for short-term offshore bank deposits in Thailand, through the tailoring of financial instruments to be perfectly attuned to hedge fund preferences as with the Russian GKO treasury bills, through discriminatory capital controls that favor short-term capital and oppose long-term capital in the Republic of Korea.

There is also a kind of bias in favor of short-term capital created by the government provision of exchange rate guarantees whose duration can never be absolutely certain and which therefore encourage the inflow of short-term capital. And so it seems appropriate to frame the question of how we can encourage policy regimes that will not discourage short-term capital but will discourage the inappropriate encouragement of short-term capital that has led to such large problems.

There's a rich and varied debate, and the right answer will differ from situation to situation, as with Chilean-style controls. But in most of the cases that we look at countries are actually on the other side of it, creating a bias for short-term capital to save costs. How can they be encouraged to make better choices that recognize that short-term capital is also liquidity? It is sometimes the only kind you can get.

I don't think we have all the answers, and I think we will find that the question of exchange rate regimes will be particularly important in this regard—with an increasing conviction that the optimum may lie toward more flexible regimes or more heavily institutionalized pegged arrangements.

## 3. How can financial crises be resolved?

It has become clear that without policy change and without strong policies, crises are unlikely to be resolved in any country. Crises typically follow a period of very substantial capital outflow. And the provision of liquidity, without changing the conditions that led to the capital outflow, is likely to lead to the outflow of the liquidity, leaving only debt behind.

At the same time, it is very clear in each of the major episodes we have all studied that there came a moment when the investors' calculus shifted from the long-run fundamentals of the country—was policy sound?—to a comparison of the quantity of reserves available with the quantity of short-term debt coming due in the next few months. At that moment the situation worsened very dramatically and no longer became amenable to a simple fix through the restoration of policy to restore confidence.

We obviously want to find ways—and this goes back to short-term capital flows—of making it as unlikely as possible that countries will find themselves in such situations. But when they do, there are very difficult questions involving finding the right provision of public sector liquidity and private sector involvement.

Bagehot's use of the term "lender of last resort" suggested an early appreciation of the concept of dynamic consistency, and we do not as yet have a clear doctrine. Indeed, one of the doctrines in this area held by some is that it is a bad idea to have a clear doctrine—calculated ambiguity and all that—for the respective roles of the private and public sectors.

What is clear and now agreed is that this is an area where the answer cannot be extreme. Appropriately conditioned finance has and no doubt will have a constructive role to play in crisis resolution. A stable and healthy financial system cannot be based on the principle that in any and all situations those who extend credit will be repaid—certainly not when those who extend credit have been compensated with very substantial risk premia. And so a critical task before the international community will be to come to greater understandings. We believe that this is most appropriately done case by case because crises differ in how they will be resolved.

## 4. How do we best put into practice our shared sentiment that appropriate attention to the vulnerable is morally right, politically necessary, and internationally prudent in time of crisis?

It is easy to enunciate that as a convincing proposition. But it seems the questions that need to be reflected on in putting into practice that sentiment—which I haven't seen reflected on as fully as they might be—include the following.

First, is this a call for more and larger deficits to support more social spending systematically in time of crisis? Or is it a call for different budget priorities? If it is a call for different budget priorities, what spending that is currently maintained is thought to be unwisely maintained in crisis and should be systematically reduced?

Second, how does one square the critique that it is important to focus conditionality as much as possible to avoid resentment from host-country governments with the critique that it is necessary to have a far-reaching investigation of spending priorities?

Third, how does one confront the issue of fungibility in providing support? Is the appropriate approach to support laudable social objectives and leave the rest to take care of itself? Or is the right approach to condition that support on some broadly appropriate reformulation of public expenditure priorities?

Fourth, how does one square the imperatives of crisis resolution with long-standing social imperatives? Although I am no expert on the question, it is my impression that the poorest and most vulnerable in any society are usually also the most voiceless—and not the most likely to upset political and social stability in time of crisis.

To what extent is a crisis, therefore, a time when assistance should be focused on them because they are most vulnerable? And to what extent is a crisis a time when the focus of policy should be on those whose lives have been most disrupted by the crisis, even if they are not objectively the poorest?

This list of questions could be continued, but it seems to me that it is high time for the international community to move beyond what surely are appropriate sentiments, and in many cases significant actions, to think through a little more carefully what our doctrines and approaches should be in this area.

5. HOW CAN WE IN THE INTERNATIONAL COMMUNITY SUBSTITUTE OR BEST PRODUCE THE SOCIAL CAPITAL THAT IS ULTIMATELY IMPORTANT FOR CONTINUING A SUCCESSFUL ECONOMY?
I don't think anybody completely understands—certainly I don't—the problems of states of the former Soviet Union, or the problems of Indonesia, or the problems in many African countries. And the problems obviously differ in very profound ways. But as I reflect on them, I am convinced that there is a common element of a lack of social connection—a lack of links between people because governments have preempted not just all the political and economic space, but also much of the social space. These are low-trust societies—societies in which the basis for the most rudimentary enforcement of law is often lacking.

It is much easier, it seems to me, to frame the problem than to solve it. Without secure property rights, there will not be commerce. Contract enforcement is crucial to business—to business connections. It is much easier to frame the problem than to know what the international community can do about it—to produce tangible results very quickly. It is perhaps inevitable that support efforts focus on problems that can be solved—whether those problems are macroeconomic stabilization or the eradication of particular diseases. But that doesn't mean that the lack of effective institutions is not at the center of the problem.

Whether the right approach is to work to develop stronger institutions or to work around the lack of effective institutions, it seems to me that we don't know the answer. But here, too, if we're going to make our efforts as effective as we can, it is appropriate to reflect on this rather carefully.

6. HOW WILL OUR THINKING DIFFER 30 YEARS FROM NOW?
I am no expert on the history of economic thought, but I have been struck that discredited doctrines are less stupid than ideas that fit one time and not a subsequent time. I am told by those who are knowledgeable about Malthus's theory that it was

actually a rather accurate description of the dynamics of population and food supply in the several hundred years that preceded his enunciating it. It was not the obvious fallacy that it is held to be in today's elementary economics textbooks.

It is not difficult to understand, studying the history of the 1930s, why the economists of the 1940s and 1950s developed a set of doctrines that were heavily centered on the achievement of more aggregate demand as the central objective of economic policy.

It is not difficult to understand—looking at the manifest failure of the American and British economies during the 1930s and their tremendous success in the Second World War, and looking at the success of the Latin American economies during the 1940s when they were cut off from international trade—why a rather dirigiste economic doctrine came to be established after the Second World War. And it is not hard to understand, looking at the experiences of the last 25 years, why the right doctrine for this time emphasizes markets, emphasizes openness, emphasizes the benefits of competition. But history should remind us—just as the World Bank's celebrated 1979 report on the Romanian economic miracle should remind us: is there some profoundly different change in process that leads one to think that nothing is being produced today that will look as foolish 20 years from now as the Romanian economic miracle report of 1979? I doubt it.

As we think this through, we have no alternative as policymakers but to operate within our best guesses and our most accurate judgments about how the world works today. But particularly for those of you who focus on research, it seems to me appropriate to reflect on the fact that there will probably be some quite substantial changes in doctrine over the next 30 years. There certainly have been over most 30-year periods in the past.

That is why it is important to anticipate what those changes will be. If one thinks about most past changes in doctrine—whether away from the hard-core Keynesian policies or away from the more dirigiste orientation—if they had come somewhat sooner rather than somewhat later, most of us would judge that the world would be a better place. So we need to apply that same kind of rigorous scrutiny to what we hold as conventional wisdom today.

KEYNOTE ADDRESS
# Whither Reform? Ten Years of the Transition

*Joseph E. Stiglitz*

*What lessons have we learned in the 10 years since the beginning of the transition? Broadly speaking, most observers would conclude that China's transition has been a success so far, while Russia's has not. The failure of reforms in the Russian Federation and in most of the countries of the former Soviet Union are not simply the result of poor implementation of sound policies. The failures go deeper, to a misunderstanding of the foundations of a market economy and of the basics of an institutional reform process. Reform models based on conventional neoclassical economics are bound to underestimate the untoward consequences of information problems, opportunistic behavior, and human fallibility—and those consequences are now plainly visible. A process of institutional reform modeled on shock therapy ignores the lessons extracted by Hayek and Popper from (ironically) the Bolshevik Revolution. The promise of quick economic transformation based on voucher privatization with investment funds has proven illusory. An alternative strategy of decentralization is to push economic decisionmaking down to the level at which stakeholders have a better chance to protect their own interests, without presupposing elaborate legal machinery that will take much longer to evolve.*

Ten years since the transition began in the former Soviet Union, how do we assess what has happened? What are the lessons? What happened there is one of the most important experiments in economics ever to take place, a revolutionary change in the rules of the game that occurred almost overnight. As rapidly as countries announced the abandonment of communism, Western advisers marched in with sure-fire recipes for a quick transition to a market economy.

A decade since the transition in Eastern Europe and Central Asia and two decades since reform began in China, the picture is mixed. Each country came to transition with a different history, a different set of human and physical endowments. Some had been under the yoke of central planning and authoritarianism for

Joseph E. Stiglitz is senior vice president, Development Economics, and chief economist at the World Bank.

most of the century; others came under communism only in the aftermath of World War II. The countries bordering Western Europe that had good prospects of integration with the European Union were clearly in a different position from landlocked countries such as Mongolia and the former Soviet republics in Central Asia.[1]

Counterfactual history—what would have been but for the policies that were pursued—is always problematic. Yet the disparity between the successes and failures is so large that it would be irresponsible not to attempt to derive some lessons from it. In any case, the public debate has already begun.

The contrast between the strategies—and results—in the two largest countries, the Russian Federation and China, is instructive. Over the decade beginning in 1989 China's GDP nearly doubled, while Russia's fell by almost half. Russia's GDP, which was more than twice that of China at the beginning of the decade, was a third smaller by the end of the decade (figure 1).[2] Not only has Russia stagnated during the past decade, but it succeeded in turning the theoretical tradeoff between equity and growth on its head: in the process of shrinking its GDP, Russia also doubled its level of inequality, as measured by the Gini coefficient (figure 2).

The titles of some recent books by leading advisers in the transition process—*How Russia Became a Market Economy, The Coming Boom in Russia*—are telling. Those who advised Russia regularly predicted that it was on the verge of success—virtually declaring victory just a short while before the recent crash—but the shortfall should have been apparent. Yes, Russia succeeded in privatizing much of its industry and natural resources, but the level of gross fixed investment—a far more

**Figure 1. Russian and Chinese GDP, 1989–97**

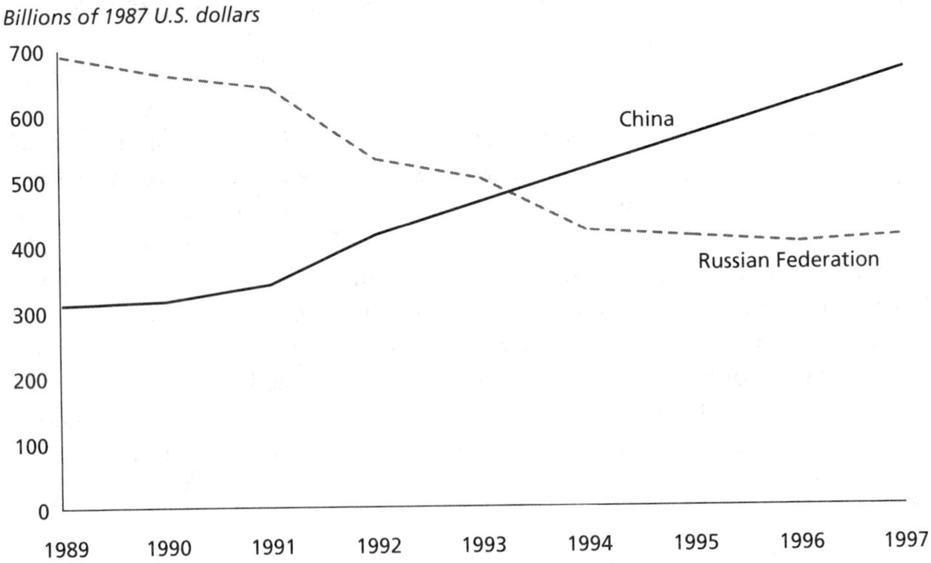

*Billions of 1987 U.S. dollars*

*Source:* World Bank data.

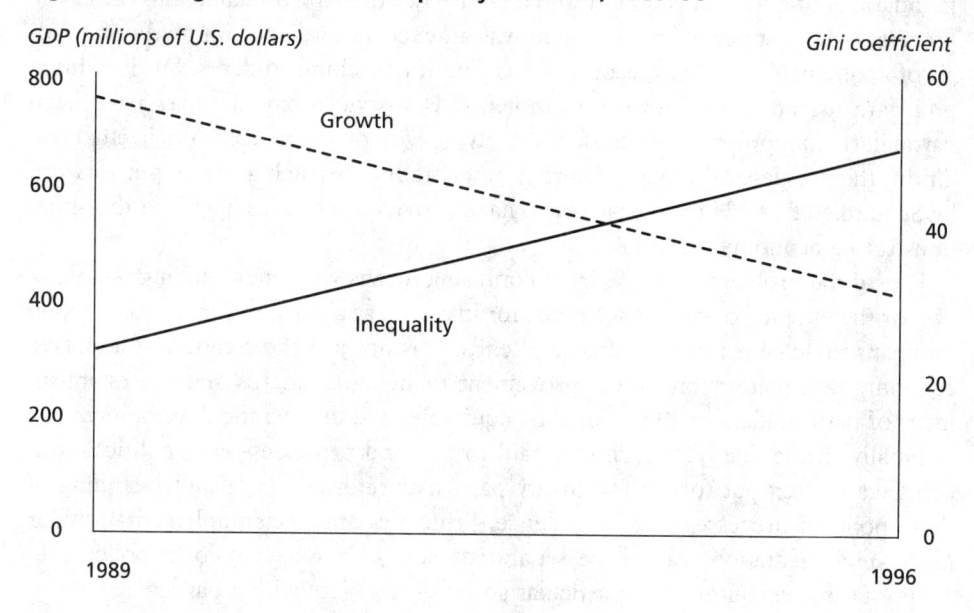

**Figure 2. Changes in GDP and Inequality in Russia, 1989–96**

*GDP (millions of U.S. dollars)* — *Gini coefficient*

*Note:* The GDP is measured in constant 1987 U.S. dollars and the figure represents generated trendline between 1989 and 1996 data points.
*Source:* World Bank 1999.

important sign of a burgeoning market economy—fell dramatically between 1992 and 1997 (EBRD 1998). Russia was fast becoming an extractive economy, rather than a modern industrial economy.

In marked contrast to these failures has been the enormous success of China, which created its own transition rather than applying a blueprint created by Western advisers. China succeeded not only in growing rapidly but in creating a vibrant, non–state-owned collective enterprise sector. While investment in manufacturing stagnated in Russia, it grew by leaps and bounds in China. Critics of such comparisons point out the marked difference in starting points, noting that China's income was far lower, providing more opportunities for catch-up. I would argue that China's difficulties were greater than Russia's, for it had to manage the challenges of transition and development simultaneously. China did better than countries with comparable income, while the countries of the former Soviet Union and Eastern Europe, by and large, did worse. Why?

Not surprisingly, those who advocated shock therapy and rapid privatization argue that the problem was not too much shock and too little therapy, but too little shock. Reforms, they argue, were not pursued aggressively enough. Never mind that the West had been jubilant over the restoration of democracy and that democratic processes repeatedly rejected the prescribed medicine. Other defenders of the recommended reform programs argue that the failures were not in design but in implementation. One Russian reformer recently quipped that there was nothing wrong with the laws they enacted except the inability to enforce them.

The failures of the reforms go far deeper—to a misunderstanding of the very foundations of a market economy and a failure to grasp the fundamentals of reform processes. At least part of the problem was an excessive reliance on textbook models of economics. Textbook economics is fine for teaching students, but it is inappropriate for advising reform governments. U.S.-style textbooks may have been particularly inappropriate, because they rely heavily on a particular intellectual tradition, the neoclassical model, ignoring other traditions (such as those put forward by Schumpeter and Hayek) that might have provided more insights into the situations facing economies in transition.

Part of the problem also rose from confusing means with ends—taking privatization or the opening of capital accounts, for instance, as a mark of success rather than as means to achieve more fundamental ends. It is not just the creation of a market economy that matters but the improvement of living standards and the establishment of the foundations of sustainable, equitable, and democratic development.

Finally, while due obeisance was paid to political processes—and political concerns were often put forward to justify particular reforms—little understanding of these political processes was in evidence. Principles and their implementation (or likely implementation) cannot be separated. Policy advisers put forth policy prescriptions in the context of a particular society—a society with a particular history, a certain level of social capital, a particular set of political institutions, and political processes affected by (if not determined by) the existence of particular political forces. Interventions do not occur in a vacuum. How policy recommendations are used, or abused, is not an issue from which economists can simply walk away—especially when one of the arguments for reform is the failure of the political process or the impact of reform on the political process itself.[3] It is time for the doctors to rethink the prescription.[4]

This address reviews the major ways in which the Washington consensus doctrines of transition (a term I use for want of a better one) failed in their understanding of the core elements of a market economy. It then focuses on the sequencing and pacing of the reform strategy.

## Misunderstanding Market Economies

In my book *Whither Socialism?* (1994), I argue that the failure of market socialism reflects a failure to understand what makes an actual market economy function—a failure arising in part from the neoclassical model itself. If the Arrow-Debreu (1954) model had been correct, market socialism might have fared far better. But while the Arrow-Debreu model captures one essential aspect of a market economy—the information conveyed by price signals and the role of price signals in coordinating production—it ignores many other information problems addressed by the economy. Prices do not convey all relevant information.

Those who advocated shock therapy, with its focus on privatization, failed because they failed to understand modern capitalism. They, too, were overly influenced by the excessively simplistic textbook models of the market economy. But we should be less forgiving of those failures. Early in the 20th century Hayek and Schumpeter developed alternative paradigms, but their views were not well integrated into the mainstream of the Anglo-American tradition. By the time the postsocialist economies faced their transition, however, the modern theory of information economics had shown the striking limitations of the Arrow-Debreu model and used the tools of modern economic analysis to illustrate forcefully the problems of corporate governance about which Marshall (1897), Keynes (1963 [1926]), Berle and Means (1932), Galbraith (1952), March and Simon (1958), Baumol (1959), Marris (1964), and many others had written.

## Competition and Privatization

Standard neoclassical theory argues that for a market economy to work well (to be Pareto efficient), there must be both competition and private property (the Siamese twins of efficient wealth creation). Clearly, if policymakers could wave a magic wand and instantaneously institute both, they would presumably do so. If they cannot have both, however, should they proceed with privatization alone?

Advocates of privatization point with pride to the large fraction of state enterprises that were turned over to private hands. These privatizations were dubious achievements, however. After all, it is easy to simply give away state assets—especially to one's friends and cronies. The incentives for doing so are especially strong if the politicians conducting the privatization can obtain kickbacks, either directly or indirectly, as campaign contributions. Indeed, if privatization is conducted in ways that are widely viewed as illegitimate and in an environment that lacks the necessary institutional infrastructure, the longer-run prospects of creating a market economy may actually be undermined. Worse still, the private property interests that are created contribute to the weakening of the state and the undermining of the social order, through corruption and regulatory capture.

Consider the incentives facing the oligarchs in Russia. They may have reasoned that democratic elections would eventually produce a government that concludes that their wealth was ill-begotten and so attempts to recover it. This assessment may have induced them to pursue a twofold strategy, using their financial power to gain sufficient political influence to reduce the likelihood of such an event and—recognizing the inherent risk of such a strategy—taking at least a significant part of their wealth out of the country. Indeed, the "reform" advisers facilitated such a process by encouraging— in some cases even insisting on—the opening of capital accounts.[5] Thus the failure of privatization to provide the basis of a market economy was not an accident but a predictable consequence of the manner in which privatization occurred.

## Alternative Forms of Privatization

Those advocating rapid privatization were faced with the problem that there were no legitimate sources of private domestic wealth for accomplishing privatization. Governments thus had essentially four alternatives: selling national assets abroad, voucher privatization, taming "spontaneous" privatization, or privatization based on lending by state or government-chartered banks, which all too frequently proved an easy route for corruption, illegitimizing the privatization initiative. Such was the route Russia chose after 1995 in the notorious loans-for-shares scheme (Lieberman and Veimetra 1996). In this setup the government allowed private entrepreneurs to create banks, which could lend money to private parties to buy the enterprises or lend money to the government, with shares of government enterprises used as collateral. Whoever acquired the banking license received a license to print money—and the license to print money is a license to acquire government enterprises. Corruption was roundabout—the process was less transparent than if the government had simply given the nation's assets to its friends—but there is little difference between the two processes.

Since the whole process was widely viewed as illegitimate, this robber baron privatization may have brought market capitalism into even greater disrepute than had the indoctrination of the communist era. And since there was no presumption that those who acquired the assets were particularly good managers, there was no reason to hope that the assets would be better deployed than they previously had been. To be sure, some who advocated privatization worried little about either political impact or managerial incompetence: they believed that strong incentives were at work to create an "aftermarket," so that assets would eventually be sold to those who could best manage these enterprises. The hope was that these new robber barons would at least conduct a good auction.

This process failed, for several reasons. First, there remained the underlying problem: where were the internal managerial teams with the requisite capital? Worse still, the declining confidence in the economy and the government made Russia even less attractive to foreign investors than it had been. The oligarchs found that they could accumulate more wealth from asset stripping than from redeploying assets in ways that would establish the foundations for wealth creation.

Voucher schemes were hardly more successful. The Czech Republic (at first perceived as a model) provides the clearest illustration of the underlying problem of corporate governance—that corporate management is a public good. Those who seized control of the enterprises (or of the holding companies that seized control of the enterprises) again used those powers to strip assets (to *tunnel* them out of the enterprises, to use the term that became fashionable there) rather than to create wealth.

In both cases, a kind of pseudo-capitalism was created: institutions that had the superficial appearance of those of capitalism, but without the substance (for example, capital markets that failed to perform the essential functions of raising *new* capital, allocating it efficiently among competing uses, and monitoring).

Perhaps trying to discipline spontaneous privatization might have offered the greatest hope. I turn later to the possibility that breaking up the large enterprises into smaller units might have provided a basis for more effective governance by stakeholders.

## Creative Destruction

An essential part of the transition to a more efficient economy is the redeployment of resources from less productive to more productive uses. Moving workers from low productive employment to unemployment does not, by itself, increase productivity. Indeed, productivity is reduced—some productivity is better than none. Creation of unemployment is a costly and inefficient intermediate stage that can be defended only if there is no better way of moving workers from low productivity to higher productivity jobs. A crude form of Say's law was often put forward (with little empirical basis): a large supply of idle workers will create demand for labor, partly by facilitating downward pressure on wages.

But any student of the process of enterprise creation and entrepreneurship would have expressed concerns, especially in regions like the former Soviet Union, where there was little history of market-oriented entrepreneurship. For entrepreneurship to succeed, certain skills need to be developed—skills that citizens of the former Soviet Union had no opportunity to hone. They had acquired skills in evading government regulations, in arbitraging away some of the inefficiencies in government regulations for private profit, and in operating at the interstices between the legal and illegal worlds. But those are far different from the skills needed to create new businesses capable of competing in the international market place.

Entrepreneurship also requires capital. Few people had the necessary capital, especially after inflation eroded what little savings people had accumulated. The banking system had no experience in screening and monitoring loans; in fact, it is incorrect to think of these "banks" as banks in the Western sense (the term confused both those in the former Soviet Union and Western advisers). In any case, few of these banks actually got into the business of providing funds to small new enterprises. And given the high interest rate policies that were pursued to maintain exchange rates at overvalued levels or push inflation to lower and lower levels, even if banks had been interested in lending to new enterprises, few enterprises would have been interested in borrowing. Thus even under the best of conditions, entrepreneurship was stifled. Where, then, were the new jobs for those forced out of employment going to come from?

Bankruptcy, or the credible threat of it, is a crucial feature of a market economy. Like entrepreneurship, the institution of bankruptcy had little or no precedent in the socialist countries and had to be created. Various models for bankruptcy codes have evolved over centuries in the market economies, each integrated into the specific context of its economy. A transplant to an alien environment could hardly be expected to take root quickly—particularly in the absence of an independent and competent judiciary trained in and sympathetic to the basic tenets of bankruptcy. Those who hoped that newly drafted and installed bankruptcy codes would drive industrial restructuring have been deeply disappointed.

Moreover, as is often the case, there is no one best way. All bankruptcy systems involve tradeoffs between creditor and debtor rights; all systems need to be tailored to the local environment.[6] One relevant feature, for instance, is the speed with which assets can be productively redeployed. In countries with little entrepreneurship, weak social safety nets, and little tradition of labor mobility, we must expect a tilt toward debtor-oriented bankruptcy.[7] Moreover, we should not expect much industrial restructuring to come out of bankruptcy courts—real restructuring is usually done to keep companies out of formal bankruptcy. I later consider a range of such restructuring actions.

Entrepreneurship and bankruptcy, entry and exit, are two sides of the same coin of economic change. A prescription to "just enforce the bankruptcy laws" or "just harden the budget constraint" is not good advice where there is little culture of new business creation. Both parts of Schumpeter's phrase "creative destruction" must be remembered.[8] Even long-standing market economies do not pull themselves out of deep depressions by forcing large numbers of firms into bankruptcy. Vigorous programs that create and maintain employment—through promotion of entrepreneurship or through Keynesian stimuli—must accompany, if not precede, bankruptcy-induced restructuring.

### Social and Organizational Capital

It has long been recognized that a market system cannot operate solely on the basis of narrow self-interest. The informational problems in market interactions offer many chances for opportunistic behavior. Without some minimal amount of social trust and civil norms, social interaction would be reduced to a minimum of tentative and distrustful commodity trades. Behind these social norms stands the machinery of the law, which itself stands apart from the market. As Kenneth Arrow (1972, p. 357) wrote:

> Property systems are in general not completely self-enforcing. They depend for their definition upon a constellation of legal procedures, both civil and criminal. The course of the law itself cannot be regarded as subject to the price system. The judges and the police may indeed be paid, but the system itself would disappear if on each occasion they were to sell their services and decisions. Thus the definition of property rights based on the price system depends precisely on the lack of universality of private property and the price system.... The price system is not, and perhaps in some basic sense cannot be, universal. To the extent that it is incomplete, it must be supplemented by an implicit or explicit social contract.

The information requirements of, and transactions costs involved in, implicit and explicit contract enforcement are typically different, so that the two types of enforcement are better thought of as complements than substitutes. The problem in the economies in transition was that both enforcement mechanisms were weak: the state's legal and judicial capacities were limited, while the very process of transition—high institutional turnover, high shadow interest rates, and short time horizons—impaired the effectiveness of implicit contracts. Thus even if institutions did not need to be created, the very process of transition impedes the workings of a market economy.

Arrow (1972), Hirschman (1992), Putnam (1993), Fukuyama (1995), and others have argued that the success of a market economy cannot be understood in terms of narrow economic incentives: norms, social institutions, social capital, and trust play critical roles.[9] It is this implicit social contract, necessary to a market society, that cannot be simply legislated, decreed, or installed by a reform government. Some social glue is necessary in any society. One of the most difficult parts of a transformation is the transformation of the old implicit social contract to a new one. If "reformers" simply destroy the old norms and constraints in order to clean the slate without allowing for the time-consuming processes of constructing new norms, the new legislated institutions may well not take hold. In this case, the reforms will be discredited and the "reformers" will blame the victims for not correctly implementing their ill-considered designs.

One variation on this theme is to blame the failure of the shock therapy reforms on corruption and rent seeking at every turn without recognizing the role of the institutional blitzkrieg in destroying but not replacing the old social norms—and thus in removing the last restraints against society-threatening levels of corruption. This is analogous to using a flamethrower to burn off an old coat of housepaint and then lamenting that the new paint could not be applied because the house had burned down.

Because the social and organizational capital needed for the transition cannot be legislated, decreed, or in some other way imposed from above, people need to take an active role in their own transformation.[10] To a large extent, they need to be in the driver's seat, to use the currently fashionable cliché. If they are not, the reform regime is only using bribes and threats to induce outward changes in behavior (insofar as behavior can be monitored)—but that is not transformation.[11]

In market economies, firms may be seen as local nonmarket solutions to collective action problems, where transaction costs inhibit coordination by market contracts (Coase 1937). In the new postsocialist market economies, as in the established market economies, the primary example of extensive (that is, beyond the family) social cooperation in daily life is found in the workplace. Thus entrepreneurial efforts that arise out of existing enterprises may be particularly effective in postsocialist societies in preserving "lumps" of social and organizational capital. Once dissipated, organizational capital is hard to reassemble, particularly in environments with little entrepreneurial experience. Other social organizations that might incubate and support entrepreneurial efforts include unions, schools, clubs, churches, professional associations, veterans associations, mutual aid associations, local township governments, extended family groups, consumer, credit, producer cooperatives, and housing.[12] Creativity and experimentation should be the order of the day to remobilize social resources, particularly in the slow-starting transition economies of the former Soviet Union.[13]

## Postsocialist Separation of Ownership and Control

Given the difficulties in reassembling organizational capital once it has been dissipated or destroyed, it is particularly important to promote entrepreneurial restructuring in existing enterprises. The need for fundamental enterprise restructuring has not been lost on Western advisers, but their advice has sometimes contributed as much to the problem as to the solution.

In retrospect, one of the remarkable features of the body of Western advice given to postsocialist economies, especially with regard to privatization, is the absence of attention to the separation of ownership and control. The intellectual framework often seems to be a curious pre–Berle-Means (1932) world in which private ownership and control of the enterprise are essentially the same thing—as if the small or medium-size closely held corporation were the norm.[14]

Yet the salient feature of the large companies in the Anglo-American economies has been what Berle and Means called the separation of ownership and control. As Keynes (1963, p. 314) noted in 1926:

> One of the most interesting and unnoticed developments of recent decades has been the tendency of big enterprise to socialize itself. A point arrives in the growth of a big institution—particularly a big railroad or big public utility enterprise, but also a big bank or a big insurance company—at which the owners of the capital, i.e., the shareholders, are almost entirely dissociated from the management, with the result that the direct personal interest of the latter in the making of the great profit becomes quite secondary.

The divergence of interests between managers and shareholders in large publicly traded corporations has been a major source of the economics of agency (Ross 1973; Stiglitz 1974, 1985, 1987). Yet despite much discussion of the corporate governance problem, the hard lessons of the separation of ownership and control—and the resulting agency problems—have received insufficient attention in the standard Western prescription provided to the transition economies. Let me give a few examples of fine phrases.

"CLEARLY DEFINED PRIVATE PROPERTY RIGHTS." Instead of trying to control managers in state-owned companies through better incentive contracts, the standard advice is to privatize and let private property rights provide the natural incentives—"like in the West." Yet the separation of ownership and control in large Western companies means that having "clearly defined property rights" does not resolve the problem of incentives. The ownership of shares, like the ownership of bonds, is indeed clearly defined—the shareholder can buy, sell, or hold those rights. But those rights do not add up to real ownership-based control of the company when the shareholders are atomized and dispersed.

One way to express this point is to recognize that the management of a publicly held company with dispersed ownership is a public good—and as in the case of any public good, it will be undersupplied (Stiglitz 1982). Put another way, the market for managers—the process of takeovers—is highly imperfect and does not in general guarantee that the company will be managed by those who will ensure that the assets yield the highest returns.[15]

"CONTROLLING PRIVATE OWNER." When the problems of dispersed shareholding were recognized, the suggested solution was usually to create a controlling private owner in the form of an investment fund. This was the standard form of voucher privatization promoted by the Washington consensus, essentially modeled on the

Czech program. One obvious problem with this solution is that the voucher investment funds had an even greater corporate governance problem than the companies in their portfolio. The funds' shares were held by a broad cross-section of the population. Thus shareholders' influence on fund management was essentially nil. Yet the controlling investment fund idea was sold by the standard Washington consensus as a solution (rather than an exacerbation) of the corporate governance problem.

"NATURAL INCENTIVES OF PRIVATE OWNERSHIP." In economics, as in politics, it is a good idea to follow the money. Who has the economic interests (cash flow rights) normally associated with corporate ownership? The standard theory is that economic interests are attached to share ownership. Shareholders enjoy the economic return to ownership in two ways: by earning dividends on shares they own and by reaping capital gains on shares they sell. But when there is a separation of ownership and control, the controlling agent is partly or almost wholly disconnected from those natural incentives of ownership. The effects of the separation are aggravated when there is pyramiding.

A case in point is the Czech voucher privatization scheme. Voucher investment funds were limited to a maximum stake of 20 percent in a company, and the funds were controlled by fund management companies receiving 2 percent of the asset value under management. The fund management company's economic interest in the portfolio company was thus 0.4 percent (20 percent x 2 percent). If two funds with the same management company each had a 20 percent interest in a company, the management company thus had a 0.8 percent economic interest. Other variations allowed 30 percent maximum holdings and 3 percent fund management fees, giving fund management a 0.9 percent economic interest. These returns are gross to the fund manager. If the fund manager expended any money—say, in devising and implementing a restructuring plan for a portfolio company—those costs would be subtracted to obtain the net return to the fund management company.

Let me ask you: if you had control of an economic asset but could extract only, say, 0.9 percent through a certain channel, would you use that channel, or would you find a more efficient channel for extracting value? At least in retrospect, no one should be surprised that the Czech investment funds found other channels to extract, or tunnel, value out of the portfolio companies.[16] After all, one does not need sophisticated economics to figure out that if the controlling interest must pay more than a 99 percent tax on money taken out one door, there will be a determined search for another door through which to extract the money.

"BETTER MANAGEMENT CONTRACTS." Perhaps, some will argue, the answer lies with better regulations and well-designed incentive contracts for the controlling fund managers. But let us step back and take stock. If a government has the monitoring and enforcement powers to design and implement such policies, why not apply those powers directly, in corporatized state-owned enterprises, and then privatize later, in a better thought-out way?

One of the main reasons for privatization was to use the natural incentives of private ownership instead of the more contrived incentives of management contracts. Yet we have come full circle. We have seen that the rapid privatization schemes promoted by the standard Western advice (voucher privatization with investment funds) did not establish or lead to controlling owners who were motivated to restructure enterprises to enable them to enjoy long-term economic success. Current advice has ended up focusing on better regulations and management contracts to get those in control to act like private owners—something the standard form of privatization failed to do. It is time to rethink that standard type of privatization.

### Reducing Agency Chains: Stakeholder Privatization

A modern market economy is based on highly developed agency relationships. One of the most important ways in which real economies diverge from textbook models is in the problems of asymmetric information, imperfect monitoring, and opportunistic behavior. Accordingly, some of the most important economic institutions arise to alleviate agency problems. These include the legal machinery to enforce shareholder and other stakeholder rights, liquid stock markets and open-end investment funds (which enable investors to vote with their feet), the legal framework of competition policy, the entire monitoring system of accounting and auditing, and the ethos of managerial professionalism. In the more stable and developed market economies long multistage chains of agency relationships have developed. For example, workers are agents for managers, who are agents for shareholders, such as mutual funds, whose shares are held by pension funds, which act as agents for their beneficiaries, which include workers. But in earlier stages of development, market economies had much shorter agency chains.

Agency institutions need to grow incrementally and evolve over decades. If one tries to set up a market economy overnight with such extended and concatenated agency relationships, the superstructure may collapse. That is what has happened in the former Soviet Union. In many cases the elites who have represented broad constituencies have not been able to resist grabbing what they can (Shleifer and Vishny 1998; Wedel 1998). They have betrayed society's trust on a massive scale. Those who would enforce the agency relationships and other legal obligations are too often themselves part of the problem.

For this reason it is time to rethink the elaborate agency chains Western advisers have been trying to install in the former Soviet Union. Think for a moment about why we condemn oligarchs and managers for asset stripping and looting that leads to the demise of an enterprise. One might say that they are within their legal rights as shareholders. Yet we nonetheless condemn them because of the direct impact on the livelihoods of workers and the indirect impact on the economic life of the local community and related parties, such as suppliers and customers. By bringing in the interests of these other parties, we are in effect identifying these other parties as stakeholders in the enterprise. The stakeholders all have implicit contracts signifying long-term relationships with the enterprise. It is these stakeholders who are ultimately harmed as an externality of the agents' betrayal of the extended agency relationships in the transition economies.

If the pyramided agency relationships are not functioning and it will take many years to build the supporting institutions, it may be best to shorten the relationships so that those who are monitoring are the ultimate stakeholders who would be hurt by looting and malfeasance. Instead of A trying to get B to get C to do something for A, A could try to get B to do something for A. The most dramatic and self-enforcing arrangement is the unification of principal and agent so that A is directly helping A. Then corporate governance becomes a more manageable, if not a solved, problem. There is no corporate governance problem with unified principal and agent on the family farm or in small owner-operated businesses. In general, we might reason that the shorter the agency chain, the easier it is to resolve the corporate governance problem.

This strategy of privatization to stakeholders could be seen as a way to generalize the owner-operated business or family farm to medium-size and larger firms (see below on decentralizing large firms).[17] Since stakeholders, by definition, have a long-term relationship with the enterprise, they have broader interests in and another channel through which to exert their corporate governance on management.[18] Because their cooperation is necessary for the firm to function, this hold-up power gives the stakeholders a way to exercise corporate governance as part of their day-to-day business relationships, rather than through external legal machinery. They are not unrelated absentee shareholders who see the enterprise only as a property (perhaps to be quickly harvested) or who are dependent on agency chains and intermediary institutions to exert their influence.[19]

This general strategy would push toward decentralization. The idea is to push decisionmaking responsibility down to the levels at which people can more directly control their agents or at which peer-monitoring can operate—without presupposing the elaborate institutions of monitoring and enforcement, which will take many years to develop. Corruption usually exists at decentralized levels as well, but centralization keeps control too removed from the discontents that can lead to change. As David Lilienthal (1949, pp. 89–90), past Chairman of the Tennessee Valley Authority, put it:

> [C]entralization to avoid unsavory local influences surely deprives the people of the chance to draw their issues locally and to clean up their own local inadequacies. The fundamental solution is to crowd more, not less, responsibility into the community. Only as the consequences of administrative errors become more localized can we expect citizens to know which rabbit to shoot.

This strategy would also entail energizing some of the more subdued segments of the population, such as workers and their unions. If oligarchs or managers are looting an enterprise and destroying people's future jobs, national pride in being long-suffering is misplaced. Those who are being hurt should have the information and the organizational capacity to vigorously protect their interests, not just depend on some reform elite to act in their best interest.[20] The same holds for local governments, suppliers, and customers, all of whom are stakeholders in the enterprise being looted. The cooperation of the stakeholders is necessary for the enterprise to function, and the interests of the stakeholders are harmed when the enterprise is looted. Therefore stakeholder privatization coupled with stakeholder empowerment will tend to reunite the de facto control rights and de jure ownership rights in a self-enforcing system of corporate governance.

## *Restructuring and Bankruptcy*

Since the strategy of shortening agency chains leads in the direction of devolution to ultimate stakeholders, let us step back and look at the role of decentralization in bankruptcy and restructuring—particularly in larger firms. Industrial restructuring to improve competitiveness has proven one of the most difficult and intractable parts of the transition process. Hopes that privatization would lead to restructuring by the market have been widely dashed. Part of the blame, as I have noted, should be assigned to privatization methods that created little incentive for restructuring as opposed to tunneling value out of firms. But part of the blame should also be assigned to the failure to understand the nature of the restructuring process in the context of economies in transition.

One fundamental error is the failure to distinguish between what is required to restructure a single firm within a well-functioning market economy and what is required to restructure an entire economy, or at least the manufacturing sector of an economy. When a single firm is restructured in an economy operating at full employment, firing underemployed workers has beneficial effects, partly because those workers are quickly redeployed to more productive uses. When, however, there is already massive unemployment, firing workers moves them from a situation of underemployment to one of no employment—not necessarily a transfer that leads to an overall increase in the productivity of the economy, though it may improve the balance sheet of a particular firm.

The economies in transition had inherited the results of many bad investment decisions. But the issue facing a country in the short run was not whether it wished it had a different capital stock; there was no magic wand for converting inefficient steel mills into efficient aluminum smelters. The question, given its capital stock, was how best to employ its workers. To be sure, even in the short run some rearrangements in the labor force were desirable—some firms should be hiring workers, some firing workers. This is an ongoing part of the process of any dynamic economy. But it cannot be the case that all firms are overstaffed—except if at the same time new firms can be and are being created to absorb the workers let go.[21]

There was no reason to believe that the financial structure of the firms in the economy at the beginning of the transition process had any inherent merit, because finance under the socialist regime played a completely different role than it does in a market economy. Banks did not screen or monitor borrowers. Thus a high debt-equity ratio—leading a firm to a situation in which it could not meet its obligations—carried no informational value, even about the competence of the chief financial officer.[22]

By the same token, when there is systemic bankruptcy, selling off assets may make little sense: who will buy them? And even when some firm could use the assets more effectively, it may not be able to obtain the funds to purchase the assets if capital market imperfections are severe. The rearrangement of assets in the case of a systemic problem is thus far more difficult than in the case of an isolated weak firm.

Thus financial restructuring was necessary, but a weak financial position had far different implications than in an ongoing market economy. And in the presence of systemic bankruptcy, the prospects of fundamental improvements in the underlying structure of the economy from disposing of assets were far bleaker.

## Restructuring through Decentralization, Reconstitution, and Recombination

One form of restructuring—restructuring to decentralize decisionmaking—was important. But, with few exceptions, such restructuring was not the focus of attention. Indeed, I believe that there is a general model of restructuring that suitably describes successes in a wide variety of contexts: decentralization, reconstitution, and recombination.

Consider a centralized organization—a unit of government, an economic enterprise—that is consistently failing in its tasks. The "iron law of oligarchy" has done its work, so the organization is centralized, ossified, and stagnant (Michels 1962 [1915]). Those who have power in the organization want to maintain its structure to preserve their power and perquisites.

New and complex situations call for many experiments. The need for many parallel experiments to see what works implies decentralization, so that smaller units can operate with some independence.[23] Risk is diversified, since a bad decision by one unit does not necessarily affect other units. Decentralization involves vertically or horizontally disintegrating a large firm into separate semiautonomous teams or profit centers within a federal structure or the splitting of a large firm into more independent business units (such as spinoffs, which could be confederated or partly owned by the mother firm) (Handy 1996). Decentralization can improve accountability and incentives (by linking actions of individuals and smaller units to rewards), and it can harden budget constraints (by eliminating the cross-subsidies common in large organizations).

New managers are needed in the decentralized units. Devolution of power to these units is the hardest part of the process, because it entails central management giving up a good part of its power to the decentralized or spun-off units run by younger middle managers. Yet it is key. Restructuring for a market economy entails a sea change away from the strategy of keeping or conglomerating the largest units possible in order to be more successful in lobbying for subsidies. Instead of the slogan "united we stand, divided we fall," the slogan might be "centralized, we go to the ministry; decentralized, we go to the market."

Pressure for the center to cede power to the decentralized units to begin the process of re-constitution should come before bankruptcy.[24] Ideally, it should come from constituent stakeholders (workers, creditors, and other parties with stable relationships to the enterprise), those who will lose if the organization is not successfully restructured. Their participation and involvement in restructuring decisions will lead to better execution of the restructuring plans (since stakeholders will have more buy-in and ownership of a plan they help devise).

Much of the relevant knowledge is, in fact, decentralized. The well-recognized failures of central planning—related at least in part to the inability of the central planner to gather and disseminate relevant information—can apply with equal force to a large organization. Simply calling the organization a firm does not provide the constituent parts with incentives to transmit information to the center, endow the "firm" with the ability to process that information, provide a clear mechanism for the central headquarters to convey instructions to its constituent parts, or provide incentives for those parts (and the individuals within them) to respond in the desired manner.

Following decentralization, the new units can experiment to probe their environment, test their capabilities, and accumulate local knowledge. Decentralization tightens the connection or loop between experiment and feedback, so the learning process can proceed apace. Benchmarking and world quality standards provide a Hirschmanian pacing mechanism to drive learning.[25] Real decentralization within an enterprise means that units can buy supplies and sell their output outside the firm; they are no longer in effect restricted as monopoly suppliers or buyers within the firm. It also means the new units should bear the costs of their failure, just as they may reap the fruits of their success. These competitive possibilities will expose vulnerabilities within the various units to induce learning and change. Thus decentralization—along with benchmarking and outside competition (like "export promotion" in the international arena)—can be seen as a social learning mechanism to drive the process of recombination and restructuring.[26] Thus the horizontal discussions between units should be seen not simply as best practice forums but as part of the "constitutional" process of rebuilding the organizational relationships from the ground up—a process emphasized by John Stuart Mill, Walter Bagehot, James Bryce, John Dewey, Frank Knight, and Charles Lindblom (1990). This is the process of rebuilding social capital, to which so little attention was paid in the process of transition.

I have so far illustrated the general model of restructuring through decentralization, reconstitution, and recombination by applying it to a large and presumably distressed firm. The model helps explain why successful restructuring is so rare in postsocialist countries (and elsewhere). The center refuses to decentralize power to start the new process of learning and reconstitution, clinging to the hope that some new master restructuring plan (or new technology) will solve the problem. If the government is to foster restructuring in troubled firms, it might find ways to promote restructuring through decentralization, reconstitution, and recombination at least as the last option before bankruptcy proceedings. Where enough constituent units have the leadership (in the form of middle managers) and initiative to strike out on the restructuring path, the government can help devise ways to lift the dead hand of the center so that renewal can go forward.

## Misunderstanding the Reform Process

Early in the decade, there was much discussion about the proper pacing and sequencing of reforms in the transition economies. Political and economic considerations were invoked to justify alternative strategies. I have already referred to some of the debates concerning key economic issues—such as corporate governance—in which the neoclassical model has been found wanting. But traditional economic theory has even less to say about the dynamics of transition than it has to say about equilibrium states—and it was issues of dynamics of transition that were central to the debate over pacing and sequencing.

### Sequencing and Pacing of Reforms

Despite the facile recommendation that everything is important and everything should be done at once, choices are always necessary given the limitations on any government's time, focus, and resources. One theory was to start with the low-hanging fruit (the easy tasks) to build up the momentum of reform before taking on the harder tasks. More generally, it can be concluded that governments will tend to pick the easy pieces first anyway. In any case, this approach was widely used.

Consider the issue of sequencing in the context of privatization. There were three different perspectives. The first recommended that privatization proceed as quickly as possible, without regard at all to how it was done, arguing that it is more important that privatization occur than how it occurs. The second recommended that privatization proceed as soon as a restructured framework for privatization was in place, without waiting for an appropriate legal structure, including a regulatory and competition framework, to be adopted (since government failure is much more important than market failure). The third approach recommended proceeding with full privatization only after an appropriate legal framework was in place.

Underlying the first two approaches was the Coasian idea that the initial private owners did not matter too much, because the market would soon reallocate the assets to the efficient owners. One of the strong arguments for rapid privatization was that it would create powerful political forces that would move forward the broader agenda of economic reform. Given the fear of a reversion to a communist state, one needed not only to lock up what successes one could but also to create a political force in favor of the market economy. Waiting until a legal structure was in place would result in long delays. Privatization, at least in a formal sense, could be done quickly, while it would take years to build up the regulatory framework for competition and the legal system to enforce it. One needed to slip through the window of opportunity in every way one could.

Underlying the third approach was the view that reforms have strong complementarities. Privatization is no great achievement—it can occur whenever one wants (if only by giving away property to one's friends). Creating a private, competitive market economy is a great achievement, but doing so requires an institutional framework, a set of credible and enforced laws and regulations. Politically sensitive privatizations of large firms could be implemented when the needed institutional infrastructure was ready; in the meantime stakeholder-oriented privatization of small and medium-size firms (which have less potential for abuse and require simpler regulatory structures) could go forward apace.

Those who worried about the sequencing and pacing of reforms were also concerned that without the appropriate reform strategy the likelihood of success was limited and that failure of reform could undermine its sustainability. Success, rather than speed, was of the essence. Indeed, failures could be reinforcing: if reforms were not viewed as sustainable, investors would not have an incentive to make the long-term commitments required for growth. Economies could get caught in a low-level equilibrium trap. Successful transition strategies had to have the property of time consistency, including political sustainability.

What have we learned in practice? Some of the most telling lessons relate to the political process itself. One problem with the privatize first theory is that interest groups do not sit still during a reform process. The early reforms, the low-hanging fruit, might create new interest groups that would then add their weight to block later reforms. It is no doubt easier to start the process of privatizing banks by privatizing the early ones to domestic groups, for example. The new domestic private banks would then be able to stabilize themselves before the government allowed foreign competition. The problem is that the private groups owning the first privatized banks will use their political clout to prevent foreign sales or entry.

Many countries adopted a "privatize now, regulate later" policy. Early privatizations into an essentially unregulated environment created a strong vested interest to block later attempts at regulation. (This problem went beyond sequencing to misunderstandings of market economics itself. Instead of seeing private property and competition as the Siamese twins of efficient wealth creation, privatization became a major fetish, while competition policies and other market regulations were seen as afterthoughts.)

Privatization was supposed to tame political intrusion in market processes. In fact, it provided an additional instrument by which special interests, and political powers, could maintain their power. For instance, in a variety of dubious arrangements, political allies of the reformers "bought" assets (sometimes with money borrowed from the government or from banks chartered by the government), with part of the "profits" generated thereby recycled to support the political campaigns of the "reformers."

The Coasian outcome of a quick reallocation of assets to efficient producers failed to materialize in part because there was no genuine secondary market—for the same reasons that there was no real primary market—so that assets were looted more than resold. But there was another problem. Property rights must not only be clarified, they must be clarified in a way that ensures that reform will be sustainable. Suppose several parties have ill-defined claims to pieces of a pie. One strategy would be to assign clear property rights to some party (probably on political grounds) and then let the parties trade. But the other parties would probably reject the assignment and sabotage the solution. This "solution" circumvents the process of discussion and agreement that could achieve buy-in so that the agreed-on property rights might be respected. In a settlement negotiated by the stakeholders, the exact disposition shares would be unclear in advance, but all parties would have an incentive to come to some agreement that could then be sustained, so that business could go forward. When those who received "clear" property rights by fiat or connivance did not view those rights as secure—and could not, since there was little perceived legitimacy to them—it made more sense for them to engage in asset stripping than in wealth creation. And that was precisely what happened.

## The Grabbing Hand of the State, the Velvet Glove of Privatization

One of the theories used to promote privatization independently of a competitive (or well-regulated) environment was the "grabbing hand" theory of the government (Shleifer and Vishny 1998). The state is seen as the primary source of problems, interfering in state firms and preying on private firms. The emphasis is on government failure, not market failure.[27] Privatization of enterprises and depoliticization of economic life are the overarching policy goals. As Shleifer and Vishny (1998, p. 11) note, "The architects of the Russian privatization were aware of the dangers of poor enforcement of property rights. Yet because of the emphasis on politics, the reformers predicted that institutions would follow private property rather than the other way around."[28]

Not only were regulatory and corporate governance institutions supposed to arise on their own, the proponents of this theory thought, it was actually happening in Russia. "Institutions supporting corporate governance, such as the banking sector and capital markets, are also developing rapidly, in part because of the profit opportunities made available by the privatized firms" (Shleifer and Vishny 1998, p. 254).

Banks did develop, but historians may well wonder how the programs implemented by the architects of the Russian privatization could have led to the present system of economic oligarchy and disorganization. The grabbing hand theory sees the state as irredeemably corrupt, while viewing the private sector through rose-colored glasses. Yet the resulting program of transferring assets to the private sector without regulatory safeguards ("depoliticization") has succeeded only in putting the grabbing hand into the velvet glove of privatization. The grabbing hand keeps on grabbing, and there is less hope than ever of public restraint.

The rapid liberalization of capital accounts allowed the "banking" sector to spirit tens of billions of dollars out of Russia each year, while the architects of capital account liberalization negotiated billions of dollars of new international debt. Economic and political forces—incentives—are at play, with far different outcomes than predicted by the proponents of the grabbing hand theory (some of whom are still arguing that 10 years after the beginning of the process, with output plummeting and inequality soaring, we are being too hasty in reaching a judgment).

Why should we be surprised? It is not the first time that strong vested interests have used political processes to maintain and strengthen their economic interests. What is remarkable about this episode is that economists, who should have known better, helped create these interests, believing somehow—despite the long history to the contrary—that Coasian forces would lead to efficient social outcomes.

Clothing the grabbing hand in a velvet glove does not solve the underlying problem of irresponsible power, public or private. That is where a strategy of decentralization comes in, to push power down to the levels at which people can use local institutions (enterprises, associations, local governments) to protect their own interests and marshal their resources to incrementally rebuild functioning institutions on a broader scale.

### *The Modern Debate: Shock Therapy or Incrementalism*

The Washington consensus took what Hirschman (1973) called an ideological, fundamental, root-and-branch approach to reform as opposed to an incremental, remedial, piecemeal, adaptive approach. I have no great quarrel with shock therapy as a measure to quickly reset expectations, say, in an anti-inflation program. The controversy is more about its use to install institutions—an approach that might more aptly be called a blitzkrieg approach. Historically, the blitzkrieg approach to changing institutions is associated with Jacobinism during the French Revolution and (ironically) Bolshevism during the Russian Revolution.

There is a tradition of criticism of the Jacobin-Bolshevik approach to institutional change. Karl Popper's criticism (1962) of utopian social engineering and Friedrich Hayek's (1979) critique of the Jacobinic ambitions of scientism gave this tradition its modern Austrian flavor, but the roots go back at least to Edmund Burke's (1937 [1790]) attack on Jacobinism in the French Revolution. Peter Murrell (1992) has explicitly used that tradition in his critique of the shock therapy approach. A major theme in my work is that informational problems coupled with human fallibility make the world we live in strikingly different from that described by the models of conventional neoclassical economic theory (see Stiglitz 1994 and the references cited there). I have long had misgivings about the shock therapy component of the Washington consensus, at least as applied to institutional change.

The irony of it all is that the modern critique of utopian social engineering was based on the problems with the Bolshevik approach to the transition from capitalism to communism. The shock therapy approach tried to use many of the same principles for the reverse transition. It is almost as if many of the Western advisers thought the Bolsheviks had the wrong textbooks instead of the wrong approach. With the right textbooks in their briefcases, the "market Bolsheviks" would be able to fly into the postsocialist countries and use a peaceful version of Lenin's methods to make the transition back to capitalism.

But we fail to do the issue justice by seeing it only as an intellectual question of overlooking the Austrian or information economics critique of utopian social engineering. One deeper origin of what became known as the shock therapy approach to the transition was the moral fervor and triumphalism left over from the Cold War. Some economic cold warriors appear to have seen themselves on a mission to level the evil institutions of communism and to socially engineer in their place (using the right textbooks this time) the new, pure textbook institutions of a private property market economy. Only a blitzkrieg approach through the brief opening provided by the confusion of transition would allow the changes to be effected before entrenched groups had a chance to organize to protect their old vested interests. This mentality is a reincarnation of the spirit and mindset of Bolshevism and Jacobinism.

For better or worse, and partly because economic theory has so little to say about processes of societal change, much of the great debate about reform has been carried on in metaphorical terms. I summarize the battle of the metaphors in table 1.

Historically, the Chinese were not immune to the Bolshevik mentality, but they seem to have gotten it out of their system in the Great Leap Forward and the Cultural Revolution. They learned the hard way where that mentality would lead. In choosing a path to a market economy, they opted for the path of incremental-

**Table 1. Shock Therapy or Incrementalism: The Battle of the Metaphors**

| | Shock therapy | Incrementalism |
|---|---|---|
| Choosing continuity or discontinuity | Discontinuous break or shock—razing the old social structure in order to build the new. | Continuous change—trying to preserve social capital that cannot be easily reconstructed. |
| Dealing with initial conditions | The first-best socially engineered solution is adopted that is not "distorted" by initial conditions. | Piecemeal changes (continuous improvements) take initial conditions into account. |
| Applying knowledge | Explicit or technical knowledge of end-state blueprint. | Local practical knowledge can be applied only by those who know local conditions. |
| Knowing-not knowing what you are doing | Knowing what you are doing. | Knowing that you don't know what you are doing (Benziger 1996). |
| Crossing the chasm | Leaping the chasm in a single bound (you can't cross a chasm in two steps). | Build a bridge across the chasm. |
| Repairing the ship | Rebuilding the ship in dry dock. The dry dock provides the Archimedian point outside the water, so the ship can be rebuilt without being disturbed by conditions at sea. | Repair the ship at sea (Elster, Offe, and others 1998). There is no dry dock or Archimedian fulcrum for changing social institutions from outside a society. Change always starts with the given historical institutions. |
| Transplanting the tree | All-at-once transplantation in order to seize the benefits and get over the shock as quickly as possible. | Preparing and wrapping the major roots one at a time (*nemawashi*) to prevent shock to the whole system and improve chances of successful transplantation (Morita 1986). |

ism ("crossing the river by groping for stones") and nonideological pragmatism ("the question is not whether the cat is black or white but whether it catches mice") (Lin, Cai, and Li 1996). Chinese policymakers had the wisdom to know that they did not know what they were doing, so they did not jump off a cliff after being assured by experts that they would clear the chasm in just one more great leap forward.[29]

In contrast, the Russians have tended toward a more Jacobinic reform regime, guided by prophets bearing clean textbook models. They learned the hard way to appreciate the old saying "it's not so much what you don't know that can hurt you—but what you know that ain't so."

### *The Comprehensive Development Framework and the Presumption for Participation*

What is the alternative strategy for change? Because social and organizational capital turns out to be fragile—and, like Humpty-Dumpty, hard to put back together again—it is best to start with existing social institutions and try to induce their incremental transformation rather than try to eliminate these institutions and start with a clean slate. As Lilienthal (1944, p. 198) notes:

> An unwillingness to start from where you are ranks as a fallacy of historic proportions.... It is because the lesson of the past seems to be so clear on this score, because the nature of man so definitely confirms it, that there has been this perhaps tiresome repetition throughout this record: the people must be in on the planning; their existing institutions must be made part of it; self-education of the citizenry is more important than specific projects or physical changes.

Why were reformers so unwilling to start from where they were? Perhaps the simplest explanation is that the post-Soviet reformers saw anything that grew organically out of Soviet or Russian reform attempts as still bearing the stigma of communism. They wanted to make a clean break and jump over the abyss to an "advanced model" like that described in Western textbooks.

The Gorbachev-era *perestroika* reforms furnish a good example of incremental institutional reforms. For decades before the collapse of communism in 1989–90, reformers worked in Eastern Europe and the Soviet Union to decentralize power away from the state. Various models of decentralized socialism were promoted, starting in Yugoslavia in the early 1950s. In the late 1980s "destatization" and decentralization spread to the Soviet Union. Some measures of independence and "self-accounting" were extended to state enterprises. New ownership forms, such as cooperatives and collective ownership by work collectives, were legalized. "The Law on Leasing set up a legal basis for gradual evolution of state ownership: work collectives could now lease enterprises from the state and run them as more or less private entities, according to market logic" (Plekhanov 1995, p. 38). These ownership forms were not imposed on managers and workers by the state. They represented the results of experimentation and collective efforts to wrench more control over their lives from the state.[30] By the beginning of 1992, some 10,000 enterprises had become leasehold enterprises (Frydman, Rapaczynski, and others 1993).

Reformers who recognized that real transformation requires participation and involvement would have welcomed this reform momentum and would have helped it push all the way to full privatization. Yet the Western-oriented reformers took the opposite course. In Russia the leasing movement was stopped dead in its tracks in favor of voucher privatization. Throughout the former Soviet Union, official announcements emphasized that voucher privatization was necessary to speed up the process, while unofficial and private admissions called for halting the leasing movement in order to have something left to go into the voucher auctions.

The leasehold firms, like the town and village enterprises in China, were far from perfect by Western standards. Rather than working to improve these ownership forms, prevent abuses, and channel these spontaneous energies, however, reformers in country after country tried to stop the imperfect bottom-up movements in favor of top-down voucher programs based on textbook models of publicly traded joint stock companies. In the voucher model real corporate governance of the firms would reside in the voucher investment funds, sometimes staffed by the political allies of the reformers. In the later loans-for-shares scheme, this theme of privatizing to provide favors for political allies was perfected—even if corporate governance was not.

More research, particularly from the more dispassionate viewpoint of history, is needed to understand the turbulent decade we have just been through. But we can already draw some lessons about the methods inducing institutional change. There are certain areas of macroeconomic management in which government-initiated action should be the norm. At the other extreme, there are vast domains of institutional transformation that cannot be achieved simply by the dictates of a proclamation from the central government. Unfortunately, economic development and transition are a matter of institutional transformation.

## Conclusion

The century coming to a close has been marked by two great economic experiments. The first—the communist experiment that dominated much of the century—is now virtually over. The lessons from that experiment appear clear.

We are in the midst of the second great experiment—the transition from the communist economy to the market economy. That experiment has not proceeded in the way many economists predicted a decade ago. To be sure, the process of transition is far from over. But it has not been an easy decade for most of the countries. Even China, despite its successes, faces difficult challenges.

Russia is a resource-rich country with enormous potential. We know that for societies to function, the state must provide a certain basic level of services and that it takes resources to provide those services. In all societies taxes are collected only because governments enforce tax laws (through the right to seize property in the event of failure to comply). Russia and the other countries in transition must show a resolve to enforce the tax laws in order to provide the basic services of the state. With compliance, government revenue problems will be resolved—and one of the main challenges facing the countries will be effectively addressed. Without compliance, governments need to take control of previously privatized assets as they would in any other advanced industrial country. They would then face the opportunity to address some of the key issues associated with privatization once again. This time, one would hope, those issues would be addressed with a better understanding of the broader principles of the market economy and the reform process. Policymakers—and their advisers—may have learned something from the many bitter and disappointing failures and the few successes of the past decade.

## Notes

1. Gallup and Sachs (1999) emphasize the importance of geography as a determinant of a country's economic prospects.

2. By some accounts this is a slight overstatement of the decline, since some informal sector activity is not included. By other accounts this is a significant understatement of the decline, since market prices, not shadow barter prices, are used to value output. See Gaddy and Ickes (1998) for a discussion of some of these issues. Social indicators (which must be taken with a grain of salt) do not reveal a rosier picture. The eighth round of the Russia Longitudinal Monitoring Survey, conducted in late 1998, showed that the number of people living below the poverty threshold had increased from 36 percent in 1996 to 39 percent in 1998 and the number of children under the age of six living below the poverty line had increased sharply, from 45 percent to a staggering 56 percent.

3. "Grand privatizations are likely to be frustrated by quarrelsome members of parliament, foot-dragging ministries, stubborn local politicians, cautious and/or confused law enforcement authorities, opportunistic managers, entrenched unions, rebellious workers, sullen and resentful citizens, bankrupt companies, illiquid banks, revolving-door governments, and the general chaotic nature of post-socialism, plus an occasional *deus ex machina*.... How robust is a privatization plan against such distortions? If the plan's implementation is distorted, will the plan lose only a small amount of effectiveness, or will the plan dissolve into a mess? This design criterion of robustness-against-chaos is quite important in Eastern Europe, but it is even more crucial in the former USSR" (Ellerman 1993, 25–26).

4. The *Transition* newsletter, sponsored by the World Bank and several other institutions, has been one forum for discussion, debate, and rethinking of the policy prescription. See http://www.worldbank.org/html/prddr/trans/WEB/trans.htm.

5. Yingyi Qian (in this volume) argues forcefully that closed capital accounts in China played a critical role in its success, not only enabling the financial system to provide a major source of income for the government (which it could not have done with full openness) but also limiting the incentives and scope for asset stripping.

6. See Balcerowicz, Gray, and Hoshi (1998) for a discussion of the various exit procedures used in the leading transition economies.

7. There is a long legal tradition that sees courts as evolving gradually and falteringly toward principles of (rough) efficiency, or at least perceived efficiency. From this perspective, one should expect independent courts in an economy with significant underutilization of resources to be sympathetic to "solutions" that provide for the continued utilization of

resources. U.S. Supreme Court Justice William O. Douglas noted that "underlying all of our bankruptcy laws is the philosophy expressed by Henry Clay in 1840: 'I maintain that the public right of the State in all the faculties of its members, moral and physical, is paramount to any supposed rights which appertain to a private creditor'" (1954, p. 289).

8. See Spicer, McDermott, and Kogut (1998) for a discussion of the processes of enterprise creation and destruction in the Czech Republic.

9. One must guard, however, against the fallacy that social institutions that arise to address the market failures from imperfections of information are necessarily welfare enhancing. The conditions under which decentralized social institutions lead to Pareto-efficient allocations (Arnott and Stiglitz 1991) are as restrictive as those under which decentralized economic institutions lead to Pareto efficiency (Greenwald and Stiglitz 1986). For a nontechnical discussion of these points in the context of privatization and the transition, see Stiglitz (1993, 1994); for a more technical treatment, see Sappington and Stiglitz (1987).

10. For recent research on this topic, see Knack and Keefer (1997). For a review of the extensive literature on social capital, see Woolcock (forthcoming).

11. See Wolfensohn (1997, 1998, 1999) on the Comprehensive Development Framework.

12. For examples of local township governments, see the township-village enterprises in China (Weitzman and Xu 1994; Lin, Cai, and Li 1996; see also the article by Qian in this volume).

13. See Blanchard and Kremer (1997) and Gaddy and Ickes (1998) for descriptions of current efforts. It is thus perhaps not an accident that China's successful development was based on township and village enterprises, which make use of the pre-existing social capital of the commune.

14. See Berle and Means (1932) and the huge literature following it, including Roe (1994); Kaufman, Zacharias, and Karson (1995); Edlin and Stiglitz (1995); and Stiglitz (1982, 1985, 1994).

15. For an early discussion of the theory of takeovers, see Stiglitz (1972). Perhaps the most dramatic illustration was provided by Grossman and Hart's (1980) analysis of takeovers: takeovers by value-enhancing management teams would never be successful, since each shareholder has an incentive to retain shares (so as to fully participate in the increased returns); while, if each shareholder believes that others will tender their shares, value reducing, asset stripping takeovers will be successful.

16. See Ellerman (1998) for an institutional analysis and Weiss and Nikitin 1998 for an econometric analysis of this phenomenon.

17. Two examples of stakeholder privatization are the Polish privatization by liquidation (mostly leasing management and employee buyouts) and the Chinese township and village enterprises. That some people object to considering these enterprises as private shows what a surreal fetish privatization has become. Chinese managers and workers are immobilized in these enterprises, so these barriers to exit lead to a logic of commitment, which together with a hard budget constraint yields a de facto private firm (Kagono and Kobayashi 1994). In contrast, Polish firms held by the national investment funds (in effect, parastatal holding companies) are considered private simply because the parastatal holding companies floated their shares on the stock market. What matters is not the semantics, but incentives and behavior.

18. The Japanese view shareholding as symbolic of an underlying business relationship rather than itself the relationship. "A high proportion of the holders of Japanese equity have more to gain from the other business they do with the company whose shares they hold than from profits or capital gains on the shares themselves. They are 'committed' in interest terms because they have a stake in the actual long-term growth of the company" (Dore 1987, p. 113). Thus corporate governance has a natural economic basis. (See Blinder 1995 for a suggestion that the former socialist countries look to Japan and East Asia for ideas.)

19. Perhaps the main stakeholder group comprises the workers and managers in an enterprise. In a perceptive article, Martin Weitzman (1993, p. 267)—unlike the most prominent Western advisers, a scholar of Soviet-style economies—put forth a pragmatic argument for the worker ownership version of stakeholder privatization. "Under worker ownership, the workers themselves, or their agents, will have to control pay and negotiate plant shutdowns. The most acute 'us vs. them' stalemates may be avoided. Ownership is more concentrated relatively close to management decisions and can put more immediate pressure on performance. Regulatory capture may be avoided. Hard budget constraints may be more acceptable. There is less opportunity for financial manipulation."

20. In other words, in large corporations, all stakeholders, not just shareholders, face public good–management problems: individually, stakeholders feel powerless to affect outcomes, and to the extent that they can affect outcomes, most of the benefits accrue to others.

21. To be sure, all firms in a sector can face a financial crisis if the sector has been being subsidized by other sectors or has accumulated liabilities on which interest is due. Such financial crises require financial adjustments.

22. This is doubly so in those cases in which interest rates increased in ways that could not have been anticipated. In contrast, some firms were left with too little debt, so that the inefficiencies arising from excessive managerial discretion were given free rein. The role of debt as an incentive device has been emphasized in much of the literature on corporate governance of the past quarter century (see Jensen and Meckling 1976).

23. See Stiglitz (1994) for an extended discussion of decentralization in various contexts. For a discussion of the related principle of subsidiarity in government, see Begg and others (1993); for a discussion of subsidiarity in a company, see Handy (1996).

24. In the West, the splitting up of a firm often takes place only in the context of bankruptcy (such as the reorganization bankruptcy of Chapter 11 under the U.S. Bankruptcy Code), when much of the organizational capital and many of the key people and market opportunities have already vanished, so that little can, in fact, be saved. Thus most reorganization bankruptcies end up as liquidation bankruptcies. The moral is that when the reorganization has to be enforced in a bankruptcy court, it is probably too late to save much of the business as a going concern.

25. See bootstrapping reforms in Sabel (1995) and experimental decentralization in Sabel and Prokop (1996) for similar approaches. See Hirschman (1958) for the original discussion of low fault-tolerance technologies as mechanisms to induce or pace social learning.

26. For a description of examples, see McDermott (1998) on the Czech Republic, Stark (1996) on Hungary, and Stark and Bruszt (1998) on Eastern Europe generally.

27. Indeed, as Shleifer and Vishny note, the Russian privatization program "deemphasized corporate governance precisely because the intent was to reduce the damage from government failure rather than from market failure" (1998, p. 11). For a related discussion, see Dyck (1999).

28. The failures of the "reformers" was more profound, as the privatization really had no hope of depoliticization—even if the grabbing hand at the federal level had not simply been transformed into the velvet glove of privatization, local political forces were allowed even wider sway by the reforms.

29. Not only did they chart their own course, but many of their policies (and the order in which reforms occurred) differed markedly from the advice the IMF was prescribing elsewhere (with far poorer results). China put new enterprise creation before the restructuring of previously existing enterprises, it put in place a two-tier price system, it still has not liberalized its capital account, and while it promoted exports, it was slow in trade liberalization.

30. To be sure, cooperative equilibrium among local players does not ensure a national Pareto-efficient outcome if externalities extend beyond the players. But surely these externality problems seem far smaller than the free rider corporate governance problems created under the alternative strategy.

# References

Arnott, R., and J. Stiglitz. 1991. "Moral Hazard and Non-Market Institutions: Dysfunctional Crowding Out or Peer Monitoring." *American Economic Review* 81 (1): 179–90.

Arrow, Kenneth. 1972. "Gifts and Exchanges." *Philosophy and Public Affairs* 1 (4): 343–62.

Arrow, Kenneth, and G. Debreu. 1954. "Existence of an Equilibrium for a Competitive Economy." *Econometrica* 22: 265–90.

Åslund, Anders. 1995. *How Russia Became a Market Economy.* Washington: Brookings Institution.

Balcerowicz, Leszek, Cheryl Gray, and Iraj Hoshi, eds. 1998. *Enterprise Exit Processes in Transition Economies.* Budapest: CEU Press.

Baumol, W.J. 1959. *Business Behavior, Value and Growth.* New York: Harcourt Brace.

Begg, David, and others. 1993. *Making Sense of Subsidiarity: How Much Centralization for Europe?* London: Centre for Economic Policy Research.

Benziger, V. 1996. "The Chinese Wisely Realized That They Did Not Know What They Were Doing." *Transition.* 7 (July–August): 6–7.

Berle, A., and G. Means 1932. *The Modern Corporation and Private Property.* New York: MacMillan Company.

Blanchard, Olivier, and Michael Kremer. 1997. "Disorganization." *Quarterly Journal of Economics* 112 (4): 1091–126.

Blinder, Alan S. 1995. "Should the Formerly Socialist Economies Look East or West for a Model?" In Jean-Paul Fitoussi, ed., *Economics in a Changing World: Economic Growth and Capital and Labour Markets.* New York: St. Martin's Press.

Burke, Edmund. 1937 (1790). "Reflections on the French Revolution." In Charles Eliot, ed., *The Harvard Classics: Edmund Burke.* New York: Collier.

Coase, R. H. 1937. "The Nature of the Firm." *Economica* 4 (November): 386–405.

———. 1960. "The Problem of Social Cost." *Journal of Law and Economics* 3: 1–44.

———. 1988. *The Firm, the Market, and the Law.* Chicago, Ill.: University of Chicago Press.

Dore, Ronald. 1987. *Taking Japan Seriously.* Stanford, Cal.: Stanford University Press.

Douglas, William O. 1954. *An Almanac of Liberty.* Garden City: Doubleday.

Dyck, Alexander. 1999. "Privatization and Corporate Governance: Principles, Evidence and Challenges for the Future." World Bank, Washington, D.C.

EBRD (European Bank for Reconstruction and Development). 1998. *Transition Report: Financial Sector in Transition.* London.

Edlin, A., and J. Stiglitz. 1995. "Discouraging Rivals: Managerial Rent-Seeking and Economic Inefficiencies." *American Economic Review* 85 (5): 1301–12.

Ellerman, David. 1993. "Management and Employee Buy-Outs in Central and Eastern Europe: Introduction." In D. Ellerman, ed., *Management and Employee Buy-Outs as a Technique of Privatization.* Ljubljana: Central and Eastern European Privatization Network.

———. 1998. "Voucher Privatization with Investment Funds: An Institutional Analysis." Policy Research Report 1924. World Bank, Washington, D.C.

Elster, J., C. Offe, and others. 1998. *Institutional Design in Post-communist Societies: Rebuilding the Ship at Sea.* Cambridge: Cambridge University Press.

Frydman, R., A. Rapaczynski, and others. 1993. *The Privatization Process in Russia, Ukraine, and the Baltic States.* Budapest: Central European University Press.

Fukuyama, Francis. 1995. *Trust.* New York: Free Press.

Gaddy, C. and B. Ickes. 1998. "Beyond the Bailout: Time to Face Reality About Russia's 'Virtual Economy.'" *Foreign Affairs* 77: 53–67.

Galbraith, Kenneth. 1952. *American Capitalism*. Boston, Mass.: Houghton Mifflin.

Gallup, J. L., and J. Sachs, with A. Mellinger. 1999. "Geography and Economic Development." In Boris Pleskovic and Joseph E. Stiglitz, eds., *Annual World Bank Conference on Development Economics 1998*. Washington, D.C.: World Bank.

Greenwald, B., and J. Stiglitz. 1986. "Externalities in Economies with Imperfect Information and Incomplete Markets." *Quarterly Journal of Economics* 101: 229–64.

Grossman, S. J., and O. Hart. 1980. "Takeover Bids—The Free Rider Problem and the Theory of the Corporation." *Bell Journal of Economics* 11: 42–64.

Handy, Charles. 1996. *Beyond Certainty*. Boston, Mass.: Harvard Business School Press.

Hayek, Friedrich. 1979. *The Counter-Revolution of Science: Studies on the Abuse of Reason*. Indianapolis, Ind.: Liberty Fund.

Hirschman, Albert O. 1958. *The Strategy of Economic Development*. New Haven, Conn.: Yale University Press.

———. 1973. *Journeys Toward Progress*. New York: Norton.

———. 1992. *Rival Views of Market Society*. Cambridge, Mass.: Harvard University Press.

Hoff, K., A. Braverman, and J. Stiglitz, eds. 1993. *The Economics of Rural Organization: Theory, Practice, and Policy*. New York: Oxford University Press.

Jensen, Michael C., and William H. Meckling. 1976. "Theory of the Firm: Managerial Behavior, Agency Costs and Ownership Structure." *Journal of Financial Economics* 3 (4): 305–60.

Kagono, Tadao, and Takao Kobayashi. 1994. "The Provision of Resources and Barriers to Exit." In Kenichi Imai and Ryutaro Komiya, eds., *Business Enterprise in Japan*. Cambridge, Mass.: MIT Press.

Kaufman, A., L. Zacharias, and M. Karson. 1995. *Managers vs. Owners*. New York: Oxford University Press.

Keynes, J. M. 1963 [1926]. *Essays in Persuasion*. New York: Norton.

Knack, Stephen, and Philip Keefer. 1997. "Does Social Capital Have an Economic Payoff? A Cross-Country Investigation." *Quarterly Journal of Economics*: 1251–88.

Lieberman, Ira, and Rogi Veimetra 1996. "The Rush for State Shares in the 'Klondyke' of Wild East Capitalism: Loans-for-Shares Transactions in Russia." *George Washington Journal of International Law and Economics* 29 (3): 737–68.

Lilienthal, David. 1944. *TVA-Democracy on the March*. New York: Harper.

———. 1949. *This I Do Believe: An American Credo*. New York: Harper.

Lin, Justin Yifu, Fang Cai, and Zhou Li 1996. *The China Miracle: Development Strategy and Economic Reform*. Hong Kong: Chinese University Press.

Lindblom, Charles. 1990. *Inquiry and Change*. New Haven, Conn.: Yale University Press.

March, J. G., and H. A. Simon. 1958. *Organizations*. New York: Wiley.

Marris, R. K. 1964. *The Economic Theory of Managerial Capitalism*. New York: Free Press.

Marshall, Alfred. 1897. "The Old Generation of Economists and the New." *Quarterly Journal of Economics* (January): 115–35.

McDermott, Gerald. 1998. "The Communist Aftermath: Industrial Networks and the Politics of Institution Building in the Czech Republic." Ph.D. diss. Massachusetts Institute of Technology, Political Science, Cambridge, Mass.

Michels, Robert. 1962 (1915). *Political Parties: A Sociological Study of the Oligarchical Tendencies of Modern Democracy*. New York: Collier.

Morita, A. 1986. *Made in Japan.* New York: E.P. Dutton.

Murrell, Peter. 1992. "Conservative Political Philosophy and the Strategy of Economic Transition." *Eastern European Politics and Societies* 6 (1): 3–16.

Piore, Michael, and Charles Sabel. 1984. *The Second Industrial Divide.* New York: Basic Books.

Plekhanov, Sergey. 1995. "The Road to Employee Ownership in Russia." In John Logue, Sergey Plekhanov, and John Simmons, eds., *Transforming Russian Enterprises.* Westport, Conn.: Greenwood Press.

Popper, Karl R. 1962. *The Open Society and Its Enemies: The High Tide of Prophecy: Hegel, Marx, and the Aftermath.* New York: Harper and Row.

Putnam, Robert. 1993. *Making Democracy Work.* Princeton, N.J.: Princeton University Press.

Roe, Mark J. 1994. *Strong Managers, Weak Owners: The Political Roots of American Corporate Finance.* Princeton, N.J.: Princeton University Press.

Ross, Stephen. 1973. "The Economic Theory of Agency: The Principal's Problem." *American Economic Review* 63 (May): 134–9.

Sabel, Charles. 1994. "Learning by Monitoring: The Institutions of Economic Development." In Lloyd Rodwin and Donald Schön, eds., *Rethinking the Development Experience: Essays Provoked by the Work of Albert O. Hirschman.* Washington, D.C.: Brookings Institution.

———. 1995. "Bootstrapping Reform: Rebuilding Firms, the Welfare State, and Unions." *Politics & Society* 23 (1): 5–48.

Sabel, Charles, and Jane Prokop. 1996. "Stabilization through Reorganization?: Some Preliminary Implications of Russia's Entry into World Markets in the Age of Discursive Quality Standards." In Roman Frydman, Cheryl Gray, and Andrzej Rapaczynski, eds., *Corporate Governance in Central Europe and Russia.* Budapest: CEU Press.

Sah, R., and J. Stiglitz. 1991. "Quality of Managers in Centralized and Decentralized Economic Systems." *Quarterly Journal of Economics* 106: 289–96.

Sappington, S., and J. Stiglitz. 1987. "Privatization, Information and Incentives." *Journal of Policy Analysis and Management* 6 (4): 567–82.

Shleifer, Andrei, and Robert Vishny. 1998. *The Grabbing Hand: Government Pathologies and Their Cures.* Cambridge, Mass.: Harvard University Press.

Spicer, A., G. McDermott, and B. Kogut. 1998. *Entrepreneurship and Privatization in Central Europe: The Tenuous Balance Between Destruction and Creation.* Working Paper 98-18. University of Pennsylvania, Wharton School, Philadelphia, Penn.

Stark, David. 1996. "Networks of Assets, Chains of Debt: Recombinant Property in Hungary." In Roman Frydman, Cheryl Gray, and Andrzej Rapaczynski, *Corporate Governance in Central Europe and Russia.* Budapest: CEU Press.

Stark, David, and Laszlo Bruszt. 1998. *Post-Socialist Pathways: Transforming Politics and Property in Eastern Europe.* New York: Cambridge University Press.

Stiglitz, Joseph. 1972. "Some Aspects of the Pure Theory of Corporate Finance: Bankruptcies and Take-Overs." *Bell Journal of Economics* 3 (2): 458–82.

———. 1974. "Incentives and Risk Sharing in Sharecropping." *Review of Economic Studies* 41 (April): 219–55.

———. 1982. "Ownership, Control and Efficient Markets: Some Paradoxes in the Theory of Capital Markets." In Kenneth D. Boyer and William G. Shepherd, eds., *Economic Regulation: Essays in Honor of James R. Nelson.* Ann Arbor, Mich.: University of Michigan Press.

———. 1985. "Credit Markets and the Control of Capital." *Journal of Money, Banking, and Credit* 17 (2): 133–52.

———. 1987. "Principal and Agent." In J. Eatwell, M. Milgate, and P. Newman, eds., *The New Palgrave: Allocation, Information, and Markets.* New York: Norton.

———. 1993. "Some Theoretical Aspects of the Privatization: Applications to Eastern Europe." In Mario Baldassarri, Luigi Paganetto, and Edmund S. Phelps, eds., *Privatization Processes in Eastern Europe.* New York: St. Martin's Press.

———. 1994. *Whither Socialism?* Cambridge, Mass.: MIT Press.

———. 1998. "More Instruments and Broader Goals: Moving Toward the Post-Washington Consensus." *WIDER Annual Lectures* 2 (January).

Wedel, Janine. 1998. *Collision and Collusion.* New York: St. Martin's Press.

Weiss, Andrew, and Georgiy Nikitin. 1998. *Performance of Czech Companies by Ownership Structure.* Washington, D.C. World Bank.

Weitzman, Martin. 1993. "How Not to Privatize." In Mario Baldassarri, Luigi Paganetto, and Edmund S. Phelps, eds., *Privatization Processes in Eastern Europe.* New York: St. Martin's Press.

Weitzman, Martin, and Chenggang Xu. 1994. "Chinese Township-Village Enterprises as Vaguely Defined Cooperatives." *Journal of Comparative Economics* 18: 121–45.

Wolfensohn. J. D. 1997. *Annual Meetings Address: The Challenge of Inclusion.* World Bank, September 23, Hong Kong. [www.worldbank.org/html/extdr/am97/jdw_sp/jwsp97e.htm].

———. 1998. The Other Crisis: 1998 Annual Meetings Address. World Bank/International Monetary Fund Annual Meetings, October 6, Washington, D.C. [http://www.worldbank.org/html/extdr/am98/jdw-sp/index.htm].

———. 1999. "A Proposal for a Comprehensive Development Framework." World Bank, Washington, D.C.

Woolcock, Michael. Forthcoming. *Using Social Capital: Getting the Social Relations Right in the Theory and Practice of Economic Development.* Princeton, N.J.: Princeton University Press.

World Bank. 1999. *World Development Indicators.* Washington, D.C.

# Economic Architecture

# Short-Term Capital Flows

*Dani Rodrik and Andrés Velasco*

*This article provides a theoretical and empirical framework for evaluating the effects of short-term capital flows. A simple model of the simultaneous determination of the maturity and cost of external borrowing highlights the role of short-term flows in self-fulfilling crises. The model also specifies the circumstances under which short-term debt is socially excessive. The empirical analysis shows that the ratio of short-term debt to international reserves is a robust predictor of financial crises and that large short-term flows are associated with more severe crises when capital flows reverse. Higher per capita income and ratios of M2 to GDP are associated with shorter-term external debt. And there does not appear to be any relationship between the volume of international trade and levels of short-term debt—suggesting that trade credit plays little or no role in driving short-term capital flows. The policy analysis focuses on how countries can avoid the illiquidity associated with large short-term flows.*

Almost all the countries that suffered financial turmoil in recent years had one thing in common: large ratios of short-term foreign debt to international reserves. In Mexico in 1995, Russia in 1998, and Brazil in 1999 the debt was owed by governments. In Indonesia, the Republic of Korea, and Thailand in 1997 most of the debt was owed by private banks and firms. But in all cases the combination of large short-term liabilities and scarce internationally liquid assets made these countries extremely vulnerable to crises of confidence and reversals of capital flows.

The capital account reversal in East Asia caused a collapse in asset prices and exchange rates. The financial panic fed on itself, causing foreign creditors to call in

---

Dani Rodrik is professor of international political economy at Harvard University, research associate at the National Bureau of Economic Research and research fellow at the Centre for Economic Policy Research. Andrés Velasco is professor of economics at New York University and research associate at the National Bureau of Economic Research. The authors are grateful to Arminio Fraga, who was slated to be a coauthor on this article before other responsibilities arose, for his early contributions. The authors are also grateful to Ken Froot and Carmen Reinhart for useful comments, to Roberto Chang and Aaron Tornell for stimulating conversations, to William Cline for furnishing the data and helping us with its interpretation, and to Vladimir Kliouev and Joanna Veltri for excellent research assistance.

*Annual World Bank Conference on Development Economics 1999*
©2000 The International Bank for Reconstruction and Development / THE WORLD BANK

loans and depositors to withdraw funds from banks—magnifying the illiquidity of domestic financial systems and forcing yet another round of costly asset liquidation and price deflation. In Indonesia, Korea, and Thailand domestic financial institutions (and in Indonesia, nonfinancial firms) came close to defaulting on their external short-term obligations. Korea and Thailand avoided default through emergency reschedulings of liabilities. Indonesia had to halt debt service by its corporations in January 1998—with tremendous output costs.

There is growing consensus that excessive short-term debt was one of the main causes of the recent crises, particularly in East Asia. Different analyses place different weights on different factors, including corruption and cronyism, lack of transparency, misguided investment subsidies and loan guarantees, poor financial regulation, real exchange rate misalignment, large external deficits, and fixed exchange rates that were maintained for too long. But few analysts doubt that large exposure to short-term debt left East Asian countries vulnerable to sudden changes in market sentiment and financial panic (Furman and Stiglitz 1998; Radelet and Sachs 1998; Corsetti, Pesenti, and Roubini 1998a). Indeed, Furman and Stiglitz (1998, p. 51) write: "The ability of this variable, by itself, to predict the crises of 1997, is remarkable."

Yet there is little theoretical and empirical work linking short-term debt, vulnerability, and crisis. This article offers progress on both fronts. On the theoretical front we offer an extremely stylized model of how excessive short-term debt can leave borrowing countries vulnerable to sudden shifts in lender expectations—shifts that can become self-fulfilling. Banks, firms, and governments tend to borrow short-term funds because such funds are "cheaper." But the term structures of interest rates are determined by the riskiness of debt maturities, and these maturities should reflect the possibility of crisis associated with illiquid portfolios.

Thus the role of short-term debt in generating a crisis can only be analyzed in a model that simultaneously determines debt maturity and the term structure of interest rates. Using such a model, we find that the desirable share of short-term debt depends on a host of factors—including the cost of early investment liquidation, the probability that a run on short-term debt will occur if one is possible (something that depends, among other things, on the borrowing country's credit history), and the likelihood and cost of debt defaults. At the same time a number of plausible distortions could lead local borrowers to prefer short-term loans beyond the socially desirable level.

On the empirical front we analyze the causes and consequences of short-term foreign debt. Using data from the Institute of International Finance for 32 emerging markets in 1988–98, we show that the ratio of short-term debt to international reserves is a robust predictor of financial crises. Countries whose short-term liabilities to foreign banks exceed reserves are three times more likely to experience a sudden and massive reversal in capital flows. Greater short-term exposure is also associated with more severe crises when capital flows reverse. And shorter-term maturities of external debt are associated with higher per capita income and ratios of M2 to GDP. There does not appear to be any relationship between the volume of international trade and the level of short-term debt—suggesting that trade credit has played little or no role in driving short-term capital flows during the 1990s.

Thus theory and empirics suggest that policymakers should keep a watchful eye on the composition of debt and on the ratio of short-term liabilities to liquid assets. There is a strong case for discouraging short-term inflows during an upswing in the lending cycle. Controls applied by countries such as Chile, Colombia, and Malaysia changed the maturity composition of foreign loans without—at least in Chile and Colombia—reducing the volume of flows. By lengthening average maturities, countries can reduce their vulnerability to crises. Yet restraining short-term borrowing is no panacea, because in some cases governments and private borrowers may have sound reasons for wanting to take on short-term liabilities.

Our analysis has implications not just for crisis prevention, but also for crisis management. Traditional, current account–driven currency crises typically require a real depreciation and a contraction of demand. Illiquidity-driven crises may call for different solutions. The emphasis should be on preventing the coordination failure that causes lenders to head for the exits. Negotiated debt rollovers and temporary suspensions of payments can benefit all parties. In the parlance of recent policy debates "bailing in" foreign lenders is preferable to bailing them out. Multilateral lenders have a role to play in arranging such coordinated outcomes, while also monitoring borrowers to prevent moral hazard.

## Short-Term Capital Flows in the 1990s

The 1990s were a boom period for international lending. The outstanding debt of emerging market economies roughly doubled between 1988 and 1997, from $1 trillion to $2 trillion.[1] Although medium- and long-term debt grew quickly, short-term debt surged the most during this period.

The debt buildup was concentrated in Latin America and East Asia (figure 1). Latin America experienced rapid growth in external debt until 1994, when the tequila crisis hit. One consequence of that crisis was that Latin America and East Asia began to diverge in their debt profiles. In Latin America short-term debt stabilized at its 1994 level. But in East Asia short-term debt grew even faster. The two regions also differ in terms of short-term lending by commercial banks. Short-term foreign liabilities to commercial banks exploded in East Asia in the 1990s, but they played a much smaller role in Latin America. One reason is that commercial banks had been burned in Latin America in the 1980s.

East Asia stands out as well in the maturity composition of its debt. In 1996 its share of short-term debt in total debt was much larger than any other region's (table 1). The share of short-term debt owed to banks was especially large in East Asia, at nearly twice the level in Latin America (29 percent compared with 15 percent).

But regional averages mask a lot of detail, and not every East Asian country binged on short-term capital inflows. Still, among the five East Asian countries hit hardest by the 1997 crisis—Indonesia, Korea, Malaysia, the Philippines, and Thailand—only Malaysia had a ratio of short-term debt to reserves of less than 1

**Figure 1. Outstanding Debt of Emerging Market Economies by Region, 1988–97**

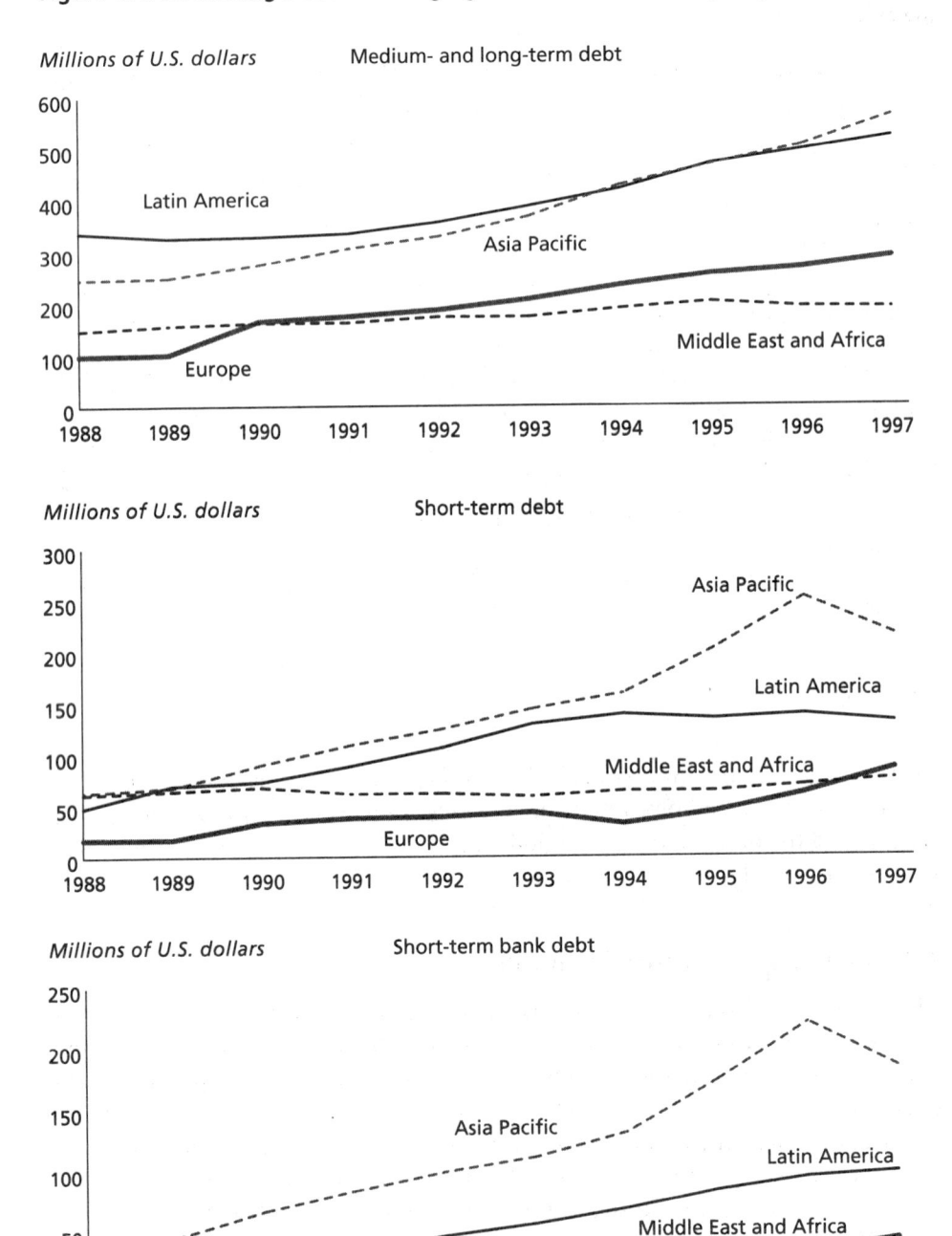

*Source:* IIF 1998.

**Table 1. Maturity Composition of Foreign Debt by Region, 1988–97**
(percent)

| Region/type of debt | 1988 | 1989 | 1990 | 1991 | 1992 | 1993 | 1994 | 1995 | 1996 | 1997 |
|---|---|---|---|---|---|---|---|---|---|---|
| **Asia/Pacific** | | | | | | | | | | |
| Short-term bank debt | 13.6 | 14.8 | 18.7 | 20.3 | 22.0 | 21.8 | 22.4 | 26.0 | 29.2 | 23.8 |
| Other short-term debt | 6.8 | 6.6 | 6.0 | 6.0 | 5.4 | 6.4 | 4.7 | 4.3 | 4.2 | 4.0 |
| Medium- and long-term debt | 79.6 | 78.6 | 75.2 | 73.7 | 72.5 | 71.8 | 72.9 | 69.8 | 66.6 | 72.2 |
| **Latin America** | | | | | | | | | | |
| Short-term bank debt | 9.3 | 8.0 | 8.9 | 8.5 | 10.3 | 11.1 | 12.4 | 13.9 | 15.0 | 15.2 |
| Other short-term debt | 3.1 | 9.6 | 9.4 | 12.5 | 12.7 | 14.0 | 12.4 | 8.3 | 6.9 | 4.9 |
| Medium- and long-term debt | 87.6 | 82.4 | 81.7 | 79.0 | 77.0 | 75.0 | 75.2 | 77.8 | 78.1 | 79.9 |
| **Europe** | | | | | | | | | | |
| Short-term bank debt | 9.7 | 10.0 | 9.4 | 9.9 | 9.5 | 10.3 | 6.4 | 7.9 | 10.0 | 11.9 |
| Other short-term debt | 5.3 | 4.6 | 7.4 | 7.9 | 7.8 | 7.0 | 5.6 | 6.6 | 8.7 | 11.0 |
| Medium- and long-term debt | 85.1 | 85.5 | 83.2 | 82.2 | 82.7 | 82.7 | 88.0 | 85.5 | 81.2 | 77.1 |
| **Africa/Middle East** | | | | | | | | | | |
| Short-term bank debt | 19.0 | 18.9 | 17.7 | 14.7 | 14.4 | 14.0 | 14.8 | 13.4 | 15.7 | 16.1 |
| Other short-term debt | 10.3 | 10.2 | 11.9 | 12.8 | 12.0 | 11.5 | 10.6 | 10.8 | 11.1 | 12.6 |
| Medium- and long-term debt | 70.7 | 70.9 | 70.4 | 72.5 | 73.6 | 74.5 | 74.6 | 75.9 | 73.2 | 71.4 |

Source: IIF 1998.

(figure 2). Indonesia and Korea had built up extremely large short-term debt relative to reserves—with the ratio in Korea exceeding 3 by the end of 1997—which left them vulnerable to self-fulfilling crises of confidence. As discussed below, this ratio is a key measure of potential illiquidity.

## A Simple Model of Short-Term Debt

These data suggest that East Asian borrowers took on too much short-term foreign debt. But what is too much or too little? And how should borrowers determine the maturity profile of their foreign debt? The following model can help answer such questions.[2]

Imagine a small open economy that contains a representative investor-consumer who lives for three periods: 0 (the planning period), 1, and 2. The investor has access to the following fixed-size investment project: investing $k$ units of the single tradable good in period 0 yields $Rk$ units of the good in period 2, where $R > 1$. But the project is illiquid, in the sense that if an amount of size $l \leq k$ is "liquidated" in period 1, it yields only $\rho l$ units, where $\rho < 1$.

To finance the project, the local investor can borrow abroad, where the riskless world interest rate is zero. Foreign lenders are risk neutral and willing to make loans for two maturities: short-term, which last one period, and long-term, which last two

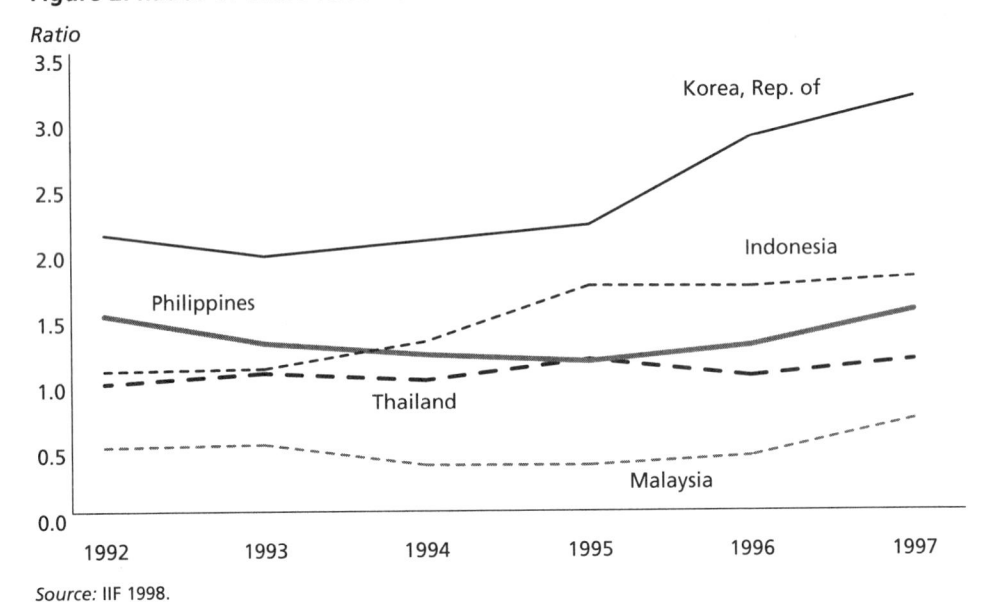

**Figure 2. Ratios of Short-Term Debt to Reserves in East Asia, 1992–97**

*Source:* IIF 1998.

periods. Assume also that all foreign lending must be collateralized by capital holdings: the investor cannot borrow more than $k$ in period 0, and the principal debt cannot be larger than the residual investment (the portion not liquidated) in any subsequent period.

Suppose that in period 0 the investor takes on $d \leq k$ of short-term debt and $k - d$ of long-term debt. When $d > 0$, lenders may choose not to roll over this short-term debt in period 1. If that happens, we say that a "run" on short-term debt has occurred.

Consumption occurs only in period 2. At that point the investor collects the proceeds of the investment, pays whatever portion of the initial loan was not repaid in period 1, and consumes. To keep matters manageable, assume that utility is linear in consumption.

We have described the model as being applicable to private debt only. But plausible interpretations make this a model of public debt as well. Imagine, for instance, that private local investors have limited access to international capital markets and that the government optimally borrows abroad on their behalf and then relends the funds domestically. In that case a run on short-term debt would prompt the government to demand early repayment from domestic borrowers (or, equivalently, to raise taxes)—again causing costly liquidation of local investment projects.

### *The Potential for Self-Fulfilling Debt Runs*

This simple model has all the ingredients needed for multiple equilibria: liquid liabilities, illiquid assets, and hence the potential for a liquidity crunch caused by self-fulfilling expectations. To see that point most simply, take the amount $d$ of short-term debt as exogenous. (We will endogenize it below.) Suppose also that the investor is charged the world real interest rate of zero on both long-term and short-term loans. (This is a rational move for lenders if the possibility of runs is zero or close to it; see below.)

What are the possible outcomes? There is an "optimistic" equilibrium in which lenders roll over loans $d$ in period 1, so that none of the investment needs to be liquidated in that period. In period 2 the investor has income of $Rk$ and debt of $d + (k - d) = k$. The investor repays in full and consumes $(R - 1)k$.

But unless $d$ is very small, that is not the only possible outcome. Suppose that in period 1 lenders call in their loans, anticipating that if they rolled the loans over they would not be repaid in period 2. When and how does this pessimistic expectation turn out to be self-fulfilling? With no rollover the investor has to liquidate $l = d/\rho$ in order to service short-term debt in period 1. This means that in period 2 the investor will only have income of $R(k - d/\rho)$ and debt of $(k - d)$. If the debt quantity is larger—something that requires $d > [(R - 1)/(R - \rho)] \rho k$—then the investor will not have sufficient resources to repay lenders of long-term debt, and lenders of short-term debt will be happy that they got out in period 1. The domestic firm will be bankrupted, leaving behind unpaid debt and no profits.

This second outcome is welfare inferior for all involved. Long-term lenders are not fully repaid. And the investor consumes nothing, in contrast with the positive consumption in the optimistic equilibrium. Hence runs on short-term debt have real effects—effects that can have important welfare consequences.

The physical liquidation cost in the model is simply a metaphor for the many costs related to illiquidity and the associated macroeconomic disarray. Projects can be left unfinished and depreciate quickly. A lack of working capital may paralyze ongoing ventures. And sharp swings in demand and relative prices can bankrupt otherwise viable enterprises overnight. All these weaknesses have been present in recent liquidity crises in emerging markets.

## The Term Structure of Interest Rates

How is $d$ determined? Our initial conjecture was that the relative costs of short- and long-term loans should affect this choice. But contractual interest rates can only deviate from the zero world rate if loans to the investor's country are risky, in that runs and crises happen with positive probability.[3] To keep matters simple, assume that with probability $p$ foreign lenders panic and refuse to roll over outstanding loans in period 1; one can think of this as a generalized panic that becomes self-fulfilling. With probability $1 - p$, on the other hand, lenders remain calm and agree to a rollover (though not necessarily at the same interest rate as before). Assume, finally, that the illiquid technology is sufficiently productive, in that $R(1 - p) > 1$.

How are the two interest rates, the maturity profile of the debt, and the vulnerability of this economy to runs and sudden capital outflows jointly determined? Let $r_S$ be the interest rate on short-term debt and $r_L$ on long-term debt; both depend on the size of $d$.

Suppose first that $d \leq \rho k$ and that $r_S = 0$. If there is a run in period 1, total claims on the investor are $d$ and maximum potential liquid assets are $\rho k$, so there is always enough to service short-term debt in the event of a run. Hence short-term debt carries the world riskless interest rate, and $r_S = 0$. What about the long-term interest rate? If $d$ is very small ($d \leq [(R-1)/(R-\rho)\,\rho k]$), then the investor can fully repay long-term debt obligations in period 2 even if a run occurs in period 1. Then $r_L = 0$ as well. If $d$ is larger $[(R-1)/(R-\rho)\,\rho k] < d \leq \rho k$, then the long-term interest rate is given by the requirement that the expected return on this loan equal the world rate:

$$(1) \qquad (1-p)(1+r_L) + p q_L (1+r_L) = 1$$

where $q$ is the probability of being repaid in the event of a run—a probability that we assume is equal to the ratio of available resources to claims:

$$(2) \qquad q_L = \frac{R\left(k - \dfrac{d}{\rho}\right)}{(1+r_L)(k-d)}.$$

Combining equations 1 and 2 yields the long-term interest rate:

$$(3) \qquad 1 + r_L = \left(\frac{1}{1-p}\right)\left[1 - \frac{pR\left(k - \dfrac{d}{\rho}\right)}{k-d}\right] > 1.$$

Consider now the case of $d > \rho k$. Obviously not all short-term debt can be repaid in the event of a run. Hence $r_S > 0$, and this interest rate is determined by:

$$(4) \qquad (1-p)(1+r_S) + p q_S (1+r_S) = 1.$$

The probability of being repaid in period 1 is now

$$(5) \qquad q_S = \frac{\rho k}{(1+r_S)d}.$$

Combining equations 4 and 5 yields:

$$(6) \qquad 1 + r_S = \left(\frac{1}{1-p}\right)\left[1 - \frac{p\rho k}{d}\right] > 1.$$

In addition, in a run all liquid resources are spent servicing short-term debt to claimants in period 1 (people who hold debt that matures in period 2 get nothing). Hence $1 + r_L = (1 - p)^{-1}$.

Thus we have an endogenous term structure that depends on the maturity of the debt chosen by the investor. If $d > [(R - 1) / (R - \rho)] \rho k$, short-term debt is indeed cheaper (in a contractual sense) than long-term debt: $r_L > r_S$.

Note that the chosen quantity of short-term debt affects both short- and long-term interest rates. This is because large volumes of short-term obligations reduce the probability that holders of long-term claims will be repaid. In a more general model in which borrowers with short and long maturities are different agents engaged in different economic activities, this would mean that the actions of short-term borrowers have an external effect on long-term borrowers. This externality could operate, for instance, through the availability of reserves at the central bank: an increase in short-term foreign debt might shrink the stock of reserves that agents anticipate will be available to service long-term claims, thereby making long-term obligations riskier.

## Choosing Debt Maturity

Does the existence of a yield curve, with long-term debt more expensive, mean that short-term debt will always be chosen? Not necessarily. It depends on how well lenders can distinguish among domestic investors and on the extent to which the representative local investor internalizes the dependence of the term structure on the chosen debt maturity.

Consider first the case in which the investor takes into account this endogeneity, including equations 3 and 6. Then it is easy to show that if $d \leq \rho k$, expected investor consumption is given by $(R - 1) k - p (R - \rho) (d/\rho)$, while if $d > \rho k$, the equivalent expression is $(R - 1) k - p (R - \rho)k$. Expected consumption falls with $d$ for $d \leq \rho k$ and is independent of $d$ for $d > \rho k$. It is maximized at $d = 0$.

Thus an investor who realizes that the contractual interest rates depends on the level of short-term debt chosen will choose to take on no short-term debt, even though $r_S \leq r_L$. The intuition is simple. Lenders have rational expectations and charge a premium to cover possible losses. Thus short-term debt is cheap in the contractual sense but not in the expected value sense. At the same time short-term debt is potentially dangerous because it requires costly liquidation in the event of a run, and runs happen with positive probability.

That is the optimal market outcome. But there are ways for market failure to occur in this context. It is easy to imagine reasons why debt choices by individual borrowers might be distorted, so that private and social incentives do not coincide:[4]

- Individual borrowers fail to take into account the damage to country risk ratings that may result from their higher borrowing.
- Because of information limitations, foreign lenders cannot distinguish among borrowers from the same country, and so consider them all equally risky. Indeed, the "sovereign ceilings" policy followed by rating agencies—under

which no company can have a rating higher than that of the government of its country—suggests that this often occurs.
- Local taxes and regulations may inadvertently stimulate short-term borrowing.
- The expectation of a bailout, rational or not, can encourage reckless behavior.
- Reckless borrowing may make a bailout more likely, thereby having external effects.

To illustrate, consider a case in which the short maturity of foreign debt is due to borrowers' failure to internalize the social effects of reducing their liquidity. Suppose that there are not one but many local investors, each of whom solves the same problem as in the previous section but with one crucial difference: each investor takes both interest rates as given and expects $r_S < r_L$. In that case the expected consumption of the representative investor is $(1 - p) [Rk - (1 + r_L) (k - d) - (1 + r_S)d]$,[5] so that this expectation is increasing in $d$ if $r_S < r_L$. Thus the investor's optimal decision is to set $d = k$. In that case (recall equation 6), in equilibrium $1 + r_S = [(1 - p\rho)/(1 - p)]$, while $1 + r_L = (1 - p)^{-1}$. Hence the expectation $r_S < r_L$ turns out to be rational, and each investor is pleased to have chosen only short-term debt.[6] This outcome is individually, but not socially, optimal.

### Short-Term Debt As a Precommitment Device

The preceding analysis may seem to imply that short-term debt has no useful role. But in fact borrowing short can be socially beneficial: short-term loans may help distribute risk between borrowers and lenders or give lenders more control over borrowers' actions and so reduce the risk of default. The point is not just academic, for if some kinds of short-term debt are socially beneficial, policies that discourage such borrowing may have costs as well as benefits.

Consider a case in which default is possible and short-term debt serves as a kind of precommitment device that ameliorates the default problem. (Jeanne 1998 builds a model with a similar mechanism.) Assume that there are two kinds of governments: orthodox governments that always repay foreign debt and permit private debtors to do the same, regardless of circumstance; and populist governments that may choose to repudiate their debt or impose exchange rate controls that prevent private debtors from repaying their foreign loans. A populist government behaves opportunistically, repaying debt only if it is in its short-term interest (or that of the local borrower) to do so.

To make the story interesting, in the sense that populists do not always cause a default, assume that default is costly. If in period 2 the government defaults on its outstanding loans, a portion $\alpha < R^{-1}$ of the income produced by the project is lost. Default costs may include sanctions, litigation and other transactions costs, and so on. Hence, in the event of a default the investor ends up with $R(k - l)(1 - \alpha)$ units of consumption.

Timing is as follows. Between periods 0 and 1 an orthodox government is always in office. Late in period 1 there is an election. With probability $\pi$ a populist leader wins; with probability $1 - \pi$ an orthodox leader wins. Election results become known before lenders choose whether to roll over their debt at the end of period 1. Then a run occurs with probability $p$ if $d$ is large enough to make a run feasible. But even if a run does not occur, rational lenders may choose not to roll over short-term debt if a populist government has been elected. Crucially, rollover decisions are made once election results are known but before the new government takes office, so that short-term debt will always be repaid to the extent that available resources permit.[7]

The interesting case occurs if a populist government is elected and no generalized run or panic occurs. In that case whether lenders refuse to roll over loans depends on whether they expect the government to cause a default. Government incentives to default depend largely on the maturity structure of debt. In this context short-term debt can have desirable incentive effects.

To see this, consider the options facing a newly elected populist government if no run occurs. If the government can assure lenders that loans will be repaid—say, by depositing project income in an international escrow account—short-term debt will be rolled over, and consumption by the representative local borrower is $Rk - (1 + r_S) d - (1 + r_L) (k - d)$. If the newly elected government cannot (or does not want to) reassure lenders, holders of short-term debts will refuse to roll them over, and some early liquidation of the project will occur. Having nothing to lose, the new government will decree a default on entering office. In that case consumption by the representative local borrower is $R (k - d/\rho) (1 - \alpha)$.

The newly elected government will choose the escrow account option if consumption by the representative borrower is larger in that case. The choice depends on the amount of short-term debt.[8] For the sake of brevity, consider just the polar cases of $d = 0$ and $d = k$. If $d = 0$, then no runs can take place and $r_S = 0$. Will a default occur? With default the representative borrower consumes $Rk (1 - \alpha)$; without it the borrower consumes $(R - 1)k$. Since we have assumed that $\alpha < R^{-1}$, consumption is higher under no payment, and the opportunistic government will prefer a default. With rational expectations $d = 0$ will cause $1 + r_L = (1 - p)^{-1}k$, since after a populist triumph in the elections, holders of long-term debt get nothing. If no short-term debt is chosen in period 0, then expected consumption by the representative borrower is $(R - 1)k - \pi\alpha k$.

If, on the other hand, only short-term debt is chosen and $d = k$ default can never occur in equilibrium: the expectation of a default would cause all debt to be redeemed in period 1, and early liquidation of the entire investment would leave nothing for the borrower to consume. But runs can clearly occur in equilibrium, so that $1 + r_L = (1 - p)^{-1}$ and $r_S$ is given by equation 6 evaluated at $d = k$. With that information it is easy to calculate expected consumption by the representative borrower, which is equal to $(R - 1) k - p (R - \rho)k$.

Comparing the two expressions for expected consumption, we see that having no short-term debt is better ex ante only if the probability of electing a populist government and the cost of the potential associated default are sufficiently small: $\pi\alpha < p (R - \rho)$. The intuition is clear: the positive incentive effect of short-term debt is most useful in countries prone to populist policies. This benefit shows up in lower contractual interest rates, since debt with a sufficiently short maturity reduces the risk of default. In such an environment eliminating all short-term borrowing would be socially harmful.

## *Implications*

The model sketched out in this section has several important implications:
- Runs can occur only when investors take on sufficiently large amounts of short-term debt.
- The larger is the stock of short-term debt, the larger is a run.
- The larger is the stock of short-term debt, the greater are the real consequences—in terms of costly liquidation and reduced output and consumption—of a run.
- Distorted incentives can cause investors to take on short-term debt even when doing so is socially costly. Hence there may be a reason to discourage short maturities through public policy.
- In some cases short-term debt can play a useful role—for instance, by serving as a precommitment device. Hence policies that sharply reduce short-term flows can have costs as well as benefits.

## An Empirical Analysis of Short-Term External Debt

Short-term capital flows involve a wide range of financial transactions: trade credits, commercial bank loans with a maturity of less than one year, and short-term private and public debt (in local and foreign currencies) issued abroad or sold to nonresidents.

Statistical coverage of these transactions and of outstanding stocks is imperfect. The Organisation for Economic Co-operation and Development (OECD), Bank for International Settlements (BIS), World Bank, and International Monetary Fund (IMF) provide data on short-term debt for developing and transition economies, but there are gaps.[9] In what follows we rely on data from the Institute of International Finance (IIF 1998). Most of these data come from national sources and in principle include all forms of supplier credits, nonresident holdings of government bills (including debt issued in local currency), and liabilities to commercial banks and other foreign currency–denominated borrowing.[10] The IIF data distinguish between medium- and long-term debt and short-term debt, and within short-term debt between debt owed to banks and other debt. The main shortcoming of the IIF data is that coverage is limited to 37 emerging market economies. For our purposes, however, this is not a major concern, as these countries constitute the relevant sample for the analysis.

A caveat is that, because comparable data are not available, we do not consider short-term domestic public debt—even though a run on such debt can cause illiquidity and crisis. For the East Asian crisis countries (Indonesia, Korea, Thailand) this is unlikely to be an important omission.[11] But public debt has played a role in other episodes. For example, the Mexican government's inability to roll over its considerable short-term debt (in particular, the infamous Tesobonos) helped trigger the financial crisis in December 1994. More dramatically, Brazil's massive internal debt seems to have been a major cause of the country's current predicament.

## Debt Maturity and Crises

As noted, short-term debt exposure figures prominently among the many causes of the East Asian financial crisis. Yet few studies have established a close empirical link between currency or balance of payments crises and short-term debt. Kaminsky, Lizondo, and Reinhart's (1998) comprehensive survey of the empirical literature uncovers no real evidence that the maturity profile of external debt matters for currency crises. The literature focuses on the level of reserves, the real exchange rate, credit growth, credit to the public sector, and inflation—but not short-term debt.

One reason, noted by Furman and Stiglitz (1998, p. 51), is that few of these studies have focused on the composition of foreign debt. Three exceptions are Sachs, Tornell, and Velasco (1996); Frankel and Rose (1996); and Eichengreen and Rose (1998). The first of these finds weak evidence that the share of short-term capital flows in total flows helps predict which countries suffered from the tequila effect in 1995. The second finds no statistically significant relationship between the share of short-term debt and the incidence of currency crises. And the third concludes that a larger share of short-term debt actually decreases the probability of banking crises.

To our knowledge, Radelet and Sachs (1998) is the only study that presents systematic evidence on the culpability of short-term debt. These authors provide a probit analysis for 19 emerging markets covering 1994–97. Their crisis indicator is a binary variable that takes a value of 1 when a country experiences a sharp shift from capital inflow to capital outflow between year $t - 1$ and year $t$. Radelet and Sachs classify nine such cases: Turkey and the República Bolivariana de Venezuela in 1994, Argentina and Mexico in 1995, and Indonesia, Korea, Malaysia, the Philippines, and Thailand in 1997.

Radelet and Sachs measure short-term debt exposure using the ratio of short-term debt (to foreign banks) to central bank reserves. They find that this ratio is positively and significantly associated with crises (as is the increase in the ratio of private credit to GDP in the previous three years). They find no evidence that crises are associated with corruption. And they find only weak evidence for the role of the current account deficit and, more surprising, no evidence for the role of real exchange rate appreciation.

In the spirit of Radelet and Sachs we present an exercise extending their analysis in two directions. First, we use the IIF database (IIF 1998), and so can distinguish between short-term debt owed to foreign banks and other short-term debt, as well as between short-term and medium- and long-term debt. By contrast, the BIS data on which most recent analyses have relied provide information only on short-term debt owed to foreign banks.[12] Second, the IIF database allows us to expand the scope of the empirical analysis: we cover 1988–98 and 32 emerging market economies, giving us a much larger sample as well as more crises.[13]

In defining a financial crisis, we focus on the proximate cause: a sharp reversal in capital flows. Hence we follow the definition of Radelet and Sachs (1998) rather than that of the earlier literature, which emphasized currency depreciations, reserve reductions, or both. We assume that there is a crisis when net private foreign capital flows ($B_t$) fall by 5 percentage points of GDP or more.[14] Operationally, our crisis variable is a 0–1 variable that takes the value 1 in any year when $B_{t-1} > 0$ and $(B_{t-1} - B_t)/Y_{t-1} > 0.05$. The value of crisis is set to missing for the two years following a year when crisis = 1 (again following Radelet and Sachs).[15]

This exercise yields 16 instances of crises (table 2). The sample includes all but two of the cases identified by Radelet and Sachs as well as many others. The two crises in Radelet and Sachs that do not meet the 5 percentage point threshold are Argentina (in 1995) and Malaysia (in 1997). Note that Malaysia is listed instead as having had a crisis in 1994, when private capital flows dropped by a whopping 20 percent of GDP (following the imposition of capital controls on inflows in January 1994; see below). Additional crisis countries include Bulgaria, Hungary, and the Philippines (1990), Uruguay (1990 and 1993), and Ecuador (1996).

**Table 2. Summary Indicators on Sharp Reversals in Private Capital Flows to Emerging Markets, 1990–98**

| Country | Year | Size of reversal (percentage of GDP) | Short-term bank debt Ratio to reserves | Short-term bank debt Share of total debt (percent) | Other short-term debt Ratio to reserves | Other short-term debt Share of total debt (percent) |
|---|---|---|---|---|---|---|
| Bulgaria | 1990 | 5.99 | 2.95 | 25 | 1.73 | 14 |
| Hungary | 1990 | 9.41 | 1.74 | 11 | 0.29 | 5 |
| Philippines | 1990 | 7.35 | 1.99 | 9 | 0.30 | 6 |
| Uruguay | 1990 | 5.36 | 1.29 | 9 | 0.02 | 1 |
| Uruguay | 1993 | 5.43 | 2.25 | 15 | 0.07 | 3 |
| Malaysia | 1994 | 19.90 | 0.30 | 22 | 0.00 | 0 |
| Turkey | 1994 | 11.05 | 1.70 | 16 | 0.09 | 3 |
| Venezuela, R. B. | 1994 | 5.53 | 0.18 | 4 | 5.91 | 23 |
| Mexico | 1995 | 5.71 | 3.64 | 14 | 0.21 | 15 |
| Ecuador | 1996 | 18.80 | 0.20 | 2 | 1.26 | 12 |
| Hungary | 1996 | 7.19 | 0.17 | 6 | 0.10 | 2 |
| Indonesia | 1997 | 5.02 | 1.41 | 26 | 5.78 | 38 |
| Korea, Rep. of | 1997 | 10.99 | 2.82 | 62 | 0.91 | 6 |
| Philippines | 1997 | 7.08 | 0.95 | 19 | 0.84 | 7 |
| Thailand | 1997 | 10.53 | 0.95 | 36 | 2.92 | 14 |
| Russia | 1998 | — | 1.35 | 11 | 5.04 | 36 |
| Average | | 9.02 | 1.49 | 18 | 1.59 | 12 |
| Average for other cases[a] | | — | 0.76 | 11 | 0.71 | 8 |

— Not available.
a. Other cases are noncrises cases.
*Note:* Debt ratios are lagged one year.
*Source:* IIF 1998 and authors' calculations.

Some of these cases are arguably not crises in the sense of financial collapse and instead seem related to idiosyncratic developments (such as the transition from socialism in Bulgaria and Hungary in 1990). But rather than exercise discretion, which leaves the empirical results open to interpretation, we rigidly follow the 5 percentage point rule. One exception is that we include Russia (1998) in the sample even though we did not have complete data on private capital flows for 1998 at the time of this writing. The results reported below are robust to the exclusion of Russia or of any other country from the sample, as well as to changes in the definition of a crisis. We are fairly confident that our findings on the importance of short-term debt are not an artifact of arbitrary decisions on thresholds, sample coverage, or other methodological choices.

As table 2 shows, countries experiencing sharp reversals in capital flows tend to have large shares of short-term debt in total. But where these countries really stand out is in ratios of short-term debt to reserves—the average ratio is twice that in noncrisis cases (1.49 compared with 0.76 for short-term debt owed to banks, and 1.59 compared with 0.71 for other short-term debt). At the same time there have been crises even when short-term exposure was quite low (as in Ecuador in 1996 and the República Bolivariana de Venezuela in 1994).

The relationship between short-term capital flows and financial crises is examined more systematically in table 3, which presents probit regressions. Columns 1 and 2 are bivariate probits, where crisis is regressed solely on an indicator of short-term debt exposure. The first indicator is a dummy variable that takes a value of 1 whenever the (lagged) ratio of short-term debt (to foreign banks) to reserves exceeds unity. The estimated coefficient is statistically highly significant, indicating that countries for which this ratio is higher than unity have a 10 percentage point higher probability of experiencing a crisis (relative to countries for which the ratio is less than 1). Given that the average probability of crisis in our sample is 0.06, this roughly corresponds to a tripling of the probability of crisis (from 0.06 to 0.16). Column 2 shows that there is also a tight bivariate relationship between crisis and the share of short-term debt in total debt.

In the remaining regressions of table 3, we introduce simultaneously the ratios of three types of debt to reserves (all in continuous form rather than as a dummy): short-term bank debt, other short-term debt, and medium- and long-term debt. Both types of short-term debt enter with positive and statistically significant coefficients (except for other short-term debt in column 9). The point estimates reveal that short-term borrowing from banks has a larger impact. Interestingly, medium- and long-term debt enter with a small, negative, and statistically significant coefficient, indicating that longer-term borrowing is associated with a lower probability of crisis (even when holding the short-term debt stock constant). One interpretation is that the medium- and long-term debt stock is correlated with omitted country attributes that increase creditworthiness and reduce the risk of crisis.

The probit estimates also indicate that the probability of crisis increases with the overall debt burden (as measured by the ratio of debt to GDP), the current account deficit (as a percentage of GDP), and the appreciation of the real exchange rate (as

**Table 3. Probit Estimates of the Determinants of Capital Flow Crises, 1988–98**

| Variable | 1 | 2 | 3 | 4 | 5 | 6 | 7 | 8 | 9 |
|---|---|---|---|---|---|---|---|---|---|
| Dummy for short-term bank debt/reserves > 1 | 0.101 (3.79) | | | | | | | | |
| Short-term bank debt/total debt | | 0.216 (3.02) | | | | | | | |
| Short-term bank debt/reserves | | | 0.052 (3.52) | 0.053 (4.26) | 0.041 (4.20) | 0.041 (3.78) | 0.030 (3.77) | 0.042 (3.89) | 0.033 (3.38) |
| Other short-term debt/reserves | | | 0.014 (1.91) | 0.014 (2.76) | 0.014 (3.80) | 0.012 (2.61) | 0.012 (2.61) | 0.013 (5.43) | 0.000 (–0.04) |
| Medium- and long-term debt/reserves | | | –0.006 (–3.22) | –0.008 (–4.41) | –0.006 (–4.78) | –0.008 (–2.83) | –0.008 (–2.83) | –0.003 (–2.98) | –0.003 (–2.03) |
| Debt/GDP | | | | 0.112 (3.33) | 0.087 (3.18) | 0.105 (2.55) | 0.105 (2.55) | 0.048 (2.04) | 0.078 (2.18) |
| Current account balance/GDP | | | | | –0.475 (–2.67) | –0.543 (–2.74) | –0.543 (–2.74) | –0.357 (–2.77) | –0.396 (–1.87) |
| Real exchange rate appreciation (previous three years) | | | | | | 0.036 (4.84) | | | |
| Budget deficit/GDP | | | | | | | –0.003 (–1.32) | | |
| M2/reserves | | | | | | | | –0.003 (–1.57) | |
| Increase in credit/GDP (previous three years) | | | | | | | | | 0.000 (–0.72) |
| Number of observations | 271 | 271 | 271 | 271 | 271 | 190 | 229 | 255.00 | 98 |
| Pseudo $R^2$ | 0.072 | 0.036 | 0.168 | 0.246 | 0.276 | 0.263 | 0.320 | 0.27 | 0.337 |

*Note:* The dependent variable takes a value of 1 in cases of sharp reversal in capital flows; see the text for an explanation of the dependent variable. Coefficients shown are the changes in the probability of crisis associated with changes in the independent variable (evaluated at the mean). Numbers in parentheses are the z-statistics associated with the underlying coefficient being zero. The regressions were estimated using maximum likelihood and correcting for within-group correlation. All independent variables are lagged one year unless specified otherwise.
*Source:* IFF 1998 and authors' calculations.

measured over the previous three years). These results are consistent with previous empirical work. By contrast, budget deficits, the ratio of M2 to reserves, and increases in the ratio of credit to GDP do not appear to have a statistically significant relationship with crises. Indeed, once the debt ratios are included, all three of these variables enter with the "wrong" sign.

These results remain essentially unchanged when 1997 and 1998 observations are excluded from the sample, restricting attention to reversals in capital flows prior to the East Asian crisis and the Russian meltdown. In particular, ratios of short-term debt to reserves continue to enter with highly significant coefficients. Thus the perils of short-term capital flows do not appear to be of recent vintage. Moreover, substituting BIS data on short-term debt (to commercial banks) for the IIF data yields almost identical results.

In short, these results provide strong support for the idea that potential illiquidity—in particular, the ratio of short-term foreign debt to reserves—is an important precursor of financial crises that are triggered by reversals in capital flows. Our evidence is consistent with the idea that illiquidity makes emerging market economies vulnerable to panic. It bears repeating, however, that such crises remain highly unpredictable. The overall "fit" of the probits is poor and of little use for predictive purposes, even when applied in-sample. For instance, the in-sample predicted probabilities of crisis in 1997 are 0.54 for Korea, 0.24 for Thailand, and 0.19 for Indonesia. The corresponding out-of-sample probabilities are 0.31, 0.17, and 0.13. Empirically, a high ratio of short-term debt to reserves is neither a necessary nor sufficient condition for financial panic.

## Short-Term Debt and the Severity of Crises

As noted, exposure to short-term debt is also likely to affect the severity of the shock once a crisis erupts. When confidence disappears and debt rollovers become difficult, a country's entire stock of short-term foreign debt may have to be paid back within a year. Thus a country whose short-term debt is equal to 15 percent of GDP could, in principle, have to pay 15 percent of GDP to its creditors in a single year.

Generating an external transfer of this magnitude is likely to be quite costly not only to domestic absorption, but also to real activity as a result of a costly liquidity squeeze, the effects on balance sheets of the drop in asset values and the currency depreciation that accompany the crisis, or traditional Keynesian multiplier effects. The costs incurred, conditional on having a crisis, might then be expected to be proportional to the preexisting stock of short-term foreign debt. A range of evidence suggests that this expectation is accurate.

The severity of a crisis seems to be influenced more by the ratio of short-term foreign debt to reserves than by the ratio of debt to GDP. Within-country contagion helps explain why. Imagine that in a crisis all the holders of short-term debt—including M1, the short-term domestic debt of the public sector—come to fear that international reserves will be exhausted by the servicing of short-term foreign debt. Such debt holders will attempt to flee as well and will succeed in doing so as long as there are dollars in the central bank or as long as the capital account remains open. With low reserves the turnaround in capital flows (relative to GDP) can be much higher in a panic.

There is a close relationship between the magnitude of the change in growth (conditional on having experienced a crisis in capital flows as previously defined) and preexisting short-term foreign debt exposure (measured relative to reserves; figure 3). In our sample of 16 crises, growth fell by an average of 4.1 percentage points in the year of crisis (relative to the previous year). But countries with extremely high short-term debt—like Turkey in 1994 and Mexico in 1995—suffered much greater collapses in real economic activity. Within the sample, an increase from 0.5 to 1.5 in the ratio of short-term debt (owed to foreign banks) to reserves is associated with a reduction in growth of 2.3 percentage points (with the associated t-statistic being a highly significant –3.8).

This relationship is partly explained by the greater downward pressure on the exchange rate in highly illiquid economies. A collapse in the exchange rate caused

**Figure 3. Changes in Growth and Ratios of Short-Term Bank Debt to Reserves, Various Countries, 1990–98**

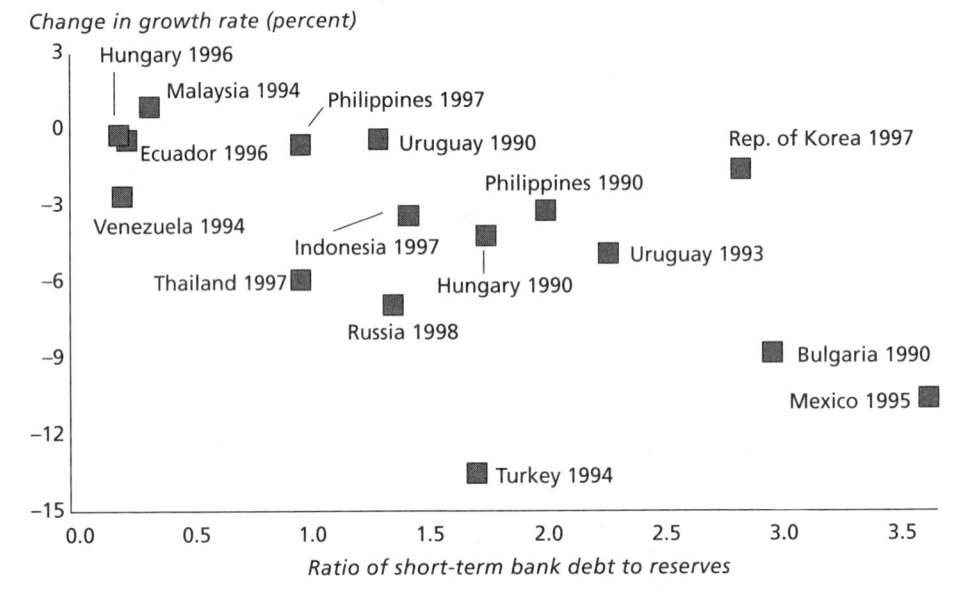

*Change in growth rate (percent)*

[Scatter plot with x-axis "Ratio of short-term bank debt to reserves" ranging from 0.0 to 3.5, and y-axis ranging from -15 to 3. Data points labeled: Hungary 1996, Malaysia 1994, Philippines 1997, Ecuador 1996, Uruguay 1990, Rep. of Korea 1997, Venezuela 1994, Philippines 1990, Indonesia 1997, Thailand 1997, Hungary 1990, Uruguay 1993, Russia 1998, Bulgaria 1990, Mexico 1995, Turkey 1994.]

*Note:* Debt ratios are lagged one bank year. Each observation corresponds to a year of sharp reversal in private capital flows, as defined in table 2.
*Source:* IIF 1998.

by financial panic wreaks havoc on private sector balance sheets and absorption, imparting strong recessionary effects in the short run. In East Asia, for example, there was a close correlation between the amount of short-term debt and the extent of currency depreciation after the Thai peg collapsed in July 1997 (figure 4). During the second half of 1997 currencies plummeted to greater depths in Korea, Indonesia, and Thailand (the countries with the region's highest ratios of short-term debt to reserves) than they did in the Philippines, Malaysia, and Taiwan (China). Korea, Indonesia, and Thailand also suffered greater reductions in economic activity.

As noted, the buildup of short-term debt in East Asia is a recent phenomenon. Thus another way of illustrating the downside of short-term debt exposure under crisis conditions is to compare the recent experience of East Asia with previous balance of payments crisis in the region. For this purpose, table 4 shows the evolution of macroeconomic indicators in Korea during the recent crisis as well as during the crisis of 1980. (Indonesia and Thailand did not experience external crises of a comparable magnitude in the past 20 years and so do not allow a similar comparison.)

The external shocks experienced by Korea in 1979–80, while originating more on the current account than the capital account, were severe by any measure (table 4). These shocks included a hike in oil prices, higher world interest rates, and a global recession that reduced demand for Korean exports. The balance of payments cost of the first two shocks alone totaled 6 percent of GDP (Aghevli and

## Figure 4. Ratios of Short-Term Bank Debt to Reserves and Currency Depreciations in East Asia, 1997

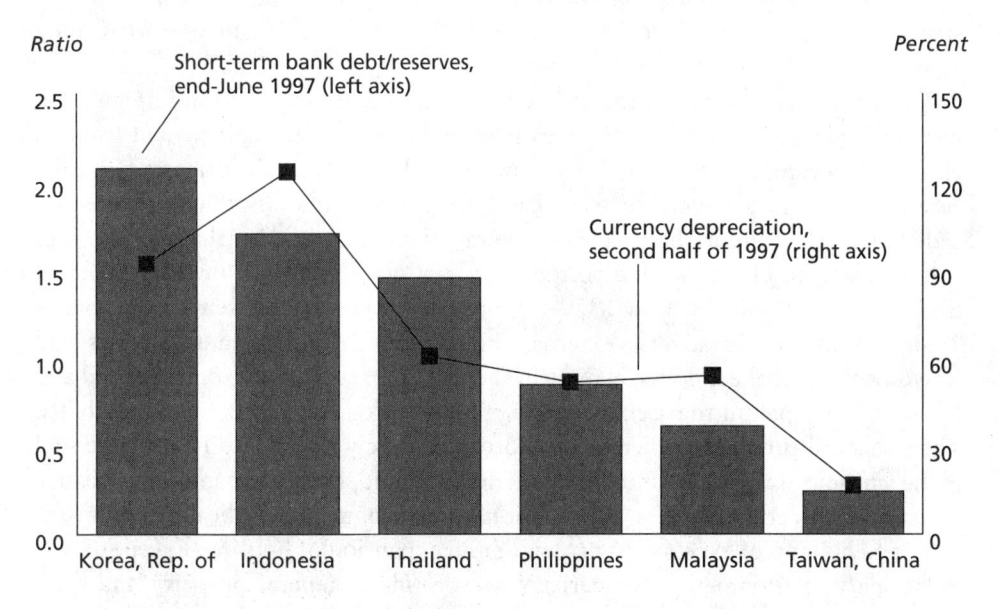

Short-term bank debt/reserves, end-June 1997 (left axis)

Currency depreciation, second half of 1997 (right axis)

Korea, Rep. of; Indonesia; Thailand; Philippines; Malaysia; Taiwan, China

Source: IIF 1998.

## Table 4. Comparison of two crises: Republic of Korea in 1997 and 1980
(percent)

| Variable | \multicolumn{4}{c}{Current crisis} |
|---|---|---|---|---|
| | 1995 | 1996 | 1997 | 1998 |
| Current account deficit/GDP | −1.9 | −4.7 | −1.8 | 13.2 |
| Real GDP growth | 8.9 | 7.1 | 5.5 | −7.0 |
| Depreciation of nominal exchange rate | −1.8 | 9.0 | 100.8 | −29.0 |
| Total debt/GDP | 26.1 | 31.7 | 34.6 | — |
| Short-term debt/GDP | 15.6 | 20.0 | 15.0 | 10.3 |
| Short-term debt/reserves | 217.6 | 284.1 | 325.2 | 59.5 |

| | \multicolumn{4}{c}{Earlier crisis} |
|---|---|---|---|---|
| | 1978 | 1979 | 1980 | 1981 |
| Current account deficit/GDP | −2.2 | −6.4 | −8.5 | −6.6 |
| Real GDP growth | 9.7 | 7.6 | −2.2 | 6.7 |
| Depreciation of nominal exchange rate | 0.0 | 0.0 | 36.3 | 6.2 |
| Total debt/GDP | 28.4 | 31.3 | 43.4 | 46.5 |
| Short-term debt/GDP | 6.3 | 8.4 | 15.0 | 14.7 |
| Short-term debt/reserves | 64.0 | 96.7 | 143.8 | 148.7 |

— Not available.
Source: Authors' calculations from various national sources.

Marquez-Ruarte 1985, p. 5). In addition, the economy faced a large reduction in agricultural output (amounting to a loss of more than 4 percent of GNP) and considerable political turbulence due to the assassination of President Park Chung Hee.

During the second half of the 1970s Korea borrowed heavily from foreign commercial banks to finance an ambitious investment program, implemented through close collaboration between the government and the *chaebol*. In many ways the recent crisis bears considerable resemblance to the 1980 crisis. Both crises were preceded by a debt buildup, limited exchange rate flexibility, some real appreciation of the currency, deceleration of export growth, real wage increases, negative terms of trade shocks (the oil shock in 1979–80, the fall in the price of semiconductors in 1996–97), and other adverse external shocks (world interest rate increases and slowdown of global economic activity in the first case, contagion from Thailand and the slump in Japan in the second)—all against a background of political instability. The structural problems afflicting the Korean economy in the late 1970s were said to be chronic excess demand for bank loans, rapid credit expansion, excessive investment in certain sectors, an inflationary environment, duplication of investment and buildup of excess capacity, and rapid expansion of housing. Except for the inflationary environment (and perhaps substituting a general property and asset price boom for the housing boom), all the other factors have been mentioned in relation to the recent crisis. The current account deficit was 2.2 percent of GDP in 1978 and 6.4 percent in 1979—similar to the deficits of 1.9 percent in 1995 and 4.7 percent in 1996.

But the debt that Korea piled on during the 1970s was mostly medium- and long-term, which sharply limited potential capital flow reversals when the crisis came. On the eve of the stabilization program of January 1980 short-term debt stood at 8 percent of GDP and 97 percent of reserves. By contrast, in late 1997 short-term debt stood at 15 percent of GDP and 325 percent of reserves.

Thus the key difference between the two episodes is that Korea became illiquid in 1997 and vulnerable to creditors' panic. Unable to roll over its short-term debt, the country had to generate a huge current account surplus, at substantial real cost to the economy. In 1980 the Korean economy faced no such difficulty. In fact, Korea was able to run an even larger current account deficit in 1980 than in previous years. It did so by relying heavily on short-term borrowing. The shift toward short-term borrowing was partly due to the hesitation of creditors to commit long-term funds in the face of political and economic uncertainty. Thus during 1980–81 Korea's short-term debt increased considerably and the maturity structure of its debt shortened significantly (see table 4). In 1997 short-term liabilities were an instigator of the crisis and could hardly play the role of savior. Instead Korea had to generate a mammoth current account surplus of 13 percent of GDP (compared with a deficit of 9 percent in 1980). The currency depreciation was commensurately larger, as was the decline in economic growth.

The moral of the Korean comparison is clear. Regardless of fundamentals, large exposure to short-term debt increases the costs of a crisis because it magnifies the current account adjustment and currency depreciation that have to be undertaken.

## Determinants of the Maturity Structure of Debt

Do systematic factors account for the maturity structure of foreign debt across countries and over time within countries? In 1997, for example, 58 percent of Uruguay's foreign debt was short term where 3 percent of Morocco's was short-term debt (IIF 1998).

There are several possible determinants of maturity structures. First, as noted, short-term debt can foster efficient financial intermediation—and, indirectly, investment and growth. For this and other (potentially less benign) reasons, the demand for and supply of maturity transformation services should increase with financial sophistication. As the productivity and financial depth of an economy increase, the ratio of short-term debt should increase as well, other things being equal. Second, at least some short-term capital flows, including supplier credits and other types of credit to importers, are trade related. Thus the volume of short-term debt should increase with the openness of an economy. Third, corruption and cronyism in debtor countries, generating expectations of bailouts, can result in inadequate internalization of the risks of short-term borrowing. Hence we might expect short maturities to be associated with high corruption.

Finally, governments have at their disposal a wide range of financial and regulatory policies that influence the maturity structure of capital flows. Regulatory policies often stimulate short-term capital flows. Basle capital adequacy standards, for example, encourage short-term, cross-border lending to non-OECD economies by attaching lower risk weights to short-term loans than to long-term loans. The Bangkok International Banking Facility, set up by the Thai government in 1993, sought to attract short-term funds from abroad. And the Korean government is often blamed for encouraging short-term inflows by making longer-term investments in Korea (such as equity investment or purchase of government bonds) difficult for foreigners. But policies can also reduce short-term capital inflows. Examples include limits on the short-term foreign liabilities of domestic banks, deposit requirements on capital inflows, and restrictions on the sale of short-term securities to foreigners.

Econometric evidence on the determinants of foreign debt maturities support some but not all of the above hypotheses (table 5). Cross-country and panel regressions (with fixed effects) for the IIF sample of 32 emerging market economies show a consistent and robust relationship between per capita income levels and ratios of M2 to GDP on the one hand and short maturities on the other. This relationship holds across countries and within countries over time. That is, as economies get richer and financial markets deepen, external debt shifts toward short-term liabilities. In addition, the overall debt burden (as measured by the ratio of debt to GDP) is positively correlated with short-term borrowing in the time series (but not in the cross-section). One interpretation is that countries that

**Table 5. Cross-Country and Panel Estimates of the Determinants of the Maturity of External Debt**

|  | Cross-country (1995) |  |  |  | Panel with fixed effects (1988–97) |  |  |
|---|---|---|---|---|---|---|---|
| Variable | 1 | 2 | 3 | 4 | 5 | 6 | 7 |
| Log income per capita | 0.083* | 0.078* | 0.105** | 0.083* | 0.143* | 0.196* | 0.216* |
|  | (3.05) | (2.85) | (2.71) | (2.85) | (2.66) | (3.33) | (3.17) |
| M2/GDP | 0.169** | 0.160** | 0.217** | 0.176** | 0.301* | 0.263* | 0.302* |
|  | (2.45) | (2.22) | (2.70) | (2.43) | (3.28) | (2.84) | (2.73) |
| Debt/GDP |  | −0.042 |  |  |  | 0.131* | 0.177* |
|  |  | (−0.96) |  |  |  | (2.64) | (3.00) |
| Transparency International corruption index |  |  | 0.025 |  |  |  |  |
|  |  |  | (1.20) |  |  |  |  |
| Imports/GDP |  |  |  | −0.053 |  |  | −0.17 |
|  |  |  |  | (−0.47) |  |  | (−1.13) |
| Number of observations | 32 | 32 | 32 | 31 | 296 | 296 | 263 |
| $R^2$ | 0.34 | 0.34 | 0.36 | 0.33 | 0.23 | 0.27 | 0.30 |

\* Significant at the 1 percent level.
\*\* Significant at the 5 percent level.
*Note:* The dependent variable is the ratio of short-term debt to total debt. Numbers in parentheses are t-statistics calculated using robust standard errors. Fixed-effect regressions include fixed effects for both countries and years. R-squares for the fixed effects regressions refer to R-square (within).
*Source:* IIF 1998 and authors' calculations.

go on a borrowing binge are forced to shorten the maturity of their external liabilities in the short run.

We also find a positive but statistically insignificant relationship between short-term borrowing and corruption, using Transparency International's corruption index (column 3).

Surprisingly, we found no relationship between short-term debt and trade. In fact, the estimated coefficient on the ratio of imports to GDP is negative, suggesting that more open economies do less short-term borrowing. This finding is puzzling given the idea that short-term borrowing is partly driven by trade credits, but there is a possible explanation.[16] Suppose that more open economies tend to be more creditworthy (because they have more to lose from defaulting or can provide more collateral to their creditors). They will be less credit-rationed in the market for long-term finance. Hence they will have higher ratios of long-term debt to GDP. Even if such economies also have higher levels of short-term debt, the net effect on the maturity composition of the debt would be ambiguous. The evidence provides partial support for this interpretation. In our sample, more openness (as measured by the ratio of imports to GDP) is associated in a statistically significant way with higher ratios of long-term debt to GDP but not with higher ratios of short-term debt to GDP. The inescapable conclusion is that short-term debt levels are related only weakly, if at all, to trade flows. Whatever drives short-term capital flows, it is not international trade.

The regressions in table 5 do not explain a lot of the variance in the maturity composition of external debt. One reason is that it is difficult to quantify the myriad policies and regulations that directly affect short-term capital flows.[17]

## Policy Implications

Financial markets—domestic and international—are susceptible to herd behavior, panics, contagion, and boom and bust cycles. There have been banking crises in 69 countries since the late 1970s, and 87 currency crises since 1975.[18] Such crises have become much more common in the past 10 years. After the recent meltdowns in Asia, Eastern Europe, and Latin America, no observer can be surprised at the apparent instability of financial markets.

The debate on the causes of these crises will continue for a long time. Bad luck (in the form of shocks from abroad and natural disasters) and bad policy (in the form of poor regulation and imprudent macroeconomic policies) undoubtedly carry some of the blame. But there is more to the story. As this article has made clear, the potential for illiquidity was at the center of recent crises, and short-term debt is a crucial ingredient of illiquidity.

The reaction to the crises—particularly from multilateral lenders but also from Wall Street—has been to call for more prudent monetary and fiscal policies and greater supervision and transparency in local financial markets. Although prudence and transparency are important, macroeconomic policies and financial standards can go only so far in reducing risks.

There is limited agreement on what macroeconomic policies are appropriate in this context. Analysts of the Asian episodes, for instance, seem to be evenly divided between those who think that countries like Indonesia and Thailand held on to fixed exchange rates for too long and those who claim that exchange rate pegs were not defended staunchly enough.

Moreover, the current emphasis on strengthening domestic financial systems glosses over the practical difficulties of doing so. Implementing prudential and regulatory controls to prevent moral hazard and excessive risk-taking in the domestic banking system is a lot easier said than done. Even the most advanced countries fall considerably short of the ideal, as their bank regulators will readily admit. Indeed, banking crises have recently befallen countries as rich as Japan and Sweden. Similarly, the collapse of long-term capital in the summer of 1998 revealed a gaping hole in U.S. financial regulation. If such problems occur in OECD countries, imagine the issues facing bank regulators in Ecuador, India, or Turkey.

The moral of the story is that financial crises are as difficult to avoid as they are to understand. There is no magic fix that will make them go away. Our incomplete understanding of how financial markets work, along with fads and disagreements on what constitutes sound economic policy in developing economies, should make us wary of attempts to impose a one-size-fits-all agenda on borrowing countries (Rodrik 1999). What is needed is a pragmatic and flexible approach that works on several fronts at once—including increasing liquidity and discouraging short-term debt.

## Crisis Prevention

One obvious, if not particularly useful, solution is to require financial systems to always be liquid. But liquidity is costly to maintain, and countries attempting to prevent crises face unpleasant tradeoffs. Chang and Velasco (1999b) and Feldstein (1999) discuss some of the options. On the asset side, using fiscal policy to build a "war chest" or securing contingent credit lines abroad—or doing both in times of trouble—are useful but not without problems. On the liability side, increasing foreign currency reserve requirements for banks' liquid liabilities (perhaps making the size of the requirement an inverse function of maturity) can discourage short-term bank debt. Lengthening the average maturity of public debt, as Mexico did after the 1995 crisis, is also crucial to preventing illiquidity.

In addition, there is a case for instituting across-the-board disincentives to short-term foreign borrowing, as Chile, Colombia, and Malaysia, among many others, have done. The potential role of such disincentives in preventing a possible liquidity crisis should be clear from the earlier theoretical analysis. Critics complain that such controls are ineffective and costly and that they fail to protect an economy from panic by all relevant players. Are these objections valid?

INEFFECTIVENESS. Any claim about the ineffectiveness of capital controls must be tempered by the observation that the most vehement opponents are the very market participants whose actions the controls are supposed to influence. Perhaps bankers and arbitrageurs denounce such taxes and ceilings (which they can presumably avoid with a simple keystroke) out of simple public-mindedness or a deep-seated reluctance to break the law—we have no way of knowing.

Whatever the motive, there is an obvious contradiction between emphasizing the need for better prudential regulation and increased transparency and maintaining that capital controls cannot work because they can easily be evaded through corruption, financial engineering, or other mechanisms. If financial markets can evade capital controls, they can surely also evade prudential regulation. Regulatory ineffectiveness may undercut the argument for capital controls, but it undercuts even more seriously the emphasis on financial standards that pervades the G–7's approach to the international financial architecture.

Moreover, there is growing evidence that controls can be effective in managing short-term inflows—as in Chile and Malaysia.[19] In June 1991 the Chilean authorities imposed a non–interest-bearing reserve requirement of 20 percent on all external credit. Equity investment was exempt. The reserves had to be held at the Central Bank for a minimum of 90 days and a maximum of one year. As an alternative to the reserve requirement medium-term creditors were allowed to make a payment to the Central Bank equivalent to the financial cost of the reserve requirement. In May 1992 the reserve requirement was raised to 30 percent and extended to time deposits in foreign currency and to Chilean stock purchases by foreigners. In addition, the deposit period was lengthened to one year (Agosin and Ffrench-Davis 1998). The authorities eventually began to closely monitor foreign direct investment flows to ensure that short-term flows were not disguised as equity investments. In 1998, faced with capital outflows, Chile relaxed and eventually set the required reserve to zero. While it was in force, the reserve requirement created a severe disincentive for short-term capital inflows. With a London interbank offered rate (LIBOR) of 5 percent, for example, the annualized cost of the policies was 3.9 percent on a one-year loan, but 11.0 percent on a three-month loan (Agosin and Ffrench-Davis 1998, table 3).

Data on Chile's external debt indicate that the policies had the intended effect. In 1991, the year the deposit requirement was imposed, the share of short-term debt in total debt fell sharply (figure 5). The ratio bounced back in 1992, but after the reserve requirement was tightened, it fell steadily through 1997. This informal conclusion is confirmed by more systematic evidence. Valdés-Prieto and Soto (1996); Larrain, Laban, and Chumacero (1997); Budnevich and Le Fort (1997); and Montiel and Reinhart (1997) find that the restrictions affected the maturity composition of flows, though not their overall volume or the course of the real exchange rate.

Malaysia's experience is less well known. In January 1994 the government prohibited nonresidents from buying a wide range of short-term securities (including bankers' acceptances, negotiable instruments of deposit, Bank Negara bills, treasury bills, and other government securities with a maturity of one year or less). These restrictions were widened in February to cover swap transactions in the currency

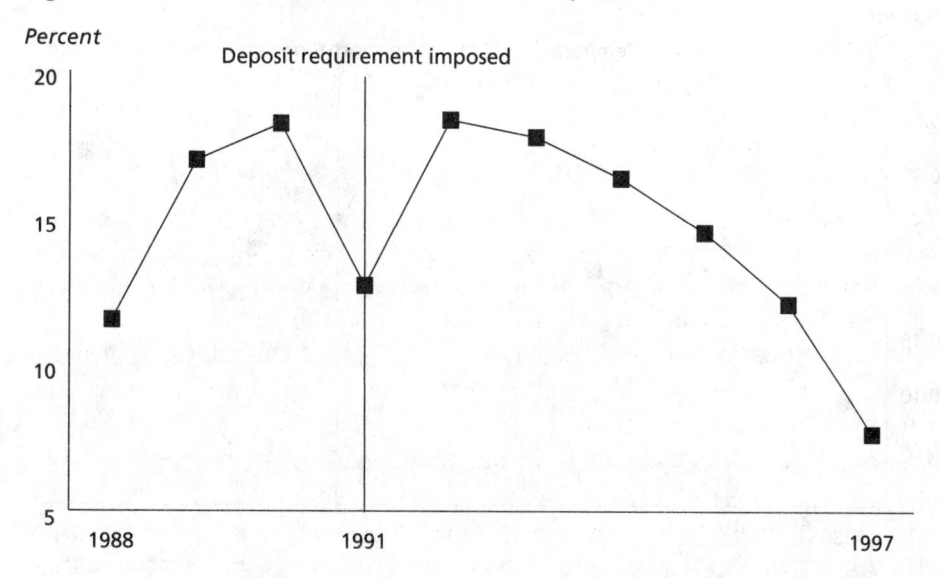

**Figure 5. Short-Term Debt in Total Debt in Chile, 1988–97**

Source: IIF 1998 and authors' caluculations.

market and complemented by an interest charge on short-term deposits placed in domestic commercial banks by foreigners. The restrictions began to be lifted in August 1994 and were largely eliminated by the end of the year.

These restrictions were motivated by a huge surge of short-term speculative capital inflows in late 1993 following a surprise 6 percent depreciation of the ringgit. The Malaysian market was flooded by hedge funds and others expecting a quick recovery in the currency. The result was a sharp increase in short-term liabilities, which peaked at 37 percent of total debt at the end of 1993 (figure 6). But the restrictions imposed in early 1994 were remarkably effective. (So effective, in fact, that the colossal turnaround in short-term capital flows in 1994 led us above to classify Malaysia in 1994 as a case of crisis.) The share of short-term debt in total dropped to 26 percent in 1994 and to 23 percent in 1995, recovering only in 1996. The overall debt burden fell as well, from 59 percent of GDP in 1993 to 41 percent in 1995.

These policies did not, however, prevent Malaysia from getting into serious trouble a few years later. One possible explanation is that the controls were lifted too soon. The ratio of short-term debt to reserves rose between 1995 and 1997 (see figure 2), and the same happened to the share of short-term debt in total debt (see figure 6).

Chile and Malaysia illustrate the importance of policy in influencing the maturity structure of foreign debt. But policy is not all-powerful. One constraint comes from the growing role of derivatives in international capital flows. As Garber (1998) emphasizes, derivatives can help circumvent controls and make it difficult to interpret standard balance of payments categories. But it is not clear that derivatives can always undo the

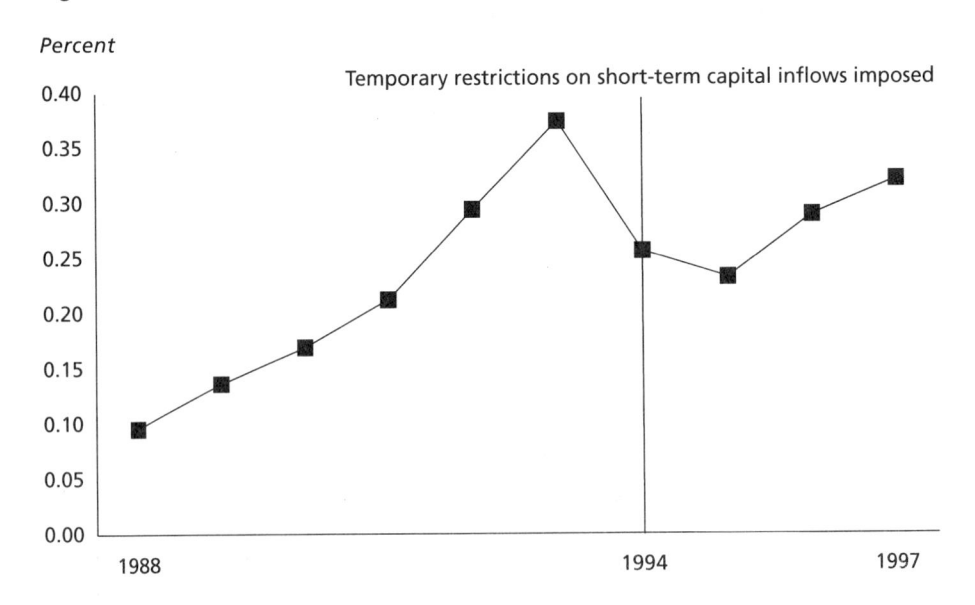

**Figure 6. Short-Term Debt in Total Debt in Malaysia, 1988–97**

*Source:* IIF 1998 and authors' caluculations.

intended effects of policy. As Garber, p. 20, writes: "Market sources ... report serious, though as yet unsuccessful, financial engineering research efforts to crack directly the Chilean tax on capital imports in the form of an uncompensated deposit requirement."

COSTLINESS. What about the costs of capital controls? In theory controls prevent risk-spreading through the global diversification of portfolios. They result in an inefficient global allocation of capital. And they encourage irresponsible macroeconomic policies at home. Is there evidence to support such presumptions?

One of us has examined this issue systematically (Rodrik 1998), relating capital account liberalization to three indicators of economic performance: per capita GDP growth, investment (as a share of GDP), and inflation. The indicator of capital account liberalization used was the portion of years for which the capital account was free of restrictions (according to IMF classifications). The study, which covered about 100 countries after 1975, found no evidence that countries without capital controls have grown faster, invested more, or experienced lower inflation.[20]

Furthermore, specific episodes of capital controls do not reveal significant real costs. Chile has had one of the most successful developing economies of the 1990s, in no small part because it has avoided the destabilizing influence of short-term capital flows. Even in Malaysia, where restrictions imposed in January 1994 caused a massive turnaround in capital flows, growth was unaffected. (In fact, the Malaysian economy grew faster in 1994–95 than in 1993.)

OTHER CLAIMANTS. The other important caveat is that foreigners are not the only short-term creditors. Hence imposing controls and reducing short-term foreign debt is neither necessary nor sufficient for ruling out crises. As Krugman (1999) emphasizes, inflow controls still leave all domestic holders of claims on commercial and central banks ready to run. There is an important distinction, however, between this type of capital flight and a reversal in short-term external flows. Under IMF rules governments are allowed to close the foreign exchange window to prevent capital outflows by domestic residents. Hence a run on a country's domestic short-term liabilities can in principle be prevented by legal means. Refusing to pay back short-term foreign debt, by contrast, would abrogate debt contracts and put the country into default. In any case we view this not as an argument against capital controls but rather as a plea to complement them with other policies. Bank regulation and the exchange rate regime are central in this regard (see Chang and Velasco 1999b and Feldstein 1999).

## Crisis Management

The presence of short-term debt makes possible a coordination failure among lenders. Hence a main task of crisis management is to attempt to coordinate lenders' behavior on the "good" outcome. In the model described above, the key is to avoid the real costs (liquidation and others) imposed by early repayment. Thus a simple suspension of payments that preserves the present value of creditors' claims makes everyone better off.

In practice, of course, lenders are wary of such a response. From New York or London it is hard to distinguish payments moratoriums that are justified by liquidity considerations from those that are thinly veiled attempts at default. When in doubt lenders are likely to suspect a default. There is also the logistical problem of coordinating the actions of many bondholders.

But the difficulty of the task should not keep policymakers from attempting it. Payments reprogrammings that are accompanied by serious macroeconomic adjustments and signals of creditworthiness (such as fiscal retrenchment) may prove more palatable. In Korea, for instance, U.S., European, and Japanese banks agreed in December 1997 to an orderly rollover of short-term loans. Major creditor countries helped by anticipating the disbursement of a portion of the bailout package the IMF had just approved. These two measures effectively ended the financial panic that had gripped Korea for several months.[21]

Multilateral lenders can also help. Just as after appropriate surveillance and conditionality they place their seal of approval on countries that follow sound macroeconomic policies, international financial institutions could publicly endorse temporary payments suspensions or reschedulings where these are justified. Such endorsements could overcome the perception of illegitimacy that surrounds changes in debt repayment terms, however justified. Multilateral lenders could also lend "into arrears" to boost confidence in a borrower's prospects. Finally, they could encourage the adoption of clauses in international bond covenants that facilitate negotiations between debtors and creditors even when debt service is suspended. Such proposals were endorsed by the G–10 in 1995 but have yet to be fully implemented (Kenen 1999).

Encouraging other kinds of capital flows may also be useful in times of trouble. In the model above much of the problem comes from the local investor's inability to sell rather than liquidate illiquid assets in the event of a squeeze. That assumption is realistic insofar as, during a crisis, there are few domestic agents with the cash in hand to buy the real capital. But foreigners are in a different position. In principle, everyone would be better off if liquidation could be avoided through foreign direct investment—even if the price is that of a fire sale, below the present value of capital's real yield in the future.[22] Thus foreign direct investment could be encouraged for such purposes. Debt-equity swaps involving foreign creditors played an important role in the resolution of the 1980s debt crisis and could be useful again in the current context as part of a broader strategy that includes the elements discussed above. At the same time a series of financial crises that become the occasion for the sale of national assets to foreigners at bargain-basement prices is unlikely to do much for the reputation of the international financial system.

## Notes

1. This group covers 11 countries in the Middle East and North Africa, 10 in Latin America, 8 in Asia, and 8 in Europe. Unless otherwise noted, all debt statistics in this article come from IIF (1998).

2. Chang and Velasco (1998, 1999a, b) also discuss the role of debt maturity in generating self-fulfilling crises. Obstfeld (1994), Calvo (1995), and Cole and Kehoe (1996) focus on short-term government debt, but without endogenizing the choice of maturity.

3. Here loans can be risky even if the principal of the initial loan is fully collateralized. There are two reasons. First, liquidating domestic capital is costly, so the resources available in period 1 are less than the $k$ initially borrowed. Second, the local investor must pay interest, not just principal.

4. For a list and discussion, see Furman and Stiglitz (1998). Some of the points that follow are theirs.

5. Note that this expectation includes only the consumption level if there is no run, because in the event of a run consumption is zero: all resources go to paying foreign creditors.

6. There is a second possible, though implausible, equilibrium. Suppose that the investor expects $r_S = r_L$, so that expected consumption is independent of $d$. Suppose also (implausibly) that, since $d$ is not determined, the investor sets $d = 0$. Then the expectation $r_S = r_L$ turns out to have been correct, and we have an equilibrium with no short-term debt. The problem, of course, is that the investor is unlikely to set $d = 0$. If the investor randomized, for instance, across all possible $d \in [0,k]$, the probability associated with hitting zero exactly would also be zero.

7. This is a realistic assumption. There is often a bunching of amortizations in the window between elections and the corresponding transfer of power.

8. To evaluate which consumption level is higher, one must pin down the value of the relevant interest rates. These rates, in turn, depend on the size of $d$. One could readily calculate, as we did in an earlier section, $r_S$, $r_L$, and expected borrower consumption for each $d$, and then use the results to identify the socially optimal level of short-term debt.

9. These organizations recently pooled their resources to provide a unified set of quarterly statistics on external debt The data are available at *http://www.oecd.org/dac/debt/*. The short-term debt stocks reported by these agencies cover liabilities to nonresident banks, official or officially guaranteed trade credits, and debt securities (money market instruments, bonds, and notes) issued abroad. The data are compiled largely from creditor and market sources. Coverage is poor or nonexistent for non–officially guaranteed supplier credits not channeled through banks, private placements of debt securities, domestically issued debt held by nonresidents, and deposits of nonresidents in domestic institutions.

10. We are grateful to William Cline of the IIF for making the data available, as well as for clarifications on sources and coverage.

11. Except for Brazil, public debt has also not been a major problem recently for comparable Latin American countries. Mexico managed to extend the maturity of its public debt after the 1994 collapse. In September 1994 short-term domestic federal debt was equivalent to $26.1 billion; by June 1997 it was less than $8.5 billion. Argentina, Chile, and Peru have not issued domestic short-term debt in any substantial magnitude.

12. There is a high correlation—typically on the order of 0.9—between the data on short-term debt to commercial banks provided by the two sources.

13. The IIF database also includes five oil-exporting countries, which we have excluded from the analysis.

14. Private capital flows are loans from commercial banks and other private credit, excluding equity investments.

15. In addition, we have excluded from the sample a few data points with extremely high ratios of short-term debt to reserves (greater than 5). Russia (in 1991) and Côte d'Ivoire (in 1992), for example, had ratios of short-term debt (to banks) to reserves of 312 and 217. Retaining such observations would result in outliers in the probit analysis that would cloud the interpretation of the results.

16. We thank Aaron Tornell for suggesting this possibility.

17. See Montiel and Reinhart (1997) for an effort to do so. Focusing on different types of capital flows in 15 countries, the authors find that capital controls tend to reduce the share of short-term flows, while sterilized intervention increases it.

18. The number of banking crises comes from Caprio and Klingebiel (1996). A banking crisis occurs, in their definition, when the banking system has zero or negative net worth. The figure excludes transition economies which, by their estimate, would add at least 20 crises to this period. The number of currency crises comes from Frankel and Rose (1996), who define such a crisis as a year when the currency depreciates by more than 25 percent, and this depreciation is at least 10 percentage points larger than the previous year's.

19. For studies on Chile, see Valdés-Prieto and Soto (1996); Larrain, Laban, and Chumacero (1997); Budnevich and Le Fort (1997); Agosin and Ffrench-Davis (1998); and Edwards (1998).

20. Policy choices on the capital account are endogenous, so there is a potential for reverse causation. But to the extent that this is a problem, it biases the results in the direction of finding a positive relationship between open capital accounts and good performance: countries are more likely to remove capital controls when their economies are doing well.

21. This description follows Corsetti, Pesenti, and Roubini (1998b). The authors also note that loan rescheduling was much more daunting in Indonesia, where there were many lenders and borrowers.

22. In the model above, because the world interest rate is zero and one unit of healthy capital yields $R$ units of the tradable good in period 2, the "fundamental" price of capital in period 1 is $R$. But any price smaller than $R$ and bigger than $\rho$ makes the borrower better off (relative to liquidation), while giving the foreign investor an abnormally high rate of return.

## References

Aghevli, Bijan, and Jorge Marquez-Ruarte. 1985. "A Case of Successful Adjustment: Korea's Experience during 1980–84." Occasional Paper 39. International Monetary Fund, Washington, D.C.

Agosin, Manuel R., and Ricardo Ffrench-Davis. 1998. "Managing Capital Inflows in Chile." Revised draft of paper prepared for UNU/WIDER (United Nations University/World Institute for Development Economics Research) project on Short-Term Capital Movements and Balance of Payments Crises, May 1–2 1997, Sussex.

Budnevich, Carlos, and Guillermo Le Fort. 1997. "Capital Account Regulations and Macroeconomic Policy: Two Latin American Experiences." Working Paper 6. Central Bank of Chile, Santiago.

Calvo, Guillermo. 1995. "Varieties of Capital Market Crises." Working Paper 15. University of Maryland, Center for International Economics.

Caprio, Gerard, and Daniela Klingebiel. 1996. "Bank Insolvency: Bad Luck, Bad Policy, or Bad Banking?" In Michael Bruno and Boris Pleskovic, eds., *Annual Bank Conference on Development Economics 1996*. Washington, D.C.: World Bank.

Cárdenas, Mauricio, and Felipe Barrera 1997. "On the Effectiveness of Capital Controls: The Experience of Colombia during the 1990s." *Journal of Development Economics* 54 (1): 27–57.

Chang, Roberto, and Andrés Velasco. 1998. "Financial Crises in Emerging Markets: A Canonical Model." NBER Working Paper 6606. National Bureau of Economic Research, Cambridge, Mass.

———. 1999a. "Banks, Debt Maturity, and Financial Crises." Federal Reserve Bank of Atlanta and New York University.

———. 1999b. "Illiquidity and Crises in Emerging Markets: Theory and Policy." Paper prepared for the 1999 National Bureau of Economic Research Macroeconomics Annual, April, Cambridge, Mass.

Cole, Harold L., and Timothy J. Kehoe. 1996. "A Self-Fulfilling Model of Mexico's 1994–1995 Debt Crisis." *Journal of International Economics* 41 (3–4): 309–30.

Corsetti, Giancarlo, Paolo Pesenti, and Nouriel Roubini. 1998a. "What Caused the Asian Currency and Financial Crisis? Part I: A Macroeconomic Overview." NBER Working Paper 6833. National Bureau of Economic Research, Cambridge, Mass.

———. 1998b. "What Caused the Asian Currency and Financial Crisis? Part II: The Policy Debate." NBER Working Paper 6834. National Bureau of Economic Research, Cambridge, Mass.

Edwards, Sebastian. 1998. "Capital Flows, Real Exchange Rates and Capital Controls: Some Latin American Experiences." NBER Working Paper 6800. National Bureau of Economic Research, Cambridge, Mass.

Eichengreen, Barry, and Andrew Rose. 1998. "Staying Afloat When the Wind Shifts: External Factors and Emerging Market Banking Crises." NBER Working Paper 6370. National Bureau of Economic Research, Cambridge, Mass.

Feldstein, Martin. 1999. "A Self-Help Guide for Emerging Markets." *Foreign Affairs* March–April.

Frankel, Jeffrey A., and Andrew K. Rose. 1996. "Currency Crashes in Emerging Markets: Empirical Indicators." *Journal of International Economics* 41 (3–4): 351–67.

Furman, Jason, and Joseph E. Stiglitz. 1998. "Economic Crises: Evidence and Insights from East Asia." Brookings Papers on Economic Activity 2. Brookings Institution, Washington, D.C.

Garber, Peter M. 1998. "Derivatives in International Capital Flow." NBER Working Paper 6623. National Bureau of Economic Research, Cambridge, Mass.

IIF (Institute of International Finance). 1998. *Comparative Statistics for Emerging Market Economies.* Washington D.C.

Jeanne, Olivier. 1998. "The International Liquidity Mismatch and the New Architecture." International Monetary Fund, Washington, D.C.

Kaminsky, Graciela, Saul Lizondo, and Carmen M. Reinhart. 1998. "Leading Indicators of Currency Crises." *International Monetary Fund Staff Papers* 45 (1): 1–48.

Kenen, Peter. 1999. "Comment on Radelet and Sachs." In the forthcoming NBER Conference Volume, based on the Conference on Currency Crises held in Cambridge, Mass., February 6 and 7.

Krugman, Paul. 1999. "Balance Sheets, the Transfer Problem and Financial Crises." In *International Finance and Financial Crises: Essays in Honor of Robert P. Flood, Jr.* Washington, D.C.: International Monetary Fund.

Larrain, Felipe, Raul Laban, and Romulo Chumacero. 1997. "What Determines Capital Inflows? An Empirical Analysis for Chile." Development Discussion Paper 590. Harvard Institute for International Development, Cambridge, Mass.

Montiel, Peter, and Carmen M. Reinhart. 1997. "Do Capital Controls Influence the Volume and Composition of Capital Flows: Evidence from the 1990s." Paper prepared for UNU/WIDER (United Nations University/World Institute for Development Economics Research) project on Short-Term Capital Movements and Balance of Payments Crises, May 1–2, Sussex.

Obstfeld, Maurice. 1994. "The Logic of Currency Crises." *Cahiers Economiques et Monétaires* 34.

Radelet, Steven, and Jeffrey Sachs. 1998. "The East Asian Financial Crisis: Diagnosis, Remedies, Prospects." Paper prepared for the Brookings Panel March 26–27, Washington, D.C.

Rodrik, Dani. 1998. "Who Needs Capital Account Convertibility?" Essays in International Finance 207. Princeton University, Department of Economics, International Finance Section.

———. 1999. "Governing the World Economy: Does One Architectural Style Fit All?" Prepared for the Brookings Institution Trade Policy Forum conference on Governing in a Global Economy, April 15–16, Washington, D.C.

Sachs, Jeffrey, Aaron Tornell, and Andrés Velasco. 1996. "Financial Crises in Emerging Markets: The Lessons from 1995." *Brookings Papers on Economic Activity 1*. Washington, D.C.: Brookings Institution.

Valdés-Prieto, Salvador, and Marcelo Soto. 1996. "The Effectiveness of Capital Controls in Chile." Catholic University of Chile, Santiago.

# The Underpinnings of a Stable and Equitable Global Financial System: From Old Debates to a New Paradigm

*Joseph E. Stiglitz and Amar Bhattacharya*

*Misguided deregulation policies have been at the center of many of the weaknesses in East Asian and other developing countries. Indeed, eliminating capital controls across the board and relying exclusively on imperfect capital adequacy requirements to curtail the risk exposure of the financial sector may actually lead to increased instability and to a higher likelihood of systemic crises. To avert such crises, which have devastating effects on the poor, developing countries need to create regulatory structures that encourage safe and sound financial institutions while at the same time calling for increased transparency and accountability of decisionmakers in both the private and public sector. Improved disclosure is a necessary, though not sufficient, condition to overcome information asymmetries, which lie at the root of many of the problems and failures of modern market economies. There is a clear role for governments to adopt measures that mitigate incentives for excessive unhedged borrowing both by banks and by corporations directly. Inadequate bankruptcy laws and financial market restructuring have proved to be among the most critical institutional weaknesses in the East Asian economies hit by the recent crises. To reduce the impact of financial crises on the poor, greater attention should be paid to the distributional implications of macroeconomic stabilization policies. Efficient social safety net programs are needed to insure the poor against the risk of loss of income during crises and to respond flexibly to their needs without creating perverse incentives that could contribute to long-term dependency.*

What a long distance political discussions of the global economic architecture have come in the past two years. Two years ago the focus of discussion was how to advance capital market liberalization. Today, we recognize that some restraints on the flow of short-term capital may be required for economic stability, especially for small, less developed economies. When the finan-

---

Joseph E. Stiglitz is senior vice president, Development Economics, and chief economist at the World Bank. Amar Bhattacharya is senior advisor, Poverty Reduction and Economic Management Network, at the World Bank.

Annual World Bank Conference on Development Economics 1999
©2000 The International Bank for Reconstruction and Development / THE WORLD BANK

cial crisis struck, attention initially focused on weaknesses in the borrowing countries. The suggestion was that, by pursuing unsound policies and indulging in "crony capitalism," these countries had brought the ills on themselves. Today, we recognize that the original indictment was unfair, that it paid undue attention to the problems originating in the developing countries and ignored the fact that for every borrower there is a lender with as much responsibility for bad loans as the borrowers have. Not only that, even countries with sound economic policies can be buffeted by the turbulence in international markets, though to be sure, countries with weaker economic policies are, almost by definition, likely to suffer more.

But while events have in less than two years moved policy discussions a distance they might otherwise have taken years to traverse, the intellectual foundations have not changed—and have not needed to change—nearly as much, and in this there is an important lesson. Many of the positions taken earlier were based not on sound theory or econometric evidence but, depending on one's perspective, on ideology, special interests, or economic models of a bygone era. The Annual World Bank Conference on Development Economics, which has sought over the years to narrow the gap between policy and economic science, provides an opportune occasion to address perhaps the most cataclysmic set of events to face the world economy since the Great Depression. This article seeks to put the debate in a broader perspective, linking it to ongoing strands in economics.

Two basic ideas should inform our thinking about these issues. The first is the modern theory of market failures, focusing on incomplete markets, incomplete contracts, and incomplete information. While the failure of the communist regimes reinvigorated confidence in the market economy, in some quarters there was a loss of perspective. The socialist experiment arose in part to address glaring failures in the market economy: its seeming failure to deliver growth to vast portions of the globe, the periodic crises that plagued capitalism, and the poverty to which so many even in the "successful" countries seemed condemned. Even apologists for market capitalism have not—at least in recent years—suggested that markets alone could generate socially acceptable distributions of income (though some maintained, even in the face of the evidence, a belief in the notion that a rising tide lifts all boats). But Adam Smith's argument of an invisible hand guiding markets to efficient resource allocations has had enormous influence. The past 15 years have shown how circumscribed are the conditions under which Smith's invisible hand theorem holds. In particular, whenever markets are incomplete and information is imperfect—that is, essentially always—markets are not even constrained-Pareto optimal.

The second basic idea is that financial markets play a key role in allocating capital and monitoring its use, a role that is essentially informational. As such, market failures are endemic, and there is a large role for government in regulating financial markets.

## What Is the Appropriate Role for Government?

While these advances in economic theory make it clear that there should be a role for government, it is not always clear what that role should be. The recent debate is not, for the most part, between free market advocates and those advocating a *dirigiste* regime. Rather, it is about the particular interventions that governments and the international community should undertake.

Should the government intervene to stabilize exchange rates—an intervention that is expensive and requires that government bureaucrats outguess markets about the level of the equilibrium exchange rate? Even when the necessary expenditures are sustained by loans from the international community, it is not taxpayers in the industrial countries that foot the bill. They will be repaid. It is the taxpayers in developing countries, especially workers, that bear the burden, as free capital mobility ensures that capital can flow out to avoid the imposition of the taxes required to repay the billions of dollars of loans. Consensus is growing that managing exchange rates is extraordinarily difficult and that billions of dollars were "wasted" in trying to defend indefensible exchange rates.

Consider the very words used to describe the crisis—*contagion* and *illiquidity*. Both are concepts that simply do not appear in the lexicon of perfect markets. Contagion suggests that there are externalities, and externalities need to be addressed by corrective taxation or regulation. Illiquidity suggests that there are borrowers who are good risks—but that the market does not judge them to be so.

Should government bureaucrats at the international or national level substitute their judgment for that of the market? But if markets can make mistakes in not lending when they should, is it not conceivable that they can make the opposite mistake and lend when they should not? If that is the case, is it not possible that part of the problem facing many countries is a sudden change in sentiment, which imposes high costs on a country, especially given that risk markets are imperfect? And if that is the case, is it not possible that government actions should be more symmetric—providing liquidity when the market does not and restricting liquidity when the market demonstrates a dangerous level of irrational exuberance, or at least restricting leverage when such irrational exuberance can have macroeconomic consequences?

Consider, too, the new mantra of reform: improved transparency, a call for government intervention to provide more information and to require more information from the private sector, a seeming recognition that market mechanisms—in which supposedly all relevant information is conveyed by prices—are insufficient to attain efficient outcomes. But there is no theorem that asserts that when prices do not convey all relevant information, the only interventions should be disclosure requirements. There is not even a theorem that asserts that more information will lead to either less market volatility or less severity of credit rationing, as discussed later in this article.

The most troubling aspect of intervention has to do with macroeconomic impacts and conflicts among objectives. For 60 years governments have assumed responsibility for helping the economy maintain full employment. This is not the place to rehearse the arguments, and evidence, for the proposition that markets do not always quickly adjust to maintain full employment—even most free marketeers recognize that there was a Great Depression and that whatever the role of monetary policy in inducing the shock, markets failed to adjust. Most governments see maintaining full employment as a first priority. To be sure, eventually the unemployment rate stabilizes and, we hope, returns to the pre-downturn levels. The role of government is seen as reducing the magnitude of the downturn and its duration.

The most recent crises raise several questions about government policies:

- Did governments choose policies that put the objective of minimizing the depth and duration of the downturn at the center of economic policy?
- To what extent were other objectives—such as preventing defaults on international debt held by firms within their economy—given equal or greater weight?
- To what extent do the different objectives conflict, and if they do, how did the political processes resolve these conflicts?
- Standard macroeconomic theory has argued for loosening monetary and fiscal policy in the face of a threatened downturn in the economy. Did the tightening of monetary and fiscal policy reflect judgments that these economies were not going to face a decline in aggregate demand? Or was it based on giving priority to other objectives or on new economic models that argue that the way to maintain full employment in the face of economic downturn is to reverse the usual policy prescriptions?
- Is there evidence that deeper economic downturns lead to better long-term performance in developing countries? Such evidence would contrast markedly with the evidence for more developed countries, which strongly suggests that any economic downturn has long and persistently undesirable effects. There is no or little detectable mean reversion, so that the best policy for maintaining long-term growth is maintaining short-term output.

## Improving Transparency and Disclosure

Recent problems in East Asia have spurred widespread calls for greater transparency by international financial institutions, national authorities, corporations, and financial institutions in recipient countries.[1] Beyond *more* information, transparency implies *better* information as well, in terms of relevance, quality, and reliability. (We put aside the broader meaning that *transparency* has sometimes assumed—and to which it is clearly related—that is, lack of corruption.)

The call for greater transparency in corporations and financial institutions reflects a set of market failures that has been well recognized in the economics literature, market failures that relate to the provision of information. The concern for greater transparency has been buttressed by changes in the characteristics of financial markets, in particular, the substitution of securitized instruments for bank lending, the greater use of financial derivatives, the changing boundaries between institutions, and the growing integration of domestic and international financial markets.

As a result, there is greater reliance on market prices in the allocation of risk, putting more emphasis on public disclosure of information than on the traditional bank-client flow of information. Systemic risks and the presence of externalities suggest that there are benefits to disclosure that accrue to parties other than the firms and financial institutions providing market information. These indirect benefits mean that more public disclosure may be appropriate, that disclosure by a much wider range of institutions is needed, and that the desirable level of disclosure may be greater than the level that corporations and financial institutions would provide on their own.

There is thus a role for public policy. Even with well-designed government interventions, though, information will remain imperfect. Greater transparency *may* reduce the frequency and depth of crises (although even this is somewhat problematic), but it will not eliminate them.

Governments are not subject to the discipline that the market provides in the production, dissemination, and processing of information. Thus special attention needs to be focused on openness in government at every level, from subnational to national and even international. Recent research has pointed out that lack of transparency is related to both corruption and poor economic performance. There is thus a high return and a special responsibility for increased openness in the public sector.

Calls for increased transparency are now at the heart of discussions of reform of the international financial architecture—partly because transparency seems to be virtue incarnate, and consensus can therefore be formed in its support, and partly because transparency reforms impose relatively little cost, especially on those calling for them. But several claims have been put forth suggesting that increased transparency may not achieve the desired results:

- Increased transparency (in the form of disclosure requirements) is not needed, since markets provide optimal incentives for disclosure, balancing out costs and benefits.
- Requirements for increased transparency are likely to be ineffective unless they are comprehensive, because they will simply induce markets to move transactions to venues in which reporting requirements do not apply. Partial information (say, about the magnitude of short-term foreign indebtedness) is of little value in itself, unless a systematic relation can be shown between the observed information and the relevant information (for example, aggregate exposure).
- Increased transparency does not necessarily increase stability or reduce credit rationing.
- Requirements for increased transparency may be counterproductive (especially if they are not comprehensive), since regulatory arbitrage (moving from venues in which reporting requirements and regulatory oversight are greater to ones in which they are weaker) may actually increase risk. Hence more transparency may even increase market volatility.
- Increased transparency reduces the rents that those who gather information garner in return for information acquisition costs and therefore may result in a lower level of information.

The validity of these claims is explored below.

## The Need for Greater Transparency

Markets provide incentives for both concealing and disclosing information (especially information that will be viewed favorably by the market). Under highly restrictive conditions, market forces will balance the marginal benefits and marginal costs of additional information disclosure (acquisition) (see Grossman 1981). But under more general conditions markets alone will not generate efficient levels of disclosure, information production, or acquisition.[2]

Governments have responded to these market failures in a variety of ways. In some cases they have recognized the public good nature of information and engaged in information acquisition (monitoring). Government supervision of banks can be viewed in part from this perspective. In most countries governments impose disclosure requirements, as in the case of securities or product labeling.

Disclosure requirements are not enough, however. Anti-fraud laws and active government enforcement are also needed to ensure that information disclosures are not deliberately misleading. Just as firms may have an incentive not to disclose all relevant information, they may also have an incentive to disclose information in ways that make it difficult to process. It is therefore essential to establish accounting standards that facilitate the interpretation of the information that is made available. For the same reasons, there are considerable advantages to establishing international standards. In the United States the government enforces standards, but the standards are set by an independent board. However, even in the United States governments in recent years have reduced the level of transparency in accounting standards in response to political pressure.[3]

Governments and firms have at their disposal a variety of mechanisms for obfuscating relevant information. In the United States in the 1980s, for instance, to put off dealing with an impending crisis in the savings and loan industry, firms were allowed to treat good will as capital, in effect creating phantom capital. Firms also obfuscate through information overload, providing much irrelevant information along with the relevant. Thus the desire to hide information—the desire for lack of transparency—is evident even in advanced industrial economies with sophisticated institutions.[4] Indeed, such economies may be in an even better position to hide what is really going on than developing countries, precisely because of their greater sophistication in accounting and finance.

New financial instruments have made it more difficult to provide accurate and timely assessments of the net worth of firms and financial institutions. Not only are many derivatives not regularly reported on balance sheets, but their market value can change markedly in response to small changes in external circumstances. In many cases there are no agreed-on ways of valuing a derivative position.

There is a striking inconsistency between the current emphasis on improved information on the one hand and the dogmas of financial market and capital account liberalization based on pure free market principles on the other. According to the standard theorems of welfare economics that underlie such doctrines, all relevant information is conveyed in prices. If the models that underlie the calls for financial and capital market liberalization were correct, there would be no need for government intervention in information disclosure. Calls for such involvement recognize not only that information is imperfect and that all relevant information is not reflected in prices but also that market mechanisms deal with information problems only imperfectly.

There is no theoretical or empirical basis to the argument that government intervention should, in such situations, be limited to disclosure requirements.

The kind of information that is now being called for—information about aggregate levels of short-term debt, for example—is not normally collected by government, even in the process of tax administration. Many firms would view disclosure of such information as an intrusion into their private transactions. There may be a compelling case for such intrusion, based on the externalities associated with the aggregate levels of, say, short-term indebtedness, but such externalities provide a rationale for government actions that go beyond information disclosure.

Even with disclosure requirements, information is likely to be highly imperfect, at best, because of the myriad forms that intertemporal obligations (the effects of which are similar if not identical to short- or long-term indebtedness) can take. The development of sophisticated derivatives complicates matters significantly.

Information on a significant portion of formal short-term indebtedness—that incurred by or on behalf of financial institutions, especially banks—can be had at relatively low marginal costs because of its relevance to bank regulators. But such information will be insufficient, as evidenced by the significant part of Indonesia's "problem" that is foreign-denominated corporate short-term indebtedness.

### The Benefits of Improved Disclosure

Even partial information may significantly improve the functioning of markets through improved resource allocation, enhanced efficiency, and a stronger foundation for corporate governance and accountability. As such, greater transparency can promote more resilient financial systems and prevent growing vulnerability by encouraging more rigorous discipline in risk taking by lenders and borrowers and inducing swifter adjustment in government policies.

In the recent crisis in East Asia many suppliers of funds were unable to distinguish between good and bad borrowers and so restricted credit to all borrowers or charged extremely high risk premiums. (Note that good borrowers have private incentives for disclosure, which reduces borrowing costs and may even lead to greater access to credit.) In effect, they grouped all borrowers together. More generally, improved information may facilitate the functioning of capital markets by convincing suppliers of capital that they are operating on a level playing field. Improved information and auditing standards have been an essential part of the development of modern capital markets (Greenwald and Stiglitz 1992).

Improved information may also reduce contagion effects, as lenders are able to distinguish the financial circumstances facing different countries. While such discrimination typically does emerge in the weeks and months after the onset of a crisis, better information up front might speed the process along.

It should be recognized, however, that much of the relevant information was available before the onset of the crises in East Asia. Much, if not most, of the relevant data concerning Thailand was available in the months preceding the crisis. Even the factor now frequently cited as primary—the real estate boom, financed by short-term foreign borrowing—was well known. Indonesia's corruption was well documented. The high debt equity ratios of firms in the Republic of Korea were well known.

The problem seems to be the inability to process currently available information. (Alternatively, the critical piece of information—how other market participants react—cannot be obtained from the disclosures themselves.) Outside rating agencies did not downgrade the debt of many of the East Asian countries until well after the onset of the crisis. The discrete revisions are inconsistent with most models of Bayesian updating, and the timing of such revisions does not coincide with the release of what would appear to be significant news warranting such large revisions. The large discrete revisions, of course, themselves exacerbated the crisis. Similarly, forecasts by reputable sources (some with access to private information) did not reveal good assessments of the risks, at least as they developed.

That the ratings and forecasts came with caveats was of limited value, since similar caveats were attached to ratings and forecasts for many countries that did not experience crises. The forecasts and ratings represented the best summary statistic, but they did not accurately reflect evolving circumstances. Crises, especially exchange rate crises, are inherently difficult to forecast, since economic theories predict that such variables will behave according to a random walk (although there may be systematic factors that can affect the variance, particularly a large downward movement). Presumably only variables that are systematically related to crises would provide information relevant to predicting and preventing crises. The lack of consensus that there are such variables makes us modest in our hopes of a significant improvement in our ability to anticipate, let alone ward off, crises.

Similarly, to the extent that currency crises are simply runs on a country's currency (analogous to bank runs), an understanding of fundamentals will not yield insights into when currency crises might occur, although research into social behavioral psychology might be instructive. The major crises that occurred before the East Asian crises—in Mexico and the Scandinavian countries, countries with the highest transparency ratings—suggest that transparency by itself may be of only limited help.

Under some circumstances information disclosure can exacerbate fluctuations and trigger crises, even when such information has little intrinsic value. Calling attention to some variables may create a coordinating mechanism (what is called a sunspot equilibrium) that precipitates a crisis, especially if market participants do not fully understand what is going on. Thus focusing attention on a variable like the ratio of short-term indebtedness to reserves may make that variable a trigger for crisis, since whenever the ratio exceeds a particular level, people will think that a crisis is imminent—or that others will believe that, so that the beliefs are self-fulfilling. Some have claimed that the crisis in East Asia was aggravated, if not precipitated, by repeated announcements about aspects of the economy that were, in some cases, already well known. People began to believe that those aspects were far worse than they had thought and contributed in far more important ways to the crisis.

Improved capabilities of processing and transmitting information may lead to more, not less, variability in the price of an asset. Lack of information may serve to average good and bad events. Empirical evidence on this relation remains inconclusive. Similarly, a direct empirical link between transparency and financial stability is difficult to establish, partly perhaps because transparency is hard to measure.[5] The high degree of corruption associated with a lack of transparency has been cited as an important contributing factor in the East Asian crisis. Evidence linking corruption (as measured by perception surveys conducted by Transparency International, the *International Country Risk Guide,* and the *World Competitiveness Yearbook*) to crises in East Asia is weak (Furman and Stiglitz 1998). Furthermore, low corruption is not enough to avert a crisis. Countries with no corruption may have little transparency in their banking systems if regulations do not require disclosure. While corruption and absence of rule of law make it difficult to achieve transparency, they do not measure transparency.

On the whole, and subject to the imperfections that attend measurement of transparency, the evidence does not support the hypothesis that a lack of transparency caused the crises. But lack of transparency may exacerbate crises. Better disclosure might avert runs on some banks if investors could distinguish healthy banks from insolvent ones. In general, the evidence suggests that more information strengthens market discipline, provided the information is reliable and that other regulatory instruments are employed to improve the incentives to use information.

## Effect of the Economic and Political Environment on the Costs and Benefits of Disclosure

The economic and political environment affects both the costs and the benefits of improved disclosure. Developing countries are typically in more volatile situations, with less capacity for auditing, monitoring, and processing relevant information. Economic policies can affect both the information available and the information required for economic stability. Liberalization of financial and capital markets may increase the informational requirements for economic stability enormously. For instance, asset price volatility associated with real estate lending means that reducing restrictions on such lending increases the potential for financial fragility as well as the information required to ensure financial viability. Capital account liberalization increases the potential for large short-term capital flows, with concomitant changes in short-term debt to reserve ratios. This contributes to financial fragility and increases the information required to ensure stability.

Economic reforms that eliminate rents can temporarily increase uncertainty (about the net worth of various enterprises, for example). In the absence of good information systems that allow people to assess the magnitude of these effects on individual enterprises, such reforms may have significant adverse short-term economic impacts that have to be weighed against the long-term benefits. The adverse informational consequences are likely to be significantly higher where firms and financial institutions are already at the brink of survival. The same arguments apply to other policies, such as large changes in interest rates, even if short lived, if they have large effects on asset prices—as they typically do.

## The Role of Policy

Governments and those who advise them, we noted above, have to be cognizant of the impact of policies (reforms) on the information requirements of the economy, especially in developing economies, where institutions and the capacity for information generation, dissemination, and processing are limited. Arguably, insufficient attention was paid to these considerations in the past. The government also has an important role to play in regulating the disclosure and provision of information, even about its own policies. In general, disclosure regulation that mandates or encourages transparency may be justified when there are information externalities. However, the decision to introduce disclosure regulation warrants careful consideration (Vishwanath and Kaufmann 1999).

First, an assessment should be made of whether more transparency would necessarily improve economic outcomes. In some instances more information may instead cause speculation and greater market volatility (Hirshleifer 1971). A recent empirical study (Bushee and Noe 1999) found that firms with improved disclosure practices experienced subsequent increases in the volatility of their stock in financial markets.[6]

Disclosure may also undermine the effectiveness of policy. Arguments in favor of central bank secrecy in matters of monetary policy are well known, but they are seldom subject to theoretical and empirical scrutiny. Recently, some researchers have argued that greater transparency of central bank policies increases the sensitivity of the bank's reputation and credibility to its actions and thus improves social outcomes (Blinder 1998). But there are also examples of transparency worsening outcomes; if the central bank's reputation is largely unjustified and only loosely related to its success, greater "transparency" may result in less confidence in the central bank and greater (subjective) uncertainty, with potentially adverse effects on overall macroeconomic performance.[7]

Privacy laws and confidentiality agreements that limit full disclosure of information reflect the notion that there is a judicious balance between privacy and transparency. There is some concern that "excessive transparency" will inhibit open discussions. But there is little evidence of any adverse effects from the policies of greater transparency adopted by the United Kingdom's central bank. Greater transparency may even force central bank authorities to provide better rationales for their decisions.

To be sure, even when disclosure regulation is justified, articulation of appropriate disclosure policies requires a careful weighing of costs and benefits. What information should be disclosed and with what precision? When should it be disclosed? Who provides the information and verifies the quality? What are the enforcement requirements?

Governments can also use a variety of mechanisms to induce revelation of information. For example, requiring the use of subordinated, uninsured debt has been used to improve private incentives to acquire information and monitor banks. Involving local communities in monitoring government services has been shown to foster transparency and reduce corruption.

Uncertainty about government economic policies is itself a major source of information failure in the economy. Some of this uncertainty is an inherent consequence of democratic governments' inability to make commitments that are binding on successive democratically elected governments. This uncertainty can be reduced by ensuring that policies and reforms have widespread domestic ownership and represent a consensus in society that is not likely to be upset by a change in administration. Accordingly, policies imposed from the outside without such ownership and consensus may weaken democratic institutions and increase economic uncertainty, thereby undermining some if not a substantial part of the desired welfare gains. (Such policies are sometimes imposed by multilateral institutions as conditionalities, particularly during crises, when countries are in weakened bargaining positions and there is little time for consensus building.)

Indeed, without such a consensus building process, there will be widespread criticism within the country, which will be interpreted negatively abroad as suggesting, perhaps rightly, that such policies may not be sustainable. So even if adopted, the policies would not have the desired confidence building effects. The answer is not to suppress democratic discussion but to engage actively in consensus building and to limit conditionality at times of crisis to issues that are essential to the problems at hand (a principle all too frequently violated in East Asia).

But while much policy uncertainty is inherent in democratic processes, some of it is unnecessary. Thus most central banks routinely do not disclose fully and in a timely way the nature of their policy discussions and votes on key policy matters. There is no evidence that such discussions would substantially increase market volatility, while there is some theoretical analysis suggesting that more regular disclosure of such information would help stabilize markets. Even if disclosure of more information in a more timely way does lead to more market instability (a proposition that would undermine current calls for more disclosure and transparency), societies need to balance the possibly small economic costs of such instability against the possibly large costs of undermining open democratic processes. The changes in the practices of the Bank of England represent a marked step forward, with no evidence of untoward consequences.

## Transparency and Corruption

Lack of transparency on the part of governments provides an opportunity for hiding corrupt practices, and corruption has been shown to be systematically related to lower levels of investment and slower economic growth. But the economic incentives for secrecy on the part of bureaucrats and government officials go beyond a desire to hide corruption. They extend to a desire to hide mistakes and to create information and political rents. Lack of information restricts political competition by creating a barrier to meaningful entry into the political process. Like other forms of artificially created scarcity, lack of information creates (information) rents that can be exchanged for political favors and (even in seemingly less corrupt societies) favorable news coverage, which is of immeasurable value to politicians and bureaucrats.

The changing presumption in favor of citizens having a right to know what their governments are doing shows a movement in the right direction. Just as governments have imposed disclosure requirements on the private sector, they need to impose such requirements on themselves. Laws such as the U.S. Freedom of Information Act stand in marked contrast to the "official secrets" acts restricting public disclosure in many countries.

The need for such disclosure requirements is greater in public than in private institutions, not only because of the absence of market incentives for disclosure and the presence of political incentives for secrecy but also because of the absence of the "exit" option. Voice takes on a more important role, and voice can be meaningfully exercised only with information. Information is an essential part of public accountability. But just as there are many ways for the private sector to obscure information, so, too, can the public sector. Most governments try to "pluck the goose without making it hiss," keeping the tax burden and incidence at least partially hidden.

Transparency presents a special burden for international institutions, because typically they are not even directly accountable to electorates. They report indirectly, through government ministries, which themselves may not be totally transparent and may reflect the interests of their "clients" more than the general interest. There should be a strong presumption, if not an outright prohibition, against secret concordats between governments and international organizations. Where there is no firm commitment to forswear secret agreements, a climate of distrust grows because participants in the political process cannot know whether an agreement has been made that commits the country to a particular course of action. Such secrets undermine democratic processes. Any agreement kept secret because the government does not want to disclose it to the people is unlikely to be sustainable. If popular support is lacking, the government should undertake to build consensus. If it is believed that a loan, for example, cannot be justified without a particular action and the government is unwilling to make public a commitment to take that action, then the loan should not proceed.

Conflicts of interest may arise when government operating agencies are also involved in producing and analyzing statistical data. Thus the close affiliation of ministries of labor with workers may make the ministries less attuned to correcting biases in cost of living indices. When policies fail, agencies may attempt to shift blame to others, with data interpretation and analysis becoming an essential part of such shifting of blame. That is why many governments have established independent statistical agencies that are not linked with any operations. The advantages of such separation outweigh the disadvantages arising from potential economies of scope in data gathering, analysis, and operations. More broadly, the organization of the provision of information is a question that requires careful scrutiny, given the potentially large consequences of information disclosure and the obvious incentive issues that those consequences raise.

Governments and international agencies need to take into account the fact that the data they gather and highlight will affect behavior. Simply making certain data available may result in market participants focusing on that variable, so that it becomes a coordinating mechanism for crises. In the event of a crisis, market participants will always claim that they have insufficient information. They are not likely to take the blame on themselves, admitting that the failure arose from their analysis of the data. Thus governments cannot use as a criterion for the adequacy of their data collection and dissemination efforts either the occurrence of crises or the prevalence of complaints about data adequacy.

So far we have delineated roles for government in establishing information standards (auditing), imposing disclosure requirements, enacting and enforcing fraud laws, and promoting transparency in its own operations. Because many aspects of information partake of key properties of pure public goods, the role of government may need to extend into other areas. For instance, there is a role for government in monitoring financial institutions, establishing and enforcing risk-adjusted capital adequacy standards, and restraining certain types of behavior, such as insider lending, accumulation of excessive foreign exchange–denominated liabilities, and excessive speculative real estate lending or lending on margin for the purchase of stock.

While recent research has helped delineate the relations among transparency, corruption, and economic growth, little or no research, theoretical or empirical, has been done in most of the areas discussed above. Recognition of the importance of transparency and disclosure suggests an important place for further research—in identifying the likely consequences of increased disclosure requirements and alternative information standards, for example.

## Reducing Incentives that Encourage Excessive Unhedged Borrowing

Many analysts agree that "excessive" unhedged short-term foreign exchange–denominated borrowing leaves a country vulnerable to shocks and was an important contributor to the recent financial crises. What causes these excessive unhedged positions, and what can government do to address the problem?

The basic premise is that market failures, including problems at the interface between international lenders and domestic borrowers, are more pervasive in developing countries. This can be attributed to several factors. Information asymmetries are greater, and susceptibility to market irrationalities may be greater, as may their costs. Market imperfections—information imperfections, including those associated with agency problems, and imperfections in risk markets—may also be greater, giving rise to a larger divergence between private and social risk and returns.

Against this backdrop macroeconomic policies can have an important effect on incentives for (unhedged) external borrowing. Reliance on monetary policy (high interest rates) to curb aggregate demand pressures associated with incipient capital flows, combined with a commitment to a stable nominal exchange rate, may, it is alleged, encourage short-term unhedged external borrowing. These allegations are themselves as much evidence of market failures as they are of government failures, except where there is a government guarantee (as is implicitly the case for government-insured bank deposits).

With well-functioning markets, interest rate arbitrage ensures the identity of borrowing costs, once the risks of devaluation are taken into account—and a truly fixed exchange rate does not really exist. "Fixed" exchange rates are simply rates that change suddenly, typically in large amounts. These are precisely the kinds of risks for which insurance markets typically work well. If the risk of devaluation were low (and markets worked well), the premium on such insurance would be low and risk-averse firms should presumably have purchased it themselves. Moreover, while macroeconomic policies need to take these potential incentive effects into account, there may be limited alternatives where capital market have been liberalized. When confronting a surge of capital and trying to avoid overheating, it may not be feasible to adjust tax rates, and it may not be possible (or desirable) to contract public expenditures on education, health, or infrastructure.

Some critics of East Asian economies have focused on alleged deficiencies in corporate governance. Improved corporate governance would presumably reduce the scope for "excessive" borrowing. But this claim, too, needs to be looked at with some care. The intuition behind the notion is that "bad" managerial decisions resulting from bad corporate governance lie behind excessive borrowing. But one needs to distinguish between bad decisionmaking caused by incompetent managers or irrational behavior and systematic weaknesses arising out of inadequacies in underlying incentives associated with, say, corporate governance.

To be sure, failures in corporate governance can result in poor business decisions, including excessive corporate borrowing. We already noted one instance of bad decisionmaking: the failure of many corporate entities to obtain cover. This decision cannot be justified simply on the basis of a quasi-fixed exchange rate, as some analysts have attempted to do, but it does not seem related to problems of corporate governance. The charge of weak corporate governance is usually leveled by those who have faith in the market system; the contention seems to be that there is a flaw in the underlying legal or institutional structures that systematically gives rise to mistakes (as a result of misguided incentives, for example).

The usual corporate governance problem is the conflict between ownership and control, a problem emphasized by Berle and Means (1933) and more recently by Stiglitz (1982, 1985) and others. The irony is that corporate governance issues traditionally arise from separation of ownership and control, but ownership (as defined as residual rights to income flows) and control were not separated in Korean firms. Corporate governance problems do arise with disperse ownership and weak legal structures, such as those associated with the voucher privatization schemes urged on the Czech Republic and other transition economies by the international financial institutions. There is no evidence that the lack of protection of minority shareholders, for instance, played a significant role in the crisis, although worries about minority shareholder rights may indeed have played a role in limiting the growth of equity markets, forcing greater reliance on debt.

At the same time, it needs to be recognized that outside of the United States and United Kingdom, relatively few countries have sufficiently strong legal systems for equity ownership to be a major source of new funds; even in the United States and the United Kingdom most funds are raised through retained earnings and borrowing. In many other countries, growth has been limited to what could be funded by retained earnings. As a result, while debt equity ratios have been kept at much lower levels, growth has been limited.

Given the apparent difficulty in establishing legal structures that provide sufficiently strong protection to minority shareholders, it is not apparent that the Republic of Korea, for instance, made a mistake in pursuing a high leverage strategy: while the strategy entailed high risk, it also facilitated high growth. (The mistake was pushing excessively rapid financial and capital market liberalization on Korea, paying inadequate attention to the features of its economy that made such policies particularly inappropriate.) Overall, looking at its performance over three decades, the "gamble" paid off. Still, a strategy strengthening the legal structures to facilitate more equity financing could facilitate growth with stability.[8]

A final lesson focuses on policies that encourage, or do not discourage, unhedged foreign short-term borrowing. Some policies would likely have reduced the excessive unhedged position. These included removing any tax bias that may encourage financial institutions or firms to rely on foreign funding, as was the case with Thailand; changing banking regulations, including establishing capital adequacy standards that discourage uncovered positions and impose greater risk weights on short-term lending (thus Basle standards, implemented and enforced in industrial countries, contributed to the crisis); and moderating asset and spending booms associated with periods of large capital inflows, possibly by raising capital gains taxes, adjusting bank regulations (on collateral or capital adequacy requirements, for example) or introducing luxury or other surtaxes. In addition, bankruptcy laws, bond provisions, and practices concerning standstills all effect the incentives of lenders to engage in due diligence. (Other policies in industrial countries, such as those that give rise to forced quick sales of debt that is downgraded by credit rating agencies, contributed to the crisis. We discuss these provisions later in this article.)

In addition, reductions in the taxation of the financial system and improvements in the efficiency of financial intermediation more generally would help lower the costs of domestic funding and thus further reduce the bias toward off-shore funding. Financial restraint—limiting deposit rates—may also serve this purpose.[9]

Lending transactions (including the terms of loans) are affected by incentives and circumstances facing both lenders and borrowers. Bail-outs and inadequate, misguided, and badly implemented regulatory structures in lending countries can result in lenders offering terms to borrowers that are "too good" for them to refuse and encourage short-term lending at the expense of long-term loans. Thus even if there were no distortions in the borrowing country, a bias can arise from distortions in the lending countries or from distortions arising from bailouts. Given the seeming unwillingness of many lending countries to address the problems that arise from their practices, borrowing countries—which bear the brunt of the cost of any crisis—must adjust their regulatory structures to offset distortions in lending countries.

In the discussion below, we focus on two issues facing developing countries: the regulation of their financial institutions and the regulation of corporate borrowing, especially through capital controls and taxes. We focus not on the measures that can be taken in the very short run—when a crisis has already occurred—but on the medium-term measures that should be undertaken now, measures that hold open the prospect of reducing the likelihood of a crisis in the future.

## Regulating Financial Institutions

Misguided deregulation policies are at the center of many of the weaknesses in East Asia and other developing countries. Indeed, such policies have been shown to be systematically related to the occurrence of crises. The focus should have been not on deregulation but on achieving the right regulatory structure, one that would encourage safe and sound financial institutions and competition while providing a modicum of consumer protection.[10] Encouraging the development of such institutions and competition requires a robust portfolio approach—one that considers both incentives and constraints and is tailored to the circumstances of the country and its supervisory capabilities.

Developing countries typically face greater risks and have less regulatory capacity than industrial countries. Moreover, the process of liberalization exacerbates these problems by increasing the incentives for risk taking (since it may reduce one of the major forms of a bank's capital, its franchise value) at the same time that regulatory capacity actually decreases, as the private sector bids away the few highly trained individuals. Accordingly, developing countries may need to impose tighter restraints than those imposed in industrial countries.

Especially given the deficiencies in risk adjustment and accounting practices in developing countries, a portfolio approach will be far more effective than excessive reliance on capital adequacy standards. The attempt to impose high capital adequacy standards quickly in crisis conditions was especially questionable. In most crisis-affected countries, capital markets are likely to have dried up; obtaining private capital injections may be extremely difficult, even for banks willing to move in that direction. As a result, the only banks able to comply are typically those that can obtain capital injections from the government. In this respect, enforcing more stringent capital adequacy criteria may further crowd out private banks while boosting state ownership of banks. More fundamentally, the basic rationale in terms of incentives for the owners and managers is called into question: how is government-as-owner better than government-as-regulator?

Even outside of crises, overly rigid capital adequacy standards may be counterproductive. Insisting on higher capital adequacy standards may even lead to less prudent behavior by banks because of adverse effects on franchise value (Hellmann, Murdock, and Stiglitz 1999). While it is widely recognized that proper risk adjustments are essential, in practice risk adjustments are deficient. Without appropriate risk adjustment, banks may even be induced to increase risk taking. Furthermore, and of particular relevance to developing countries, there need to be cyclical adjustments, without which capital adequacy standards result in built-in destabilizers. This is especially problematic in countries without safety nets and tax systems that act as automatic stabilizers.

To what extent capital adequacy standards should be made less rigid is clearly controversial: forbearance can be a risky and costly policy. Letting banks operate with a weak, or sometimes nonexistent, capital base increases the moral hazard that banks will venture into riskier lending, eventually exacerbating the problem. But that is precisely why these polices of more gradual adjustments in capital must be accompanied by tighter regulatory oversight, including possibly reimposing regulations (such as restrictions on speculative real estate lending) that had been lifted in the excessive exuberance of financial market liberalization.

REDUCING FOREIGN EXCHANGE EXPOSURES OF FINANCIAL INSTITUTIONS. There is a growing belief that authorities should adopt more stringent measures on the degree of foreign exchange exposure by financial institutions. A number of specific steps can be taken to manage foreign exchange exposure:
- Limits can be set on the net open positions financial institutions can take in the foreign currency market and on the amount of gross foreign currency liabilities (as a fraction of total liabilities or as a ratio to equity). (Many industrial countries also limit the maturity mismatches on foreign exchange liabilities and assets.)
- Banks can be required to hold a higher ratio of liquid assets to liabilities for foreign exchange liabilities than for domestic currency liabilities. Such a measure would reduce indirect foreign exchange exposure and provide banks with a source of liquidity that is less likely to dry up during periods of stress in the domestic financial markets.
- Guidelines on internal risk management systems and tight monitoring of the internal risk management systems of financial institutions can be improved, providing sanctions for poor systems.
- Supervision of borrowers can be tightened. Borrowers, for example, could be required either to have the capacity to repay foreign exchange loans or to put in place a hedge.

Important as these steps are, we should be aware of their limitations. Ascertaining the extent of exposure (particularly of borrowers) is difficult. Some Korean banks, for instance, believed that they had purchased cover, only to find that when they needed it, the counterparty had gone bankrupt. Those ascertaining risk exposure require information not only about contracts but also about the risk profile of those providing cover, including knowledge of the correlation of credit and market risks to which the financial institution and the firms to which it has lent are exposed. This is a heavy burden, one which banks and their regulators even in industrial countries seem to have had a hard time shouldering.

REDUCING OTHER EXPOSURES. There is merit in strengthening the prudential regulation of banks with regard to other exposures as well. In particular, a strong case can be made for a cyclical component to risk-based capital adequacy. During periods of capital inflows, the system would take into account the higher risk to sectors such as real estate and to highly leveraged firms. This may not be sufficient, however. Sectoral limits for real estate, consumer finance, and stock market–related lending may also be necessary. Governments may also want to consider speed limits that would automatically restrict excessive credit growth at the institutional level. Rapid credit growth has been shown to be systematically related to the likelihood of financial weakness (Demirgüç-Kunt and Detragiache 1997).

Restricting real estate exposures can take various forms: caps on the share of portfolios that can be allocated to real estate or on credit growth rates, maximum loan-to-value ratios, maximum individual loan sizes, prohibitions on certain forms of real estate lending, minimum requirements for the share of equity finance for developers, and so forth. Many of these limits are already in place, but several can be strengthened, in terms of the relative levels of the limits, the degree of disclosure, and the implementation and monitoring of rules.

Margin lending, lending against stock and other assets, consumer lending, and connected lending are other areas in which lending limits, (re)valuation rules (such as the frequency of marking-to-market assets), and disclosure requirements can be strengthened over time. Concentration rules (single lending limits and group lending limits) also need to be strengthened in many Asian countries, particularly in the supervision of compliance.

Other measures can also help reduce exposure. Well-designed risk-based capital adequacy and deposit insurance premiums, for example, may induce banks to adjust interest rates to discourage such exposure and leverage. But regulatory structures even in industrial countries are not equal to this task.

Requiring subordinated debt to be provided in tranches may provide helpful information to regulators. It could also enhance bank incentives and buffer the government against bank failures.

Deposit insurance, too, can play a role. The argument that deposit insurance is the source of the problem, rather than part of the solution, is erroneous. Without such insurance, bank runs can (and frequently have) occurred. Furthermore, incentives for gambling can arise even without such insurance; governments typically bail out large banks even when there is no formal insurance, and the public goods nature of monitoring implies that reliance on private monitoring is inefficient.[11]

### Curtailing Excessive Borrowing by Corporations

That two-thirds of short-term foreign-denominated borrowing in Indonesia was by corporations suggests that "excessive" borrowing needs to be addressed in that sector directly, not just within the financial sector. In the same way that putting a finger in the hole of a dike will simply redirect water pressure toward other weaknesses, misguided incentives to borrow from abroad are likely to show up elsewhere in the system if changes are made in the financial sector alone.

Restrictions on banks borrowing abroad can be evaded if corporations are set up that borrow from abroad and on-lend to banks. And the impact of high levels of foreign short-term indebtedness by firms to which the banks have lent money can be as devastating as direct borrowing by the banks themselves.[12]

What are the market failures that might lead to excessive borrowing by corporations, or more generally, to excessive cross-border capital flows? And what are the policies that can address the problem? Note that the standard explanation for excessive borrowing in the financial sector—the existence of deposit insurance without appropriately adjusted premiums (implying that the government is providing insur-

ance for risk taking but not charging appropriately)—does not apply here. Still, three arguments used to justify government intervention in the financial sector apply with almost equal force here:
- *Some borrowers are too big to fail.* Systemic borrowing, or even borrowing by a few large firms, places the entire economy in jeopardy in the face of a potential currency crisis, in particular by tying the hands of the government—by forcing it, for instance, to attempt to defend the currency by raising interest rates, at great costs to others. Such borrowing has huge potential externalities. The IMF's insistence that exchange rates be defended, lest there be adverse balance sheet effects from depreciation, has exacerbated this problem.
- *Prudential actions are costly.* Currently, countries must maintain reserves equal to aggregate short-term foreign denominated liabilities if they are to be viewed as pursuing prudential policies. There are high opportunity costs to maintaining such reserves; those borrowing should be made to pay for those costs.
- *Borrowing rates have externalities.* If markets view the country's aggregate foreign denominated short-term liabilities as a risk factor in determining interest rates, additional borrowing by one party exerts a negative externality on others. The party causing the externality should have to pay for it.

The systemic risks imposed by cross-border capital flows—risks that have had enormous social consequences and that by themselves argue for intervention—are by now well recognized. Another class of arguments, based on information externalities, has also recently been put forward. The recent crisis revealed that information problems in cross-border lending are severe and that lending in the form of highly liquid claims is susceptible to bandwagon effects, both euphoria and panic. In this context, portfolio allocation decisions made by individual investors can have large and adverse external effects through the impact of their actions on the decisions made by other agents and thus on the magnitude of the financial shocks experienced by small capital-importing countries. Because these information effects are likely to be especially severe in an environment in which information is scarce—as it is in most developing countries—the rationale for government intervention on this account is strong.

Several policy instruments can address the issue of excessive corporate borrowing:
- Inflow taxes, such the Chilean tax on capital inflows.
- Limitations on tax deductibility of foreign-denominated short-term debt.[13]
- Exit taxes. While it is too early to reach a definitive judgment on the Malaysian exit tax, the international community should be open to learning from this and other experiments aimed at stabilizing capital flows, especially when such experiments are market friendly (that is, take the form of tax interventions rather than outright controls) and pay due attention to the needs of long-term capital as they attempt to dampen short-term speculative flows.
- Bank regulations, such as regulations on the exposure of firms to which the bank has lent money. Imposition of appropriate risk-adjusted capital ade-

quacy standards would mean that loans to firms with high foreign exchange exposure would be given a higher risk weight. This would provide banks with an incentive to charge higher interest rates for firms with greater exposure, thereby reducing the firms' incentive to take on such exposure.

All of these measures can be imposed in flexible ways, directed at stabilizing the flows—ways that need not interfere with long-term capital movements, foreign direct investment, or trade credit. If these measures are imposed in this adaptive way, the arguments that over the long run they are evaded or that in the short run they are imperfect are unpersuasive: such interventions may still stabilize capital flows. While the existence of derivatives makes the implementation of interventions more difficult, it also highlights the need for such interventions, since such instruments can themselves contribute to volatility. Requiring registration of such derivatives (in order for them to be enforceable in courts) would be an easy way both to increase transparency and enhance stability.

Some have argued that there may be a need to go farther than these relatively market-friendly measures. Such proposals take several forms. One is to limit the class of firms allowed to raise debt finance offshore. Firms raising funds offshore could be required to be rated by an international or domestic rating agency or to be listed on the domestic stock exchange. A more controversial measure would be to impose prudential ratios for borrowing firms, such as a minimum equity to liability ratio, a maximum foreign to domestic currency liability ratio, or a maximum net or gross foreign exchange open position. These criteria could be combined and differentiated based on the type of offshore funding and sector. In addition, restrictions could be imposed on the terms of loans.

Actions need to be taken in both industrial and developing countries. We have already noted how badly designed financial regulations can contribute to excessive short-term foreign borrowing and how inadequate enforcement of regulations can lead to loan terms that are too good to pass up. Abrupt changes in financial regulatory stances can contribute to the volatility of short-term flows. In the past such changes may have contributed to instability. Policies that induce a credit contraction in an industrial country, for example, can have spillover effects on developing countries to which its banks have lent money.

Contract provisions that contribute to the instability of capital flows (such as the provisions that in effect convert a long-term loan into a short-term credit in times of crisis, just when the funds are most needed) should be discouraged. And fiduciary requirements imposed in industrial countries that require the immediate sale of assets when they are downgraded by rating agencies need to be changed, as such provisions clearly contributed to market volatility in the recent crises.[14]

## Dealing with the Lack of Liquidity

A set of issues that has moved front and center in the policy debates in the past few months—from lender of last resort to contingent finance—involves the issue of liquidity. While frequently referred to, the concept of liquidity is seldom well defined.

Emphasis is often placed on the distinction between liquidity and net worth. Central banks are told to bail out illiquid but not insolvent firms. The distinction is evidence of the belief that markets do not work in the manner described by the neoclassical model, in which any firm with positive net worth can gain access to credit.

There are at least four sets of circumstances in which liquidity issues may arise:

- For some commodities, such as housing, in which heterogeneity is important, selling an asset quickly yields a lower price; such an asset is said to be illiquid. The problem here is associated with the time that search takes to match the asset with a buyer. This is typically not the case for the financial assets that are at the center of recent crises.
- When there is a probability of default, credit may be rationed (Weiss and Stiglitz 1981). Thus some borrowers may not be able to gain access to funds at any interest rate. This is a real liquidity problem. Despite the borrower's positive net worth, it is unable to borrow, because the supplier of credit cannot appropriate large enough returns to compensate for the risk borne.
- When there are large differences in beliefs between lenders and borrowers, at the interest rate required to compensate the lender the borrower believes it is paying a usurious return. This is not strictly a case of liquidity, except to the extent that the borrower believes that, over time, information it possesses but cannot credibly make available to the lender will become available. The belief that there are large asymmetries of information may itself cause a liquidity problem of the second type, as lenders' beliefs about the credit worthiness of borrowers deteriorate as more attractive terms are offered (these Akerlof-Greenwald-Stiglitz "adverse selection effects closing market" arguments seem more persuasive in the context of equity markets than in the context of debt markets).
- Multiple equilibria—such as those exhibited in the Diamond-Dybvig (1983) model—may give rise to illiquidity. Individuals, believing that others are going to withdraw their money, do so, causing a bank that would have been solvent to become insolvent. The provision of temporary funds can restore the bank to solvency. Even better, the belief that there are funds available eliminates the incentive to withdraw funds, thus preventing the liquidity crisis altogether.

What are the implications of these different forms of illiquidity for interventions? Many recent interventions seem to have been in response to the third type of illiquidity—international bureaucrats have been driven by the belief that they have better judgments than the market about the ability and willingness of a country (or companies within a country) to repay a loan. We have already commented on the profound implications that such a perspective has on market interventions more generally.

There is little evidence that bureaucrats' judgment is superior to that of the market; their record in ascertaining equilibrium exchange rates is hardly impressive. Moreover, it remains hard to understand why assessing countries' creditworthiness should be the only instance in which their judgment should replace that of the market.

Many more recent proposals are premised on a slightly different "market failure"—namely, the inability of the private sector to make credible commitments to make credit available under certain circumstances (in a crisis) at prescribed interest rates (or interest rate formulae). One of the reasons for this is presumably the reason that markets cannot provide business cycle insurance: these are systemic shocks, and many of the firms that might provide such insurance will themselves go bankrupt (or face liquidity constraints) in the event of a crisis. The liquidity constraints facing many of the suppliers of funds to the emerging markets in the aftermath of the Russian default bear testimony to the importance of this possibility. (In some cases, the issue is the price at which such insurance is made available. In that case this argument is equivalent to the third argument above, a difference in views about the appropriate price.)

International financial institutions may face different circumstance from private sector borrowers with respect to the second set of liquidity problems—the enforcement of claims. As senior creditors, the international financial institutions can count on greater compliance than private sector creditors. This raises two issues: the impact of the provision of such credit on the price and availability of credit by private lenders and the possibility that such credit could itself precipitate a crisis, or at least cause it to occur earlier than it would otherwise have occurred.

Modigliani-Miller (1958) type analysis suggests that the provision of credit by the international financial institutions with their preferred creditor standing may reduce the return on nonpreferred credit, reducing the amount of lending that nonpreferred creditors will make available. Moreover, the anticipation that a preferred creditor loan will be made could lead to credit rationing at an earlier date. The availability of such a credit line could thus cause crises to occur earlier (and possibly more frequently) than otherwise. Moreover, it could (indeed would be anticipated to) lead to higher interest rates on nonpreferred credit. Thus the country as a whole may save little if anything in overall borrowing costs. (Note that if capital markets were perfect—as IMF ideology often seems to assume—there would be no savings in overall capital costs.) To be sure, if the international financial institutions' interventions were believed to lead to better policies or policies that reduced the risk of default, all of these effects could be reversed. That such contingent lending leads to earlier or more frequent crises may not by itself be an argument against such loans: the adverse consequences of crises are highly nonlinear in their size, and delay may lead to crises of greater magnitude.

The multiple equilibria model raises the most interesting prospects for contingent loans, for the belief that funds are available in the event of an attack against a currency may actually stave off the attack. Among the key questions is whether the volume of funds available is likely to be sufficient, especially once it is recognized that pressure on a currency may come from domestic capital flight as well as a direct speculative attack. If funds are insufficient to stave off an attack, the availability of more funds to defend a currency actually enhances the incentives for an attack. Remember, to a first-order approximation, speculative attacks represent zero-sum games: speculators gain at the expense of others.

Who are these others? In the past, government support of exchange rates has provided a large supply of funds to speculators; by increasing the "food" available to feed speculators, the profitability of speculation is increased. To be sure, recent rhetoric has focused on governments allowing their exchange rates to fluctuate. But such talk is somewhat hollow: if exchange rates were really left to fluctuate freely, there would be no need for stabilization funds. Today it is sometimes argued that government should limit itself to ensuring that exchange rates do not overshoot—whatever that means and however such policies could be implemented in practice. But any such intervention provides food for a speculative frenzy.

This discussion of illiquidity is not meant to settle the issue; indeed, it is intended to be unsettling—and to emphasize that willingness to discuss liquidity indicates recognition not only that there are market imperfections but that they are of first-order importance. Once one admits that, however, one needs to broaden the discourse to address the full range of desirable interventions, not only once a liquidity crisis occurs, but before. And one needs to address not only the most disastrous consequences of these market imperfections, which manifest themselves in crises, but the less disastrous but nonetheless real consequences that may occur, in more subtle forms, in more normal times as well.

## Dealing with Systemic Distress

It is now widely recognized that recovery from the crises that struck East Asia in 1997 will require much more widespread corporate reorganizations than have occurred and that the financial sector is the highest priority among structural issues to be addressed as part of the crisis response. Two issues in particular—bankruptcy and financial sector restructuring—require attention.

### *Bankruptcy*

Without addressing the bankruptcy issue it will be hard to fully resolve the weaknesses in the financial sector. Doing so is essential if the flow of credit that underpins a healthy economy is to be restored. By some accounts, more than 60 percent of Indonesia's firms and more than 25 percent of Thai firms cannot meet their debt obligations and are now effectively bankrupt. Nonperforming Thai banking loans peaked at just under 50 percent in 1998. More than two and half years after the onset of the crisis, close to 40 percent of loans were still nonperforming.

If firms remain in bankruptcy, the incidence of nonperforming loans will remain high, and it will be difficult even to ascertain the full magnitude of capital infusions necessary to restore these institutions to viability. It will also be hard to rekindle investment, and there remains a real danger off asset stripping. Inadequacies in the bankruptcy laws and their implementation through judicial processes have slowed the process of corporate reorganization and have often been cited as one of the underlying institutional weaknesses in the East Asian economies.

ISOLATED BANKRUPTCY. As economies in Asia and elsewhere approach the task of designing bankruptcy laws, they need to think carefully about some of the basic underlying principles, which all too often have been ignored, both in the popular press and by the visiting firemen from the industrial countries proffering advice and counsel. First, the central role of bankruptcy in modern capitalist economies needs to be recognized. Modern capitalism could not have developed without limited liability corporations, and limited liability implies bankruptcy. Accordingly, bankruptcy should not be viewed as "letting borrowers off the hook" or "allowing debtors to unilaterally abrogate contracts." Indeed, so important is bankruptcy for the functioning of modern capitalism that firms are typically not allowed to write contracts that override the provisions of the bankruptcy code.

Second, it should be recognized that there is no single bankruptcy code that can be packaged and adopted around the world. Bankruptcy provisions need to be tailored to the situation of the country and the circumstances in which it finds itself, although countries should recognize the great advantage of adhering to widely accepted standards. Different bankruptcy provisions do have different consequences for debtors and creditors in different situations; questions of efficiency and equity are central. But there is no single bankruptcy code that is unambiguously best for everyone in society (to use economists' jargon, there is no single "Pareto dominant" bankruptcy code)—although badly written codes may actually make everyone (debtors, creditors, and others) worse off (in economists' jargon, some codes are "Pareto inferior"). That is why bankruptcy codes are typically the subject of such intense political debate—as witnessed during the recent furor over revisions in the U.S. bankruptcy code. This has strong implications for policymaking: bankruptcy codes cannot be imposed from outside, and one should be suspicious of bankruptcy codes designed by interested parties (such as lenders) or those representing their interests.

Third, bankruptcy affects not only lenders but also other stakeholders, particularly workers. There is thus an important externality: the resolution of bankruptcy disputes between lenders and borrowers affects innocent bystanders, people not party to the agreement. But it is not just that workers are affected: workers have rights that must be recognized during the bargaining between lenders and borrowers. There is typically an implicit commitment between workers and firms. If the worker continues to work effectively, the firm will not only continue to employ him or her, it will also pay wages commensurate with the worker's abilities and effort. There are, of course, limitations to this commitment: if the firm's sales decline precipitously, workers, as well as the firm's shareholders, bear some of the risk. The commitment is typically not explicit, simply because it is impossible to write down all relevant conditions. Anglo-American common law recognizes these implicit commitments: in bankruptcy proceedings, a payment due to workers for work already performed has seniority over other senior creditors. But there are broader, and typically unresolved, issues concerning other obligations toward workers (those embedded in the implicit contract) and other creditors.

Fourth, bankruptcy law typically provides a backdrop against which bargaining between creditors and debtors takes place. It is worth noting that bankruptcy law does not provide a simple formula that can automatically be invoked. Judges—in the United States specialized in handling the intricacies of such matters—are called upon to interpret bankruptcy law in different circumstances. Often the priorities of different creditors are ambiguous and the interests of other stakeholders need to be taken into account. In simple models of bankruptcy, when the firm cannot meet its obligations, all residual value is turned over to creditors. In practice, the original equity owners generally retain a significant share of the value of the firm. There is often disagreement over the equity value of the firm, and therefore the adequacy of compensation for the creditors, with the original owners claiming the market has simply temporarily undervalued their shares. Thus while equity owners may believe that creditors have received more than the value of their claims, creditors may believe that they have been inadequately compensated. Of course, if markets worked perfectly, such disputes would not exist—but neither would "liquidity" problems, which are often at the root of bankruptcies. Because it affects the likely outcome if a dispute has to be resolved by the courts, bankruptcy law affects the outcome of the bargaining process, which is typically designed to avoid the uncertainty and delay of relying on court-mandated resolutions.

Fifth, it is important for the bankruptcy rules of the game to be as clear as possible. Ambiguity can give rise to a risk premium. As long as there is clarity, interest rates will adjust to reflect the probability of default, but the higher interest paid merely offsets lower payments in bankruptcy states and accordingly need not have a significant adverse effect on capital flows. More generally, arguments that more creditor-friendly bankruptcy codes are necessary to maintain the flow of capital need to be looked at with suspicion. In any case, some moderation of the flow of short-term capital might reduce the externalities associated with those flows.

SYSTEMIC BANKRUPTCY. Most important, it is imperative to distinguish between systemic bankruptcy and isolated bankruptcy. In the midst of the crisis, the countries of East Asia faced systemic bankruptcies; bankruptcy codes designed to deal with isolated bankruptcy simply would not do. Some of the reasons for this should be obvious. When a single firm goes bankrupt, there is a reasonable inference that the firm itself did something wrong and there is typically a large supply of managerial teams. There is normally little concern about macroeconomic consequences (although occasionally a firm is so large that the "too big to fail" doctrine is invoked). None of these conditions was true in the East Asian crisis.

There is a simple solution to this problem: a new "Super Chapter 11" to be imbedded in every country's bankruptcy code. In the U.S. bankruptcy code, Chapter 11 is distinguished from Chapter 7 in that under Chapter 11 management proposes a continuation of its own control of the firm. Existing management or controlling shareholders typically receive more than their due—that is, shareholders are not totally wiped out, even if creditor obligations are not fully satisfied, simply because doing so would erode the management structure, and hence, efficiency, of the firm. This was brought home forcefully by the reorganization of Long-Term Capital Management, the U.S. hedge fund that had an exposure of more than $1 trillion and thus presented (at least in the view of some supporters of the private bail-out) a systemic risk to the global financial system. Even as the firm was being bailed out by lenders, the principal equity owners (who under straight bankruptcy proceedings should have received nothing unless creditors were fully satisfied) retained a 10 percent equity share.

Chapter 11 is designed for a quick resolution of bankruptcy disputes, but even under Chapter 11, proceedings typically take a year or more. To protect against waste or mismanagement of assets in the interim, courts typically take on a strong trusteeship role. With systemic bankruptcy, not only is the cost of delay greater—as unemployment mounts and financial institutions weaken—but the effectiveness of interim monitoring is reduced. There simply are not an adequate supply of bankruptcy trustees—even in the United States, with its wealth of experience in sophisticated bankruptcy law—to meet the challenge.

What is required is a Super Chapter 11, modeled after Chapter 11, that addresses the problems brought on by systemic bankruptcy, particularly systemic bankruptcy caused by massive macroeconomic disturbances, such as major economic contractions, huge increases in interest rates, and sharp devaluations. As in Chapter 11, the presumption would be that management would stay in place and that there would be a debt-to-equity conversion.

Super Chapter 11 would differ from Chapter 11 in three important ways, however. First, given the importance of speed of resolution, the time within which the courts would have to rule would be shortened considerably; a stronger burden would be placed on those attempting to delay. Second, there would be a stronger presumption in favor of management staying in place and on management proposals that, in the reorganization, give management or old shareholders enough of an equity interest to have adequate incentives. In other words, a higher burden of proof would be placed on creditors to demonstrate that the management proposal was grossly inequitable. Third, to facilitate quick resolution, a wider set of default or guideline provisions would be specified. These would be aimed at ensuring fairness in the protection of other claimants (such as workers) and in balancing the claims of creditors with claims denominated in foreign and domestic currency in an environment of rapidly changing exchange rates.

Such a Super Chapter 11 might be an effective way out of the seeming impasse, which is so costly to everyone in countries facing systemic bankruptcy. To be sure, such a bankruptcy code might lead to somewhat higher interest rates, especially by short-term foreign lenders. But that might be all to the good, causing them to focus more clearly on the risks inherent in such lending—risks that extend well beyond those party to the transaction to innocent bystanders, that is, the workers and small businesses that have been badly hurt under the current financial regime. Such a bankruptcy regime would accordingly be fairer than the current one, especially if it were known in advance. Adjustments in interest rates charged would compensate lenders for any changes in risk assumed.

Even under current circumstances, it could be argued that a movement to this new code would be fair. So much of the burden of the delay is being borne by third parties, and the current regime gives too much power to creditors, who were frequently already well compensated for the risks they bore. Even ignoring the systemic benefits, the quick resolution provided by such a provision would have distinct efficiency advantages: it would end the waste associated not only with the unemployment of resources but also with the stripping of assets.[15]

A change of bankruptcy code along these lines would also reduce the need for public funds in the corporate reorganization process. Once firms reorganized and the economy started working again, capital markets would be willing to provide funds to firms with projects with high returns. It should be remembered: corporate reorganizations are simply a rearrangement of claims on the assets of the firm. To be sure, such rearrangements, if not done or done badly, have strong implications for the performance of firms. But the reorganization process itself does not require funds—except when costly and litigious bankruptcy proceedings are resorted to. The Super Chapter 11 would reduce the incentives for such litigation.

Recently, there have been proposals for an injection of funds from public agencies to provide a "carrot" to induce faster reorganization. Such proposals, originating as they have from governments of creditor countries, are hardly surprising. Discussing such proposals is counterproductive, for they provide an incentive to delay reorganization in the hopes that such delay will reap some part of the public largesse. There are far better ways to spend scarce public funds—focusing on high multiplier, job-creating programs with benefits targeted especially to the poor.

A Super Chapter 11 could also eliminate some of the "bad" equilibrium in a world of multiple equilibria (Miller and Stiglitz 1999). Incentives for faster bankruptcy resolution may be needed, but these should take the form of sticks rather than carrots. The fear that such sticks, aimed at creditors, will cause the future supply of capital to dry up are almost surely unfounded. First, with its high savings rate, East Asia does not need a foreign supply of capital. Second, lenders look at future prospects, not past results. A clearly defined bankruptcy regime, a well-functioning economy (with a high level of employment), the lack of the kind of social and political unrest that inevitably accompanies extended periods of unemployment—all of these are of first-order importance, and all of these would be enhanced by the new bankruptcy code. Given these enhanced opportunities and increased certainties, creditors would be better able to ascertain the interest rates to be charged to compensate themselves adequately for the risks they face. The historical experience has confirmed these theoretical propositions: lenders returned relatively quickly even after the massive defaults that have periodically plagued Latin America. Interest rates may well rise, but the increase only serves to bring private costs of borrowing more in alignment with social costs.

## Financial Sector Restructuring

Even before the nature of financial sector vulnerabilities and the dynamics of their likely evolution in East Asia were adequately appreciated, the attention of governments and the international community focused on the financial sector as the highest priority among structural issues to be addressed as part of the crisis response. The concentration on the financial sector was surely justified. Unfortunately, there is now a general awareness of some of the problems in the policy responses. In order to avoid similar mistakes in the future, we need to ask why they occurred.

One hypothesis is that policy responses on these interrelated fronts were hampered by the absence of a coherent analytical framework based on requisite microfoundations, a framework that integrates effectively, for instance, the financial and real sectors. Much of the knowledge about lags and irreversibilities, persistence and asymmetries, and the relations between financial markets and economic activity was not effectively brought to bear on the policy designs.

In East Asia, as in other developing countries that have suffered from systemic financial distress, a large proportion of financial institutions are illiquid and many are potentially insolvent. The strategy for dealing with financial restructuring has to be designed to mitigate, not exacerbate, the economic crisis. A key goal must be to maintain credit flows. Typically, as an economy faces a crisis, credit flows are impeded. The bankruptcy of one firm has adverse effects on suppliers and customers, which curtail the availability of normal trade credit. Similarly, banks facing declining net worth and worsening prospects reduce the flow of credit. These normal reactions in an economic downturn are exacerbated in financial crises. Weak banks—banks that fail to meet the basic capital adequacy standards and are on the verge of insolvency (or beyond it)—often need to be restructured. This restructuring can be done in better or worse ways. In particular, it can be done in ways that impede the already limited flow of credit and thus contribute to the economy's decline.

The way financial restructuring was conducted in the United States' saving and loan crisis in the 1980s and recently in Indonesia provide examples of such success and failure. In the United States, relatively few savings and loan institutions were closed. Most were merged with stronger institutions, typically over a weekend so that customers barely noticed the change in management. In Indonesia, by contrast, 16 private banks were closed, there were intimations that other weak banks might be shut down, and depositors were put on notice that they were at risk. The resulting run on the remaining private banks was no surprise, especially as there were safer alternatives: state banks (which many believed had the government's implicit guarantee) and foreign banks (which many believed were sounder). But even if these safe havens had not been available, depositors could have taken out their money and put it into foreign banks (thereby also avoiding the risk of devaluation). As private banks were thus weakened, the contracting supply of credit contributed to the downward spiral of the economy.

In one sense, it is understandable why the IMF made these mistakes. Weak banks had played a critical role in bringing on the crisis, and so it was natural to try to strengthen the banks, and to do so quickly. What is less understandable was the failure to see that the strengthening of the banks had to be done in ways that maintained the flow of credit. After all, the multitude of financial (banking) crises had provided ample lessons for anyone who wished to grasp them.

Two additional observations about financial restructuring are worth noting. First, the costs of restructuring can be divided into two parts. One arises from the fact that the net worth of many banks is negative because of the high level of bad loans. With deposit insurance, the government must fill the gap. This redistribution from taxpayers to depositors needed to fill that gap has a fiscal cost, but it is a transfer payment. It does not use real resources and, in that sense, is not inflationary. Moreover, while the government may have committed itself to repay depositors, it typically has not made a commitment on the interest rates it must pay. It may, for instance, contemplate restricting withdrawals and limiting the interest rate paid on deposits; alternatively, it can allow deposit withdrawals but restrict transfer of capital abroad. These are examples of ways in which the costs of fulfilling the government's commitments may be contained—ways that are less distortionary than the perhaps more traditional ways of inflating away the value of monetary claims.

The second part of the cost of restructuring consists of the finance required to "restart" the banking system. This can be funded in ways that entail low interest costs, such as by borrowing from banks at low interest rates and investing back in the banking firms. While such financial transactions may meet standard capital adequacy standards, they do not resolve incentive issues. They may, however, restore confidence. It is also important to note that in terms of the government's budget, these financial transactions rightly belong in the capital account, not the current account, and therefore should not crowd out other output-, growth-, or equity-enhancing forms of public expenditure. Unfortunately, if costly ways are employed to finance the restructuring of the banks and if the distinction between capital and current budgets is not made, there is a real danger that restructuring expenditures will crowd out others, to the detriment of economic recovery. Thus a careful analysis that balances the benefits of alternative ways of spending scarce public funds is necessary. Moreover, the restructuring should not proceed under the assumption that but for the crisis at hand, capital markets work perfectly, so paying a "less than market rate" will mean huge distortions.

The second observation relates to the phenomenon in which as an economy goes into recession and lending is discouraged by the economy's seemingly weak prospects, there is sometimes an increase in liquidity of the banking system among banks that do not face massive withdrawals. Some economists, worried about inflation, naively argue for mopping up the liquidity. However, governments typically have only blunt instruments for doing so. As a result, banks without excess liquidity are affected as well. Finding their constraints tightened further, these banks decrease their lending, exacerbating the downturn. More generally, worries about inflation—in the face of massive excess capacity—are likely to be misplaced. In this regard, it is also worth noting that the relation among aggregate economic variables (including that between monetary aggregates and output) may be greatly disturbed in an economy with a disrupted financial sector. This was a lesson that the U.S. Federal Reserve learned in the early 1990s, at significant expense to the economy.

Simplistic models are likely to lead to misguided policies. But if governments refuse to provide new capital, the insistence on banks quickly meeting capital requirements actually contributes to instability. When a crisis hits countries that are at their limit and capital adequacy standards are rigidly enforced, defaults rise and bank net worth declines. New capital sources have to be found or lending must decrease. But the midst of crisis is hardly an ideal time for raising new capital. As a result, lending typically contracts, further weakening the economy by leading to more bankruptcies, more nonperforming loans, and perhaps an even greater shortfall in capital adequacy.

This chain of events dramatically emphasizes the difference between policies designed to deal with a systemic crisis and policies affecting an individual institution. Rigorous enforcement of capital adequacy standards in the case of an isolated bank facing troubles is markedly different from the rigorous enforcement of those standards in the case of a systemic crisis. In a systemic crisis, a better alternative is to accept lower capital with more stringent supervision and tighter regulation of lending. The objective is restructuring the financial system in ways that do not interrupt credit flows but rather lead to higher-quality lending.

One must acknowledge that it is difficult if not impossible to restore the strength of the financial system in the middle of a recession; sustained recovery requires simultaneous progress on corporate and financial restructuring, as well as "reflation" of the economy. Indeed, in view of the large exchange rate devaluations in East Asia, the necessary redeployment of economic resources across sectors requires substantial availability and flow of credit.

## Reducing the Impact of Crises on the Poor

The disruption and very large social costs witnessed in the aftermath of economic crises, even for middle-income countries, have highlighted the extent of social vulnerability of developing countries in the new financial environment. The recent crises have also shown that the impact can be extremely diverse across countries, locations, sectors of employment, genders, and levels of wealth and income.

The magnitude of the social impact of the recent financial crises can be attributed to four interrelated factors: very large swings in exchange rates, interest rates, and asset prices; sharp declines in aggregate demand; banking and corporate sector distress; and cuts or breakdowns in public services. The immediate and dominant impact of these factors on most households is through reduced labor demand. Unemployment doubled in Thailand and tripled in the Republic of Korea in just a year during the recent crisis. In Indonesia and Malaysia, and to some degree Thailand, most of the adjustment appears to have taken place through falling real wages and the movement of workers into low-paying informal sector jobs (Atinc and Walton 1998). The loss of jobs and decline in wages led to huge declines in standards of living: 25 percent in Indonesia, 22 percent in the Republic of Korea, and 14 percent in Thailand (Jimenez and Ruedi 1998).

While income inequality generally tends to rise during periods of economic contraction, the incidence and severity of the impact in the recent crisis has varied. Among the crisis-affected countries of East Asia, the Republic of Korea saw the largest proportional increase in poverty, largely among the urban unemployed. In Thailand suburban and rural areas, including the traditionally poorer areas of the north, were more affected.

Those most affected by unemployment or lower wages have tended to be lower-skilled workers working in small- and medium-size enterprises. These enterprises accounted for almost half of the increase in unemployment in Thailand and 60 percent of the increase in the Republic of Korea. Although the impact of the crisis was most severe and broad based in Indonesia, it was the urban nonpoor that bore the brunt there; poverty in Indonesia increased by far less than originally expected. (Many of the country's poor lead a subsistence life that is relatively unaffected by markets.)

If effective programs are to be designed to contain the social costs of crises, the differential impacts on people facing different circumstances—income sources, consumption patterns, and access to public services—must be taken into account. Thailand illustrates the various channels through which the poor are affected. It is not just the direct impact of closed factories and lost jobs as a result of reduced aggregate demand. With flexible wages, the decline in aggregate demand may lead to markedly reduced incomes rather than much higher unemployment. Migration to the rural sector would have lowered income there, even if nothing else had changed. And even if Thailand had not had a financial crisis, its farms would have suffered from lower commodity prices. Indeed, the much vaunted recovery (the bounce back of the exchange rate)—combined with falling agricultural prices partly resulting from the global slowdown—did more to immiserate the farms than the crisis itself.

In addition to the short-term impact, financial crises can have long-term and irreversible effects on the poor. Many of the children who were pulled out of junior secondary schools in Indonesia will permanently lose out on educational opportunities. The increased prevalence of malnutrition at crucial stages of childhood can have permanent effects on physical and mental development. And social and political strife and the loss of social capital can have long-lasting effects in terms of increased crime and violence, as evident from the experience of Latin America following the debt crisis of the 1980s. Although it has complex roots, the downward social spiral in Indonesia was triggered by, and is being exacerbated by, the ongoing economic crisis.

A lesson that has been underscored by the recent Asian crisis is that minimizing the risks and severity of economic downturns is probably the most important step that the international community, and developing countries, can take to contain the social costs of the crises. This, in turn, has two implications. First, there is a high premium to reducing vulnerability, including through appropriate management of volatile capital flows. Second, policy responses to crises need to be designed so that they do not lead to large declines in aggregate demand and unemployment.

### Adopting Appropriate Macroeconomic Policies

Macroeconomic policies are the most important determinant of the level of economic activity. They thus constitute the most important tool with which to support employment and incomes in the aftermath of crises. Designing appropriate macroeconomic responses in crisis situations is a complex and difficult task, because the usual uncertainty about impact and lags is greatly heightened and the effects are inherently asymmetric and nonlinear. A relatively small shock to the economy may be self-correcting, but a larger shock may plunge the economy into recession. Hence the wrong policies can result in virtually unbounded harm, while the right policies will only keep the economy operating normally.

There is abundant evidence that a major economic downturn can be translated into a prolonged period of higher unemployment and slower growth. This can occur because of the dissipation of physical and organizational capital and because firms respond to bad times by reducing their investment in research and development. Furthermore, long-term unemployed workers lose their job-searching skills and become stigmatized by employers—an effect economists have called *hysteresis*. Many economists place some of the blame for high European unemployment in the past 15 years on hysteresis.

The social consequences of a downward economic spiral can be highly uneven. Even if everyone shares the losses, the effects on the poor, who have just enough to survive, are enormous compared with the effects on the better off. Moreover, the burden of adjustment is typically not shared equally: a disproportionate share of the increase in under- or unemployment is concentrated among the least well off. As a result, these innocent bystanders, who played no part in the causes leading up to the crisis, bear the greatest burden. There is thus much merit in avoiding large downturns and in ensuring equitable sharing of losses between external creditors and domestic nationals and between taxpayers and owners of banks and firms.

These considerations have an important bearing on the balance of risks and the design of macroeconomic policies. Three other aspects are also important. First is the role of expectations. The macroeconomic policy response needs to be designed to restore confidence in the economy in the face of a crisis. In this regard, austerity measures are not necessarily appropriate. If there is a prospect of a collapse in private demand, more expansionary macroeconomic policies geared to maintaining the strength of the economy will help preserve confidence.

Second is the recognition of the growing importance of macrofinancial linkages. Theory and empirical evidence over the past two decades have established the importance of financial markets, their links with the macroeconomy, the role that financial crises play in economic downturns, and the fact that economic downturns precipitated or accompanied by banking and currency crises are deeper and longer than, say, downturns associated with inventory cycles. Macroeconomic policy thus needs to be formulated to take into account the close linkages with the financial sector, in particular, the effects of macroeconomic swings on the financial structures of banks and corporations and the associated risks. Examples of the importance of these linkages abound. Large increases in interest rates have large adverse effects on asset values, reducing firms' ability and willingness to absorb risk; shifting the aggregate supply curve to the left, thereby exacerbating the downturn through a channel quite different from that emphasized in traditional Keynesian analysis; and contributing to corporate distress, especially among highly leveraged firms. They may thus contribute to the further weakening of the already weak banking sector.

Third is the distributional impact and the adequacy of coping mechanisms. Devaluations have been shown to have a positive impact on the poor in Sub-Saharan

Africa, because they tend to be net producers of tradable goods. But if the poor relied on imported food, the effects would be negative. Similarly, the net effects of monetary policy on different groups vary from country to country depending on institutional practices in both the private and public sectors. In most economies, high interest rates tend to restrict borrowing and investment by small and medium-size enterprises much more than large firms. Substantial evidence from several countries has documented that higher interest rates can have an especially large adverse effect on farmers' access to credit. The distributional effects of changes in interest rates, however, depend on the degree to which different credit markets are segmented and the existence of government programs to help different groups gain access to credit. In Brazil, for instance, government programs and financial market practices have, to a large degree, delinked the interest rate faced by many farmers from the key monetary policy interest rates. In contrast, Indonesia's credit markets are tightly linked, and an increase in policy interest rates rapidly translates into higher interest rates across the board.

The design of policies and the analysis of risks must also take into account the ability of the economy—its workers and others within society—to absorb various shocks, including under- and unemployment. The lack of social safety nets in East Asian economies suggests that the social costs of an economic downturn there would be an order of magnitude greater than in Finland, where the huge increase in unemployment as a result of its financial crises was mitigated by its strong social welfare system.

The downside risks of macroeconomic policies are thus large. Given the high degree of uncertainty in a crisis environment, macroeconomic policies need to be flexible and adaptable, taking into account the specific circumstances of a country, the balance of risks, and new information. If capital outflows are very large, a combination of new money and voluntary or involuntary "bailing-in" of the private sector may be needed to create the room for macroeconomic maneuver. In extreme circumstances, temporary capital controls or interventions to tilt incentives against concerted withdrawal of capital may be the only course. There are large externalities associated with such flows, which provide a rationale for public intervention.

## Achieving Better Balance in Structural Policies

Many of the same considerations that apply to the macroeconomic policy responses to crisis situations also apply to structural policy responses. Indeed, we are increasingly recognizing that there is no clear separation between macroeconomic and structural issues. Structural weaknesses—such as weaknesses in financial systems or widespread corporate bankruptcies—have macroeconomic consequences; mistakes in macroeconomic policy can have profound effects on economic structure that will take years to undo. Like macroeconomic policies, structural policies entail a complex balancing of different objectives. Policies need to be designed with four interrelated considerations in mind: ex ante incentives, ex post incentives, distributional equity and fairness, and macroeconomic consequences.

To give one illustration, financial regulation needs to ensure that borrowers and lenders have the ex ante incentive to behave prudently. After a crisis, however, the financial structure of banks and corporations changes, and policies will imply a different set of ex post incentives. Considerations of equity—including who continues to have access to credit as well as whose money bails out whom—should also be important.

The balance of these considerations depends on the circumstances. In good times, the macroeconomic implications of structural policies may be less important, since any contractionary consequences may be easy to offset with more expansionary macroeconomic policies. As the economy shifts from downturn to recession to depression, however, the balance of these objectives shifts, and ex post incentives—incentives facing firms in the current situation—and macroeconomic consequences become the overriding concerns.

In recent years, wide-ranging long-term structural reforms have been at the heart of many crisis programs. There are two possible justifications for such an emphasis. The first is that a crisis may present a unique opportunity to undertake reforms whose desirability has long been recognized but for which there is little political will in noncrisis periods. The second is that to the degree that these structural weaknesses are perceived as having caused the crisis, even reforms with only long-run economic benefits might immediately improve confidence and thus help restore economic strength.

Not all long-term structural reforms, however, make sense in the midst of a crisis. In particular, there are three reasons why we should be cautious. The first is that responding to a crisis is extremely difficult and often requires the full attention of the scarce personnel of both the crisis country and the international institutions working with it. Overloading the reform program may distract attention from the immediate problems.

Second, some reforms that are beneficial in the long run may actually harm the economy in the short run. Eliminating distortions that create rents, although beneficial in the long run, may weaken the economy in the short run, exacerbating the problem of bankruptcy. If the distortionary tax preferences for housing had been eliminated in the midst of the U.S. savings and loan crisis, for example, the United States might have been confronted with a full-scale financial crisis. Similarly, under some circumstances, improving transparency in the midst of a crisis may reveal that the problems are much worse than anyone had realized, thus exacerbating the crisis.

Third, to the degree that unnecessary structural reforms are pushed into the programs by outsiders, domestic political support for the entire program may be undermined, including support for the parts that are essential for addressing the crisis at hand. For this reason, there was reluctance in the United States to move to more transparent, more efficient bank accounting standards and risk adjustments in the midst of its banking crises in the 1980s.

Reforms included as part of the crisis response must be genuinely desired by the crisis country, not imposed from outside. They should also be related, at least in terms of perception, to the crisis itself. Finally, reforms must not have contractionary effects in the short run.

## Building Better Social Safety Nets

Even with sound macroeconomic and structural policies, a country is unlikely to escape a serious balance of payments or banking crisis without a period of slower growth or even economic contraction. Experience also shows that income inequality often rises in periods of economic crises, structural adjustment, and output contractions. Both the lower level of income and the shift in income distribution increase the number of people living in poverty.

We must recognize, however, several attributes of developing countries that make establishing social safety nets inherently more difficult and have an important bearing on their design. Because of their smaller size and less diversified structure, developing economies are inherently more susceptible to shocks. They thus experience much more variability in incomes and real wages in the wake of crises. At the same time, the informal sector tends to dominate, so that formal social insurance, even if well functioning, covers only a small proportion of the population, especially among the poor. Demographic structures of developing countries are also typically quite different from those in industrial countries, with children constituting a much larger proportion of the population. Moreover, few households have easy ways to cushion their expenditures. Large reversals in rural-urban migration following economic downturns such as those seen in Thailand and Indonesia act as a buffer in some respects, but they also have important implications for policy response and program design.

Developing country governments are also much more constrained in their ability to respond to crises. The ability to use budgets countercyclically in the face of downturns is much more limited. (In the East Asian crisis, the insistence at early stages on balanced budgets only made matters worse.) Constrained budgets suggest tight targeting, but the difficulty of measuring household incomes in developing countries makes means-tested programs very hard to implement. As a result, indirect indicators have to be used, but even this may be difficult because of the paucity of information. Food subsidies, which could be confined to foods consumed mainly by the poor, may indeed be critical to avoid malnutrition. Education subsidies can also be key to avoiding interruptions in schooling (as some reports indicate they have in Indonesia). Nevertheless, problems in delivery mechanisms are likely to pose constraints in shaping an effective response to deal with the social consequences of crises.

In certain countries, especially middle-income countries, it may make sense to develop or expand the unemployment insurance system, especially if large numbers of workers in the formal sector remain without coverage. Such programs are often criticized for their adverse incentive effects, but these effects may be negligible in periods of severe recessions.

In general, though, limiting social costs and improving resilience to crises will require a much broader approach in developing countries than just establishing formal safety nets. We are learning how to design better interventions to mitigate social costs. Public expenditure programs should not only protect core social and poverty-oriented programs, they should also be geared to increasing expenditures where multiplier effects are likely to be greatest (construction of rural roads, low-income housing, and small-scale environmental infrastructure are some possibilities). Governments and international agencies need to learn to take a more sophisticated approach to budgeting. Not all "expenditures" pose the same inflationary threat—some might more rightly be considered capital transactions.

We noted earlier that there are less—and more—expensive ways of recapitalizing the banking system. Advocates of the "more" expensive ways typically employ models of the capital market that ignore the increased understandings of these markets of the past two decades. In particular, they act as if capital markets are perfect, so that any support at below-market rates reduces overall efficiency. Countries—and especially the poor—have had to pay a high price for these misguided views. Actions to fix the supply side should also focus on areas with high multiplier effects (by relieving bottlenecks in export credit, for example, especially for small and medium-size enterprises).

Fiscal policies that protect spending on education and health can prevent cuts in services the poor use and protect their ability to build up human capital. (Of course, the elimination of unproductive expenditures may help keep social spending at its pre-crisis levels. But some countries have eliminated much of these expenditures, with those categories surviving having political support that makes their elimination difficult at best.) Tilting education and health expenditures toward activities that are more beneficial for the poor, such as basic education or primary healthcare, or have high externalities, such as vaccinations and vector control, will increase the impact on poverty and social objectives. In Indonesia expenditures on primary education have increased by more than 50 percent in real terms. As a result, the number of school dropouts has been much lower than feared at the outset of the crisis. Other public investments that affect the productivity of the poor—most notably, investments in rural infrastructure and the provision of microfinance—should also be protected.

In addition to modulating and protecting core public expenditures, a well-designed safety net can substantially mitigate adverse effects by providing an insurance function. Such safety nets should be established before a crisis to be effective in a timely way.

Three key principles should guide the design of effective safety nets. First, they should insure the poor against the risk of loss of income, responding flexibly to their needs. Second, they should not provide perverse incentives that could contribute to dependency. Third, they should be efficient and well governed (at the margin, money spent on these programs should be as effective at raising the welfare of the poor as money spent on other programs) (Ravallion 1999).

Experience in a number of countries suggests that programs that provide employment for those able to work and targeted transfers for those who cannot or should not work have proved effective in protecting the poor during crises. (The key problem, of course, is distinguishing among these categories of individuals.) Workfare programs targeted to geographic areas that are most adversely affected can benefit the poor both through direct employment benefits and through the positive spillovers of the project. In the design of such workfare programs, it is often necessary to set wages at levels that lead to self-selection by the poor. Good models of this type of program are the Argentine Trabajar scheme for middle-income countries and the Maharashtra Employment Guarantee Scheme for low-income countries.

Workfare programs may need to be complemented by even more carefully targeted programs to provide educational grants, basic health support, food, and even cash. The key and difficult challenge is to set up systems that can be scaled up and down quickly and to design programs that can be targeted (through self-selection mechanisms, for example). A good example of a scheme to keep children in school is the Bolsa Escola scheme in Brazil, which offers scholarships to families who send all their children to school. Such targeted programs would mitigate the impacts of increases in the cost of education and prevent long-term losses in educational attainment and earning potential.

## Concluding Remarks

We have touched on a wide range of issues concerned with international financial markets. There is a common theme: the problems that have arisen are evidence of market failures and irrationalities, interpreted in the broadest sense.

This article is a plea for intellectual consistency and integrity. Some might say that admitting the existence of these market failures opens up a Pandora's box—one that market conservatives are keen to keep shut. Their objective is to narrow the scope of government actions as much as possible. If government regulation of financial markets is required, they support the most rule-bound and simple form of regulation (rigidly enforced capital adequacy standards, for example). According to them, governments should either not intervene in the foreign exchange market at all or pursue a blind commitment to a fixed exchange rate regime. Governments should force information disclosure but not impose further restrictions.

By contrast, we would argue that that is the wrong way to approach the issues. The question should be, given the market failures as well as the limitations of government, what is the best set of interventions—by industrial countries, by developing countries, and by the international community—taking due account of the distributional consequences of different forms of interventions? Even the term *interventions* may be inappropriate: policies, institutions, and laws are all important. Every economy needs to have bankruptcy laws and financial market regulations. Thus the question is not whether there should be such laws and regulations but what form they should take.

## Notes

1. The most significant effort in the wake of the East Asia crisis is reflected in the 1998 Report of the G-22 Working Group on Transparency and Accountability. See http://www.imf.org/external/np/g22/taarep.pdf.

2. The discrepancy between private and social returns has been recognized for a long time (see Hirshleifer 1971 or Stiglitz 1975). Market participants may actually have incentives to obfuscate information (see Edlin and Stiglitz 1995).

3. This has occurred, for instance, in the reporting of off–balance sheet items. The most recent controversy centered on the disclosure of stock options. While there is some uncertainty in the valuation of such options, implicitly setting a value of such options at zero is clearly wrong. The Financial Accounting Standards Board proposed a more transparent form of disclosure, but it was eventually forced to retreat under political pressure—including pressure from the U.S. Treasury, which has been among those calling most loudly for increased transparency. There exist ways of providing minimum estimates of the value of the outstanding options.

4. Similarly, decisions in the United States not to require bank disclosure on the basis of marking to market and not to use risk adjustments that reflect market risk adversely affected transparency.

5. See, for example Vishwanath and Kaufmann (1999). The empirical literature has developed some proxy indicators. In an empirical study of industrial and developing countries, Demirgüç-Kunt and Detragiache (1997, 1998) identify many factors associated with banking crises. They find that institutional factors, as measured by inefficient bureaucracy, weak rule of law or contract enforcement, and an index of corruption, increase the likelihood of banking crises. However, their correlation is only weakly significant. In addition, extending such a finding to transparency is valid only to the extent that achieving transparency requires enforcement.

6. Transparency or disclosure is measured by the annual ranking of a firm's disclosure published by the Association of Investment and Management Research. Several researchers have used this ranking as a proxy for overall levels of disclosure.

7. See Faust and Svensson (1998). Their analysis is based on a theoretical model and has not been empirically tested.

8. Berle and Means (1933) and Stiglitz (1985) have argued that in countries with widely diversified share holdings, banks play an important role in corporate governance. Thus had the Republic of Korea (or some of the other East Asian countries) widely diversified its stock ownership, it might still have had a corporate governance problem, simply because of the problems in the financial sector to which we have already alluded.

9. Financial restraint, which has been shown to have positive (or at least nonnegative) effects on growth and investment, needs to be distinguished from financial repression. Implementation of financial restraint requires careful attention to provisions for opening capital accounts and opening up markets to foreign financial institutions.

10. A further objective of regulation may be to ensure that underserved groups have access to capital. In the United States, section 711of the recently enacted Gramm-Leach-Bliley Act establishes annual reporting and public disclosure requirements for certain written agreements between insured depository institutions or their affiliates and nongovernmental entities or persons (including business entities) made pursuant to, or in connection with, the fulfillment of the Community Reinvestment Act of 1977 (CRA requirements).

11. As our colleague Jerry Caprio has put it, there are two kinds of countries: those that have formal deposit insurance and those that have deposit insurance and don't know it.

12. To be sure, strong regulations effectively implemented against bank lending to corporations with large exposure will limit both corporate exposure and the country's vulnerability to changes in exchange rates, especially if there are good bankruptcy laws.

13. Enforcing such limitations may actually be easier than implementing the Chilean scheme. Attention has to be paid to attempts to evade these provisions through derivatives, but with appropriate transparency (which can be encouraged by making unregistered derivative contracts unenforceable in courts), these problems can almost surely be addressed.

14. In addition, it would be desirable if credit rating agencies did a somewhat better job of providing information about the deteriorating state of a country's economy in advance, rather than abruptly changing credit ratings just before or as the country plunges into crisis.

15. Such a provision also has advantages in terms of incentives before bankruptcy: there is now considerable evidence that firms facing a high probability of imminent bankruptcy may engage in value-decreasing risk-taking behavior, which enhances equity values in the event the disaster does not occur but decreases asset values in the event it does occur. Typically, the prospects of a firm look good at the time loans are made, but especially in the world of rapid financial movements and changes in investment sentiment, these prospects can change dramatically, providing considerable scope for these perverse incentives. A Super Chapter 11 provision would reduce such perverse incentives.

## References

Atinc, Tamar Manuelyan, and Michael Walton. 1998. *Social Consequences of the East Asian Financial Crisis*. Working Paper for the World Bank Annual Meetings Program of Seminars, September, Washington, D.C.

Berle, A. A., and G. C. Means. 1933. *The Modern Corporation and Private Property*. New York: Macmillan.

Blinder, Alan. 1998. *Central Banking in Theory and Practice*. Lionel Robbins Lectures. Cambridge, Mass.: MIT Press.

Bushee, Brian, and Christopher Noe. 1999. "Disclosure Quality, Institutional Investors, and Stock Return Volatility." Harvard Business School Working Paper 00–033. Cambridge, Mass.

Demirgüç-Kunt, Asli, and Enrica Detragiache. 1997. "The Determinants of Banking Crises: Evidence from Industrial and Developing Countries." Policy Research Working Paper 1828. World Bank, Development Research Group, and International Monetary Fund, Research Department, Washington, D.C.

———. 1998. "Financial Liberalization and Financial Fragility." Policy Research Working Paper 1917. World Bank, Development Research Group, and International Monetary Fund, Research Department, Washington, D.C.

Diamond, Douglas W., and Philip H. Dybvig. 1983. "Bank Runs, Deposit Insurance, and Liquidity." *Journal of Political Economy* 91 (3): 401–19.

Edlin, A., and Joseph E. Stiglitz. 1995. "Discouraging Rivals: Managerial Rent-Seeking and Economic Inefficiencies." *American Economic Review* 85 (5): 1301–12.

Faust, Jon, and Lars E. O. Svensson. 1998. "Transparency and Credibility: Monetary Policy with Unobservable Goals." Centre for Economic Policy Research Discussion Paper 1852. London.

Furman, Jason, and Joseph E. Stiglitz. 1998. "Economic Crises: Evidence and Insights from East Asia." In *Brookings Papers on Economic Activity* 2. Washington, D.C.: The Brookings Institution.

Greenwald, Bruce, and Joseph E. Stiglitz. 1992. "Information, Finance and Markets: The Architecture of Allocative Mechanisms." *Industrial and Corporate Change* 1 (1): 37–63.

Grossman, Sanford J. 1981. "The Informational Role of Warranties and Private Disclosure about Product Quality." *Journal of Law and Economics* 24 (3): 461–83.

Hellmann, Thomas, Kevin Murdock, and Joseph E. Stiglitz. 1999. "Liberalization, Moral Hazard in Banking and Prudential Regulation: Are Capital Requirements Enough?" *Industrial Organization and Regulation* 3 (17).

Hirshleifer, J. 1971. "The Private and Social Value of Information and the Reward to Inventive Activity." *American Economic Review* 61 (4): 561–74.

Jimenez L., Luis Felipe, and Nora Ruedi A. 1998. "Determinants of Inequality among Urban Households." *CEPAL Review* 66: 53–72.

Miller, M., and Joseph E. Stiglitz. 1999. "Bankruptcy Protection against Macroeconomic Shocks: The Case for a 'Super Chapter 11'." World Bank Conference on Capital Flows, Financial Crises, and Policies, April 15, Washington, D.C.

Modigliani, F., and M. H. Miller. 1958. "The Cost of Capital, Corporation Finance, and the Theory of Investment." *American Economic Review* 48 (3): 261–97.

Ravallion, Martin. 1999. "Appraising Workfare." *World Bank Research Observer* 14 (1): 31–48.

Stiglitz, Joseph E. 1975. "Information and Economic Analysis." In J .M. Parkin and A. R. Nobay, eds., *Current Economic Problems*. Cambridge: Cambridge University Press.

———. 1982. "Ownership, Control, and Efficient Markets: Some Paradoxes in the Theory of Capital Markets." In Kenneth D. Boyer and William G. Shepherd, eds., *Economic Regulation: Essays in Honor of James R. Nelson*. Lansing, Mich.: Michigan State University Press.

———. 1985. "Credit Markets and the Control of Capital." *Journal of Money, Banking, and Credit* 17 (2): 133–52.

———. 1999. "What Have We Learned from the Recent Crises: Implications for Banking Regulation." Paper presented at the conference Global Financial Crises: Implications for Banking and Regulation, Federal Reserve Bank of Chicago, May 6, Chicago, Ill.

Weiss, A., and Joseph E. Stiglitz. 1981. "Credit Rationing in Markets with Imperfect Information." *American Economic Review* 71 (3): 393–410.

Vishwanath, Tara, and Daniel Kaufmann. 1999. "Towards Transparency in Finance and Government." World Bank Institute, Governance, Regulation, and Finance, Washington, D.C.

Working Group on Transparency and Accountability. 1998. *Report of the Working Group on Transparency and Accountability*. G-22 Meeting, October 2.

# Comment on "Short-Term Capital Flows," by Dani Rodrik and Andrés Velasco, and "The Underpinnings of a Stable and Equitable Global Financial System: From Old Debates to a New Paradigm," by Joseph E. Stiglitz and Amar Bhattacharya

*Kenneth A. Froot*

These insightful articles present a lot of useful information about international financial flows and their role in shocks and crises. Here I comment on them in turn.

## Interpretations and Implications of Short-Term Debt

Dani Rodrik and Andrés Velasco accurately assess the association between short-term debt and recent crises in developing countries. The authors offer some interesting theoretical and empirical findings that raise useful policy questions.

On the theoretical side, this is a model of runs—that is, a model in which there are deadweight costs associated with trying to harvest capital early. If short-term loans have been extended, they may have to be harvested. If that harvesting occurs, deadweight costs will be incurred in proportion to the value of the short-term debt.

This is a compelling story. As with bank runs, there is the possibility of an externality, in the sense that short-term borrowers may not take into account the effects of their borrowing on overall deadweight costs, in the form of passing on higher costs to long-term borrowers. Thus excessive short-term borrowing can lead to outcomes that are not socially optimal.

So why does short-term borrowing occur? What function does it have for, say, optimal contracts? Rodrik and Velasco suggest that short-term debt can serve as a precommitment device that lowers the adverse selection costs of default on long-term commitments. That is certainly possible.

Another possibility, as Joseph E. Stiglitz and Amar Bhattacharya mentioned, is the "tight leash" fallacy. Say that a firm or a country has borrowed and perhaps raised money in equity markets. But then negative shocks develop, and all of a sudden the borrower defaults on the debt. Once that happens, if there is a need for additional cash before the uncertainty is resolved, the firm or country will try to access sources of capital that are more junior or that stand beneath existing claims. But it is

---

Kenneth A. Froot is Andrè A. Jakurski Professor of Business Administration at Harvard Business School.
*Annual World Bank Conference on Development Economics 1999*
©2000 The International Bank for Reconstruction and Development / THE WORLD BANK

extremely difficult to access such sources. It is difficult for a company to issue equity, for example, in the hopes that it will be able to get equityholders' cash to guarantee bondholders' payments.

As a result many companies move in the opposite direction, working up the pecking order and issuing more senior claims. The term *structure of debt* becomes increasingly short term, and increasingly tightens from a leash to a noose.

On the empirical side, Rodrik and Velasco do an excellent job of nailing down the association between short-term debt and recent crises. The ratio of short-term debt to reserves convincingly and powerfully explains large changes in capital flows, as well as the severity of the crises, changes in capital flows, changes in GNP, and changes in exchange rates. Moreover, the findings on the maturity composition of flows are compelling because they take into account financial development factors. For example, trade openness does not seem to be related to short-term borrowing. While these findings are compelling, they raise the issue of causality. Is short-term debt really the villain?

I do not think so. Indeed, short-term borrowing offers benefits. It can serve as an escape hatch for a firm or country if negative shocks occur and a mechanism is needed to promise available collateral at a more senior level, in order to keep going. In that sense, short-term debt is a good thing.

Financial distress is costly for a lot of reasons, many of which are independent of short-term debt. Renegotiation, default, the uncertainties associated with committing to plans—all are costly, and the problem is not short-term debt. The problem is financial distress, and short-term debt can actually lower some of these costs.

Thus the policy implications depend on how one views short-term debt. There are three crucial differences between short-term debt and portfolio flows, for example. First, with bank flows there is a strong outflow associated with crises, while with portfolio flows there was no real outflow from crisis countries during, say, the tequila crisis. Before the crisis foreign equity investors in emerging markets were buying about one basis point of market capitalization a day. That one basis point average sunk to about zero as the crisis approached and turned slightly negative at the time of the crisis, but that was the extent of the change. Moreover, the change in dollar terms was considerably smaller than the change in the intermediated flow. Thus the intermediated flow is distinctly different. Analysts sort of expect that, because equity prices adjust and because that tends to constrain flows. But it does not negate the fact that equity flows adjust. Although there is less adjustment, there is still some adjustment—despite the fact that there are also price changes.

The second difference is that cross-sectional comovement seems to be much lower for portfolio flows, particularly equities, than for bank flows. Thus there is less contagion among disintermediated debt flows than among intermediated flows.

Finally, while equity flows tend to persist on a daily or monthly basis, they are much less persistent than debt flows. Debt flows seem to be harder to turn around—but when they do turn around, they turn around with much greater force.

## Flows, Shocks, and Financial Systems

That leads me to some thoughts about the article by Stiglitz and Amar Bhattacharya. They have built a story by considering country experiences and by thinking about the theory of market failures and how to deal with shocks.

But consider an opposite example, in an area where there is stunning resilience to shocks in capital flows—the San Francisco peninsula. What features are most important in distinguishing that area from a lot of crisis countries? Over the past 30 years it has experienced 5 kinds of revolutions.

Early on there was aerospace. Then in the 1970s and early 1980s there were computers. From the early to late 1980s there were semiconductors. Software was intermingled in all those developments, and now there is the Internet. All five phases saw strong capital shocks, but the region and its companies have been able to deal with them. How?

Obviously many things distinguish the San Francisco peninsula from countries in crisis, but a few are especially important. First, while the area does not have its own currency, it has seen a real appreciation in living costs. But what might have happened if, with the booms and busts that have occurred, the area had a floating exchange rate? If there was a floating rate, market risks—that is, changes in the exchange rate—would be pretty highly correlated with credit risks. And that correlation between market risks and credit risks is crucial in many crisis countries.

To digress for a moment, consider Grupo Sidek, a large conglomerate in Mexico. It had two parts. One was a manufacturing firm that sold to world markets in dollars and borrowed in dollars. The manufacturing side appeared fairly well hedged, with minimized exposures on the currency side. The other part, a real estate firm that sold to Mexicans and borrowed in pesos, appeared fairly unhedged. And when Mexico's 1994 crisis came, the manufacturing firm did fine, while the real estate firm was devastated. Why? Because the drop in the peso set off a lot of economy-wide effects, the ripples of which destroyed the credit quality of people who borrowed to finance real estate purchases. Thus a lot of complex effects intermingle into exchange rates that go way beyond market risks.

Back to the difference between the San Francisco peninsula and emerging markets. Besides the issue of an independent currency, labor mobility might seem a second point of departure. However, labor mobility is often oversold. There is a lot of labor mobility in and out of the San Francisco peninsula, of course, but there are still lower-income towns. East Palo Alto remains a working class area, looking no better or worse today than it did 30 years ago. Many people keep their jobs through booms and busts, so it is not clear that labor mobility is an important feature making the Bay Area so resilient.

Third, financing of Bay Area firms does not involve much short-term debt. Of course, there is hardly any debt. Equity markets dominate. Moreover, financing is not very intermediated—it comes directly from the marketplace, so there is an ability to adjust. That is not to say that firms do not get into trouble. In the late 1970s and in 1986, for example, it looked like Intel might go out of business. There were large run-ups and run-downs in its net cash position, as well as large run-ups in its short-term debt as it tried to buy or borrow its way through bad times—which it did. Thus the uses of short-term debt may not be that different from what happens in crisis countries, in the sense that Intel was in crisis. What was different was the preponderance of financing that was quite flexible, both in price and in source.

One explanation is the financial system. The financial system of the San Francisco peninsula does not look like anything in crisis countries. In particular, it is not balkanized. Crisis countries tend to have concentrated intermediation, both through governments and through financial sectors, and that becomes dangerous, because credit risks become difficult to evaluate. Yet it is crucial to do so, because in most cases loans are being extended to a small group of people.

So one challenge is to disintermediate the intermediaries in these countries, to free up the whole approach. And of course, that effort leads to a policy orientation very different from that offered by Stiglitz and Bhattacharya. The goal I am referring to is one of building something that can take the speed, rather than impose speed limits that might undermine the ability to deal with the underlying problems.

Perhaps mine is an extreme view. But the prudential issues in crisis countries are a major problem, and we have not yet found a good way to deal with them. In a world of high capital flows and opportunity, the concentration of intermediation in crisis countries creates difficulties in sorting out credit risks. We need to break the logjam; to free up trade in financial services and intermediation activities. Markets may not be perfect, but the Asian crisis serves as yet another example that the alternatives can be even less so.

# The Changing Corporate Governance Paradigm: Implications for Developing and Transition Economies

*Erik Berglöf and Ernst-Ludwig von Thadden*

*The rapidly growing literature studying the relationship between legal origin, investor protection, and finance has stimulated an important debate in academic circles. It has also prompted many applied research projects and strong policy statements. This article discusses the implications of this literature, particularly for developing and transition economies. It concludes that its focus on small investors is too narrow when applied to these countries. This group of investors is unlikely to play an important role in most developing and transition economies. External investors may still be crucial, but they are more likely to come in as strategic investors or as creditors. The article proposes a broader paradigm, encompassing other stakeholders and mechanisms of governance, to help improve the understanding of the corporate governance problems facing these countries and lead to policy recommendations that compensate for the weaknesses of capital markets.*

Corporate governance has dominated policy agendas in developed market economies for more than a decade, lately in continental Europe and Japan especially. In the transition economies corporate governance took some time to rise to the top of the policy agenda, but since the mid-1990s it has been among the most hotly debated issues. In the wake of the Asian crisis corporate governance has also become a catchphrase in the development debate. Governments and stock exchanges are competing to produce corporate governance guidelines, and the Organisation for Economic Co-operation and Development (OECD) is about to publish its own principles.

---

Erik Berglöf is director of the Stockholm Institute of Transition Economics and East European Economies (SITE), Stockholm School of Economics and research fellow of the Centre for Economic Policy Research (CEPR). Ernst-Ludwig von Thadden is professor of economics at the Université de Lausanne and a CEPR research fellow. The authors are grateful to the Center for Advanced Study in the Behavioral Sciences, Stanford, California, for providing such a stimulating environment for writing this article, and to Masahiko Aoki, Bernard Black, Florencio Lopez-de-Silanes, Joseph Stiglitz, and two anonymous referees for their comments.

*Annual World Bank Conference on Development Economics 1999*
©2000 The International Bank for Reconstruction and Development / THE WORLD BANK

But how important is corporate governance? Some rank it among the most important policy issues; others claim that its effects are of the second order. These differences in opinion may reflect the fact that people mean different things by the term. Another explanation could be that corporate governance is not always important, but that when it matters, it matters very much. Corporate governance certainly seems to be more important in some phases of a firm's life cycle than in others. It is also likely to matter more in some contexts or some phases of economic development than in others.

Ultimately, of course, when and how much corporate governance matters is an empirical question. A recent series of articles has begun to address these issues from a comparative empirical perspective, promising more precise definitions of the corporate governance problem and better measures of its impact on economic growth (La Porta and others 1997, 1998, and 1999b; for simplicity, we refer to these three main articles as La Porta and his coauthors where a more precise reference is unnecessary). The authors of these articles—Rafael La Porta, Florencio Lopez-de-Silanes, Andrei Shleifer, and Robert Vishny—raise important questions about the interaction between law and finance and, more broadly, about the role of institutions in economic development.

The articles by La Porta and his coauthors have already given rise to a cottage industry of research on the interaction between law and finance. Recent contributions analyze the effects of legal rules protecting investors and of the general quality of the legal system on, for example, the development of the financial system (Levine, Loayza, and Beck 1998), the impact of macroeconomic shocks (Johnson and others 1998), the cost of capital (Lombardo and Pagano 1999), and corporate behavior and industrial growth (La Porta and others 1999a; Rajan and Zingales 1998; Carlin and Mayer 1999). In many cases the explanatory power of the legal variables is very strong, suggesting important implications for policy.

La Porta and and his coauthors document statistically and explain theoretically cross-country variations in ownership concentration and financing arrangements. Their main argument is that when the legal framework does not offer sufficient protection for outside investors, entrepreneurs and original owners are forced to maintain large positions to align their incentives with those of other shareholders (Shleifer and Vishny 1997). Thus countries with poor shareholder protection would be expected to have more concentrated ownership structures. La Porta and his coauthors find support for this hypothesis, and they argue that differences in investor protection have implications for corporate behavior and economic growth.

In this article we discuss how the findings in this rapidly growing literature should be interpreted. In particular, what are their implications for developing and transition economies? Although the recent contributions have raised a range of interesting questions and expanded the empirical base from which economists form their theories and draw policy implications, the analysis is incomplete and normative conclusions are often premature. The analysis is incomplete mainly because it focuses on only one side of the tradeoff between investor protection and the provision of incentives to managers and controlling owners, and on only one group of actors in corporate governance—small outside investors. The fate of corporations is also, and possibly should be, determined by other actors, inside and outside the firm. The net of empirical investigations must therefore be cast wider. We recognize the ingenuity and importance of this first generation of empirical corporate governance papers, but so far, few general conclusions can be drawn.

## Defining the Corporate Governance Problem

The recent literature is based on the premise that the main corporate governance problem is self-interested management and weak, dispersed shareholders. The need to raise external finance determines the structure of the firm and the legal framework in which it operates. Here the literature follows a long tradition. In the quest to understand the interaction between the legal framework and corporate governance, however, the contributors have shown that the empirical context from which they derived their world view is highly unrepresentative when taken beyond the United Kingdom and the United States. A rapidly growing body of cross-sectional studies and comparable country studies demonstrates clearly that the widely held firm is a rare phenomenon in most countries (see La Porta and others 1999b and Barca and Becht 1999).

Most firms, even listed ones, have a dominant owner. Moreover, this shareholder is very often involved in the management of the firm. Sometimes, though rarely, a bank will play this role, but in most cases a family or the state holds the dominant stake. This pattern is strong on the European continent and even more pronounced in developing countries. In transition economies ownership structures still are not well established, but widely held firms are extremely rare, even in countries that opted for early mass privatization through vouchers.

The realization that the closely held firm is the dominant form of governance profoundly affects how we conceive of the corporate governance problem and its policy implications. In the debate about ownership and control the focus shifts from conflict between management and shareholders to three-way conflict among managers, minority investors, and holders of large blocks of shares. Furthermore, the identity of investors comes into play, and it becomes important who monitors them, what their incentives are, and how they are constrained by the legal framework. When the firm is closely held, the emphasis shifts from shareholder-oriented governance institutions, such as takeovers, general shareholder meetings, and boards of directors, to a broader set of devices for redesigning ownership and control, such as cross-ownership, block trading, dual-class shares, managerial networks, and pyramiding of shareholdings. And in the analysis of capital market activity the paradigm of the competitive stock market must be abandoned in favor of models of bilateral negotiations, blockholder conflicts, and market design. In particular, with closely held companies, takeover markets operate very differently. Hostile takeovers are often impossible when one owner controls the majority of the shares, and most control transactions take place outside the official exchanges.

What are the policy implications of the findings of La Porta and his coauthors? There are several possible interpretations. A naive and optimistic interpretation is that legal rules protecting minority shareholders should be strengthened. This recommendation should be particularly uncontroversial for developing and transition economies, where these laws are likely to be weakest. La Porta and his coauthors list features of rules that would achieve this result, such as forbidding deviations from the one-share-one-vote rule or allowing proxy voting by mail. Then corporations would be controlled more efficiently, or at least controlling owners would be able to sell off some of their equity, allowing them to better diversify their portfolios and making stock markets more liquid. The remaining problem would primarily be one of implementation and possibly enforcement.

A deeper, but also more pessimistic, interpretation is that protecting investors is indeed very important, but that the rules for doing so are generated by different legal systems—with the most important distinction being between civil law and common law systems—that the laws in any legal system are highly complementary, and that investor protection can therefore be improved only by reforming the entire legal system. Such reforms are complex, however, and may not be an option for many transition economies. Moreover, in most countries the choice of the legal system either is predetermined (as in many former colonies) or has already been made, if only half-heartedly and imperfectly. Finally, because the necessary legal reforms cannot be restricted to isolated changes in corporate law, important stakeholders may resist legal reform, making it even more difficult.

To make policy recommendations therefore requires defining the corporate governance problem in a particular country with respect to its prevailing institutions. The predominant corporate governance problem in a transition economy is likely to differ from that in a developing country, which in turn differs from that in a developed market economy. Corporate governance issues also vary substantially across developed market economies (see, for example, Berglöf 1997; Gugler 1998; and Barca and Becht 1999). These differences will affect the implementation of policies to improve corporate governance.

An interesting case in point is the problem of corporate transparency. According to the market-based view of corporate governance, transparency about ownership and control arrangements is unambiguously a good thing. On the basis of several measures proposed by La Porta and his coauthors, many countries are deficient in this respect. Prompted by criticism about such deficiencies, the European Commission passed its Transparency Directive in 1993 to increase corporate transparency in the European Union. But this directive appears to have achieved little, if anything (ECGN 1998). Most firms—even countries—in Europe seem to have found ways around the restrictions imposed by the commission. This outcome suggests that piecemeal introduction of legislation advocated by the market-based corporate governance view may not work in economies organized along other lines.

One reason for this difficulty is that the focus of corporate finance theory for so many years—the widely held corporation—is, as we argued above, a rare phenomenon. But the understanding of the closely held firm, corporate groups, and the markets in which controlling blocks are traded is still limited, and analysis of the mechanisms for separating ownership and control has only just begun. In particular, little is known about how to preserve the powerful incentives of owner-managers, especially in family firms, while strengthening the protection of minority shareholders. Furthermore, almost all corporate finance theory assumes that firms operate under the constraint of a functioning civil and criminal justice system. Such theories must fail in environments where large-scale fraud and theft are standard business practice, as in Russia and in some African countries.

More generally, however, an important shortcoming of the new corporate governance literature is that it restricts its attention to control by the providers of capital, and often even further to control by equity holders. In a legalistic sense this restriction may be justified, because equity holders formally "own" the firm unless it is bankrupt, in which case ownership of the firm, or of parts of it, may switch to other providers of capital. The implicit argument that those who own the firm should control it, however, is flawed in many respects. Most important—and this is, of course, at the heart of the traditional corporate governance literature—there is a big difference between *should* and *does*. More generally than in the traditional literature, however, this difference relates not only to the conflict between top management and equity holders. Other groups inside and outside the firm exert significant influence on at least some decisions by the firm. These include the employees (sometimes formally represented through worker councils or other institutions), middle and higher management, trade unions, firm-specific suppliers or buyers, other large firms that are not linked to the firm by equity stakes, the public, and the government.

In this article we therefore argue that the market-based corporate governance approach not only should be broadened to include the problem of owner-controlled firms and large blockholders, but also should be generalized to a model of multilateral negotiations and influence seeking among many different stakeholders. Such a model must integrate checks and balances between stakeholders and outside constraints and must take into account the effects of a country's legal and political system on these checks and balances.

Even if there is theoretical reason to believe in the view that ownership with all its costs and benefits belongs to equity, this view is not dominant in most economies other than the United Kingdom and the United States. So, the broader notion of corporate governance offers some hope for understanding other economies better, particularly developing and transition economies, where anonymous stock markets are unlikely to promote the necessary entrepreneurial activity and corporate restructuring. It suggests that other mechanisms, such as product market competition, peer pressure, or labor market activity, may compensate for this weakness or, more realistically, may be more promising targets for legal or political reform than the stock market. Of course, investor protection will still be important, particularly if strategic investors are needed to restructure companies, but it becomes one policy goal to be weighed against others. In the long run protecting small foreign investors may also help attract international portfolio investment, but this source of funds is highly volatile and cannot be the centerpiece of a development program.

This broadening of the perspective on corporate governance implies that the empirical focus of La Porta and his coauthors on ownership concentration and corporate law, although operationally and statistically useful, is likely to be too narrow. La Porta and his coauthors are silent on the roles of suppliers, employees, product markets, and management networks and on the bodies of law that affect the workings and interactions of these agents, such as labor or competition law. In particular, they leave corporate governance isolated from product and labor markets. Also largely overlooked is the interaction between corporate governance arrangements and the political system. In most developing countries "crony capitalism" may be a much more important problem than the protection of minority shareholders, mainly because dominant family owners of business groups are influential politically. Because powerful business families have often succeeded in influencing legislation and regulation, policy recommendations to simply change the rules may be insufficient.

## Law and Finance

La Porta and his coauthors pursue an ambitious agenda in their three main articles. They want to establish systematic, even causal, links between the legal framework and financing patterns—and, ultimately, corporate performance and economic growth (figure 1). They classify legal origins as Anglo-Saxon, French, German, and Scandinavian, or simply common law (Anglo-Saxon) and civil law (the three others). The authors view legal origin as exogenous, that is, handed down through history or imposed from outside. In their view the legal origin shapes corporate law, particularly the extent to which it protects external investors, and corporate law influences firms' choice of financial arrangements. The implicit claim is that these financial arrangements, in conjunction with the legal framework, then affect corporate behavior and performance.

La Porta and his coauthors presume that the elements of the causal chain can be quantified and observed. In particular, the authors assume that corporate law can be meaningfully reduced to a set of measures, often binomial, that capture the degree of investor protection. They offer eight indicators of shareholder protection and five of creditor protection, supplementing these measures with more or less generally accepted indices of enforcement (table 1). La Porta and his coauthors establish a strong correlation between legal origin, investor protection, and ownership concentration; when they control for investor protection, the significance of legal origin disappears, suggesting that legal origin affects finance primarily through investor protection. They also identify some potentially interesting differences between countries at different levels of development. We return to these differences later.

Many lawyers have been critical of the classification of countries by legal origin. They find the distinction between common law and civil law particularly superficial.

**Figure 1. A Casual Chain from Legal Origin to Economic Growth**

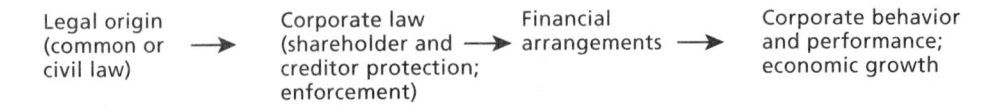

Legal origin (common or civil law) → Corporate law (shareholder and creditor protection; enforcement) → Financial arrangements → Corporate behavior and performance; economic growth

**Table 1. Indicators of Investor Protection**

| Shareholder protection | Creditor protection | Indicators of enforcement |
| --- | --- | --- |
| One share, one vote | No automatic stay | Efficiency of judicial system |
| Proxy by mail allowed | Secured creditors paid first | Rule of law |
| Shares not blocked before meeting | Restrictions on going into reorganization | Corruption |
| | | Risk of expropriation |
| Cumulative voting and proportional representation | Management required to leave in reorganization | Risk of contract repudiation |
| | | Rating on accounting standards |
| Oppressed minority | Legal reserve requirements | |
| Preemptive rights to new issues | | |
| Percentage of share capital needed to call an extraordinary shareholders meeting | | |
| Mandatory dividends | | |

*Source:* La Porta and others 1998.

Common law countries have a high degree of codification (in the United States, for example, many of the rules protecting investors are described in the Uniform Commercial Code and creditor protection is defined in part by the Bankruptcy Code of 1978), and civil law countries have developed powerful bodies of case law. In classifying countries, La Porta and his coauthors draw on an admittedly controversial standard textbook in comparative law (Watson 1974). Analysts have challenged the classifications of some countries and have emphasized the differences within the groups. But even if the labels used by La Porta and his coauthors can be legitimately criticized, the strong correlation remains to be explained. A few reclassifications would not radically change the results.

Another criticism by legal professionals is that La Porta and his coauthors use biased or misleading measures of the quality of corporate law. Qualitative judgments obviously lie behind the measures of investor protection, but in principle it should eventually be possible to agree on the appropriate characterizations. Even if the measures were accurate, the danger is, of course, that the quantifiable aspects of the law provide a biased picture or that the conceptual framework used for identifying these measures is flawed.

Different legal systems find different ways to compensate for their weaknesses. For example, mandatory dividends are rare in common law countries but common in civil law countries, particularly in the developing world, indicating that they are intended to compensate for poor protection in other respects. Moreover, the problem of investor protection could have more dimensions than the measures capture. For example, junior and senior creditors may have very different interests, and laws that protect one group may harm the other. Again, even if these biases do exist, critics must explain the systematic and strong correlation that La Porta and his coauthors establish.

Another, potentially more serious criticism relates to the causality claim: that corporate finance drives corporate law and not the other way around. It is easy to come up with examples showing how corporate law, as written and as enforced, has been shaped by financial structures. Countries with a tradition of strong bank involvement in corporate control have often found effective ways of accommodating this tradition in legal practice (as in Japan and Sweden). Similarly, in countries where closely held firms predominate, legislators and regulators have often found it unnecessary to specifically regulate the composition of boards of directors. When there are clearly identifiable controlling owners, they are believed to be better suited—and to have the right incentives—to make optimal decisions about board composition. The response of La Porta and his coauthors to this criticism is that legal origin, if not corporate law, is highly exogenous—indeed, often imposed by colonial powers. The fact that countries with one legal origin (civil law) score significantly worse on the measures the authors use must still be explained.

The causality issue brings up another possible problem with the interpretation of the results. It could be that the correlation between legal origin and financing arrangements merely reflects the influence of a third exogenous variable, such as the role of the state or the nature of the political system. In other words, the poor performance of countries with French legal origin would reflect the strong French tradition of state intervention or the French political system; what was imposed on Latin American countries was not just the legal tradition but the entire system of government. A similar underlying variable could be fundamental differences in the relationships between stakeholders in society (Roe 1999). But it is not clear how such differences are transferred across countries and cultures. All these explanations challenge the interpretation of the results, but they still leave a strong correlation between origin, however broadly defined, and investor protection and financing arrangements.

La Porta and others (1999b) follow up their previous two articles (1997 and 1998) by describing in greater detail the cross-country differences in ownership and control of listed firms in a smaller number of countries where data were available. The authors go to considerable trouble to document both direct control and indirect control (when a firm is controlled by another firm, which in turn may be controlled by a third entity, and so on). This requires information on the use of such control mechanisms as dual-class shares, pyramiding, and cross-ownership. The authors show that except in the United Kingdom and the United States, the overwhelming majority of listed corporations have a controlling owner who in many cases is actively involved in management. As expected, in countries with a common law origin firms are more widely held.

These findings are consistent with and highly complementary to those of parallel work in the European Corporate Governance Network (summarized in Barca and Becht 1999 and Gugler 1998). This network strives to establish data comparable across countries, at least for Europe. The contributors have access to better-quality data than La Porta and his coauthors do, though for a smaller number of countries. Their data allow a more detailed description and analysis of the corporate governance problem in individual countries.

The European Corporate Governance Network studies show some shortcomings in the quality and comparability of the data used by La Porta and his coauthors. The picture that emerges is nevertheless similar, with a strong concentration of ownership and extensive use of mechanisms for separating ownership and control. The studies show that banks are more—and the state less—important in corporate governance in Europe than in the world as a whole. In addition, the country studies in Barca and Becht (1999) suggest that La Porta and his coauthors underestimate bank control by missing channels for influence other than direct ownership. In some countries banks have managed to circumvent formal restrictions on ownership by establishing independent investment companies (Sweden) and informal constraints by using proxy votes (Germany). Banks' most important source of influence is typically their role as concentrated creditors.

Nevertheless, the qualitative and quantitative assessments by Barca and Becht (1999) and Gugler (1998) raise some fundamental questions about the interpretation of the findings of La Porta and his coauthors. There are undoubtedly situations where better investor protection seems highly desirable; stories of controlling owners exploiting minority shareholders abound in some countries (Italy is the favorite example in the literature; see Zingales 1995). But blockholders on the whole appear to be important monitors of management and often participate actively in management themselves (these studies suffer from an obvious problem of endogeneity: does ownership determine performance or vice versa?). The jury is out on whether concentration of ownership is good or bad for performance; in some countries, such as Austria, the Netherlands, and Spain, companies with concentrated ownership do worse than those with dispersed share holdings, while in others the reverse seems to be true (Gugler 1998). Roe (1999) raises the legitimate point that, if there are any benefits from large blockholders, better legal protection should, if anything, lead to the formation of *more* large blocks, not fewer.

It is easy to find examples of laws that seem unfair to holders of minority blocks, and the European Corporate Governance Network studies point many of them out. But the basic legal framework is seldom challenged—at least not from within the countries. Could these countries really have lived for decades or even centuries with laws that have the gross inefficiencies suggested by La Porta and his coauthors without recognizing their fundamental weaknesses? In particular, why have controlling owner-managers been willing, year after year, to absorb the large costs associated with these inefficiencies without pushing for legal reform? Are the laws protecting minorities really as hard to change as La Porta and his coauthors seem to suggest? After all, any policymaker could walk down the list in table 1 and propose reforms that supposedly would improve the protection of investors.

Implicit in the articles by La Porta and his coauthors is a political economy story in which managers and large blockholders effectively block legal reform. In some cases this interpretation seems highly plausible. For example, dual-class shares are crucial in the exercise of control in many countries (such as Sweden), and preventing deviations from the one-share-one-vote rule would seriously undermine the influence of existing holders of high-voting stock and result in substantial redistribution of wealth (voting shares typically trade at a substantial premium). Reforms applied ex post understandably meet with strong resistance, but ex ante legislation could also have important redistributive effects (see Zingales 1999 for an explanation of why inequality may feed resistance to stronger investor protection).

The political economy story may explain why inefficient laws remain in place for long periods, but the many remaining puzzles suggest that we need to better understand the conceptual framework underlying the studies by La Porta and his coauthors before interpreting their observations and drawing policy conclusions.

## Corporate Governance and the Firm

Corporate governance can be defined as the set of mechanisms that translate signals from product and input markets into firm behavior. This definition focuses on two elements: the signals generated outside the firm and the control structures inside the firm to execute decisions based on those signals. The definition is deliberately broader than the more traditional ones, which focus on the conflict between outside investors and top management (for example, those of Shleifer and Vishny 1997 or Tirole 1998). It reflects the importance of recognizing at the outset that control over a firm's course involves more than these two groups of actors.

Despite its theoretical flavor, this definition of corporate governance has important practical implications. It opens the firm, and its management, to pressures from sources other than shareholders. It also emphasizes the need to look at corporate governance within the wider context of product market competition and corporate links. The definition further suggests that the various forces that affect a firm's behavior may be substitutes as well as complements in pushing the firm toward efficiency. In this section we place La Porta and his coauthors' view of corporate governance in the broader context of this definition and relate it to the modern theory of the firm.

Samuelson (1957) once remarked that in a competitive economy it would not matter whether capital hires labor or labor hires capital. Indeed, if inputs are homogeneous and the only signals from markets are competitive prices that leave no quasi-rents to producers, the only function of corporate ownership is to determine a profit-maximizing production plan and distribute firm revenues according to marginal productivity. In reality, the signals from factor and product markets are richer and more ambivalent than that, the operation of firms generates substantial quasi-rents, at least in the short run, and labor input in particular is heterogeneous and difficult to control. So ownership does matter.

But even if the focus is limited to the ownership arrangement most common in most economies—ownership by capitalists—the analysis of corporate governance is less straightforward than often claimed. There are two extreme forms of capitalist ownership: the widely held firm and the firm fully controlled by a family with no outside ownership. In between is a continuum of firms with more or less concentrated ownership. The corporate governance problem of the widely held firm has been studied extensively, both theoretically and empirically; Roe (1994) has characterized it in the United States as one of "strong managers, weak owners." This type of firm relies on anonymous finance using primarily arm's-length contracts and third-party intervention through the market for corporate control.

The family firm has a different corporate governance problem. Although there may be conflicts between owners and hired managers, these problems are probably of minor importance; owners are generally believed to be well equipped to control the operations of their firm. The corporate governance problem in the family-held firm arises precisely because there is no outside interest in the firm. Owner-managers sometimes fail to recognize business opportunities or pitfalls, particularly in times of change, where outsiders would see them and intervene; the fall of such well-known firms as Wang in the United States and Grundig in Germany can be attributed to this type of governance failure. Corporate governance also becomes an issue when there is a succession problem or when the firm decides to raise funds outside the family. In these important but rare situations the lack of links to the capital market may significantly reduce the value of the firm if outsiders are reluctant to buy assets of which they know little and over which they have little control. The corporate governance problem in the pure family firm can therefore be characterized as one of "strong managers, no outsiders."

The corporate governance problem in the closely held firm is again different. The main conflict is that between the controlling owner and the minority shareholders. The financing pattern mixes arm's-length finance by minority investors with control-oriented finance, that is, finance by an outside investor who takes a controlling stake to directly affect investment decisions. Small shareholders will usually find it difficult to challenge large shareholders directly because of the difference in the size of their stakes. Moreover, when ownership of financial instruments is concentrated, there are fewer traders in the markets for these instruments; that makes them less liquid, which in turn reduces the value of the exit option of small shareholders (Bolton and von Thadden 1998). In the closely held firm, then, the corporate governance problem is one of "strong blockholders, weak minorities."

So far we have discussed the relationship between the firm and its shareholders, and between controlling and noncontrolling shareholders. Shareholders are only one class of investors, however. Creditors obviously also contribute funds to the firm. So do suppliers and sometimes even employees (as in Russia today). The state, too, often offers outside funding—voluntarily, by default (unpaid taxes), or through subsidies in response to stakeholder pressure.

The objectives of the law become more complex for creditor protection than for shareholder protection. There are at least four potential inefficiencies: debtor-creditor law may be too hard or too soft on management or controlling owners, and it may favor inefficient liquidation (when continuation would be optimal) or inefficient continuation (when liquidation would be optimal) (Berglöf, Roland, and von Thadden 1999). In addition, conflicts typically arise between creditors in cases of bankruptcy, depending on the types of their loans and their relationship with the firm. But conflicts may also exist much earlier if different creditors have different lending experiences and intervention capacities. Thus creditors can and will seek to influence a firm in distress in different ways and with different objectives. The simple goal of maximizing creditor protection provides little guidance for the design of corporate law.

We have focused on external finance, but internal finance is more important in most developed countries and is particularly important in countries with widely held firms (Mayer 1990). In the closely held firm, however, the distinction between external and internal finance may not be straightforward. The owner's contribution to the firm is typically viewed as internal, even if the firm and its owner are legally separated through limited liability. But when the owner-manager turns to distant family members or friends and acquaintances, at what point does internal finance become external finance? And should the finance provided by the group bank in the financial *keiretsu* in Japan or bank-led corporate groups elsewhere be regarded as internal or external?

The consideration of internal finance provides a richer perspective on corporate governance than the traditional shareholder perspective and brings us back to Samuelson's (1957) question: who owns the firm and who should own it? Internal funds are the engine of most firms' operations. They crucially influence a firm's ability to compete, invest, and grow, and at the same time they determine the rents and quasi-rents enjoyed by management, lower-level employees, and other stakeholders. According to the corporate governance model of La Porta and his coauthors, centered on external investor protection, corporate governance law should focus mainly on helping small investors get as much control over these funds as possible. But shouldn't the law also protect management and owner-managers?

Clearly, if the primary objective of policy is to protect corporate insiders, as it has been until recently in some developing countries, the answer to this question is trivially affirmative. But even if the law has subtler objectives, such as efficiency, the answer is not necessarily negative, because the protection of external investors comes at the expense of managerial incentives and discretion. As Burkart, Gromb, and Panunzi (1997) argue, when managers are tightly controlled, their willingness to exert effort and take initiative may be weaker, because controlling outsiders cannot commit to respecting managerial quasi-rents generated through managerial initiative. In the closely held firm this tradeoff also applies to the owner-manager or large blockholder. Restrictions on the discretion of these actors also are costly for efficiency, and maximum protection of minority investors is most likely to be less than optimal.

Building on the literature on ownership and control developed by Grossman and Hart (1986) and Hart and Moore (1990), one can push this argument even further. If the presumption of the corporate governance model of La Porta and his coauthors is true and top management is indeed the de facto residual claimant to corporate profits—through private benefits deriving from power, the choice of pet investment or public relations projects, or outright diversion of funds—then it may well be efficient for management to also have some of the residual control rights formally associated with ownership (Hellwig 1998). The point here is not to advocate the formal transformation of capitalist companies into labor-managed companies in the sense of Samuelson (1957), but merely to observe that modern capitalist corporations resemble labor-managed firms in this one important dimension and that this may be efficient. In this sense, legislation designed to rein in managerial power may have unwanted consequences for efficiency.

Other arguments based on similar general considerations make the same point: that outside intervention in management may reduce efficiency. It has been argued, for example, that if internal finance is such an important source of capital, management (possibly as a representative of other stakeholders) should have a role in preventing certain outside investors from grabbing internal funds. According to this popular view, outside investors do not necessarily take into account the long-term interest of the firm and financial markets are excessively oriented toward the short term. Theoretically, this argument can be shown to be sound if there are asymmetries of information in the capital market (Stein 1988; von Thadden 1995). But the empirical evidence relating to short-sightedness is mixed.

It is only logical to extend the discussion of managerial incentives to the broader group of all stakeholders. The main argument here builds on the insight that many stakeholders of a firm—particularly employees, customers, and suppliers—make firm-specific investments and that these investments are practical only if protected by implicit contracts that will not be breached (Shleifer and Summers 1988). But if the firm is owned by anonymous shareholders who can sell their stakes on the stock market, the shareholders cannot credibly commit to not breaching these contracts, because once the firm-specific investment has been made and an outsider proposes a high takeover price, it is optimal for them to sell out. According to this reasoning, stakeholders will not invest sufficiently if they are not given some protection against breaches of contract.

The stakeholder perspective clearly has its dangers, especially when taken to extremes. Deviations from the goal of maximizing "shareholder value," allow management to hide behind diffuse objectives and open possibilities for individual stakeholder groups to capture excessive rents (for a forceful critique along these lines see Jensen 1993; for a more balanced skepticism see Tirole 1998). Yet the point is not that shareholders should be disenfranchised to the benefit of another stakeholder group. The theory we have discussed suggests instead that many different stakeholder groups should play their part in corporate governance and that what counts is the delicate balance among them.

This balance typically depends on the broader legal and political environment in which firms operate—not only, as La Porta and his coauthors suggest, on the design of corporate law. Thus the entire nexus of laws affecting firms in a country matters in the analysis of corporate governance. It is no coincidence, for example, that Germany's infamously weak shareholder protection laws go hand in hand with relatively strict competition policies, far-reaching labor participation laws, two-tier boards favoring extensive managerial networks, and tax laws favoring corporate cross-ownership.

Whether or not a good normative argument can be made for a stakeholder perspective, in many countries, if not most, stakeholders do share in rents and take part in decisionmaking. This pattern is particularly striking in many transition economies, often as a result of privatization, but it is also a feature of most continental European countries. In fact, employee participation is very strong in the firms considered by many to have the most advanced corporate finance arrangement in the capitalist world, those with venture capital finance (for analyses of this arrangement in a corporate governance perspective see Aoki 1998 and Rajan and Zingales 1998). Thus the broader concept of corporate governance we have proposed here not only has theoretical appeal, but also is empirically relevant for comparative institutional analysis.

## Corporate Governance and Economic Growth

La Porta and his coauthors implicitly claim that the legal system and the protection it provides to external investors strongly influence the behavior of firms and, ultimately, corporate performance and economic growth. Figure 2 attempts to make explicit an enlarged causal model allowing for exogenous factors other than legal origin and a two-way causal relationship between the legal and financial systems. It also incorporates the influence from input and product markets suggested by our definition of corporate governance.

Few empirical studies have directly tested the claim of La Porta and his coauthors, but many have looked at individual links in the figure. This section discusses some of these empirical studies in the context of a broader model relating corporate governance to economic growth.

The discussion in the previous section focused on the balance between management and different classes of investors, but our definition of corporate governance suggests that signals from input and product markets affect investment decisions, through many channels. Obviously, the intensity of these signals should be important. The more competitive are product markets and the stronger is the bargaining power of suppliers, the more likely they are to influence the firm's behavior. But if management or the controlling owner is somehow shielded from these pressures, the strength of the signals may not matter. Corporate governance, market competition, and pressures from suppliers may be both complements and substitutes. The legal framework may thus have a double role, in reinforcing the signals and in

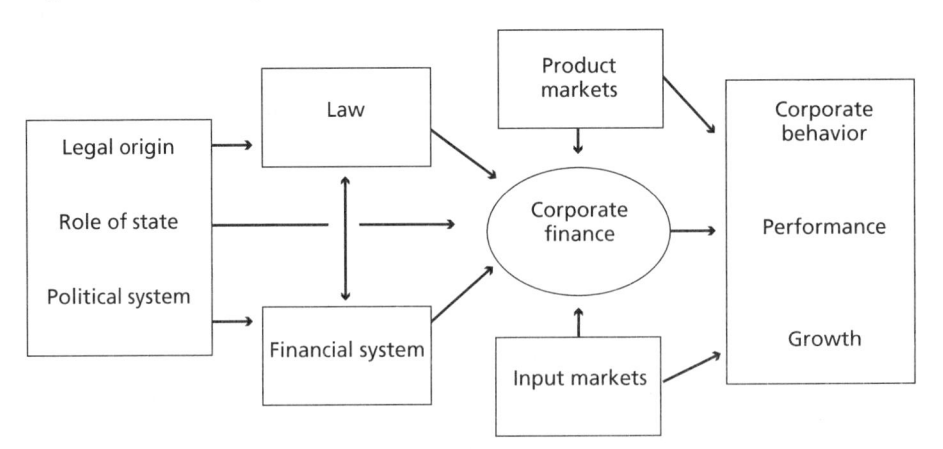

**Figure 2. Financial System and Growth—An Enlarged Causal Model**

improving the mechanism whereby they are channeled into investment decisions. In evaluating the impact of legal mechanisms and drawing policy implications, one should take both functions into account.

Whether product market competition and corporate governance are substitutes or complements is ultimately an empirical issue. Some recent research has investigated this question. Nickell (1996) and Nickell, Nicolitsas, and Dryden (1997) study the relative importance of shareholder pressure (the existence of a leading shareholder), debt pressure (measured as leverage), and intensity of competition and whether these forces substitute for or reinforce one another in a sample of British firms. They find some support for the substitution hypothesis. A study of Russian firms finds that competition has little impact—or even a negative impact—on restructuring (Earle and Estrin 1998). The authors lacked data on corporate governance, but the general impression from the study is that this mechanism was very weak at the time. Brown and Brown (1998) suggest that when the regional fragmentation of markets is taken into account, the effect of competition should be stronger. One interpretation of the Russian experience is that for competition to affect firm behavior requires at least a minimum of corporate governance. Below that minimum, the question of whether product market competition and corporate governance are substitutes or complements may not be crucial for policy as long as both have a positive impact; competition policy becomes even more important if corporate governance is weak.

Another literature has studied the impact of the financial system on economic growth. King and Levine (1993) show that among a large number of variables related to growth, measures of two aspects of the financial system are economically the most significant: the share of private institutions in financial intermediation and the size of the banking sector. Later contributions have refined these measures and attempted to better control for reverse causality (Levine, Loayza, and Beck 1998). If anything, the impact of financial variables becomes stronger when scrutinized more closely. Levine, Loayza, and Beck (1998) also attempt to link the earlier findings to those of La Porta and his coauthors. They suggest that the degree of investor (more specifically, creditor) protection explains the development of the financial sector. Indeed, the measures of creditor protection used by La Porta and his coauthors come out strongly significant.

Another set of contributions has focused on the impact of the legal and financial systems on corporate behavior rather than performance. Rajan and Zingales (1998) show that under certain assumptions industries dependent on external finance are more developed in countries with better protection of external investors. Rajan, Servaes, and Zingales (1998) present evidence that corporate governance affects the degree of diversification of firms. La Porta and others (1999a) show that firms in common law countries pay more dividends than their counterparts in civil law countries.

All these findings suggest that investor protection strongly influences firm behavior and probably economic performance and growth. Nevertheless, any policy recommendations must be country-specific, based on analysis of the dominant ownership and control structures and the larger economic system in which they operate.

## Implications for Developing Countries

Developing countries as a group are probably even more heterogeneous than developed market economies in their basic legal frameworks, corporate ownership structures, and financial systems. This heterogeneity suggests that few general implications can be drawn for these countries, but there are other important considerations in applying to the developing world the insights from the literature inspired by La Porta and his coauthors.

Although La Porta and his coauthors do not focus on the development problem, they provide data for 22 developing countries (excluding the Asian newly industrialized countries) and control for GDP per capita in their regressions. These data lead to some interesting observations. As expected, there is a development effect, with several variables, such as rule of law and quality of accounting standards, positively correlated with GDP per capita. But investor protection does not seem to improve with level of development. In fact, creditor protection is strongest in the least developed countries. La Porta and his coauthors interpret this observation as reflecting the reliance on collateral in these economies. But the crucial issue is, of course, whether the letter of the law really matters where enforcement is poor.

There are relatively few listed firms in most developing countries, and in these firms ownership and control is strongly concentrated (La Porta and others 1999b; for Asia see also Claessens, Djankov, and Lang 1998). The variation across countries is substantial, but with few exceptions firms have a controlling owner, family-controlled firms are important, and many large firms are members of business groups. Business groups are a notable feature of many developing economies (see Granovetter 1994; Khanna and Palepu 1999; or Khanna and Rivkin 1999). They are organized through extensive cross-ownership, are often dominated by a controlling family, and often have good contacts in the government (see, for example, Bhagwati 1993 on India, and Fisman 1998 for Indonesia).

Shareholder protection laws may not be a relevant criterion for assessing the workings of capital markets in such economies, because the group-based corporate structure in developing economies is usually seen as a response to lack of capital market institutions. The most comprehensive empirical study of business groups in emerging economies that we know of, Khanna and Rivkin (1999), finds that in three of the seven economies with large numbers of business groups (India, Indonesia, and Taiwan, China), group membership has a statistically significant, positive impact on firm profitability, while the impact is indistinguishable from zero in the other four (Brazil, Chile, the Republic of Korea, and Thailand). So business groups, with all their opacity, lack of outside accountability, and insider dominance, at least do not seem to harm their shareholders, given the environment in which they operate.

More generally, we believe that the corporate governance problem in our broader perspective is an equilibrium problem: the absence of organized markets and small investors gives rise to substitute constructs such as business groups, but these substitutes prevent capital markets and market-based corporate shareholdings from emerging. In such a situation, modifying corporate law according to the guidelines of La Porta and his coauthors is likely to have little effect and may even be counterproductive.

The consideration of business groups sheds light on another important aspect of the literature inspired by La Porta and his coauthors. This literature presumes that external finance constrains the growth of firms. In most developed market economies that is probably true for at least some important industries. However, internal finance is more important, and new issues of equity and debt are relatively rare events in firms, though bank debt is often used. In developing countries the actual or potential role of external finance is less clear. Finance, internal or external, will help only when firms have access to profitable projects with sufficiently low risk. But the risk premium is high in many developing countries (in part, of course, because of weaknesses in investor protection, rule of law, enforcement, and transparency). If such projects were available, firms would probably draw on internally generated funds before pursuing external sources. Here, business groups play an important role: a group, by channeling resources between its firms, relaxes the liquidity constraint at the firm level. This mechanism is enhanced if the group contains a bank, as is often the case. Again, legal reform may be harmful, if it disrupts these channels without establishing new, reliable ones (which is quite likely to be the outcome at least in the short run—see, for example, Blanchard and Kremer 1997 for the case of transition economies).

One feature that stands out in most studies of ownership and corporate control in developing countries is the close ties between business interests and government, often called crony capitalism—or as Bhagwati (1993) put it nicely for India, the economy is enmeshed in a "Kafkaesque maze of controls." Although crony capitalism is not a corporate governance problem in the traditional sense, it affects corporate governance in our broader concept, because large family owners often use their influence to limit competition, to obtain favorable finance from the government, and in other ways to alter the game in their favor. With soft budget constraints a common part of the picture, crony capitalism can be a strong deterrent to outside investors, particularly when a country is exposed to macroeconomic shocks.

Some of La Porta and his coauthors' indicators relate to rule of law capture elements of crony capitalism, but this political dimension needs to be developed further. For example, Johnson and others (1998) show that the measures for rule of law explain a significant part of the variation across countries in effects from the Asian crisis.

A question worth exploring is why the ownership structures that lead to crony capitalism in developing economies do not do so in continental Europe. The answer should be closely related to the issues addressed by La Porta and his coauthors. The strength and quality of government is likely to be part of this answer, but such features as tax law and competition law certainly also play a role. Crony capitalism requires remedies other than investor protection, but corporate law might be able to help dismantle some of these unhealthy structures by offering opportunities for broadening or phasing out current ownership.

## Implications for Transition Economies

The research program of La Porta and his coauthors was triggered largely by the transition experience; several of the authors have been deeply involved in Russian institutional reform. Yet their data set includes no transition economies. Although this omission is understandable given the state of data for these countries, it is nevertheless unfortunate. The lessons from this body of work are important for transition economies, though it is dangerous to take them at face value.

The transition economies have widely varying histories and institutional setups, but they also share important features. They all have a large sector of formerly state-owned enterprises that need to be restructured and in many cases phased out. They all need new enterprises to emerge in underdeveloped parts of the economy, particularly the service sector. And they all inherited a dysfunctional legal system, with many having to construct basic institutions from scratch.

The new enterprises have very much the same problem, or lack of problem, as those in developing countries do. Still at an early stage of the firm life cycle, they are unlikely to face the problem of intergenerational transfers anytime soon, and liquid markets are therefore relatively unimportant. These firms may not even be financially constrained. The problem of the emerging private sector is instead the lack of market signals and managerial accountability in much of the formerly state-owned sector. Many of the newly privatized enterprises need strong outside investors to execute painful restructuring, but the dominant pattern in Central and Eastern Europe and the former Soviet Union is insider control. In the absence of well-functioning laws, managers with or without shares can effectively expropriate minority investors (who often entered more or less by default through mass privatization or insider privatization schemes). In this situation protection of external investors is crucial; outsiders must be able not only to accumulate stakes but also to exercise control.

While better investor protection is likely to be very important in many transition economies, particularly in the former Soviet Union, the formal legal text is likely to matter much less than in developed market economies. The Russian corporate law provides an interesting example. The original document, prepared in collaboration with Western advisers close to La Porta and his coauthors, was strongly inspired by Anglo-Saxon thinking. The approach taken in the law is very similar to that advocated by La Porta and his coauthors—in fact, the legal text is close to perfect according to their criteria listed in table 1 (Linnarud 1998). The drafters of the law clearly recognized the limited capacity of the Russian legal system and the need for flexibility: they focused on self-enforcing legal rules and left large holes to be filled by case law (see Black and Kraakman 1996; and Hay and Shleifer 1998).

The problem is that the cumbersome procedures and weak enforcement powers of the courts deter investors from bringing suits (Russia ranks 82 out of 99 countries ranked in the 1999 Transparency International Corruption Perceptions Index). The lack of cases has left the large holes in the legal text unfilled, leading to great investor uncertainty. Furthermore, a potentially harmful conflict between the Anglo-Saxon case law doctrine and the Russian legal tradition has manifested itself in the past few years. Russian courts typically have very high evidentiary standards, relying on documentary evidence, and rarely consider circumstantial evidence adequate, unlike in the United States, for example. For this reason, Russian courts dismiss many cases that would be decided in the United States, a tendency that reinforces the other obstacles to building up a sufficient body of case law. And finally, many lower-level courts in Russia are simply corrupt, so that case law based on their rulings is often worthless.

Poor investor protection and concentration of ownership undermine the liquidity of equity markets, a problem that the designers of privatization programs in many countries appear to have underestimated. They emphasized speed and equity, expecting appropriate corporate governance structures to emerge in due course. But when markets for corporate control are illiquid, initial ownership and control structures become very sticky, something that seems to be at the core of the governance problem in many transition economies. The overwhelming finding in transition economies, at least in Central and Eastern Europe, is that outside, preferably foreign, investors are crucial in bringing about deep restructuring (for an early survey, see EBRD 1996).

Another important feature of the economic environment in many transition economies, particularly in the former Soviet Union, is the persisting, even worsening, problem of soft budget constraints (Berglöf and Roland 1998; Schaffer 1998). The large size or number of formerly state-owned enterprises often forces the government to give in to pressures to refinance the loss-making entities. Weakness in the banking sector also contributes to the lack of financial discipline. The softness of budget constraints weakens the need to seek outside finance and thus the pressure to restructure, sustaining inefficient governance structures.

The predominant corporate governance problem of the large firms in transition economies can thus be summarized as "omnipotent managers, little resistance." Improved investor protection can help to attract outside capital and force restructuring, but the overriding issues in most transition economies seem to be law enforcement and government commitment to economic reform (see Dewatripont and Roland 1997). To be effective, measures to strengthen investor protection must be combined with efforts in other areas—hardening budget constraints, eliminating government corruption, reconsidering the workings of the court system.

In fact, the Russian example suggests that such measures may not even be sufficient. There is much evidence that many large privatized firms in Russia are being run by veritable kleptocrats uninterested in managing these firms for profit. Their real goal, and their comparative advantage, is to plunder the firms' assets and transfer the loot abroad, if necessary by using brute force against opposition (see Black, Kraakman, and Tarassova 1999 for a well-informed and vivid description).

In this situation the normal paradigm of corporate governance—fine-tune the checks and balances on individual self-interest and opportunism—changes its meaning so completely that corporate finance theory no longer applies. In particular, advice to protect minority investors or increase corporate transparency seems to be largely irrelevant, as long as the society's basic rules of economic and political interaction are Leviathan. It is hard to imagine any checks on kleptocratic insiders if the entire political system has proved unable or unwilling to confront them.

## General Implications

La Porta and his coauthors have highlighted many issues crucial for understanding the relationships between laws, financing arrangements, and economic growth. The literature shows strong correlation, both statistically and economically, between variables in these areas. Although the issues of causality and the possibility that underlying factors explain these observations have not been resolved, the contributions of La Porta and his coauthors challenge academics and policymakers alike.

We defined corporate governance as the mechanisms translating signals from product and input markets into corporate behavior. The pressure generated by external investors is just one of these mechanisms. Others include monitoring by employees, suppliers, and competitors and within corporate networks; the government also influences the transmission of signals, directly or through the framework it provides for corporations. That all these stakeholders do influence decisions in firms has strong normative implications for the role of law, particularly investor protection. The pressures from different stakeholders may push corporations away from efficiency and profit maximization, in which case strengthened investor protection may be a welcome countervailing force. But these mechanisms can also substitute for, or complement, monitoring by external investors.

The law can affect these tradeoffs and the accompanying costs and benefits. But these costs and benefits are multidimensional, and the law, particularly corporate law, must be careful not to focus excessively on outside investors. The optimal governance arrangements reflect delicate tradeoffs between the costs and benefits of concentrated holdings, employee participation, management structures, corporate networks, and other institutional features of the economy. For example, concentration of ownership improves incentives to monitor management and aligns incentives of owner-managers with those of the rest of the shareholders. Its costs come from the agency problems between concentrated owners and minority owners and from the reduced liquidity of shares. Liquidity can be improved by issuing shares with different voting power. But improved liquidity comes at the cost of separation of ownership and control, and the resulting worsening of the agency problem. Table 2 brings together our (perhaps oversimplified) characterizations of the predominant governance problems in different types of firms.

The lessons of La Porta and his coauthors apply primarily to systems in which widely held firms dominate and to some extent in transition economies, where the predominant conflict is between managers and external investors. Whether the protection of external investors in Anglo-Saxon systems is too strong or too weak is hard to say, and there is likely to be important variation across countries with

**Table 2. The Corporate Governance Problem Defined—A Simple Classification**

| Widely held firm | Closely held firm | Family firm | Transition economy firm | Developing country firm |
|---|---|---|---|---|
| Strong managers Weak owners | Strong blockholders Weak minorities | Strong managers No outsiders | Omnipotent managers Little resistance | Strong managers Related investors |

Source: Authors' summary.

such systems. In many transition economies, particularly those of the former Soviet Union (excluding the Baltic countries), external investors appear excessively weak, and the law should aim to strengthen them. For improved investor protection to affect restructuring, however, budget constraints must be hardened, the courts must be more active in settling business disputes, and governments must maintain or create broad political support for economic reforms while making sure that product and factor markets work sufficiently well to provide meaningful signals to firms.

The conceptual framework underpinning La Porta and his coauthors is less well suited to the analysis of corporate governance in countries with mostly closely held firms, even though most of the measures of investor protection also apply to conflicts between controlling owner-managers and minority investors. The evidence is inconclusive on whether the protection provided is excessive or insufficient. La Porta and his coauthors find significant differences among countries with civil law systems, such as between France and the Netherlands. The literature suggests that some countries in continental Europe give too little protection to minority investors. Italy is the most frequently cited example; for other countries, such as Belgium and Sweden, the verdict seems less clear. But there is a general perception that investor protection is weak in many continental European countries. Pressure to reform corporate governance in these countries is particularly strong from U.S.–based institutions desiring to diversify their portfolios internationally. Yet, as we have argued, economic theory does not provide unambiguous guidance in this respect. So policy recommendations must be preceded by careful investigations of the web of relationships governing corporate decisionmaking.

It is less clear that investor protection is a first-order problem in most developing countries. The most important economic policy challenges in most of these countries are fostering an environment for good investment projects, strengthening human capital, accumulating physical capital, and improving government accountability. The policy mix for reforming corporate governance will then depend very much on the roles played by markets and different stakeholders. Clearly, better protected investors and functioning financial markets will be part of the solution. In some countries, such as the Republic of Korea, policies to reform corporate governance seem possible and important, while in others their urgency is less clear. In all countries, however, the problem is likely to be one of enforcement rather than of changes in the law.

In the optimistic interpretation of the findings of La Porta and his coauthors countries can achieve reforms of corporate law and investor protection by changing the text of laws and improving their enforcement. The deeper and more pessimistic interpretation is that legal origin determines investor protection and that changing this protection requires changing the basic legal system, a complex task. A similar but conceptually different interpretation is that other, more fundamental factors explain the observed correlation between legal origin, corporate law, and investor protection. If these factors involve the role of the state or deeply ingrained relationships between different stakeholders, reforms will be even harder to undertake and will certainly require changes in the society beyond those suggested by the framework of La Porta and his coauthors.

## Policy Implications

The policy implications of La Porta and his coauthors are less immediate than a superficial reading would suggest, particularly for developing and transition economies. Nevertheless, despite the constraints and caveats that we have outlined, we are convinced that there is scope for economic policy on corporate governance. Indeed, it has become very popular to adopt corporate governance guidelines. Many OECD countries have done so, and the OECD itself has issued a set of principles (most guidelines are available on the European Corporate Governance Network's Web site, at http://www.ecgn.ulb.ac.be).

The current draft of the OECD guidelines is an interesting document. Although it still focuses on minority shareholders and that rare species, the widely held corporation, it shows a clear evolution in thinking compared with earlier versions and with other documents produced by the organization. The preamble recognizes the contextual nature of corporate governance and its dependence on the legal, regulatory, and institutional environment. Moreover, the guidelines acknowledge the need to consider stakeholders other than minority shareholders; one of the five basic principles deals with this issue.

The problem with the OECD guidelines, particularly when applied to developing and transition economies, is that they cover a broad range of rules and principles without specifying clear priorities among them. And since the guidelines presume the existence of many of the institutions lacking in these countries, they also fail to provide priorities across policy areas. Moreover, even the watered-down language of these prescriptions is often too ambitious for policymakers. Nevertheless, the OECD guidelines provide a useful start. The following paragraphs therefore give our view of the priorities for developing and transition economies.

- *Any international guidelines must recognize the international differences in governance systems.* Generalizations are often more harmful than helpful. Ownership and control structures differ tremendously, and so do the roles of governance institutions and the basic mechanisms for correcting governance failures. General principles nevertheless should be articulated, particularly

when they are unlikely to be expressed locally. At the least, they will force domestic actors to make their own preferences explicit.
- *The general accounting rules and transparency requirements of the OECD guidelines should be a benchmark.* Transparency in ownership and control arrangements is desirable, particularly for improving the liquidity of shares and attracting foreign investors. It is hard to see how such disclosure can have any significant social costs, and the benefits seem substantial. The puzzle is why companies in need of external finance have not implemented these guidelines on their own, which would presumably lower their cost of capital. The failure of the Transparency Directive of the European Union also suggests much resistance or inertia. Either companies do not need (or want) outside funds, or disclosure has substantial private costs. One hypothesis is that insiders to these arrangements are concerned that their legitimacy would be undermined.
- *Protection of external investors is more important in transition economies than in developing countries.* The emphasis in La Porta and his coauthors on external investor protection is most appropriate in transition economies where many managers have entrenched themselves in formerly state-owned companies. But the pressure for change will not come from small shareholders or takeover threats in anonymous equity markets. Instead, it must come from strategic investors with large stakes, or even from the labor force, political authorities, or other groups.
- *The development effect from any program that focuses solely on the plight of small shareholders is likely to be very small.* Poor access to external funds may not be a binding constraint for most firms in developing countries. Even where it is, small, anonymous shareholdings will not be the dominant source of capital in most cases. Most finance is likely to come through family ties or, possibly, peer group arrangements. The same holds for transition economies. That is not to say that protection of small shareholders should not be part of corporate governance, only that it should not be the main focus.
- *Protection of creditors is more important than protection of shareholders in developing and transition economies.* While debt is the dominant source of external finance in developed market economies, equity is more important in developing countries. But developing country firms typically raise equity not in public markets but through family ties or personal relationships. In the short term any substantial growth in external finance is likely to take the form of debt, probably from banks. Recent studies show a strong link between creditor protection and development of the banking sector. In most transition economies companies have been unsuccessful in raising external finance, but their need for it is great. While strategic shareholders are important for restructuring, most external capital in these countries, too, is likely to come as debt.
- *The short- and medium-term emphasis in investor protection should not be on creating liquid markets for shares and corporate bonds.* The reason is not that

liquid markets and liquidity are undesirable, as is sometimes argued. Liquid markets generate information and facilitate control transactions in many developed market economies. In developing economies liquidity is most important when families have to sell out, but this does not seem to be a first-order problem in the short and medium term. In some transition economies liquid equity markets could help strategic investors build positions, but it is not clear that insiders will play their part by issuing shares.

- *In the long term liquid securities markets can be important for attracting foreign portfolio investment.* These markets are hard to create, take time to develop, and are difficult to sustain. In most countries they are not an important source of finance. The recent problems in Asia and Russia have shown how volatile these markets are, but the vulnerability of countries to this volatility seems to be closely related to how well protected external investors are. Foreign portfolio investment may be the type of investment where investor protection matters most. It has important benefits in relieving domestic capital constraints, and its lure can provide important incentives in implementing governance reform.

- *Reforms focusing on enforcement are more important—and more difficult—than changes in the letter of the law.* This obvious point needs to be made. Enforcement is the outcome of a large set of interrelated formal and informal institutions. Unfortunately, our knowledge of how these institutions interact, to what extent they are substitutes or complements, whether they can be successfully transplanted from one country to another, and the like is still limited.

- *Reforms must recognize the complementarity of different parts of the law and of different political institutions.* In countries with weak law enforcement the legal protection and legal obligations of economic actors must differ from those in countries with strong enforcement. The efficiency of legal procedures, such as the scope of criminal or civil law in business court cases or the use of circumstantial evidence in court, will depend on the country's overall legal framework and political structure.

- *In many contexts the most immediate concern is to protect stakeholders other than shareholders.* In many transition economies, especially Russia, the main governance problem is entrenched managers' outright theft from, or at least failure to pay, the government and employees. Ruthless managers also exploit suppliers and customers locked into inherited relationships. In many developing countries weak labor laws discourage firm-specific investment by employees and may also undermine general skill formation. An approach favoring nonfinancial stakeholders could allow managers and individual stakeholders to exploit blurred corporate objectives and paralyze decisionmaking. But corporate governance reform must strike a balance between financial and nonfinancial stakeholders and recognize the needs and the potential value added of stakeholders other than shareholders.

- *Implementation and enforcement of fundamental corporate governance reform will in many cases require external conditionality.* Governments in developing and transition economies are generally weak. This weakness has many sources, but an important one, particularly in transition economies, is the political deadlock over key reforms arising from their distributional effects. External conditionality can relieve these political constraints. The European Union has played a crucial role as an outside anchor to the institutional reform in Central and Eastern Europe. Unfortunately, EU membership has not been in the cards for most of the former Soviet Union. Conditionality from the international financial institutions should be systematically used, though it can never have the same leverage. Explicit or implicit conditions from foreign investors are also important, but this pressure is likely to be less consistent and less coordinated. Here OECD and other guidelines may be useful.

- *Effective corporate governance reform will often require a combination of threats and co-optation of the main actors.* Given the weakness of governments and the absence of credible outside anchors in most developing and transition economies, fundamental reform will not take place against the will of the main actors. Pivotal groups will somehow have to be co-opted. Threats may even be necessary. In the extreme case of Russia renationalization of strategic assets followed by renewed privatization may be the only way to break the resistance to reform. This strategy has obvious reputational consequences, however, and the government may not be strong enough to act on such a threat.

## References

Aoki, Masahiko. 1998. "A Theoretical Foundation for Comparative Corporate Governance." Stanford University, Department of Economics and Center for Economic Policy Research, Stanford, Calif.

Barca, Fabrizio, and Marco Becht, eds. 1999. "Ownership and Control: A European Perspective." Free University of Brussels, European Centre for Advanced Research in Economics.

Berglöf, Erik. 1997. "Reforming Corporate Governance: Redirecting the European Agenda." *Economic Policy* 24 (April): 93–123.

Berglöf, Erik, and Gérard Roland. 1998. "Soft Budget Constraints and Banking in Transition." *Journal of Comparative Economics* 26: 18–40.

Berglöf, Erik, Gérard Roland, and Ernst-Ludwig von Thadden. 1999. "The Hypothetical Creditors' Bargain." Stockholm Institute of Transition Economics and East European Economies, Stockholm School of Economics.

Bhagwati, Jagdish. 1993. *India in Transition: Freeing the Economy.* Oxford: Clarendon.

Black, Bernard, and Reinier Kraakman. 1996. "Self-Enforcing Model of Corporate Law." *Harvard Law Review* 109: 1911–81.

Black, Bernard, Reinier Kraakman, and Anna Tarassova. 1999. "Russian Privatization and Corporate Governance: What Went Wrong?" Stanford University, Stanford Law School, Stanford, Calif.

Blanchard, Olivier, and Michael Kremer. 1997. "Disorganization." *Quarterly Journal of Economics* 112 (November): 1091–26.

Bolton, Patrick, and Ernst-Ludwig von Thadden. 1998. "Blocks, Liquidity, and Corporate Governance." *Journal of Finance* 53 (February): 1–25.

Brown, Annette, and David Brown. 1998. "Does Market Structure Matter?" SITE Working Paper. Stockholm School of Economics, Stockholm Institute of Transition Economics and East European Economies.

Burkart, Mike, Denis Gromb, and Fausto Panunzi. 1997. "Large Shareholders, Monitoring and the Value of the Firm." *Quarterly Journal of Economics* 112 (August): 693–728.

Carlin, Wendy, and Colin Mayer. 1999. "Finance, Investment and Growth Finance, Investment and Growth." CEPR Discussion Paper 2233. Centre for Economic Policy Research, London.

Claessens, Stijn, Simeon Djankov, and Larry H.P. Lang. 1998. "Who Controls East Asian Corporations?" Policy Research Working Paper 2054. World Bank, Financial Sector Practice Department, Washington, D.C.

Dewatripont, Mathias, and Gérard Roland. 1997. "Transition as Large-Scale Institutional Change." In David Kreps and Ken Wallis, eds., *Advances in Economic Theory*. Cambridge: Cambridge University Press.

Earle, John, and Saul Estrin. 1998. "Privatization, Competition, and Budget Constraints: Disciplining Enterprises in Russia." SITE Working Paper. Stockholm School of Economics, Stockholm Institute of Transition Economics and East European Economies.

EBRD (European Bank for Reconstruction and Development). 1996. *EBRD Transition Report*. London.

———. 1998. *EBRD Transition Report*. London.

ECGN (European Corporate Governance Network). 1998. "Corporate Governance and Disclosure in a Transatlantic Perspective." Centre for Economic Policy Research and European Corporate Governance Network, Brussels.

Fisman, Raymond. 1998. "The Incentives for Rent-Seeking: Estimating the Value of Political Connections." Harvard University, Harvard School of Business, Cambridge, Mass.

Granovetter, Mark. 1994. "Business Groups." In Neil J. Smelser and Richard Swedberg, eds., *Handbook of Economic Sociology*. Princeton, N.J.: Princeton University Press.

Grossman, Sanford, and Oliver Hart. 1986. "The Costs and Benefits of Ownership: A Theory of Vertical and Lateral Integration." *Journal of Political Economy* 94 (August): 691–719.

Gugler, Klaus. 1998. "Corporate Governance and Economic Performance." Department of Finance, University of Vienna.

Hart, Oliver, and John Moore. 1990. "Property Rights and the Nature of the Firm." *Journal of Political Economy* 98 (December): 1119–58.

Hay, Jonathan R., and Andrei Shleifer. 1998. "Private Enforcement of Public Laws: A Theory of Legal Reform." *American Economic Review* 88 (May): 398–403.

Hellwig, Martin. 1998. "On the Economics and Politics of Corporate Finance and Corporate Control." University of Mannheim, Department of Economics, Germany.

Jensen, Michael. 1993. "The Modern Industrial Revolution, Exit and the Failure of Internal Control Systems." *Journal of Finance* 48 (July): 831–80.

Johnson, Simon, Peter Boone, Alisdair Breach, and Eric Friedman. 1998. "Corporate Governance and the Asian Financial Crisis." Massachusetts Institute of Technology, Sloan School of Business, Cambridge, Mass.

Khanna, Tarun, and Krishna Palepu. 1999. "Emerging Market Business Groups, Foreign Investors, and Corporate Governance." NBER Working Paper 6955. National Bureau of Economic Research, Cambridge, Mass.

Khanna, Tarun, and Jan W. Rivkin. 1999. "Estimating the Performance Effects of Networks in Emerging Markets." Harvard Business School, Harvard University, Cambridge, Mass.

King, Robert, and Ross Levine. 1993. "Finance and Growth: Schumpeter Might Be Right." *Quarterly Journal of Economics* 108: 717–38.

La Porta, Rafael, Florencio Lopez-de-Silanes, Andrei Shleifer, and Robert Vishny. 1997. "Legal Determinants of External Finance." *Journal of Finance* 52: 1131–50.

———. 1998. "Law and Finance." *Journal of Political Economy* 106: 1113–55.

———. 1999a. "Agency Problems and Dividend Policies around the World." Harvard University, Department of Economics, Cambridge, Mass.

———. 1999b. "Corporate Ownership around the World." *Journal of Finance* 54: 471–517.

Levine, Ross, Norman Loayza, and Torsten Beck. 1998. "Financial Intermediation and Growth: Causality and Causes." World Bank, Washington, D.C.

Linnarud, Christina. 1998. "Corporate Governance and Shareholder Rights in the Russian Law." MA thesis, Stockholm School of Economics, Department of Finance.

Lombardo, Davide, and Marco Pagano. 1999. "Legal Determinants of the Cost of Equity Capital." Paper presented at the 1999 Journal of Financial Intermediation Symposium, Cornell University, Ithaca, N.Y.

Mayer, Colin. 1990. "Financial Systems, Corporate Finance, and Economic Development." In R.G. Hubbard, ed., *Asymmetric Information, Corporate Finance, and Investment*. Chicago and London: University of Chicago Press.

Nickell, Stephen. 1996. "Competition and Corporate Performance." *Journal of Political Economy* 104 (August): 724–46.

Nickell, Stephen, Daphne Nicolitsas, and Neil Dryden. 1997. "What Makes Firms Perform Well?" *European Economic Review* 41 (3–5): 783–96.

OECD (Organisation for Economic Co-operation and Development). 1999. "OECD Principles of Corporate Governance." Paris.

Rajan, Raghuram, and Luigi Zingales. 1998. "Financial Dependence and Growth." *American Economic Review* 88 (June): 559–86.

———. 1999. "The Tyranny of the Inefficient: An Inquiry into the Adverse Consequences of Power Struggles." University of Chicago, Graduate School of Business.

Rajan, Raghuram, Henri Servaes, and Luigi Zingales. 1998. "The Cost of Diversity: Diversification Discount and Inefficient Investment." University of Chicago, Graduate School of Business.

Roe, Mark. 1994. *Strong Managers, Weak Owners: The Political Roots of American Corporate Finance*. Princeton, N.J.: Princeton University Press.

———. 1999. "Political Preconditions to Separating Ownership from Control: The Incompatibility of the American Public Corporation with Social Democracy." Columbia University, School of Law, New York.

Samuelson, Paul. 1957. "Wages and Interest: A Modern Dissection of Marxian Economic Models." *American Economic Review* 47: 884–912.

Schaffer, Mark. 1998. "Do Firms in Transition Economies Have Soft Budget Constraints? A Reconsideration of Concepts and Evidence." *Journal of Comparative Economics* 26: 80–103.

Shleifer, Andrei, and Lawrence Summers. 1988. "Breach of Trust in Hostile Takeovers." In A.J. Auerbach, ed., *Corporate Takeovers: Causes and Consequences*. Chicago and London: University of Chicago Press.

Shleifer, Andrei, and Robert Vishny. 1997. "A Survey of Corporate Governance." *Journal of Finance* 52: 737–83.

Stein, Jeremy. 1988. "Takeover Threats and Managerial Myopia." *Journal of Political Economy* 96: 61–80.

Tirole, Jean. 1998. "Corporate Governance." CEPR Discussion Paper 2086. Centre for Economic Policy Research, London.

von Thadden, Ernst-Ludwig. 1995. "Long-Term Contracts, Short-Term Investment, and Monitoring." *Review of Economic Studies* 62 (213): 557–75

Watson, Alan. 1974. *Legal Transplants.* Charlottesville: University of Virginia Press.

Zingales, Luigi. 1995. "What Determines the Value of Corporate Votes?" *Quarterly Journal of Economics* 110: 1047–73.

———. 1999. "Legal Systems and Financial Development." University of Chicago, Graduate School of Business.

# Does the Invisible Hand Need a Transparent Glove? The Politics of Transparency

*Ann M. Florini*

*Transparency is on the rise, touted as the solution to such disparate problems as financial volatility, environmental degradation, money laundering, and corruption. But transparency faces much opposition, particularly from those under scrutiny, who have strong incentives to avoid providing information. The key to increasing transparency is to create incentives for governments and corporations to provide information. The international financial institutions can do some good directly, by modeling the advantages of transparency through their own behavior and by applying conditionality under some circumstances. Little will change unless large national and international constituencies for transparency emerge, however.*

The "invisible hand" of the market depends heavily on the support of a thick "glove" of rules, norms, and institutions, including governments. But too often the glove is opaque, obscuring flows of information essential to the efficient and equitable functioning of both markets and the national and international institutions that regulate them. Recently, demands to make both institutions and markets transparent have reached a fevered pitch. Many of the arguments over the creation of a new global financial architecture put calls for increased transparency front and center.[1]

The rising clamor for transparency in economic, financial, and business discussions reflects a global trend. Scholars, policymakers, and activists have called for transparency in such varied contexts as banking, auditing, and accounting standards; national fiscal practices; control of drug trafficking; pollution control; anticorruption efforts; multilateral development assistance; and private sector environmental and labor practices.[2] In politics promoters of democracy have come to realize that elections alone cannot provide accountability; citizens must also be able to monitor the actions of the officials they elect. In environmental issues a whole field of pollu-

---

Ann M. Florini is senior associate at the Carnegie Endowment for International Peace. She is grateful to Nancy Birdsall, Stephen Flynn, Virginia Haufler, David Lipton, Daniel Morrow, Sunil Sharma, Nadeem Ul Haque, and two anonymous reviewers for their helpful comments on earlier versions of this article.

tion regulation based on public disclosure by firms is developing, one that relies on public pressure rather than government sanctions to induce firms to clean up (Tietenberg and Wheeler 1998). In arms control the last years of the Cold War accustomed major powers to the practice of inviting highly intrusive mutual scrutiny of one another's military forces, a practice now broadening to include many more governments and large swaths of the private sector. The Chemical Weapons Convention, for example, now subjects the chemical industry to both regularly scheduled and surprise inspections at thousands of facilities around the world (Florini 1997).

The demands for transparency are increasing in large part because of globalization. As the world becomes more tightly integrated, many people are affected by, and thus want a say in, what used to be other people's business. As goods, capital, environmental degradation, drugs, people, and ideas cross political boundaries in ever greater quantities, events in one place have significant impact elsewhere. Countries under pressure to attract foreign investment demand information from their firms and government agencies. International financial institutions, which are major promoters of economic integration, are beginning to make strong recommendations about what information governments should demand from citizens and firms.

There are good reasons to believe that increased transparency is frequently beneficial, often indispensable, and sometimes a moral imperative. Consistent transparency can smooth the operation of financial markets, and it may attract the investment that fosters growth. It provides a means of detecting, and thus correcting, errors in the policies of governmental and international institutions—errors that in the era of economic integration can wreak havoc on bystanders if left uncorrected. Most important, as democratic norms spread, it is harder and harder to maintain societal consensus on decisions reached in secret by small elites. Publics have proved willing to accept painful reforms, but only when they have been fully consulted and kept fully informed.

Despite the benefits of transparency, increasing it is difficult. Doing so often requires the power to induce disclosure, either by coercion or by restructuring incentives, and the information thus revealed can shift power from the former holders of secrets to the newly informed. Moreover, even when a government or corporation finds it in its institutional interest to be transparent, individuals within such institutions may prefer secrecy—to cover up incompetence, to protect opportunities for rent-seeking, or simply to avoid the bother of public scrutiny (Stiglitz 1998). When a corporation or government is generating externalities—by secretly dumping toxic substances, for example, or lying about its financial reserves (thus risking a financial crisis that could prove costly to others)—it has obvious incentives to conceal its actions.

The key to increasing transparency is to create incentives for governments and corporations to provide information. Such incentives are necessary because, with rare exceptions, transparency depends on the more or less "voluntary" provision of information. The European Union becomes more transparent only when its bureaucrats make their files accessible. National and corporate accounts become transparent only when governments and corporations publish them.

Because increasing transparency generally requires institutions and individuals to release information they are accustomed to withholding, transparency will rarely come about unless pressures can be brought to bear. International organizations such as the World Bank and International Monetary Fund (IMF) can serve as important sources of pressure to encourage transparency. Toward that end they should analyze the benefits of transparency and consider how they can help bring it about.

## The Meaning and Value of Transparency

Although the term *transparency* seems ubiquitous these days, it is rarely defined with much rigor. Of whom is information being demanded? What specific information is needed, and for what purposes? One reason for the lack of precision is that the term is being used in so many different issue areas. In politics, transparency refers to enabling citizens to learn what their governments are up to by obtaining information provided by the government. The term has been especially widespread in discussions within the European Community. In economics and finance, transparency has been defined very broadly as "a process by which information about existing conditions, decisions, and actions is made accessible, visible and understandable" (IMF 1998b). The national security and arms control field defines transparency relatively narrowly as involving the systematic provision of information on specific aspects of military activities under informal or formal international arrangements (United Nations 1991).

These varied definitions agree that transparency is always closely connected to accountability. The purpose of calls for transparency is to permit citizens, markets, or governments to hold others accountable for their policies and performance. Transparency can thus be defined as the release by institutions of information relevant to evaluating those institutions.

Because transparency is a tool to permit evaluation, much of its value lies in its role in overcoming the principal-agent problem (that is, the difficulties principals have in ensuring that their agents do what the principals want them to do rather than acting in their own interests). In the corporate world, firm managers are supposed to be agents of the stockholders. Without transparency, however, stockholders cannot determine whether the company is being well managed, and investors are unable to determine whether to become stockholders. Lack of transparency can also contribute to herd behavior by fund managers if they have few signals other than the actions of other investors on which to base their judgments. In the realm of politics, where governments are supposed to act as the agents of their citizens, the wave of corruption scandals in the 1990s indicates that too many government officials serve private rather than public ends when no one is looking. Thus transparency can provide very practical means of improving the functioning of markets and governments.

The demands for transparency also have a moral dimension. Principals have the right to know a great deal about their agents, even—or especially—when the agents are governments or international organizations and the principals are the general public. Citizens have the right to know how their government performs. Consumers and investors have the right to receive honest information about the products they buy and the companies in which they invest. And because economies cross national borders, so do those rights.

Nevertheless, it is important to be pragmatic about when it is worthwhile to push for transparency, because that push is costly and not always worth the cost. Transparency merely lets people see streams of facts. It neither enables people to do anything about those facts nor conveys any understanding of their meaning. Demands for transparency make sense only if two conditions are met. First, the targets of the calls for transparency must be able and willing to provide the requisite information. Second, recipients of the information must be able to use it to evaluate the provider of the information according to some accepted standard of behavior.

## Incentives for Transparency

It can be surprisingly difficult to compile economic and financial information, especially in developing countries, which almost by definition are short on the human capital and institutions needed. Expansion of programs to help public sector entities learn how to compile and transmit information could increase transparency.

Once actors are able to provide information, however, what makes them willing to do so? What inherent incentives for transparency exist, and what carrots or sticks must be applied to induce such "willingness"? The answer depends on whether the information will be used to deter misbehavior or signal good behavior. Shining a spotlight on miscreants can deter them from misbehaving if they are convinced that misbehavior will be spotted and penalized. The flip side of deterrence is reassurance. Reassurance enables actors to prove that they are abiding by a standard. Such reassurance can be crucial for stockholders deciding whether to hold or sell their shares or for countries trying to prove that they are not about to attack their neighbors.

The incentives for providing information differ dramatically depending on whether transparency is being used for deterrence or reassurance—that is, whether the target wants to be held accountable. If transparency is being used to deter a particular behavior, some actors will misbehave in the absence of transparency. These actors will find it in their interest to stonewall or lie about their behavior. In such cases the incentive to deceive must somehow be overcome, and ways must be found to verify the information that is released. In cases of reassurance, the incentive problem does not exist. Transparency will flourish as long as the institutions providing the information are credible.

For deterrence to be legitimate and for reassurance to work, however, providers and recipients of information must agree on what the released information means. Transparency matters because it is coupled with some form of accountability. But such accountability requires the prior existence of a *shared* standard of behavior.

Businesses and governments object to demands by nongovernmental organizations (NGOs) for transparency in large part because NGOs sometimes use the information to chastise them for failing to meet standards those firms and governments never agreed to meet.

Such standards, in turn, depend on shared understandings of the meaning of the information conveyed by transparency. Transparency, after all, conveys facts, not knowledge about causal connections.[3] Recipients of information react to that information based on theories about its meaning. Transparency can create reassurance only if the providers and recipients of the information agree that the information provided in fact describes a desirable situation. The same announcement of workforce layoffs that can propel stock prices to new highs in the United States, where such layoffs are seen as signs of greater efficiency, can force the resignation of corporate leaders in Japan, where layoffs are seen as threats to the social order.

## Can There Be Too Much Transparency?

Even if all these conditions are met, increasing levels of transparency can sometimes have negative effects. International organizations, governments, firms, financial markets, NGOs, and others may use information for purposes other than informing the public or facilitating mutually beneficial economic exchange. In arms control, for example, the same information that reassures other countries that your military forces are not massing for attack can enable them to locate and attack your forces. In economics, misinterpretation or deliberate misuse of information by national or corporate rivals can spark unfavorable headlines, plunges in stock prices, and capital flight. Moreover, transparency does not always redistribute power from the strong to the weak. Secrecy can be the refuge of the weak against the strong, as human rights organizations working in repressive countries have found.

It is also possible to have too much transparency. Too much disclosure can produce a white noise effect, making it difficult to know what is significant or even to sort through all the data. Indeed, one way of concealing information is to bury it in a flood of data. Disclosing information also requires time and effort, a burden that may be difficult for some institutions to bear. Corporations, for example, are being bombarded with demands to make their environmental and labor practices transparent. Such calls are often paired with demands to permit third-party certification of their compliance with "voluntary" corporate social responsibility standards (Haufler forthcoming).

If transparency is to be used successfully, it must be used judiciously. Careful attention must be paid to minimizing the burden created by the demand for information and to formatting information in user-friendly ways that minimize the white noise effect.

Transparency is expected to improve the efficiency and fairness of markets and corporations and to enhance the accountability and legitimacy of national governments and intergovernmental organizations. This is a heavy burden for a relatively new buzzword, raising two fundamental questions that cross issue areas and actors. First, would increased transparency actually do much good? Second, can transparency be increased, given problems with both incentives and the ability to provide information?

## Transparency in the Global Economy

Can transparency ameliorate such downsides of the globalization of financial markets as the increase in volatility and money laundering and the avoidance of necessary fiscal reforms? Many people seem to think it can; nowhere are calls for transparency louder than in the debate over the new financial architecture. In part, this emphasis on transparency reflects the efforts of investors to shift the blame for their poor investment decisions (Furman and Stiglitz 1998). But it also reflects an increase in investors' desire to identify investment opportunities across national borders, as well as pressures by countries well endowed with capital, particularly the United States, to smooth their path. Demands for transparency are arising because of the growth in the number of investors wanting the means to assess the quality and risks of portfolio investments across a broad range of countries.[4]

Financial markets, more than others, depend on information to function well. For investors to know who will most productively use their capital, they must have some basis for discriminating among vying claimants. Mechanisms for such discrimination include personal trust, reputation, the existence of well-functioning legal systems to prosecute fraud (Greenwald and Stiglitz 1991), and insurance systems to enable investors to recover some of their money when they make bad judgments (Haufler 1997). Such systems do not seem to be working well in the rapidly evolving global financial system, especially for portfolio investment flows. Reputations, where they exist, can be unreliable. Legal systems find it hard to stretch enforcement powers across national borders. And insurance systems raise as-yet-unresolved issues of moral hazard.

Would substantial increases in transparency prevent or ameliorate the kinds of crises that have afflicted so much of the world in the past few years? Most observers assume that it would and have called for increased information from both firms and governments (IMF 1998b). As Barry Eichengreen (1999, p. 10) has noted, greater transparency could reduce the incidence of financial crises: "Better information on the economic and financial affairs of governments, banks, and corporations will strengthen market discipline (encourage lenders to ration credit to borrowers who fail to take the steps needed to maintain their financial stability) and help policymakers to identify the need for corrective action." It is certainly plausible that better information would enable investors, governments, and international financial institutions to improve the reliability of risk assessment, leading to better investment decisions and better government policy.

Transparency by itself will not suffice, however, in part because it is never absolute and in part because lack of information is not the only cause of financial meltdown. Scandinavia, which has some of the most transparent systems in the world, was not protected from financial trauma a decade ago (Furman and Stiglitz 1998). Under some circumstances transparency could even be harmful, leading, for example, to the closure of temporarily shaky financial institutions that might otherwise have recovered (Furman and Stiglitz 1998).[5] Overall, however, regular and consistent transparency would promote economic efficiency and reduce the "lumpiness" of negative information that can create such large adjustment costs.

## Transparency within Firms

Corporate disclosure varies greatly across countries. In recent decades some transnational associations have attempted to develop standards of disclosure that could be followed globally. Since its founding in 1973 the International Accounting Standards Committee (IASC) put forward rather flexible standards. Several developing countries have found it is easier to adopt those standards than to develop their own (Jones 1998). In the 1990s, responding to pressures from institutional investors for better data, the IASC developed a more rigorous set of standards, which it hopes will be endorsed by the International Organization for Securities Commissions.

Incentives to adopt and enforce the new corporate disclosure standards may be lacking. The United States, for example, which already has rigorous standards, is unwilling to accept universal standards weaker than its own. Many Continental European countries have also been ambivalent about the new IASC standards, which they believe reflect too much U.S. and British influence (Jones 1998).

Even if improved transparency standards for firms are adopted, transparency may not increase. As the G-22 Working Group acknowledged, the big problem is behavior, not laws: "Poor disclosure practices stem from inadequate compliance with and enforcement of existing standards" (IMF 1998b, p. vi). Firms in poor countries may find the proposed standards too rigorous and complex. If they fail to comply with recent standards, why should more disclosure standards matter?

The hope appears to be that once a standardized format is available so that investors can compare firms across countries, market forces will impel compliance by channeling investment to more transparent companies. Indeed, some research indicates that firms are finding that transparency attracts investment (*Financial Post* December 6, 1997). The Basle Committee on Banking Supervision (1998) argues that the market provides incentives for banks to want to be perceived as conducting their business in an efficient and prudent manner. Well-run banks should thus welcome the opportunity to provide reassurance through greater transparency. For banks that are not well run, transparency could act as a deterrent: "To the extent a bank's management knows its activities and risk exposures will be transparent ... investment decisions and other business decisions [by market participants] can provide a strong incentive for bank management to improve risk management practices and internal controls" (p. 6). Effective deterrence depends heavily on a credible threat that banks will be unable to avoid such public disclosure, however—a threat that many governments may be unable to enforce.

## Transparency within Government

It is widely argued that *countries* also need to become transparent to attract investment and that governments must provide timely and complete information about macroeconomic developments and policies in order to ensure such transparency. The variety of emerging standards for transparency on a range of governmental economic and financial data is impressive (IMF n.d.).

In March 1996 the IMF unveiled its Special Data Dissemination Standard for countries having or seeking access to international capital markets (IMF 1996). (For other countries, the IMF has created the General Data Dissemination Standard.) The Special Standard specifies what economic performance and policy data should be made available to the public and how often, how widely, and how it should be distributed. Since September 1996 the IMF has maintained an electronic Dissemination Standard Bulletin Board (http://dsbb.imf.org), from which anyone can download information on the more than 40 countries that have subscribed to the Special Data Dissemination Standard. The bulletin board also provides hyperlinks to data available on national Internet sites. In April 1998 the Interim Committee adopted a Code of Good Practices on Fiscal Transparency, and the IMF is developing a Manual on Fiscal Transparency (IMF 1998a). Other efforts at creating global disclosure standards for governments include the accounting standards for the public sector put forward by the International Federation of Accountants and the international standards for government auditing set by the International Organization of Supreme Audit Institutions.

Although such disclosures are intended to help countries attract foreign investment, the standards would have domestic political effects as well. Indeed, as the G-22 Working Group argues, because one of the primary responsibilities of national governments is to maintain macroeconomic stability, accountability of national authorities demands that such information be provided (IMF 1998b). Citizens need to know how the economy is doing and what the government is doing about it so that they can, if necessary, demand changes in policies or officials.

Government incentives *not* to be transparent could hardly be more evident. And when it comes to macroeconomic policies, governments have all sorts of ways to muddy the waters. As Alesina and Perotti (1996) argue, the complexity of the budgets of modern economies is partly artificial, created to help politicians hide taxes, overemphasize the benefits of spending, and conceal government liabilities. Governments obfuscate in several ways. They present overly optimistic projections of growth and tax revenues, which then result in "unexpected" deficits. They inflate baseline projections, making future budgetary increases appear smaller than they actually are. They keep some items off budget and use multiyear budgeting that postpones all hard decisions to out-years. With these and other tools of opacity at governments' disposal, the current and proposed standards for governmental disclosure clearly face enormous obstacles.

Both carrots and sticks could help overcome the incentives for continued opacity by government (and firms). The international financial institutions could help make compliance with transparency requirements an easy signal for investors to read. The IMF Working Group on Transparency and Accountability has proposed that the IMF issue country-specific transparency reports summarizing the degree to which a national economy meets internationally recognized disclosure standards.[6] If enough countries and firms abide by such standards and their compliance is widely reported, mere compliance with the transparency requirement may serve as a powerful seal of approval—even if the underlying data are not particularly impressive. The international financial institutions could also make compliance with disclosure standards a condition of loans.

## Transparency by Investors

Up to this point the discussion of transparency in the global financial system has left out one very important actor. All these calls for transparency are aimed at making life easier for investors. But some of the investors that have wreaked the greatest havoc, such as hedge funds, are themselves among the least transparent of actors. Although their decisions can make or break national economies, they are largely unaccountable.

Standard assumptions about the working of financial markets hold this opacity to be a virtue rather than a drawback. Financial firms have strong incentives to object to any disclosures that could lead to a competitive disadvantage. Hedge funds, for example, do not want to disclose their positions in various markets because those positions may be taken as signals by other investors. Anonymity for investors is important for the liquidity of financial markets (Eichengreen and others 1998). Is it reasonable, though, to expect high standards of transparency from everyone in the international financial system except investors?

## The Problem of Criminality

When self-interested behavior veers into outright criminality, does transparency still have a role to play? Illegal activities, such as money laundering or corruption, can threaten the stability and efficiency of the global financial architecture (Tanzi 1996). Illicit activities are inherently very difficult to measure, but both money laundering and corruption appear to be large problems. All estimates of money laundering start in the hundreds of billions of dollars—on a par with mid-size national economies and many of the largest global industries (Flynn 1999). As for corruption, a rapidly growing literature demonstrates the high economic and political costs of this pervasive problem (Mauro 1997; Rose-Ackerman 1997).

If transparency could be made to work in such cases of criminality, there seems little doubt that it would change behavior. If evidence of criminal activities could be gathered, the guilty could be held accountable through prosecution. In the case of corruption, even if criminal prosecutions did not occur, tainted officials could be forced from office. Criminals and corrupt officials have overwhelming incentives to resist disclosure of information about their activities, however. Transparency must thus target a very broad range of actors and activities in order to eliminate the shadows in which illegal activities take place.

## Money Laundering

Many of the proposed solutions to the problem of money laundering take just such an approach. At the 1989 Paris Summit meeting, the G-7 established the Financial

Action Task Force, headquartered at the Organisation for Economic Co-ooperation and Development (OECD), to examine measures to combat money laundering.[7] Of the 40 recommendations issued by the task force in 1990 (and revised in 1996), some half dozen relate directly to a form of transparency that has come to be known as a "know-your-customer" requirement. These recommendations call on financial institutions to identify their customers accurately, determine what activities are normal for those customers, pay special attention to large or unusual transactions or patterns of transactions, and report to the authorities any suspicions that funds stem from criminal activities. Most task force members have implemented requirements for mandatory reporting of suspicious transactions (Financial Action Task Force 1998).

The Core Principles for Effective Banking Supervision issued by the Basle Committee in September 1997 lays down similar rules. According to these principles, banks should "have adequate policies, practices, and procedures in place, including strict 'know-your-customer' rules, that promote high ethical and professional standards in the financial sector and prevent the bank being used, intentionally or unintentionally, by criminal elements" (Basle Committee 1998).

It is not clear, however, that transparency will significantly constrain money laundering unless it is pressed much farther. In most cases the reporting obligation extends only to financial institutions. Even when it applies more broadly, almost all reports are made by financial institutions, particularly banks (Financial Action Task Force 1998). Not surprisingly, money launderers have shifted to using nonbank financial institutions and nonfinancial businesses. Such transparency measures as reporting requirements may be hard pressed to keep up with the shifting patterns of money laundering activities.

The limitations of reporting requirements have spurred calls for even greater transparency. One analysis calls for restructuring the interbank payments system so that wire transfers document the originator and beneficiary of the transaction and for regularly publishing an "Accessories to Transovereign Crime Report," spotlighting "governments, business institutions, or individuals who routinely fail to abide by regional and international crime control conventions" (Flynn 1999, pp. 119–20).

But just as the backlash against globalization is triggering calls for transparency, transparency has the potential for spurring its own backlash, even from those engaged in purely legitimate activity. The U.S. government unleashed a firestorm of wholly unexpected public protest in 1998 when it published a proposed regulation establishing uniform and mandatory know-your-customer banking procedures. The American Bankers Association protested that the rules did not apply to other financial institutions, such as broker-dealers, insurance agencies, and securities dealers. Others strongly objected to monitoring the accounts of individuals who were not suspected of committing illicit activities, considering that to be a gross invasion of privacy. One member of the U.S. Congress dubbed the proposal the "spy on your neighbor" rule and sponsored a bill to kill the proposal should it be adopted (*Insight on the News* 22 February 1999).

These objections suggest that even law-abiding institutions may need incentives to allow themselves to be monitored. Such monitoring runs counter to deeply embedded suspicions of authority in some countries. Elsewhere, where objections have not yet been voiced, problems may arise if the information is misused. If transparency is to play a significant role in controlling illegal flows of capital, a major public education program will be required to convince people of the need for transparency. And safeguards will have to be designed to protect against the abuse and misuse of personal financial information.

## Corruption

Corruption—the abuse of public office for private gain—would seem to be a problem tailor-made for the transparency solution. In most countries it is both illegal for public officials to accept bribes and highly embarrassing for them to be caught doing so.

During the 1990s, citizens in all parts of the world, from Italy to Brazil to Pakistan to Zaire, made it clear that corruption is heavily penalized. In the first half of the 1990s government ministers in Argentina, India, Japan, Switzerland, and the United Kingdom were forced to resign in the wake of corruption charges (Naim 1995). Shining the spotlight on corruption may not always topple governments or put politicians behind bars, but it has done so often enough that the prospect of transparency is likely to have a significant deterrent effect. Transparency is not always effective—the campaign finance system in the United States, for example, seems impervious to any degree of revelation—but it generally helps reduce corruption.

The incentives against transparency are obvious. Corrupt officials rarely confess—they get caught. However, although corrupt officials have every incentive to keep their dealings opaque, others have incentives to increase the transparency of governmental processes. Honest officials welcome and promote transparency.

Demands for greater transparency to deal with corruption generally come from two sources: newly empowered information media that have discovered the profit potential of corruption scandals (Naim 1995) and an international community of donors and NGOs fed up with the diversion of development funds into private coffers. Donors and NGOs have come up with some innovative techniques for spotlighting corruption that get around the obvious disincentives to transparency. Transparency International's annual corruption perceptions index, which ranks countries on how corrupt they are perceived to be according to surveys of businesspeople, political analysts, and the public, put both corruption and Transparency International on the map. This highly visible information often becomes headline news and the subject of parliamentary debates. In 1999 Transparency International released a second index spotlighting the supply side of international corruption by identifying countries that are home to the corporations most likely to offer bribes.

## Increasing the Transparency of International Financial Institutions

In short, increasing transparency will be key to the future success of economic integration. Only with transparency will it be possible to deter corruption, crack down on money laundering, and foster efficiency in the allocation of investments across companies and countries. Moreover, economic integration will have little legitimacy among the public as long as it remains a mysterious, unaccountable process.

But increasing transparency will be no easy task. Transparency comes up against obstacles ranging from the legitimate privacy concerns of individuals to the desire of rent seekers to hide their ill-gotten gains. Transparency also runs counter to entrenched beliefs in many parts of the world that governments need not be accountable on an ongoing basis to their citizenry. Similar beliefs prevail among much of the world's economic policy elite, who argue that they should not be publicly accountable.

Overcoming such obstacles to transparency should constitute a major part of the future agenda of the World Bank and the IMF. But are these institutions themselves sufficiently transparent to credibly lead the campaign for transparency? For their first several decades, both the World Bank and the IMF were highly secretive. Both institutions answered (sometimes with less than complete candor) only to their member governments and provided little information to the public.

## The World Bank

No international organization has faced more vociferous demands to open up than the World Bank. Beginning in the early 1980s, a wide range of NGOs began pressuring the Bank to be more forthcoming about its plans and policies, arguing that "if development bank project planning and design were open and transparent ... fewer disastrous projects would be approved and a greater opportunity to promote development alternatives would exist" (Udall 1998, p. 391). Three different transnational civil society networks—on poverty, environment, and structural adjustment—have coalesced around opposition to World Bank projects and procedures (Nelson 1996).

The proponents of World Bank transparency are right. In the days when the Bank remained cloaked in secrecy, too often government officials in both borrowing and donor countries were less concerned with the quality of the projects being funded than with such considerations as the political imperatives of channeling funds to particular governments or the opportunities for personal enrichment or political power. Although at least some of the actors now demanding transparency from the Bank undoubtedly have their own agendas, if the Bank becomes truly transparent all agendas will have to be contested openly.

These pressures for transparency have had an impact, in part because the argument has resonated so effectively with U.S. policymakers. Members of Congress proved willing to hold funding for the Bank hostage to the establishment of new Bank disclosure policies (Udall 1998). Under the disclosure policy established a decade ago and revised in 1993, the Bank releases a project information document on every project. Also available are final staff appraisal reports, environmental impact statements, and other documents.

Whether meaningful transparency has been achieved—or can be achieved—remains unclear. As is virtually always the case, policies from above to promote transparency within an institution provide only a starting point. Whether project information documents actually contain information that make it possible for outsiders to comment meaningfully on projects in the early stages of planning will depend on the incentives World Bank staff face. If staffers are rewarded primarily for getting large projects through the pipeline quickly, they will have every incentive to make those documents as bland and meaningless as possible, in order to ward off objections to their projects. If, however, Bank staff are held accountable for the ultimate success of projects, they will have every incentive to permit widespread participation in the planning and preparation of projects in order to be able to anticipate problems and ensure that stakeholders in the borrowing countries support rather than oppose those projects. In short, the disclosure policy by itself means little. It can be just another bureaucratic hurdle, or it can be a useful and welcome tool.

Beyond this question of the utility of transparency as a means of helping the Bank do its job better lies a moral issue. The Bank is not an end in itself. It exists to provide certain services. It was constituted by national governments, but its avowed goal is to help the world's poor. In other words the Bank is an agent, but it answers to two quite different principals: those affected by the projects it helps to finance and the governments of its member states. Governments are in turn supposed to be agents for their citizens. When governments use Bank funds in ways that are not in the interests of their citizens and those citizens complain to the Bank about those uses, should the Bank withhold information from affected citizens on the grounds that only their governments—their supposed agents—are entitled to see that information?

## The International Monetary Fund

The IMF is beginning to face similar demands that it provide information about its plans, policies, and decisionmaking procedures and the effectiveness of its programs. As one NGO has argued, it is not enough for the IMF to provide information to its member governments because institutions like the IMF "can directly affect the welfare of large groups of the world's population" (Center of Concern 1998, p. 5), some of whom are not well represented or well served by the governments with whom the IMF negotiates. Without such public assessment, the IMF may be hard pressed to bolster its legitimacy around the world. And without that legitimacy, it will be difficult for the IMF to sustain its work. As the IMF has learned through bitter experience, programs secretly arrived at in consultation with government officials only and imposed without adequate involvement and understanding by the public are likely to prove ineffective.

The IMF has already begun to increase efforts to inform the public directly about the nature of and rationale for its programs, rather than relying on governments to do so. For the most part, however, the IMF leaves it up to governments to decide whether information is to be publicly released. The IMF could easily push much harder, making publication of many of its documents a condition of lending. The IMF should certainly not hide behind the façade of market sensitivity as a rationale for keeping its own Executive Board minutes secret for 30 years.

## The Future of Transparency

Transparency can play an important role in future efforts to manage global problems. Whether it does so will depend on a growing demand for transparency and the emergence of a culture of transparency that can counterbalance incentives for continued opacity.

### *Understanding the Demand for Transparency*

The calls for transparency that have been voiced to date are probably only the leading edge of a tidal wave of such demands. Part of the reason that demands for transparency are likely to increase is globalization—as people become more interdependent, they need to know more about each other. But other factors, including changing technology, democratization and the development of civil society at both the national and global levels, and the role of the United States as the world's leading power, are also at work.

TECHNOLOGY. Thanks to the revolution in information technology, the costs of becoming transparent have plummeted. Surveillance systems, broadcasting systems, data processors, and telecommunications technologies are rapidly becoming less expensive and more capable, and they are increasingly able to interact with one another.

Information is being reduced to the same basic form in all these systems: bits of electronic data that can travel from one technology to another. And because the technologies interact, progress in one stimulates developments in the others. Data collection systems, including everything from supermarket checkout scanners to satellite-based remote sensors, gather vast quantities of raw data. Computers turn those enormous data streams into usable information. Telecommunications systems have become inexpensive enough that a significant share of the world's population now has access to that usable information and can send it to others.

Put it all together and the result is a massive stream of information flowing around the world. Some of this information is wholly new: Three decades ago no one could monitor consumers' buying habits or gather global data on land-use patterns. Some of this information, such as the highly classified data flowing from superpower spy satellites, used to be available only to small groups. Although the information revolution needs to be put in historical context—it began, in a sense, more than 500 years ago with the printing press, and every development since then from the telegraph to the telephone has been greeted with predictions of imminent global transformation—the current technological convergence really does seem to represent something quantitatively and qualitatively new.

It would be hard to exaggerate the pace of this revolution:
- In 1999 a private company launched a commercial remote-sensing satellite capable of detecting objects as small as one meter—detection nearly as accurate as that possible with spy satellites. Once all the planned commercial and

government systems reach orbit over the next few years, anyone with a few hundred dollars will be able to purchase detailed satellite imagery of any spot on the planet (Center for Global Security and Cooperation 1999).
- On the ground, both governments and citizens are making extensive use of surveillance cameras (Brin 1998). Soon, cameras too small to be seen from any distance will be widely available (Florini 1998).
- Computing power now doubles about every 18 months, and the pace shows no signs of slowing.
- Telecommunications is connecting more and more people and allowing them to share larger quantities of information. Several companies are launching constellations of satellites that will permit wireless "roaming" anywhere on the planet (Evans 1998).

While none of these technologies is guaranteed market success, the pattern is clear: The quantity and scope of data being transmitted, the capacity to manipulate the data, and the number of people connected are all skyrocketing. All this technology does more than just reduce the direct costs of transparency. It also facilitates global integration and, by decentralizing information, empowers civil society.

DEMOCRACY AND CIVIL SOCIETY. The spread of democratic ideals and democratic forms of government has contributed greatly to demands for transparency. Newly empowered citizens want to know what their newly elected officials are doing. Newly elected officials have greater incentives than their unelected predecessors to keep their constituents informed, or at least to stay in contact with them.

But those officials also have incentives to maintain secrecy, to avoid controversy over policies, and to conceal incompetence and corruption. Government officials everywhere try to avoid scrutiny, even honest officials in well-established democracies. The holding of regular free and fair elections does not always bring with it the government's willingness to report on its activities. Despite many promises and the release of a protransparency White Paper by the current government, for example, the United Kingdom has yet to promulgate a freedom of information act allowing public access to information about the government's activities.

The European Union is also struggling with transparency. Under the Amsterdam Treaty, all citizens and legal persons in the European Union acquired the right of access to documents of the European Parliament, the European Council, and the European Commission—a fairly significant change in the way the European Union has operated. Transparency is as popular a catchphrase in the European Union as it is at the World Bank and the IMF, frequently mentioned by EU officials in speeches and scattered throughout EU documents. But practice lags well behind promise.

Even more significant to the future of transparency than the spread of electoral systems is the rise of civil society: organized groups that in many cases sustain the pressure for transparency. NGOs are not only monitoring governments and firms within certain countries, they are increasingly linking themselves into transnational networks that collectively can impose powerful demands for information (Florini forthcoming). In virtually every international issue area, such nongovernmental actors, particularly in the form of NGOs, are becoming more numerous and more effective in their demands for greater transparency from governments, international organizations, and the private sector. As civil society grows more vigorous around the world—facilitated by information technology, democratization, and not least the growing funding it is receiving from governments, international organizations, and foundations—its demands for transparency will escalate. (Interestingly, civil society itself has been largely exempt from the spotlight, although recent critiques of the unaccountability of NGOs indicate that such pressures are beginning to build (Simmons 1998).)

THE ROLE OF THE UNITED STATES. At a time when the need for new tools to manage global integration is so obvious, the world's leading power is one whose ideology, values, and experiences lead it to favor transparency (Lee and Parker 1984; Stiglitz 1999). It is not only in the economic area that the United States has supported high standards of transparency. Beginning in the 1950s, the United States argued vociferously that the advent of nuclear weapons gave their possessors new responsibilities to provide information about their military capabilities and intentions—a perspective the Soviet Union came to share in the Gorbachev period (Florini 1996). In the 1980s, the United States became the first country to pass a law mandating that companies that emit certain quantities of certain toxic chemicals report publicly on those emissions—a law intended to shame companies into reducing their emissions. This precedent is now being imitated around the world.

This is not to suggest that the United States is a paragon of unselfish transparency. The toxic chemical law passed Congress by a single vote. U.S. demands for military information from the Soviet Union combined U.S. security interests with an opportunity to score propaganda points against a relentlessly secretive adversary. And there are strong signs that the U.S. government's propensity to impose transparency on others may be running headlong into American suspicion of government and demands for protection of privacy, as the outcry over the proposed regulation imposing mandatory know-your-customer banking procedures revealed. Overall, however, the presumption in U.S. governance favors transparency on the part of corporations and governments, and Americans now tend to apply that perspective to international problems as well.

## Fostering a Culture of Transparency

Despite the many factors facilitating transparency, it will not be easy to overcome the incentives that corporations, governments, financial institutions, and intergovernmental organizations all have to withhold or distort information. Doing so will require sustained effort toward entrenching a norm favoring transparency among these many actors. The idea of fostering a culture of transparency may sound vague, even idealistic, but it is actually a concrete call for changing not only the incentives people face but the way they think about those incentives. There is powerful historical evidence that even highly resistant actors can be induced over time to change their views of transparency.

One of the reasons the Cold War ended peacefully is that a norm of transparency came to prevail in the relationship between NATO and the Warsaw Pact (Florini 1996). Countries now expect to provide information on their military capabilities and plans, even—perhaps especially—to their adversaries, to prove their benign intentions. By the time the Soviet Union ceased to exist, East and West had enmeshed themselves in a web of treaties requiring highly intrusive inspections of one another's most sensitive military installations. Allowing such openness conflicts sharply with millennia of military strategy, because the information provided is just as useful for targeting as it is for reassuring. Yet somehow, a norm of transparency was fostered even in this most inhospitable of settings.

Establishment of transparency between East and West was no accident but the result of years of consistent effort. For three decades the United States did everything in its power to promote the novel idea that the only reason the Soviet Union would insist on secrecy about its military capabilities was that it was concealing sinister plans. This demand for transparency was purely self-interested, of course—the United States was desperately trying to obtain whatever information it could on its adversary. As the United States was a far more open society than the Soviet Union, at best the proposals for intrusive arms control inspections and mutual overflights could even the balance of information between the two; at a minimum, calling for transparency would score propaganda points. After decades of adamant Soviet rejection, in the mid-1980s, to nearly everyone's great surprise, the Soviet Union suddenly began to accept such proposals, even outbidding the United States on the degree of transparency proposed. The Soviet Union simply changed its mind about transparency, deciding that the reassurance value outweighed the risks.

If a culture of transparency can be fostered in so unlikely a setting, can it be fostered among the much wider range of actors involved in the global economy and within governments throughout the world? Achieving such an ambitious goal will require consistent effort over a long period of time, often in the face of what appears to be strong resistance. One step is to change the immediate costs and benefits of transparency for governments and corporations by providing rewards for transparency and imposing penalties for opacity, thereby making the targets accountable for being transparent. So far it is not clear to what degree markets will provide these incentives. To make it easier for them to do so, the World Bank and IMF should maintain transparency registries. The international financial institutions could also make transparency a condition for receiving loans. The stick of conditionality is a blunt instrument, however, that tends to raise the hackles of the countries to which it is applied, making it an imperfect means of changing minds. Persuasion may work better, especially to the degree that the World Bank and the IMF make themselves fully transparent institutions, providing important demonstrations through their own behavior that transparency, despite its discomforts, is a highly effective means of improving an institution's legitimacy and functioning.

But a culture of transparency will not come about solely as the result of hectoring (or even conditionality) by the international financial institutions. If it is ever to come to seem normal for corporations and governments to reveal the kinds of information discussed here and if the information revealed is to do any good, it will be necessary to develop local constituencies for transparency. Experience in several issue areas—including calls for transparency at the World Bank, in the environmental field, and in domestic politics—suggests that civil society is crucial to the creation of systems of transparency-based governance. Policy research institutes must be able to serve both as reviewers of existing policies and as fonts of policy innovation (Stone 1996). NGOs must also continue to play a role. By relentlessly advocating transparency, NGOs can make the costs of opacity higher than the costs of transparency.

Constituencies for transparency are already emerging in the form of the information media, policy research institutes, and civil society organizations in many parts of the world. But too often these are poorly funded and widely scattered organizations trying to operate in settings in which both human and social capital are sorely lacking. Moreover, only a handful of these organizations are themselves as transparent as they call on governments, corporations, and intergovernmental organizations to be, threatening their own legitimacy in the long run. The World Bank's substantial program of support for the development of human and social capital should be explicitly aimed at creating domestic constituencies that can effectively demand transparency within their own societies.

## Conclusion

Transparency plays many beneficial roles in both markets and governance, roles that merit greater attention by the World Bank and the IMF. It appears to increase the efficiency with which markets operate and may reduce the likelihood of financial crises (although the evidence here is surprisingly thin, and further research is required). It is logically necessary for accountability in governance, the political equivalent of the efficiency generated by competition between firms. Since political authorities are monopolies, "competition" occurs among ideas rather than organizations. Transparency makes such open competition of arguments and policies possible.

Achieving transparency is no easy task. It requires going beyond disclosure standards, creating incentives for corporations and governments. Although the international financial institutions can do some good directly—by modeling the advantages of transparency through their own behavior and by applying conditionality under some circumstances—little will change unless large national and international constituencies for transparency emerge. Such constituencies exist in embryonic form. Most lack meaningful resources, however, and will need help to develop.

As the World Bank transforms itself from a provider of financial capital to a knowledge bank and the IMF struggles to develop effective approaches to managing the global financial system, one of the most useful contributions these institutions could make would be to promote the norm of transparency. Such promotion would start with a renewed push to ensure that the World Bank and the IMF themselves operate in a highly transparent manner. It would also involve conscious planning for incorporating the norm of transparency systematically into World Bank and IMF programs.

The World Bank and IMF have a right—indeed, an obligation—to promote transparency wherever and however they can. Their role as agents for both their member governments and all those affected by their programs oblige them to make information on their own processes and policies accessible to all concerned. Their roles as central players in the management of the global economy oblige them to promote the use of tools, such as transparency, that can contribute to global governance in the absence of global government.

Such governance must be transparent because, as many governments and international organizations have found to their dismay in recent years, secretive decisionmaking by small elites can no longer be sustained. Contrary to the claims that decisionmaking on technical or complex subjects is best left to experts, without informed participation by all those affected policy decisions will fail to take into account important information and interests and will lack the legitimacy that only public voice can bring. Decisionmakers should not try to sneak even good public policy past the public.

## Notes

1. See, for example, G-7 Leaders' Statement 1998; Declaration of G-7 Finance Ministers and Central Bank Governors 1998; Ostry 1997; IMF 1998b; Sutherland 1998. For useful cautions about the limits of transparency in prevention or resolving financial crises, see Eichengreen (1999).

2. On banking, see Basle Committee (1998) and Reinicke (1998). On auditing and accounting standards, see Jones (1998) and Wippurfurth (1998). On national fiscal practices, see Kopits and Craig (1998). On control of drug trafficking, see Flynn (1999). On pollution control, see Tietenberg and Wheeler (1998). On corruption, see Dye and Stapenhurst (1998); Naim (1995); and Vogl (1998). On multilateral development banks, see Udall (1998). On private sector practices, see Haufler (forthcoming).

3. The term *transparency* is sometimes used to refer to such knowledge creation. In her discussion of the need for transparency as part of a potential new regime for foreign direct investment, for example, Sylvia Ostry (1997) contends that greater knowledge about the number and range of foreign investment initiatives would itself constitute an increase in transparency—a quite different use of the term from the one employed here.

4. In part because of its extensive experience with corporate financial disclosure, the United States is particularly prone to see transparency as a major and essential element of global financial regulation. Early in this century, large numbers of small investors put substantial political pressure on the government to protect them from deceit and insider dealings. Disclosure became mandatory after the Depression-era creation of the Securities and Exchange Commission. Since that time, companies whose securities are listed on national securities exchanges have been required to file periodic reports, whose form and content is determined by the SEC (Cochrane 1984). Demand for the disclosure of fuller, more reliable, and more comprehensible financial data has continued, driven by the growth of both small shareholders and institutional investors. The United States is not alone in having relatively high standards for corporate financial disclosure. Great Britain experimented with disclosure laws beginning in the mid-eighteenth century (Lee and Parker 1984). The United States and Great Britain are unusual in the degree to which their firms rely on equity financing rather

than bank loans, but given the degree to which equity financing is spreading, their experiences may hold some useful lessons.

5. There are no good measures of transparency, making it very hard to correlate economic stability and the degree of transparency, much less argue about causation. The availability of better data a few years from now may allow researchers to disentangle the effects of varying degrees of transparency from other causes of economic inefficiencies. Various proposals for international standards of transparency are being proposed for all sorts of data relevant to global finance. If some of these proposals are adopted (in particular the G-22's Working Group's recommendations concerning "transparency about transparency"), good data should become available about which firms and countries are relatively transparent and which are not. Such data should make it possible to determine what types of transparency have what types of effects.

6. Such a certification of compliance with transparency standards sidesteps the problems the IMF has with releasing too much information about the economies of its member countries. These problems are caused by the dual nature of the IMF's mandate: It both provides advice to individual governments and serves as a certifier of good economic practices by those same governments. If the IMF releases information about specific countries, those governments have every incentive to conceal bad news, making it difficult for the IMF to provide well-informed advice.

7. The Financial Action Task Force has 26 member governments (mostly OECD countries, plus China) and two member regional organizations (the European Commission and the Gulf Cooperation Council). Delegations to the task force are drawn from many fields and government agencies, including ministries of finance, justice, and interior and external affairs; financial regulatory authorities; and law enforcement agencies (Financial Action Task Force 1998). Originally scheduled to last until 1999, the task force has now been extended until 2004.

## References

Alesina, Alberto, and Roberto Perotti. 1996. *Budget Deficits and Budget Institutions.* Washington, D.C.: International Monetary Fund.

Basle Committee on Banking Supervision. 1998. *Enhancing Bank Transparency: Public Disclosure and Supervisory Information that Promote Safety and Soundness in Banking Systems.* Basle.

Brin, David. 1998. *The Transparent Society: Will Technology Force Us to Choose between Privacy and Freedom?* Reading, Mass.: Addison-Wesley.

Center for Global Security and Cooperation, Science Applications International Corporation. 1999. "Implications of Commercial Satellite Imagergy on Arm Control." McLean, Va.

Center of Concern. 1998. *IMF Study Group Report: Transparency and Evaluation.* Washington, D.C

Cochrane, G. 1984. "The Auditor's Report: Its Evolution in the USA." In T.A. Lee and R.H. Parker, eds., *The Evolution of Corporate Financial Reporting.* New York: Garland Publishing.

"Declaration of G-7 Finance Ministers and Central Bank Governors." 1998. Paris.

Dye, Kenneth M., and Rick Stapenhurst. 1998. *Pillars of Integrity: The Importance of Supreme Audit Institutions in Curbing Corruption.* Washington, D.C.: World Bank, World Bank Institute.

Eichengreen, Barry. 1999. *Toward a New International Financial Architecture: A Practical Post-Asia Agenda.* Washington, D.C.: Institute for International Economics.

Eichengreen, Barry, Donald Mathieson, Bankim Chadha, Anne Jansen, Laura Kodres, and Sunil Sharma. 1998. *Hedge Funds and Financial Market Dynamics.* IMF Occasional Paper 166. Washington, D.C.: International Monetary Fund.

Financial Action Task Force on Money Laundering. 1998. *Annual Report 1997–1998.* Paris.

Florini, Ann M., ed. 1996. "The Evolution of International Norms." *International Studies Quarterly* 40: 363–89.

———. 1997. "A New Role for Transparency." *Contemporary Security Policy* 18 (2): 51–72.

———. 1998. "The End of Secrecy." *Foreign Policy* 111: 50–63.

———. Forthcoming. *The Third Force: The Rise of Transnational Civil Society.* Tokyo and Washington, D.C.: Japan Center for International Exchange and Carnegie Endowment for International Peace.

Flynn, Stephen. 1999. "The Global Drug Trade vs. the Nation-State: Why the Bad Guys Are Winning." In Maryann Cusimano, ed., *Beyond Sovereignty: Issues for a Global Agenda.* New York: St. Martin's Press.

Fox, Jonathan A., and L. D. Brown. 1998. *The Struggle for Accountability: The World Bank, NGOs, and Grassroots Movements.* Cambridge, Mass.: MIT Press.

Furman, Jason, and Joseph E. Stiglitz. 1998. "Economic Crises: Evidence and Insights From East Asia." Paper presented at Brookings Panel on Economic Activity, September 3–4, Washington, D.C.

Greenwald, Bruce C., and Joseph E. Stiglitz. 1991. *Information, Finance, and Markets: The Architecture of Allocative Mechanisms.* Cambridge, Mass.: National Bureau of Economic Research.

"G-7 Leaders' Statement on the World Economy." 1998. London.

Haufler, Virginia. 1997. *Dangerous Commerce: Insurance and the Management of International Risk.* Ithaca, N.Y.: Cornell University Press.

———. Forthcoming. *Should Business Make the Rules?: International Business Self-Regulation and the Intersection of Private Interest and Public Policy.* Washington, D.C.: Carnegie Endowment for International Peace.

IMF (International Monetary Fund). n.d. "International Standards Related to Fiscal Transparency." Washington, D.C.

———. 1996. "IMF Launches the Dissemination Standards Bulletin Board on the Internet." Press Release 96/47. Washington, D.C.

———. 1998a. "Manual on Fiscal Transparency—Draft." www.imf.org/external/np/fad/trans/manual/index.htm.

———. 1998b. *Report of the Working Group on Transparency and Accountability.* Washington, D.C.

Jones, Mike. 1998. "The IASC: Twenty-Five Years Old This Year." *Management Accounting–London* 76 (5): 30–32.

Kopits, George, and Jon Craig. 1998. *Transparency in Government Operations.* Washington, D.C.: International Monetary Fund.

Lee, T. A., and R.H. Parker, eds. 1984. *The Evolution of Corporate Financial Reporting.* New York: Garland Publishing.

Mauro, Paolo. 1997. "The Effects of Corruption on Growth, Investment, and Government Expenditure: A Cross-Country Analysis." In Kimberly A. Elliot, ed., *Corruption and the Global Economy.* Washington, D.C.: Institute for International Economics.

Naim, Moises. 1995. "The Corruption Eruption." *Brown Journal of World Affairs* 11 (2): 245–59.

Nelson, Paul J. 1996. "Internationalising Economic and Environmental Policy: Transnational NGO Networks and the World Bank's Expanding Influence." *Millennium: Journal of International Studies* 25 (3): 605–33.

Ostry, Sylvia. 1997. *A New Regime for Foreign Direct Investment*. Washington, D.C.: Group of Thirty.

Reinicke, Wolfgang H. 1998. *Global Public Policy: Governing without Government?* Washington, D.C.: Brookings Institute.

Rose-Ackerman, Susan. 1998. "Corruption and Development." In Boris Pleskovic and Joseph E. Stiglitz, eds., *Annual World Bank Conference on Development Economics 1997*. Washington, D.C.: World Bank.

Scholte, Jan A. 1998. "The IMF Meets Civil Society." *Finance & Development* 35 (3): 42–45.

———. 1999. "Civil Society and Democracy in Global Finance." Paper prepared for the annual conference of the International Studies Association, February 16–20, Washington, D.C.

Simmons, P. J. 1998. "Learning to Live with NGOs." *Foreign Policy* 112: 82–96.

Stiglitz, Joseph E. 1998. "Distinguished Lecture on Economics in Government: The Private Uses of Public Interests: Incentives and Institutions." *Journal of Economic Perspectives* 12 (2): 3–32.

———. 1999. "On Liberty, the Right to Know, and Public Discourse: The Role of Transparency in Public Life." Paper prepared for the Oxford Amnesty Lecture, January 27. [www.worldbank.org/html/extdr/extme/jssp012799.htm].

Stone, Diane. 1996. *Capturing the Political Imagination: Think Tanks and the Policy Process*. Portland: Frank Cass.

Sutherland, Peter D. 1998. *The 1998 Per Jacobsson Lecture: Managing the International Economy in an Age of Globalisation*. Washington, D.C.: International Monetary Fund.

Tanzi, Vito. 1996. *Money Laundering and the International Financial System*. IMF Working Paper 96/55. Washington, D.C.: International Monetary Fund.

Tietenberg, Tom, and David Wheeler. 1998. "Empowering the Community: Information Strategies for Pollution Control." Paper presented at the "Frontiers of Environmental Economics Conference," Airlie House, October 23–25, Virginia.

Udall, Lori. 1998. "The World Bank and Public Accountability: Has Anything Changed?" In Jonathan A. Fox and L. D. Brown, eds., *The Struggle for Accountability: The World Bank, NGOs, and Grassroots Movements*. Cambridge, Mass.: MIT Press.

United Nations. 1991. *Study on Ways and Means of Promoting Transparency in International Transfers of Conventional Arms*. UN Document A/46/301. New York.

Vogl, Frank. 1998. "The Supply Side of Global Bribery." *Finance & Development* 35 (2): 30–33.

Wipperfurth, Heike. 1998. "U.S. and International Rule Makers Seemed Headed for Showdown that May Well Decide the Fate of an International Accounting Standard." *Investment Dealers Digest*. August 31.

# Comment on "The Changing Corporate Governance Paradigm: Implications for Developing and Transition Economies," by Erik Berglöf and Ernst-Ludwig von Thadden, and "Does the Invisible Hand Need a Transparent Glove? The Politics of Transparency," by Ann M. Florini

*Florencio Lopez-de-Silanes*

Recent research in economics has increasingly focused on the importance of institutions to economic development (North 1981; Olson 1993; Greif and Kandel 1995; Knack and Keefer 1995). The articles by Erik Berglöf and Ernst-Ludwig von Thadden and Ann M. Florini are part of a recent effort to understand how institutions, legal rules, regulations on transparency, and enforcement make a difference. They also set out an agenda for continuing research.

I want to focus on a central point of this agenda: investor protection as a key corporate governance mechanism. Fostering competition in product markets and protecting the property rights of stakeholders are essential for economic performance, but they cannot solve the problem of corporate governance, narrowly defined. Investor protection, through laws, regulations fostering transparency, and enforcement, is essential for the development of capital markets and indirectly for growth. And although governance arrangements differ across countries, investor protection is necessary everywhere to enable firms to get access to external finance. All types of investors—small, large, shareholders, or creditors—need such laws, and external capital markets can play an essential role.

## The Meaning of Corporate Governance

Narrowly defined, corporate governance is the set of mechanisms that ensure a firm's suppliers of finance of getting a return on their investments. The question addressed by this narrow definition is: How do security holders (shareholders and creditors) make sure they get money back? Particularly, how do they make sure that it is not stolen or expropriated? La Porta, Lopez-de-Silanes, Shleifer, and Vishny (1997, 1998) use this definition in their analysis of the development of capital markets across countries.

A much broader definition of corporate governance equates it with the set of mechanisms transmitting signals from product and input markets to firm behavior.

---

Florencio Lopez-de-Silanes is associate professor of public policy at the John F. Kennedy School of Government, Harvard University.

Annual World Bank Conference on Development Economics 1999
©2000 The International Bank for Reconstruction and Development / THE WORLD BANK

Which definition one uses might depend on one's interests. Berglöf and von Thadden use the broad definition in questioning the impact of corporate governance on economic growth and performance. In particular, they elaborate on the impact of product market competition and input markets (represented by employees and suppliers) on economic outcomes. But if this is the focus, analysis needs to take account of many other factors that determine growth and economic performance, such as property rights, political rights, trust among people, religion, cultural attitudes toward savings, geography, education, ethnolinguistic fractionalization, the origin of the country's laws,[1] and so on. Therefore, although we care about economic growth, we do not want to blur the picture by adding too many factors.

Using the narrower definition of corporate governance, we can focus on the simpler policy problem of the size of capital markets and why some countries have larger capital markets than others. Does this have any real consequences for economic growth? Investor protection matters for the size of capital markets and therefore for growth, but it is not the only thing that matters for economic performance. For this reason, I will use the narrower definition of corporate governance as it helps us separate areas that can ultimately affect economic performance.

## Expropriation and Corporate Governance

The narrow definition of corporate governance is closely connected to the ideas in Florini's article and in La Porta and others (1998). They argue that transparency, and regulation in general, should be closely connected to accountability by the agent to the principal. Agency relationships in the firm are the source of the main problem in corporate governance: the expropriation by managers and controlling investors of minority investors' money.[2]

Extensive expropriation severely undermines the effectiveness of a financial system. Potential investors, fearful of expropriation, are unlikely to finance even attractive investment projects. The projects most likely to be financed, then, are those of firms with sufficient internal funds to make the investment. Overall, then, too few projects are financed and those that are are not necessarily the right ones, at least from a social welfare perspective. When investment is insufficient and misallocated, productivity and economic growth suffer.

In most countries the relevant agency problem in corporations is not that between managers and shareholders (Jensen and Meckling 1976), but that between controlling shareholders and minority investors. La Porta, Lopez-de-Silanes, and Shleifer (1999) show that outside the richest common law countries, Berle and Mean's image of the widely held corporation disappears. In the rest of the world firms are typically controlled by one large investor. Sometimes that investor is the state, sometimes a financial institution, but most often it is a family, usually the firm's founder and descendants. The top management of these firms is also usually part of the controlling family. In practice, then, the main problem in corporate governance outside very developed capital markets is not the expropriation of small investors by management, but the expropriation of small investors by controlling investors.

We need to understand this kind of expropriation better before we can propose mechanisms to control it. Much of the literature, much of it U.S.–based, analyzes some forms of expropriation from minority investors, including management compensation and perquisites (Jensen and Meckling 1976) and the pursuit of non-profit maximizing projects that simply entrench management or the controlling investor (McConnell and Muscarella 1986; Kaplan and Weisbach 1992). We still do not know whether these forms of expropriation exhaust the mechanisms used by controlling investors or whether they are just the tip of the iceberg. We lack a taxonomy of expropriation mechanisms across countries.

Moving beyond the United States, we find an array of expropriation forms not yet properly studied. Some of these forms are illegal nearly everywhere, such as accounting fraud or insider trading. Others are more prevalent in certain countries because their legal system allows them. In countries that allow different types of shares, controlling shareholders may not need to resort to huge compensations or perquisites, but can instead pay themselves special dividends. Selling output cheaply to a company owned by the controlling shareholder is said to be quite common among firms in the Russian oil industry. Simple asset stripping is another form of expropriation. *The Economist* (June 1995) reports that Korean chaebols sometimes sell their subsidiaries to the relatives of the chaebol founder at bargain basement prices. There is also evidence that some Italian firms sell assets at high prices to other firms with many small shareholders (Zingales 1994). In some countries firms have purchased assets at above-market prices from firms owned by the controlling investors. This may also lower profits and ease pressure to pay high dividends.

Other forms of expropriation have to do with actions that entrench controlling investors. Among these are targeted share repurchases or targeted share issues. Firms issue shares to parties friendly to the controlling investor to dilute the value of the shares of other shareholders or potential troublemakers. Granting services, contracts, or executive posts to firms owned by controlling investors or to their offspring, as in SK Telecom in Korea (see below), is another example. And the Asian crisis of 1997–98 has made painfully evident the negative effects of credit guarantees to related firms. To close the list, I would mention a subtle form of expropriation. There is scattered international evidence to suggest that violations of the corporate opportunities doctrine are occurring: controlling shareholders not only engage in non-profit maximizing projects at the expense of financiers, they also make the company pass on good projects and opportunities, so that they can exploit them with their own firms.

The recent case of SK Telecom in Korea, the telecommunications arm of the famous Korean SK Group, shows some of these forms of expropriation at work. *The Financial Times* (February 24, 1998) reported that several U.S. institutional investors had alleged that SK Telecom tried to provide low-interest loans to SK Securities, which suffered heavy losses on overseas derivatives trading. Under pressure, SK Telecom agreed to call back $216 million in loans to affiliates of the SK group (*Wall Street Journal*, September 29, 1998). To head off an attack from shareholders, various members of the family of the chairman of SK Group donated their

30 percent ownership stake in Taehan Telecom to SK Telecom. Taehan Telecom was suspected of being used as a channel for diverting some of SK Telecom's profits. Taehan Telecom was also a preferred consulting company for SK Telecom for many years (*Korea Herald,* March 27, 1998). The Fair Trade Commission found that SK Telecom had paid inflated prices for equipment and services from its affiliates as a way of transferring assets to them. This transaction lowered SK Telecom's operating profits—from 31 percent of sales in 1994 to 14 percent in 1996—and eased pressures to pay higher dividends and corporate taxes (*Business Week,* February 23, 1998). Finally, the president of the group apologized to minority shareholders for illegal insider trading (*Asia Pulse,* March 27, 1998).

The question in circumstances such as these is how to find efficient ways—governance mechanisms—to control expropriation. Berglöf and von Thadden suggest that different countries have developed different governance mechanisms. They argue that, through the political process and specific actions by firms, continental Europe, for example, has developed institutions providing effective investor protection, including product market competition, pressure from other stakeholders, ownership structures, and government interventions.

One of the more widespread governance forces cited in the literature is product market competition. This may be a powerful force for economic efficiency, but it is unlikely by itself to solve the problem of expropriation of noncontrolling investors. Capital is, to a large extent, sunk and specific. Therefore, those who put capital into the firm need to be assured that they will get a return on it. Corporate governance mechanisms try to foster this assurance. Product market competition, by cutting the returns on capital, may reduce the amount of money that managers and controlling investors can expropriate, but it can hardly prevent them from expropriating the competitive returns after the capital is sunk.

Stakeholders other than shareholders and creditors have also been advanced as a potential force providing governance. Berglöf and von Thadden suggest that stakeholders, like suppliers, employees, or governments, may play a role in monitoring management and controlling owners. Protecting the property rights of workers, shareholders, creditors, suppliers, or the state is important for economic growth and performance. We all agree on that. But although workers and other stakeholders might be important for social capital, it is unlikely that they will be successful in preventing expropriation and fostering transparency.

Some of my skepticism comes from systematic and anecdotal evidence from developing and developed countries. Contracts with stakeholders differ markedly around the world. So does the role of workers. Countries like Sweden and Japan place considerable emphasis on workers as stakeholders of firms; the United States places less emphasis on workers. And there is no clear correlation between the size of capital markets and the emphasis placed on workers as stakeholders.

One explanation may be that stakeholders are co-opted by management and controlling investors. Indirect evidence along these lines comes from privatized firms in Mexico. Privatized firms that gave workers decision power significantly underperformed other privatized firms in efficiency improvements and profitability, even though they had not performed significantly worse than other state firms before privatization (Lopez-de-Silanes 1997; La Porta and Lopez-de-Silanes 1999). One of the most pervasive findings of privatization in the transition economies of Eastern Europe is that firms privatized to insiders (workers and managers) substantially underperformed other firms (Frydman and others 1999). Finally, in most cases where employees and managers contribute positively to corporate governance, as in leveraged buyouts in the United States, they do so in their role as shareholders.

Since product market competition and stakeholders other than investors are unlikely to solve the problem of corporate governance, we have to look elsewhere.

## Investor Protection: Measurement and Consequences

Recent evidence on the "legal approach" to corporate governance suggests a common element to explanations of why some countries have broader and more valuable stock markets than others and why firms in some countries can borrow more easily than firms in others. The common element is *investor protection* in the form of laws, regulations, and their enforcement. Investor protection is a key governance mechanism for controlling expropriation from investors in as much as it increases the effectiveness of their control rights and fosters transparency connected to accountability, as Florini argues. To be effective, investor protection should include punishment for expropriation and misrepresentation and protection of the weak against the strong.

La Porta and others (1998) assembled a data set of key legal rules on the rights of investors and the quality of enforcement for 49 countries with publicly traded companies. Laws are typically not written from scratch, but transplanted—intentionally or not—from a few legal families or traditions. In general, *commercial* laws come from two broad traditions: common law and civil law. Most English-speaking countries belong to the common law tradition; the rest of the world belongs to the civil law tradition, rooted in Roman law, with three main branches: the French, based on the Napoleonic Code of 1804; the German, based on Bismarck's Code of 1896; and the Scandinavian, which scholars describe as less derivative of Roman law but "distinct" from the other two families. La Porta and others (1998) group the 49 countries according to the origin of their investor protection laws (table 1). Rules protecting investors come from different sources, some of the most important being company laws and bankruptcy laws. Though there are many potentially measurable differences among countries in their company and bankruptcy laws, La Porta and others (1998) focus exclusively on the basic rules that scholars believe are essential to corporate governance, especially those that can be interpreted as pro-investor.

Shareholders have residual rights over the cash flows of the firm, and their right to vote is their main source of power. The shareholder rights index measures how strongly corporate law protects shareholders' voting rights and the rights that support voting mechanisms—and thus how strongly it protects minority shareholders against expropriation by controlling shareholders. The index covers shareholders' rights to receive advance notice of shareholders meetings and to vote by mail, to

**Table 1. Indices of Investor Protection**

| Country group | Shareholder rights index (0–6) | Creditor rights index (0–4) | Efficiency of the judicial system index (0–10) | Accounting standards index (0–10) |
|---|---|---|---|---|
| Common law family (18 countries) | 4.00 | 3.11 | 8.15 | 6.96 |
| French civil law family (21 countries) | 2.33 | 1.58 | 6.56 | 5.12 |
| German civil law family (6 countries) | 2.33 | 2.33 | 8.54 | 6.27 |
| Scandinavian civil law family (4 countries) | 3.00 | 2.00 | 10.00 | 7.40 |
| World average (49 countries) | 3.00 | 2.30 | 7.67 | 6.09 |

Source: La Porta and others 1998.

participate in the meetings, to elect directors that represent their views, to subscribe to new issues of securities on the same terms as controlling shareholders, to call extraordinary shareholders meetings, and to sue directors for suspected wrongdoing, including expropriation. A country scores one point on the index for each pro-investor right its corporate law grants.

Common law countries—with an average index of 4—provide significantly better shareholder protection than do French or German civil law countries—both with an average score of 2.33. With an average index of 3, Scandinavian civil law countries offer less shareholder protection than do common law countries but outperform the other civil law families.

The index of creditor protection, based on bankruptcy law, measures the ability of creditors to use the law to force companies to meet their credit commitments. The index scores creditor rights in both reorganization and liquidation, in part because almost all countries rely to some extent on both procedures. The creditor rights assessed are those of senior secured creditors, in part because they account for much of the debt in the world. Creditor protections relate largely to bankruptcy procedures. They include creditors' rights to take possession of collateral, to protect their seniority, and to decide whether to fire management. And they include measures that make it harder for firms to seek court protection in reorganization without creditors' consent. Like the shareholder rights index, the creditor rights index includes one point for each pro-investor right granted by law.

On average, common law countries offer creditors stronger legal protection than civil law countries do. The average creditor rights score for common law countries is 3.11, compared with a mere 1.58 for French civil law countries. German civil law countries are more pro-creditor than French, averaging a score of 2.33. Countries with a Scandinavian legal origin have an average index of 2—a statistically insignificant difference from the score for those with a French or German legal origin.

The results thus far show that corporate and bankruptcy laws differ a great deal across countries in different legal families. Common law countries protect shareholders and creditors the most, and French civil law countries protect them the least. German and Scandinavian civil law countries fall somewhere in the middle.

Legal rules are only part of investor protection, however. Enforcement is just as important, if not more so. Good laws that are not enforced cannot be effective. But strong enforcement can compensate for weak rules. An efficient judiciary system can redress management expropriation, protecting investors despite bad laws.

An index measuring the efficiency of the judicial system serves as a proxy for the quality of enforcement. This index also shows significant differences across countries. But in contrast with legal rules, which do not appear to depend on a country's level of development, the quality of enforcement is markedly better in wealthier economies.[3] Still, legal origin seems to matter: when per capita income is held constant, French civil law countries score lowest on legal enforcement among the four legal families.

A final index measures the quality of accounting standards for publicly traded firms. Disclosure and accounting standards, usually imposed by securities exchanges, are central to corporate governance. They provide investors with the information they need to exercise their rights and allow courts to resolve disputes among investors. On this index, too, French civil law countries score lowest.

Together, the four indexes show that investor protection, through laws and their enforcement, varies significantly and systematically across countries according to legal origin. The question is: Does it matter and if so how?

The legal approach would predict that countries that protect investors better would have broader and more highly valued capital markets than countries that offer less protection. Some indices of capital market development confirm this prediction, showing that countries with greater investor protection have more valuable stock markets, more listed securities relative to population size, and more initial public offerings (table 2). For example, in 1994 the ratio of external stock market capitalization (shares owned by noncontrolling shareholders) to GDP averaged 60 percent in common law countries and 19 percent in French civil law countries (the world average was 40 percent). Common law countries had an average 2.23 initial public offerings per million people annually, while French civil law countries had only 0.28 (the world average was 1.02). Similarly, countries that protect creditors better have a higher ratio of private debt to GDP. This ratio was 68 percent in common law countries, 56 percent in French civil law countries, and 97 percent in German civil law countries.

To the extent that corporate decisions respond to agency problems, these decisions too should differ across countries. Recent studies have shown that in countries with less investor protection, dividends are lower (La Porta and others 2000), firms have more concentrated ownership (Claessens, Djankov, and Lang 1999; La Porta and others 1998; La Porta, Lopez-de-Silanes, and Shleifer 1999) and lower valuation multiples (La Porta and others 1999a), and the voting premium is higher (Nenova 1999). And drawing an ingenious connection, Johnson and others (1999) show that investor protection explains a significant part of the cross-country variation in exchange rate depreciation after the Asian financial crisis of 1997–98.

**Table 2. Indices of Capital Market Development, 1995**

| Country group | External market capitalization as a percentage of GDP | Firms listed on stock exchanges per million people | Initial public offerings per year per million people | Total debt as a percentage of GDP |
|---|---|---|---|---|
| Common law family (18 countries) | 60 | 35.45 | 2.23 | 68 |
| French civil law family (21 countries) | 19 | 11.89 | 0.28 | 56 |
| German civil law family (6 countries) | 46 | 16.79 | 0.12 | 97 |
| Scandinavian civil law family (4 countries) | 30 | 27.26 | 2.14 | 57 |
| World average (49 countries) | 40 | 21.59 | 1.02 | 59 |

*Note:* The statistical significance of the differences in the table holds in a regression analysis controlling for various country characteristics.
*Source:* La Porta and others 1997.

## Which Investors Need Protection?

An interesting question is which investors need protection. Berglöf and von Thadden suggest that although poor protection is likely to deter small investors, such investors are unlikely to play an important role everywhere. That might lead us to believe that investor protection is unnecessary in countries where small investors are unimportant. But lack of legal protection need not deter only small investors. All noncontrolling investors—large or small—need their rights protected.

Poor investor protection deters strategic investors and both modest and large shareholders. Although large shareholders can monitor management more closely and thus solve the free-riding problem that affects small investors, to be effective they still need legal protection of their voting rights. In developing countries it is common practice for foreign strategic investors entering into a joint venture to require a shareholders' agreement to protect their rights. But unless they can expect the courts to enforce the agreement, they will be unwilling to share their technological know-how. And in Russia a foreign investor holding 30 percent of the shares of a firm can be rendered ineffective by management tricks, such as removing the investor's shares from the books under the claim that they are illegal.

Poor investor protection also deters creditors, who need clear bankruptcy procedures and courts that enforce the law in order to take possession of collateral. Creditor protection therefore matters for the development of the financial sector. Levine (1997) shows that moving from the lowest quartile of countries ranked by quality of creditor protection to the next quartile translates into a 20 percent increase in financial development, accelerating long-run growth by almost one percentage point a year. La Porta and others (1997) show that creditor protection leads to large debt markets. Creditors are less effective in many French civil law countries because the procedures for turning control over to banks are unclear. And such countries as Greece, Mexico, and the Philippines, which have poor creditor protection and enforcement, have small and concentrated debt markets as a result. Thus the implication of the legal approach to corporate governance is that a method of financing develops when financiers are protected by the law and its enforcement.

## And Which Countries Need Capital Markets?

Berglöf and von Thadden raise another interesting question: Do countries need equity markets, or can they rely on banks and private equity? One might argue that developing countries have no real need for a stock market, because firms typically raise external finance from the controlling investor's family and friends. But just because external capital markets are not used does not mean that they are not needed. A better explanation for the absence of these markets may well be poor legal protection (La Porta and others 1997).

The emphasis on family and bank financing overshadows the important role that external financing through markets can play in an economy. As Hart (1995) argues, growth opportunities cannot be easily financed with debt because it is poorly suited for high-risk projects. External financing may become essential, then, for promoting new firms. For venture capitalists, external capital markets provide an exit option, critical for encouraging financing from this source. In addition, equity markets allow easy diversification.

Recent research has shown that the absence of developed capital markets disproportionately hurts capital-intensive sectors. In non-capital-intensive industries, Rajan and Zingales (1998) find, family funds play a role, but for capital-intensive industries, lack of external capital markets is burdensome. External funds may not be needed for textile manufacture, but they are for steel production.

Some of the recent literature suggests that the inability of firms to raise external funds may be an important obstacle to growth (King and Levine 1993; Levine and Zervos 1998; Demirgüç-Kunt and Maksimovic 1996; Levine 1997; Carlin and Mayer 1999). Several studies show that an exogenous component of financial market development, obtained by using legal origin as an instrument, predicts economic growth. Financial development accelerates economic growth by enhancing savings, channeling savings into real investment and thus fostering capital accumulation, and improving the efficiency of resource allocation (Beck, Levine, and Loayza 1999; Wurgler 1999; and Morck and others (1999).

## Legal Reform and Enforcement

Clearly, improving corporate governance and transparency should top the policy agenda in many countries. A natural response to all the evidence on the state of corporate governance is to call for wholesale legal reform. Creditors and shareholders would benefit from mechanisms to prevent expropriation, and there is plenty of room for improving disclosure requirements.

But the politics of legal reform are difficult. Changes in corporate and bankruptcy law will lead to transfers of wealth from controlling to minority investors (La Porta and Lopez-de-Silanes 2000). Faced with this loss of private benefits, controlling investors will oppose reform. As Florini argues, transparency faces opposition from those in power. Good rules may not be exercised because those hurt by the rules may threaten to hurt those charged with enforcing them. That is probably what has happened to the Transparency Directive of the European Commission.

Legal reform will require creativity. The design of reform needs to reflect the reality that in most developing and transition economies the quality of enforcement is low and could remain so for some time. An extensive legal reform could include, for example, adoption of an oppressed minority mechanism similar to Chile's, which minimizes the involvement of the courts—even if the more mechanical process leads to outcomes that are less fair. And in countries with weak legal institutions, where enhanced disclosure requirements may be insufficient, institutional investors could be allowed to invest only in companies that meet minimum corporate governance standards as determined by an independent commission.

Reform of creditor rights could emphasize bankruptcy procedures that also minimize court involvement. The United Kingdom's bankruptcy system, for example, centers on an administrative procedure that puts most of the discretion in the hands of commercial banks rather than the courts. In another departure from current practice in bankruptcy, market forces could be introduced by auctioning off bankrupt firms, in much the same way that state-owned enterprises are privatized (Hart and others 1997).

A central issue in my discussion and in the articles by Berglöf and von Thadden and Florini is the overwhelming importance of the quality of enforcement. That is one of the reasons why the evidence I have presented speaks not to the rules, but to the quality of the rule of law, the level of corruption, and the efficiency of the judicial system. Enforcing rules is much harder than making them. Putting enforcement mechanisms in place, reforming the judicial system, and reducing corruption are all extremely difficult. Improving enforcement is a great challenge for all those of us interested in corporate governance and an area where more work is desperately needed.

## Notes

1. The origin of a country's laws, as defined in La Porta and others (1998), plays a role in determining economic performance not only because of the investor rights associated with that origin, but also because of the associated degree of interventionism in political systems, as Berglöf and von Thadden argue. Using legal origin as a proxy for political systems, La Porta and others (1999c) find that legal origin is an important determinant of various measures of the quality of government and development.

2. Unlike workers and suppliers, whose continuous involvement with the firm's activity makes them less vulnerable to expropriation, investors who provide finance to the firm are very susceptible to expropriation because they sink their investments when they provide the funds and can only hope to get a return.

3. For statistical evidence on this point and others see La Porta and others (1998).

## References

Beck, Thorsten, Ross Levine, and Norman Loayza. Forthcoming. "Finance and the Sources of Growth." *Journal of Financial Economics.*

Berle, Adolf, and Gardiner Means. 1932. *The Modern Corporation and Private Property.* New York: MacMillan.

Carlin, Wendy, and Colin Mayer. 1999. "Finance, Investment and Growth." University College, London.

Claessens, Stijn, Simeon Djankov, and Larry H.P. Lang. 1999. "The Separation of Ownership and Control in East Asian Corporations." World Bank, Financial Sector Strategy and Policy Department, Washington, D.C.

Demirgüç-Kunt, Asli, and Vojislav Maksimovic. 1998. "Law, Finance, and Firm Growth." *Journal of Finance* 53: 2107–39.

Easterbrook, Frank, and Daniel Fischel. 1991. *The Economic Structure of Corporate Law.* Cambridge, Mass.: Harvard University Press.

Frydman, Roman, Cheryl Gray, Marek Hessel, and Andrzej Rapaczynski. 1999. "When Does Privatization Work? The Impact of Private Ownership on Corporate Performance in the Transition Economies." *Quarterly Journal of Economics* 114 (4): 1153–91.

Greif, Avner, and Eugene Kandel. 1995. "Contract Enforcement Institutions: Historical Perspective and Current Status in Russia." In *Hoover Institution Book.*

Hart, Oliver. 1995. *Firms, Contracts, and Financial Structure.* New York: Oxford University Press.

Hart, Oliver, Rafael La Porta, Florencio Lopez-de-Silanes, and John Moore. 1997. "A New Bankruptcy Procedure That Uses Multiple Auctions." *European Economic Review* 41: 461–73.

Jensen, Michael, and William Meckling. 1976. "Theory of the Firm: Managerial Behavior, Agency Costs, and Ownership Structure." *Journal of Financial Economics* 3: 305–60.

Johnson, Simon, Peter Boone, Alasdair Breach, and Eric Friedman. 1999. "Corporate Governance in the Asian Financial Crisis, 1997–98." Massachusetts Institute of Technology, Cambridge, Mass.

Kaplan, Steven, and Michael Weisbach. 1992. "The Success of Acquisitions: Evidence from Divestitures." *Journal of Finance* 47: 107–38.

King, Robert, and Ross Levine. 1993. "Finance and Growth: Schumpeter Might Be Right." *Quarterly Journal of Economics* 108: 717–38.

Knack, Stephen, and Philip Keefer. 1995. "Institutions and Economic Performance: Cross-Country Tests Using Alternative Institutional Measures." *Economics and Politics.*

La Porta, Rafael, and Florencio Lopez-de-Silanes. 1999. "The Benefits of Privatization: Evidence from Mexico." *Journal of Finance* 54: 471–517.

———. 2000."Creditor Rights and Bankruptcy Reform." In Simeon Djankov and Joseph E. Stiglitz, eds., *Systemic Corporate Distress and Its Resolution.* Washington, D.C.: World Bank Institute.

La Porta, Rafael, Florencio Lopez-de-Silanes, and Andrei Shleifer. 1999. "Corporate Ownership Around the World." *Journal of Finance* 54 (2): 471–517.

La Porta, Rafael, Florencio Lopez-de-Silanes, Andrei Shleifer, and Robert Vishny. 1997. "Legal Determinants of External Finance." *Journal of Finance* 52: 1131–50.

———. 1998. "Law and Finance." *Journal of Political Economy* 106: 1113–55.

———. 1999a. "Investor Protection and Corporate Valuation." Harvard University, Cambridge, Mass.

———. 1999b. "The Quality of Government." *Journal of Law, Economics and Organization* 15: 222–79.

———. Forthcoming. "Agency Problems and Dividend Policies around the World." *Journal of Finance*.

Levine, Ross, and Sara Zervos. 1998. "Stock Markets, Banks and Economic Growth." *American Economic Review* 88: 537–58.

Lopez-de-Silanes, Florencio. 1998. "Determinants of Privatization Prices." *Quarterly Journal of Economics* 112: 966–1028.

McConnell, John, and Chris Muscarella. 1986. "Corporate Capital Expenditure Decisions and the Market Value of the Firm." *Journal of Financial Economics* 14: 399–422.

Morck, Randall, Bernard Yeung, and Wayne Yu. Forthcoming. "The Information Content of Stock Markets: Why Do Emerging Markets Have Synchronous Price Movements?" *Journal of Financial Economics*.

Nenova, Tatiana. 1999. "The Value of a Corporate Vote and Private Benefits: A Cross-Country Analysis." Harvard University, Cambridge, Mass.

North, Douglass. 1981. *Structure and Change in Economic History*. Cambridge: Cambridge University Press.

Olson, Mancur. 1993. "Dictatorship, Democracy and Development." *American Political Science Review*.

Rajan, Raghuram, and Luigi Zingales. 1998. "Financial Dependence and Growth." *American Economic Review* 88: 559–86.

Wurgler, Jeffrey. 1999. "Financial Markets and the Allocation of Capital." Harvard University, Cambridge, Mass.

Zingales, Luigi. 1994. "The Value of the Voting Right: A Study of the Milan Stock Exchange." *Review of Financial Studies* 7: 125–48.

———. 1995. "Inside Ownership and the Decision to Go Public." *Review of Economic Studies* 62: 425–48.

# Social Issues

# Crime, Violence, and Inequitable Development

*François Bourguignon*

Too much inequality may generate economic inefficiency and slow economic development. Can this occur through the influence of inequality on crime and violence? The answer seems to be yes: crime and violence may result from excessive relative poverty and inequality, along with more sociological factors, and have sizable economic and social cost. This article reviews theoretical arguments and the limited empirical evidence on such a relationship. The analysis suggests that reducing crime and violence may be one of the substantial social benefits of ensuring that economic development takes place evenly and equitably.

Increasing interest has focused on the idea that too much inequality may generate economic inefficiency and slow economic development. The recent literature has examined different hypotheses about this relationship (see Benabou 1996; Bertola 2000; Bourguignon 1999; Piketty 2000; and Bardhan, Bowles, and Gintis 2000). For example, analysts have considered the role of credit market imperfections and the effect of income distribution on public decisionmaking about capital taxation and public spending. But empirical evidence favoring one or more of these hypotheses is weak, and the policy implications of this burgeoning literature remain ambiguous.

This article explores a more direct link between inequality and economic efficiency, and possibly economic development. The analysis here involves the potential effect of inequality on private and collective violence and the substantial economic loss these social ills may cause. Some authors have investigated the dangers of excess inequality for political stability and social peace, and the harm that political instability and social upheaval can cause to social welfare and growth. Although debatable, there seems to be evidence of such a direct link.[1] But much less work has been done on the more elementary stage of this process—that is, situations where inequal-

François Bourguignon is professor at the Ecole des Hautes Etudes en Sciences Sociales and research fellow in the Département et Laboratoire d'Economie Théorique et Appliquée (DELTA) in Paris. This article draws on Bourguignon (1998a). The author is grateful to Serguei Soares for assistance with the victimization part of the 1988 Brazilian Household Survey (PNADE).

Annual World Bank Conference on Development Economics 1999
©2000 The International Bank for Reconstruction and Development / THE WORLD BANK

ity or poverty produce private rather than collective violence, essentially through crime and the development of illegal activity. This lack of analysis seems somewhat surprising given that some of the early work on the economics of crime in industrial countries emphasized the role of poverty and inequality in explaining spatial differences in criminality (see Ehrlich 1973).

The analysis here is motivated by the considerable and increasing crime and violence in developing countries—particularly in Latin America—known for their high inequality and poor growth performance (see Fajnzylber, Lederman, and Loayza 1998 and Londoño and Guerrero 1998). Is the unusually high crime and violence in these countries the result of poverty and inequality? Are these countries caught in a vicious circle whereby violence undermines the social and economic climate and weakens economic incentives and development factors, leading to more violence? Or is crime mainly due to other sociological or cultural factors that are more or less orthogonal to economic factors? This article answers those questions using a blend of economic theory and empirical evidence. As it turns out, excess inequality and high relative poverty can foster crime that imposes high social and economic costs. Thus there may be much to gain from policies that ease inequality, alleviate relative poverty, and control crime and violence.

## Crime and Development: Some Orders of Magnitude

Police reports are the most common source of data on crime. But for various reasons, many crimes are not reported to the police. Thus police reports are likely to underestimate criminality and to unevenly cover different areas and types of crime.[2] When available, victimization surveys are a more reliable, less biased source of crime data. In such surveys a representative sample of individuals are asked whether they have been victims of a crime, at what cost, and in what circumstances.

Although their number is increasing, such surveys are available in only a limited number of countries and often at a single point in time. Moreover, victimization surveys are far from perfect. In particular, they tend to miss crime and violence not directed toward ordinary people but taking place among criminals or marginal groups such as gangs. As a result international and intertemporal comparisons must rely primarily on data from police reports.

This section mainly relies on a United Nations database compiled from national police reports. Because of the biases just mentioned, this database is probably more accurate for serious crimes like intentional homicides and major robberies.[3] Series data on intentional homicides are available for quite a few countries, at least for some periods. These data are apparently consistent in the sense that no abnormal changes in orders of magnitude occur in the series. Yet these series are unavailable for some countries or are only available for periods that are too short or too distant to be of much interest. Series for major robberies are available for fewer countries and sometimes show inconsistencies over time, suggesting changes in definition or coverage. Still, it is possible to identify a subsample where data look approximately consistent. Series for less serious crimes—thefts, burglaries, fraud—are less reliable and so are not used here.

Crime rates in various regions during 1985–95 are shown in table 1. The table shows the mean and median rates in each region. It may be thought that the median is more reliable than the mean because it is insensitive to possibly inconsistent extreme values. But in fact, the overall picture is not that different whether one uses the median or the mean. Big differences across regions may indicate that international police report data are not comparable. But this should be less the case for homicides, which seem easier to record.

Before examining these data in detail, it is useful to keep in mind some orders of magnitude. Because data are more reliable there, it seems natural to take high-income countries as a basis for comparing crime rates. Among them the United States lies at the upper extreme, with robberies averaging nearly 250 per 100,000 inhabitants and homicides averaging 7.2 per 100,000 inhabitants in 1985–95. Crime is much lower in other high-income countries, with the United Kingdom at the lower end of the range for large countries—its robbery rate is about 60 per 100,000 inhabitants and its homicide rate is fewer than 2 per 100,000 inhabitants. But all these figures are national averages. Crime would be higher if only major metropolitan areas were considered. For instance, the homicide rate in New York City—13 per 100,000 inhabitants—is nearly twice the U.S. average.

Among other regions, crime is strikingly high in Latin America and the Caribbean. Reported robbery rates are comparable to those in the United States—about 200 per 100,000 inhabitants, and higher in some countries. Homicide rates are generally

**Table 1. Crime Rates by Region, 1985–95**
*(number of crimes per 100,000 inhabitants)*

| Region | Number of countries | Major robberies Regional mean | Major robberies Regional median | Intentional homicides Regional mean | Intentional homicides Regional median |
|---|---|---|---|---|---|
| Africa | 8 | 36.0 | 34.4 | 5.1 | 2.5 |
| Asia | 10 | 13.4 | 7.6 | 5.4 | 2.1 |
| Latin America and the Caribbean | 17 | 200.5 | 172.0 | 14.0 | 8.5 |
| Eastern Europe and Central Asia | 15 | 28.3 | 23.0 | 6.8 | 7.1 |
| Western Europe | 16 | 54.4 | 54.0 | 4.4 | 3.8 |
| Other high-income economies | 8 | 87.3 | 54.0 | 3.2 | 2.2 |
| United States | | 248.7 | | 7.2 | |

*Note:* The data for Africa cover Botswana, Burundi, Ethiopia, Madagascar, Malawi, Mauritius, Rwanda (until 1992), and Zimbabwe. The data for Asia cover Bangladesh, China, India, Indonesia, Republic of Korea, Malaysia, Nepal, Philippines, Sri Lanka, and Thailand. The data for Latin American and the Caribbean cover Argentina, Bolivia, Brazil, Chile, Colombia, Costa Rica, Dominican Republic, Ecuador, Honduras, Jamaica, Mexico, Nicaragua, Panama, Peru, Trinidad and Tobago, Uruguay, and República Bolivariana de Venezuela. The data for Eastern Europe and Central Asia cover Armenia, Azerbaijan, Belarus, Bulgaria, the Czech Republic, Estonia, Hungary, Kazakhstan, the Kyrgyz Republic, Latvia, Lithuania, Poland, Romania, the Russian Federation, and Slovak Republic. The data for Western Europe cover Austria, Belgium, Denmark, Finland, France, Germany, Greece, Israel, Italy, the Netherlands, Norway, Portugal, Spain, Sweden, Switzerland, and United Kingdom. The data for other high-income economies cover Australia, Canada, Hong Kong, Japan, Kuwait, New Zealand, Singapore, and the United States.
*Source:* United Nations.

higher than in the United States, but there are many disparities. Argentina and Costa Rica experience nearly 5 homicides per 100,000 inhabitants, but the República Bolivariana de Venezuela has more than 10 and Brazil and Mexico have nearly 20—while Colombia has a staggering 66 homicides per 100,000 inhabitants. Again, these figures severely understate urban crime. In 1995 the homicide rate was estimated to be 80 per 100,000 inhabitants in Rio de Janeiro (Brazil) and 52 per 100,000 inhabitants in Caracas (República Bolivariana de Venezuela), compared with national averages of 20 and 14. Recent victimization surveys showing the portion of adults who have been victims of armed robbery in the past year reach 9 percent in Rio and 17 percent in Caracas (Londoño and Guerrero 1998)—more than 10 times the highest police-reported robbery rates in the region. But as noted, the definitions of crime used by these various sources are not necessarily consistent.

Crime appears to be much less rampant in other regions (except for homicides in Eastern Europe and Central Asia). Homicide rates are comparable to levels in high-income countries, and robbery rates are lower. Robberies may be seriously underreported in many regions, however. In addition, there may be considerable diversity behind the means or medians in table 1. For instance, low means and medians for Asia do not mean that crime is uniformly lower there than in the rest of the world. The homicide rate in Thailand was 10 per 100,000 inhabitants during the period under analysis, and the rate in India was comparable to that in the United States.

Given the lack of comparability of crime rates across countries, the time dimension may be more relevant than the cross-sectional dimension. From that perspective, figures 1 and 2—which are based on the same type of information presented in

**Figure 1. Median Robbery Rates by Regions, 1970–94**

*Robberies per 100,000 inhabitants (logarithmic scale)*

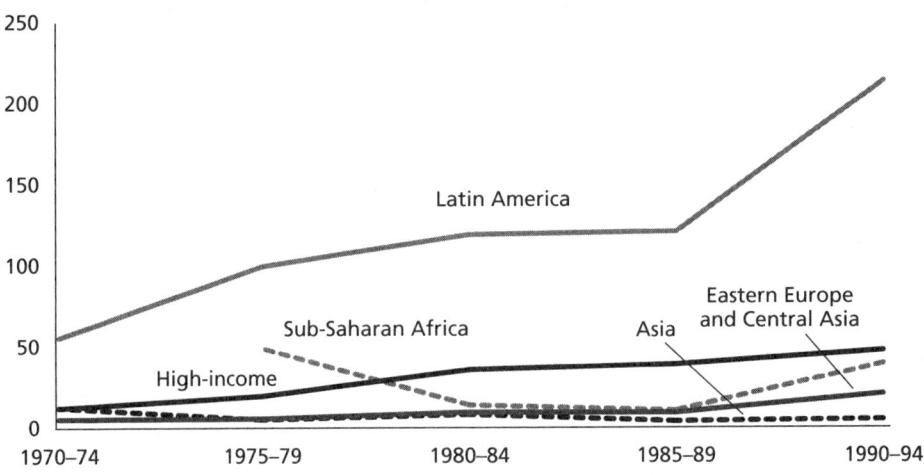

*Source:* United Nations.

**Figure 2. Median Homicide Rates by Regions, 1970–94**

*Homicides per 100,000 inhabitants*

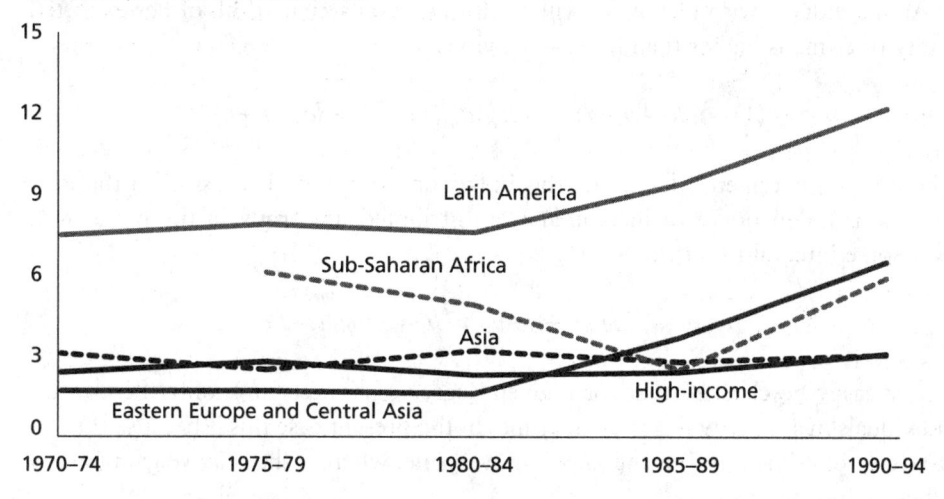

[Chart showing homicide rates from 1970–74 to 1990–94 for Latin America, Sub-Saharan Africa, Asia, Eastern Europe and Central Asia, and High-income regions]

*Source:* United Nations.

table 1—show a clear upward trend in crime since the early 1980s. This trend is most notable for Latin America and for Eastern Europe and Central Asia, where homicides and robberies doubled between the early 1980s and early 1990s. Such an evolution suggests that crime is not a purely structural characteristic of society that changes slowly with economic, social, and cultural development. Thus it is important to examine the possible factors behind this evolution.

## What Economic Theory Has to Say about Crime, Poverty, and Inequality

The canonical theoretical model of the economics of crime dates to Becker (1968) and was first given empirical content by Ehrlich (1973). The basic argument behind this model is summarized here using a simple general framework that incorporates an elementary representation of the distribution of income or wealth. The section then discusses the implications of the model and considers possible extensions likely to modify them.[4]

### The Basic Model

Assume that society is divided into two classes: the poor ($p$) and the nonpoor ($r$), with resources $w$ (say, income) such that $w_p < w_r$. Let $n_p$ and $n_r$ be the demographic weights of these two classes. Assume that the utility function of income is logarithmic—that is, unitary relative risk aversion—and let criminal activity be represented in the following manner. Engaging in crime pays a benefit equal to x with probability $(1 - q)$ and yields a loss $F = f_w$ with probability $q$. Thus $q$ is the probability of being caught, in which case a sanction $F$ proportional to initial resources is due. Criminal activity is taken here to be an all-or-nothing decision.

An individual $i$ with income $w_i$ will opt for criminal activity if his or her expected utility of crime is higher than in legal activity:

(1) $$(1 - q) \log(w_i+x) + q \log[w_i (1 - f)] > \log w_i + h_i$$

where $h_i$ is a parameter describing this individual's honesty. It is assumed that this variable is independent of income and is distributed uniformly in the population over some interval $[0, H]$. Rewriting equation 1 as:

$$(1 - q) \log (1 + x/w_i) > h_i - q \log(1 - f)$$

it may easily be checked that for a given degree of honesty ($h_i$), only the poorest individuals in society will engage in crime. In the present case this is because the relative cost of crime $(1 - f)$ is the same for everyone, whereas the relative gain $(x / w_i)$ is higher for the poorest.

This simple model could be generalized in many directions. For instance, the "loot" variable ($x$) could explicitly refer to the mean income of the population—an assumption made below—or that of the rich class. The probability of being caught ($q$) could be made a decreasing function of initial wealth to reflect the possibility opened by corruption. Risk aversion could be made an explicit parameter of the model. Although these modifications could allow the model to describe a wider array of possibilities, it is unlikely that they would substantially alter its main implications. Note also that the preceding framework may not be appropriate for describing the mechanics of violence and crime in countries with significant idiosyncrasies. The influence of guerrillas and militias on crime—especially kidnapping—in Colombia is an obvious example of such an exceptional case.

To further simplify the model, consider the case in which the honesty interval $[0, H]$ and the parameters $q$ and $f$ are such that condition 1 may only hold for poor people if they are sufficiently dishonest.[5] The crime rate, or percentage of criminals in the population, is then given by:

(2) $$c = C (n_p, x/w_p, f, q, H) = [(1 - q) \log (1 + x/w_p) + q \log (1 - f)]\, n_p/H.$$

According to this model, the crime rate depends positively on the extent of poverty as measured by the proportion of poor people ($n_p$) and on the potential relative gain ($x/w_p$) that these people receive from engaging in crime. The crime rate depends negatively on crime deterrent variables—that is, the probability of being caught ($q$) and the size of the sanction ($F$) relative to initial income ($f$). In addition, the crime rate depends negatively on the cultural or sociological attitude toward crime and the extent of honesty within society as represented by $H$.

The probability of crime detection ($q$) can hardly be taken as a given and so independent of the crime rate. It seems more natural to assume that it depends on the amount ($P$) that the community is spending on crime prevention and detection per inhabitant and the actual number of crimes ($c$). That relationship can be denoted by:

(3) $$q = G(P, c).$$

$G(\ )$ is a kind of production function of police activity. It may be assumed to be increasing with $P$ (at a decreasing rate) and decreasing with $c$ (at an increasing rate). Of course, this function is a reduced form for various phenomena reflecting the efficiency of the police. In particular, a given level of expenditures ($P$) may be associated with more or less efficiency depending on the extent of corruption—or more precisely, on the incentives for honesty in the police force (that is, the wage paid to the police and the loot of criminals). At the limit, an increase in $P$ may be ineffective in increasing the probability of detection and conviction ($q$). This case of mostly ineffective police is considered below.

Substituting the preceding production function in equation 2 and solving with respect to $c$ yields a new crime function:

(4) $$c = C^*(n_p, x/w_p, f, P, H).$$

In the list of arguments of the crime function, the probability of being caught ($q$) has simply been replaced by police expenditures per inhabitant ($P$).

To complete this theoretical framework, we now evaluate the social loss due to crime. This loss has four components: the direct cost of crime—that is, the pain and suffering of the victims; the cost of crime prevention ($P$) and of the judicial system; the cost of sanctions to convicted criminals ($F$), typically forgone earnings due to imprisonment; and the negative indirect effects of crime on economic activity. Assuming that the cost of pain is a proportion ($s$) of the economic cost of crime ($x$), the social loss amounts to:

(5) $$L = csx + P + cqj + cqF + cIC$$

where $q$ and $c$ are given by equations 3 and 4 and $j$ is the average cost of criminal justice per criminal. Note that the actual economic cost of crime ($x$) does not appear as such in equation 5. This is because it may be considered equivalent to a transfer from victims to criminals and therefore not a social loss. Some authors, however, include the economic cost of crime in the calculation of $L$ because $x$ should also correspond to the opportunity cost of criminals—for instance, the time spent outside market work. The term $IC$ in equation (5) corresponds to all the external effects that crime may have on economic activity after some critical level has been reached. These involve, for instance, the insecurity felt by all citizens, regardless of whether they are victims of a crime, as well as investment disincentives or negative effects on tourism and foreign investment. But these effects are extremely difficult to evaluate.[6]

## Implications of the Model

Despite its simplicity, the preceding model has interesting implications for the analysis of crime. To better understand them, it is important to keep in mind that the preceding economic argument is better suited to property crime or illegal activity (drug dealing, illegal gambling, prostitution) that offers economic gain than to crimes against people. It certainly cannot be ruled out that homicides, intentional or not, are more common among poor and less educated people and in areas where police are less present. In addition, part of intentional homicides and physical violence is directly linked to property crime or illegal activity. Thus the homicide rate in a given area may be determined by many of the same variables as the property crime rate. But given the exceptional nature of homicide, the relationship with these variables is most likely to be weaker than for property crime.

From the perspective of economic policy, the first two arguments in the general crime function (equation 4) are the most interesting. These arguments correspond to the direct effect that the distribution of income and other economic resources may have on criminality. This effect occurs through two channels: the proportion of poor people ($n_p$) and the potential relative gain that these people receive from engaging in crime ($x/w_p$).[7] Over time or across countries, the gain from crime is likely to be a function of the general affluence of society—that is, the mean or the median of the distribution of income. Thus the second argument of the crime function appears to be a measure of income inequality at the bottom of the distribution or, in other words, of relative poverty.[8] Interpreted in those terms, one could say that the basic model of crime could predict that the crime rate should be a function of both the relative poverty headcount ($n_p$) and the relative poverty "shortfall" ($\bar{w}/w_p$ or $w^M/w_p$, with $\bar{w}$ and $w^M$ being respectively the mean and the median of the income distribution) up to a simple transformation.[9] Note that these concepts differ from standard measures of inequality (such as the Gini coefficient) that take into account the entire income distribution.

According to the preceding argument, economic development that is accompanied by an increase in relative poverty should lead, other things being equal, to an increase in crime. Equivalently, in two societies at the same level of development less crime should be observed in the society with less relative poverty. These points do not imply that crime should be an increasing function of inequality between the very rich and the rest of the population or that it should increase with absolute poverty. Presumably, these seem to be testable hypotheses.

The preceding argument about the relevance of relative poverty has a long-term orientation. From a shorter-term view it may be noted that, according to the general crime function C( ), any increase in absolute poverty (through an increase in $n_p$ or a drop in $w_p$), will likely increase the crime rate. This is because the anticipated gain from crime ($x$), as well as all the other arguments of the function, will likely be somewhat rigid in the short term. Thus severe economic recessions may be expected to be accompanied by a surge in crime. What is more, if there is hysteresis in this process, then the volatility of economic activity may be thought of as an aggravating factor of crime—another interesting and testable hypothesis.[10]

The third and fourth arguments of the general crime function refer to the direct control that policymakers may have over crime through the severity of the sanctions handed down by the judicial system and the probability of crime detection, which is determined by police spending. These look like standard exogenous or policy variables. Thus it should come as no surprise that much of the literature on the economics of crime has focused on these punishment and crime deterrence issues. Rather than repeating what has been said elsewhere, and in line with the main theme of this article, I want to point out why these variables are also likely to be influenced by the distribution of income and well-being within the population. This approach may provide a second important, although indirect, link between crime and inequality.

Rather than considering the crime deterrence parameters ($f$ and $P$) as exogenous, consider them as the endogenous result of public decisionmaking. Suppose that the amount of police spending ($P$) is determined by some voting mechanism, possibly a degenerated one in which only the richest citizens participate. Under the simplifying temporary assumption that there is no possible crime prevention other than public police, we may reasonably assume that the private benefit from public police is an increasing function of the income of potential victims. Thus majority voting by the entire population should lead to the standard result in the redistribution literature that police spending depends on the distribution of income in the population.In the present case, however, it is necessary to assume nonconstant risk aversion for this result to hold. The direction in which police spending depends on the income distribution then varies according to the way risk aversion changes with income.[11] In any case the result obtained within a majority voting framework could be reversed in nondemocratic societies, where votes at the top of the distribution of income and wealth may have more weight than others. The important point is that through this political economy of spending on crime deterrence, economic and social inequality may have an indirect effect on crime, on top of the direct incentives they represent for criminals.

Having said this, it is not clear whether more inequality will lead to a larger or smaller budget to fight crime. Risk aversion, the income structure of society, and the political weight of various classes are important here. But so too are the social geography of the city and the private and public technology of crime prevention. We can easily imagine circumstances where the public decisionmaking mechanism for spending on crime protection leads to extensive protection in rich neighborhoods and business districts and relatively little spending in poor neighborhoods or on more general crime disincentives.

Another point to take into account is the possibility for part of the population to buy private protection through alarm systems, private guards, and strict residential segregation that improves the capacity to spot intruders and would-be criminals. If the social class that can afford this type of private security can influence political decisions, nothing substantial may be done to increase public security despite mounting crime. An extreme example of this situation is the development of private militias and paramilitaries in Colombia.

Private protection against crime modifies the relationship between poverty and inequality and crime. The possibility of self-protection against criminals logically eases the relationship between poverty and the crime rate. This works as follows. Potential victims anticipate that more poverty and inequality, due for instance to unbalanced development, increase crime risks. These people buy additional protection, which may reduce the actual change in crime. But the marginal social cost of poverty and inequality going directly or indirectly through crime remains the same. In equation 5 for this loss, the effect of a marginal increase in the crime rate ($c$) is simply replaced by a change in the private protection part of $P$.

When private and public crime protection benefit the rich, the relative poverty that may initially be responsible for criminality has an additional social cost: whatever crime remains will necessarily be directed toward the middle class and the poor. In other words, the negative social externality arising from excessive relative poverty through criminal activity is distributed in a regressive way. Thus both criminals and victims would have to be found in the lower range of the income distribution.

We now come to the last argument of the general crime function (equation 4). This is certainly the most difficult part of the function for an economist to discuss. For simplicity this argument was referred to as an honesty parameter ($H$). But it should include all the variables—ethnicity, religion, family structures, residential segregation—that may explain that in front of some cost-benefit ratio of crime and some characteristics of judicial and police systems, the crime rate may vary by city and country.

Some of these variables may be related to economic phenomena. For instance, the increase in the proportion of single-parent families in urban areas, which is linked to increased juvenile crime and violence, is probably not foreign to labor market conditions. Similarly, residential segregation reproduces existing economic inequalities (Benabou 1996). The variable $H$ in the general crime function thus provides a third channel through which economic cycles or the equalizing or unequalizing nature of the development process may affect crime and violence. This effect goes through the influence of economic conditions on some of the sociological factors that influence individuals' propensity to commit crime (Hagan 1994). Analyses based on the concept of social capital may be relevant here.

### Extensions of the Model

This analysis of the relationship between income distribution and crime may be objected to on the grounds that it takes too much of an economist's view of criminal behavior and so may be misleading for policy. In particular, many observers insist that violence in big cities is often not directed toward the property of others but toward specific segments of society in the poorest areas. An obvious example is violence related to the control of illicit activity like gambling, prostitution, or drug dealing and trafficking. In many violent parts of today's cities such activity—rather than more conventional burglary or robbery—seems to be the main cause of the increase in violence and the surge in homicides. Another departure from the canonical model might lie in the low probability of crime detection and sanction in many marginalized urban areas of developing countries. In many Latin American cities, for example, the probability of being arrested and incarcerated for murder is estimated to be less than 10 percent.[12]

In effect, however, this view of criminality may be seen as an extension of some of the previous arguments. Consider the limit case in which the rich class is able to protect itself against crime. In this case the potential gain from property crime shrinks and would-be criminals must rely on the market for the illicit activity cited above. Suppose in addition that people engaged in such activity run no big risk of being arrested and prosecuted. Crime then becomes a matter of industrial organization and occupational choice.

The main difference between this type of crime and other economic sectors and occupations is that there are likely to be no market rules for the illicit activity. As a result individuals engaging in such activity must rely on their capacity to physically neutralize potential competitors. At some stages of the organizational development of this sector in a given local environment, "nonmarket" competition is strong and is responsible for high violence among people or gangs. At other stages or in a different environment, the sector may be fully controlled by organized crime—with, paradoxically, some drop in violence (Fiorentini and Peltzman 1995). In that case the analysis of crime and violence linked to illicit activity turns to the conditions under which some type of organization of this activity predominates over others.

This view of the causes of violence does not deeply modify the nature of the initial model of crime and the role of the various factors discussed above. It seems natural to consider that the premium ($x$) of becoming involved in illegal activity continues to be related to the affluence of the economy, but it modifies the nature of the risk ($q$) involved and potential sanction ($F$) incurred in doing so. The risk is no longer determined exogenously by public spending on crime deterrence. Such spending is supposed to be too small for deterrence to be effective. The risk is now endogenous and depends on the organization of the illegal sector—for instance, it may be the probability of being killed by a competitor seeking to control a given territory for drug dealing. In any case, the main economic factor pushing toward crime remains the income that people may get if they remain in legal activity relative to the expected utility of illegal activity. In the current framework, as in the original model, any drop in this level of income (that is, an increase in relative urban poverty) increases the incentives to switch to illegal activity.

The preceding analysis is essentially static. In a dynamic framework the prospect of permanently rather than transitorily low relative income may be the main factor pushing some individuals toward crime and illegal activity. This adds another dimension to the relationship between crime and inequality. Namely, at a given point in time the absence of income and social mobility—which arises from poverty traps like credit market imperfections—may be as important as relative poverty in explaining criminality at the bottom of the income distribution.

## Evidence on the Relationship between Crime and Inequality and Poverty

The main conclusion of the preceding analysis is that urban inequality and poverty may be the main economic determinants of crime and violence. The relationship may be direct, as more inequality and poverty make crime more profitable at a given level of crime deterrence. It may also be indirect, going through the amount that a society spends on crime deterrence. But is there evidence of such a relationship between crime and inequality and poverty?

For two reasons this question is extremely difficult to answer. First, as noted, sociological factors could be responsible for the violence observed in a society—but these factors are statistically difficult to observe and quantify. Even though there is little doubt that economic disadvantage has always been an important cause of crime, it is certainly not a sufficient cause of high crime rates in a given social group.[13] The second difficulty is purely statistical. As we have seen, it is difficult to get reliable data on crime and violence across countries and cities, and even over time in a given country or city. It is even more difficult to draw conclusions on the relationship between these data and data on international or intertemporal differences in poverty and inequality.

Time series analysis is feasible only for a few industrial countries. But such analyses are usually inconclusive on the relationship between crime and inequality because few countries have experienced distributional changes that are likely to have significantly affected the crime rate.[14] Here we mostly consider cross-sectional evidence.

Figures 3 and 4 compare crime data from the United Nations database with inequality data from Deininger and Squire (1996). Crime rates are averaged over 1985–95, while inequality figures refer as much as possible to the mid-1980s. The samples for major robberies and intentional homicides each include 50 observations.

**Figure 3. Cross-sectional Relationship between Inequality and Robbery Rates, 1990–94**

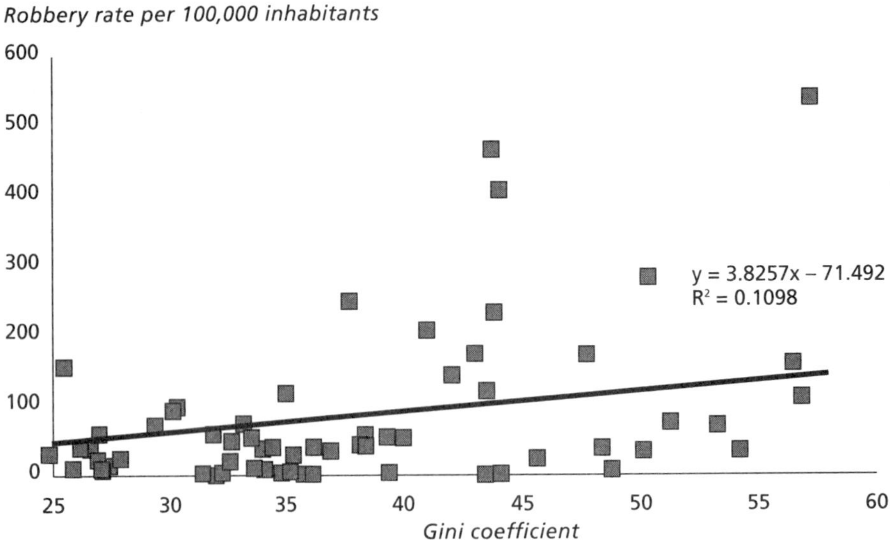

*Robbery rate per 100,000 inhabitants*

$y = 3.8257x - 71.492$
$R^2 = 0.1098$

*Source:* United Nations and Deininger and Squire 1996.

**Figure 4. Cross-sectional Relationship between Inequality and Homicide Rates, 1990–94**

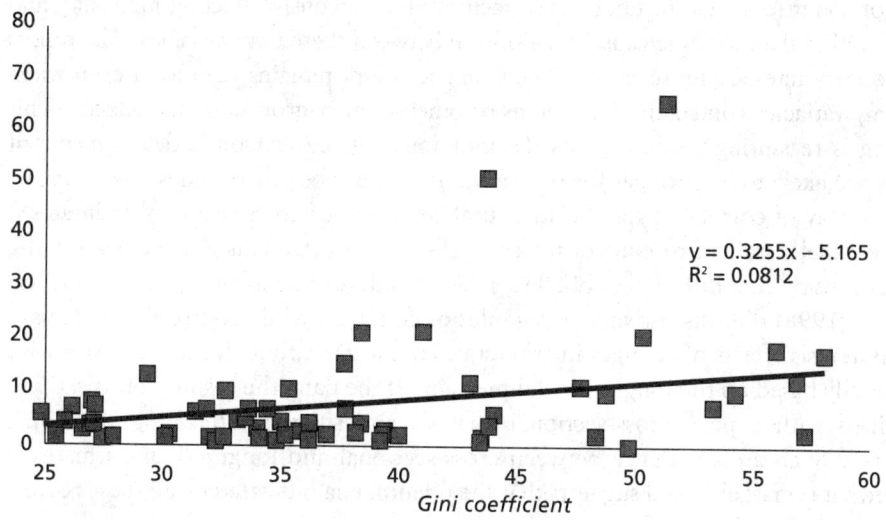

*Homicide rate per 100,000 inhabitants*

$y = 0.3255x - 5.165$
$R^2 = 0.0812$

Gini coefficient

*Source:* United Nations and Deininger and Squire 1996.

The preceding section explained the complex and subtle ways in which the distribution of income and wealth may affect the crime rate in a given economy. In particular, the direct effect of that distribution on crime was more likely to be related to the bottom of the distribution and the concept of relative poverty than to the top of the distribution and the income share of the richest. Thus it may be somewhat surprising that simple scatter diagrams like figures 3 and 4, relating crime rates and Gini coefficients, show a positive relationship and—in line with intuition—a stronger relationship for robberies than for homicides.

Even though this finding is reminiscent of Ehrlich's early attempt to draw conclusions on the role of relative poverty in explaining crime across U.S. states, most cross-sectional evidence is ambiguous and fragile. Figures 3 and 4 are no exception. In fact, when a few Latin American countries known for their high crime and inequality are removed from the sample, the relationship between these two variables weakens considerably.

A complete cross-sectional analysis based on the same data is offered by Fajnzylber, Lederman, and Loayza (1998). Core independent variables are urbanization, average education, GNP per capita, the Gini coefficient, and variables controlling for the prevalence of drug use. Among them, the Gini coefficient is the only variable that is systematically significant. Moreover, its effect is sizable. A 5 point increase in the Gini coefficient—not an unlikely change in a country experiencing genuine shifts in income distribution—would produce an average 15 percent increase in homicides, and two or three times that for robberies.

As before, however, the corresponding coefficient becomes insignificant when a dummy variable is introduced for Latin America in the homicide regressions. This result may suggest that the significance of inequality as a determinant of crime in a cross-section of countries is due to unobserved factors simultaneously affecting inequality and crime rather than to some causal relationship between these two variables. The results for robbery rates are more robust. The Gini coefficient remains significant even when dummy variables controlling for regions or other country groups are introduced. This finding is reassuring because it fits the intuition that the economic determinants of crime are likely to be stronger for property crimes than for other crimes.

One way of correcting for the structural weakness of cross-sectional estimates is to use panel data and to control for country-fixed effects. This is done by running regressions on first differences of all variables of interest. Fajnzylber, Lederman, and Loayza (1998) did this for smaller samples of countries while controlling for possible hysteresis effects of changes in crime rates (table 2). Although the regressions are essentially based on the longitudinal dimension of the data, the results confirm those obtained with a pure cross-sectional analysis and suggest interesting additional effects.[15] Such a coincidence between cross-sectional and longitudinal estimates is somewhat remarkable and suggests that the phenomena indicated by all these regressions are more robust than expected.

This is true, first of all, for the effect of income inequality on criminality. This effect is significant and substantial for homicides and robberies. In the short run (less than five years) a 1 point increase in the Gini coefficient produces a 3.6 percent increase in the homicide rate and a 1.1 percent increase in the robbery rate for the

**Table 2. Panel Regressions of Crime Growth Rates: First Difference Auto-Regressive Models**

| Explanatory variable | Homicide growth rate | Robbery growth rate |
|---|---|---|
| Gini coefficient [a] | 0.036 | 0.011 |
|  | (0.000) | (0.009) |
| Urbanization rate | 0.004 | 0.011 |
|  | (0.063) | (0.000) |
| GNP per capita (log) | −0.207 | −0.045 |
|  | (0.000) | (0.035) |
| GDP growth rate- | −0.036 | −0.072 |
|  | (0.001) | (0.000) |
| Drug possession crime rate | 0.001 | 0.001 |
|  | (0.047) | (0.019) |
| Secondary enrollment rate | 0.009 | 0.002 |
|  | (0.000) | (0.191) |
| Lagged crime rate | 0.640 | 0.839 |
|  | (0.000) | (0.000) |
| Number of observations (countries) | 54 (20) | 50 (17) |

*Note:* Numbers in parentheses are p-values. Second lags and third lags of dependent and independent variables were used for all variables except the lagged crime rate, for which the third lag was used.
a. Strictly exogenous.
*Source:* Fajnzylber, Lederman, and Loayza 1998 (estimates obtained by using the generalized method of moments).

countries in the sample. This effect is much stronger in the long run because of the compounding effect of hysteresis in crime rates. The coefficients of the lagged crime rate are such that the effect of inequality would be multiplied by three for homicides and by seven for robberies.[16] These orders of magnitude are higher than those suggested by the pure cross-sectional results mentioned above.

Table 2 exhibits other interesting features. Of special relevance is the role of short-run variations in GDP and the substantial hysteresis in the evolution of criminality. Here again, and as would be expected, these trends are more pronounced for robberies than for homicides. For the variations in GDP, a simple calculation based on the coefficients shown suggests that a major recession leading to a sudden 5 percent drop in GDP would produce an instant 50 percent increase in the robbery rate. The hysteresis effect is such that the crime rate would practically remain at this level until the initial GDP loss is fully compensated by faster growth.[17] These orders of magnitude are only indicative. But recessions leading to a 5 percent drop in GDP are not uncommon in developing countries, and the lasting increase in crime caused by a temporary surge in poverty may add considerably to their social cost.

Because they are based on a restricted number of observations and countries, the preceding results are not truly representative. It turns out that fixed effects are less a problem for homicides than for robberies, so for homicides alternative specifications may be estimated on larger samples. The results reported by Fajnzylber, Lederman, and Loayza (1998) lead to the same general conclusions as above. In addition, they confirm that crime deterrence variables—essentially police levels and conviction rates—have a significant negative influence on homicides.

Convergent findings are reported by Londoño and Guerrero (1998), who ran fixed effect regressions on homicides in 17 Latin American countries during 1970–95. The specification that the authors chose to estimate is not as complete as that by Fajnzylber, Lederman, and Loayza, so a detailed comparison is not possible. But Londoño and Guerrero also find that poverty and inequality have important effects on homicide, with a 1 percentage point increase in the poor population producing an instant 2.5 percent increase in the number of homicides. This finding is similar to the orders of magnitude seen above.

Although they seem to be convergent, these estimates must be taken with considerable care. As noted, pure cross-sectional exercises have natural limitations. Introducing fixed effects to samples that pool different countries at different periods certainly leads to more robust conclusions. Here, however, the studies by Fajnzylber, Lederman, and Loayza and by Londoño and Guerrero draw on samples are limited to 20 countries. Thus final estimates may be strongly influenced by a small number of observations. This shortcoming points to the need for better and more consistent data on crime and victimization, both across countries and within countries over time.

Still, it remains somewhat remarkable that with both cross-sections and panel data the distribution of income appears to be a significant determinant of international and intertemporal differences in crime rates. This finding suggests that some of the mechanisms envisaged in the preceding section to explain the influence of distributional phenomena on crime may indeed be at work. But identifying more precisely these mechanisms—and in particular, whether the effect of the distribution of crime is direct, as in the canonical model, or indirect, through policy and other structural variables—seems impossible with available data.

## The Social Cost of Crime and Inequality—and the Scope for Equitable Development Policy

Given the likely positive association between crime and poverty and inequality, we now measure the social cost of crime and the part of the social cost of inequality that goes through crime. Though rough, these estimates give an idea of the surprising scope for policies aimed at reducing inequality and poverty in urban areas.

Crude estimates of the components of the social cost of crime in the United States and Latin America are shown in table 3. The table follows equation 5 and draws on Freeman (1996) and Londoño and Guerrero (1998). Estimates for other countries or regions may be obtained by scaling these estimates up or down depending on observed crime rates.

The first row of the table shows a straight estimate of the monetary amount of property crime (robberies, thefts, burglaries, fraud, and the like). For the United States the estimate comes from national crime victimization surveys. For Latin America the estimate is based on a survey of six countries (Brazil, Colombia, El Salvador, Mexico, Peru, República Bolivariana de Venezuela) conducted as part of a research project sponsored by the Inter-American Development Bank. Assuming that the average amount involved in property crime is proportional to per capita income, the rate of property crime in Latin America is three times that in the United States, which seems reasonable.[18]

Note that this first row is called "transfers" and is not included in the social cost of crime. This view corresponds to the theoretical model above, where property crime appears as a simple exchange of property and so as a transfer of wealth or income from victims to criminals. But part of this wealth may be destroyed in the

### Table 3. Estimates of the Social Cost of Crime in the United States and Latin America
*(percentage of GDP)*

| Component | United States | Latin America |
|---|---|---|
| Transfers (monetary amount of property crime) | 0.5 [a] | 1.5 [a] |
| Monetary cost (medical expenses, opportunity cost of time) | 0.2 | 0.6 |
| Nonmonetary cost (pain and suffering resulting from property crime) | 0.7 | 2.1 |
| Human capital loss (homicides) | 0.4 | 1.7 |
| Opportunity cost of incarceration | 0.6 | 0.1 |
| Criminal justice and police | 1.3 | 1.6 |
| Private crime prevention | 0.6 | 1.4 |
| Total | 3.8 | 7.5 |

a. These data are not included in the totals.
*Source:* Freeman 1996; Londoño and Guerrero 1998; author's calculations.

transfer. This part appears in the second row of table 3 as the monetary cost of crime. This item also includes the actual costs incurred by victims in addition to what they lost—that is, medical expenses in cases of violent robbery, property repair in cases of burglary, time spent dealing with the police or justice personnel, and so on. There is no direct estimate of the monetary cost for Latin America.[19] The figure in table 3 was obtained by assuming the same proportionality factor to the United States as for transfers.

To these monetary costs are added the nonmonetary cost of pain and suffering in cases of property crime, and the loss of human capital in cases of homicides. The nonmonetary cost of pain and suffering is based on jury estimates in the United States. Again, the same proportionality factor as for transfers was applied to Latin America, leading to a cost of 2.1 percent of GDP.[20] Londoño and Guerrero (1998) calculated the human capital loss in Latin America based on the average life expectancy of homicide victims and unskilled wage rates. The resulting cost is substantial: 1.7 percent of GDP. The figure for the United States was obtained through its homicide rate relative to that of Latin America.

Other costs arise through crime prevention and punishment. The opportunity cost of the incarceration time of U.S. prisoners is estimated by Freeman (1996) to be 0.6 percent of GDP. Assuming that this cost is proportional to the incarceration rate—that is, the number of incarcerated people per inhabitant—leads to a figure of just 0.1 percent of GDP for Latin America. Spending on criminal justice and police compensates for some of this difference; such spending amounts to 1.6 percent of GDP in Latin America and only 1.3 percent in the United States. Latin America also spends more on private crime prevention (security guards, alarm systems, armored cars). As a result total spending on crime prevention and sanction accounts for a larger portion of GDP in Latin America than in the United States, though the ratio between these two figures is lower than that for crime rates.

Summing all these components leads to a social cost of crime equal to 3.8 percent of GDP in the United States and a stunning 7.5 percent in Latin America. Although both figures are rough, their order of magnitude is probably about right. As noted, by world standards the countries covered by this analysis have very high crime rates. In most European and Asian countries the same calculation would likely result in figures below 2 percent of GDP.

The preceding calculation is at the aggregate level and does not take into account the potential social cost arising from the fact that crime victims may not be distributed uniformly within the population. The basic crime model reviewed above, in the section on economic theory suggests that the probability of being a victim should increase with income. But the opposite might occur where there is private protection against crime or a high income bias in policing.

The 1988 Brazilian Household Survey (PNADE)[21] seems to confirm both hypotheses (table 4). For theft and robbery the victimization rate clearly increases with income—the slope of that function becomes significant only in the top half of the income distribution. For assault, however, no significant tendency seems to be present. This finding may reflect the combination of two phenomena. Victimization rates are

**Table 4. Distribution of Urban Crime in Brazil by Income Decile, 1988**
*(crime rates in percent)*

| | Men | | Women | |
|---|---|---|---|---|
| Decile[a] | Theft and robbery | Assault | Theft and robbery | Assault |
| 1 | 4.0 | 1.2 | 3.6 | 1.3 |
| 2 | 4.9 | 2.1 | 3.8 | 1.1 |
| 3 | 5.0 | 1.7 | 3.7 | 2.0 |
| 4 | 5.1 | 1.3 | 3.8 | 0.7 |
| 5 | 5 | 1.3 | 3.8 | 1.3 |
| 6 | 6.4 | 1.6 | 4.0 | 0.7 |
| 7 | 7.6 | 1.3 | 5.2 | 1.0 |
| 8 | 7.8 | 1.4 | 6.1 | 0.8 |
| 9 | 10.0 | 1.9 | 7.6 | 1.1 |
| 10 | 13.4 | 1.7 | 9.7 | 0.9 |
| Total | 6.9 | 1.6 | 5.1 | 1.1 |

a. Deciles are defined on the distribution of equalized household income among all individuals in the population.
*Source:* Author's calculations based on 1988 Brazilian Household Survey (PNADE) data.

high in the top half of the income distribution because the motivation to commit assaults is essentially the same as for theft and robbery. But victimization rates are also high in the bottom half of the distribution because of youth violence in low-income urban areas. The data do not, however, allow us to further test this hypothesis.

Putting together the various estimates discussed in this section and the previous one, we find a strikingly high order of magnitude for the portion of the social cost of poverty and inequality that may go through crime and violence in Latin America. Consider, for example, the elasticity of crime rates relative to inequality and poverty suggested by the coefficient in table 2. As noted, a 5 point increase in a country's Gini coefficient might increase crime by 50 percent. A similar effect may be expected from a recession that causes a 5 percent drop in GDP.

The portion of the social cost of such backslides that might go through crime can be inferred from table 3. If nothing is done to increase crime deterrence, then the bottom half of the table will not change—but the top half will likely increase in proportion to the crime rate. In high-crime countries, like many of those in Latin America, the additional cost would be more than 2 percent of GDP. Moreover, if we take into account the fact that the increase in crime will likely be concentrated in large urban areas, the local social cost of crime in these areas will be much higher. These are not small effects.

An active crime deterrence policy could lower the cost of inequitable development or recessions. In that case the bottom half of table 3 should be modified depending on the efficiency of crime deterrence. But there might not be much to gain, as shown by the United States in the 1980s. According to Freeman (1996), the increase in crime that could be expected from the dramatic drop in the real incomes of low-skilled workers during the 1980s was likely offset by a drastic jump in the incarceration rate, which more than doubled between 1980 and 1992 (and has increased by 50 percent since then). If this estimate is accurate, about half of the opportunity cost of incarceration, as well as the part of the criminal justice budget that covered the direct costs of incarceration policy—such as the cost of prisons—must be considered a price that society had to pay for increasing inequality. As the bottom half of table 3 indicates, the resulting figure is probably not far from the hypothetical cost that would have been incurred if crime had increased.

It is worth remembering that many of these estimates and conclusions rely on Latin America's unique experience. The potential cost of inequitable development going through crime is probably much lower in Asia or Africa. Still, when the estimates above are made proportional to reported crime rates, this cost is still significant in several Asian countries. It is lower in Africa because of the predominance of the rural population. The problem there may be to to avoid having urbanization lead to crime rates as high as in Latin America. A final cost to consider is the potential negative effect of high crime on economic efficiency and growth. Attempts to introduce the crime data from the United Nations database in a conventional cross-sectional growth regression failed to yield significant coefficients. This analysis was done for 1985–95, a period when the deviation from long-run growth was so large that a relationship between crime and growth might be difficult to substantiate. What is needed is a more comprehensive time series framework in which both economic growth and crime would be endogenous. There is, however, no reliable database for such an analysis.

## Conclusion

Crime and violence are likely to be socially costly byproducts of, among other factors, uneven or inequitable economic development. Economic theory shows how property crime and, more generally, the violence associated with illegal activity may in part be consequences of excessive inequality and poverty. Limited evidence suggests that an increase in relative poverty or income inequality generally leads to a rise in crime. Similarly, by increasing the extent of poverty, major recessions may inspire a sharp jump in crime. Moreover, hysteresis in the way crime changes over time may magnify these effects considerably.

It follows that through crime and violence, inequality, poverty, and macroeconomic volatility may have a large social cost. In countries where crime is already high, severe recessions (like those recently experienced by many developing countries) or major increases in inequality (comparable to what occurred in many countries during the 1980s) could generate social losses as high as 2 percent of GDP. This loss is even greater if we consider only urban areas—where most of the increase in crime is likely to occur\.

Regional differences in crime are consistent with this analysis. Latin America is the region with by far the most crime, and is also the region where the income distribution is generally more unequal than elsewhere and economic growth has been extremely volatile. The recent surge of crime in some Central European and Central Asian countries can probably be analyzed in the same way. But such an evolution also raises the issue of the social control of crime. High inequality or increases in relative poverty need not lead to higher crime if crime deterrence is simultaneously strengthened.

Strengthening crime deterrence to mitigate the effects of high inequality or increases in relative poverty may not be a simple task, however. First, in a political economy framework, crime deterrence may itself be the consequence of existing inequality—so, for example, a highly unequal society may have a low propensity to invest in police and crime prevention. Second, even if increased crime deterrence measures prevent an increase in inequality and so avoid higher crime, such measures are costly.

## Notes

1. See Alesina and Perrotti (1996) for the relationship among income inequality, political instability, and investment. The negative effect of political instability and violence on growth was put forward in Barro (1991).

2. It may also be in the interest of police to report inaccurate data. In particular, crime will be overreported if there is a need to hide inefficient performance.

3. Robbery refers to taking away a person's property and overcoming resistance through force or threat of force. For countries lacking data on homicides, the database is complemented by World Health Organization data on causes of death.

4. See Eide (1997) for a brief survey and exhaustive bibliography of the theoretical and empirical literature on crime, with a focus on industrial countries.

5. In other words, condition (1) is not satisfied with $h_i = 0$ when $i = r$, but it holds when $i = p$.

6. There may also be benefits associated with illegal activity. In some cases drug trafficking or smuggling may contribute to national welfare. These are not the kind of crimes considered here, however.

7. A more general representation of the income distribution—that is, the portion of people below some income threshold on the one hand and the mean income of these people on the other—would lead to a similar characterization of the distribution's effect on the crime rate. However, the income threshold defining poverty would itself be a function of all the parameters of the model rather than arbitrarily defined.

8. Absolute poverty would matter here only if the gain from crime (x) could be defined in absolute terms without any reference to a society's level of development. But this does not seem to be a reasonable assumption.

9. Rigorously the relative poverty shortfall should be the relative distance from the mean or the median, that is $1 - w_p/\bar{w}$ or $1 - w_p/w^M$.

10. One channel this hysteresis may go through is the anticipation by would-be criminals of the probability (q) of being caught. Crime increases during recessions because of the first two arguments of equation 4, while police spending remains the same. It follows that the crime rate increases and the detection rate falls. When the economy recovers, the anticipated probability of crime detection by criminals and therefore the crime rate may fail to readjust to their initial level. For such an expectational model of crime, see Sah (1991).

11. If we denote $t$ the (proportional) tax rate needed to finance policy expenditures, writing equation 1 for the victim rather than the criminal may show that expected utility is separable in $w$, $(1 - t)$, and $q$ whenever the cost of crime (x) is proportional to income. It follows that the preferred tax-policy expenditure combination is independent of income. This would remain true even if the (constant) risk aversion were different from 1.

12. Londoño and Guerrero (1998, p. 37) report a rate of 8 percent for El Salvador. This figure was less than 6 percent in the Colombian city of Cali in 1983, and probably of the same order of magnitude in other big metropolitan areas in Colombia.

13. In industrial countries, for instance, there are well-documented differences in crime rates among ethnic minorities that are equally discriminated against; see Tonry (1997).

14. From that point of view, the United States is an exception. However, evidence there on the effect on crime of the surge in relative poverty in the 1980s is still much debated.

15. The samples used for cross-section and panel analysis differ because of distinct data requirements.

16. These multiplicative factors are simply the inverse of $1 - \lambda$, where $\lambda$ is the coefficient of the lagged crime rate in table 2.

17. The dynamics of aggregate criminality may be more complex than is postulated in this model. However, there are not enough observations in the time dimension of the sample to estimate a richer time structure.

18. United Nations data indicate a comparable robbery rate in Latin America and the United States and a homicide rate in Latin America that is twice that in the United States. But these data are probably affected by a stronger negative bias in the case of Latin America.

19. Londoño and Guerrero (1998) report just 0.2 percent of GDP for medical expenses and a much higher amount than is shown in table 3 for productivity losses.

20. Londoño and Guerrero (1998) give a much larger estimate for this component—5.3 percent of GDP—based on reported willingness to pay for safety. That figure, however, seems artificially high in comparison with the U.S. figure.

## References

Alesina, Alberto, and Roberto Perotti. 1996. "Income Distribution, Political Instability, and Investment." *European Economic Review* 40: 1203–28.

Bardhan, Pranab, Samuel Bowles, and Herbert Gintis. 2000. "Wealth Inequality, Wealth Constraints and Economic Performance." In Anthony Atkinson and François Bourguignon, eds., *Handbook of Income Distribution*. Amsterdam: North-Holland.

Barro, Robert. 1991. "Economic Growth in a Cross Section of Countries" *Quarterly Journal of Economics* 106: 407–43.

Becker, Gary. 1968. "Crime and Punishment: An Economic Approach." *Journal of Political Economy* 101: 385–409.

Benabou, Roland. 1994. "Human Capital, Inequality and Growth: A Local Perspective." *European Economic Review* 38: 817–26.

———. 1996. "Inequality and Growth." *NBER Macroeconomics Annual 1996*. Cambridge, Mass.: MIT Press for the National Bureau of Economic Research.

Bertola, Giuseppe. 2000 "Macroeconomics of Distribution and Growth." In Anthony Atkinson and François Bourguignon, eds., *Handbook of Income Distribution*. Amsterdam: North-Holland.

Bourguignon, François. 1998a. "Crime As a Social Cost of Poverty and Inequality: A Review Focusing on Developing Countries." Background paper prepared for *World Development Report 1999/2000*. World Bank, Washington, D.C.

———. 1998b. "Inefficient Inequalities: Notes on the Crime Connection." World Bank, Washington, D.C.

———. 1999. "Distribution, Redistribution and Development: Where Do We Stand?" Desarollo y Sociedad.

Deininger, Klaus, and Lyn Squire. 1996. "A New Data Set Measuring Income Inequality." *World Bank Economic Review* 10(3): 565–91.

Ehrlich, Isaac. 1973. "Participation in Illegitimate Activities: A Theoretical and Empirical Investigation." *Journal of Political Economy* 81: 521–65.

Eide, Erling. 1997. "Economics of Criminal Behavior: Survey and Bibliography." Law and Economics Working Paper 5. University of Oslo, Norway.

Fajnzylber, Pablo, Daniel Lederman, and Norman Loayza. 1998. *Determinants of Crime Rates in Latin America and the World: An Empirical Assessment.* Latin American and Caribbean Studies. Washington, D.C.: World Bank.

Fiorentini, Gianluca, and Sam Peltzman, eds. 1995. *The Economics of Organised Crime.* Cambridge: Cambridge University Press.

Freeman, Richard. 1996. "Why Do So Many Young American Men Commit Crimes and What Might We Do About It?" *Journal of Economic Perspectives* 10 (1): 25–42.

Glaeser, Edward 1999. "An Overview of Crime and Punishment." Harvard University, Cambridge, Mass.

Hagan, J. 1994. "Crime, Inequality and Efficiency." In Andrew Glyn and David Miliband, eds., *Paying for Inequality: The Economic Cost of Social Injustice.* London: IPPR/Rivers Oram Press.

Londoño, Juan Luis, and Rodrigo Guerrero. 1998. "Epidemología y costos de la violencia en America Latina." Report for the Inter-American Development Bank, Washington, D.C.

Perotti, Roberto. 1994. "Income Distribution and Investment." *European Economic Review* 38 (3–4): 827–35.

Piketty, Thomas. 2000. "Theories of Persistent Inequality and Intergenerational Mobility." In Anthony Atkinson and François Bourguignon, eds., *Handbook of Income Distribution.* Amsterdam: North-Holland.

Sah, Raaj. 1991. "Social Osmosis and Patterns of Crime: A Dynamic Economic Analysis." *Journal of Political Economy* 99: 1272–95.

Tonry, Michael. 1997. *Ethnicity, Crime and Immigration.* Chicago: University of Chicago Press.

United Nations. Various years. "World Crime Surveys of Crime Trends and Operations of Criminal Justice." United Nations Centre for International Crime Prevention, Vienna. [www.uncjin.org].

# Comment on "Crime, Violence, and Inequitable Development," by François Bourguignon

*Mauricio Rubio*

As Colombia suggests for Latin America, and as Kosovo and other recent conflicts show for Eastern Europe, violence can seriously undermine economic growth. Thus François Bourguignon's article is quite relevant for policy in developing countries. Here I will comment on a few of the many interesting issues Bourguignon raises—data problems, theoretical considerations, implications for policy—drawing heavily on Colombia's experience.

## Data on Crime and Violence

As Bourguignon points out, data on crime are often unavailable or of poor quality. His table 1 shows how important these problems can be. According to this table, Africa's crime rate for major robberies is about two-thirds of that for Western Europe, and Africa's homicide rate is lower than the U.S. rate. These data make little sense for a continent where almost half the countries have experienced violent conflict in recent years, resulting in almost 15 million displaced people (Michailof 1999). It is not surprising that only eight African countries report their crime statistics. In Colombia, and in Latin America generally, less available and lower-quality data are associated with more crime and violence.

Data problems are far more serious for property crime than for homicides. In countries like Colombia, police records tell nothing about variations in property crime, in time or in space. There are two reasons. First, the reporting rate is negatively associated with real crime rates. Second, police records tend to link reporting to performance. For 1975–95 Colombian police records show a long-term decrease in property crime that does not correspond to the findings of victimization surveys. Furthermore, this decline is strongly correlated with convictions. It is hard to think of a social phenomenon for which the relationship between what is spent on gathering data and the phenomenon's social cost is as unfavorable as it is for crime and violence.

Mauricio Rubio is associate researcher in the Paz Pública at the Universidad de Los Andes, Bogotá, and associate professor at the Instituto Universitario de Derecho y Economía (IUDEC), Universidad Carlos III, Madrid. All references to Colombian evidence can be found in Rubio (1999).

*Annual World Bank Conference on Development Economics 1999*
©2000 The International Bank for Reconstruction and Development / THE WORLD BANK

## Interesting Issues

Bourguignon's article advances economic thinking on crime in a way that is of interest to developing countries. Several novel aspects stand out. First is his effort to endogenize public decisions on safety. In Colombia the idea that poverty and inequality are the main causes of violence has been conventional wisdom throughout the 20th century. For several reasons, this type of thinking has weakened the criminal justice system:
- This issue is raised whenever there are legislative efforts to reform the penal code.
- It is part of the ideological discourse that led to different—and quite favorable—legal treatment for political violence.
- It is a common excuse for bad performance among the police, the judiciary, and even the military. Among all these agencies there is a common view that without "social justice" it is impossible to even think of reducing crime.

The second novel issue for developing countries is the discussion of different access to private security. In Colombia rich households spend more on security than do poor households. There even seems to be different security technology in different income groups.

A third issue that is not very well developed in the article but is worth mentioning is the effort to introduce a geographic dimension of crime. One of the main characteristics of violence in Colombia is its strong concentration and persistence in a few specific areas, and even within cities.

## Overlooked Issues

Bourguignon's model and, in general, the economic approach to crime overlook a few issues that seem relevant for analyzing crime and violence in developing countries. The first is the need to emphasize individuals rather than organizations. Related to this is the lack of different treatment for leaders and followers. My impression is that the behavioral model for the leaders of strong illegal organizations is rather weak—and this is the behavior that one wants to be able to predict.

Consider two recent opinions about Yugoslav President Slobodan Milosevic. The first is from the U.S. ambassador to FYR Macedonia: "One of the most irrelevant questions in Yugoslavia today is who is second in charge. There's only one guy. So you have to crawl into his head and move around a lot of cobwebs there to figure out what decision the Yugoslav state is going to take" (*Newsweek*, April 26, 1999, p. 84). The second is from a NATO officer, quite surprised by Milosevic's reaction to the air strikes: "It's hard for a rational person to predict the reaction of irrational people" (Jaime Shea, quoted in *El País*, April 6, 1999, p. 3).

The relevance of a few powerful leaders comes from the fact that criminal activities usually involve increasing returns to scale that lead to some sort of natural monopoly. This is particularly the case for serious, violent crime. The capacity to make credible lethal threats strongly benefits from an established violent reputation. In violent areas an implicit assumption of the economic theory of crime—that there is a state that has a monopoly on coercion and makes policy decisions—may not hold. Thus a useful extension of the distributional crime model proposed by Bourguignon might include another social class: rich, successful criminals.

Another relevant point for developing countries is that the scale and scope of private protection against crime change significantly with violent crime. Inefficient or corrupt authorities may lead citizens or businesses to establish private protection contracts with paramilitary or militia groups. Private protection may extend to private justice. This usually means revenge—and more violence.

In addition, social costs are higher for violent crime. Such costs may become unrelated to real crime rates. Even citizens and businesses that are not victimized become insecure. Production, transaction, and investment decisions may be affected. The two biggest threats to economic performance seem to be very violent crime and the influence of illegal armed organizations. Both phenomena are associated with high homicide rates.

Finally, a weakness in current knowledge about the relationship between inequality and violence is the lack of a convincing body of behavioral theory. Most thinking by economists on this association deals with property crime and with labor market opportunities for the rich and the poor. Bourguignon recognizes this fact. The extension of the argument to more serious crimes, like homicides, is unconvincing—especially when what is going on is young poor men killing young poor men.

A persuasive explanation for this relationship is given not by economics but by evolutionary psychology. The essence of the argument is that competition for resources among young men can only be violent when there is disequilibrium in the mating market. Poor young men kill young poor men when competing for resources only if mating opportunities are scarce and the lack of resources can jeopardize reproductive success (Daly and Wilson 1988). This type of reasoning also addresses one of the best-known facts about violence, and one that has been ignored by economic theory: strong and almost universal gender differences.

## Policy Considerations

My main concern about Bourguignon's article is its implications for public policy. Essentially, there are two types of policy options to deal with crime: government spending (the carrot) and law enforcement (the stick). Although the economic theory of crime has traditionally emphasized law enforcement, in developing countries the general recommendation is for more government spending and less law enforcement.

There is an economic argument for this recommendation. Government spending provides positive externalities for policymakers in terms of political rewards. It will be oversupplied. Law enforcement is essentially a public good. It will be undersupplied. In addition, government spending fits the general recommendation that it is better to prevent than to punish. Even among academics there is a tendency to apologize when showing empirical results that favor law enforcement. Moreover, some more radical views propose that too much law enforcement—that is, political oppression—is one of the main causes of violence.

As Bourguignon argues, there might be some sort of endogenizing of decisions about public safety. Government spending may diminish the desire for law enforcement. In addition, criminal organizations may be powerful enough to prevent more law enforcement. In fact, they may claim that the only way to avoid violence is through more government spending and less law enforcement. I would not want an article like Bourguignon's to end up in the hands of guerrilla groups in Colombia.

For these reasons it is easy to predict that, in terms of policy, the practical implication of Bourguignon's model in developing countries will be more government spending and less law enforcement. More specifically, government spending will be a function of the level of violence. Violent communities will get priority in terms of public transfers at the expense of poor, peaceful communities. This approach distorts incentives and may lead to a vicious circle between violence and government spending. Colombia's experience over the past 10 years suggests this kind of perverse scenario.

I will conclude with a story about a society that has been recognized as a model in terms of institutional design favorable to economic growth. A thousand years ago—long before Adam Smith or concerns about poverty—William the Conqueror began setting up a strong criminal justice system. He showed particular concern for reducing lethal violence. For centuries homicide was considered a tort that could be compensated by an economic retribution, the *wergild,* or blood money, paid to the family of the victim. Revenge was only justified when the wergild was not paid.

William the Conqueror assumed a more active public role against homicide. He outlawed private revenge and began to view violent deaths as an offense against the crown. He even made local communities accountable for the death of any Norman. The *hundreds,* groups of about 100 households, were established as local entities responsible for setting up juries to investigate homicides and report the facts to the royal court.

William's son, Henry I, strengthened royal justice even more. He established the *eyres,* ambulant courts that traveled the kingdom collecting fines for criminal offenses from local communities. These fines were an important fiscal resource for the crown. And although homicide fines were only a small portion of this income, homicides were intensively investigated because the king received the property of convicted felons. A local agent of the crown, the *coroner,* had to investigate every death (Daly and Wilson 1988). It is not easy to determine the model behind these public decisions. But one thing is clear. The English crown not only applied the stick (law enforcement) but also managed to get carrots (government funds) to apply it.

## References

Daly, Martin, and Margo Wilson. 1988. *Homicide.* New York: Aldine de Gruyer.

Michailof, Serge. 1999. "The New Forms of Conflicts in Sub-Saharan Africa." Paper presented at the World Bank workshop on Civil Conflicts, Crime, and Violence in Developing Countries, 22–23 February, Washington, D.C.

Rubio, Mauricio. 1999. *Crimen e impunidad: Precisiones sobre la violencia.* Bogotá: Tercer Mundo–Uniandes.

# Social Exclusion and Ethnic Groups: The Challenge to Economics

*Glenn C. Loury*

*This article discusses the concept of social exclusion with an eye to assessing its utility in the study of ethnic and racial group inequality in the modern nation state. A brief review of the literature and some methodological discussion are offered. The article then examines race-based social exclusion in the United States, showing how race and ethnicity can inhibit the full participation of individuals in a society's economic life. The concept of social capital—the role of nonmarket relations in aiding or impeding investments in human skills—is stressed. The article concludes with a discussion of the legitimacy of race-based remedies for the problem of exclusion.*

The concept of social exclusion has gained wide currency in recent years. But is this concept useful in studying racial and ethnic inequality? Social divisions between racial and ethnic groups—along economic, cultural, and political lines—are a central feature of public life throughout the world. The problem spans geographic and political boundaries and reflects universal social dynamics. Accordingly, much can be learned from comparing such tensions across national boundaries. Inequality and conflict between groups entail not just economic but also, and centrally, sociological and political factors.

Morals and ethics play an essential role in this area. Indeed, a cursory review of the recent literature on social exclusion reveals that normative matters are the primary concern of those invoking this concept. But social exclusion is a loaded term. Use of the term can be a political move—a bid to define the debate in a way that favors progressive, "inclusive," and socially democratic policy. Concerns about the status of minorities, immigrants, women, the unemployed, and indigenous peoples fit nicely into this school of thought. This observation is not intended to signal a lack of sympathy for such political programs. A thorough analysis of the concept of social exclusion simply requires that one attend to its rhetorical as well as its social-scientific dimension.

Glenn C. Loury is professor of economics and director of the Institute on Race and Social Division at Boston University.

## A Brief History of the Concept of Social Exclusion

Use of the term *social exclusion* arose in Europe in the wake of prolonged and large-scale unemployment that provoked criticisms of welfare systems for failing to prevent poverty and for hindering economic development. Silver (1994) stresses that economic restructuring in North American and European countries since the mid-1970s has given rise to such terms as *social exclusion, new poverty,* and *the underclass* to describe the consequent negative effects on the more vulnerable populations in these countries. Such phenomena also intensified the debate over the adequacy of universal social protection policies and fueled growing concern about the distributive fairness of employment and income patterns. Used first in France (Yepez-del-Castillo 1994), the concept spread quickly to the United Kingdom and throughout the European Union.

Social exclusion theorists are concerned with the dissolution of social bonds, the incomplete extension of social rights and protections to all groups, and the links between the idea of exclusion and more conventional understandings of inequality. They draw on theories of poverty, inequality, and disadvantage. In this context policies to aid the excluded have focused on subsidizing jobs and wages, providing housing, and responding to urbanization. The value added of these discussions derives from their focus on the multifaceted nature of deprivation and on analysis of the mechanisms and institutions that function to exclude people (de Haan 1998). The concept of social exclusion has encouraged scholars to consider simultaneously the economic, social, and political dimensions of deprivation. As Bhalla and Lapeyre (1997) stress, this concept encompasses the notion of poverty broadly defined, but is more general in that it explicitly emphasizes poverty's relational as well as its distributional aspects.

The focus on more sociological and institutional aspects of poverty among social exclusion scholars is evident in work on Europe. Evans (1998) explores the institutional basis of social exclusion in Europe, emphasizing the different theoretical approaches to social exclusion in France and the United Kingdom. Buck and Harloe (1998) explore the processes underlying social exclusion in London, arguing that it is best seen in terms of functioning of the labor market, access to state redistribution, and access to communal resources of reciprocity and mutual support. Similarly, Sen (1997) discusses the impact of various inequalities on individuals, focusing on the effect of unemployment on social exclusion, family crises, and lower skills, motivation, and political activity. He also discusses how massive unemployment may intensify racial and gender inequality and emphasizes that these costs will not be adequately reflected in market prices.

Although the theory and concept of social exclusion originated in developed countries, they have been applied extensively to developing countries. (The International Institute for Labour Studies has played a key role in introducing the idea of social exclusion into the developing country debate.) Properly done, such diffusion should attend closely to the context-dependent definitions and meanings involved with an idea like social exclusion. It certainly does not mean the same thing in every culture (de Haan 1998).

Rodgers, Gore, and Figueiredo (1995) is a representative collection applying the concept of social exclusion to developing countries. The papers in the volume look at both conceptual and empirical issues, covering such topics as social change in Africa, the exclusion of poor and indigenous peoples in Latin America, and patterns of inequality in India, Mexico, Russia, and elsewhere. The papers in Burki, Aiyer, and Hommes (1998), the proceedings of a 1996 World Bank conference on development in Latin America and the Caribbean, focus on poverty, inequality, and social exclusion in the region. Topics include rural poverty, the conditions of poor children, labor reform and job creation, the uneven coverage of social services, urban violence and the role of social capital, and the impoverishment of indigenous peoples in Ecuador. Thorne (1999) explores the social exclusion of indigenous peoples in Brazil and the impact on their physical and social environments of World Bank–sponsored development projects.

## Limits of Social Science to Address Social Exclusion

Many approaches have been offered to mitigate social exclusion. Those that draw on the science of economics, however, have some shortcomings worth noting. Acknowledging these shortcomings is not to dismiss economic science as being irrelevant to the problem. Rather, it is a way of urging some caution and humility among economists as we apply our analytical tools to the profound moral and political problems raised by this phenomenon. Here I suggest some reasons for proceeding cautiously, by reflecting on factors that may limit the successful application of scientific ideas.

### Is "Good Science" Good Enough?

That "good science" might prove to be an antidote to group hatred has been a hope of progressive social observers throughout the modern age. The story goes something like this. Antagonism toward a particular "race" may involve supposedly objective claims about the nature of people of that race—about their moral deficiencies or intellectual inferiority, for example. These claims can be subjected to scientific scrutiny and refuted. Confronted with these scientific arguments, rational people might then alter the beliefs on which their racial enmity rests. In this way sound science, a value-neutral enterprise, can produce the ethically desirable result of undermining racial antagonism by replacing prejudice and stereotypes with data and rigorous analysis.

This story is plausible, with ample historical precedent. It is only made more compelling when one recalls how totalitarian political regimes—particularly the Nazis—have used "bad science" to justify their racist political programs. If science falls under the influence of a political agenda and ceases to be an autonomous intellectual activity—if it becomes bad science—then it can abet the spread of racial hatred. Thus proper scientific argument can foster racial tolerance, while the abuse of science can lead to disturbing results.

Yet these outcomes are by no means guaranteed. Whether science is good or bad depends on its conformity with disciplines and methods that practitioners see as meeting their standards of evidence and argument. This essentially technical matter has relatively little moral content. In any event, scientific argument is a specialized discourse within a narrow community of investigators governed by strict norms and disciplines. Indeed, it is an indication that a field has matured as a science when its discourse takes on the quality of what might be called sociolinguistic closure. Thomas Kuhn (1962) stressed just this point in his influential work, *The Structure of Scientific Revolutions.*

On the other hand, hatred, enmity, antagonism, and conflict among racial groups are universal cultural phenomena, observable through the ages and still prevalent today. This is so despite the fact that science has more authority than ever before. In fact, although population geneticists declare that there are no "races" in an objective, biological sense, the social and political construct of race continues to reproduce itself across generations in many societies. Racial identity is a stubborn reality, one that has survived the demise of the 19th century anthropology from which it arose. So, as a cultural and historical matter, it seems safe to say that racial hatred will not be vanquished by the steady march forward of scientific discovery.

What matters most for dispelling racial hatred is not what scientists say to each other, but what the general public understands them to have said. To gain insight into the relationship between scientific argument and persistent racial conflict, one needs to focus on broad cultural appropriations of scientific understanding. Ultimately, the hope that science can dispel racial enmity is grounded in the belief that the authority of science can be conferred on a particular kind of cultural work, that good science can make people more tolerant of human difference, more open-minded, less parochial, less nationalistic, less chauvinistic, less certain about inherited cultural verities. Gauging the potential for scientific argument to have this influence requires attending to the interpretive discourses through which the results of scientific work are diffused into the larger culture. Unlike arguments within scientific communities, this cross-boundary discourse is inherently, inevitably political. As such, whatever the quality of the scientific work informing this interpretive discourse, there can be no certainty that preexisting racist ideology will not contaminate that discourse.

Does this mean that the age-old conundrum of intergroup conflict is, at its base, a problem for the humanities, not the sciences? True, humanistic inquiries are constrained by facts about the world that only structured scientific inquiry can uncover. Quantitative magnitudes cannot simply be set to whatever value one would like. But in the end, when we try to find ways to dispel racial hatred, we are engaged in an enterprise of narration, interpretation, and moral justification.

In this connection it is crucial to note that what we say about "the way society works" is itself a social datum, powerfully influencing the workings of society. For example, "capitalism is superior to socialism" may be true about a world inhabited by the kinds of people produced by late 20th century capitalism, but it need not be a law of nature, true for all times and places. The narrative rationalizations constructed by and for the inhabitants of our liberal, democratic, capitalist states partly serve to make that statement true. In this respect, today's much-derided Marxists are right to insist that while the consciousness of humans determines their existence, it is also true that the conditions of humans' social existence help determine their consciousness. (Roemer 1981, pp. 53–54, provides a typical formulation of this doctrine.)

When our formal methods in the social sciences seduce us into believing that we are engaged in a value-neutral enterprise—one with a clear separation between subject and object, as in physics or chemistry—I believe we are gravely misled. Formal rigor cannot substitute for taking responsibility for the inescapable normative dimensions of our work.

This methodological point can be illustrated with an example from my own discipline, economics, where the central metaphor is Adam Smith's unseen or invisible hand. The preeminent modern exponent of this idea was Friedrich von Hayek, who introduced the notion of spontaneous order to refer to the social products that emerge from human interaction but not from human design—the order that knows no author. As Hayek (1994, p. 56) put it, "that the division of labor has reached the extent which makes modern civilization possible we owe to the fact that it did not have to be consciously created but that man tumbled on a method by which the division of labor could be extended far beyond the limits within which it could have been planned." Spontaneous order thus refers to the unconscious collaboration of individuals through the market, leading to the solution to problems of resource allocation that would have to be consciously solved in a planned system.

Hayek's fundamental point, therefore, is that such a consciously planned solution is impossible in practice, and our best course is to rely on "spontaneous order." This is obviously a deeply political claim. It can be profoundly persuasive as a description of many economic situations. Yet, as the legal scholar Cass Sunstein (1996) has observed, for Hayek the economic argument was less important than the moral one: spontaneous order promotes his ultimate value—freedom. We need not go far to see the significance of these ideas in our daily lives. Are these scientific, philosophical, or religious claims? Are they amenable to refutation on the basis of evidence? When we hear debates about the limits of the welfare state, we can discern this Hayekian metaphor of spontaneous order, invoked by advocates who see this as a "truth" about society established through the scientific study of history. Which is to say that it is not only Marxists who fall prey to what Karl Popper (1957) called the "historicists' fallacy."

## *Is Economic Analysis Thorough Enough?*

All this supports that point that economic science without serious political reflection is a conceptually impoverished framework in which to debate social policy. In the particulars of governing, the economist's view of the world can be narrow and reductive. Policymaking involves more than simply providing technical solutions to the problems of governance. It also involves taking symbolic actions that express a people's values and beliefs. And it is about doing justice. As any good politician knows, a policy's cost-benefit effect may pale next to this communicative role. Yet what might be called the expressive content of public action—the message to the political community conveyed by the letter of a law, the behavior of a bureaucracy, or the public utterances of a political leader—has no place in conventional economic models.

For example, criminals are punished not simply to deter crime but also to signal a polity's collective abhorrence of the offending act. Conversely, punishment is sometimes mitigated or forgone—even though that might blunt the deterrent effect—to show mercy or do justice. In no jurisdiction in the world does the political viability of capital punishment turn on whether it, in fact, deters murder. The more compelling argument over the state-sanctioned killing of criminal offenders begins by asking, "What manner of people are we, who destroy human life in public rituals of revenge?" This most decidedly is not a question about incentives.

To take another example, the conservative drift of U.S. social welfare policy in recent years was driven primarily by the desire of many Americans to state, unequivocally, what they can rightly require of public assistance recipients. Whether we like it or not, for most people such beliefs—about who deserves to be helped and how we should separate public from private responsibilities—have very little to do with analytical judgments. Indeed, even with experienced analysts one often finds the influence running in the opposite direction—from basic value commitments to conclusions about cause and effect.

Conventional economic analysis has little to say about this kind of thing, starting as it does from the assumption that individual preferences among alternative courses of action are given and lie beyond the scope of respectable intellectual discussion. An alternative view, however, takes the principal objective of policy to be altering individuals' views about how to live their lives. That is, the expressive content of public action can also serve a pedagogic function—by showing citizens how to lead better lives, as individuals and together within the political community. This too is a consideration missing from the economist's conceptual toolkit.

But there is more than a conceptual poverty of economic discourse (and much other social science). There is a moral impoverishment as well. This seems an important point to raise in a discussion of social exclusion, which, as I have emphasized, unavoidably entails moral concerns. The accounts of human behavior on which we social scientists rely are clinical and abstract. The human beings in these accounts are soulless creatures—utility-maximizing buyers and sellers, behaviorally conditioned violators of the law, genetically predisposed substance abusers. This brand of social science propounds theories about human action that omit any consideration of what most makes us human—our awareness of our mortality and our fitful, uncertain, often unsuccessful attempts to give our brief lives meaning that transcends our pitifully brief existences. This omission has left social scientists less equipped to prescribe remedies for the most serious problems confronting our societies.

Consider an example. Much has been written by U.S. behavioral scientists in recent decades about how parents discipline their children and about the consequences of such behavior for the sociability of young people. Criminologists have argued that the regular provision of modest positive and negative reinforcements for good and bad actions lowers the risk of antisocial behavior as a child enters adolescence. Once allowed to develop, these antisocial behaviors are alleged to be difficult to change. So, if the character-shaping tutelage of vigilant parents is missing in early childhood, the young adult who emerges may turn out to be incorrigible.

This is a matter of no small policy significance because, in the most disadvantaged quarters of many societies, millions of children grow to maturity in the absence of conscientiously applied parental discipline. Yet many people in various civic institutions work in the most marginal communities to turn these "incorrigibles" in a different direction. These inspired activists confront young adults who did not receive proper nutrition in infancy, who experienced insufficient verbal stimulation as toddlers, who never learned to internalize the difference between right and wrong, and who have committed the kinds of acts that incorrigible, undisciplined adolescents commit. Yet despite all that, many young people are considerably aided by the activists' interventions.

What is interesting to me as a social scientist is the antideterministic character of this way of thinking. Most social science theories say, in effect, that material conditions mediated by social institutions cause us to behave in a certain way. Yet surely it is more plausible to hold that material and institutional givens can at best establish only a fairly wide range in which behavior must lie and that specific actions in this range depend on factors of motivation, will, and spirit—that is, on factors having to do with what a person takes to be the source of meaning in life, with what animates that person at the deepest level.

If this is correct, then the crucial implication is that the behavior of freely choosing, socially situated, spiritually endowed human beings will in some essential way be unpredictable, even mysterious. For if human behavior is largely a consequence of what people understand to be meaningful, then the social interaction and mutual stimulation that generate and sustain patterns of belief in human communities become centrally important. But these processes of persuasion, conformity, conversion, myth construction, and the like are open-ended. They are at best only weakly constrained by material conditions.

That is, while what we believe about the transcendent powerfully shapes how we act in a given situation, these beliefs are not a necessary consequence of our situation. We can always agree to believe differently or more fervently—particularly if those with whom we are most closely connected are undergoing a similar transformation. Religious revivals and reformations can sweep through our ranks and change our collective view of the world almost overnight. We can be moved to make enormous sacrifices on behalf of abstract goals. As former Czech President Vaclav Havel (1992, p. 145) has said, "the essential aims of life are present naturally in every person. In everyone there is some longing for humanity's rightful dignity, for moral integrity, for free expression of being and a sense of transcendence over the world of existences."

I admit to being deeply moved by this fact about human experience—that we are spiritual creatures, generators of meaning, beings that must not and cannot "live by bread alone." One can readily see the power for good—and for ill—of communal organization acting through collectivities that share understandings about the meaning of their lives. This all-too-human search for meaning and significance often results in ethnic or racial solidarity and its complement—intergroup conflict and antagonism. Any social science that does not treat this aspect of the human drama with utmost seriousness will fail to do justice to its subject of study and to the national communities that look to it for advice on a host of social ills.

## "Race" and Social Exclusion in the United States

I now wish to carry forward this discussion in the context of a specific example—that having to do with "race" in the United States. I rely on this case because it is most familiar to me, and permits me to speak with some specificity about the mechanism of exclusion and the extent to which factors of race, ethnicity, and identity are an important aspect of the problem. In doing so, however, I want readers not to lose sight of the fact that similar processes are at work in many other social contexts in both developing and industrial nations. I see the value of the discussion that follows, then, as being suggestive of the more general dynamics underlying social exclusion in many societies.

### *Broadening the Focus beyond "Discrimination"*

The economic literature on discrimination tends to focus on the different treatment of individuals—based on race, gender, or ethnicity—in labor, credit, and consumer goods markets. This is obviously a serious matter, and there is ample evidence in the United States and elsewhere that such disparities are real and quantitatively important as a source of intergroup economic inequalities (Modood and others 1997; Wilson 1996). Nevertheless, when considering ethnic group inequality, economists should look beyond what happens in markets.

Of course, economists tend to focus on how markets work or fail. Economic theory suggests that discrimination based on gender or racial identity should be arbitraged away in markets of competitive sellers, employers, and lenders. But such discrimination is readily observed in society, and this anomaly attracts attention. Critics of neoclassical economics seize on it, and defenders of that orthodoxy seek to explain it away. Thus evidence that wage differences between the races or sexes have declined, after controlling for worker productivity, is supposed to vindicate the economist's belief in market forces.

This way of approaching the problem is too narrow. With wages, for example, the usual focus is on the demand side of the labor market—employers either have a "taste" for discrimination or use race as a proxy for unobserved variables that imply lower productivity for minorities. The primary normative claim in this approach is that such discrimination is morally offensive, a legitimate object of regulatory intervention, and a significant contributor to racial and gender inequality. But implicit in this claim is the notion that if inequality were due to supply-side differences—in the skills presented to employers by blacks and whites, for example—the resulting disparity would not raise the same moral issues or give a comparable warrant for intervention. There is a comparable view in housing markets—that residential segregation induced by the discriminatory behavior of realtors is a bigger problem than segregation that comes about because of the freely made decisions of market participants.

I propose a shift in emphasis. In the United States market discrimination against blacks still exists, but such discrimination is not as significant an explanation for racial inequality as in decades past. This calls into question the conventional wisdom on equal opportunity policy—that eliminating racial discrimination in markets will eventually resolve racial economic inequality. Much evidence supports the view that the substantial gap in skills between blacks and whites is a key factor accounting for racial inequality in the labor market. Yet this skills gap is itself the result of social exclusion processes that deserve explicit study and policy remediation. The gap reflects social and cultural factors—geographic segregation, deleterious social norms and peer influences, poor education—that have a racial dimension (Cutler and Glaeser 1997; Akerlof 1997). Group inequality such as that between blacks and whites in the United States cannot be fully understood, or remedied, with a focus on market discrimination alone.

There is a long history of justified concern that focusing less on employer discrimination and more on skill differences could foster dangerous stereotypes and undermine arguments for policies to narrow the racial wage gap. In the decade after U.S. antidiscrimination laws were enacted in the 1960s, researchers like Wilson (1978) who began to find evidence of a decline in labor market discrimination were sometimes criticized for giving aid and comfort to political conservatives. But this reaction accepts the implicit normative assumption that racial inequality based on skill disparities is not as important a moral problem, warranting as vigorous a corrective intervention, as inequality based on wage discrimination in the labor market. That assumption is not compelling—and should be challenged.

## The Importance of Social Networks

Economic analysis begins with a depersonalized agent who acts more or less independently to make the best of the opportunities at hand. This way of thinking has been fruitful for economics, but it cannot fully capture the ways that racial inequality persists over time. Individuals are embedded in complex networks of affiliations: they are members of nuclear and extended families, they belong to religious and linguistic groupings, they have ethnic and racial identities, they are attached to particular localities. Each individual is socially situated, and one's location within the network of social affiliations substantially affects one's access to various resources.

Opportunity travels along these social networks. Thus a newborn is severely handicapped if its parents are uninterested in (or incapable of) fostering intellectual development in the first years of life. A talented adolescent whose social peer group disdains the activities that must be undertaken for that talent to flourish is at risk of not achieving his or her full potential. An unemployed person without friends or relatives already at work in a certain industry may never hear about the job opportunities available there. An individual's inherited social situation plays a major role in determining economic success.

In earlier work I have suggested an extension of human capital theory designed to provide a richer context in which to analyze group inequality (Loury 1977, 1981, 1987). This theory builds on observations about the importance of family and community background to individual achievement. A person's investment in productive skills depends on position in the social structure, because imperfect capital markets for education loans necessitate reliance on finance through personal ties, social externalities are mediated by residential location and peer associations, and psychological processes shape a person's outlook on life. As a result familial and communal resources—social and cultural capital—explicitly influence the acquisition of human capital. In this view an important part of racial inequality arises from the way that geographic and social segregation along racial lines makes an individual's opportunities to acquire skills depend on skill attainments by others in the same social group.

The literature offers fairly strong support for this view of the lagging economic position of blacks in the United States. Akerlof (1997) provides a theoretical argument, supported by a wealth of evidence from social anthropology, for the notion that concerns for status and conformity are primary determinants of education attainment, childbearing, and law-breaking behavior. Anderson (1990) provides an ethnographic account of life in inner-city Philadelphia, where peer influences significantly constrain the acquisition of skills by adolescents. Waldinger (1996), in a study of immigrant labor in New York City, concludes that poor blacks suffer less from the racism of employers than from their lack of access to the ethnic networks through which workers are recruited for jobs in construction and service industries. Cutler and Glaeser (1997), comparing U.S. cities with varying concentrations of different races, find blacks to be significantly disadvantaged by residential segregation. The authors estimate that a 13 percent reduction in segregation would eliminate about one-third of the black-white gap in schooling, employment, earnings, and unwed pregnancy rates. Mills and Lubuele (1997, p. 735) argue that a central problem for students of urban poverty is explaining why "low income black residents actually or potentially eligible for jobs that have moved to suburbs [have] not followed such jobs to the suburbs."

All this suggests the inadequacy of seeing discrimination or antidiscrimination efforts only within a market framework. Conventional economic discrimination against minority groups is rarely the primary source of group disparities. Moreover, available methods for fighting such discrimination have little power to reduce the economic gap between groups. Given the information asymmetry between employers and enforcement agents, there are limits to how aggressive antidiscrimination policy can be before significant efficiency costs arise (Coate and Loury 1993a). If the concern is economic inequality between groups, then looking mainly through the lens of wage and price discrimination is unlikely to bring the problem into focus.

In the United States there is another, more fundamental reason to broaden the discussion of group inequality beyond market discrimination. In cities across the country and in rural areas of the Old South the situation of the black underclass and, increasingly, of the black lower working class, is bad and getting worse. This is certainly a race-related problem. But the plight of the underclass should not be seen as another (albeit severe) instance of economic inequality, American-style—conventional market discrimination is only a small part of it.

These black ghetto-dwellers are a people apart, susceptible to stereotyping, ridiculed for their cultural styles, socially isolated, experiencing an internalized sense of helplessness and despair, with limited access to communal networks of mutual assistance (Anderson 1990; Wilson 1996). Their purported criminality, sexual profligacy, and intellectual inadequacy are frequent objects of public derision. They suffer a pariah status (Goffman 1963). This is social exclusion with a vengeance. It does not require extraordinary powers of perception to see how this degradation relates to the history of black-white race relations in the United States.

Here is where the implicit normative model that accompanies the emphasis on market discrimination is most seriously flawed. Given social segregation along racial lines, the effects of past discrimination can persist over time by adversely affecting the skills acquired by the offspring of those discriminated against. Moreover, discrimination in one market can leave its victim less well prepared to compete in another. Ethically, the cumulative impact of an act of discrimination—over time and across markets—should be no less problematic than was the original offense.

The U.S. civil rights struggle, which won for blacks the right to be free of discrimination, failed to secure a national commitment to eradicating the effects of discrimination that had already occurred. When those effects manifest themselves in patterns of behavior among poor blacks that lead to seemingly self-imposed limits on their acquisition of skills, many observers who think only in terms of market discrimination argue that society is not at fault. This is the grain of truth in the insistence of some observers that, while overt racism was the problem in the past, behavioral differences lie at the root of racial inequality in today's United States (Thernstrom and Thernstrom 1997).

But the deeper truth is that, for quite some time, the communal experience of the descendants of African slaves has been shaped by political, social, and economic institutions that by any measure must be seen as oppressive. When we look at "underclass culture" in the U.S. cities of today, we see a product of that oppressive history. In the face of the despair, violence, and self-destructive behavior of these people, it is morally obtuse and scientifically naïve to argue, as some conservatives do, that if "those people" would just get their acts together we would not have such a horrific problem. Yet for the same reason it is a mistake to argue, as some liberals do, that the primary causes of continuing racial inequality are ongoing market discrimination.

Significant market failures, having little to do with economic discrimination as conventionally understood, play a powerful role in perpetuating racial inequality. Consider the problem of residential segregation (Massey and Denton 1993). Compelling theoretical arguments (Schelling 1978, ch. 4) and recent computer simulations (Wayner 1998) show that even a mild desire among people to live near members of their own race can lead to a strikingly severe degree of segregation. Adding class concerns to these models only strengthens their predictions of geographic clustering. Moreover, residential location is not the only venue in which segregation occurs. Linguists studying speech patterns in urban centers have uncovered strong evidence of race and class separation (Labov 1982). Ethnic group differences in communication styles seem to play an important role in accounting for the adverse labor market outcomes of low-income blacks (Lang 1986; Cornell and Welch 1996; Charles 1997; Wilson 1996).

Even though social segregation and exclusion based on race and ethnicity may be a natural result of nondiscriminatory market interactions, the consequences could still be morally disturbing. And even if those consequences manifest themselves mainly on the supply side of the labor market, a strong case could still be made for doing something about them. That case need not be based solely on equity grounds. Indeed, once it is admitted that preferences and investment in skills of market participants are influenced by social and psychological externalities, the conventional results in welfare economics on the efficiency of market outcomes are no longer generally valid.

As an example of a social externality, consider the dissonance associated with holding values at some distance from one's peers. If groups help sustain norms, with individuals looking to the apparent preferences of their peers to infer appropriate behavior, then there is a possibility of multiple self-sustaining norms (Akerlof 1997). Generalizations about differences among groups in attitudes toward work, family life, criminal participation, and the like may thus be empirically correct but morally irrelevant. Moreover, with multiple self-sustaining norms, acting to shift the norm can lead to Pareto improvements in welfare (Sunstein 1996).

A psychological externality can occur when individuals draw on their own encounters with the market, and on the encounters of others to whom they are socially connected, to reach conclusions about, say, the extent to which effort accounts for market rewards—as opposed to ability or luck. In this scenario the degree to which an individual believes that bad personal outcomes are due to inadequate personal "effort" can depend on the aggregate experience of other members of the group. Self-fulfilling pessimism about the returns to effort for certain activities, like academic pursuits, are possible in a model like this (Steele 1992).

I am not suggesting that these social and psychological externalities are the primary explanation for racial inequality. But they are not implausible accounts of how social segregation might support behavior patterns that lead to skill gaps between racial groups. Furthermore, these scenarios (and others that could be sketched) suggest that policies directed at reducing skill gaps might be just as morally required, and even more effective, than policies directed against such market discrimination as may still exist.

## "Exclusion" in the U.S. Inner City

Most social analysis of "race" in U.S. life goes on at a macroscopic level, citing the changing population composition, the loss of jobs in core industries in central cities, and the incidence among blacks and whites of various indicators of disadvantage. The perspective of these analyses is aggregative and systemic, generalizing from broad patterns. University of Pennsylvania sociologist Elijah Anderson (1990, 1999) takes a different approach, and his work is worthy of close attention. His research method involves careful and extensive observation of the face-to-face interactions of inhabitants of inner-city neighborhoods, with due attention to the larger economic and political context in which these encounters occur. His work provides a participant-observer's account of social life in a U.S. urban community mixed along racial and class lines. This is ethnographic work in the fine tradition of William Whyte's *Street Corner Society* (1943) and Elliot Liebow's *Tally's Corner* (1967). Surpassing these other works, however, Anderson's great achievement is to weave together the data of ethnographic observation with a coherent theory of how people encounter each other in public places.

In *Streetwise* (1990) Anderson builds on the work of the great sociologist Erving Goffman's *The Presentation of Self in Everyday Life* (1959). Anderson presents a theory revolving around the problem of "decoding" that all social actors must solve when meeting others in public (see, for example, the related work in economics of Cornell and Welch 1996). One cannot be entirely certain of the character or intent of "the other"; assessments have to be based on the processing of information gleaned from an examination of the visible behavior of those being encountered. The context of the meeting—time of day, physical setting, whether the individual is alone or in a group, and so on—will affect how these external clues are read. As an encounter unfolds, communication between the parties, ranging from a meeting of eyes (or the avoidance of same) to an exchange of greetings, permits further inferences to be drawn. Race and ethnic identity—often easily and instantly ascertainable characteristics—can be expected to play a large role in this game of inference. Social class—as conveyed by dress, manner, occupation, speech—will also be important. An individual's experience of the social environment will be governed by how those encountered in public negotiate these meetings.

Anderson describes in elegant detail the rules of public etiquette, norms of mutual expectation, conventions of deference, methods of self-protection, strategies of turf-claiming, signals of intention, and deciphering of cues, mistakes, biases, bluffs, threats, and self-fulfilling prophecies implicit in the interactions he observes. He identifies social roles, public routines, and behavioral devices common to the encounters he chronicles. All these routines are key features of how racial groups interact in the modern U.S. city.

More recently, Anderson's (1999) work has focused on face-to-face social interactions in a low-income, racially segregated African-American community. His book, *The Code of the Streets*, presents the results of this investigation. The analysis relies heavily on the concept of "the streets," the social environment where people live and interact. These are poor communities—dilapidated, dirty, noisy, and unsafe. But there is a high degree of sociability: the neighbors know each other, and people are often in the street. Most jobs are menial, with low wages. Drugs are a major source of income. Welfare, aid from the state, is also important. Men, especially in the roles of husbands and fathers, are scarce.

These are tough places. Money is in short supply. The games and scams that people play can lure and ensnare those who are not streetwise. One boy may try to take another's sneakers or his jacket. Another boy may flaunt his gold chain, wearing it openly, daring someone to try to take it as a way of signaling his toughness. There is an air of incivility, especially at night. Some of the older residents are distressed by that, more committed to values of "decency" than are many of the young. But their influence in setting the tone of the community seems to be waning.

There is what one might call, and this is my term, a "moral ecology" of the streets. One of the most important insights from Anderson's work is that ghetto neighborhoods are highly heterogeneous places (for further evidence in this regard, see Newman 1999). There are people of different generations, different family structures, different degrees of economic stability. Clashes of values result from this heterogeneity. "Street" versus "decent" values is how Anderson poses the opposition. There is a complex interaction or tension between these value systems, especially for the young. Young men and women, boys and girls, want to be thought of as "hip," not socially "lame." And yet, being hip may mean taking on "street values."

Adolescent peer groups are crucial in Anderson's account. Children sometimes raise themselves. There are many single parents, and even when parents are married, they are working and away from home much of the time. Children spend a lot of time on the street. They may be more influenced by their peer group than by what goes on in the family, especially in families driven by so-called street values. Nevertheless, there is a culture of decency, connected with close, extended families: families where the work ethic is important, where getting ahead is important, where religious influences remain. Parents are seen struggling for the hearts and minds of their children as the tensions between decent and street values exert influence.

Role models of decency are in short supply. The "old heads" about whom Anderson wrote in *Streetwise*—mature, stable, and influential residents looked up to by the young—are not as important in these communities as they once may have been. The new role models—young drug dealers—are increasingly influential, and the scarcity of work is taken to be central to this transformation. As Anderson (1999, p. 325) writes:

> A vicious cycle has thus been formed. The hopelessness many young innercity black men and women feel, largely as a result of endemic joblessness and alienation, fuels the violence they engage in. This violence then serves to confirm the negative feelings many whites and some middle-class blacks harbor toward the ghetto poor, further legitimizing the oppositional culture and the code of the street for many alienated young blacks. But when jobs disappear and people are left poor, highly concentrated, and hopeless, the way is paved for the underground economy to become a way of life, an unforgiving way of life organized around a code of violence and predatory activity.

Moreover, Anderson finds in his ethnographic investigations that without work, stable family relations are no longer a credible source of a man's self-esteem. Young men come to emphasize sexual prowess and conquest, in reference to their male peer group, as the source of their sense of worth. They congregate on street corners boasting of their exploits. In this way they build each other up by boasting of what they have managed to gain in their interactions with young women. "Casual sex with as many women as possible, impregnating one or more and getting them to have your baby, brings a boy the ultimate in esteem from his peers and makes him a man. Casual sex, therefore, is fraught with social significance for the boy who has little or no hope of achieving financial stability and, hence, cannot see himself taking care of a family" (Anderson 1999, p. 177). This becomes a "game," a game in which girls are lured by older boys who promise love and marriage. Boys want prestige among their peers, lots of sex, lots of women. Girls want what Anderson calls "the Dream." Girls dream of a husband, of security, of the middle-class life.

Sex often results in pregnancy in this world. Girls may not actively be trying to prevent it. With the dream of a mate, a girl may be indifferent to the possibility of pregnancy, even if it is not likely that pregnancy will lead to marriage. A large part of the girl's identity is provided by the baby and the peer groups among the girls in these communities. Becoming a mother can, Anderson says, be a strong play for authority, maturity, and respect in these communities. "The baby may bring her a certain amount of praise, (in the past) a steady welfare check, and a measure of independence...As she becomes older and wiser, she can use her (welfare) income to turn the tables, attracting her original man or other men" (1999, p. 178)

The girl's outlook is crucial to describing what her behavior will be. Important factors include her education, her self-respect, her wisdom, and whether she has had mentoring from "decent" role models within "decent" families, where there may be a husband and wife present or a strong single mother getting support from her extended family. The parents may be able to instill some sense of hope, a positive sense of the future, a healthy self-respect. Siblings who have succeeded may also help to achieve this. Ministers and teachers can play this role by communicating the expectation that girls do something with their lives.

But where such expectations are not communicated, where some sense of hope or possibility about the future is not present, the prospect of having a baby outside of marriage, far from being regarded as a negative, may be seen as a positive. And that can be reinforced not only by the financial benefits that might come from the state, meager as they are, for support for the child, but perhaps more important in the world being described, by the status these girls gain with their peers, by the extent to which they are affirmed in the peer group for having the child.

## Positive Discrimination: Group-Based Remedies for Social Exclusion

What should be done about the inequality that arises due to exclusion from opportunities for human development associated with race and ethnicity? Some observers suggest that special assistance should be targeted to individuals in the excluded groups—that, in effect, they should be the beneficiaries of "discrimination" in their favor, to offset the effects of historically practiced discrimination against them. This policy is controversial. Many critics object that "two wrongs do not make a right"—that while we cannot undo the exclusionary practices of the past, we should not add to this injustice with present-day discrimination, however noble its purpose. I take issue with this position, and in the discussion that follows explain how remedial discrimination can be justified.

### Should "Color Blindness" Be the Goal?

There are two key distinctions to emphasize in the debate about whether distributive goals intended to reduce group inequality should be pursued through "positive discrimination": instruments are not ends in themselves, and the public use of group-based instruments does not determine whether citizens embrace group-based identity and consciousness. The color blindness sought by antipreference crusaders deals with the instrumentality in public action (and, admittedly, there may be reasons for these instruments to be color blind in some cases). But equating such a consideration with whether the society is color blind entails a serious conceptual error. Accordingly, I reserve the term *color blind* to refer to eschewing the use of race when implementing a policy and use a different term—*color neutral*—to indicate unconcern about race when determining the goals of policy action. For example, if a school admissions or employment selection rule depends only on traits that are identity-independent, it is a color blind policy—for it can administered in the absence of racial information.

Color neutrality is morally the more fundamental notion, for it assesses a policy in terms of its consequences for the members of racial groups. In the United States the so-called War on Drugs has been color neutral with a vengeance. But has it been just? University of Minnesota criminologist Michael Tonry, in his book *Malign Neglect* (1995), suggests not. In fact, Tonry denounces the blatant color neutrality of U.S. drug policy—a policy adopted without any apparent concern for its racial impact.

His point, expressed by means of an analogy, is something that everybody knows: prostitution takes place "by the docks." One does not look for prostitutes on the streets of wealthy communities, though certainly many of their patrons live there. One looks by the docks. Likewise, where else but in the bombed-out, abandoned buildings of undersocialized and disconnected communities of despair, where else but among the brutalized and oppressed, where else but among the underclass would one expect illicit drug traffic to take place? Thus, if the government undertakes as a matter of policy to incarcerate everyone found trafficking drugs on the streets, it is a predictable consequence that the results will be racially disparate—massively so. Given that this is knowable, should the government decide not to attend to it, Tonry argues, it will have practiced a form of malign neglect. But in so doing, no color blind norms have been violated. The policy can be administered without racial information.

This example shows that the key moral issue is often about color neutrality, not color blindness. The deepest ethical questions bearing on racial group inequality are not about whether instruments of public action use racial information, but about whether appropriate concern has been taken for the disparate racial consequences of what may be color blind actions. Yet those who insist on color neutrality (as a corollary of their commitment to color blindness) avoid making the most relevant arguments when the question is framed entirely in terms of whether administrative procedures are color blind. They escape having to explain why society should be indifferent if one-third of young black men in inner cities are in prison. They forgo the need to defend a regime in which the hedonism of a privileged middle class engenders a public response that imposes most of its costs on a vulnerable and weak minority population—balancing the cultural budget on the backs of the poor, so to speak. They avoid the need to justify why historically determined racial stigmas should be reproduced in our enlightened time through race-neutral public action.

## Reasons to Care Explicitly about Group Inequality

RACIAL IDENTITIES MATTER. In 1996 the conservative U.S. federal judge Richard Posner, ruling in the case of *Wittmer v. Peters,* upheld the preferential hiring of a black prison guard in an Illinois boot camp for young offenders. He argued that, with an inmate population that was three-quarters black, and given that "aversive training" methods familiar to Marine enlistees were to be used at the boot camp, the state might have a compelling and thus constitutionally justifiable interest in providing for racial diversity in the camp's officer corps.

Faced with such examples, supporters of color blindness invariably reply that race here simply serves as a proxy for some nonracial trait—like the ability to win the trust of black inmates. But this response is insufficient, for the crux of the matter is not the state's use of race as a proxy for some desirable characteristic in an employee, but rather the tendency of some citizens to view the world through a racially tinted lens. In the boot camp young inmates are bullied mercilessly by guards who either have their best interests at heart or do not. If black youths refuse to believe that this bullying is for some useful purpose when none of the guards are black, then successful training requires a racially diverse staff. This is true no matter how sophisticated the prison personnel office may be at discovering, without using race, whether an applicant truly cares about his prospective charges.

GROUP IDENTITY CONVEYS INFORMATION. Another reason to care about racial inequality is that race is an important source of information in many situations. Race is an easily observable trait that is correlated with some hard to observe traits about which employers, lenders, police officers, and others are concerned. Evidence from employer interviews indicates that both black and white employers are reluctant to hire young black urban males who exhibit lower-class behavioral styles. Racial identity is also used as information by police in a variety of ways. Some evidence indicates that it shapes their law enforcement decisions. Indeed, the dramatic disparity between races in rates of arrest and incarceration for criminal offenses must be taken into account when discussing racial differences in the labor market experiences of males, thought the direction of causality is difficult to untangle.

Racial-statistical discrimination can be quite damaging to both the efficiency of market allocations and to equity. This is due to the real possibility that the empirically valid statistical generalizations lying at the heart of such discrimination can become self-fulfilling. There is an information externality present whenever decisionmakers take actions based on group inferences. It is not difficult to provide straightforward economic accounts of how this process might work in a variety of contexts.

Suppose only a few taxi drivers will pick up young black men after a certain hour. Given that behavior by taxi drivers as a class, it is plausible through a process of adverse selection that the "types" of young black men attempting to hail taxis during those hours include a large portion of potential robbers. This makes it rational to avoid them. But if most drivers willingly picked up young black men, it might induce a less threatening set of black males to select taxi transportation after dark, confirming the rationality of the drivers' more tolerant behavior.

Or, suppose employers believe that blacks are more likely to be low-effort trainees than are whites. They will set a lower threshold for blacks on the number of mistakes needed to trigger dismissal because they will be quicker to infer that black workers have not tried hard enough to learn the job. But knowing that they are more likely to be fired for making a few mistakes, more black employees may elect not to exert high effort during training, thus confirming the employers' initial beliefs.

Or, if car dealers believe that black buyers have higher reservation prices than do whites, dealers will be tougher when bargaining with blacks than with whites. Given this experience of tough bargaining, a black buyer anticipates less favorable alternative opportunities and higher search costs than does a white buyer, and so may rationally agree to a higher price. This behavior confirms the dealers' initial presumption that racial identity predicts bargaining power.

Such stories have a ring of truth about them. The key to all these examples is their self-reinforcing nature: they begin with racial beliefs that then bring about their own statistical confirmation. These examples are not unrelated to historical problems of race as they have developed in U.S. society. Race is an easily discernable characteristic that has salience in our culture, making it operate powerfully in many venues because it is common knowledge that people are taking it into account.

SOCIAL NETWORKS (AGAIN) AFFECT OPPORTUNITIES. Yet another reason to care about group inequality is that race influences the social networks open to individuals, and these networks have a major effect on individuals' opportunities. Two observations are key to this argument. First, all societies exhibit significant social segmentation. People make choices about whom to befriend, whom to marry, where to live, to which schools to send their children, and so on. Factors like race, ethnicity, social class, and religious affiliation influence these choices of association.

Second, the processes through which individuals develop their productive capacities are shaped by custom, convention, and social norms and are not fully responsive to market forces or reflective of people's innate abilities. Networks of social affiliation are usually not the result of calculated economic decisions. Nevertheless, they help determine how resources important to the development of people's productive capacities are made available to individuals.

One can say that adult workers with a given degree of personal efficacy have been "produced" from the "inputs" of education, parenting skills, acculturation, nutrition, and socialization to which they were exposed in their formative years. While some of these inputs can be bought and sold, some of the most crucial "factors of production" are only available as by-products of social affiliation. Parenting services are not sold on the market, but accrue from the social relations between custodial parents and their child. The allocation of parenting services among a prospective generation of adults is thus the indirect consequence of social activities undertaken by members of the preceding generation. An adolescent's peer group is similarly a derivative consequence of social networking.

Though this is an artificial way of thinking about human development, the artifice is useful—because it calls attention to the critical role of social and cultural resources in the production and reproduction of economic inequality. The relevance of such factors, as an empirical matter, is beyond doubt. The importance of networks, contacts, social background, family connections, and informal associations has been amply documented by students of social stratification.

I can put this somewhat less abstractly. There is one view of society in which we are atomistic individuals, pursuing our paths to the best of our abilities given the opportunities available in the marketplace. Some of us work harder, some are luckier, some are more talented than others, so the outcomes are not equal. But this is a false, or at least incomplete, view of how society works. The fact is that we are all embedded in a complex web of associations, networks, and contacts. We live in families, we belong to communities, and we are members of collectivities of one kind or another. We are influenced by these associations from the day we are born. Our development—what and who we are and become—is nourished by these associations.

It is a severe disadvantage to be born to parents who are not interested in your development. It is a great impediment for a talented youngster to be embedded in a social network of peers whose values do not affirm the activities the youngster must undertake to develop that talent. Children do not freely choose their peers. To a significant degree they inherit these associations as a consequence of where they live, what their parents believe, what social group they belong to, and so on.

In U.S. society, given our history, racial identity is an important component of the complex of social characteristics that define the networks in which we live. Opportunity travels along these networks. We learn about what we can do with our talents from the conversation over dinner, from the family friend who says "your kid should do this," from the business owner who offers a summer job. These kinds of opportunity-enhancing associations are not just out there in the marketplace to be purchased by the highest bidder. Nor are they allocated randomly to create some kind of level playing field. They are, rather, the product of a racially conditioned social structure. And when they work to systematically hold back a group of people from participating in a society's venues of human development, that society has failed to achieve racial justice.

## *Is Racial Justice a Coherent Idea? Philosophical Considerations*

What do I mean by racial justice? Suppose that there are certain norms of social justice—requiring, for example, that the distribution of opportunities to develop talents affords some minimal threshold of possibility for all people and gives rise to economic and social arrangements that avoid unfair and exploitive relationships. If, because of race relations in U.S. society, members of certain groups are disproportionately excluded from the benefits of otherwise socially just institutions, if they do not have the chance to achieve their full human potential, if they are stigmatized and do not enjoy the dignity and social standing presumptively extended to others—if, in other words, welfare rolls are oversubscribed by blacks, if the places of hopelessness and despair in society are occupied predominantly by blacks, if one can put a color on urban despair—then these social arrangements violate the standards of racial justice.

Kids develop from infancy into adulthood in a situated process of interaction with those around them. The situations and the opportunities for interaction are defined to some degree by racial identity. Consider the racial geography of U.S. cities. Where do people live? With whom do they come into contact? Continue through a more psychological consideration of how individual identities are formed. Who are kids' heroes? What do they take to be worthy projects? And so on. People's inclinations, when acting on their own account, should be included in a consideration of whether a regime is racially just. Because when social processes encourage the development of self-destructive behavior among a (racial) group of people, questions of (racial) justice necessarily arise.

This is not to say that individuals have no responsibility for the bad choices they make. Rather, it is to recognize a deep dilemma—one that does not leave any good choices. Confronted with someone who behaves self-destructively or violently toward others, we must hold such a person accountable; the acts are judgable. But when an entire community is overrun with such people, and they reproduce themselves over time within a society and economy and polity, one deals with matters of justice. And when those structures are substantially based on race, one deals with matters of racial justice.

So now we have a harder problem. If we tell a ghetto-dwelling kid "you're a victim of the dynamics of history, which is why you are toting around an automatic weapon," not only do we serve ourselves poorly, we also patronize that kid and deny his humanity. But if we are not cognizant of the history and the ongoing social structures that produce such people, we have blinded ourselves to matters relevant to a consideration of social justice. This is a dilemma; it is hard to know how to act morally in such a circumstance.

Here is a youngster to whom one says, "Why don't you marry the girl you got pregnant? Why don't you work in a fast-food restaurant instead of standing on the street corner hustling? Why don't you go to community college and learn how to run one of the machines in the hospital?" And his answer is not, "I have done my sums and the course you suggest simply does not pay." Rather, his answer is, "Who, me?" He cannot see himself thus. When the young man answers in this way, have we heard an individual speaking? Or have we heard a call from a corner, a margin, of society—from a social space that can only be understood if seen in racial terms? And if we refuse to heed this call, can we possibly be pursuing social justice? I think not.

Consider two 12-year-olds. One has grown up in an affluent, suburban, two-parent family with wholesome neighbors, attending good schools. The other's circumstances were less felicitous. When it comes time to allocate state-funded opportunities for the intellectual development of these two youngsters, need we pretend that they come with numbers of their foreheads—say, 97 versus 89—such that the kid with the higher number "merits" the greater developmental opportunity?

Under my conception of racial justice, such a pretense would be unacceptable. I am almost moved to say that children do not have merit—though that is only a rough formulation of the relevant moral claim. Children are children—a reflection in large measure of things that lie outside themselves. This is really a shorthand formulation of a more sophisticated argument about the extent to which the application of meritorious criteria early in personal development reifies and locks in structures exogenous to the individuals in question. If such an application of meritocratic principle is defended in the name of individualism, when in fact it is a projection onto individuals of larger social structures, then one has made an ethical error.

My concern for racial justice turns on the fact that inalienable, nonmarketed social and cultural resources, made available to people partly on the basis of their racial identities, are critical in the production and reproduction of economic inequality. In this context it is crucial to realize that, contrary to the libertarian's view, even the values, attitudes, and beliefs held by an individual—of central importance for attaining success in life—are shaped by the cultural milieu in which that person develops. Whom one knows affects what one comes to believe, and in that way influences what one can do with one's God-given talents. Do we as a society have any responsibility for the debilitating, even pathological cultural milieus that exist among the socially marginalized in our midst? This is an important component of today's racial inequality. Are these subcultures of despair mere reflections of the nature of "those people," toward whom the rest of us have no obligations whatsoever? Or are they products of a history in which society as a whole is implicated?

My claim here is that the social pathology observed in some quarters of U.S. society did not come out of thin air but is largely a consequence of historical practices—including, in the case of blacks, the practice of racial oppression. Moreover, the ongoing racial segmentation of U.S. society—most visible in the isolation of urban black poor—is an important inequity that perpetuates the consequences of our troubled racial history. This analysis has an essential ethical implication: because the creation of a skilled workforce is a social process, the meritocratic ideal—that in a free society individuals should be allowed to rise to the level of their competence—should be tempered with an understanding that no one travels that road alone.

We should not embrace the notion that individuals have "merit" entitling them to be rewarded without some cognizance of the processes through which that "merit" is produced. Theses are social processes with a racial dimension. It should be evident that, notwithstanding the establishment of laws requiring equal opportunity, historically engendered economic differences between racial groups could persist into the indefinite future—and not, as some have argued, perniciously, because of the genetic inferiority of blacks. Thus the pronounced racial disparities in U.S. cities are at least partly the product of an unjust history, propagated across generations by segmented social structures of our race-conscious society. This is what I mean by the problem of racial injustice.

For this reason I would argue that, as a matter of social ethics and social science, there should be collective public effort to mitigate the economic marginality of blacks who languish in U.S. ghettos. That is, public goals should not be formulated in color neutral terms—even if the instruments adopted for pursuing those goals are themselves color blind. Prevailing social affiliations, including the extent of racial segregation, influence the development of intellectual and personal skills among young people. As a result patterns of inequality—among individuals and between groups—must embody, to some degree, the social and economic disparities that existed in the past. To the extent that past disparities reflect overt racial exclusion, the propriety of the contemporary order is called into question.

This is not an argument for reparations. I am not saying that some individuals are due something because of what was done to their ancestors. Neither is this a group entitlement argument, in which racial collectivities are seen as having rights that take precedence over those of individuals. Indeed, my argument here is entirely consistent with individualism as a core philosophical premise. I am simply acknowledging the fact that in society, people are not atoms. Rather, they are situated in systems of mutual affiliation. And in U.S. society these systems are partly defined by race.

Taking note of these systems and understanding their historical roots leads me to some recognition of race as a legitimate factor when thinking about social justice. When people's development prospects depend on the circumstances of those with whom they are socially affiliated, and when social affiliation reflects a tendency toward racial segregation, even a minimal commitment to equality of opportunity for individuals can require a willingness to take into account racial identity. In the divided society of the United States, given our tragic past, this implies that public efforts to counter the effects of historical disadvantage among blacks are not only consistent with but indeed are required by widely embraced, individualistic, democratic ideals.

## Costs of Racial Preferences

This criticism of color blind absolutism is not meant as an unqualified defense of positive discrimination in all cases. In certain contexts the costs of using racial preferences will outweigh the benefits. One reason for questioning the wisdom of affirmative action in certain contexts is that the widespread use of preferences can logically be expected to erode perceptions of black competence. This point is often misunderstood, so it is worth spelling out. The argument is not a speculation about the feelings of people who may or may not be the beneficiaries of affirmative action. Rather, it turns on the rational, statistical inferences that neutral observers are entitled to make about the unknown qualifications of persons who may have been preferred, or rejected, in a selection process.

The main insight is not difficult to grasp. Let there be two racial groups, A and B, and suppose that A's are advantaged while B's are to be aided through affirmative action. Let some employer use a lower threshold of assessed productivity for the hiring of B's than A's. The preferential hiring policy defines three types of individuals in each of the two racial groups: "marginals," "successes," and "failures." Marginals are those whose hiring status is altered by the policy—either A's not hired who otherwise would have been, or B's hired who otherwise would not have been. Successes are those who would be hired with or without the policy, and failures are those who would be passed over with or without the preferential policy. Let us consider how an outsider who can observe the hiring decision, but not the employer's productivity assessment, would estimate the productivity of those subject to this hiring process.

Note that a lower hiring threshold for B's causes the outside market to reduce its estimate of the productivity of B's who are successes since, on average, less is required to achieve that status. In addition, B's who are failures, seen to have been passed over despite a lower hiring threshold, are thereby revealed as especially unproductive. On the other hand, a hiring process favoring B's must enhance the reputations of A's who are failures, as seen by outsiders, since they may have been artificially held back. And A's who are successes, hired despite being disfavored in selection, have thereby been shown to be especially productive.

We have thus reached the result that, among B's, only marginals gain from the establishment of a preferential hiring program. Moreover, among A's only marginals are harmed by the program. In practical terms, since marginals are typically a minority of all workers, the outside reputations of most B's will be lowered, and that of most A's enhanced, by preferential hiring. The inferential logic that leads to this arresting conclusion is particularly insidious, because it can legitimize otherwise indefensible negative stereotypes about B's.

Another reason to be skeptical about affirmative action is that it can undercut the incentives for B's to develop their competitive abilities. For instance, preferential treatment can lead to the patronization of B workers and students. By patronization I mean the setting of lower standards of expected accomplishment for B's than for A's because of the belief that B's are not as capable of meeting a higher common standard. Coate and Loury (1993b) show how this kind of behavior can be based on a self-fulfilling prophesy. That is, observed performance among B's may be lower precisely because B's are being patronized, a policy that is undertaken because of the need for an employer or admissions officer to meet affirmative action guidelines.

Furthermore, consider a workplace in which a supervisor operating under some affirmative action guidelines must recommend subordinate workers for promotion. Suppose further that the supervisor is keen to promote B's wherever possible, and monitors performance and bases recommendations on these observations. Pressure to promote B's might lead the supervisor to deemphasize deficiencies in the performance of B subordinates, recommending them for promotion when he would not have done so for A's. But such behavior could undermine the ability of B workers to identify and correct their deficiencies. They are denied honest feedback from their supervisor and encouraged to think that one can get ahead without attaining the same degree of proficiency as A's.

Alternatively, consider a population of students applying to professional schools. The schools, due to affirmative action concerns, are eager to admit a certain percentage of B's. They believe that to do so they must accept B applicants with test scores and grades below those of some A's whom they reject. If most schools follow this policy, the message being sent to B students is that the performance needed to gain admission is lower than that which A students know they must attain. If B and A students are, at least to some extent, responsive to these different expectations, they might achieve grades and test scores reflective of the expectation gap. In this way the schools' belief that different admissions standards are necessary becomes a self-fulfilling prophecy.

### Developmental Affirmative Action

The common theme in these two examples is that the desire to see greater B representation is pursued by using different criteria to promote or admit B and A candidates. But the use of different criteria reduces the incentives for B's to develop needed skills. This argument does not presume that B's are less capable than A's. It is based on the fact that an individual's need to use his or her abilities is undermined when that individual is patronized by an employer or an admissions committee.

This problem could be avoided if, instead of using different selection criteria, employers and schools sought to achieve their desired level of B participation through a concerted effort to enhance performance, while maintaining common standards of evaluation. Call it "developmental" as opposed to "preferential" affirmative action. Such a targeted effort as performance enhancement among B's is definitely not color blind behavior. It presumes a direct concern about group inequality and involves allocating benefits on the basis of group identity. What distinguishes it from preferential hiring or admissions, though, is that it takes seriously the fact of differential performance and seeks to reverse it directly, rather than trying to hide from that fact by setting different expectations for the performance of B's.

For example, in the U.S. context, given that black students are far scarcer than white and Asian students in math and science, encouraging their entry into these fields without lowering standards—through summer workshops, support for curriculum development at historically black colleges, or the financing of research assistantships for promising graduate students—would be consistent with my distinction between preferential and developmental affirmative action. Also consistent would be the provision of management assistance to new black-owned businesses, which would then be expected to bid competitively for government contracts, or the provisional admission of black students to a state university, conditional on their raising their academic scores to competitive levels after a year or two of study at a local community college. The key is that the racially targeted assistance be short-lived and preparatory to the entry of its recipients into an arena of competition where they would be assessed in the same way as everyone else.

## References

Akerlof, George. 1997. "Social Distance and Social Decisions." *Econometrica* 65 (5): 1005–28.

Akerlof, George, and Rachel Kranton. 1998. "Economics and Identity." Paper presented at an Institute on Race and Social Division workshop, Boston University, January, Boston, Mass.

Anderson, Elijah. 1990. *Streetwise: Race, Class, and Change in an Urban Community.* Chicago, Ill.: University of Chicago Press.

———. 1999. *Code of the Streets.* New York: W.W. Norton.

Appasamy, P., S. Guhan, R. Hema, M. Majumdar, and A. Vaidyanathan. 1996. "Social Exclusion from a Welfare Rights Perspective in India." International Institute for Labour Studies Research Series 106. International Labour Organization, Geneva.

Applebaum, Arthur Isak. 1996."Racial Generalization, Police Discretion and Bayesian Contractualism." In John Kleinig, ed., *Handled with Discretion: Ethical Issues in Police Decision Making.* Lanham, Md.: Rowman & Littlefield.

Arrow, Kenneth J. 1972. "Models of Job Discrimination." In Anthony H. Pascal, ed., *Racial Discrimination in Economic Life.* Lexington, Mass.: D.C. Heath.

Becker, Gary S. 1957. *The Economics of Discrimination.* Chicago: University of Chicago Press.

Bhalla, Ajit, and Frederic Lapeyre. 1997. "Social Exclusion: Towards an Analytical and Operational Framework." *Development and Change* 28 (3): 413–33.

Buck, Nicholas-Hedley, and Michael Harloe. 1998. "Social Exclusion in London." University of Essex, Institute for Economic and Social Research.

Burki, Shahid Javed, Sri-Ram Aiyer, and Rudolf Hommes, eds. 1998. *Annual World Bank Conference on Development in Latin America and the Caribbean 1996: Poverty and Inequality: Proceedings of a Conference Held in Bogota, Colombia.* Washington, D.C.: World Bank.

Charles, Kerwin. 1997. "Diversity in Managerial Markets: The Rule of Expertise, Information Quality and Miscommunication." University of Michigan, Department of Economics.

Coate, Stephen, and Glenn Loury. 1993a."Anti-Discrimination Enforcement and the Problem of Patronization." *American Economic Review Papers and Proceedings* 83 (2): 92–98.

———. 1993b. "Will Affirmative-Action Policies Eliminate Negative Stereotypes?" *American Economic Review* 83 (5): 1220–40.

Cornell, Bradford, and Ivo Welch. 1996. "Culture, Information, and Screening Discrimination." *Journal of Political Economy* 104 (3): 542–71.

Crane, Jonathan. 1991. "The Epidemic Theory of Ghettos and Neighborhood Effects on Dropping Out and Teenage Childbearing." *American Journal of Sociology* 96 (5): 1126–59.

Cutler, David, and Edward Glaeser. 1997. "Are Ghettos Good or Bad?" *Quarterly Journal of Economics* 112 (August): 827–72.

de Haan, Arjan. 1998. "Social Exclusion: An Alternative Concept for the Study of Deprivation?" *IDS Bulletin* 29 (1): 10–19.

de Haan, Arjan, and Simon Maxwell. 1998. *Poverty and Social Exclusion in North and South.* University of Sussex, Poverty Research Unit.

Duclos, Jean-Yves. 1998. "Social Evaluation Functions, Economic Isolation and the Suits; Index of Progressivity." *Journal of Public Economics* 69 (1): 103–21.

Eckstein, Harry. 1984. "Civic Inclusion and Its Discontents." *Daedalus (Journal of the American Academy of Arts and Sciences)* 113 (4): 107–45.

Evans, Martin. 1998. "Behind the Rhetoric: The Institutional Basis of Social Exclusion and Poverty." *IDS Bulletin* 29 (1): 42–49.

Goffman, Erving. 1959. *Presentation of Self in Everyday Life.* Garden City, N.J.: Doubleday.

———. 1963. *Stigma: Notes on the Management of Spoiled Identity.* New York: Simon and Schuster.

Harriss, John, K.P. Kannan, and Gerry Rodgers. 1990. *Urban Labour Market Structure and Job Access in India: A Study of Coimbatore.* Geneva: International Institute for Labour Studies.

Havel, Vaclav. 1992. "The Power of the Powerless." In *Open Letters: Selected Writings 1965–1990.* New York: Vintage Books.

Hayek, Friedrich A. von. 1994. *The Road to Serfdom.* Chicago, Ill.: University of Chicago Press.

Holzer, Harry J. 1994. "Black Employment Problems: New Evidence, Old Questions." *Journal of Policy Analysis and Management* 13 (4): 699–722.

Horowitz, Donald. 1985. *Ethnic Groups in Conflict.* Berkeley, Calif.: University of California Press.

Jargowsky, Paul A. 1997. *Poverty and Place: Ghettos, Barrios, and the American City.* New York: Russell Sage Foundation.

Jayaraman, R. 1981. *Caste and Class: Dynamics of Inequality in Indian Society.* Delhi: Hindustan Pub. Corp.

Kuhn, Thomas. 1962. *The Structure of Scientific Revolutions.* Chicago, Ill.: University of Chicago Press.

Kumcu, M. Ercan. 1989. "The Savings Behavior of Migrant Workers: Turkish Workers in W Germany." *Journal of Development Economics* 30 (2): 273–86.

Labov, William. 1982. *The Social Stratification of English in New York City.* Washington, D.C.: Center for Applied Linguistics.

Lang, Kevin. 1986. "A Language Theory of Discrimination." *Quarterly Journal of Economics* 101 (2): 363–82.

Liebow, Elliot. 1967. *Tally's Corner: A Study of Negro Streetcorner Men.* Boston, Mass.: Little Brown.

Loury, Glenn C. 1977. "A Dynamic Theory of Racial Income Differences." In P.A. Wallace and A. Lamond, eds., *Women, Minorities and Employment Discrimination.* Lexington, Mass.: Lexington Books.

———. 1981. "Intergenerational Transfers and the Distribution of Earnings." *Econometrica* 49 (4): 843–67.

———. 1987. "Why Should We Care about Group Inequality?" *Social Philosophy and Policy* 5 (autumn): 249–71.

———. 1995. *One by One from the Inside Out: Essays and Reviews on Race and Responsibility in America.* New York: The Free Press.

———. 1996. "The Divided Society and the Democratic Idea." University lecture. Boston University, Boston, Mass.

———. 1997. "How to Mend Affirmative Action." *The Public Interest* 127 (spring): 33–43.

———. 1998a. "An American Tragedy: The Legacy of Slavery Lingers in Our Cities' Ghettos." *The Brookings Review* 16 (2): 36–40.

———. 1998b. "Discrimination in the Post-Civil Rights Era: Beyond Market Interactions." *Journal of Economic Perspectives* 12 (2): 117–26.

———. 1998c. "Human Intelligence and Social Inequality." In Lee Rouner, ed., *Is There a Human Nature?* Notre Dame, Ind.: University of Notre Dame Press.

———. 1998d. "Integrating the Historically Disadvantaged into the World of Work." In M. Archer and E. Malinvaud, eds., *The Right to Work: Towards Full Employment.* Vatican City: Pontificiae Academiae Scientiarum Socialium Acta (Pontifical Academy of Social Sciences).

———. 1999. "Conceptual Problems in the Enforcement of Anti-Discrimination Laws." In Kenneth Arrow, Samuel Bowles, and Steven Durlauf, eds., *Meritocracy and Economic Inequality.* Princeton, N.J.: Princeton University Press.

Mandel, Ruth. 1993. "Foreigners in the Fatherland: Turkish Immigrant Workers in Germany." In Camille Guerin-Gonzales and Carl Strikwerda, eds., *The Politics of Immigrant Workers: Labor Activism and Migration in the World Economy since 1830.* New York and London: Holmes and Meier.

Massey, Douglas S., and Nancy Denton. 1993. *American Apartheid: Segregation and the Making of the Underclass.* Cambridge, Mass.: Harvard University Press.

Mills, Edwin S., and Luan Sendé Lubuele. 1997. "Inner Cities." *Journal of Economic Literature* 35 (2): 727–56.

Modood, Tariq, Richard Berthoud, Jane Lakey, James Nazroo, Patten Smith, Satnam Virdee, and Sharon Beishon. 1997. *Ethnic Minorities in Britain: Diversity and Disadvantage.* London: Policy Studies Institute.

Neal, Derek A., and William R. Johnson. 1996. "The Role of Pre-market Factors in Black-White Wage Differences." *Journal of Political Economy* 104 (5): 869–95.

Newman, Katherine. 1999. *No Shame in My Game: The Working Poor in the Inner City.* New York: Knopf/Russell Sage.

Popper, Karl. 1957. *Poverty of Historicism.* London: Routledge, Kegan and Paul.

Reid, Donald. 1993. "The Politics of Immigrant Workers in 20th Century France." In Camille Guerin-Gonzales and Carl Strikwerda, eds., *The Politics of Immigrant Workers: Labor Activism and Migration in the World Economy since 1830.* New York and London: Holmes and Meier.

Rodgers, Gerry. 1989."Urban Poverty and the Labour Market: Access to Jobs and Incomes in Asian and Latin American Cities." International Labour Office, Geneva.

Rodgers, Gerry, Charles Gore, and José B. Figueiredo, eds. 1995. *Social Exclusion: Rhetoric, Reality, Responses.* Geneva: International Institute for Labour Studies.

Roemer, John. 1981. *Analytical Foundations of Marxian Economic Theory.* Cambridge: Cambridge University Press.

Schelling, Thomas C. 1978. *Micromotives and Macrobehavior.* New York: W.W. Norton.

Sen, Amartya. 1997. "Inequality, Unemployment and Contemporary Europe." *International Labour Review* 136 (2): 155–72.

Silver, Hilary. 1994. "Social Exclusion and Social Solidarity: Three Paradigms." *International Labour Review* 133 (5–6): 531–78.

Smith, Yvonne. 1997. "The Household, Women's Employment and Social Exclusion." *Urban Studies* 34 (8): 1159–77.

Steele, Claude M. 1992. "Race and the Schooling of Black Americans." *The Atlantic Monthly* 269 (4): 67–78.

Sunstein, Cass R. 1996. "Social Norms and Social Roles." *Columbia Law Review* 96 (4): 201–66.

Thernstrom, Stephan, and Abigail Thernstrom. 1997. *America in Black and White: One Nation, Indivisible.* New York: Simon and Schuster.

Thorne, Eva. 1999. "The Politics of Policy Compliance: The World Bank and the Social Dimensions of Development." Ph.D. diss. Massachusetts Institute of Technology, Department of Political Science, Cambridge, Mass.

Tonry, Michael. 1995. *Malign Neglect: Race, Crime, and Punishment in America.* New York: Oxford University Press.

Waldinger, Roger. 1996. *Still the Promised City: African-Americans and New Immigrants in Postindustrial New York.* Cambridge, Mass.: Harvard University Press.

Waldorf, Brigitte S., Adrian X. Esparza, and James O. Huff. 1990. "Behavioral Model of International Labor and Nonlabor Migration: The Case of Turkish Movements to West Germany, 1960–1986." *Environment and Planning* 22 (7): 961–73.

Wayner, Peter. 1998. "Basic Geometry May Explain Segregation's Intractability." *The New York Times,* CyberTimes section, 22 January.

Whyte, William Foote. 1943. *Street Corner Society: The Social Structure of an Italian Slum.* Chicago, Ill.: University of Chicago Press.

Wilson, William Julius. 1978. *The Declining Significance of Race: Blacks and Changing American Institutions.* Chicago, Ill.: University of Chicago Press.

———. 1987. *The Truly Disadvantaged: The Inner City, the Underclass, and Public Policy.* Chicago, Ill.: University of Chicago Press.

———. 1996. *When Work Disappears: The World of the New Urban Poor.* New York: Alfred A. Knopf.

Yepez-del-Castillo, Isabel. 1994. "A Comparative Approach to Social Exclusion: Lessons from France and Belgium." *International Labour Review* 133 (5–6): 613–33.

Yinger, John. 1995. *Closed Doors, Opportunities Lost: The Continuing Costs of Housing Discrimination.* New York: Russell Sage Foundation.

# Prospects and Strategies for Land Reform

*Abhijit V. Banerjee*

*Redistributive land reform may promote both equity and efficiency. Implementing such reform can be costly, however, and may not be the best way to achieve redistribution. If land redistribution is to be implemented, it should be based on a uniform land ceiling that can be exceeded if landowners are willing to pay a high enough price to do so. Owners of redistributed land should be permitted to rent out their land. Sales of redistributed land should, however, be restricted, though not banned: sales that respect the land ceiling should be permitted, and a government body should be empowered to buy land back from those who need to sell. Land reform programs should be accompanied by agricultural extension and emergency income support programs. Where traditional (coercive) land reform is not possible, market-assisted reforms and tenancy reforms can be considered, but while they are easier to implement, they have important disadvantages.*

Writing on a topic with as much emotional resonance as land reform is difficult. It is made all the more difficult by the multiple meanings of the term, from land reclamation to reforestation to a host of policy actions that affect land. To make the task more manageable, this analysis will limit *land reform* to its narrow definition of redistributing land to the rural poor. But even in this circumscribed definition, the case for land reform is multifaceted. And how we make the case influences what we think should be appropriate policy.

The case for land reform rests on two distinct arguments: first, that a more equitable distribution of land is desirable and second, that achieving more equitable distribution is worthwhile even after a careful consideration of the costs associated with redistributing land and the alternative uses to which the resources could have been put. Each of these arguments is explored in turn.

---

Abhijit V. Banerjee is professor of economics at the Massachusetts Institute of Technology. He is grateful to Klaus Deininger, Karla Hoff, and Jonathan Morduch for their very helpful comments and to Robert Campe Goodman and Pitiporn Phanaphat for excellent research assistance.

*Annual World Bank Conference on Development Economics 1999*
©2000 The International Bank for Reconstruction and Development / THE WORLD BANK

## The Case for More Equitable Land Distribution

At the heart of the argument for more equitable land distribution is the observation that small farms in developing countries tend to be more productive than larger farms. Evidence for this relationship between size and productivity dates back to the 1940s and 1950s for India (Bhagwati and Chakravarty 1969). Berry and Cline (1979) summarize more recent evidence from a range of countries in Asia and Latin America (see also the many studies cited in Binswanger, Deininger, and Feder 1995).

The magnitude of the productivity difference is substantial. In Punjab, Pakistan, productivity on the largest farms (as measured by value added per unit of land) is less than 40 percent of that on the second smallest size group, while in Muda, Malaysia, productivity on the largest farms is just two-thirds of that on the second smallest size farms (Berry and Cline 1979). In the semi-arid region of India, profit-to-wealth ratios are at least twice as high on the smallest farms as on the largest farms (Rosenzweig and Binswanger 1993).

### *Scale Effects in Agriculture*

Scale affects agricultural productivity in several ways. Technological factors appear to cause increasing returns to scale. Incentive effects tend to cause decreasing returns to scale.

SOURCES OF INCREASING RETURNS. From a purely technological point of view, the bias in agriculture is, if anything, toward increasing returns. It takes a certain minimum amount of land to make full use of a tractor or a harvester combine; even a draught team can be underused if there is too little land. Increasing returns may also emerge at the processing or marketing stage. Sugarcane crushers, for example, which are large (it takes thousands of acres of sugarcane to keep a single crusher fully employed), give large plantations an obvious advantage. Tea requires special marketing skills, which small farmers might have difficulty acquiring.

Some of the disadvantages of small size can be mitigated by clever contracting arrangements or better institutional design. The rental market for farm machinery and bullock teams, for example, allows small farmers to take advantage of better technologies without having to purchase them. Cooperatives allow sugar farmers to own crushers collectively, spreading the cost among many farmers. Contract farming, in which a single marketing organization contracts to purchase and market products from a large number of farmers, has been used in the fruit industry to allow farmers to take advantage of increasing returns in marketing.

On balance, however, small size probably remains a handicap, especially because the effectiveness of these alternative arrangements tends to be limited by agency problems and other transactions costs (see Banerjee and others 1998). Compounding the technological advantages of large farms is the fact that larger farms tend to have better access to credit and other inputs, partly because of increasing returns in lending. Larger farmers are also often able to capture more than a proportionate share of inputs that are politically regulated.[1]

Another potential source of increasing returns is occupational choice. It seems reasonable to assume that the more technologically savvy or talented farmers will want to work with more land. Other things being equal, then, larger plots ought to be more productive than smaller plots (Lucas 1978). The extent of increasing returns from this source should, however, be much more limited in agriculture than in most other industries, for two reasons. First, the pace of technological change in agriculture tends to be slow, and a substantial fraction of new technologies are both developed and promoted through public extension systems. Second, talent is probably less important for success in agriculture (at least in areas where cultivation has a long history) than in most other industries

SOURCES OF DECREASING RETURNS. Incentive problems loom large in agriculture: by its very nature, agricultural work resists supervision. People work alone and at some distance from others. The work, while usually straightforward, often demands care and attention.

A potential source of decreasing returns is the fact that larger farms hire labor whereas smaller farms tend to be farmed by family members. Hired labor will be less productive than family labor unless it is effectively supervised (which may be very costly) or given the right incentives.

Agency theory helps us identify the conditions under which hired labor will face weaker incentives than those (implicitly) faced by family labor. A simple example is a situation in which there is a limit to how little someone can be left with. This limit could be physical (one cannot take away what someone does not have), social (most societies do not allow bonded labor, for example), or imposed by what is enforceable. Forcing tenants to give up more than this limit may be counterproductive—they may rebel or run away, making it costly to collect what they owe.

Such a limit sets a lower bound on how effectively a farm laborer can be punished for failure. Of course, workers could still be provided with the right incentives by offering them rewards for success, but rewards cost money. A rational landowner may choose to offer only a small reward in order to avoid having to pay it, settling instead for lower productivity.

This argument can be rephrased as follows: Ideally, landowners would like to sell hired laborers the right to be residuals (in other words, they would prefer fixed-rent tenants). The problem is that at the beginning of the season tenants are too poor to pay the rent landowners would like to charge. The alternative for landowners is to wait until after production, when tenants will have more money (at least on average). But production is uncertain; when crops fail, landowners still face the limit on how much they can collect from their tenants. This limit will set the bound on the fixed rent they can charge (for a fixed rent to be meaningful, tenants have to be able to pay it even when their crops fail). If this lower bound is low enough, the landowners may not want a fixed rent; they would be better off charging their tenants more when the crop does well (and tenants are able to pay more) than when it fails. What emerges is a version of sharecropping, a contract by which landowners impose what is, in effect, a tax on their tenants' output. Tenants will react by putting less effort into production, and productivity will be lower than on smaller farms that use only family labor. (For a theory of sharecropping along these lines, see Banerjee, Gertler, and Ghatak 1998.)

Thinking about the problem of incentives in this way makes it clear that the problem is not a missing market for credit or land. The landowner in our example has the option of offering the tenant a loan that the tenant could use to pay the rent. Providing credit simply shifts the problem from one of collecting rent to one of collecting on a loan, however. Unless limits on loans differ from limits on rents, the same limit on how much can be extracted from the tenant that made the rent contract unprofitable will now make the loan unprofitable.

Land markets do not help for much the same reason. In this model, landowners would like to sell their land to their tenants. The problem is that the price the tenants can afford is too low. Landowners could lend their tenants the money to buy the land, but they would then face the problem of collecting on the loan.

Agency problems can also arise in the absence of constraints on how much people can be made to pay. From the point of view of incentives, the ideal situation occurs when the tenant or laborer becomes the residual claimant. Unfortunately, this also means that tenants bear all the risk. If they are risk averse, they may not want to take on all of the risk, preferring to share the risk with landowners. As a result, it will be in both tenants' and landowners' interests to move away from a fixed-rent contract toward risk-sharing and lower incentives. (For a model of share tenancy based on these ideas, see Stiglitz 1974.)

Do these theories support the case for land reform? The two views of the agency problem seem superficially similar but are in fact quite different. In the first model, the size-productivity relationship is a direct consequence of the fact that owner farmers (who are the ones who crop small farms) face very different incentives from tenant farmers or hired laborers (who crop large farms). Landowners in this model are not doing anything useful; doing away with them thus has clear benefits and no costs.

In the second, risk aversion–based, model, landowners are indeed useful—they are acting as insurers to their tenants. To generate a size-productivity relation in this model, we need to assume that the demand for insurance (generated by the extent of risk aversion) varies among farmers. Owner farmers clearly tolerate much more risk than tenant farmers; we need to explain why they are prepared to do so. One explanation is that owner farmers and tenant farmers have different characteristics. Owner farmers are those who are willing to accept more risk in return for higher returns; tenant farmers settle for the relative safety of working for somebody else. (See Kihlstrom and Laffont 1979 or Kanbur 1979 for theories of entrepreneurship based on these considerations.) A second explanation recognizes the endogeneity of risk aversion, positing that owner farmers are those who happen to own some land and are therefore less risk averse.

The two versions of the risk aversion–based model have quite different implications for the effect of land reforms on productivity. Under the first, purely selection-based, view land reform should not affect erstwhile tenants' incentives. Like the previous landowners, the new owners will simply find someone with whom to share risk and returns; productivity will be unchanged. Under the second view, the new owners will be richer after land reform and therefore willing to take on more risk. Productivity will therefore rise.

It is important to emphasize that in all of these agency models, the incentive effect of redistribution occurs because land reform increases tenants' net worth. Incentives improve because tenants are richer, and it is easier to give incentives to richer tenants. *Any other way of making tenants richer could work just as well as redistributing land.* The fact that former tenants actually own the land after land reform is, in some sense, beside the point.

OWNERSHIP EFFECTS. In the world of complete contracts we have been describing, ownership in itself has no incentive effect; some contractual incompleteness is necessary if there is to be a pure ownership effect. To see how that might work, consider the following rather commonsense variant on the agency story. Imagine that the input the agent chooses is not immediately useful, as we have been assuming, but pays off only after some time. Tenants who expect to be on the land for only a year or two would not purchase that input unless they were paid to do so by the landowner.[2] If the investment is difficult to contract—caring for a pump set, for example, keeping a well clean, not over-watering the land—the fact that tenants lack security of tenure will clearly affect their incentive to invest. The landowner could, of course, promise the tenant long-term tenure on the land. But without a legal system effective enough to enforce long-term contracts that specify both the length of tenure and the rents to be charged in the future, such a system would be problematic. Making the tenant the owner of the land clearly circumvents many of these problems and may therefore promote investment.

It is possible that the effect of ownership goes even farther. The arguments above implicitly assume that landowners make the best possible use of the land (given the various incentive constraints). In fact, people often own land for reasons other than making money from it. In India, where agricultural incomes are not taxed, land is a potential tax shelter. In Brazil land is an important form of collateral. In some rural societies land is a source of political power and social prestige. In some areas of India, for example, the person who controls the agricultural work teams reportedly also controls their votes (Elkins 1975). Such landowners may not try very hard to get the most out of their land.

Legal restrictions may also prevent landowners from making optimal use of their land. One important institutional reason why the largest estates may use wage labor even when it is suboptimal is the fear of potential land reforms, which are generally applied retroactively. Land reform laws often exempt land that is self-cultivated. As a result, large landowners who employ sharecroppers may face immediate legal problems or fear losing their land in the future if land reform is instituted. In addition, there may be a psychological dimension to owning land that may make tenants react more strongly to the transition to ownership than standard incentive theory would predict. In all of these cases efficiency of land use may be substantially enhanced by transferring ownership to someone directly involved in making the most productive use of the land.

## Other Explanations of the Size-Productivity Relationship

LANDLORD-SUPPLIED INPUTS. Even in a world in which agricultural inputs could be monitored perfectly and incentives for tenants were irrelevant, there would likely be a variety of contracts between landowners and tenants. After all, tenants can be very different from one another. Some may own their own farm implements and draught teams; others may want to use tools that belong to the landowner. Some may require credit from the landowner or benefit from the landowner's technical expertise. As a result of these differences, contracts with tenants are likely to vary. In particular, it seems plausible that tenants will be more likely to be fixed-rent farmers or to buy out the land when they do not need anything from their landowners, and to work as hired laborers or sharecroppers when they need the landowner's help.

How do these factors affect the relation between size and productivity? One plausible explanation is that tenants who are more independent are also more productive. Land redistribution in such a setting will have no effect on tenants' incentives. It may, however, affect tenants' ability to acquire all the inputs they need. Former landowners who once lent their tenants money or machines may now refuse to do so. If there are fixed costs of enforcing contracts, landowners may stop dealing with tenants once the main land-based nexus is broken. Landlords may feel more vulnerable in their dealings with a former tenant because they can no longer threaten expulsion from the land. As a result, they may be unwilling to extend credit to former tenants.

If land redistribution makes former tenants less able to acquire inputs, productivity could fall as a result of reform. New owners could try to sell their land back to the former owners and restore the old equilibrium, but this may not always be possible. If land reform includes a ceiling on ownership, for example, former owners may now be unable to acquire more land. Even without a ceiling, fear that additional reforms may cause them to lose newly purchased land may make landowners unwilling to buy land in the new regime.

FARMER CHARACTERISTICS AND LAND QUALITY. This article has already suggested as a potential explanation of the size-productivity relationship a correlation between farmers' productivity and the characteristics that make them willing to be owner farmers. However, Rosenzweig and Binswanger (1993) find that the relation survives even when we control for fixed farmer characteristics. They estimate a relation between farmers' wealth and profits based on the ICRISAT data set from Central India. Since they have panel data at the level of the farmer, they can estimate a specification that includes fixed farmer effects. They find that the profit-to-wealth ratio for the smallest category of farmers is always at least twice that for the largest farmer.

An alternative theory of why small farms may be more productive is premised on the idea that small farmers own better land (in the sense that crop failure is less likely). Because small farmers place a higher value on security, they may purchase land on which the likelihood of crop failure is low. If small farms are, in fact, on better land, productivity comparisons need to control for exogenously given differences in land quality. The study by Rosenzweig and Binswanger (1993) does not directly control for differences in land quality across size categories, but differences in land values should have been taken into account in the calculation of the profit-wealth ratio. As long as the land values correctly reflect differences in land quality, the fact that smaller farmers have better land should not bias the estimate. This, however, remains something of an issue: since the land market is at best imperfect, it is possible that the best quality land may be undervalued, which would then make the small farmers look excessively profitable.

Bhalla and Roy (1988) and Benjamin (1995) do try to look at the size-productivity relationship after controlling properly for land quality. Benjamin shows that once he instruments for farm size using variables uncorrelated with land quality, the inverse relationship is entirely eliminated. The fact that average farm size is very small substantially limits the scope of his results, however. Bhalla and Roy use direct measures of farm quality and estimate the relationship district by district for their study in India. They eliminate the inverse relationship in 71 percent of the 176 districts for which they have data. It is not clear how damaging this is for the inverse-relationship view, however. Since they average only about 150 observations per district, it is not too surprising that they do not find a significant relationship.[3]

## Direct Evidence on the Effects of Tenancy

Shaban (1987) makes a more direct attempt to measure the effect of tenancy. Using the same ICRISAT data that Rosenzweig and Binswanger (1993) use, he compares the amounts of inputs (including their own labor) that farmers put into land that they own with the amounts the same farmers put into land that they sharecrop. Like Rosenzweig and Binswanger, Shaban is therefore able to control for any fixed farmer characteristics that affect productivity. Shaban also has detailed measures of plot quality variables from ICRISAT, which he uses to control for differences in land quality of owned and sharecropped land.

Shaban finds that farmers use 10–47 percent fewer inputs on land they do not own than on land they do own. His point estimate for the resulting loss in productivity is 16 percent after controlling for differences in land quality and 32 percent without controlling for such differences. Land quality differences are in part exogenous, but they also reflect investments made on the land, which are affected by who owns the land. These two point estimates thus represent lower and upper bounds on the true productivity loss.

It is important to note that these figure apply only to sharecroppers who also own some land. If mixed sharecroppers are richer than pure sharecroppers (and therefore face stronger incentives), these figures may overestimate the effect of ownership among pure sharecroppers. Alternatively, the fact that these sharecroppers own some land and still continue to sharecrop may suggest that they are more risk averse than the average sharecropper and perhaps therefore less productive.

A very different approach to this question is to look at the effect of an exogenous change in tenants' incentives on productivity on the same plot. Using this approach, Lin (1992) examines the effects on productivity of decollectivization in China. Between 1978 and 1984, Chinese agriculture went from a system based entirely on collective incentives to one based almost entirely on individual incentives. Lin studies the productivity consequences of this reform, taking advantage of the fact that the reform spread at different speeds in different districts. Based on a production function analysis of a district-level panel, he finds that productivity increased 14 percent. This effect seems modest, especially given the inefficiency of collective farming. One reason the increase in productivity was not greater may be that the poorest areas in China moved away from collective incentives first. The long-run increase in productivity may be greater than 14 percent because it may take time before the effect on investment shows up in the data.

Banerjee, Gertler, and Ghatak (1998) apply a similar methodology to Operation Barga, a large-scale tenancy reform carried out in West Bengal in the late 1970s and early 1980s. As a result of land reform, the proportion of sharecroppers paying 50 percent or more of their revenues to landowners fell from 90 percent to 58 percent and tenants were given more secure land tenure.[4] They estimate that the productivity of the average sharecropper rose almost 60 percent—a much larger increase than that found by Lin for China. As in most studies based on aggregate data, there is some question about whether other factors may have contributed to the productivity increase. While Banerjee, Gertler, and Ghatak control for improvement in public infrastructure, for example, they cannot control for changes in agricultural extension services available to farmers, which may have contributed to the productivity increase.

The various attempts to measure the efficiency loss due to tenancy do not tell us whether the loss is a result of forgone investment or insufficient current incentives. This is to be expected, since the same reasons that make investments and current inputs noncontractible make them difficult to measure.

Little can be said a priori about the effect of tenancy on efficiency. On the one hand, many of the more obvious forms of investment (such as irrigation) ought to be contractible, which limits the scope of the investment effect. On the other hand, institutional and psychological factors could make the effect of a transfer of ownership to the tenant greater than basic theory would predict. As we have no measure of the size of these effects, nothing definitive can be said about this question. This is unfortunate, as policymakers cannot avoid dealing with the question of whether the correct response is to enrich tenants (to improve their incentives) or to make them landowners (to encourage investment). We await further empirical work on this point.

## The Case for Redistributing Land

Redistribution is a goal in itself, quite apart from any efficiency gains that might result from a more equitable land distribution. The rural poor are among the poorest segments of the population in any country. Giving them any assets must therefore promote equity. Recent work has suggested that a more equitable distribution of wealth can promote efficiency (Galor and Zeira 1993; Banerjee and Newman 1993). With more assets the poor are able to obtain more credit and better insurance coverage, which helps them invest more effectively. The children of the beneficiaries of land reform may have better health and more education, which may make them more productive. They may also be better able to start small businesses of their own by using their land as loan collateral.

There is also a political economy argument that favors redistribution. It has been argued that when the poor have too little stake in the economy, they are liable to impose inefficient taxes on the rest of the economy (taxes here may be a metaphor for crime, riots, and, in extreme cases, civil wars; Alesina and Rodrik 1994; Persson and Tabellini 1994). It is certainly difficult to avoid the impression that there is a correlation between left-wing insurgency and extreme inequity in the distribution of wealth, especially in rural areas. (The rise of the Shining Path in Peru and the Naxalites in Bihar are obvious examples.)

None of this, however, implies that we ought to redistribute land. There are substantial costs of implementing redistribution, even if landowners are not compensated. Moreover, the opportunity cost of land redistribution might be high, since the government could expropriate the land, resell it, and redistribute the proceeds. In fact, giving these funds to the poor or using them to make public investments in education and health might benefit the poor more than redistributing land.

## *Why Give the Poor Land?*

Regrettably, the current state of empirical knowledge is too primitive to allow us to compare the social benefits of investment in health or education with the benefits of land redistribution. On the question of whether we should redistribute land rather than money, the instinctive answer among economists is that redistributing money must be better, all else being equal, since beneficiaries could always use the money to purchase land. In fact, if the only reason the rural poor do not buy land is that they are too poor to do so, all poor rural residents would use a cash distribution to buy land and the productivity gains from land reforms would be realized. The case for redistributing land could thus be based on the belief that all beneficiaries want land and that redistributing land directly would eliminate some transactions costs. In all other cases, one could argue, it would be better to distribute money.

Redistributing money may not always be the best option, however, for several reasons. One is that land reform may help keep people in rural areas instead of moving to cities. Giving the poor assets that are useful only in rural areas would be one way of discouraging migration. The problem with this argument is that the debate over whether cities are too large has been inconclusive. Until this issue is settled, it is hard to base an argument on this premise.

A more compelling argument is that land can be a permanent source of income for poor families. Heads of families may not always act in the collective interest of their families. If there are conflicts of interest within the family or between current and future generations, the goal of redistribution may be better served by giving the family an asset other than money. Doing so might, for example, prevent a husband from decamping with financial assets, leaving his wife and children destitute. Moreover, land may be a particularly good asset to inherit, because fewer skills are needed to make use of that asset than other fixed assets, such as factories or shops. Whichever family member is left with the land could probably earn a living from it (Agarwal 1996).

These arguments are obviously highly speculative. In the absence of better empirical support, they make what is at best a very tentative case for land redistribution as a way of benefiting the rural poor.

### Why "Tax" Landowners?

It is possible to take a very different view of land reform, as simply an effective way of taxing the rural rich. The immediate goal of land reform is not to redistribute land to the poor but simply to raise resources. These resources could be given to the rural poor in the form of land, but there need not be a connection; the resources collected could go to the urban poor (or for that matter, to the urban rich). Conversely, resources to finance land transfers to the rural poor could be financed out of other taxes. The key here is to find the best way to raise resources.

One argument for using land reform as a tax is that taking land away from the rich, (perhaps) unlike taking factories away from the rich, has no direct efficiency cost. Moreover, as a tax on sunk capital, confiscating land has no short-run incentive costs. If the government can credibly commit not to redistribute land again, the long-run costs of reform may also be limited.

A second argument for taxing landowners is based on the price effects of redistributing land. Large-scale land reform may be an effective way to convince landowners that there will be no more special subsidies for large farmers in the future (because the constituency of large farmers will be much depleted) and therefore to make them more willing to sell out. The importance of land ownership as a source of status and political influence may also be greater when there are many large landowners than when there are a few.

"Taxing" landowners can also have coordination benefits. One potential benefit of land reform is that it may forestall peasant unrest. In settings in which this is important, landowners who sell their land to peasants may be doing a favor to landowners who do not. It is possible as a result that in equilibrium too little land will be sold. A coordinated program of land transfers may therefore be in everyone's interest.

Although the potential benefits of land reform are compelling, actually redistributing land is difficult. The difficulty might seem counterintuitive. Land is, after all, the ultimate fixed asset—it can neither be hidden nor taken abroad. Land ownership is often less transparent than ownership of capital or other assets, however, partly because land records are often incomplete. Moreover, the structure of social relationships in many rural communities is such that the formal ownership of land is often irrelevant: Landowners can formally give away their land to members of their extended family, or even to farm servants, and yet retain effective ownership. Corruption in the bureaucracy entrusted with carrying out land reform is yet another problem. Landowners can simply pay the bureaucrats to look the other way. For all of these reasons, as Binswanger, Deininger, and Feder (1995, p. 2683 ) note, "Most large-scale land reforms were associated with revolts . . . or the demise of colonial rule . . . . Attempts at land reform without massive political upheaval have rarely succeeded in transferring much of a country's land."[5] The recent thrust in a number of countries, including Brazil, Colombia, and South Africa, toward market-assisted land reforms, in which the government uses general tax money to help the poor buy land, is perhaps the clearest proof that "taxing" agriculture has not proved easy.

## The Design of a Land Reform Program

How should a land reform program be designed to achieve the efficiency and equity goals that are its ultimate justification? This section examines design issues that pertain to traditional land reform.

### *Should Land Reform Be Permanent?*

Reforms differ in the extent to which they affect the long-term distribution of land. At one extreme are rules banning all transfers of redistributed land except through inheritance. More common and less extreme are permanent land ceiling regulations, which, if properly enforced, restrict the number of acres a landowner can own. At the other extreme are one-shot efforts that redistribute land without imposing any constraints on subsequent transactions. These programs could end up with the largest farmers eventually owning all of the land.

Permanent land reform is desirable for several reasons. First, permanent reform is less likely than a one-shot reform to be undone. Second, permanent reform reduces uncertainty. Following a one-shot reform, landowners fear future changes since other reforms can always follow if the distribution of land becomes too unequal. Lack of certainty about reform holds back investment. Moreover, fear of another round of reforms with possibly different rules may discourage landowners from renting out their land, even when doing so represents the most efficient choice. Third, permanent reform encourages the rural population to remain in rural areas.

Finally, and perhaps most important, if land has a natural tendency to become concentrated (as Binswanger, Deininger, and Feder 1995 have argued), the government should recognize that unless it takes steps to make the current reform permanent, there will be pressure for more redistribution in the future, when the current generation of beneficiaries are dead. Demands for such reform may be difficult to resist, since there is no obvious ethical reason why the next generation should suffer because their parents' generation managed to lose their land. Taking the cost of such future redistribution into account clearly strengthens the case for permanent reform. It is worth noting, however, that the government can limit the tendency toward land concentration in other ways. If, as Binswanger, Deininger, and Feder (1995) claim, distress sales are the main reason for increasing land concentration, preventing such sales by offering emergency income support programs (such as food-for-work programs) could help. Removing the distortions in the current system of taxes and transfers, which encourages the formation of large estates, would also counteract a tendency toward land concentration.

The most obvious objection to permanent reform is that it limits the extent of redistribution. The family that gets the land may be better off selling it or at least selling a part of it. But if, as argued above, long-term equity is better served by not allowing the sale of redistributed land, this tradeoff could be made more palatable by combining land reform with emergency income assistance, such as a food-for-work program. Such a policy, effectively implemented, would make it less likely that the peasant would need to sell land in an emergency.

Another potential disadvantage of a permanent reform is that it can stand in the way of efficient reallocation of land. In this respect, a land ceiling is less obtrusive than a ban on all sales, because it allows reallocation among landowners who own less than the maximum allowable acreage. A uniform ceiling on the amount of land that can be held may still discourage talented people from taking up farming, however. Setting a ceiling also potentially limits the extent to which the system can benefit from the talents of those who do participate in the sector.

A land ceiling could also prevent farmers from taking advantage of any increasing returns to scale. Increasing returns do not appear to be common in agriculture in developing countries, however. Moreover, banning land sales to large farmers does not imply that the use of the land cannot be transferred. Reverse tenancy—renting or leasing land to a large farmer on a yearly or even half-yearly basis—is still permissible and is widely practiced in many areas with enforced land ceilings. Given that large farmers who want extra land tend to have good access to credit and insurance, the efficiency loss from reverse tenancy should be relatively small in most settings (and indeed most of the reverse tenancy contracts tend to be fixed-rent contracts).[6]

It is possible, however, that increasing returns could become more important in agriculture in developing countries. If they do, the fact that a dynamic farmer could not come in, buy the needed land, and make the necessary investments could hold back productivity growth. It should be possible, however, to limit the loss from this source by making it easier for current owners to make necessary investments. Publicly funded research on agricultural technology and agrobusiness, better extension services, public investments in infrastructure and marketing, and improvements in credit access should all be a part of a broader program that includes land reform. These investments would also make the redistributed land more valuable, thereby enhancing the extent of redistribution.

It may also be optimal to allow some land sales that exceed the land ceiling by setting a high minimum price for such transactions. The goal of discouraging land transfers to the rich would be served, while talented and dynamic entrepreneurs (for whom the land would be worth purchasing even at a high price) would still be able to purchase land. In fact, the best way to self-select talented producers (rather than those who want land for rent-seeking purposes) is to charge more than the market price but to offer some discounts based on output, perhaps through a tax rebate.

Yet another problem with a permanent restriction on land transfers is that it makes it difficult or impossible to use land as collateral. Since land is typically the only asset the rural poor possess, banning the sale of land restricts their ability to obtain credit to finance consumption smoothing or investment. It is possible to limit the cost of such a restriction by providing alternative ways of smoothing consumption, such as food-for-work programs. Moreover, imposing a land ceiling rather than a ban on land sales would make it easier to use land as collateral, especially if lenders are permitted to hold on to the collateralized land for some period following a default, after which they must sell the land to someone who has not reached the land ceiling. (Selling the land immediately after default may be difficult, however, because defaults often occur as a result of shocks that are correlated across the area.) The government could agree to buy all land acquired in this way at a fixed price, thereby guaranteeing lenders a reasonable return. The government could then redistribute the land.

Finally, perhaps the most important problem with permanent reform is the need for a permanent bureaucracy. Land ceilings must be enforced and land sales monitored by bureaucrats, who would constantly be exposed to bribes. Any bureaucracy would find the task difficult. The limited bureaucratic resources available in developing countries make the task particularly difficult.

If, however, the alternative to permanent reform is implementing new land reforms every few years, permanent reform may nevertheless be desirable. While getting bureaucrats to monitor land transfers on an ongoing basis is difficult, it may be even harder to get them to carry out large-scale land transfers with the knowledge that their efforts will soon be undone. It may be possible to limit the bureaucratic demands of permanent reform by changing the style of enforcement. One possibility is to make greater use of the court system. Instead of monitoring all land transfers, the government could require that courts not enforce transfers that violate the land ceiling. Landowners who sell land to buyers who already own the maximum holding would be given the right to reclaim the land without refunding the purchase price. Implementing such a policy would discourage potential buyers from exceeding the land ceiling.

Another option is to have the government stand willing to buy back any redistributed land at an attractive price, to be paid in the form of a guaranteed income. The government could then resell the land. If the price paid were high enough, it would attract a large fraction of true distress sales, thereby limiting the number of transactions the bureaucracy has to monitor.

## What Land Should Be Targeted?

Traditional land reform programs have almost always established a ceiling on the amount of land a man, woman, or family can own. While ceilings can be justified on equity grounds, they are not necessarily the most efficient approach to reform. A better approach would be to use a direct measure of productivity. The problem is that measuring productivity (after controlling for land quality, climate, and so on) is difficult, and it is hard to imagine that the political system would ever have enough faith in productivity estimates to base policy decisions on such information. There are, however, ways to use information about productivity. One possibility is to tie expropriation to the absence of the landowner, on the grounds that the talents of landowners who do not live on their farms cannot matter very much if their presence is not necessary.[7] (Decisions that can be made from afar, such as suggesting new crops or technologies, could perhaps be made by government extension agents.) And most land reform programs do attempt to discriminate on the basis of landowners' participation in agriculture. This may be defensible if past participation is being rewarded, especially if the landowners are themselves peasants with no other skills or assets. However, even in this case it is important to ensure that the law is implemented effectively. Appu (1996) claims that during the long process of negotiation over land reform in India, many landowners got wind of what was coming and quickly began to cultivate their own land. Numerous tenants lost their land rights in the process. If such exceptions are to be made, reforms need to be implemented rapidly or the law should apply retroactively, with absenteeism defined as absences over the past several years.

Less defensible is the so-called right of resumption, the clause in many reform laws that grants landowners special exemptions if they resume cultivation of the land. In many cases landowners can exercise this right without actually living in the village. Especially in such cases the right of resumption is an open invitation to convert tenanted estates into estates for cultivation using farm labor. If the resumption represents a true conversion of the land from a tenanted estate into an estate using farm labor, the change presumably diminishes the efficiency of land use (since otherwise the land would not have been tenanted).[8] But if the conversion is merely nominal, with tenants simply bullied into describing themselves as farm laborers, there will be no effect on land use. In either case the main result is that a large number of tenants lose some of their land rights. Attempts to protect tenants by exempting tenanted land from the domain of this law have often been frustrated because tenants have been induced (often by threat of violence) to "voluntarily" surrender their land (Appu 1996). It is not surprising that these exemptions have often been viewed as part of a deliberate strategy of creating loopholes in order to emasculate the reform.

Many land reform laws grant exemptions for certain kinds of farms (such as commercial farms or farms growing certain types of crops). In the Philippines, for example, the Aquino reform laws included special dispensations for new crops, such as mangoes and coffee. In India almost all the states made special allowances for rubber, tea, coffee, cardamom, and cocoa plantations. These kinds of exemptions will distort the effects of land reform. Large farmers will move into crops and organizational forms with generous exemptions—even when they do not represent the most productive options. In the process of converting the land, landowners may actually reduce the amount of labor used (by throwing out sitting tenants, for example), which presumably hurts the poor. Wurfel (1988) estimates that the number of people thrown off the land as a result of the Marcos reforms in the Philippines exceeded the number of new owners those reforms created. The cumulative effect of such reform-induced conversions could be enormous.

## Should Landowners Be Compensated?

A key dimension of any land reform is compensation of landowners. At one extreme are programs of pure expropriation, as implemented in the post-revolutionary period in the Soviet Union and China. At the other extreme are programs in which landowners are generously (sometimes even excessively) compensated, as in Tsarist Russia or in the Philippines under Aquino, where landowners received 133 percent of the market value of their land (Riedinger 1995).

The tradeoff here is clear: landowners will resist reform less if they are generously compensated, but redistribution will be more limited if compensation must be paid. Reducing resistance to reform is beneficial; the landowner class tends to be well represented in the ruling elites of most countries, giving them enormous political power that they can use to block, stall, or undermine efforts to carry out land reforms. Generously compensating landowners clearly limits the benefits from the program, however. If the beneficiaries of reform pay the bulk of the compensation, the extent of effective redistribution—and therefore the equity gains from the reform—will be limited. Efficiency gains may also be limited, because from the point of view of the basic (complete contracting) agency model, what counts is not land ownership but the net asset position of the tenant. If tenants' net position changes only slightly because compensation payment liabilities have to be deducted from the value of the extra land they have acquired, their incentives and hence their productivity will also change little. Essentially, tenants will want to trade away a part of their share of the profits in order to reduce their borrowing costs or risk exposure. The fact that tenants' net asset position has not changed much also implies that their ability to borrow (and to take risks more generally) will not change much. We should not therefore expect to see large changes in other indicators, such as the health or education of tenants' children.

This is not to say that land reform cannot have a beneficial effect if the compensation payments that beneficiaries have to make are relatively generous. We have already argued that transfer of ownership can, by itself, have positive effects on productivity. Moreover, as already suggested, carrying out land transfers on a large enough scale could lower the price of the land and, more generally, make landlords more willing to reduce their landholdings.

The discussion so far assumes that beneficiaries pay most of the compensation, as the emancipated serfs did in Russia. But many modern reforms have included significant state subsidies. Often the state pays the compensation up front, with beneficiaries paying off the compensation over time, usually at a subsidized rate of interest. Since peasants often default on their amortization payments, which are then written off, the effective subsidy tends to be even larger than the nominal subsidy. Riedinger (1995), for example, reports that no more than 10 percent of the beneficiaries of the Marcos reforms were current on their amortization payments in the mid-1980s.

Subsidies, while they can enhance efficiency and equity benefits, are very costly. The extent of reform will be limited by the government's ability to mobilize additional resources from the rest of the economy.[9] In a country in which agriculture contributes 25 percent to GDP, the value of the nation's land may represent close to 25 percent of the national wealth. Redistributing land on any substantial scale and paying for it out of public resources will therefore require a very large transfer from the rest of the economy to the agricultural sector. (The problem here is not one of financing the transfer—which, in any case, can be facilitated by a loan from abroad—but of imposing a substantial and ongoing cut in the consumption stream of the nonagricultural sector.) A priori it is not clear that the political and economic costs of making such transfers are lower than those associated with simply expropriating the land. Indeed, even if it were politically feasible, it is not obvious that the rural poor would be better off if the government paid for land reform by imposing an extremely heavy tax burden on the rest of the economy or by cutting back government spending. Moreover, once the government agrees to pay part of the compensation, the reform can turn into a bonanza for the landowner class if the government sets compensation too high.

The tradeoffs here are all unpleasant. Compensated reforms will tend to be politically easier but potentially less effective (and, if the government has to pay for them, less extensive) than uncompensated reforms. Some element of prior coalition building, which would make it easier to implement a less generously compensated reform, may have to be an integral part of a truly effective land reform.

## Alternatives to Land Redistribution by the State

Redistributing land from those who own it to those who do not is not the only way of achieving land reform. Alternatives to traditional land reform can achieve the same goals without involving the state in physically redistributing land.

### Market-Assisted Land Reform

Market-assisted land reform has emerged in recent years as a noncoercive alternative to traditional land reform in a number of countries, including Brazil, Colombia, and South Africa.

The basic idea is simple: the state gives qualified landless people a grant or a subsidized loan with which to buy land. Superficially, market-assisted land reform is therefore similar to a fully compensated land reform, with the government paying for a substantial part of the compensation. There are, however, key differences. First, market-assisted reform includes neither a fixed time-scale nor explicit targets for the kind of land distribution that will eventually be achieved. This probably means that the change in the land distribution will be less coordinated—both in time and in space—than in the case of a (successful) conventional land reform. For this reason, the coordination benefits of a market-assisted reform are likely to be smaller than those of a large-scale traditional land reform.

A second disadvantage of market-assisted reform is the uncertainty about how many landowners will sell. As a result, no landowner may want to be the first to sell out. Indeed, it is plausible that the price of land will go up when such a reform is introduced.

Supporters of market-assisted reform stress that it is demand driven. Instead of the government deciding who will benefit, potential beneficiaries decide whether they want to go through the various bureaucratic processes necessary to purchase land. This, presumably, generates better targeting, at least along some dimensions. People who want the land most and who know where to find the kind of land they are looking for should come forward first (although the fact that most of these programs do not forbid immediate resale may also attract buyers who have no interest in farming). Market-assisted reform may also raise productivity and placate the politically most volatile sections of the rural population, at least if there is some restriction on immediate resale. (It is less clear that this kind of procedure is the best way to promote equity; there is some reason to suspect that the nature of the bureaucratic process tends to discourage the weakest sections of the population. Encouraging and subsidizing NGOs to help those who would not otherwise be able to apply, as the South African program does, may resolve this problem.)

Another advantage of market-assisted reform is that beneficiaries pay a part of the price for the land, thereby presumably having stronger incentives for negotiating a low price than a bureaucrat entrusted to negotiate a compensation acceptable to the landowner. In this sense market-assisted land reform should be substantially less costly than a fully compensated traditional land reform. The market-assisted approach also avoids the substantial political costs of traditional reform.

The most important drawback of the market-assisted approach is one that it shares with traditional land reform programs that pay generous compensation—it is expensive (albeit not necessarily as costly as a fully compensated traditional program). The high cost of market-assisted reform means that it cannot be expected to achieve very substantial redistribution in the near future. (In the longer run, as the rest of the economy grows and agriculture becomes a less important part of the national product, making such transfers will be easier, albeit possibly less valuable.) Market-assisted reform may nevertheless be a useful policy tool, especially where the bureaucratic and political constraints are such that a traditional approach to land reform is doomed to failure. In particular, market-assisted reforms can be a way of giving some extra land to the most dynamic or volatile elements in the agricultural sector, thereby bringing about some measure of political peace in rural areas. Unlike ambitious traditional reform programs, however, market-assisted reform can only be a part of a much larger program for alleviation of rural poverty.

## Tenancy Reform

Unlike land reforms, tenancy reforms do not attempt to change the pattern of ownership of land. They simply give tenants additional rights on the land. The typical tenancy reform law sets a bound on how much the landowner can demand from the tenant as rent or a share of output and restricts the rights of landowners to evict tenants who have paid their due rents or shares. For obvious reasons, these two elements need to be combined: In the absence of a rent ceiling the restriction on evictions has no bite—the landowner can always persuade the tenant to leave by raising the rent high enough. Conversely, a tenant who can be evicted at will probably could not insist on the legal rent ceiling because the landowner could use the threat of eviction to force the tenant to agree (secretly) to a higher rent.

Why should tenancy laws and land redistribution have similar effects? Our reasoning so far has tied productivity gains to increases in tenants' net asset position. It is not clear why tenancy laws would significantly alter that position. To explain the effect of a reform law within the framework of the agency model, we need to invoke another ingredient—tenants' outside option. Tenants' outside option matters because it determines how costly tenants will be for the landowner. In the agency model landlords offer low incentive contracts because tenants must be paid more if they have strong incentives. If, however, tenants are already well paid, relatively little is saved by dulling their incentives. In other words, under certain plausible conditions, the worse the tenants' outside option, the less efficient will be the use of their labor (Banerjee, Gertler, and Ghatak 1998).

Tenancy reforms work in part by making tenants more expensive. The first effect of a reform is to change the distribution of power between landowners and tenants by giving tenants the option of holding out for the share of the output guaranteed by the reform law. This share now represents tenants' outside option; landowners must offer tenants something that is at least comparable. By making tenants more expensive, tenancy reform increases their incentives and the productivity of the land.

This is not the only effect of tenancy reform. The ban on evictions makes it impossible to use the threat of evictions as an incentive, which should reduce productivity. The ban gives tenants a long-term stake in the land, however, which encourages investment in a world of incomplete contracts.

Tenancy reform has other, longer-run effects. The rights such reform creates are typically not tradable, which means that land is effectively tied to a single family. This may not have any costs in the short run if landowners in the pre-reform period had picked the best possible tenants. In the longer run, however, current tenants retire; their children may not be the best people to farm the land. In many places, including West Bengal, tenancy laws do not build in mechanisms that would allow an efficient turnover of the land in this situation (Banerjee, Gertler, and Ghatak 1998). The one provision they typically include is to allow tenants to buy the land they farm at a subsidized price. It is not clear, however, that tenants can raise enough money to pay for the land. Moreover, to generate turnover, tenants who purchase land will have to resell it (which is sometimes allowed and sometimes not) and so will have to find a buyer with enough money to buy the land.

An interesting alternative way of generating turnover was built into the Sri Lankan tenancy reform of 1958. That reform allowed tenants to sell their right of tenancy, but only to local cultivation committees. The condition discouraged landowners from trying to coerce the tenants to sell their land rights, but it also kept the committee from reallocating land rights to the best possible person. Setting effective criteria for how the land should be reallocated—perhaps by allowing bidding among potential tenants as long as they satisfy certain criteria—may make this system more effective.

The net effect of tenancy reform on productivity may be positive or negative.[10] It can also make tenants better off without improving their productivity. Using data from India, Besley and Burgess (1998) find no positive effect of tenancy reform on productivity but a strong effect on poverty reduction. Banerjee, Gertler, and Ghatak's (1998) work, based on a tenancy reform in West Bengal in the late 1970s and early 1980s, shows that the effect on productivity was substantial and positive. One reason for the discrepancy between these results is that the reforms in West Bengal were effectively implemented, whereas many of the reforms examined by Besley and Burgess (1998) were not.

There is clearly not enough evidence to conclude that tenancy reforms are an effective substitute for land reforms. If, however, increasing the cost of tenant labor can bring about better incentives, then a range of interventions—what elsewhere are called empowerment strategies—(including but hardly confined to tenancy reform) will become relevant. Other programs, such as food-for-work and other rural employment schemes, may have some of the same effects by improving the bargaining position of tenants.

## Conclusion

After all these arguments and counterarguments, what are we left with? Although the evidence is hardly definitive, redistributive land reforms appear to promote equity and efficiency. Were implementation not a constraint, traditional (coercive) land reform would have a number of clear advantages over alternative types of land reform. Such reform will almost certainly be more extensive than noncoercive (market-assisted) reform. It also probably costs less and has a stronger effect on productivity. Implementation is a constraint, however, and may indeed be the binding constraint in many cases. In such cases, market-assisted reforms or tenancy reforms may provide better outcomes.

Where policymakers want to implement traditional reform, they should apply certain principles. Land reform programs should be accompanied by effective agricultural extension programs and by emergency support programs and other empowerment strategies. Such programs limit the need for emergency land sales, increase peasants' willingness to take risks, and improve the bargaining power of peasants who remain tenants. The government also needs to create an appropriate institutional environment for farmers cooperatives and contract farming. Reform beneficiaries should be permitted to rent out redistributed land. Land ceilings and any other laws applicable to tenancy should not discriminate on the basis of choices landowners can make (such as whether they return to cultivation, what crops they grow, and so on). Discrimination on the basis of past choices may be a good idea if the reform is implemented effectively and quickly. Tax distortions and distortions in the market for inputs that discriminate in favor of large farmers should be removed as a prelude to land reforms. Quick and coordinated implementation of the land transfer process may make it easier to commit to not reinstituting these or other distortions.

Though the evidence is substantially weaker, there may be a case for supporting restrictions on the sale of redistributed land, such as a permanent land ceiling or a ban on sales by individual beneficiaries. Some violations of the land ceiling may be desirable, however, as long as violators pay a higher than market price for the additional land. Tenancy reforms may also be useful policy instruments.

Finally, we need to know more. Making policies that may change the lives of large numbers of people is always daunting, but it is all the more so when it is based so heavily on speculation.

## Notes

1. Few historical phenomena share the remarkable uniformity found in the history of agrarian relations. The state, it appears, has intervened always and everywhere in the markets for land, agricultural labor, and other agricultural inputs and outputs in order to make life easier for larger farmers. See the appendix to Binswanger, Deininger, and Feder (1995) for an erudite account of this history.

2. The fact that tenants' incentives are distorted will mean that landowners may not want to pay for the input, even if, in a first-best world, doing so would be worthwhile (Braverman and Stiglitz 1986).

3. They do not report the point estimate for these cases and nor do they mention whether they ever find a positive significant relationship.

4. In fact, tenants were more or less certain that they would never be evicted. The effect of this knowledge is ambiguous. On the one hand, freedom from eviction is likely to make tenants more willing to make long-term investments. On the other hand, inability to evict tenants restricts landowners' ability to use eviction threats as an incentive device.

5. Bell (1990) also argues for pessimism about land reform in "normal" times. Peacetime reforms tend to fail for at least two reasons. First, landlords are probably more powerful in times of peace; by definition, revolts represent the times when the masses have managed to coordinate their efforts to resist. Second, peacetime reforms tend to respect de jure ownership—a problem because landlords may own much more land than legal records indicate. In contrast, during revolutionary times redistribution may be based on de facto ownership.

6. The efficiency loss could be exacerbated by banning the renting out of redistributed land, as the land ceiling act in Maharastra, India, does (Behuria 1997). The best argument for restricting rentals may be that rentals can be a way of making secret land sales.

7. Residence requirements of this type were a part of the successful postwar land reforms in Japan, which banned ownership of tenanted land by absentee landowners. In India some states (such as West Bengal and Maharastra) give resident landowners extra protection from tenancy reforms, but the National Guidelines on Ceilings on Agricultural Holdings in India do not include additional penalties for absentee landowners (Behuria 1997). Land reform laws in the Philippines also fail to distinguish between resident and nonresident landowners (Riedinger 1995).

8. The exception is where the conversion induces landlords to give up their alternative occupations. In this case, farm output may rise even though the overall social surplus declines.

9. In the short run, governments often finance these programs by issuing special bonds. This is a natural strategy if the reform is expected to generate productivity gains—the reform can, in effect, pay (at least in part) for itself. Some governments have also adopted the strategy of paying landlords, at least in part, with bonds. This approach gives landlords a stake in the success of the reform, since a failed reform and associated peasant unrest may cause the bonds to be devalued. Landlords are often reluctant to accept bonds from a government they do not trust, however. For this reason, at least in some situations, it may be better to pay cash to landlords by selling the bonds or obtaining an external loan.

10. For a negative assessment of tenancy reform, see Bell (1990).

## References

Agarwal, B. 1996. *A Field of Her Own: Gender and Land Rights in South Asia.* Cambridge: Cambridge University Press.

Alesina, A., and Dani Rodrik. 1994. "Distributive Politics and Economic Growth." *Quarterly Journal of Economics* 109: 465–90.

Appu, P. S. 1996. *Land Reforms in India.* New Delhi: Vikas Publishing.

Banerjee, A., and A. Newman. 1993. "Occupational Choice and the Process of Development." *Journal of Political Economy* 101: 274–98.

Banerjee, A., P. Gertler, and M. Ghatak. 1998. "Empowerment and Efficiency: The Economics of Agrarian Reform." Department of Economics, Massachusetts Institute of Technology, Cambridge, Mass.

Banerjee, A., D. Mookherjee, K. Munshi, and D. Ray. 1998. "Inequality, Control Rights, and Rent Seeking: Sugar Cooperatives in Maharashtra." Department of Economics, Massachusetts Institute of Technology, Cambridge, Mass.

Behuria, N. C. 1997. *Land Reforms Legislation in India: A Comparative Study.* New Delhi: Vikas Publishing.

Bell, C. 1990. "Reforming Property Rights in Land and Tenancy." *World Bank Research Observer* 5 (2): 143–66.

Benjamin, D. 1995. "Can Unobserved Land Quality Explain the Inverse Productivity Relationship?" *Journal of Development Economics* 46: 51–84.

Berry, R. A., and W. R. Cline. 1979. *Agrarian Structure and Productivity in Developing Countries.* Baltimore, Md.: Johns Hopkins University Press.

Besley, T., and R. Burgess. 1998. "Land Reform, Poverty Reduction and Growth: Evidence from India." London School of Economics.

Bhagwati, J., and S. Chakravarty. 1969. "Contributions to Indian Economic Analysis: A Survey." *American Economic Review* Supplement (September).

Bhalla, S. S., and P. Roy. 1988. "Mis-specification in Farm Productivity Analysis: The Role of Land Quality." *Oxford Economic Papers* 40: 55–73.

Binswanger, H., K. Deininger, and G. Feder. 1995. "Power, Distortions, Revolt, and Reform in Agricultural Land Relations." In J. Behrman and T. Srinivasan, eds., *Handbook of Development Economics.* Vol. III. New York: Elsevier.

Braverman, A., and J. Stiglitz. 1986. "Landowners, Tenants and Technological Innovations." *Journal of Development Economics* 23: 313–32.

Elkins, D. 1975. *Electoral Participation in a South Indian Context.* Durham, N.C.: Carolina Academic Press.

Galor, O., and J. Zeira. 1993. "Income Distribution and Macroeconomics." *Review of Economic Studies* 60: 35–52.

Kanbur, S. M. 1979. "Of Risk Taking and the Personal Distribution of Income." *Journal of Political Economy* 87: 769–97.

Kihlstrom, R. E., and J. J. Laffont. 1979. "A General Equilibrium Entrepreneurial Theory of Firm Formation Based on Risk Aversion." *Journal Political Economy* 87: 808–27.

Lin, J. Y. 1992. "Rural Reforms and Agricultural Growth in China." *American Economic Review* 82: 34–51.

Lucas, R. E. 1978. "On the Size Distribution of Business Firms." *Bell Journal of Economics* 9: 508–23.

Persson, T., and G. Tabellini. 1994. "Is Inequality Harmful for Growth?" *American Economic Review* 84: 600–21.

Riedinger, J. M. 1995. *Agrarian Reform in the Philippines: Democratic Transitions and Redistributive Reform.* Stanford, Calif.: Stanford University Press.

Rosenzweig, M. R., and H. P. Binswanger. 1993. "Wealth, Weather Risk and the Composition and Profitability of Agricultural Investments." *Economic Journal* 103: 56–78.

Sengupta, S., and H. Gazdar. 1997. "Agrarian Politics and Rural Development in West Bengal." In J. Dreze and A. Sen, eds., *Indian Development: Selected Regional Perspectives.* New York: Oxford University Press.

Shaban, R. A. 1987. "Testing between Competing Models of Sharecropping." *Journal of Political Economy* 95: 893–920.

Stiglitz, J. E. 1974. "Incentives and Risk Sharing in Sharecropping." *Review of Economic Studies* 41: 219–55.

Wurfel, D. 1988. *Filipino Politics: Development and Decay.* Ithaca, N.Y.: Cornell University Press.

# Comment on "Prospects and Strategies for Land Reform," by Abhijit V. Banerjee

*Karla Hoff*

In the past three decades the introduction of moral hazard, incomplete contracts, and other "frictions" into the frictionless model of neoclassical economics has radically changed economists' beliefs about the way markets work. Mainstream economics has also begun to incorporate political factors into formal models. Abhijit V. Banerjee's article considers the implications of these developments for how we should think about redistributive land reform.

Banerjee makes two main points: that a redistributive land reform is likely to increase productivity, but that whether it is the best way to increase rural productivity and help the poor is a question that remains almost entirely unsettled.

I agree with Banerjee. What I want to do in this comment is to unpack his arguments by linking them to several distinct economic models. Each focuses on one set of factors to the exclusion of others and thereby generates implications for policy. The limitations in our understanding of whether a redistributive land reform would be desirable, or even feasible, in a given setting reflect, in large part, the limitations in our understanding of the weight to assign to the forces analyzed in each of these models.

To illustrate the central issue Banerjee raises, it is helpful to begin with a simple case. Consider two individuals, Farmer A and Farmer B, each of whom efficiently manages a small farm. A dictator takes over and redistributes land from Farmer A to Farmer B and thereby creates one large farm, which Farmer B is not capable of managing efficiently. One's first intuition might be that Farmer B will then lease or sell the land back to Farmer A. (This intuition would be correct in a model with complete markets or perfect Coasian property rights.) In that way Farmer B would obtain a profit from the efficient reallocation above and beyond the gain from the dictator's transfer of land.

In fact, this kind of experiment has occurred all over the world. In many countries the highly unequal distribution of land arose originally not from market transfers but from the allocation of land to politically privileged groups (Binswanger, Deininger, and Feder 1995). *Can the market undo this land distribution if it is not*

Karla Hoff is visiting assistant professor at Princeton University.
Annual World Bank Conference on Development Economics 1999
©2000 The International Bank for Reconstruction and Development / THE WORLD BANK

*efficient?* A key implication of recent work, to which Banerjee is an important contributor, is to put that idea to rest: neither tenancy markets nor land markets are adequate to restore efficiency. That is because the historical redistribution of land tends to create agency problems in the landless class—an impoverished group of decisionmakers highly vulnerable to downside risk—and also to create a political coalition that may be able to use its power to extract further political and economic advantages. Both factors contribute to maintaining the new distribution of land.

## Five Models

That is Banerjee's key message. My comments link Banerjee's arguments on the value of land reform to five economic models.

### Wealth Effects on Incentives

The central idea of models of wealth effects on incentives is that when a principal (in our case, a landlord) uses an agent (a tenant) to do a task (cultivate the land), it is easier to give incentives to richer agents (tenants). Examples include Sappington 1983 and Mookherjee 1997; Hoff 1996 surveys the literature. This provides an argument for policies that would increase tenants' wealth.

In general, an agricultural tenant has discretion over some set of actions that are not observable by the landlord. Suppose that what is not observable is the tenant's level of effort $e$, and for simplicity, suppose that there are only two possible outputs from the tenant's effort: "good" ($y^g$) and "bad" ($y^b$). Higher effort by the tenant increases the probability $\pi$ of the good outcome: that is, $\pi = \pi(e)$, with the derivative $\pi' > 0$.

If the tenant's cost (disutility) of effort is represented by the function $D(e)$, then the expected joint gains to the landlord and the tenant, for any given level of effort can be written as:

$$(1) \qquad \text{expected joint gains} \equiv \pi(e)y^g + [1-\pi(e)]y^b - D(e).$$

The efficient level of effort—the effort at which the joint gains in equation 1 are at a maximum—occurs where, at the margin, the joint gain from higher effort is just equal to the cost:

$$(2) \qquad \text{joint marginal gain} = (y^g - y^b)\pi' = D' = \text{marginal cost}.$$

The landlord and tenant enter into a contract that can be completely described by a pair of values ($w^g$, $w^b$), with the tenant earning $w^g$ if the good outcome occurs and $w^b$ otherwise. A tenant who is risk neutral will choose an effort level that maximizes the expected return and satisfies:

$$(3) \qquad \text{tenant's marginal gain} = (w^g - w^b)\pi' = D' = \text{tenant's marginal cost}.$$

Comparison of equations 2 and 3 shows that the tenant will choose the efficient level of effort only if $y^g - y^b = w^g - w^b$; that is, only if the payment for land is a fixed rent—the same regardless of the output.

But a landlord will choose the contract that maximizes the landlord's own income, subject to the constraint that the tenant wants to and is able to comply with the contract. Figure 1 depicts the case of a fixed payment $F$, in which the "bad outcome" entails losses to the tenant: $w^b < 0$. If the landlord requires payment of the rent in advance, a low-wealth tenant would not be able to pay. If the landlord agrees to payment after the harvest and the harvest turns out to be bad, the contract would be unenforceable.

This model helps to convey a simple insight: the principal's ability to provide incentives—a large gap between the tenant's income in the good and bad states—that do not come out of the landlord's own income depends on the agent's ability to pay in the case of a bad outcome and, therefore, on the agent's wealth. When the agent is poor, the ability to absorb losses in the case of failure is low. It can be shown that, in general, it is not in the landlord's interest to offer a contract that would elicit the level of effort at which the *joint* gains are at a maximum. Adequate incentives for a low-wealth tenant to put in appropriate effort would mean allowing the tenant a very high income in the good state, and that would reduce the landlord's income.

This model can explain the persistence of sharecropping contracts among the poor in developing countries. Under a contract in which the tenant receives a share $s$ of output and pays a fixed fee $F$, the tenant earns $w^g = sy^g - F$ if the harvest is good and $w^b = sy^b - F$ if the harvest is bad. Any contract ($w^g$, $w^b$) can be written in terms of $s$ and $F$, with

$$(4) \quad s = \frac{w^g - w^b}{y^g - y^b}.$$

With a pure rental contract ($s = 1$) the tenant receives the joint marginal gains from effort, which elicits the efficient level of effort. With a sharecropping contract ($0 < s < 1$) the tenant receives less than the marginal product of effort and so chooses inefficiently low effort. Figure 2 depicts a sharecropping arrangement where $s = 1/2$ and $F = 0$; the small gap between $w^g$ and $w^b$ indicates that the tenant has weak incentives to expend effort.

Will a landlord nonetheless offer a sharecropping contract to a low-wealth tenant? In general, a pure rental contract with the rent set so low that the tenant could always pay will be less profitable to the landlord than a sharecropping arrangement in which the tenant makes a higher payment to the landlord when the harvest is good than when it is bad. This increases the landlord's share of the expected joint gains—share of the pie—at the cost of reducing the pie.

One test of this model was undertaken in a rural area of Tunisia by Laffont and Matoussi (1995). In this area the main economic activity is farming, and landlords contract with tenants to cultivate the land. Tenant farmers have incentive contracts in the form of the share of output that they retain (the remaining share being paid

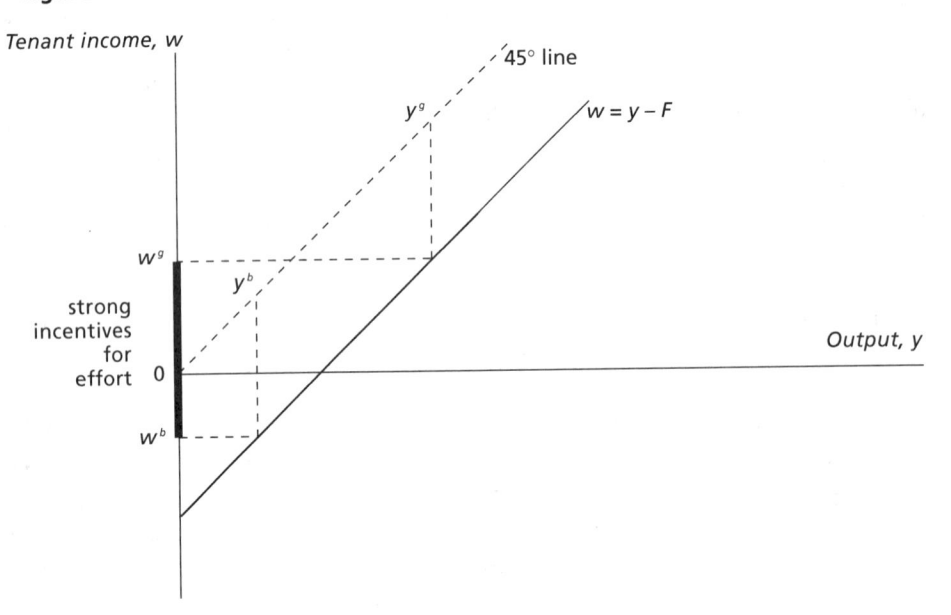

**Figure 1. Tenant Income with a Pure Rent Contract**

*Note:* A pure rent contact, characterized by $w^g - w^b = y^g - y^b$, provides appropriate incentives, but $w^b < 0$ will be infeasible for poor tenants.
*Source:* Author's analysis; see text.

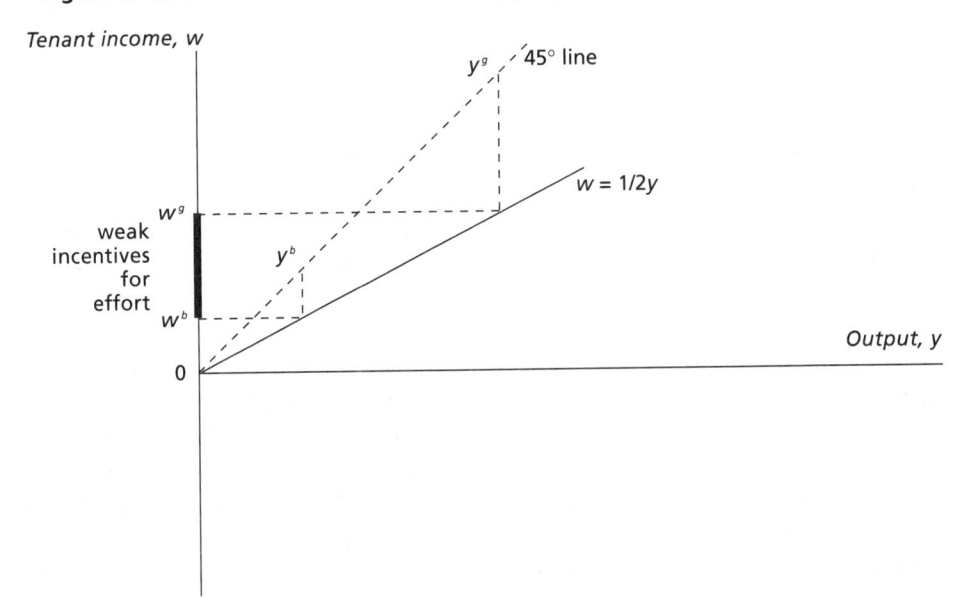

**Figure 2. Tenant Income with a Sharecropping Contract**

*Note:* A sharecropping contract, characterized by $w^g - w^b < y^g - y^b$, reduces tenants' incentives for effort.
*Source:* Author's analysis; see text.

to the landlord). The tenants' output share was observed to take one of four values: 1/2, 2/3, 3/4, or 1. Laffont and Matoussi establish two results. First, the higher the tenant's wealth, the closer the tenant's contract was to a rent contract; that is, fixed rents are observed as long as the tenant is sufficiently wealthy. Second, holding constant all observed inputs, the effect of moving from a sharecropping contract to a nonshare contract increases output by 50 percent.

Laffont and Matoussi interpret the increase in output as reflecting differences in incentives for high effort between the two kinds of contracts.[1] The implication is that cultivators with low wealth produce less output than cultivators with greater wealth because their limited wealth, working through the resulting contractual structure and pattern of incentives, means that they have limited incentives to work hard. Admittedly, there are empirical issues in this result: more skilled farmers may have the highest inherited wealth or may be the most willing to choose a rental contract. But these findings are consistent with Shaban (1987), who finds that output by a given farmer on land that is rented or owned is greater than output on land that is sharecropped.

To sum up, this model has three implications:
- An increase in the net worth of the tenant, or in the tenant's claims to output share, will increase total output.
- In itself the tenant's ownership of land (rather than some other form of wealth) does not matter.
- The landlord is useless, and doing away with the landlord would have no costs.

## Incentives and Risk Aversion

Another model of sharecropping, the incentives and risk aversion model (Stiglitz 1974), supports the first two implications but not the third. In this model the focus is on risk-sharing or income-smoothing as the motivation for sharecropping. The model captures the idea that low-wealth cultivators have limited access to insurance and credit and therefore that landlords offer these services as part of the land tenancy contract. Now the landlord has a role—providing insurance.

The share contract that the tenant chooses represents a tradeoff between incentives and insurance. There is strong evidence that higher-wealth individuals are less risk averse (Rosenzweig and Binswanger 1993 provide striking results for India). Individuals who own land are less risk averse for this reason. In light of this evidence a land reform that increases the net worth of the tenant should increase the tenant's willingness to bear risk and so should give rise to a different land tenancy contract with higher risk-bearing on the part of the cultivator and greater incentives to produce.

This model also highlights one reason why land reform programs should be accompanied by measures to help tenants bear risk, as Banerjee emphasizes. If a "land to the tiller" program is put in place without any complementary investments and supporting services to provide insurance and credit, tenants might be no better off. Through distress sales of land, landholding might be reconcentrated over time in the hands of the wealthiest farmers.[2]

It is sometimes said that the exception proves the rule. There is an interesting exception to the general rule that sharecropping has an incentive bias. In a study of sharecroppers in Thailand, Sadoulet, Fukui, and de Janvry (1994) find that two classes of sharecroppers are efficient: those who are poorest and face high risk and those in a long-term relationship of gift exchange with their landlords. In the first category are farmers facing so much risk of falling below subsistence that they follow a safety-first strategy, leading to very high effort. In the second category are tenants in contracts that are repeated over time and in which the tenants earn a return above their best alternative opportunity. The risk of losing that relationship can induce the tenant to take account of the landlord's interest and to act in a way that achieves the efficient output.

Recalling the second implication above, the two models considered so far do not provide a rationale for redistributing wealth through land per se: redistribution through any other asset would be as good. The next two models do provide a rationale for land redistribution.

## Nonunitary Household Model ("Selfish Parents")

Until recently a standard assumption in economic models was that the head of the family acts in the collective interest of all its members. In the past 10 years empirical work on allocations within the household has thoroughly undermined that presumption. If parents are selfish, there is justification for redistributing wealth through land and for proscribing its resale: a redistribution in the form of a money transfer could be spent for the sole benefit of the household head, whereas a permanent land transfer provides benefits to the children and future generations.

But a permanent land redistribution may come at the price of efficiency. Land may no longer be put to the best use. Land loses much of its value as collateral that can be pledged against credit, since it cannot be transferred, and some of its value as insurance, since it cannot be sold in times of distress. Banerjee's article offers some interesting proposals to address each of these problems.

## Incomplete Contracts

Models of incomplete contracts provide another, distinct justification for land transfers to poor cultivators. These models show that ownership of an asset matters when contracts are incomplete and thus subject to renegotiation (Hart and Moore 1990).

Suppose that in order to realize the full benefits of the land, a tenant must make a sunk investment in it, for example, by improving soil quality. Suppose also that the landlord and tenant cannot write a contract for long-term improvements to the soil. Then the tenant, anticipating that the landlord will increase the land rent in future periods to reflect the soil improvements, will choose a level of investment that is too low. Rather than equating marginal cost to the overall marginal benefit, the tenant will equate marginal cost only to that portion of the benefit the tenant can be expected to capture. In this view, redistributive land reform will mitigate an inefficiency in "noncontractible" investments.

### Political Economy

The last class of model that underlies Banerjee's arguments are political economy models. These models take account of the fact that land ownership in developing countries is often a source of political power. While agricultural technology is probably neutral to scale above some minimum farm size—and may even favor small farms—the political environment is not.[3] As Bardhan (1999) observes, if the political gain from owning 100 hectares is larger than the combined political effect accruing to 50 new buyers owning 2 hectares each, then the offer price of numerous small buyers may not compensate a large landowner for the loss of political rents.[4]

One particular political source of increasing returns to landownership is that landlords may control the votes of their workers. In general, the single vote of a peasant is not pivotal electorally, whereas the votes controlled by a large landlord might be. This idea is formalized in Baland and Robinson (1999).

An interesting extension of this kind of model sheds light on the possible advantages of a large- rather than a small-scale program of land reform. One source of a landlord's political power is the political bloc of large landlords. If all other large farms are broken up, the political power of the remaining large landlord may be negligible. Under these circumstances, if a large-scale land reform occurs, the cost of expropriation with compensation at market prices will fall. Thus the per farm cost of redistribution may be much smaller under a large-scale reform than under a small-scale one.[5]

Scale effects can operate in another way. In many countries a gain anticipated from a large-scale redistributive land reform is an end to civil strife. If each landlord believes that the government can carry out a large-scale land reform, each landlord may support it as the price of peace, yet would not support a small-scale, local land reform, which would not deliver domestic peace. Land reform becomes a kind of assurance game; coordinated land redistribution from large to small farmers may make everyone better off, whereas uncoordinated land redistribution would not.

### Conclusion

There is yet another reason why redistributive land reform, as a policy tool, attracts development economists, even though its merits relative to alternative policies (say, increased funds for education for the poor) are unsettled even among this group. Cross-section regression analysis points to strong correlations between initial inequality in land assets and subsequent growth. Deininger and Squire (1998) find that only 2 of the 15 developing countries with a Gini coefficient for the distribution of land above 0.7 managed to grow at more than 2.5 percent a year over the 1960–92 period. At first blush such findings convey a simple message: redistributive land reform is a means to increased growth. But in fact the regressions relate one endogenous variable (growth) to another endogenous variable (land distribution). They do not identify a policy lever—an exogenous factor—through which higher growth might be obtained.

The tortuous history of redistributive land reform in many places suggests that policies that attempt to change land distribution can be counterproductive if the underlying political forces that sustain political inequality remain in place. I mention one cautionary tale (based on de Janvry and Sadoulet 1993). Colombia enacted its first land reform law in 1936. The law used the threat of expropriation of lands that were unproductive to induce landlords to modernize their farming practices. In response, a new landlord class of large-scale entrepreneurs emerged with political influence over the state. This group used its influence to weaken the land reform law and to direct public expenditures on infrastructure, irrigation, and credit subsidies to larger farmers. As violence by the landless increased in the countryside, Colombia passed a redistributive land reform law in 1961 aimed at creating a family farm sector. But by then yields were higher on large farms than on small ones, and high market prices for large farms made expropriation with full compensation impossible. Land concentration actually increased in the decade after 1961. In 1972 Colombia declared the end of redistributive land reform. Land reform efforts had resulted in neither an efficient reallocation of ownership nor a reduction in poverty, but rather in greater uncertainty, political turmoil, and the creation of a highly capital-intensive agriculture on large estates subsidized by heavy public expenditures.

## Notes

1. An alternative explanation that Laffont and Matoussi consider and reject is that the more able tenants have earned more in the past, have more working capital, and so are more likely to obtain rental contracts. When they eliminate this effect by restricting the analysis to young tenants, they obtain similar results.

2. A model of how technological progress can contribute to distress sales is Braverman and Stiglitz (1989).

3. The relationship between wealth inequality and the evolution of political and economic institutions is beginning to attract the attention of economists. Besides the work of Binswanger, Deininger, and Feder (1995), see the studies of the New World economies in Engerman and Sokoloff (1997) and Engerman, Haber, and Sokoloff (1999). These two papers contrast the evolution of institutions in the 13 colonies and Canada with their evolution in Latin America, and explore the thesis that plantation agriculture, which enhances inequality, in turn shapes a set of institutions that tend to perpetuate and enhance the privileges of the elite at a cost in economic growth.

4. Three other factors that may raise the price of land held by a large landowner above its capitalized value for even a more productive small farmer are the value of land as collateral, as an inflation hedge, and as a tax shelter. Note that land that is mortgaged has no value as collateral (Binswanger, Deininger, and Feder 1995).

5. A tenancy reform that increases the tenant's output share but does not break up large farms can indirectly achieve this end through its effect on voluntary market transactions. A successful tenancy reform reduces the present value of the land to the landowner and increases the purchasing power of the tenant class. Both effects tend to increase land sales

from large to small farmers. Rawal (1998) reports some evidence for this and also finds instances in which landlords gave title on one-half of their sharecropped land to the sharecropper in exchange for the sharecropper's promise not to claim official tenancy rights on the remaining one-half of the land.

## References

Baland, Jean-Marie, and James Robinson. 1999. "Land and Power." Facultes des Sciences Economiques et Sociales, Namur, Belgium.

Banerjee, Abhijit, Paul Gertler, and Maitreesh Ghatak. 1998. "Empowerment and Efficiency: The Economics of Agrarian Reform." Massachusetts Institute of Technology, Department of Economics, Cambridge, Mass.

Bardhan, Pranab. 1999. "Distributive Conflicts, Collective Action, and Institutional Economics." University of California, Department of Economics, Berkeley, Cal.

Binswanger, Hans P., Klaus Deininger, and Gershon Feder. 1995. "Power, Distortions, Revolt, and Reform in Agricultural Land Relations." In Jere Behrman and T. N.Srinivasan, eds., *Handbook of Development Economics*. Vol. 8. Amsterdam: Elsevier.

Braverman, Avishay, and Joseph E. Stiglitz. 1989. "Credit Rationing, Tenancy, Productivity and the Dynamics of Inequality." *The Economic Theory of Agrarian Institutions*. Oxford: Clarendon Press.

Deininger, Klaus, and Lyn Squire. 1998. "New Ways of Looking at Old Issues: Growth and Inequality." World Bank, Development Research Group, Washington, D.C.

de Janvry, Alain, and Elisabeth Sadoulet. 1993. "Path-Dependent Policy Reforms: From Land Reform to Rural Development in Colombia." In Karla Hoff, Avishay Braverman, and Joseph E. Stiglitz, eds., *The Economics of Rural Organization*. New York: Oxford University Press.

Engerman, S. L., and K. Sokoloff. 1997. "Factor Endowments, Institutions, and Differential Paths of Growth Among New World Economies: A View from Economic Historians of the United States." In Stephen Haber, ed., *How Latin America Fell Behind*. Stanford, Cal.: Stanford University Press.

Engerman, S. L, S. H. Haber, and K. Sokoloff. 1999. "Inequality, Institutions, and Differential Paths of Growth among New World Economies." University of California, Los Angeles.

Hart, Oliver, and John Moore. 1990. "Property Rights and the Theory of the Firm." *Journal of Political Economy* 98 (6): 1,119–58.

Hoff, Karla. 1996. "Market Failures and the Distribution of Wealth: A Perspective from the Economics of Information." *Politics and Society* 24 (4): 411–32.

Laffont, Jean-Jacques, and Mohamed Matoussi.1995. "Moral Hazard, Financial Constraints, and Sharecropping in El Oulja." *Review of Economic Studies* 62 (3): 381–99.

Mookherjee, Dilip. 1997. "Informational Rents and Property Rights in Land." In John E. Roemer, ed., *Property Relations, Incentives and Welfare*. IEA Conference Volume 115. New York: St. Martin's Press.

Rawal, Vikas. 1998. "Agrarian Reform and Land Markets: A Study of Land Transactions in Two Villages of West Bengal, 1977–1995." Indira Gandhi Institute of Development Research, Mumbai, India.

Rosenzweig, Mark R., and Hans P. Binswanger. 1993. "Wealth, Weather Risk, and the Composition and Profitability of Agricultural Investments." *Economic Journal* 103 (January): 56–78.

Sadoulet, Elisabeth, Seiichi Fukui, and Alain de Janvry. 1994. "Efficient Share Tenancy Contracts under Risk: The Case of Two Rice-Growing Villages in Thailand." *Journal of Development Economics* 45 (2): 225–43.

Sappington, David. 1983. "Limited Liability Contracts between Principal and Agent." *Journal of Economic Theory* 29 (1): 1–21.

Shaban, Radwan Ali. 1987. "Testing between Competing Models of Sharecropping." *Journal of Political Economy* 95 (5): 893–920.

Stiglitz, Joseph E. 1974. "Incentives and Risk Sharing in Sharecropping." *Review of Economic Studies* 41: 219–55.

# Why Is Inequality Back on the Agenda?

*Ravi Kanbur and Nora Lustig*

*After a period of relative neglect in the 1980s, inequality—and distribution more generally—has come to the fore in the development discourse. Contributing to this renewed visibility are several key aspects of inequality, including a new look at the tradeoff between efficiency and equality, new information on the trends in inequality within and between countries, and new insights on the complexity of the determinants of inequality. These different strands of analysis ensure that inequality will remain prominent on the development agenda in the decade to come.*

Relatively neglected during the 1980s issues of inequality and distribution are back at the center of discussions on economic policy and development. In the introduction to *Handbook of Income Distribution*, the first ever published, Atkinson and Bourguignon (2000, p. 2) write, "There was a time in the postwar period when interest in the distribution of income had almost vanished.... Today, the position is different." A few years earlier Atkinson (1997) wrote of "Bringing Income Distribution in from the Cold."

In this article we examine five factors that may account for this resurgence of interest: the professionwide debate on the separation of efficiency and equity, the role of the Kuznets curve, changes in inequality between the 1980s and the 1990s, the complex micro-patterns of distributional change that occur in developing countries even when overall indices of inequality do not change much, and inequality between countries.

---

Ravi Kanbur is T.H Lee Professor of World Affairs and professor of economics at Cornell University. Nora Lustig is chief of the Poverty and Inequality Advisory Unit at the Inter-American Development Bank and nonresident senior fellow of the Brookings Institution. The authors are grateful to Francisco Ferreira, Karla Hoff, Branko Milanovic, Martin Ravallion, and Jaime Ros for their helpful insights and to two anonymous reviewers for their comments. They also wish to thank Janet Herrlinger, Heather McPhail, Jose Antonio Mejia, and Luis Tejerina for their valuable assistance.

Annual World Bank Conference on Development Economics 1999
©2000 The International Bank for Reconstruction and Development / THE WORLD BANK

## Efficiency and Equity

One strand of research that speaks to the question of why inequality is now back on the agenda is welfare economics. The fundamental theorems of welfare economics give precise form to Adam Smith's invisible hand. The first theorem states that any equilibrium in competitive markets is Pareto efficient; the second states that, under certain conditions, any Pareto-efficient allocation can be attained as a competitive equilibrium. There is thus a tight connection between market equilibrium allocations and efficiency.

But what about distribution? One of the conditions for the second theorem is the availability of lump-sum transfers through which endowments can be redistributed. Because any Pareto-efficient outcome can be described as an equilibrium of perfectly competitive markets, outcomes can be egalitarian or nonegalitarian. Efficiency and equity are thus separable. Policy recommendations to redistribute assets while keeping markets as free and as competitive as possible reflect the fact that efficient allocations need not be egalitarian. (A lucid account of this debate is found in Meade 1964.)

The framework developed by Arrow and Debreu and their followers, which describes the precise conditions under which the invisible hand does its work, was refined and sharpened in the 1950s and 1960s. Such refinement highlighted the severity of the conditions required—no increasing returns, no monopolies, a complete set of markets for present and future goods, complete insurance markets, fully available and symmetric information, lump-sum transfer instruments, and so forth. In the 1970s and 1980s reaction set in, and a number of economists began relaxing these assumptions. Joseph Stiglitz, George Akerlof, Michael Spence, and others took the implications of imperfect information head on. This line of research questioned the efficiency of market equilibrium. Greenwald and Stiglitz (1986), for example, showed that when information is imperfect, the competitive equilibrium is not even constrained Pareto efficient.

### Nonseparability of Efficiency and Equity

Much of the literature in this vein is devoted to describing features of equilibria under conditions that approximate reality better than the Arrow-Debreu model or demonstrating the inefficiency of market equilibria. Particularly relevant is the result that shows that once the Arrow-Debreu conditions are relaxed, efficiency and equity are no longer separable. With imperfect information, lump-sum redistribution of endowments can increase efficiency (in the sense of making at least one person better off without making anyone else worse off) under certain conditions and decrease efficiency under others (Hoff 1994). In the absence of lump-sum instruments, market interventions may reduce efficiency but improve equity. Whether they are substitutes or complements, efficiency and equity are inseparable and must be addressed simultaneously.

This nonseparability has been analyzed in detail in a growing number of contributions. Mirrlees (1971) shows that lack of lump-sum transfer instruments makes equity and efficiency substitutes. Examining the classic tradeoff between progressive income taxation and the incentives to work, he shows that the appropriate policy depends on the degree of egalitarianism and the characteristics of the labor supply. The large literature that followed Mirrlees's contribution (see the survey in Dixit and Besley 1997) helped us better understand the nature of this tradeoff.

Another line of research emphasizes the complementarity between equity and efficiency. Boadway and Keen (2000, p. 699) survey the literature and show how the lack of separability affects capital markets:

> Lenders' informationally constrained responses to the possibilities that borrowers will default on their loans or simply abscond with the funds are likely to lead to levels of investment that depart from the first best. Differing models give different predictions as to whether there will be under- or overinvestment: lenders may ration investments below the first best, for example, or borrowers may borrow excessively to take advantage of being able to default if things go badly. In either event, however, a redistribution of wealth towards borrowers is likely to move investment closer to the first best, so increasing aggregate income: incentive problems will be mitigated insofar as greater wealth enables (or obliges) investors to rely more heavily on their own funds rather than borrowed funds tainted with the lender's mistrust.

Bardhan, Bowles, and Gintis (2000) review and elaborate on a large and growing literature along these lines, looking explicitly at issues such as common property resource problems and socially optimal levels of risk taking. Although they identify both complementarities and tradeoffs, they conclude that distribution and efficiency are inextricable. Aghion, Caroli, and García-Peñalosa (1999) also conclude that the relationship between equality and growth is positive.

## Effects of Different Specifications

Once the conditions that give rise to the separability of efficiency and equity are abandoned, much depends on the specifics of the situation at hand; very different results can be obtained with different specifications. To grasp the point, consider the debate on adjustment and equity in Africa in the 1980s. The macroeconomic shocks of the late 1970s revealed major weaknesses in African economies, particularly on the trade front. Grossly overvalued exchange rates and a plethora of trade controls, it was argued, were highly inefficient distortions that needed to be removed through stabilization and adjustment measures. But what about the distributional consequences of this adjustment (setting aside the effects of the stabilization phase)?

Kanbur (1987) and others have argued that these consequences would be benign. Kanbur's analysis proceeds from a stylized characterization of adjustment as increasing the returns to activities producing internationally tradable goods and services relative to activities producing nontradable goods and services. Identifying the welfare consequences thus consists of identifying the parties that (in the short run) derive their income primarily from the tradable sector and identifying which factor (in the long run) is used more intensively in the tradable sector. Kanbur (1990) presented empirical evidence to argue that on both these counts outcomes are likely to be more equitable than the status quo: essentially, households engaged in the tradable sector, such as smallholder farms in West Africa producing cash crops for export, were poorer on average than those in the more urbanized nontradable sector.

All of this work analyzed distribution at the household level. Mainstream economic analysis and data collection in the mid-1980s rarely examined intrahousehold issues. During the past 15 years considerable work has been done on gender division within the household (for a review, see Alderman and others 1995). Since the pioneering work of Sen (1983), intrahousehold inequality has been treated much more systematically. Haddad and Kanbur (1990), for example, show how taking intrahousehold inequality into account can dramatically alter the measurement of inequality and poverty. An intrahousehold and gender perspective may also change the analysis of adjustment and equity. For example, if production is segmented by gender, household resources are not completely pooled, and women derive their income primarily from nontradable goods and services, the sort of adjustment referred to above may increase inequality by worsening women' economic position relative to men's (Kanbur and Haddad 1994). This phenomenon may explain why some of the most vocal complaints against "adjustment" have come from women's groups in developing countries.

One reason, then, that inequality is back on the agenda is the triumph of the imperfect information and imperfect markets perspective in mainstream economics in the past two decades. As a consequence distribution has become an integral part of the analysis of economic performance, not an add-on to be considered once efficiency has been established. The new perspective means that a detailed, case-by-case analysis is needed to determine whether distribution and allocative efficiency are substitutes or complements.

## Growth and Distribution

The literature on growth and distribution has gone through several interesting cycles in the past 50 years (see Kanbur 2000). Immediately before and after World War II the focus was on demand management and overall growth. Thus, for example, Rosenstein-Rodan's (1943) analysis of development problems focuses entirely on industrialization and growth, not on the distribution of growth. Most of the development and growth models of this period (Mahalanobis 1963) adopted the same approach. Change occurred in the mid-1950s, with the classic contributions of Lewis (1954) and Kuznets (1955). Lewis saw himself as reviving a "classical tradition" in which growth and distribution were organically connected (as Ricardo noted, "To determine the laws which regulate this distribution is the principal problem in political economy"). True to his classical inspiration, Lewis focused on the distribution between capital and labor, showing how this distribution affected savings, the accumulation of capital, and hence growth.

## The Kuznets Framework

In a celebrated article looking at the personal distribution of income, Kuznets' (1955) put forth his inverted U hypothesis: inequality first increases and then decreases as development proceeds and per capita income rises. Kuznets showed that growth and equity are not independent—they are first substitutes and then complements once the turning point of the inverted U is reached. (For an elaboration of the simple model, see Anand and Kanbur 1993b.) In another widely cited article Ahluwalia (1976) claimed to have found empirical support for the inverted U based on data from a cross-section of developing and industrial countries.

Widely differing policy conclusions were drawn from Kuznets's framework. To some the relationship meant that there was a sharp tradeoff between growth and equity (Fishlow 1972), a tradeoff that needed to be managed. (The need to manage the distributional consequences of growth is reflected in the title of the book that many would argue represents the culmination of this strand of thinking, *Redistribution with Growth,* by Chenery and others 1974.) To others the turning point in the U meant that rapid growth was critical: economies needed to get over the hump and into the decreasing inequality range as quickly as possible. For both sides, however, growth and distribution were inseparable.

In the 1980s the pendulum swung back, and once again growth and distribution were separated. One of the main reasons for the about face was that empirical support for the Kuznets relationship proved weak. Using the same data set as Ahluwalia (1976), Anand and Kanbur (1993a) found no empirical relationship between growth and distribution once clean data were used and appropriate econometric techniques applied. This finding was confirmed by researchers on a greatly expanded data set compiled by Deininger and Squire (1996). Li, Squire, and Zou (1998), for example, found that intracountry inequality changes very little over time (and even more persuasively, since per capita incomes do change considerably, that there is no systematic relationship between inequality and per capita income for countries over time).

## Implications for Policy Analysis

What policy implications can be drawn from the new conventional wisdom that inequality does not change very much as per capita income increases? According to Bruno, Ravallion, and Squire (1998, p. 127):

> There have been cases in which growth was associated with rising inequality, but there have been at least as many cases of falling inequality. There does not appear to be any systematic tendency for distribution to improve or worsen with growth. On average, then, absolute poverty will fall.

It is worth examining the logic behind this argument. What it seems to be saying is that growth can be pursued without fear of increased inequality because there is no systematic relationship between growth and changes in inequality. But the lack of a relationship between growth and inequality is a statement about a reduced-form relationship between per capita income and income distribution. Moreover, lack of correlation on average can conceal large differences between countries, as Bruno, Ravallion, and Squire have warned (1998). In any event the reduced-form relationship cannot provide policy guidance, because the instruments that influence growth may also influence distribution. Of course, there is a combination of policy instruments that could replicate the growth but no distribution change pattern seen in the outcomes for various countries. But reduced-form analysis cannot identify that combination. In fact, this kind of analysis can be dangerous because it can lead to the assumption that growth is distribution neutral in the structural form because it is distribution neutral in the reduced form. In other words, policy instruments that lead to growth are distribution neutral. Recent work by Lundberg and Squire (1999) shows how individual policy instruments can be highly distributionally nonneutral, even though some combination of them can lead to distribution-neutral growth. (See also the recent work of Gallup, Radelet, and Warner 1998 for a more structural approach to distributional change.)

Another type of analysis, which decomposes changes in poverty into "growth" and "redistribution" components, risks falling into a similar trap (Datt and Ravallion 1992; see also Ravallion 1999 for a comparison with Kakwani 1994). To see why, consider two income distributions, one for period $t$ and one for period $t+1$. In general the means and the level of inequality of the two distributions will differ, as will the values of given poverty indexes (such as the head count ratio), $P(t)$ and $P(t+1)$. We can construct a synthetic intermediate distribution, denoted by an asterisk, that has the mean of the $t+1$ distribution but the spread of the $t$ distribution (there are different ways of creating these distributions and different approaches to dealing with path dependence and the residual, but the basic idea should be clear). This synthetic distribution * also has a poverty number $P(*)$ associated with it. The change from $P(t)$ to $P(*)$ is referred to as the growth component of the overall poverty change between the two periods; the change from $P(*)$ to $P(t+1)$ is referred to as the redistribution component. Typically, the growth component accounts for as much as 80 percent of the overall change.

This sort of analysis is perfectly acceptable as an accounting exercise—it represents an interesting initial way of organizing and presenting the evolution of income distribution. But the power—and potential danger—of policy analysis comes from the leap to an implicit separability of policy instruments between the two components—the notion that, somehow, the growth component is independent of the redistribution component. Careful researchers warn against going beyond the accounting nature of the exercise (Ravallion 1999), but there is a danger of an easy slip into a classification of policy instruments into "growth" instruments (lower tariffs, higher foreign direct investment, privatization of state-owned enterprises) and "redistribution" instruments (food subsidies, labor-based public works, progressive taxation)—a separation for which, it is now clear, there is no justification in economic theory. It should also be clear that many if not most individual policy instruments have both growth and distributional consequences (see Lundberg and Squire 1999). Of course, there are combinations of instruments that can produce distribution-neutral growth. Identifying the right combination in each case, however, requires, among other things, a distribution-sensitive analysis of each instrument.

### Links between Initial Inequality and Subsequent Growth

Finally, a large and growing body of literature produced in the past 15 years has explored the connections between growth and distribution by investigating the possible causal link between initial inequality and subsequent growth. This literature has brought together recently developed models of endogenous growth with an earlier generation of models of credit and other market failures. It has also incorporated insights from the new political economy (see Aghion, Caroli, and García-Peñalosa 1999; Alesina and Rodrik 1994; Bénabou 1996; Bruno, Ravallion, and Squire 1998; Kanbur 2000; and Ravallion 1997).

In some of these models output depends on capital, labor, and a public good. The public good is financed through a proportional tax whose rate, given the endogenous growth specification, determines steady-state growth. Because people with higher endowments pay more in taxes than people with lower endowments, they are more likely to favor a lower tax rate. The actual rate set is determined through the political economy institutions. With majority voting the median voter theorem can be invoked under certain conditions: as the ratio of median to mean wealth rises (that is, as the measure of inequality decreases), the tax rate endorsed by voters will be lower and hence growth will be higher. The jury is still out on whether empirically there is a positive or negative causal link from inequality to growth (Fishlow 1995; Forbes 1998). Ros (2000), for example, argues that different types of inequality (wage inequality or asset inequality, for example) affect growth differently and that these differences cannot be captured by reduced-form regressions. What is clear, however, is that the assumption that growth and distribution are independent needs to be questioned seriously.

In the growth and distribution literature, much has been made of the lack of systematic correlation between per capita income and inequality at the aggregate level. The absence of a systematic relationship has sometimes been used as the basis for separating out growth and redistribution in policy discourse. But as we have argued, such reduced-form relationships have little to say about policy instruments. What is needed is empirical work on the distributional consequences of specific policy instruments. Such work is now under way (and described in the next section). The key is to find combinations of instruments that will deliver both growth and equity (see Birdsall, Ross, and Sabot 1995).

## Recent Changes in Income Inequality

Can at least some of the recent revival of interest in distribution be attributed to the increase in inequality over the past two decades? Gini coefficients for all countries for which "reliable" data[1] are available for the last decade reveal that while rising inequality is by no means the norm, very sharp increases in inequality have occurred in a number of countries (table 1). Over a period of a decade or less, the Gini coefficient rose 5–9 percentage points in 11 countries, 10–19 percentage points in 7 countries, and more than 20 percentage points in 2 countries. Clearly, monitoring the evolution of the Gini coefficient is no longer as dull as "watching the grass grow," to quote Henry Aaron (1978).

While it is true that almost all of the large increases in inequality (5 percentage points or more) occurred in transition economies, upward movements took place in countries with very different structural characteristics. Inequality rose in both countries that were traditionally more egalitarian (Thailand) and countries that were traditionally very nonegalitarian (Mexico, for example), in both rich countries (the United States and the United Kingdom) and poor countries (Panama and Ethiopia), and in both long-standing market economies (Hong Kong, China) and economies in transition (China and Russia).

A second important observation is that there is no systematic relationship between the evolution of inequality and growth performance (figure 1). In a sample of 104 observations for more than 80 countries, inequality rose in both expanding economies (Australia) and stagnant ones (Lithuania). Output growth was positive in 16 of the 34 countries in which inequality increased and in 8 of the 12 countries in which inequality declined.[2]

Analysts have attempted to explain the increases in inequality as stemming from the global effects of skilled-biased technological change and, particularly for the higher-income countries, increased trade with low-income countries whose abundant factor is cheap unskilled labor. If such changes account for the rise in inequality, however, why has inequality remained virtually unchanged in some countries (Colombia, India, Japan, Morocco, Sweden) and even fallen in a few (Bangladesh, Canada, Honduras, Tunisia)? What accounts for the difference in outcomes?

According to Atkinson (1998) differences in changes in income inequality in advanced industrial countries reflect both differences in government policies and differences in social norms. Countries in which the Gini coefficient rose between 1980 and the early 1990s (Germany, Japan, the United Kingdom, he United States) were governed by right-wing or center-right parties; countries in which the Gini coefficient fell (Canada, France, Italy) were governed by center-left social democratic governments. The question that remains is the nature of the causality. Did countries with less egalitarian social norms vote for more conservative governments? Or did inequality increase as a result of the policies of more conservative governments?

In the case of the transition economies of Eastern Europe and the former Soviet Union it is conceivable that government policy made an important difference. In three out of the four countries in which income inequality remained virtually unchanged between the period just before and just after the dismantling of the Communist regime, the governments pursued what Milanovic (1998) calls "populist" policies. In Hungary, Poland, and Slovenia—among the most egalitarian coun-

## Table 1. Comparing the Average Gini Coefficient for the 1980s and the 1990s

| Economy | 1980s | 1990s | Welf [a] | Unit [b] | Source [c] | GDP per capita [d] |
|---|---|---|---|---|---|---|
| **Inequality increased (average 1990s Gini greater than 1980s Gini)** | | | | | | |
| Australia | 29.73 | 31.70 | ID | P | LIS | + |
| Belarus [e] | 23.00 | 28.00 | I | P | M | – |
| Brazil | 57.64 | 60.90 | I | P | L/S | – |
| Bulgaria [f] | 23.00 | 34.00 | I | P | M | + |
| China [e] | 30.41 | 35.03 | I | P | D/S | + |
| Czech Republic [e] | 19.00 | 27.00 | I | P | M | – |
| Czechoslovakia | 21.13 | 24.56 | I | P | D/S | .. |
| Denmark | 32.07 | 33.20 | I | H | D/S | + |
| Dominican Republic | 46.88 | 49.00 | I | P | D/S | + |
| Estonia [f] | 23.00 | 35.00 | I | P | M | – |
| Ethiopia | 41.00 | 44.50 | E | P | WB | + |
| Finland | 20.70 | 22.30 | ID | P | LIS | + |
| Hong Kong, China | 41.49 | 45.00 | I | H | D/S | + |
| Hungary | 21.00 | 23.00 | I | P | M | + |
| Jordan | 38.45 | 40.66 | E | P | D/S | – |
| Kazakhstan [e] | 26.00 | 33.00 | I | P | M | – |
| Kyrgyz Republic [f] | 26.00 | 55.00 | I | P | M | – |
| Latvia [f] | 23.00 | 31.00 | I | P | M | – |
| Lithuania [f] | 23.00 | 37.00 | I | P | M | – |
| Mexico | 44.93 | 47.60 | I | P | L&S | + |
| Moldova [f] | 24.00 | 36.00 | I | P | M | – |
| Nigeria | 37.02 | 39.31 | E | P | D/S | + |
| New Zealand [e] | 35.31 | 40.21 | I | H | D/S | + |
| Norway | 31.69 | 33.31 | I | H | D/S | + |
| Panama [e] | 52.10 | 57.40 | I | P | L/S | – |
| Peru | 42.75 | 44.87 | E | P | D/S | – |
| Poland | 24.59 | 28.26 | I | P | D/S | – |
| Romania [e] | 23.00 | 29.00 | I | P | M | – |
| Russia [g] | 24.00 | 48.00 | I | P | M | – |
| Slovenia | 22.00 | 25.00 | I | P | M | .. |
| Taiwan (China) | 29.05 | 30.54 | I | P | D/S | .. |
| Thailand | 47.27 | 51.78 | I | P | WB | + |
| Turkmenistan [f] | 26.00 | 36.00 | I | P | M | – |
| Ukraine [g] | 23.00 | 47.00 | I | P | M | – |
| United Kingdom [e] | 27.32 | 32.35 | I | Pe | D/S | + |
| United States | 32.50 | 35.55 | ID | P | LIS | + |
| Uzbekistan [e] | 28.00 | 33.00 | I | P | M | – |
| **Inequality decreased (average 1990s Gini lower than 1980s Gini)** | | | | | | |
| Bahamas | 44.42 | 42.99 | I | H | D/S | – |
| Bangladesh | 36.86 | 34.87 | I | P | D/S | + |
| Canada | 31.54 | 27.61 | I | H | D/S | + |
| Finland | 30.30 | 26.11 | I | H | D/S | + |
| Ghana | 36.32 | 33.94 | E | P | D/S | – |
| Honduras | 59.90 | 55.53 | I | P | L/S | – |
| Indonesia | 33.44 | 32.39 | E | P | D/S | + |
| Italy | 33.42 | 32.19 | I | H | D/S | + |

*(Table continues on next page.)*

**Table 1. Comparing the Average Gini Coefficient for the 1980s and the 1990s**
(continued)

| Economy | 1980s | 1990s | Welf[a] | Unit[b] | Source[c] | GDP per capita[d] |
|---|---|---|---|---|---|---|
| Jamaica | 43.35 | 39.83 | E | P | D/S | + |
| Mauritius | 39.37 | 36.69 | E | P | D/S | + |
| Philippines | 46.08 | 45.00 | I | H | D/S | − |
| Slovak Republic | 20.00 | 19.00 | I | P | M | − |
| Spain | 32.10 | 30.60 | ID | P | LIS | + |
| Tunisia | 43.00 | 40.24 | E | P | D/S | + |
| **Inequality has not changed (average 1990s Gini approximately equal to 1980s Gini)[h]** | | | | | | |
| Belgium | 26.43 | 26.92 | I | H | D/S | + |
| Chile | 55.55 | 56.49 | I | P | D/S | + |
| Colombia | 48.30 | 49.25 | I | P | L/S | + |
| Costa Rica | 46.26 | 46.83 | I | P | L/S | + |
| India | 31.45 | 31.41 | E | P | D/S | + |
| Israel | 30.90 | 30.50 | ID | P | LIS | + |
| Japan | 35.20 | 35.00 | I | H | D/S | + |
| Lesotho | 56.02 | 57.00 | E | P | D/S | + |
| Luxembourg | 23.80 | 23.70 | ID | P | LIS | + |
| Morocco | 39.19 | 39.20 | E | P | D/S | + |
| Netherlands | 27.50 | 27.20 | ID | P | LIS | + |
| Portugal | 36.80 | 36.20 | I | H | D/S | + |
| Sweden | 31.74 | 32.48 | I | H | D/S | + |
| Venezuela, R. B. | 46.02 | 46.33 | I | P | L/S | − |
| Yugoslavia | 32.74 | 31.88 | I | P | D/S | .. |

+ Income growth.
− Income decline.
.. Data not available.
a. Whether the Gini coefficient is calculated based on income or expenditure (I = Income, E = Expenditure, ID = Disposable income [LIS own definition]).
b. Whether the base unit is the person or the household (He = Household equivalent [households are weighted by the number of people], Pe = Person equivalent [in addition to He, the effective number of members in the household is assumed to be the square root of the actual members], P = By individual, H = By household).
c. Sources: D/S: Deininger and Squire.; LIS: Luxembourg Income Study; L/S: Londoño and Szekely; M: Milanovic; L&S: Lustig and Szekely; WB: World Bank.
d. Yearly average change in GDP per capita (constant PPP 1987 US$). Growth refers to the period between the first and the last available Gini estimates.
e. Between 5 and 9 points.
f. Between 10 and 19 points.
g. 20 points or more.
h. No change indicates that the variation in the Gini coefficient was less than 1.00 in either direction.
*Source:* Deininger and Squire 1998; Luxembourg Income Study 1998; Londoño and Székely 1997; Milanovic 1998; Lustig and Székely 1997; and World Bank 1997.

tries of the old Soviet bloc—the Gini coefficient for 1993–95 hovered below 0.25, and wages, cash social transfers, and nonwage private income rose. Cash social transfers moderated the increases in inequality caused by the increase in wage inequality. According to Milanovic, governments in these countries attempted to cushion the population from the sharp contractions in GDP. At the other extreme, the countries that saw the sharpest increases in inequality, such as Russia and

**Figure 1. Growth and Inquality**

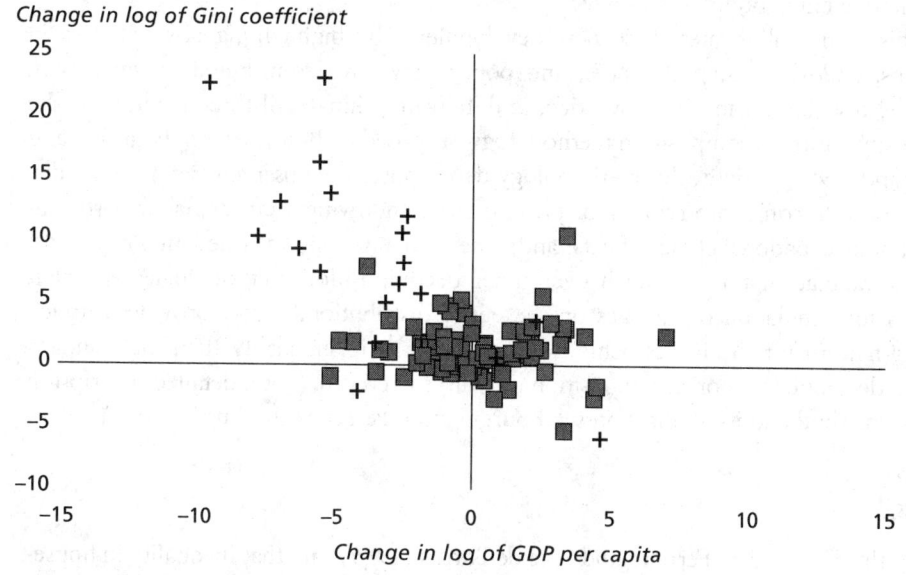

*Change in log of Gini coefficient*

[Scatter plot with x-axis "Change in log of GDP per capita" ranging from −15 to 15, and y-axis ranging from −10 to 25]

*Note:* Figure is based on 104 non-overlapping observations for more than 80 countries from the late 1970s to 1996. The fitted regression line was estimated excluding the former Soviet republics and the countries of Eastern Europe. Points marked with "+" represent data from transition economies.
*Source:* Modeled after Ravallion and Chen 1997. New data points have been added.

Ukraine, were led by governments that Milanovic calls "noncompensators" (see also Commander and Lee 1998). Not all countries led by such governments experienced the sharp increases in inequality observed in Russia and Ukraine, however.

The reason why outcomes are so different in countries that appear to share similar structural characteristics and to be subject to similar global forces may lie in the fact that the size distribution of income is the result of a number of complex forces that sometimes move in the same direction and sometimes in opposite directions, even to the point of canceling each other out. Some of these forces stem from the evolution of the distribution of endowments and their market returns, which are affected by trends in technology, openness, and decisions affecting the rate of labor market participation and occupational choice. Other forces are related to family formation decisions, such as the choice of partner and the number of children. Yet other forces are related to tax and transfer policy and how it affects after-tax income levels (or what is sometimes called "unearned" income). These forces and their interactions are addressed in the next section.

## Complex Patterns of Change in Inequality

Another reason inequality is back on the agenda is that as time series data from household surveys of developing countries have become more widely available, analysts have delved beneath the surface of Gini coefficients to explore the microeconomic structures of changes in inequality. Such detailed investigations have yielded interesting insights into income distribution processes and raised questions about alternative entry points for policy.

This section illustrates these new developments by highlighting how changes in returns, endowments, preferences, and policy may have contributed to changes in income distribution in Brazil, Mexico, and Taiwan (China). All three studies use the microsimulation decomposition methodology proposed by Bourguignon, Fournier, and Gurgand (1998). Briefly, this methodology decomposes the observed trends in the distribution of income into returns, or price, effects; endowment effects; labor participation and occupational choice effects; and, where data permit, unearned income effects. The advantage of this approach over other decomposition methodologies is that it allows for simulation of changes on the entire distribution. It also provides a much richer texture for the forces behind observed trends in inequality than the standard group decomposition or decomposition by source exercises. (For a detailed description of this method and its application see Bourguignon, Ferreira, and Lustig 1997.)

## Brazil

Using the Theil index, Ferreira and Paes de Barros (1999) find that inequality in household per capita income in urban Brazil fell from 0.79 in 1976 to 0.69 in 1996 (the Gini, however, remained constant at 0.59 over the same period). When age and gender are controlled for, the earnings-education profile for both wage earners and self-employed workers became substantially more convex over time, implying an increase in the returns to education over most pairwise comparisons. (Steeper returns to education were also observed in Mexico and Taiwan, China.) The returns to experience (measured by age) were essentially unchanged. The gender earnings gap (as measured by the "returns to being male") fell for both types of workers, but simulations indicate that the effect was not sufficient to outweigh the dispersion-increasing effect of a steeper earnings-education profile. Overall, then, the returns, or price, effects were unequalizing.

How can these results be reconciled with the decline in inequality observed in Brazil? Applying the Bourguignon, Ferreira, and Lustig (1997) methodology, Ferreira and Paes de Barro find three main equalizing factors at work in Brazil that together more than offset the unequalizing effect of increasing returns to education. The first was changes in the educational composition of the population, as the average years of schooling in Brazil rose (from 3.8 to 5.9 over the period). The simulated effect of changes in educational endowments on both the individual earnings distribution and on the distribution of per capita household income was equalizing. The second effect was demographic and was—at least in part—a secondary effect of the rightward shift in the distribution of education: higher levels of schooling (particularly for women) contributed to a noticeable reduction in family size (largely through a decline in the number of children). The average household declined from 4.3 to 3.5 persons; the dependency ratio also fell. This decline was more pronounced for poorer households, leading to a relative increase in their per capita incomes and a reduction in inequality.

The third effect was a reduction in the variance of returns to "unobserved" characteristics, which include regional location, race, and the size of the firm in which people worked, and skills unrelated to education. This effect suggests a reduction in the degree of segmentation in the Brazilian labor market during 1976–96, as well as a possible decline in regional inequalities. These trends are compatible with some of the earlier evidence from both static and dynamic decompositions of scalar inequality measures, reported by Ferreira and Litchfield (1998). They also highlight the continuing importance of investigating the evolution of discrimination and segmentation in the Brazilian labor market in a more systematic way.

## Mexico

Income inequality in Mexico rose sharply between 1984 and 1994, with the Gini coefficient rising from 0.491 to 0.549 (Bouillón, Legovini, and Lustig 1999).[3] As the Lorenz curves present no crossings, the increase is unambiguous (Lustig and Székely 1997). Applying the micro-simulation decomposition methodology described above, Bouillon, Legovini, and Lustig (1998) attempt to identify which factors lie behind the rise in inequality using a reduced-form household income regression model. Their results reveal that the widening gap in "returns" to education explains close to 50 percent of the observed increase in inequality, while the "returns" to regional location explains about 24 percent of the increase, with the south alone accounting for 15 percentage points of the change.[4] Most of the rising inequality in Mexico can thus be ascribed to increasing disparities in returns. Endowment effects—that is, the distribution of skills—account for about a fourth of the increase in inequality. In contrast to the case of Brazil and Taiwan (China), the unequalizing effect of the widening gap in the returns to skills was not compensated for by the more equal distribution of (observable and unobservable) skills.

Several explanations have been proposed to account for the sharp observed increase in the returns to education. One explanation looks at institutional changes in the labor market, such as reductions in the minimum wage, the decreasing strength of trade unions, and the declining share of state-owned enterprises. The fact that the distribution of real wages reveals no truncation around the minimum wage, however, suggests that the minimum wage was not binding during the period under consideration (Láchler 1997). In addition, there is no evidence that the distributions of union and nonunion wages differ significantly once differences in education levels are accounted for. Average wages for unionized workers did decline relative to wages for nonunionized workers over the period, a trend that should make the distribution of wage income more equal (OECD 1996).

The other explanation for the rising returns to education is that the demand for labor has become more skill biased. Based on their analysis of Mexican employment surveys, Cragg and Epelbaum (1995) conclude that the increase in wage inequality can be attributed to the rapid increase in wages for more educated and experienced workers. They conclude that this trend is caused by a shift in demand that is skewed in favor of workers with higher skills, rather than by a uniform increase in response to different elasticities of labor supply by skill.

The skill (education)-biased shift in demand for labor could be the result of several factors. Two in particular have been analyzed in the literature: trade liberalization and technical change. Hanson and Harrison (1995), for example, find that 23 percent of the increase in relative wages for skilled workers during 1986–90 could be attributed to the reduction in tariffs and the elimination of import license requirements. Revenga (1995) finds that reductions in import quota coverage and tariff levels were associated with moderate declines in firm-level employment. Her analysis suggests that there has been a slight shift in the skill mix in favor of skilled labor (nonproduction workers in her sample). Her findings also indicate that employment and wages for unskilled labor (production workers in her sample) are significantly more responsive to reductions in protection levels, a finding she attributes to the fact that unskilled workers are more heavily concentrated in industries in which protection was significantly reduced.

Tan and Batra (1997) find that investment in technology (as measured by investment in research and development and labor training) and export orientation have a large impact on the size-wage distributions for skilled workers and a smaller effect on wages paid to unskilled workers. This asymmetric impact of technology is consistent with skill-biased technical change. It is supported by the fact that in Mexico foreign-owned exporting enterprises, which operate in the most export-oriented sectors, and enterprises that adopt the technology of other enterprises appear to pay higher wages to skilled workers. Because these enterprises are in a more favorable competitive position in the world economy, they have the ability to increase production and increase in number as the integration process progresses and consolidates, especially in connection with the North American Free Trade Agreement. Even if Mexico invests in educational and training institutions, it may not be able to do so rapidly enough to counter the trends in labor demand. Demand and remuneration for skilled workers may thus continue to rise, and the wage gap between skilled and unskilled labor may continue to widen.

### Taiwan (China)

Inequality in Taiwan (China) is low and stable, with a Gini coefficient that has hovered around 0.30 for the past 30 years. Examination of the evolution of income distribution reveals that the lack of inequality by no means reflects the absence of changes in earning patterns, demographic structure, or labor choices, however. Inequality has remained stable because countervailing forces have largely cancelled each other out (Bourguignon, Fournier, and Gurgand 1998).

While overall inequality remained all but unchanged in Taiwan (China), the distribution of primary (before taxes and transfers) adult equivalent income became more unequal, implying that government policy was effective at countervailing other forces. In contrast, the distribution of income of individual earnings became more equal. Does this mean that Taiwan (China) did not experience the widening gap in returns to education observed in many other economies? If not, what forces operated in Taiwan (China) to prevent what in other economies has been at the bottom of rising overall inequality? What factors have made the distribution of primary income more unequal in spite of lower earnings inequality?

Bourguignon, Fournier, and Gurgand (1998) find that Taiwan (China) has experienced the same relative increase in returns to education at the higher end that has been experienced in the other two countries. Interestingly, the increase occurred despite the extraordinarily rapid expansion in the supply of workers with more years of education (the average number of years of schooling increased from 6.0 in 1970 to 9.5 in 1995). The unequalizing effect on the distribution of earnings implied by higher returns to education was more than offset by three other factors, however: the decline in the variance of unobserved characteristics, the change in the level and distribution of schooling among wage earners, and the fact that more women chose to participate in the labor force while some men dropped out. Because of the initial gap in earnings between men and women, these changes in labor force participation were equalizing, and the net result of all these forces was a decline in inequality in the distribution of individual earnings.

At the level of the household—that is, when earners are paired with other earners, or earnings are paired with other sources of income—inequality in overall primary (adult equivalent) income increased over time. Interestingly, changes in labor force participation and occupational choice had an unequalizing effect as a result of two phenomena. First, the negative effect of husbands' incomes on wives' participation in the labor force weakened over time, as more women married to higher-income earners chose to participate in the labor force. While the fact that the average level of education of women entering the labor force was higher than it had been had an equalizing effect on the distribution of earnings, it increased income inequality at the level of the household because better-educated women tend to live in households with higher incomes to begin with. In contrast, the equalizing effect of the expansion of education was weaker at the household level because of its negative impact on labor force participation by younger cohorts, particularly those coming from the lower end of the income spectrum.

## Forces behind the Trends

What the three case studies reveal is that behind apparently straightforward trends, major structural forces are at play. Some of these forces, such as the average number of years of schooling or the distribution of the stock of education, can be directly affected by policy, but doing so takes time. Other forces are strictly market outcomes or stem from individual preferences in labor force participation, choice of partner, or number and spacing of children. The influence of policy measures on these decisions is likely to be ambiguous. Finally, as the case of Taiwan (China) shows, tax and transfer policies can counteract observed increases in primary income inequality.

## Inequality between Countries

Yet another reason why inequality is back on the agenda is the increase in inequality between countries since 1980 (table 2). Milanovic (1999) finds that the world

Gini coefficient rose from 62.8 in 1988 to 66.7 in 1993, with the bulk of the increase reflecting between-country differences. This widening gap has led to a burgeoning literature that has, at least indirectly, put inequality back on the agenda.

If the world behaved as predicted by the simple neoclassical growth model, the per capita incomes of countries with the same preferences (that is, saving rates), technologies, government policies, and population growth would eventually converge. Differences in countries' per capita income could be explained in full by differences in steady-state per capita income and by how far per capita income diverges from the steady-state equilibrium. Initial conditions would not matter, and transitory shocks would not alter the long-run equilibrium. If, however, the world is characterized by multiple, locally stable equilibria, convergence may not ensue. Different initial conditions or transitory shocks could push countries with the same preferences, technologies, and other characteristics into permanently different long-term equilibria.

Whichever model is correct, two questions remain: Why do some countries remain stuck in the low-income club, and can something be done to move them out? Although no clear consensus has emerged on whether conditional convergence is validated by empirical analysis, ample evidence suggests that the world seems to be converging toward two clubs: the rich countries and the poor countries (see Quah 1993 and Ros 2000). More precisely, a sort of conditional convergence—that is, an inverse relationship between per capita output growth and per capita income—appears to apply to countries with per worker incomes above the world average. In contrast, economies on the other end of the spectrum seem to be caught in a poverty trap. Historically, there has been massive divergence in absolute and relative per capita incomes, with steady and nearly equal growth rates for the leaders in the long run and consistently low growth rates for the countries that are currently poor (Pritchett 1997). This phenomenon explains the difficulty of finding strong tendencies toward divergence or convergence for the entire sample of countries.[5]

A number of explanations have been put forward as to why slow growth persists at low income levels. Extensions of the simple neoclassical framework suggest that slow growth reflects differences in steady-state equilibria resulting from low investments in human capital and political instability (Barro 1991, 1997; Mankiw, Romer,

**Table 2. Coefficient of Variation of GDP Per Capita**

| Year | Coefficient of variation |
| --- | --- |
| 1980 | 0.7575 |
| 1985 | 0.7867 |
| 1990 | 0.8083 |
| 1995 | 0.8291 |
| 1996 | 0.8294 |
| 1980s | 0.7789 |
| 1990s | 0.8210 |

*Note:* The total number of countries included in the calculations is 61.

and Weil 1992). Low growth could also be the result of a protracted transition caused by a series of large adverse external shocks. Ros (1998) tries to address this issue by grouping the sample of countries used in Mankiw, Romer, and Weil (1992) into growth performance categories and estimating their steady-state per capita incomes. Ros then compares the relative position of countries in their steady states with actual income gaps. Because the steady-state gaps are much narrower than the actual income gaps, the differences would seem to arise from the fact that poorer countries are farther away from their steady state. If this were the case, however, neoclassical theory would suggest that poorer countries should be growing faster than other countries, something that is not validated by actual performance (Ros 1998).

Although this exercise is not conclusive, it does support the view that economic growth may be better characterized by multiple equilibria—that is, a world in which initial conditions matter and transitional shocks have long-run implications. In such a world, poverty traps occur as countries are pushed, either by initial conditions or external shocks, into low-level equilibria. In the development literature, particularly early on, several simple models of low-level equilibrium traps were put forward. One is the insufficient savings theory introduced by Leibenstein (1957) and subsequently formalized by King and Rebelo (1993). According to this approach, at low capital-labor ratios, per capita income is barely enough for subsistence, and savings fall below depreciation. The country is "stuck" in a low-level equilibrium trap. Although good investment opportunities may exist, the country is too poor to take advantage of them. Of course, were foreign investment or foreign aid available, profitable investments could be exploited despite the lack of domestic capital. Political risk could deter private capital flows, however, and international misbehavior, such as engaging in war or coup d'état, could deter foreign aid. Barro (1991, 1997) finds some support for convergence, albeit at a slow pace, when he controls for the role of political risk in addition to controlling for human capital differences. Ros (2000), however, finds that if countries are classified by income level, differences in the rule of law index (used by Barro) at the low end of the spectrum appear too small compared with the large differences in growth rates observed among countries in this group.

The debate on the seemingly inexorable increase in inequality between countries is affecting the development discourse in many ways. The multiple equilibria and club convergence perspectives have strong implications for policy. The club convergence view gives credence to the view that policy matters, that a country's evolution is not preordained but can be altered by intervention—a view that leads to the still unresolved debate on what exactly these interventions ought to be. Insofar as initial conditions include low levels of physical and human capital, this perspective also supports arguments for foreign aid to help poor countries break out of their low-level traps.

The most recent work on aid, however, has thrown doubts on the extent to which it has actually helped poorer countries grow. Burnside and Dollar (1997), World Bank (1998), Kanbur (1999), and a host of other recent publications point to the dismal record of aid in breaking the poverty traps identified in the growth literature.

The reason, it would seem, is that resources by themselves are not enough; how they are used is crucial. Burnside and Dollar (1997) show that aid promotes growth only when it flows into "good" policy environments—otherwise, it is at best ineffective. This is the empirical counterpart to the general theoretical proposition that in a second-best world simply expanding the resource base may do no good or may even immiserize a society. What matters, primarily, is domestic policy. The increase in inequality between economies is thus not independent of growing inequality within economies.

## Conclusion

It could be argued that interest in inequality never disappeared but was always on the agenda in one form or another. The untidy way in which academic analysis advances means that discussion of a topic almost always continues, even during times when interest in the topic has reportedly died. Clearly, however, the turn of the century has seen a resurgence of interest in inequality, and distribution more generally, as a result of the culmination of several trends in the analytical, empirical, and policy literature.

First, the separation of distribution and allocative efficiency—an immediate implication of postwar attempts to formalize Adam Smith's invisible hand—no longer holds sway. As the real world features of imperfect information and imperfect markets have been recognized and incorporated into the analytical framework, equity and efficiency are now recognized as integrally connected, and detailed analysis is required to identify and understand these connections.

Second, the empirical regularities between inequality and growth are increasingly being recognized for what they are—regularities that provide little in the way of specific policy implications. The current consensus is that there is no systematic empirical relationship between inequality and growth—but this type of separation has policy implications only if it is assumed that there are separable sets of growth and redistribution policy instruments. Once specific policy instruments are considered—and this is what policymakers are interested in—inequality is back on the agenda.

Third, aggregate measures of inequality have changed dramatically for some countries in the past decade. The fact that inequality has remained relatively stable in other countries—and has even declined in some—has raised questions about why countries facing broadly similar global circumstances have had such widely different experiences.

Fourth, recent empirical work is showing how the evolution of inequality is the outcome of a complex pattern of forces, such as the evolution of markets, assets, and institutions, overlaid on basic demographic shifts. Understanding these forces, which takes us beyond the simple lack of correlation between aggregate inequality and per capita income, represents the real challenge. Meeting this challenge will require new techniques and open up new avenues of policy analysis.

Fifth, global divergence has put the issue of inequality between nations back on the agenda. In the past decade this increase has led to a rich literature on what determines relative growth rates and whether growing inequality between nations is inevitable. This debate is also linked to the role of foreign aid in overcoming the poverty traps the literature has identified.

These five strands of the literature appear set to define the research and policy agenda in the first decade of the next century. They have already led to fruitful insights and significant policy implications, even beyond the realm of distributional analysis.

## Notes

1. We put "reliable" in quotations because, in general, available inequality measures for particular countries do not necessarily provide an accurate description of the country's degree of inequality. One source of the problem is the underreporting of income (and expenditures), which occurs more frequently at lower and higher ends of the income spectrum. As a result, an inequality measure for the same country, using the same survey and for the same year, can vary by several percentage points depending on whether the data on income were corrected for underreporting and on the method followed to do the correction. Different methods of correcting for underreporting can yield different measures of inequality. For an illustration, see Lustig and Szekely (1998).

2. Only changes in inequality of more than 2 percentage points were considered.

3. The rise in inequality is robust to the inequality measure and to adjustments to income to account for economies of scale in the household and for underreporting.

4. Because the decomposition method is applied to a reduced-form household income model, the estimated coefficients are not strictly speaking returns, as they capture not only the market returns to the corresponding characteristics but also a range of endogenous decisions such as labor force participation and occupational choice.

5. The observed patterns in the relationship between growth and income per capita may be reflecting gaps across countries in their positions relative to their steady states. The simple neoclassical framework is perfectly consistent with a country that is closer to its low steady-state income per capita level growing more slowly than a richer country that is much farther away from its steady-state equilibrium.

## References

Aaron, H.J. 1978. *Politics and the Professors.* Washington, D.C.: Brookings Institution.

Aghion, P., E. Caroli, and C. García-Peñalosa. 1999. "Inequality and Economic Growth: The Perspective of the New Growth Theories." *Journal of Economic Literature* 37 (4): 1615–61.

Ahluwalia, M. 1976. "Inequality, Poverty and Development." *Journal of Development Economics* 3: 307–42.

Alderman, H., P-A. Chiappori, L. Haddad, J. Hoddinott, and R. Kanbur. 1995. "Unitary versus Collective Models of the Household: Is It Time to Shift the Burden of Proof?" *World Bank Research Observer* 10 (1): 1–19.

Alesina, A., and D. Rodrik. 1994. "Distributive Politics and Economic Growth." *Quarterly Journal of Economics* 109: 465–90.

Anand, S., and R. Kanbur. 1993a. "Inequality and Development: A Critique." *Journal of Development Economics* 41: 19–43.

———. 1993b. "The Kuznets Process and the Inequality-Development Relationship." *Journal of Development Economics* 40: 25–52.

Atkinson, A. B. 1997. "Bringing Income Distribution in from the Cold." *Economic Journal* 107: 297–321.

———. 1998. *Equity Issues in a Globalizing World: The Experience of OECD Countries.* International Monetary Fund, Conference on Economic Policy and Equity, June 8–9, Washington, D.C.

Atkinson, A. B., and F. Bourguignon. 2000. "Introduction." *Handbook of Income Distribution.* Amsterdam: North Holland.

Bardhan, P., S. Bowles, and H. Gintis. 2000. "Wealth Inequality, Credit Constraints, and Economic Performance." In A.B. Atkinson and F. Bourguignon, eds., *Handbook of Income Distribution.* Amsterdam: North Holland.

Barro, R. J. 1991. "Economic Growth in a Cross Section of Countries." *Quarterly Journal of Economics* 106: 407–44.

———. 1997. *Determinants of Economic Growth: A Cross-Country Empirical Study.* Cambridge, Mass.: MIT Press.

Bénabou, R. 1996. "Inequality and Growth." In B.S. Bernanke and J. Rotemberg, eds., NBER *Macroeconomics Annual 11.* Cambridge, Mass.: MIT Press.

Birdsall, N., D. Ross, and R. Sabot. 1995. "Inequality and Growth Reconsidered: Lessons from East Asia." *World Bank Economic Review* 9 (3): 477–508.

Boadway, R., and M. Keen. 2000. "Redistribution." In A. B. Atkinson and F. Bourguignon, eds., *Handbook of Income Distribution.* Amsterdam: North Holland.

Bouillón, C., A. Legovini, and N. Lustig. 1999. "Rising Inequality in Mexico: Returns to Household Characteristics and the 'Chiapas Effect.'" Inter-American Development Bank, Washington, D.C.

Bourguignon F., F. Ferreira, and N. Lustig. 1997. "The Microeconomics of Income Distribution Dynamics in East Asia and Latin America." Research proposal, Inter-American Development and World Bank, Washington, D.C.

Bourguignon F., M. Fournier, and M. Gurgand. 1998. "Distribution, Development, and Education: Taiwan, 1979-94." World Bank, Washington, D.C.

Bruno, N., M. Ravallion, and L. Squire. 1998. "Equity and Growth in Developing Countries: Old and New Perspectives on the Policy Issue." In V. Tanzi and K.Y. Chu, eds., *Income Distribution and High-Quality Growth.* Cambridge, Mass.: MIT Press.

Burnside, C., and D. Dollar. 1997. "Aid Spurs Growth—In a Sound Policy Environment." *Finance and Development* 34 (4): 4–7.

Chenery, H., M. Ahluwalia, C. Bell, J. Duloy, and R. Jolly. 1974. *Redistribution with Growth.* Oxford: Oxford University Press.

Commander, S., and U. Lee. 1998. "How Does Public Policy Affect the Income Distribution? Evidence from Russia, 1992-96." World Bank, Washington, D.C.

Cragg, M., and M. Epelbaum. 1995. "Why Has Wage Dispersion Grown in Mexico? Is it the Incidence of Reforms or the Growing Demand for Skills?" *Journal of Development Economics* 51 (1): 99–116.

Datt, G., and M. Ravallion. 1992. "Growth and Redistribution Components of Changes in Poverty Measures: A Decomposition with Applications to Brazil and India in the 1980s." *Journal of Development Economics* 38: 275–95.

Deininger, K., and L. Squire. 1996. "A New Data Set Measuring Income Inequality." *World Bank Economic Review* 10 (3): 565–91.

Dixit, Avinash, and Timothy Besley. 1997. "James Mirrlees' Contributions to the Theory of Information and Incentives." *Scandanavian Journal of Economics* 99 (2): 207–40.

Ferreira, F., and J. Litchfield. 1998. "Education or Inflation? The Roles of Structural Factors and Macroeconomic Instability in Explaining Brazilian Inequality in the 1980s." STICERD DARP Discussion Paper 41. London School of Economics.

Ferreira, F., and R. Paes de Barros. 1999. "The Slippery Slope: Explaining the Increase in Extreme Poverty in Urban Brazil, 1976–96." Policy Research Working Paper 2210. World Bank, Poverty Division, Poverty Reduction and Economic Management Network, Washington, D.C.

Fishlow, A. 1972. "Brazilian Size Distribution of Income." *American Economic Review* 62: 391–402.

———. 1995. "Inequality, Poverty, and Growth: Where Do We Stand?" In Michael Bruno and Boris Pleskovic, eds., *Proceedings of the 1995 Annual World Bank Conference on Development Economics*. Washington, D. C.: World Bank.

Forbes K. 1998. "A Reassessment of the Relationship Between Inequality and Growth." Working Paper. Department of Economics, Massachusetts Institute of Technology, Cambridge, Mass.

Gallup, J. L., S. Radelet, and A. Warner. 1998. "Economic Growth and the Income of the Poor." Harvard Institute for International Development, Cambridge, Mass.

Greenwald, Bruce, and Joseph. E. Stiglitz. 1986. "Externalities in Economies with Imperfect Information and Incomplete Markets." *Quarterly Journal of Economics* 101: 229–64.

Haddad, L., and R. Kanbur. 1990. "How Serious Is the Neglect of Intrahousehold Inequality?" *Economic Journal* 100: 866–81.

Hanson, G., and Harrison A. 1995. *Trade, Technology and Wage Inequality in Mexico*. NBER Working Paper 5110. National Bureau of Economic Research, Cambridge, Mass.

Hoff, K. 1994. "The Second Theorem of the Second Best." *Journal of Public Economics* 45: 223–42.

Kakwani, N. 1994. "Poverty and Economic Growth, with Application to Côte d'Ivoire." *Review of Income and Wealth* 39: 121–39

Kanbur, Ravi. 1987. "Measurement and Alleviation of Poverty." *IMF Staff Papers* 36: 60–85.

———. 1990. *Poverty and the Social Dimensions of Adjustment in Côte d'Ivoire*. Social Dimensions of Adjustment Paper 5. World Bank, Washington, D.C.

———. 1999. "A Framework for Thinking Through Reduced Aid Dependence in Africa." Working Paper WP 99-06. Cornell University, Department of Agricultural, Resource and Managerial Economics, Ithaca, N.Y.

———. 2000. "Income Distribution and Development." In A.B. Atkinson and F. Bourguignon, eds., *Handbook of Income Distribution*. Amsterdam: North Holland.

Kanbur, Ravi, and L. Haddad. 1994. "Are Better Off Households More Unequal or Less Unequal?" *Oxford Economic Papers* 46: 445–58.

King, Robert G., and Sergio T. Rebelo. 1993. "Transitional Dynamics and Economic Growth in the Neoclassical Mode." *American Economic Review* 83 (September): 908–31.

Kuznets, S. 1955. "Economic Growth and Income Inequality." *American Economic Review* 45: 1–28.

Láchler, U. 1997. "Education and Earnings Inequality in Mexico." Mexico Country Department, World Bank, Washington, D.C.

Leibenstein, Harver. 1957. "The Theory of Underemployment in Backward Economies" *The Journal of Political Economy* 62 (2): 91–103.

Lewis, W. A. 1954. "Economic Development with Unlimited Supplies of Labour." *Manchester School of Economic Studies* 22: 139–81.

Li, H., L. Squire, and H. F. Zou. 1998. "Explaining International Inequality and Intertemporal Variations in Income Inequality." *Economic Journal* 108: 26–43.

Londoño, Juan Luis, and Miguel Székely. 1997. "Persistent Poverty and Excess Inequality: Latin America, 1970–1995." Working Paper 357. Inter-American Development Bank, Washington, D.C.

Lundberg, M., and L. Squire. 1999. "Inequality and Growth: Lessons for Policy." World Bank, Office of the Vice President, Development Economics, Washington, D.C.

Lustig, N., and M. Székely. 1997. "México: evolución económica, pobreza y desigualdad." Technical Study. Inter-American Development Bank, Sustainable Development Department, Washington, D.C.

Luxembourg Income Study. 1998. "Income Distribution Measures Based on LIS Data." [http://lissy.ceps.lu/inequality.htm].

Mahalanobis, P. 1963. *The Approach of Operational Research to Planning India*. Bombay: Asia Press.

Mankiw, G., D. Romer, and D. Weil. 1992. "A Contribution to the Empirics of Economic Growth." *Quarterly Journal of Economics* 107: 407–37.

Meade, J. E. 1964. *Efficiency, Equality, and the Ownership of Property*. London: Allen and Unwin.

Milanovic, Branko. 1998. *Income, Inequality, and Poverty during the Transition from Planned to Market Economy*. Washington, D.C.: World Bank.

———. 1999. "True World Income Distribution, 1988 and 1993: First Calculation Based on Household Surveys Alone." Policy Research Working Paper 2244. World Bank, Poverty and Human Resources, Development Economics Research Group, Washington, D.C.

Mirrlees, J. 1971. "An Exploration in the Theory of Optimum Income Taxation." *Review of Economic Studies* 38: 175–208.

OECD (Organisation for Economic Co-operation and Development). 1996. *OECD Economic Surveys 1996-1997, Mexico*. Paris.

Pritchett, Lant. 1997. "Divergence, Big Time." *Journal of Economic Perspectives* 11 (Summer): 3–17.

Quah, Danny. 1993. "Empirical Cross-Section Dynamics in Economic Growth." *European Economic Review* 37 (April): 426–34.

Ravallion, Martin. 1997. "Can High-Inequality Developing Countries Escape Absolute Poverty?" *Economic Letters* 56: 51–57.

———. 1999. "On Decomposing Changes in Poverty into 'Growth' and 'Redistribution' Components." World Bank, Development Economics Research Group, Washington, D.C.

Ravallion, M., and S. Chen. 1997. "What Can New Survey Data Tell Us About Recent Changes in Distribution Poverty?" *World Bank Economic Review* 2: 357–82.

Revenga, A. 1995. "Employment and Wage Effects of Trade Liberalization: The Case of Mexican Manufacturing." Policy Research Working Paper 1524. World Bank, Latin America and the Caribbean Region Country Unit, Washington, D.C.

Ros, J. 2000. *Development Theory and the Economics of Growth*. Ann Arbor: University of Michigan Press.

Rosenstein-Rodan, P. 1943. "Problems of Industrialization in Eastern and Southern Europe." *Economic Journal* 53: 202–11.

Sen, A. K. 1983. *Resources, Values, and Development*. Oxford: Blackwell.

Tan, H., and G. Batra. 1997. "Technology and Firm Size Wage Differentials in Colombia, Mexico, and Taiwan (China)." *World Bank Economic Review* 11: 59–83.

World Bank. 1997. *Taking Action to Reduce Poverty in Sub-Saharan Africa*. Washington, D.C.

———. 1998. *Assessing Aid: What Works, What Doesn't, and Why*. World Bank Policy Research Series. New York: Oxford University Press.

# Comment on "Why Is Inequality Back on the Agenda?" by Ravi Kanbur and Nora Lustig

*Karla Hoff*

Issues of inequality have once again become central in discussions of development. Ravi Kanbur and Nora Lustig provide a wide-ranging overview of the many reasons for the resurgence of interest. In this comment I will discuss just four of those reasons:

- *Paradigm shift.* The leading paradigm to explain growth has shifted from the neoclassical growth model, in which (assuming a linear savings function) aggregate behavior is independent of the wealth distribution, to models with imperfect capital and insurance markets, in which a reduction in wealth inequality can increase investment opportunities, productivity, and hence growth.[1]
- *Intrahousehold distribution.* Work in the past two decades, to which Kanbur has made important contributions, has shown that measured inequality and the estimated incidence of policy can be significantly altered by a focus on intrahousehold distribution.
- *Magnification effects.* There is now a rich set of models for understanding channels through which a market economy can magnify variation in individual attributes (through convex returns to skill, for example), and there is evidence for some countries of market-driven increases in inequality.
- *Endogenous policy.* Recent work suggests links between inequality and development policy. Greater equality in the distribution of land is empirically associated with the emergence of legal institutions that permit broader participation in the market economy. A higher share of income for the middle class is associated in the subsequent period with more public investment in education and sanitation.

## Paradigm Shift

I appreciated Kanbur and Lustig's characterization of the shift in economic thinking in recent decades as the "triumph of the imperfect information paradigm." This tri-

---

Karla Hoff is visiting assistant professor at Princeton University.

Annual World Bank Conference on Development Economics 1999
©2000 The International Bank for Reconstruction and Development / THE WORLD BANK

umph was not widely foreseen even 15 years ago, as I can attest from experience. During my graduate student years at Princeton, 1984–88, there was a conflict within the economics department over who would teach the first-year course in microeconomics. Should it be Hugo Sonnenschein, who would focus on the Walrasian model with a complete set of markets—for all goods and all risks in all periods? Or should it be Joseph Stiglitz, who would emphasize information economics? Information economics was the emerging catchall term for work by scholars from various fields of economics who were exploring the information problems that preclude complete markets. In 1984–85, the conflict over teaching assignments was resolved in favor of Stiglitz—perhaps by default since Sonnenschein took a sabbatical that academic year.

Two years later the place of information economics in the canon resurfaced in my graduate program in another way. Ravi Kanbur was then teaching the course in development economics. I suspect that he did not foresee how complete the triumph of information economics would be, since he put the course material on information and incentive problems under the heading "Stiglitzian economics."

Much has changed in the past decade. Information economics now represents about a third of the standard graduate textbook in microeconomic theory (Mas-Colell, Whinston, and Green 1995). The imperfect information paradigm is the leading paradigm in all recent texts in development economics (Basu 1997; Ray 1998; Bardhan and Udry 1999). Stiglitz (forthcoming) provides an assessment of this paradigm shift.

Once imperfect information is incorporated into economic analysis, it becomes apparent that an economy is bound by not one but two sets of constraints: *resource constraints,* as in the standard competitive model, and *incentive constraints,* which arise because of the problems of providing individuals with proper incentives in a setting of imperfect information. Here the key idea is that wealth often provides a way to get around these incentive constraints, resolving problems of moral hazard, adverse selection, "hold-up," and enforcement. Thus whether incentive constraints bind tightly or not in an economy depends on the distribution of wealth. Lenders, because of their limited information over the uses to which borrowers put their funds and the high costs of enforcement, may not be willing to lend to poor individuals or may do so on unfavorable terms. As a result, low-wealth individuals may be shut out of education and entrepreneurial activities. Because of risk aversion, they may be unable to make the best use of the resources they have. Farmers in semi-arid regions of India, for example, forgo fixed investments in irrigation in favor of more liquid investments in cattle, which provide some insurance. More generally, poor people tend to forgo high-return, high-risk investments in favor of those with lower risks and lower expected returns (see Morduch 1994 and the references he cites). In a wide variety of ways a person's assets play a dual role as an *input,* which is used up in production, and as a *catalyst,* which is not used up but makes it possible for an individual to obtain credit, create a business, and self-insure. Market forces can create "poverty traps" and can lead to the polarization of the population into rich and poor, with low growth in aggregate. (A recent, highly accessible treatment is Banerjee 2000.)

## Intrahousehold Distribution

Kanbur and Lustig highlight recent work on the distribution of income within the household. One important policy question to which this work contributes concerns the incidence of structural adjustment, when overvalued exchange rates are brought into line with market rates. It might appear to be sufficient to evaluate the question at the level of the household. But Kanbur and Lustig provide an example in which household-level analysis suggests that a devaluation would reduce inequality (because households producing export crops are poorer on average than those in the more urbanized nontradables sector), whereas analysis at the level of the individual suggests that devaluation would increase inequality. It is, in general, men in rural areas, not women, who earn most of the income from producing export crops. Women derive their income primarily from nontradables. When adults within the household do not pool their earnings, devaluation can exacerbate the unequal distribution of income by hurting women in rural households. Thus analysis of the distributional consequences of a policy instrument may require careful examination of intrahousehold patterns of income sharing and occupational choice.

## Magnification Effects

Analysis of the distributional consequences of policy may also require examination of externalities within and across households. One example that has recently been explored theoretically (Basu and Foster 1998) and empirically (Basu, Narayan, and Ravallion 1999) is externalities from literacy. *Isolated illiterates*—illiterate people in households with no literate members—are less likely to learn about new technologies and less likely to respond to new opportunities than *proximate illiterates*, illiterate people who live in a household with at least one literate member. Consequently, a literacy measure that captures that externality, as constructed by Basu and Foster, is likely to be better than the standard literacy measure in predicting achievements that depend on literacy.

Local interaction environments are, of course, endogenous: we choose our spouses, our neighbors, the location of our businesses. Neighborhoods may be open to anyone able to afford and find a place to live, but in fact they often exhibit tendencies to attract their own kind and to repel other kinds. When local spillover effects interact with stratification of neighborhoods, initial differences in the attributes of individuals can be magnified (a review is Durlauf 1994). I will briefly discuss two examples.

Benabou (1996) focuses on the case in which individuals differ in human capital. It is assumed that adults with high levels of human capital create spillovers that favor the production of human capital in the young. Benabou's analysis shows that market forces can lead to the formation of neighborhoods that are stratified by human capital, leading to persistent inequality and to deep cleavages in society over time. This stratification and the resulting cleavage can occur even when it is highly inefficient. In making a location decision, no household takes into account the impact of its decision on others. Thus it may move from one location to another in order to obtain a small gain, while imposing a large loss on others. The implication is that poverty traps can be self-organizing in (imperfect) market economies.

Hoff and Sen (1999) focus on the case in which individuals are identical in all respects except initial wealth. There are two interpretations of the model, one focusing on homeownership the other on entrepreneurship. Homeowners have stronger incentives for home improvement effort than renters. Similarly, entrepreneurs have stronger incentives for work effort than salaried managers. It is assumed that effort creates local spillovers and complementarities: The value of improvements to a home depends on the desirability of the neighborhood; similarly, the return to research and development may depend on knowledge spillovers from neighboring firms. In these cases individuals' efforts create spillovers that are especially advantageous to those who also expend high effort. The analysis shows that segregated equilibria may emerge. Even though the poor do not have different preferences than the rich, rich and poor may live in communities (or work in settings) that exhibit very different characteristics—the rich in a community with high levels of home ownership (entrepreneurship) and high levels of spillovers that raise each individual's return to effort, and the poor in a community with low levels of both.

Sorting of workers across firms can also give rise to magnification effects. In a discussion of changing patterns of inequality in Brazil and Mexico, Kanbur and Lustig note the contribution to within-country inequality of convex returns to education. What forces could explain that phenomenon? I will discuss one possible explanation here.

Traditional production functions allow firms to substitute quantity for quality: two low-skilled workers may be as good as one high-skilled worker. But in many processes this is not the case. Mistakes in any one of a set of tasks can dramatically reduce the value of the final output: a flaw in the design of the O-rings in the rocket boosters destroyed the space shuttle *Challenger*. Kremer's (1993) "O-ring" theory of production can explain not only why the gaps in wages across skill levels are so great within countries but also why the gaps in per capita incomes are enormous across countries. Increasing returns to skill will be realized through stratification by skill level across firms, just as in the Hoff-Sen model of neighborhood formation, discussed above, increasing returns to effort are realized through stratification between homeowners and renters across neighborhoods. But in Kremer's model the stratification is efficiency-enhancing.

The key idea in Kremer's model is the complementarity of skills within the firm. To capture that idea, Kremer supposes that there are $n$ tasks in a production process. For simplicity, let $n = 2$. Each worker has a skill $q$, where $q$ is between 0 and 1. Let $q_1$ denote the skill of the person performing the first task and $q_2$ denote the skill of the person performing the second task. A firm's production function is $y = A\, q_1 q_2$. One way to interpret the model is that $q$ is the probability that a job is done correctly. Under this interpretation the value of a firm's output if both jobs are done correctly is $A$, and the probability of that joint event is $q_1 q_2$.

Competitive equilibrium is characterized by a wage function, say $w(q)$, and an allocation of workers to firms. Given the wage function, each firm will choose $q_1$ and $q_2$ to maximize its expected income, $Aq_1 q_2 - w(q_1) - w(q_2)$. The first implication of the model is the "skill clustering theorem:" firms will select workers with similar ability levels.

To see this is straightforward. Consider any distinct values for $a$ and $b$. Since $(a-b)^2 = a^2 + b^2 - 2ab > 0$, it must be true that $a^2 + b^2 > 2ab$. If $a$ and $b$ represent the skill levels of the individuals who perform the first and second tasks, then it follows that expected output is higher when the skill levels of the workers in the two tasks are matched than when they are not. Intuitively, it does not pay to "waste" a high-probability-of-success worker through pairing with a low-probability-of-success coworker. This means that whatever the wage and skill levels, each firm will group workers of the same skill level.

This finding has strong implications for the return to skills. It implies a *convex wage schedule,* in which a doubling of skills more than doubles wages. The reason is that the value of the marginal product of an increase in skill to a given individual is proportional to the skill of the person's coworker (formally, a small increment in $q_1$ will increase output by $Aq_2$). From the skill clustering theorem, the coworker's skill is just equal to the individual's own skill level. Thus a worker with high-level skills will work with other highly skilled workers and the marginal return to skill will be high, whereas a worker with low-level skills will work with other workers with low-level skills and the marginal return to skill will be low.

## Endogenous Policy

Kanbur and Lustig raise the central questions of why some countries remain in the low-income club and what forces could pull them out. Their discussion touches on the recent literature exploring the effect of inequality on policy. Inequality—particularly the size of the middle class—affects support for education and public goods (see Benabou 1994 and Easterly 1999 and references therein). More generally, it affects political support for institutions that permit broad participation in the market. This is illustrated by recent work on the New World economies since the 1700s. Engerman and Sokoloff (1997) and Engerman, Haber, and Sokoloff (1999) find that societies that began with greater inequality tended to place greater restrictions on six factors: the franchise, the right to vote in secret, the right to create a company, the right to patent an invention and to protect that right in the courts, access to primary schooling, and access to land. Restriction of the franchise and the right to vote in secret tended to cement the political power of the elite; the other four factors tended to limit the participation of low-income groups in commercial activity. In Latin America, where initial inequality was high, the legal regime contributed to inequality and limited growth. In contrast, inequality was low in the 13 American colonies and Canada, and the political and legal institutions that emerged were more supportive of broad participation in commercial activity and, more generally, welfare and growth.

Kanbur and Lustig successfully make the case that inequality is now "back on the agenda." I have tried to suggest a few additional reasons why this agenda item now appears to be central in understanding the development process.

## Note

1. Further evidence of the extensive research activity in this area is the survey by Aghion, Caroli, and Garcia-Penalosa 1999, which appeared after Kanbur and Lustig's article was written.

## References

Aghion, Philippe, Eve Caroli, and Cecilia Garcia-Penalosa. 1999. "Inequality and Economic Growth: The Perspective of the New Growth Theories." *Journal of Economic Literature* 37 (December): 1615–60.

Banerjee, Abhijit. 2000. "The Two Poverties." Massachusetts Institute of Technology, Department of Economics, Cambridge, Mass.

Bardhan, Pranab, and Christopher Udry. 1999. *Development Microeconomics.* Oxford and New York: Oxford University Press.

Basu, Kaushik. 1997. *Analytical Development Economics.* Cambridge, Mass: Massachusetts Institute of Technology Press.

Basu, Kaushik, and James E. Foster. 1998. "On Measuring Literacy." *Economic Journal* 108 (November): 1733–49.

Basu, Kaushik, Ambar Narayan, and Martin Ravallion. 1999. "Is Knowledge Shared within Households?" World Bank Policy Research Working Paper 2261. Office of the Senior Vice President and Chief Economist, Development Economics, and Poverty and Human Resources, Development Research Group, Washington, D.C.

Benabou, Roland. 1994. "Unequal Societies." New York University, Department of Economics, New York.

———. 1996. "Equity and Efficiency in Human Capital Investment: The Local Connection." *Review of Economic Studies* 63 (April): 237–64.

Durlauf, Steven N. 1994. "Spillovers, Stratification, and Inequality." *European Economic Review* 38 (April): 836-845.

Easterly, William. 1999. "The Middle Class Consensus and Economic Development." World Bank, Development Economics, Development Research Group, Washington, D.C.

Engerman, Stanley L., and Kenneth L. Sokoloff. 1997. "Factor Endowments, Institutions, and Differential Paths of Growth among New World Economies: A View from Economic Historians of the United States." In Stephen Haber, ed., *How Latin America Fell Behind.* Stanford, Cali.: Stanford University Press.

Engerman, Stanley L., Stephen H. Haber, and Kenneth L. Sokoloff. 1999. "Inequality, Institutions, and Differential Paths of Growth among New World Economies." University of California, Department of Economics, Los Angeles.

Hoff, Karla, and Arijit Sen. 1999. "Home-Ownership, Community Interactions, and Stratification." World Bank, Development Economics, Development Research Group, Washington, D.C.

Kremer, M. 1993. "The O-Ring Theory of Economic Development." *Quarterly Journal of Economics* 108 (August): 551–61.

Mas-Colell, Andreu, Michael D. Whinston, and Jerry R. Green. 1995. *Microeconomic Theory*. Oxford and New York: Oxford University Press.

Morduch, Jonathan. 1994. "Poverty and Vulnerability." *American Economic Review* 84 (2): 221–25.

Ray, Debraj. 1998. *Development Economics*. Princeton, N.J.: Princeton University Press.

Stiglitz, Joseph E. Forthcoming. "The Contributions of the Economics of Information to Twentieth Century Economics." *Quarterly Journal of Economics*.

# Economics of Transition

# Macroeconomic Lessons from Ten Years of Transition

*Charles Wyplosz*

*Transition was never going to be easy, despite its promising long-run outlook. Not only was the process a major theoretical and policy challenge, but politics and economics were bound to interfere. With some spectacular exceptions, most transition economies are now on the right track. In hindsight, the old debate on the best approach to transition—big bang or gradualism—is more a question of feasibility, though many of the arguments favoring big bang have proven correct. Inflation has been found to be incompatible with growth, and the importance of a good microeconomic structure—especially an effective banking system—has been confirmed. The choice of an exchange rate regime, another early controversy, appears secondary to adherence to a strict monetary policy. The decline of the state is both spectacular and puzzling, combining desirable and dangerous features.*

When transition started, there was little experience to rely on. Latin America was shifting to market-friendly policies, and East Asia had embarked on its "miraculous" path of breakneck growth. But the former Soviet bloc faced different challenges. These countries had no markets, almost no private businesses, and monetary and banking systems unlike anything seen elsewhere. Moreover, they were undergoing a political revolution. In most cases productive capital was entirely publicly owned, opening the way for the largest privatization programs ever and creating from scratch a class of corporate moguls.

It should have been clear from the outset that this complex undertaking would not succeed everywhere, at least not initially. Political conditions differed vastly, affecting the range of feasible policies and the ability to forge a consensus sufficient to pursue unavoidably unsettling changes. In some countries—such as the Czech Republic and Poland—new leaders emerged from years of opposition to the com-

---

Charles Wyplosz is professor of economics at the Graduate Institute of International Studies, Geneva, and director of the program in international macroeconomics at the Centre for Economic Policy Research. The author is grateful to Dragoslav Avramovic, Danica Popovic, Richard Portes, and Boris Vujcic for useful comments.

Annual World Bank Conference on Development Economics 1999
©2000 The International Bank for Reconstruction and Development / THE WORLD BANK

munist regime, ready for dramatic change. In others—Bulgaria, Slovak Republic, the former Soviet Union—power was gained by shifting political allegiances, but old habits were not discarded. Elsewhere—Albania, Hungary, Romania—political turmoil reflected power-grabbing efforts by individuals and groups who put short-term political gains ahead of economic stability.

Not only politics mattered, though. Economists also diverged sharply. For those aiming at a fast shift to market mechanisms, the big bang approach was logically consistent. Others aimed instead at gradualism: without denying that the ultimate aim was the establishment of a Western economic system, they were concerned about the economic, social, and political costs of adjustment. Given time constraints, some sequencing of reforms was unavoidable. The literature on sequencing was developed with other experiments in mind, mainly in Latin America, and was ill suited to transition. Some economists advocated the preeminence of macroeconomic conditions, while others were more concerned with establishing property rights early on. The role of banking was also highly controversial (Pleskovic 1994). Was a well-functioning credit market indispensable at the outset, or should the state continue to oversee capital accumulation while human capital was being developed?

While privatization and a proper banking system were always considered essential by economists, there has been debate on what kind of market economy should be aimed at. In the U.S. model the bulk of corporate financing originates in stock markets, industrial policy is frowned on, and welfare programs are limited. The European model accepts social goals and relies more on large banks and the state.

Thus from the outset there were different transition paths and objectives. Given these differences, combined with political conditions and the usual dose of historical randomness, it is no surprise that outcomes have varied considerably. This article surveys the facts and distills the voluminous literature on transition to offer lessons from the variety of experiences. It reviews a territory that has been much visited recently—for example, by Åslund, Boone, and Johnson (1996); Begg (1996); Blanchard (1997); Caprio (1995); de Melo, Denizer, and Gelb (1996); Pleskovic (1994); and World Bank (1996).

## The Broad Facts

For citizens and observers of transition economies, the most important outcomes of the experience involve effects on growth, inflation, unemployment, and real wages. From these findings it is possible to identify the successes and failures of transition.

### Growth

Growth in transition economies has tended to follow a U-shape curve.[1] A number of economists—mainly in international organizations—had optimistically anticipated a J-shape curve, expecting fast growth to set in as soon as market institutions were in place. Others—mainly analysts of Eastern Europe—warned of a protracted L-shaped curve if breakneck reforms led to the instant obsolescence of accumulated capital.

The length and depth of the initial recession were not foreseen. Average growth in transition economies did not turn positive until 1994, following a cumulative 29 percent drop in GDP. The initial crash in output, the subject of considerable controversy, remains something of a mystery. It partly reflects the disorganization that followed the demise of central planning. Firms large and small suddenly had to fend for themselves, whether by adopting market rules, asking for state support, or both. In addition, international trade among transition economies, previously organized by the Council for Mutual Economic Assistance, instantly collapsed.

By 1998 only three countries—Poland, Slovak Republic, and Slovenia—had seen GDP recover to 1989 levels (figure 1). In many others GDP stood at about half of its 1989 level. Fischer, Sahay, and Végh (1996b) argue convincingly that transition data are of poor quality and underestimate post-transition GDP relative to pre-transition levels because output prices have plummeted and the underground economy has boomed.[2] Still, the general impression of a deep depression is unlikely to be misleading. The country that recovered fastest, Poland, underwent a deeper decline early on but achieved much stronger performance afterward. Russia briefly returned to positive growth (a paltry 0.8 percent) in 1997, but it relapsed in 1998.

## Inflation

Most transition economies started out with massive inflation, in some cases close to or even above Cagan's (1956) standard hyperinflation threshold of 50 percent a month (figure 2). The peak in 1992 corresponds to the burst that followed price liberalization. Only two countries, Czechoslovakia and Hungary, managed to keep

**Figure 1. GDP in 1998 as a share of GDP in 1989 in Transition Economies**

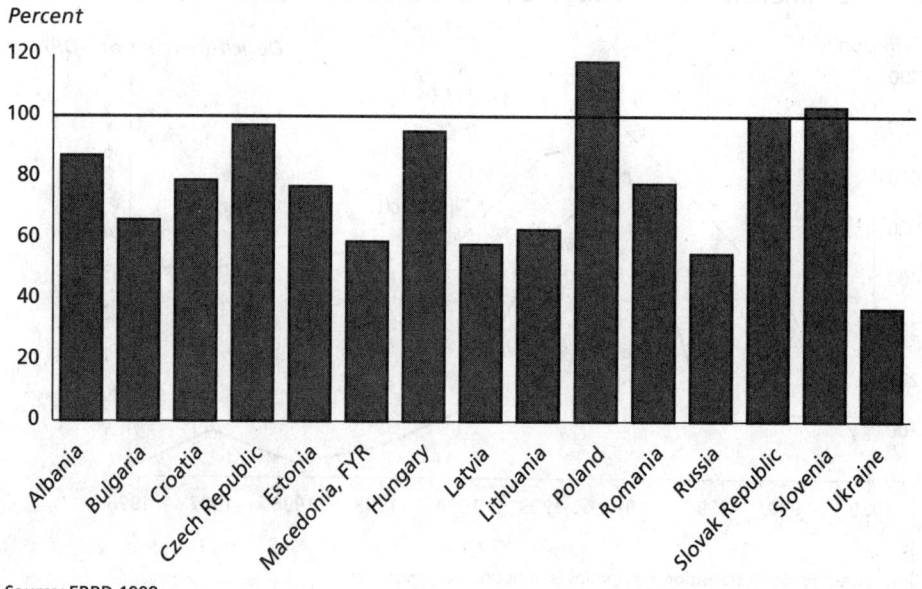

*Source:* EBRD 1998.

inflation in check, in Czechoslovakia thanks to a careful approach and in Hungary because partial liberalization had been allowed over the previous 10 years. Nine of the fifteen countries whose average is shown in figure 2 experienced annual inflation close to or above 1,000 percent. Except in Romania and Russia, inflation is now under control, in the lower double or even single digits.

Price liberalization does not cause inflation, however. It is a once-off adjustment. Its size corresponds partly to the monetary overhang inherited from the goods shortage that characterized central planning, and partly to the initial devaluation when establishing currency convertibility. Price liberalization can be amplified by indexation mechanisms and by expectations of monetary laxity.

In most cases the initial burst of inflation was not entirely unwelcome. It eliminated debts inherited from central planning that were based on wrong prices and so backed by nearly valueless collateral. Once started, however, inflation tended to continue and often increased. One reason was the widespread belief in the misleading theory of inertial inflation, which was really a fig leaf to conceal a monetary authority's unwillingness to stop ratifying price increases. Another reason was the emergence of budget deficits in some countries where the central bank had little or no independence and where debt financing was not yet possible (see figure 2).

## Unemployment

Unemployment data are problematic for all countries. But because of their often rudimentary welfare systems and large underground economies, the situation in most transition economies is much worse and should be interpreted with great cau-

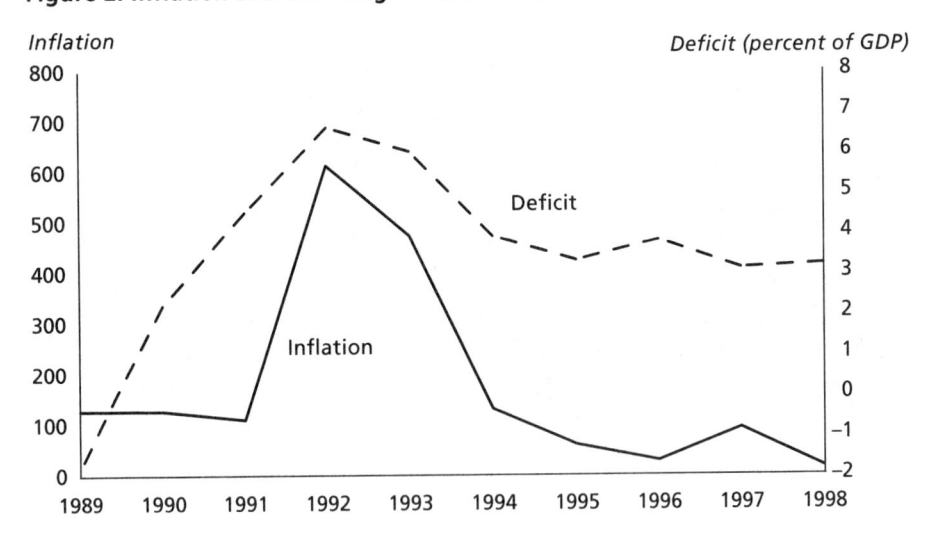

**Figure 2. Inflation and the Budget Deficit in Transition Economies, 1989–98**

*Note:* Average for 15 transition economies (see figure 1 for countries).
*Source:* World Bank various years.

tion. The broad outlines of the situation are not controversial, however. Starting from the near-zero official figures enforced under communism, unemployment immediately shot up, reaching double-digit levels within the first three years of transition—where it has remained since.

This average pattern conceals considerable variation among countries. The Czech Republic is an outlier, but other countries, like the Baltic states, have also managed to keep unemployment below double-digit levels. This is also the case in Russia and Ukraine, though in both countries the recorded figures are almost meaningless.[3] Poland's sharp decrease since 1993 is atypical.

The increase in recorded unemployment is tame compared with the decrease in output. The result, a dramatic drop in measured productivity, sharply contradicts the central aim of transition: boosting productivity. Several factors account for this pattern. To start with, the underground economy often represents a substantial portion of official GDP. Unofficial estimates for Russia, for instance, set this portion at 30–50 percent. Another explanation is that large state-owned firms were reluctant to stop providing lifelong jobs even after privatization. Instead they sought subsidies to keep workers on their payrolls.

### Real Wages

The evolution of real wages is highly contrasted from one country to another, partly reflecting starting positions. In some countries that experienced high inflation when reform was enacted, even moderately lagging wages were severely reduced in real terms.

Is there a link between unemployment and real wages? Given the number of shocks experienced in this period, one would not expect to see a clear relationship. Yet there is evidence of a negative relationship, with unemployment tending to be lower where real wages are higher relative to the first year of transition (top half of figure 3). Though this link is weak, it suggests that fast-reforming countries have low unemployment and high wages. But this conjecture is not supported by a comparison of unemployment data and the European Bank for Reconstruction and Development's liberalization index for transition economies (bottom half of figure 3).

### Successes and Failures

Transition is primarily about setting sick economies on a catchup path. On this criterion, country performance has been varied but mostly disappointing (see figure 1). This does not mean that economic welfare has declined, however, because GDP used to include goods and services—military goods, services of a repressive state, unwanted or poor-quality goods—that did not contribute to ordinary citizens' satisfaction.

Table 1 presents rough summary measures of success: GDP growth rates (averaged over 1996–98 to account for possible hiccups along the way), the purchasing power of wages (measured in U.S. dollars to represent both real wages and terms of trade),[4] and the percentage of GDP produced by the private sector (an imprecise

**Figure 3. Unemployment and Real Wages in Transition Economies**

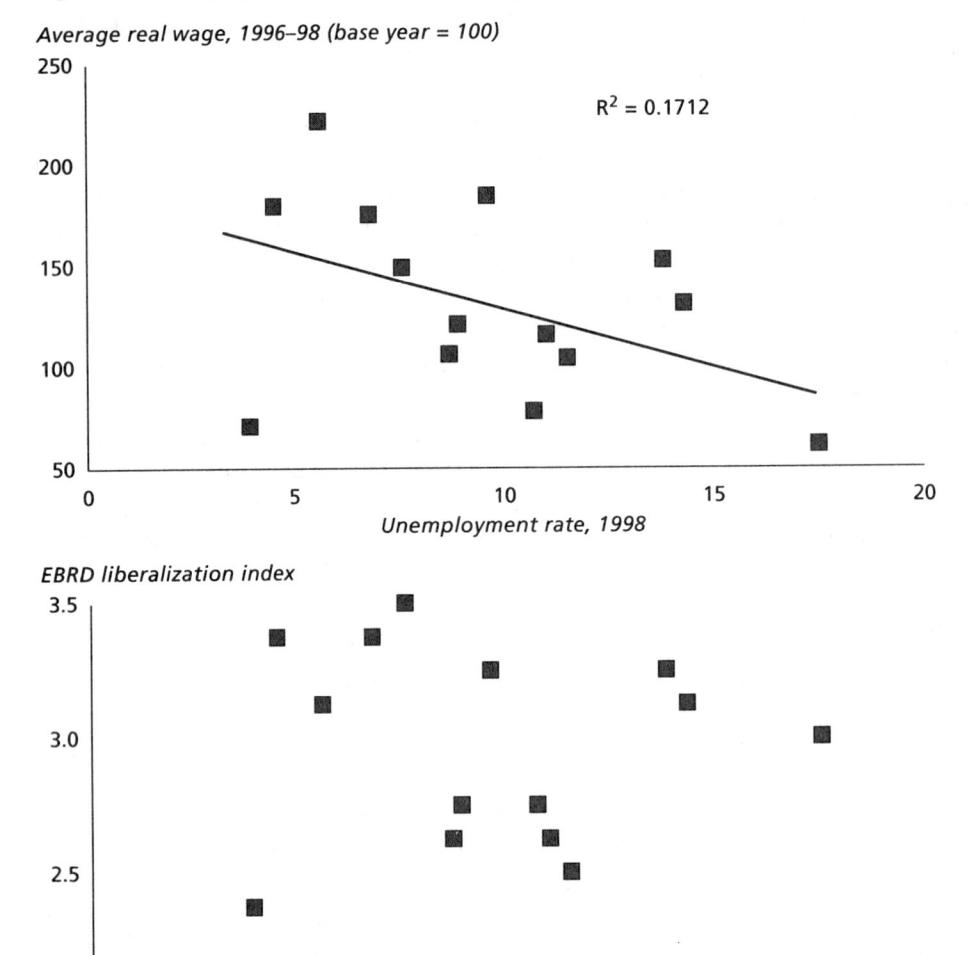

*Average real wage, 1996–98 (base year = 100)*

$R^2 = 0.1712$

Unemployment rate, 1998

*EBRD liberalization index*

Unemployment rate, 1998

*Note:* The base year for real wages corresponds to the first year of transition.
*Source:* UN Economic Commission for Europe data.

gauge of adjustment of output to demand).[5] A country that does well on one of these dimensions tends to also do well on the other two (the partial correlation of GDP growth with the dollar wage is 0.64 and with private output, 0.17). Averaging the three measures delivers an index of success shown in the table as index 1. Index 2 is obtained by dropping private output.

These ad hoc indexes attempt to formalize casual appraisals. Both tell the same story, which matches popular perceptions. One group of countries—Estonia, Hungary, Poland, Slovak Republic—has clearly turned the corner. The Czech

**Table 1. Economic Performance in Transition Economies, 1996–98**

| Country | GDP growth, 1996–98 | Dollar wage, 1998 | Private output (percentage of GDP), 1998 | Index 1 rank | Index 2 rank |
|---|---|---|---|---|---|
| Bulgaria | –6.9 | 100 | 50 | 13 | 13 |
| Croatia | 5.1 | 636 | 55 | 8 | 2 |
| Czech Republic | 1.4 | 323 | 75 | 4 | 8 |
| Estonia | 6.7 | 257 | 70 | 3 | 4 |
| Hungary | 3.4 | 309 | 80 | 1 | 6 |
| Latvia | 4.2 | 270 | 60 | 9 | 6 |
| Lithuania | 4.1 | 166 | 70 | 6 | 9 |
| Poland | 6.0 | 303 | 65 | 5 | 3 |
| Romania | –2.5 | 98 | 60 | 11 | 11 |
| Russia | –3.0 | 149 | 70 | 10 | 10 |
| Slovak Republic | 6.1 | 272 | 75 | 2 | 5 |
| Slovenia | 3.6 | 877 | 55 | 7 | 1 |
| Ukraine | –4.4 | 75 | 55 | 12 | 12 |

*Note:* Index 1 is based on the weighted average of the three first columns, with each element measured relative to the sample mean and the weights being the inverse of the index's standard deviation. Index 2 only takes into account GDP growth and the dollar wage. Sample does not include Albania and FYR Macedonia.
*Source:* EBRD and World Bank data.

Republic would have belonged to this group had it not suffered a serious blow with the May 1997 mini–currency crisis. Croatia, Latvia, and Slovenia are doing well in terms of macroeconomics, but they are lagging in terms of private output. Other countries—Bulgaria (now quickly improving), Romania, Russia, Ukraine—have failed. Lithuania sits in the middle, mainly because of a low dollar wage, reflecting adverse initial conditions rather than the transition.

Good performance tends to be achieved in all dimensions, or not at all. It could be that success breeds success, that some countries had better initial conditions, or that some elites are better able to steer transition.

## Big Bang or Gradualism?

From the outset of transition, economists have been remarkably divided on the best strategy. There was never much doubt about what had to be done: stabilize inflation, control budget deficits, liberalize prices, adopt a single exchange rate, make the current account convertible, open trade and capital movements, build banking and financial systems, establish property rights, end soft budget constraints, and create market-based welfare systems. The question was always, when should these policies be implemented?

One view was that the move from a centrally planned to a market-based economic system could only be done in one go. Lags in design, decisionmaking, and implementation meant that this approach could not literally be enacted in one day, but proponents of the big bang insisted that front-loading was highly desirable. Theorists on the other side of the fence argued that it was not only impossible to do everything at once, but also highly undesirable. Instead the gradualists proposed a sequencing of policy measures.

## The Case for a Big Bang

On the big bang side, Lipton and Sachs (1990), Balcerowicz (1994), Åslund, Boone, and Johnson (1996), and many others presented the following arguments:[6]

- *Reforms are complementary.* The alternative to a big bang is sequencing, but it is difficult to come up with a logical sequence. To be fully effective, most reforms need one another. For example, restoring the price mechanism is only useful if firms face hard budget constraints, which require clear property rights and the ability to uphold them. This in turn calls for a separation between firms and the state—that is, the end of the planning system and the phasing out of state subsidies. Unprofitable firms need to be closed and potentially profitable firms must find new sources of financing, which requires the prompt emergence of a financial system. Because price liberalization often leads to a once-off jump in prices, macroeconomic policy must prevent the price adjustment from triggering inflation. Necessarily, then, monetary policy should be shifted to control the money supply, which is impossible unless the budget is brought under control. In short, to succeed, macroeconomic stabilization and structural reforms need each other, and each part strengthens the whole.
- *Delays breed uncertainty.* Given the many actions to be taken, any lag in their implementation creates uncertainty and impedes restructuring. The delay may lead to inefficiencies, and even to perverse behavior such as asset stripping by managers before privatization, lack of investment, firing of workers in profitable firms, and so on. Perverse behavior spreads and gives the market economy a bad name. If a political backlash occurs before enough irreversible adjustments have been made, the entire transition is in jeopardy.
- *The political window of opportunity enables rapid action* (Balcerowicz 1994). Whoever rises to power in the aftermath of the collapse of communism is endowed with an unusually large stock of political capital. The population is willing to accept temporary hardship in the expectation of rewards to come. Former elites are shaken and demoralized and will take time to regroup and mount an effective opposition. New interest groups do not yet exist. It is during this period of "extraordinary politics" that reforms can be decided and implemented most easily.

## The Case for Gradualism

On the other side of the debate, proponents of gradualism have offered the following arguments:

- *It takes time to build a new world* (Nuti and Portes 1993). It is simply impossible to enact all reforms in a short period. Some can be implemented quickly (macroeconomic stabilization, price liberalization), but others require the accumulation of human capital (establishing a banking system, changing the tax system) or physical capital (the emergence of new firms), or the adoption of complex legislation (such as for commercial laws and courts). Attempting to do everything at once amounts to doing first what can be done first, not necessarily following the best sequencing. Moreover, trying to move too fast leads to policy mistakes.

- *Adjustment costs are high* (Dewatripont and Roland 1992). Rapid changes can be too costly, and can even threaten the transition process. The costs are economic—closing down inefficient firms implies an instant destruction of physical and human capital—as well as social—the pain of sudden unemployment, the dislocation of established ways of life. Efforts to force through overly rapid changes are doomed to fail and ultimately destroy the credibility of transition. When there are adjustment costs, there is an optimal speed of reform that is not a big bang. The power of this argument rests on the identification of empirically relevant adjustment costs. Four are important.

First, workers cannot move instantly from old state-owned firms to new private ones (Aghion and Blanchard 1994). Job searches are long and costly. Unduly rapid changes result in an inefficient rise in unemployment. The best approach is to close or restructure inefficient firms as new firms emerge and can absorb laid-off workers. A related argument emphasizes the need to set up a welfare system before allowing unemployment to increase.

A second issue is time inconsistency (Coricelli and Milesi-Ferretti 1993). In the presence of distortions (such as wage rigidity) that lead a government to temporarily intervene (say, by subsidizing firms to limit unemployment), the private sector may adopt perverse behavior (for example, setting wages even higher). Announcing that there will be no subsidies is not time consistent if a big bang worsens unemployment to the point at which it is socially excessive. A gradual approach is more compatible with the commitment not to provide subsidies.

Third are costly fluctuations in the real exchange rate (Abel and Bonin 1992). A big bang results in deep relative price changes that affect the real exchange rate. Large fluctuations in the exchange rate create massive uncertainty and can deter investment in the traded goods sector. Phasing in reform, by contrast, allows for small and more predictable price changes.

Finally, there are political costs (Dewatripont and Roland 1992; Murell 1992). Transition involves winners and losers. Losers are likely to form coalitions that try to block aspects of a coherent transition. Proceeding step by step makes it possible to Pareto-compensate each group of potential losers.

## A Look at the Evidence

The debate on the two approaches is not over, though country outcomes seem to be vindicating the big bang school. But the divide is less clear-cut than was initially believed. Even the most determined policymakers had to phase in big bang policies, while governments that started slowly soon had to accelerate, given inflation pressures and mounting resistance by vested interests. It used to be fashionable to pit big bang Poland against gradualist Hungary. But Poland is a laggard on privatization, while Hungary's 1991 bankruptcy law led to massive exit by firms.[7] In hindsight it is not clear whether Poland, an early boomer that got tangled along the way, differs much from Hungary, a gradualist that adopted a number of radical policies.[8]

Key to the debate are the reasons for the collapse in output and increase in unemployment that accompanied the early years of transition. Nuti and Portes (1993) argue that, absent egregious policy mistakes and the shock of the dismantling of the Council for Mutual Economic Assistance, GDP should rise, not fall. After all, transition is about enhancing productivity from well inside the production possibility frontier. Blanchard (1997) further develops this view. He concludes that output fell because of the disorganization that ensued as central planning disappeared; the collapse of the Council for Mutual Economic Assistance, which forced a reorientation of trade; and excessively rapid and possibly misguided policies, combined with adjustment costs.

This debate is primarily based on circumstantial evidence. A few studies have attempted to test econometrically for the effects of big bang. De Melo, Denizer, and Gelb (1996); Fischer, Sahay, and Végh (1996b); and Åslund, Boone, and Johnson (1996) conclude that the faster reforms were enacted, the earlier a country recovered. These results do not rule out the possibility of early adverse effects, but they suggest a tradeoff between early costs and long-run benefits. For countries that are members of the Commonwealth of Independent States, Selowsky and Martin (1997) find a negative short-term effect, though the longer-term effect is positive (but weaker than in Central and Eastern Europe).

This assessment is borne out by figure 4. The dotted line shows the unweighted average real GDP in transition economies, with year 0 set for each country on the year the reform process started (using the dating proposed by Fischer, Sahay, and Végh 1996b). The solid line does the same but is based on the year a macroeconomic stabilization program was introduced (using the dating proposed by Åslund, Boone, and Johnson 1996). Transition is clearly followed by a fall in GDP, regardless of whether reform is adopted. On average recovery occurs in the third year after reform. Importantly, recovery is faster once macroeconomic stabilization is introduced (whether at the same time as reform, or more gradually after initial and partial reform).

Further confirmation that fast-moving countries did better than gradualist ones is provided by figure 5, which shows GDP around the year of stabilization for two groups of countries: those that stabilized in 1990–91 and those that did not implement a stabilization program until 1994–95.[9] The early movers suffered a much smaller decline before stabilization. The late movers were slower to recover and, by 1998, had not achieved positive growth. GDP could be underestimated in slow-reforming countries, but it is doubtful that the conclusion would be reversed with more accurate data.

## Macroeconomic Stabilization, Inflation, and Disinflation

Inflation soared in 1992 (see figure 2). The surge in inflation occurred after prices were freed, with the peak occurring during the year of reform (figure 6). Inflation

## Figure 4. Real GDP in Transition Economies Undergoing Reform and Stabilization

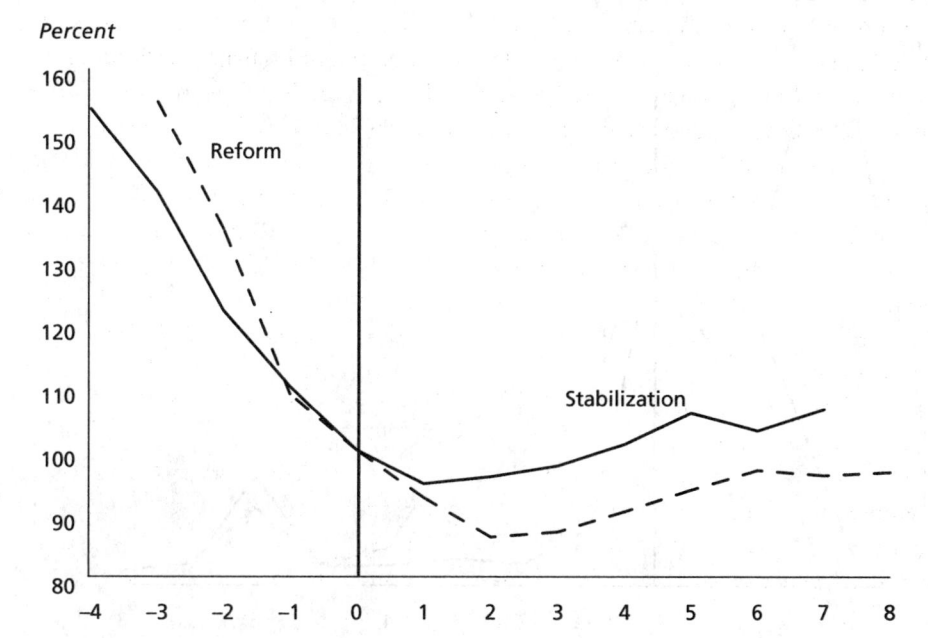

*Percent*

*Note:* Year 0 is the first year of reform or stabilization, with GDP indexed to 100.
*Source:* Fischer, Sahay, and Végh 1996b; Åslund, Boone, and Johnson 1996; author's calculations.

## Figure 5. Real GDP among Early and Late Stabilizers

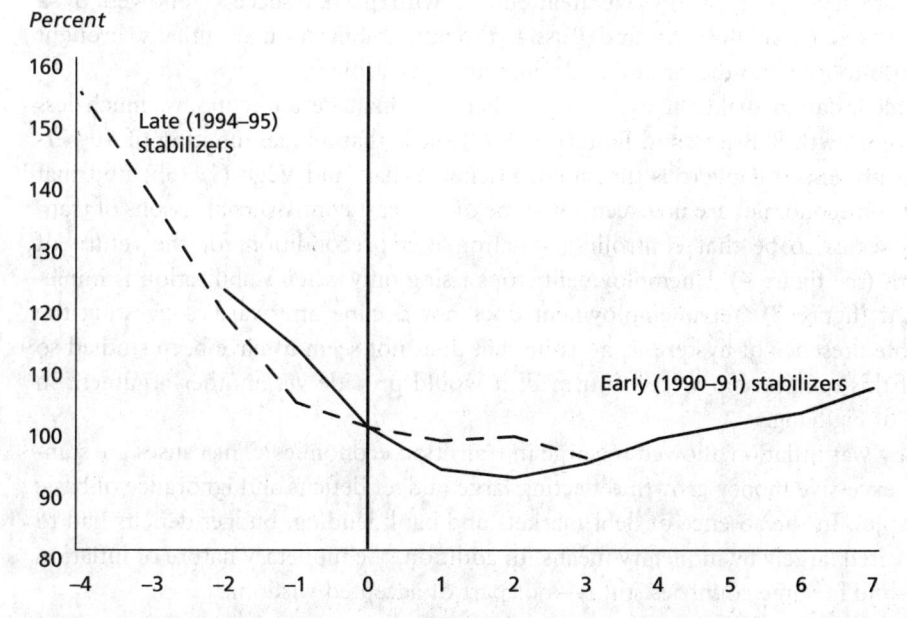

*Percent*

*Note:* The early stabilizers are Bulgaria, Czech Republic, Hungary, Poland, and Slovak Republic. The late stabilizers are FYR Macedonia, Romania, Russia, and Ukraine. Year 0 is the first year of reform or stabilization, with GDP indexed to 100.
*Source:* Author's calculations based on EBRD data.

**Figure 6. Inflation in Transition Economies Undergoing Reform and Stabilization**

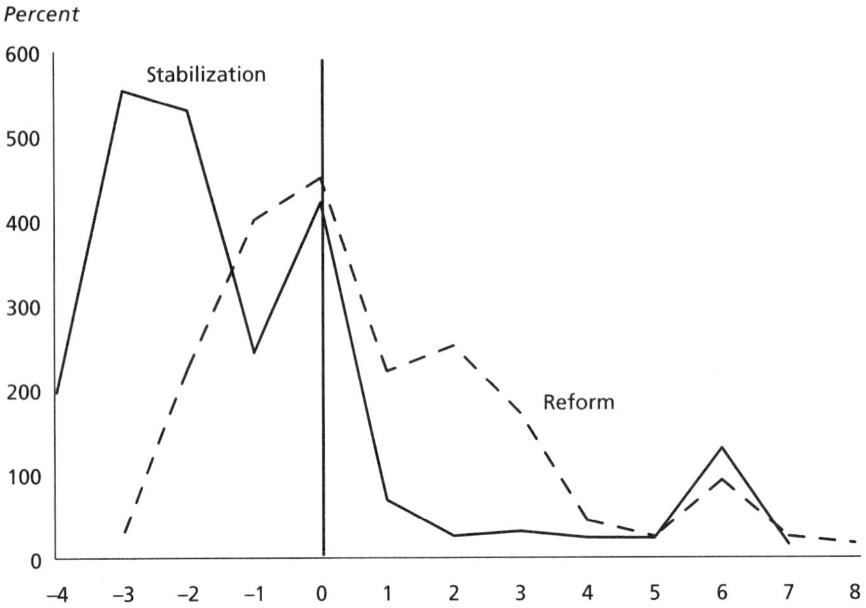

*Percent*

Note: Year 0 is the first year of reform or stabilization, with GDP indexed to 100.
Source: Author's calculations based on World Bank 1996.

often stabilized only after several attempts, with partial success followed by a relapse. Except in Bulgaria and Russia, though, stabilization eventually brought inflation to low two-digit rates, and sometimes even lower.

High inflation makes it extremely difficult to manage an economy, much less achieve growth.[10] Bruno and Easterly (1998) show that annual inflation of 40 percent represents a dangerous threshold. Fischer, Sahay, and Végh (1996b) find that transition economies are no exception. One of the least controversial lessons of transition seems to be that controlling inflation is a precondition for the return of growth (see figure 4). Unemployment stops rising only when stabilization is implemented (figure 7). Yet unemployment does not decline afterward, suggesting the possible presence of hysteresis, an issue that does not seem to have been studied so far. If this relationship were confirmed, it would provide yet another argument in favor of big bang.

Why was inflation allowed to surge in transition economies? The causes are standard: excessive money growth reflecting large budget deficits and ignorance of basic principles. In the absence of debt markets and bank lending, budget deficits had to be covered largely by monetary means. In addition, the monetary nature of inflation was—and in some countries still is—not part of accepted wisdom.[11]

Big bang, especially its macroeconomic component, once again appears to draw support from the path of inflation. Early stabilizers avoided hyperinflation, which had a devastating impact elsewhere (figure 8; see also figure 5).

**Figure 7. Unemployment in Transition Economies Undergoing Reform and Stabilization**

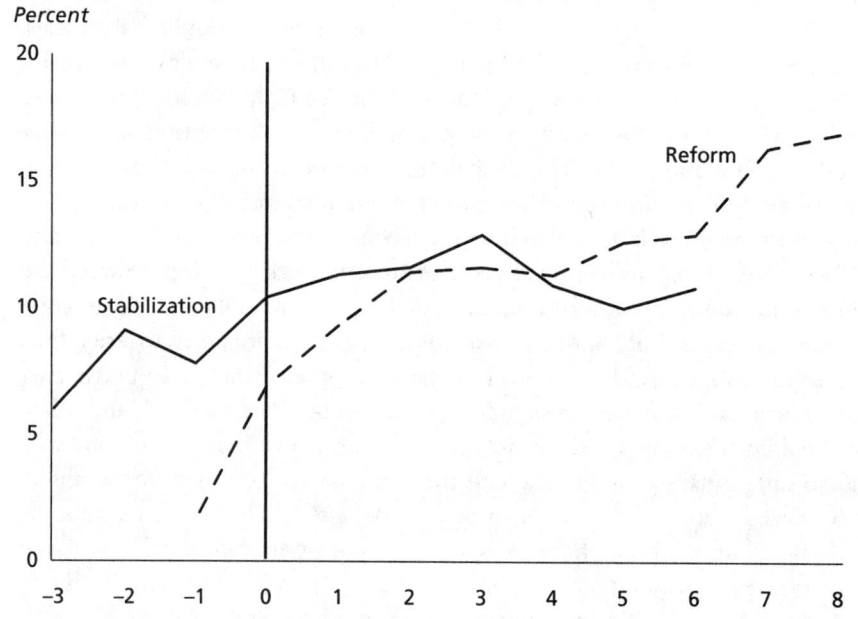

*Percent*

*Note:* Year 0 is the first year of reform or stabilization, with GDP indexed to 100.
*Source:* Author's calculations based on EBRD data.

**Figure 8. Inflation among Early and Late Stabilizers**

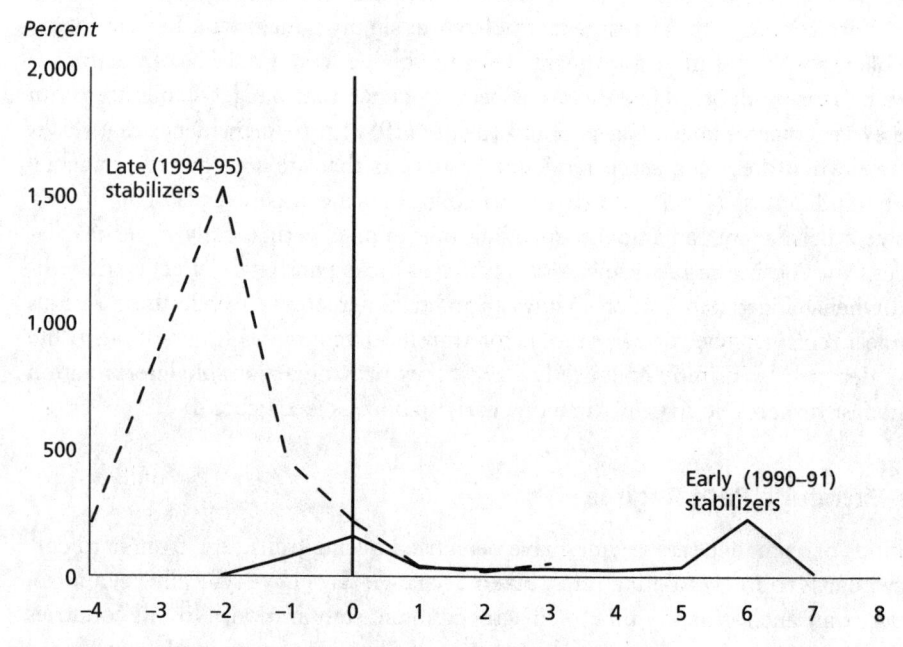

*Percent*

*Note:* Year 0 is the first year of stabilization, with GDP indexed to 100.
*Source:* Author's calculations based on World Bank various years.

But did macroeconomic policies aimed at curbing inflation contribute to the early depression? Inflation was closely related to the financing of budget deficits (see figure 2). Thus stabilization programs had to combine tight monetary and fiscal policies.

Deficits developed for good and bad reasons. Transition economies started with low incomes but could rationally expect to catch up. Accordingly, individuals and governments were justified in quickly raising spending on consumption and investment goods, private and public. The deficits that develop from such spending represent intertemporal smoothing and are not an inherent source of concern.

More worrisome is the frequently observed decline in tax revenues (Bélanger and others 1994). Part of this decline was caused by the end of the osmosis between the state and the economy. Reform of the tax structure and tax collection administration is needed but takes time. But here again, as long as steps are taken to strengthen the tax system, temporary deficits are best seen as an investment. Concern rises when tax reform is indefinitely postponed (as in Romania and Russia) and when inefficient public spending (subsidies to money-losing firms, overly generous welfare, and so on) is maintained. In the end the combination of lower taxing ability and an oversized public sector leads to unwise deficits.[12] These deficits must be closed. If, in addition, bond finance is not possible, eradicating high inflation requires that public spending be brought down to levels compatible with declining revenues—possibly even if this prevents sufficient intertemporal smoothing.

There are reasons to doubt that stabilization had a powerful, contractionary effect. Starting with monetary policy, real interest rates were typically raised (sometimes sharply) from negative to positive levels. Yet outside the former Yugoslavia, bank loans to producers or consumers were almost unheard of. Thus the standard channel for a contractionary effect of monetary policy was simply nonexistent. In terms of fiscal policy, the end of monetary financing of the budget could have a contractionary effect by closing deficits. But there has been evidence that budget stabilization can have expansionary effects. Giavazzi and Pagano (1996) provide evidence that this is the case when there is a sharp reduction in deficits that are seen as unsustainable. Alesina and Perotti (1995) find that fiscal contractions can be expansionary if they involve a permanent reduction in spending that implies permanently lower tax liabilities. And Alesina and Ardagna (1998) find that the expansionary effect is strengthened when budget stabilization involves a political agreement. While these various channels remain to be formally tested for transition economies (in addition to the effect detected by Bruno and Easterly 1998), they provide a plausible interpretation of the fast turnaround in growth among early stabilizers (see figure 4).

### The Exchange Rate Regime

All kinds of exchange rate regimes have been tried during transition, from hard currency boards to freely floating rates. Fixed exchange rates have typically been introduced as an anchor at the time of macroeconomic stabilization. Not all countries have adopted that strategy, though. Latvia and Slovenia, for example, eradicated inflation by focusing on monetary targets. But even then the exchange rate has been heavily managed, with Slovenia maintaining an implicit real exchange rate target. Several questions arise. Why did countries undergoing the same process choose different exchange rate regimes? Which ones worked better? And what difference did it make?

### Fixed or Flexible?

Because the choice of an exchange rate regime always involves tradeoffs, there is no universally ideal regime. Still, one lesson of the past 20 years seems to be that a declared parity—a fixed exchange rate or crawling band—is dangerous in the presence of capital mobility (Eichengreen 1999; Wyplosz 1998). Yet transition economies have tried both fixed and flexible approaches.

Big bang countries typically opted for limited exchange rate flexibility early on, often with a large dose of current account and capital account openness. Countries that were slow in stabilizing opted for more flexibility and various restrictions on their current and capital accounts. These countries often felt that limited exchange rate flexibility required foreign exchange reserves beyond their reach, though a deep devaluation would probably have resulted in a balance of payments surplus, which would have made it possible to adopt a peg.[13] Thus there was a virtuous circle involving stabilization, limited exchange rate flexibility, and low inflation; and a vicious circle in which exchange rate flexibility and runaway inflation resulted from the absence of macroeconomic stabilization. In extreme cases of zero credibility and weak governments—as in Bosnia and Bulgaria—currency boards have been used to not tempt the devil.

Thus it is impossible to assign a causal role to the exchange rate regime. Rather, the choice was part and parcel of the macroeconomic strategy. Still, early stabilizers with low or declining inflation have tended to maintain for too long the dangerous mix of limited flexibility and considerable capital mobility. The Czech Republic's crisis in May 1997 served as a wakeup call,[14] followed by Russia's collapse in August 1998. The lesson has been communicated, but corrective action has been slow (Begg and Wyplosz 1999b).

No study has tried to determine whether a specific exchange rate regime has worked better. Most likely, the regime makes little difference by itself. Two aspects matter here. The first is the constraint that the regime imposes on monetary policy. Especially when there is considerable capital mobility, an exchange rate commitment—explicit or implicit—imposes market-based discipline on the central bank. In countries where central banks are not independent, or lack public and political support for discipline, this outcome is desirable. What is needed is an exit strategy, the introduction of some exchange rate flexibility once capital movements grow and become a threat. Russia is a good example of a country that used an exchange rate anchor to stabilize inflation but failed to develop a consistent exit strategy.

But what about the much-feared conflict between the anchoring of the exchange rate and the need to keep the economy internationally competitive? Real exchange rate appreciation has been massive in transition economies, ranging from more than

40 percent in Hungary to nearly 600 percent in Lithuania (table 2). Appreciation is partly a catch up following massive undervaluation at the time exchange rates were unified and allowed to respond to market forces. The crucial question is whether the real appreciation goes too far and eventually results in overvaluation. A trend of real appreciation is to be expected in countries undergoing deep restructuring and fast productivity growth.[15] Estimates by Halpern and Wyplosz (1997, 1998a); Krajnyák and Zettelmeyer (1998); and EBRD (1998) indicate that by 1998 there was no case of overvaluation, though some countries are nearing that point. Yet the issue has been raised repeatedly in domestic discussions and weighs on policy choices. This illustrates a key difficulty of operating a fixed exchange rate or crawling band: the exchange rate becomes a political issue.

## Currency Boards

Currency boards have three main merits: they are robust, they establish credibility, and inflation becomes endogenous. But they also have three main disadvantages.

First, a currency board eliminates a government's ability to conduct lender of last resort operations. Because banking systems are fragile in most transition economies, this may be a serious cost—but there are solutions. For example, foreign ownership of banks, as in Estonia, transfers the responsibility for bank bailouts to bank shareholders. If the country is small, the cost of a bank rescue is well within the means of parent banks. An alternative is for the treasury to accumulate a rescue fund, as in Argentina. If either approach is adopted, and both have merits, this disadvantage largely disappears.

Second, a currency board prevents the central bank from pursuing countercyclical policies, which may result in undesirable output volatility. Small, open, and diversified economies are less sensitive to this problem. In all cases, price and wage flexibility is the best response—but one that no government can control.

**Table 2. Real Exchange Rate Appreciation in Transition Economies**
*(percentage increase in the dollar wage)*

| Country | Increase from trough or first available data | Year of trough or first available data |
|---|---|---|
| Bulgaria | 65 | 1991 |
| Czech Republic | 90 | 1993 |
| Estonia | 225 | 1993 |
| Hungary | 43 | 1990 |
| Latvia | 76 | 1994 |
| Lithuania | 558 | 1992 |
| Poland | 176 | 1990 |
| Romania | 125 | 1990 |
| Russia | 201 | 1992 |
| Slovak Republic | 61 | 1993 |
| Slovenia | 64 | 1991 |
| Ukraine | 173 | 1992 |

*Note:* Sample does not include Albania, Croatia, and FYR Macedonia.
*Source:* Halpern and Wyplosz 1998a.

Finally, a currency board is widely seen as a temporary arrangement for countries needing an exit strategy. For Central and Eastern European countries likely to soon join the European Monetary Union, sticking to a currency board for a few years is reasonable, though among them only Estonia has adopted a currency board. Other countries in the region have no reason to enter into a currency board arrangement because they have an exit strategy. For countries further away from accession to the European Union, or unlikely to ever join, there is no readily available exit strategy. This either rules out a currency board or calls for an eventual "euroization," much as Argentina has been considering dollarization.

## The Budget

Tax revenue and public spending in transition economies have followed three main patterns. First, tax revenue has generally plummeted, often starting in the years before reform. Disorganization and a general decline in discipline—or the end of fear of the state—probably explain this evolution.[16]

Second, public spending has fallen in line with tax revenue as price subsidies declined in the wake of price liberalization and governments struggled to control deficits. In some ways this development has not been unwelcome, because centrally planned governments were oversized. But in many cases spending cuts have primarily affected investment and useful social welfare.

Finally, in a number of countries deficits were already large before reform was implemented. In such cases the inherited situation has perpetuated itself.[17] Many of the countries in table 1 that appear unsuccessful belong to this category. Causality probably runs both ways.

The general impression is that the evolution of budgets again provides an argument for an early big bang. Where tax revenue had declined before reform, it has proven hard to stem the hemorrhage. Similarly, where deficits were large to start with, they have continued to be unsustainable.

## Banking, Financial Markets, and Credit

Unlike with the macroeconomic aspects discussed earlier, there is much agreement on the evolution of banking and credit in transition economies. The general view is that banking systems and stock markets are vastly undersized, that they tend to finance public deficits rather than productive investment, and that banks are not sufficiently robust (Begg 1996; EBRD 1998).

### Banks

Banks have been created by breaking up mono-banks, by transforming specialized institutions (such as the Soviet Export–Import Bank), or from scratch at the initiative of entrepreneurs or large corporations. Technical know-how has been in short supply in new private banks and at regulatory agencies. The most striking characteristic of banking during transition is that banks do very little lending to the private sector, even after taking into account their stage of development. Many countries are known for their fragile banking systems and recently experienced banking crises. Thus significant portions of outstanding credit could be valueless. And even in countries with little lending to the private sector, crises are widespread.

Banks are weak and credit undersized for well-known reasons. Until recently, bank supervision was poor. In addition, as long as inflation was high and variable, bank lending was impossible. With many firms still operating with soft budget constraints, bank lending tends to flow to inefficient but well-connected producers—a pattern that eventually results in crises and government bailouts. Small, dynamic firms tend to finance their needs through retained earnings (in all countries, not just transition economies). In some countries, especially in the former Soviet Union, property rights are poorly defined and loan repayment is far from guaranteed. In most countries banks are saddled with poor loans inherited from the mono-bank or accumulated poor loans in their startup years.

Banking crises are common in transition economies (table 3). In some countries, open crises have been avoided only by continuing state transfers. Bank portfolio restructurings and recapitalizations, often supported with public money, are familiar. These interventions have often erred in the wrong direction when balancing the need to prevent bank meltdowns with the moral hazard costs of support.

Bank lending to the private sector has long been—and sometimes continues to be—crowded out by the public sector. This occurs when inflation is too high for

**Table 3. Banking and Financial Markets in Transition Economies**

| Country | Number of banks, 1997 | Number of foreign-owned banks, 1997 | Year of bank crisis | Share of bank loans to the public sector (percent), 1998 | Year stock market started | Stock market capitalization (percentage of GDP), 1997 |
|---|---|---|---|---|---|---|
| Albania | 9 | 3 | 1996–97 | 93.1 [a] | 1996 | — |
| Bulgaria | 28 | 7 | 1996 | 62.7 | 1992 | 0 |
| Croatia | 61 | 7 | 1998 | 0 | 1994 | 22.5 |
| Czech Republic | 41 | 15 | 1997 | 21.8 | 1993 | 30.0 |
| Estonia | 12 | 3 |  | 7.8 | 1996 | 25.2 |
| Macedonia, FYR | 9 | 3 | 1995 | 3.8 | 1996 | 0.3 |
| Hungary | 41 | 30 |  | 39.0 [a] | 1990 | 36.2 |
| Latvia | 32 | 15 | 1995–96 | 29.5 | 1995 | 11.0 |
| Lithuania | 11 | 4 | 1995 | 34.9 | 1992 | 22.8 |
| Poland | 83 | 29 |  | 50.8 | 1991 | 9.8 |
| Romania | 33 | 11 |  | 53.0 | 1995 | 6.8 |
| Russia | 1,697 | 26 | 1998 | 53.1 | 1993 | 29.4 |
| Slovak Republic | 25 | 9 |  | 40.5 | 1992 | 9.7 |
| Slovenia | 34 | 4 |  | 30.7 | 1989 | 10.9 |
| Ukraine | 227 | 12 |  | 76.5 | 1992 | 6.1 |

— Not available.
a. Data are for 1996.
Source: EBRD 1998.

treasury bills to exist and foreign financing is absent. Once inflation is lowered, treasury bill markets develop, which, under proper conditions, allow banks to diversify their portfolios. Indeed, the share of loans to the public sector, which used to exceed 60 percent, has recently fallen sharply in a number of countries (see table 3).

Many loans to the private sector are nonperforming. Officially listed nonperforming loans probably vastly underestimate the true state of affairs, as was made clear during the failure in 1998 of a bank in Croatia. In addition, one lesson from the East Asian crisis is that loans that appear safe can sour in no time when a currency crisis occurs—something that is certainly possible in transition economies.

An important recent change has been the wider opening of banking to foreign ownership (see table 3). Foreign ownership has been highly beneficial in Latin America, allowing for recapitalization and transfer of technology. Foreign ownership eases the pressure on national budgets and strengthens bank oversight and regulation. More important, perhaps, it provides (to some degree) for an external lender of last resort.

## Financial Markets

Most transition economies moved quickly to establish financial markets, as a symbol of moving to a market economy. Large-scale privatization has been instrumental, but the markets remain small, with few securities actively traded except treasury bills. Most analysts believe that it will take years for these markets to become an important vehicle for corporate financing. There is some debate on whether transition economies should aim at the European model—where bank financing dominates capital market financing—or the U.S. model (Corbett and Mayer 1991). A more likely evolution, as in Western Europe, is toward the European model first, and then to the U.S. model. But this evolution is a question of decades, not years.

## The Role of the State

Because transition economies inherited enormous governments, they were expected to spin off a significant portion of the state's responsibilities. That has happened, but not to the extent anticipated. Average public spending in transition economies dropped from 53 percent of GDP in 1989 to 40 percent in 1997—still above the average among OECD countries of 39 percent. The usual presumption (Wagner law) that poorer countries have smaller governments does not seem to apply to transition economies. Begg and Wyplosz (1999a) show that, even after taking into account many economic and political characteristics, transition governments are large by international standards.

The main advantage of centrally planned economies was their extensive welfare systems, which provided citizens with low but highly stable incomes from the cradle to the grave. This legacy is difficult to demolish, even if it generates incentives that do not mix well with a market economy. Within a few years all the governments that had taken power from communists had been voted out of office—a strong indication that the population was upset with rising uncertainty. It may be that transition economies have to retain, from the outset, a welfare state that richer countries have built up over decades. In that case, competitiveness and growth will require low wages to deliver low after-tax labor costs. Failing to deal with this serious tradeoff will lead to European-style high unemployment.

Public consumption (as a share of GDP) has remained fairly stable in many transition economies, declining where taxes declined most. Credit to state enterprises (as a share of gross domestic credit) has declined, often substantially. The main item that did not decline much, at least as a share of declining spending, is transfers and subsidies. Some of these transfers correspond to welfare, but others are subsidies to declining industries. The Czech Republic is a case in point; the continuation of such transfers and subsidies may help explain why the *wunderkind* of transition is now mired in a slow-growth trap.

## Microeconomic Underpinnings

This article has focused on the macroeconomic aspects of transition. A running theme is that policies and institutions tend to be mostly right or mostly wrong. The same conclusion applies to the microeconomic aspects of transition. Microeconomic indicators of transition are positively correlated, especially those on enterprise restructuring, financial institution development, and market reforms. These three indicators are also correlated with macroeconomic indicators (especially the budget surplus) and growth performance, with a further strong link between inflation and market reforms. And as noted, inflation stabilization is a precondition for growth (EBRD 1998).

Which factors, microeconomic or macroeconomic, are more crucial for a successful transition? It is nearly impossible to answer that question, though it is easier to explain performance during 1996–98 than during 1991–98. Inflation stabilization and market reforms—including price liberalization, adjustments in trade and foreign exchange systems, and changes in competition policy—are essential. Enterprise restructuring—privatization and governance—is less important. Fiscal stabilization is never significant on its own, which suggests that it matters mostly through its effect on inflation (see figure 2). These findings also apply to 1991–98, but they are less precise.

## Conclusion

Though its long-term outlook is highly promising, transition was never going to be easy. But with a few spectacular exceptions, most countries are now on the right track. Several important lessons have emerged, though a few policy issues still need to be addressed. In addition, many unresolved issues remain on the research agenda.

### *Five Useful Lessons*

IT PAID TO START EARLY AND MOVE FAST. The big bang approach is highly desirable but impractical, while gradualism is unavoidable but should be compressed as much as possible. The countries that bit the bullet early and hard have achieved better results.

STABILIZE FIRST, GROW NEXT. Macroeconomic stabilization is a prerequisite for growth, in transition economies and elsewhere. Macroeconomic stabilization does not require eliminating budget deficits, but it is essential to sever the link between deficits and money growth.

STRUCTURAL REFORM IS IMPORTANT. Microeconomic reforms, which have often been overlooked, should be introduced as soon as possible. Essential steps include establishing property rights, hardening budget constraints, building a healthy banking system, and ensuring competition in domestic markets. Hungary pursued these goals while being too lax on the macroeconomic side, while the Czech Republic was a model of monetary and fiscal rigor but did not pay much attention to microeconomics. Hungary has made the most progress, while the Czech Republic is falling behind.

THE EXCHANGE RATE REGIME IS IRRELEVANT. The exchange rate regime does not seem to matter much. Like the debate between big bang and gradualism, the issue of the "right" exchange rate regime may have been overblown. Countries that floated their exchange rates have tightly managed them, while countries with fixed exchange rates have repeatedly devalued and often ended up floating. Some monetary targeting was needed, but it has not really mattered which target was chosen as long as it was adhered to.

IRREVERSIBLE POLICIES ARE CRUCIAL. The less stable is the economy, the more important are policies. Implementing irreversible policies early on allows governments to pursue change without undermining the transition. Otherwise, a shaky economic base provides fertile ground for policy reversals that can set back the clock for several years (as in Bulgaria, Romania, and Russia).

## Policy Issues

Most pending policy issues involve the continuation of structural reforms. Still, a few macroeconomic questions remain on the agenda.

INFLATION. Annual inflation stands at 3–15 percent in most transition economies. What is the proper inflation rate for these countries? One view is that transition economies are no different from others and should aim at a rate between, say, 0 percent and 5 percent. Another view is that higher inflation is desirable for years to come and has a limited negative effect.

Moderate inflation may make sense. Even if disinflation has not had much effect on growth—a controversial view—squeezing inflation by a few more percentage points would be painful. At this stage, the argument goes, the priority for transition economies is to embark on a robust growth path. Growth is needed for several reasons. A shaken population needs to see the promised benefits of reform. Investment to modernize the economy requires strong growth prospects. Continued restructuring is bound to be accompanied by changes in relative prices (which are easier to achieve when no price needs to decline in absolute terms). With underdeveloped tax systems the optimal inflation tax cannot be as low as in more mature economies. And fast growth facilitates social transformation by allowing relatively painless redistributive transfers.

THE EXCHANGE RATE AND CAPITAL LIBERALIZATION. If inflation is going to be higher than in the West, exchange rates will need to be adjusted to maintain external competitiveness. In addition, as one of the world's fast-growth areas, transition economies will likely face large capital inflows. What targets should be set for exchange rate regimes and for capital liberalization?

Most countries have introduced some exchange rate flexibility. Yet large fluctuations are undesirable for trade integration. Countries engaged in accession to the European Union will face growing pressure to stabilize their exchange rates relative to the euro. One solution is to maintain a heavily managed float while limiting capital mobility. Another solution is to adopt a currency board, though most countries will not want to adopt such a radical strategy. In many ways it is impossible to aim at a stable floating exchange rate, and exchange rate management will remain a permanent challenge.

One lesson from the Latin American and East Asian crises is that full capital mobility is undesirable during periods of rapid structural change. Most transition economies have retained restrictions on capital mobility, but popular economic theory and Western pressure still lead them to aim at rapid liberalization. Such a strategy should be seriously reconsidered. Countries that have fully liberalized (Czech Republic, Poland) will not—and should not—want to fully step back. But Chilean-type prudential measures aimed at lengthening the maturity of capital flows offer an appealing transitory measure on the road to membership in the European Monetary Union.

BANKING. The past few years have seen much progress in strengthening banking systems in transition economies. Still, banks are contributing far too little to the allocation of domestic resources. Financing growth through retained earnings is normal for small firms and may be sufficient in the early years of transition. The next step requires external financing.

Transition economies could skip the banking stage and move on to what appears to be the next stage, stock market financing. This approach is unlikely, though, and could even be dangerous because budding stock markets are far too volatile. Thus transition economies must establish sound banking systems. The required steps are well known, spelled out in the Basel accords.

UNEMPLOYMENT. In just three years, Central and Eastern Europe caught up with Western Europe in one sad achievement: double-digit unemployment. Perhaps much of this increase simply reflects the extraordinary depression that marked the early years of transition. But there is a serious risk of hysteresis—that temporary unemployment will turn into permanent unemployment.

Western Europe offers many lessons in this regard. Many are "don'ts": don't let labor markets become rigid through well-intended but self-destructive legislation and social practices, and don't promise quick macroeconomic policy fixes. There are also some "do's": aim at unemployment policies that provide incentives to find a job quickly, encourage labor negotiations at the firm or plant level, and beware of a generous welfare state.

## The Research Agenda

The transition experience is rich, involving many countries that, despite their differences, face the same basic challenge. As the dust settles, some of the early debates have faded. But data have accumulated and, at great last, permit formal investigations. On the macroeconomic front, a number of issues deserve special attention.

CONTRACTIONARY STABILIZATION. There is no clear understanding of why the depression was so deep and of the contribution of various factors. At the same time, evidence from Western Europe indicates that, under some conditions, fiscal stabilization does not have to be contractionary—complementing Cagan's (1956) suggestion that sharp disinflation can be achieved at little or no output cost. Transition economies that underwent massive inflation and undertook deep stabilizations offer a fascinating field for research.

DESIRABLE INFLATION. The view that inflation hurts growth when it hits 40 percent a year, and maybe much less, requires refinements. It is unlikely that the same rule applies to every country regardless of its economic structure. Transition economies share common features that may justify a different rule. Progress in this area matters a great deal for policy over the next 10 years.

ELECTIONS. Transition economies have experienced more than massive economic changes. Elections have repeatedly shaken the political establishment, regardless of the incumbent's political views. The growing literature on the link between policy and politics can be enriched by the experience in transition economies. Does the pace of change explain the short lifespan of governments, or should we also examine income redistribution, the emergence of interest groups, and the newness of democracy? Lessons in this area could be useful for much of the developing—and largely undemocratic—world.

INTEREST GROUPS. Almost from scratch, all sorts of interest groups have emerged rapidly in transition economies. In some countries these groups have been extremely effective in thwarting reforms. In other countries governments have been able to address the concerns of such groups and to continue pursuing policy goals. The speed and visibility of interest group formation offers a unique opportunity to examine an issue that explains policy failures around the world.

## Notes

1. Throughout this article, the sample of 15 transition economies covers Albania, Bulgaria, Croatia, Czech Republic, Estonia, Hungary, Latvia, Lithuania, FYR Macedonia, Poland, Romania, Russia, Slovak Republic, Slovenia, and Ukraine. The quality of data is poor, so conclusions should be taken with caution.

2. It is sometimes argued that measures of GDP adjusted for purchasing power parity (PPP) are better indicators, but it depends what one wants to measure. Given the trend real appreciation characteristic of the transition process documented in Halpern and Wyplosz (1997), using PPP-adjusted GDP would make a significant difference and show more growth. Here, however, the focus is on the quantity of output; hence the use of non-PPP-adjusted GDP. More troublesome is the underground economy, which is presumed to have grown much faster than officially recorded GDP, and which may now account for 20–35 percent of output. Some estimates can be found in Lackó (1998).

3. In most former Soviet countries, workers often remain attached to firms even though they hardly work and get paid with great delays, and often in kind.

4. Examining 1998 dollar wages overlooks initial conditions. However, most transition economies initially underwent dramatic currency depreciations, so the starting value of the dollar wage is not informative. Eventually, success means OECD-level dollar wages.

5. Higher private output does not ensure that the goods being produced are desirable if subsidies allow firms to keep producing goods for which there are no takers. Privatization, and in particular the approach used for mass privatization, is a crucial issue. The literature is too vast to be covered here, however.

6. The big bang approach has often been dubbed, mostly by its opponents, as "shock therapy." Balcerowicz (1994) explains how this expression is both misleading and a crude but efficient way of making the approach look unreasonable.

7. An important issue is the privatization method and the contrast between voucher privatization (as in Poland) and cash sales, including to foreigners (as in Hungary). The large literature on this issue is beyond the scope of this article. But the point made here is different: it concerns the exit of state-owned firms. Not all state-owned firms are necessarily inefficient, so Hungary's sweeping bankruptcy procedures may have wrongly eliminated some firms and destroyed useful capital. Against this risk lies the risk of providing subsides (with the risk of an ever-growing number of claimants), which are then hard to roll back (as in the Czech Republic), as well as the political implications of maintaining the influence of the industry-based nomenklatura (as in Russia and Ukraine).

8. For an interpretation of the Hungarian experience along these lines, see Halpern and Wyplosz (1998b). For an argument that the distinction between big bang and gradualism can be overblown, see Portes (1994).

9. Bulgaria is a special case. It first stabilization program foundered and it enacted a second, more radical, program in 1997. Lacking any better criterion, each country is listed according to the year of its first stabilization program.

10. An inflation rate of 100 percent cuts average annual growth by 3 percentage points.

11. For instance, there is still a lively debate in Russia on whether inflation is related to money or to "structural factors" such as the presence of monopolies or the decline in output (which is seen as a source of excess demand).

12. For a view on whether public spending is excessive in transition, see Begg and Wyplosz (1999a).

13. Begg (1996) argues convincingly that pegging the exchange rate is impossible unless the budget deficit has been brought under control.

14. I owe this expression to Miroslav Hrncir from the Czech National Bank.

15. One reason is the traditional Balassa-Samuelson effect. Yet this does not seem to apply well to transition economies. For an alternative theory, see Grafe and Wyplosz (1999).

16. The data are for the general budget. In Russia these data fail to reveal the dramatic decline in tax revenue suffered by the federal government, because most regional authorities have been able to uphold—and often improve—tax collection at the expense of the central budget. The decline in federal tax revenues lies directly at the roots of the 1998 exchange crisis; see Ivanova and Wyplosz (1998).

17. Hungary stands apart as having allowed its deficit to grow after reform.

## References

Abel, Istvan, and John P. Bonin. 1992. "The 'Big Bang' Versus 'Slow But Steady': A Comparison of the Hungarian and Polish Transformations." CEPR Discussion Paper 626. Centre for Economic Policy Research, London.

Aghion, Philippe, and Olivier J. Blanchard. 1994. "On the Speed of Transition in Central Europe." In Stanley Fischer and Julio J. Rotemberg, eds., *NBER Macroeconomics Annual*. Cambridge, Mass.: MIT Press.

Alesina, Alberto, and Silvia Ardagna. 1998. "Tales of Fiscal Adjustments." *Economic Policy* 27: 487–546.

Alesina, Alberto, and Roberto Perotti. 1995. "Fiscal Adjustments: Fiscal Expansions and Adjustments in OECD Countries." *Economic Policy* 21: 205–48.

Åslund, Anders, Peter Boone, and Simon Johnson. 1996. "How to Stabilize: Lessons from Post-Communist Countries." *Brookings Papers on Economic Activity 1*. Washington, D.C.: Brookings Institution.

Balcerowicz, Leszek. 1994. "Common Fallacies in the Debate on the Transition to a Market Economy." *Economic Policy* 19S: 18–50.

Begg, David. 1996. "Monetary Policies in Transition Economies." Birkbeck College, London.

Begg, David, and Richard Portes. 1993. "Enterprise Debt and Economic Transition: Financial Restructuring in Central and Eastern Europe." In Colin Mayer and Xavier Vives, eds., *Capital Markets and Financial Intermediation*. Cambridge, U.K.: Cambridge University Press.

Begg, David, and Charles Wyplosz. 1999a. "How Big A Government? Transition Economy Forecasts Based On OECD History." Paper presented at the Fifth Dubrovnik Conference on Transition Economies, 23–25 June, Dubrovnik, Croatia.

———. 1999b. "Untying Exchange Rate Hands As Transition Proceeds." Paper presented at the Fifth Dubrovnik Conference on Transition Economies, 23–25 June, Dubrovnik, Croatia.

Bélanger, Gérard, and others. 1994. "Eastern Europe: Factors Underlying the Weakening Performance of Tax Revenues." IMF Working Paper 94/104. International Monetary Fund, Washington, D.C.

Blanchard, Olivier J. 1997. *The Economics of Post-Communist Transition*. Oxford: Oxford University Press.

Bruno, Michael, and William Easterly. 1998. "Inflation Crises and Long-Run Growth." *Journal of Monetary Economics* 41 (1): 3–26.

Cagan, Philip. 1956. "The Monetary Dynamics of Hyperinflation." In Milton Friedman, ed. *Studies in the Quantity Theory of Money*. Chicago, Ill.: University of Chicago Press.

Calvo, Guillermo A., Ratna Sahay, and Carlos A. Végh. 1994. "Capital Flows in Central and Eastern Europe: Issues and Policy Options." University of Maryland, College Park.

Caprio, Gerard. 1995. "The Role of Financial Intermediaries in Transitional Economies." *Carnegie-Rochester Conference Series in Public Policy* 42: 257–302.

Corbett, Jenny, and Colin Mayer. 1991. "Financial Reform in Eastern Europe: Progress with the Wrong Model." *Oxford Review of Economic Policy* 7 (4): 57–75.

Coricelli, Fabrizio, and Gian Maria Milesi-Ferretti. 1993. "On the Credibility of 'Big Bang' Programs." *European Economic Review* 37: 387–95.

de Melo, Martha, Cevdet Denizer, and Alan Gelb. 1996. "Patterns of Transition from Plan to Market." *The World Bank Economic Review* 10 (3): 397–424.

Dewatripont, Mathias, and Gerard Roland. 1992. "The Virtues of Gradualism and Legitimacy in the Transition to a Market Economy." *The Economic Journal* 102: 291–300.

EBRD (European Bank for Reconstruction and Development). 1998. *Transition Report 1998*. London.

Eichengreen, Barry. 1999. *Towards A New International Financial Architecture*. Washington, D.C.: Institute for International Economics.

Fischer, Stanley, Ratna Sahay, and Carlos Végh. 1996a. "Economies in Transition: The Beginnings of Growth." *American Economic Review* 86 (2): 229–33.

———. 1996b. "Stabilization and Growth in Transition Economies: The Early Experience." *Journal of Economic Perspectives* 10 (2): 45–66.

Giavazzi, Francesco, and Marco Pagano. 1996. "Non-Keynesian Effects of Fiscal Policy Changes: International Evidence and the Swedish Case." *Swedish Economic Review*: 67–103.

Grafe, Clemens, and Charles Wyplosz. 1999. "The Real Exchange Rate in Transition Economies." In Mario Blejer and Marko Skreb, eds., *Balance of Payments, Exchange Rates, and Competitiveness in Transition Economies*. Dordrecht, Netherlands: Kluwer Academic.

Halpern, László, and Charles Wyplosz. 1997. "Equilibrium Exchange Rates in Transition Economies." *IMF Staff Papers* 44 (4): 430–60.

———. 1998a. "Equilibrium Exchange Rates in Transition Economies: Further Results." Paper presented at the Economic Policy Initiative Forum, 21–22 November, Brussels.

———. 1998b. "The Hidden Hungarian Miracle." In László Halpern and Charles Wyplosz, eds., *Hungary: Towards a Market Economy*. Cambridge, U.K.: Cambridge University Press.

Ivanova, Nadezhda, and Charles Wyplosz. 1998. "Arrears: The Tide that Is Drowning Russia." Paper presented at the Russian European Centre for Economic Policy's First Annual Conference, 11 September, Moscow.

Krajnyák, Kornélia, and Jeromin Zettelmeyer. 1998. "Competitiveness in Transition Economies: What Scope for Real Appreciation?" *IMF Staff Papers* 45 (2): 309–62.

Lackó, Mária. 1998. "Hungarian Hidden Economy in International Comparison: Estimation Method Based On Household Electricity Consumption and Currency Ratio." In László Halpern and Charles Wyplosz, eds., *Hungary: Towards a Market Economy*. Cambridge, U.K.: Cambridge University Press.

Lipton, David, and Jeffrey D. Sachs. 1990. "Creating a Market Economy: The Case of Poland." *Brookings Papers on Economic Activity* 1. Washington, D.C.: Brookings Institution.

Murell, Peter. 1992. "Evolution in Economics and in the Economic Reform of the Centrally Planned Economies." In Christopher K. Clague and Gordon C. Rausser, eds., *The Emergence of Market Economies in Eastern Europe*. Oxford: Basil Blackwell.

Nuti, Domenico, and Richard Portes. 1993. "Central Europe: The Way Forward." In Richard Portes, ed., *Economic Transformation in Central Europe*. London: Centre for Economic Policy Research.

Pleskovic, Boris. 1994. "Financial Policies in Socialist Countries in Transition." Policy Research Working Paper 1242. World Bank, Washington, D.C.

Portes, Richard. 1994. "Transformation Traps." *Economic Journal* 104 (426): 1178–89.

Saunders, Anthony, and Andrea Sommariva. 1993. "Banking Sector and Restructuring in Eastern Europe." *Journal of Banking and Finance* 17: 931–57.

Selowsky, Marcelo, and Ricardo Martin. 1997. "Policy Performance and Output Growth in the Transition Economies." *American Economic Review* 87 (2): 349–53.

United Nations Economic Commission for Europe. Various years. *Economic Survey of Europe*. New York.

World Bank. Various years. *World Development Indicators*. Washington, D.C.

———. 1996. *World Development Report 1996: From Plan to Market*. New York: Oxford University Press.

Wyplosz, Charles. 1998. "International Capital Market Failures: Sources, Costs and Solutions." Paper prepared for the World Bank, Washington, D.C.

# Restructuring in Transition Economies: Ownership, Competition, and Regulation

*Simon Commander, Mark Dutz, and Nicholas Stern*

*Transition requires the reallocation of resources across activities through the closure of inefficient firms and the creation of new firms. It also requires restructuring of existing firms where improvements in performance are feasible. This article examines experience in the transition economies with both processes. It shows that failure to restructure has generally been associated with failure to reallocate and that progress in restructuring has varied substantially across countries. In Central Europe incentives for private agents to start businesses, restructure, and invest have been largely set in place. Growth has increased, facilitating dynamic adjustment to earlier inadequacies in policy. Further east, soft budget constraints have been associated with privatizations that have strongly favored incumbents. The web of nontransparent links connecting government, firms, and banks has consequently not been broken. Productivity growth has been low, and structural change has been negligible. Throughout the transition economies substantial regulatory and institutional weaknesses remain.*

Ownership change through privatization, the entry of new firms, and policies to stimulate competition in markets for both products and corporate control are central to a transition from a command to a market economy. How these changes take place has consequences for restructuring and for performance. There is significant variation in these changes across transition economies. The process is still in its early stages and, indeed, has barely begun in a number of countries. Where radical changes in both resource use and the structure of output have not occurred, the evidence points to major failures in imposing hard budget constraints and raising competition. These in turn have limited any positive effects of changes in ownership on governance.

---

Simon Commander is an adviser to the chief economist at the European Bank for Reconstruction and Development. Mark Dutz is senior economist at the World Bank. Nicholas Stern is Chief Economist at the European Bank for Reconstruction and Development.

*Annual World Bank Conference on Development Economics 1999*
©2000 The International Bank for Reconstruction and Development / THE WORLD BANK

## Reallocation and Restructuring

The simplest way to think about the complex interaction of ownership, competition, and performance in transition is to think of two key elements: reallocation of resources across activities and restructuring of activities. Reallocation requires the closure of inefficient producers and the creation of new firms. Restructuring involves changes within existing firms that appear capable of achieving long-run viability. Both processes lead to productivity growth.[1]

Resource reallocation requires changes in government objectives and expenditure plans and in the rules and institutions affecting entry, exit, taxation, and other factors influencing private decisions. Restructuring implies changes in the objectives and financing constraints of existing firms, and also requires changes in regulations and institutional capabilities. In dynamic terms restructuring choices will depend on the relative values—appropriately discounted—of being in a restructured or unrestructured firm, qualified by the distribution of control rights within the firm, outside factor market conditions, and the availability of severance or other mechanisms for compensating losers. Restructuring also critically depends on the availability of external finance and hence on the banking sector (since equity markets are still underdeveloped). And because banks differ from other firms in a number of key respects, the conditions under which they should operate and fail are different.

While conceptually distinct, the processes of resource reallocation and restructuring are closely tied. The evidence shows large variations in emphasis across countries, with some emphasizing entry more than restructuring, for example. Nor can reallocation and restructuring be viewed as tidy processes uncontaminated by politics or other disturbances. Where change in ownership has been combined with hard budget constraints and increased competition, corporate governance has improved, which has generally facilitated restructuring. But in a significant number of cases change in ownership has not been accompanied by the imposition of hard budget constraints and the introduction of greater competition and has even impeded any subsequent imposition of such effects. These failures in implementation have long lasting and adverse consequences. Thus to uncover the reasons for the variations in outcomes in different countries we need to understand the political economy of ownership change and competition, and the resulting institutional and enforcement dynamics.

In Central Europe privatization has been widely implemented, though the balance between new entrants and privatized firms in new private sectors has varied considerably.[2] Conditions for entry have generally been favorable, and trade liberalization has imposed competitive discipline on domestic producers. Steps nevertheless need to be taken to restructure further and to change incentives faced by firms and banks.

In Russia, Ukraine, and many other parts of the former Soviet Union, the picture is far less rosy. Even where large-scale privatization has occurred, the results have often been at odds with original intentions. Incumbents took control of the redistribution of ownership and control rights, compounding the sorry legacy of connected lending, cronyism, and rent-seeking. Privatization has influenced and been influenced by the incestuous links connecting government, firms, and banks. These failures have imposed large costs—including the cost of sanctioning theft and corruption—and raise difficult questions about how to address them.

Some countries acted in the belief that restructuring could be left to unfettered markets, no doubt a reaction to the rigidities of the former command system. And some countries delayed restructuring because prevailing patterns of control and the associated distribution of political bargaining power led to ineffectual changes in ownership and competition. The challenge ahead is to make the right policy choices that will make the business environment become conducive to private restructuring decisions that also benefit the economy as a whole. That means addressing the obstacles that have blocked hard budget constraints and effective competition through policy changes affecting both ends of the competitive process (entry and exit). The task is complicated by the fact that some initial policy decisions are now difficult to alter.[3] Moreover, the ability to construct and enforce good regulation is one of the scarcest resources.

To examine this experience with restructuring, we begin with a theoretical analysis of the influence of ownership and competition on restructuring and performance. We put the analysis in context by reviewing evidence from OECD countries on the nature and strength of these relationships. We then present an empirical analysis of the transition economies, surveying the evidence on both the scale of reallocation and restructuring and their impact on performance. Building on these findings, we identify the main policy challenges for the coming years.

## Why Ownership and Competition Matter

Private ownership and competition are needed to increase productivity and generate growth. Establishing both in the transition economies is critical to generating increased employment, income, consumption, and innovation in the long run.

### Restructuring and Productivity

Restructuring is the implementation of significant changes in the structure of a firm's output mix. It generally includes shutting down some activities, which means significant changes in resource use. By definition restructuring is a process of radical adjustment that will affect some vested interests.

The purpose of restructuring is both to save resources and to redeploy them to more efficient uses. In market-oriented economies restructuring is usually motivated by a desire to restore or regain competitiveness and enhance long-term shareholder value in response to a radical change in the business environment or a gradual erosion of competitiveness. In the transition from command to market economies restructuring requires that profit generation become the overriding objective of the enterprise.

Restructuring encompasses both survival-driven cost-side changes aimed at reducing inefficiencies and growth-oriented revenue-side changes aimed at reorienting an enterprise's processes and products to current market requirements (see Carlin 1998 for an overview of the two-stage approach to restructuring). Survival-driven restructuring, which may involve labor shedding, plant closures, and the search for new markets for existing products, is commonly a necessary first step to deeper restructuring. Survival-driven restructuring decisions that seek to make only the minimum defensive changes necessary to avoid closure or more radical changes in output mix will generally be neither sufficient nor even desirable. Such decisions tend to tie up resources that could be more productively employed elsewhere.

Growth-oriented restructuring, in contrast, generally involves substantial new investment in fixed and human capital as well as strategic changes in product mix. Such deeper restructuring generally requires identification of profitable opportunities and access to sufficient financial resources to take advantage of them. From an economywide perspective, the successfully restructured entity will have a reconfigured asset mix that is appropriate for its environment. Resources that may have been subsidizing inefficient production can be reallocated to growing new and restructured enterprises, allowing over time better economywide resource allocation and thus higher employment, income, and consumption levels.

In practice, however, the restructuring decisions that are most desirable from an economywide or even enterprise perspective will generally not be chosen because the social benefits and costs of restructuring will almost always differ from the private net benefits that accrue to key decisionmakers. The policy challenge is to construct a business environment, including regulations, institutions, capabilities, and resources, that narrows divergences between private and social returns (Atiyas, Dutz, and Frischtak 1992).

## *Ownership and Competition with Well-Functioning Markets*

Ownership and competition are important and mutually reinforcing disciplinary devices that provide private incentives for socially desirable restructuring. Key decisionmakers must be motivated by the objective of maximizing the firm's profit and must be able to implement the decisions that are made. This depends on whether the owner is able to establish control, which in turn depends on the distribution of control rights between shareholders and creditors and potential conflicts of interest with other stakeholders. There are at least four channels through which effective corporate governance can affect restructuring (Dutz and Vagliasindi 1999a) by:

- Identifying appropriate restructuring or turnaround agents.
- Ensuring that managers take appropriate restructuring decisions.
- Attracting and retaining external finance needed for restructuring.
- Facilitating broader social and political legitimacy for the restructuring process.

There is no debate on the importance of competition for resource allocation in general and restructuring in particular. Intensity of rivalry is the engine that makes market economies work. Product market competition affects restructuring in at least four ways:

- By ensuring that appropriate restructuring takes place as price and profit signals reflect relative scarcities.
- By accelerating the decision to restructure through the closure of poorly managed firms, the reduction of managerial slack within firms, and the spurring of innovation.[4]
- By reducing the extent of political involvement in restructuring decisions (Shleifer and Vishny 1993).
- By reducing the scope for corruption, thereby improving the overall social and political legitimacy of any restructuring.

The empirical evidence from relatively well-functioning markets suggests that privatization significantly improves the operating and financial performance of divested firms. Although there is continuing debate over the extent to which improvements in performance have been exclusively driven by ownership change or associated increases in competition, the evidence points to the joint importance of strong and well-enforced ownership and control structures coupled with effective competition (see Megginson and Netter 1998; Nellis 1999; and La Porta and Lopez-de-Silanes 1997a).

## Ownership and Competition in Transition Economies

Transition economies suffer from capital and product market imperfections as well as weak regulatory and institutional regimes. These features suggest more severe underlying problems with both incumbent monopolists and incumbent managers.

Changes in ownership without adequate attention to market structure establish vested interests that are difficult to reverse. Restructuring before privatization in a manner that is consistent with improved competition is challenging (Van Siclen 1992); it becomes next-to-impossible once ownership rights to a stream of monopoly rents have been transferred and paid for by new private owners and a powerful new set of lobbying interests is created.[5] Changes in ownership without adequate attention to the distribution and subsequent exchange of control rights can impede restructuring.[6] For instance, transferring ownership to incumbent insiders without constraining their ability to appropriate resources can be worse than continued state ownership, especially if it results in capital flight and undercuts political support for reform. Similarly, the absence of minority shareholder protection enables insiders to divert resources and strip assets.

The case for competition becomes even stronger when corporate control through shareholder and creditor monitoring is weak. Competition in product markets can act as a substitute for debt-related financial pressure and external shareholder control (Nickell, Nicolitsas, and Dryden 1997).[7] To the extent that competition increases the sensitivity of profits to unit costs, more competition creates stronger incentives for cost-reducing or revenue-increasing restructuring changes (Willig 1987). Competition can also reduce agency problems and improve corporate control by moving managers closer to profit maximization, diminishing incentive problems between managers and owners or directly between managers and the market.

More competitors mean more opportunities for benchmarking or other types of comparison, which can lead to sharper incentives (Rey 1998).

By definition restructuring involves winners and losers. Without sufficient competition, especially through unencumbered entry and expansion possibilities, it becomes almost impossible to accommodate the downsizing and social dislocations that accompany restructuring. Thus social and political legitimacy are critical to restructuring and overall reform. Unless the process is perceived as legitimate, it will be difficult to attract outsiders and avoid backtracking. Some initial evidence also suggests that increases in product market competition reduce corruption in the bureaucracy (Ades and Di Tella 1995; Laffont and N'Guessan 1998). To the extent that decreased institutional corruption leads to better enforcement of regulations, competition will improve corporate incentives.

## Review of Experience in Transition Economies

What has been the actual experience of transition economies with resource reallocation and restructuring?

### Initial Conditions

The need for restructuring and resource reallocation in the transition economies stems from a number of common initial conditions:
- Ownership of firms and banks was concentrated in the hands of the state. State-owned firms operated largely with non–profit-maximizing objectives. The banking system was dominated by monolithic state banks (monobanks).
- Firms were configured in ways that did not necessarily suit the needs of a market economy. Problems, including overstaffing and choice of technology, were amplified by declining investment before transition, which resulted in a decaying capital stock.
- Managerial and entrepreneurial skills were honed to working the networks of the planned economy, including lobbying for soft supports. Real managers and entrepreneurs were in short supply. Human capital of both workers and managers tended to be highly firm specific.
- The dominance of the monobank meant that expertise in selecting and monitoring projects was very limited. Banking technology was primitive and connected lending endemic.
- The structure of production was driven by political objectives that resulted in a systematic bias toward manufacturing alongside tough restrictions on competition.
- Foreign trade was organized largely through the Council for Mutual Economic Assistance, at artificial prices.
- Firms tended to be larger and to possess more market power than in market economies. There were almost no small manufacturing firms in the Soviet Union. In Poland in 1990 the leading firm had more than 30 percent of the

market in more than 60 percent of all markets (at the three-digit industrial code level) and more than 60 percent of the market in 25 percent of markets (Newbery and Kattuman 1992). Concentration was not as great throughout the former Soviet Union, but some firms had market power in regional markets (Brown, Ickes, and Ryterman 1996; Brown and Brown 1998).
- Planned economies lacked appropriate business infrastructure. Distribution systems were inadequate, and access to services was constrained (EBRD 1996).

## Evidence on Reallocation

The linkages between restructuring and reallocation are fundamental. Policies that promote entry and result in a dynamic new private sector help attract resources away from less dynamic firms. This facilitates a smoother—albeit possibly more protracted—reduction in the size of the state sector, as China's experience shows. For restructuring to be effective, reallocation of resources must be complemented by measures to increase the pressure on state firms by hardening the budget constraint, provide an exit mechanism, and lower the value of not restructuring (and so reduce the incentive for insiders to block restructuring). And while private sector growth will facilitate restructuring, given the scale of necessary adjustment, it is unlikely that restructuring can be feasible—politically or otherwise—unless adequate safety nets are provided for those dislocated in the adjustment process.

Reallocation of resources across activities and firms requires a decline in soft supports. It also requires the closure of failing firms and the emergence of new private firms. Evidence on subsidies to firms has been unambiguous: in almost all countries explicit subsidies have declined significantly, almost across the board (EBRD 1998). Except in Russia, where subsidies remained high, subsidies to firms in transition economies ranged from 1 to 3 percent of GDP in 1997 (table 1). These figures can be misleading, however, since they neglect soft supports in the form of nonpayments or severely delayed payments and soft credits from the banking system (Commander 1998; Schaffer, Bevan, and Mochrie 1998; Carlin and Landesmann 1997). In Russia, for example, explicit subsidies and directed credits were replaced by loan rollovers, skipped payments to government and utilities, and the massive proliferation of barter and nonmonetary transacting (see below). Quasi-fiscal transfers to firms have replaced on-budget subsidies, with large-scale net credit creation to firms provided through utilities and other publicly controlled institutions.

In the core Central European countries—Czech Republic, Hungary, and Poland— hard budget constraints were imposed on the bulk of firms relatively early in the transition. Although the scale and speed of closure have varied widely, bankruptcy rules have generally been introduced, if only selectively implemented, not least because of institutional weakness and problems in the design of bankruptcy procedures.[8] In contrast, hard budget constraints have not been imposed in Bulgaria, Romania, and most of the former Soviet Union.[9] The result has been slower restructuring and some crowding-out of the new private sector. Bankruptcy and exit procedures have remained weak at best, nonexistent at worst.

**Table 1. Budgetary Subsidies to Firms, 1994–97**
*(percent of GDP)*

| Country | 1994 | 1995 | 1996 | 1997 |
|---|---|---|---|---|
| *Eastern Europe and the Baltic States* | | | | |
| Bulgaria | 1.3 | 1.2 | 0.8 | 0.8 |
| Croatia | 2.0 | 1.8 | 1.9 | 1.9 |
| Czech Republic | 3.1 | 2.7 | 2.2 | 2.4 |
| Estonia | 0.9 | 0.5 | 0.4 | 0.3 |
| Hungary | 4.5 | 3.8 | 3.9 | 3.3 |
| Latvia | 0.2 | 0.4 | 0.3 | 0.4 |
| Lithuania | 1.7 | 1.1 | 1.3 | 0.9 |
| Poland | 3.3 | 2.9 | 2.5 | 2.4 |
| Romania | 3.8 | 4.1 | 4.3 | 2.6 |
| Slovak Republic | 3.2 | 2.8 | 2.4 | 2.2 |
| Slovenia | 1.6 | 1.6 | 1.2 | 1.3 |
| *Commonwealth of Independent States* | | | | |
| Armenia | 12.8 | 0.9 | 0.1 | 0.4 |
| Azerbaijan | 5.4 | 2.2 | 2.1 | 0.7 |
| Belarus | 6.3 | 3.4 | 2.9 | 1.3 |
| Georgia | 13.8 | 1.1 | 1.0 | 1.5 |
| Russia | — | — | 6.2 | 6.4 |
| Uzbekistan | 1.9 | 3.4 | 4.0 | 3.2 |

— Not available.
*Source:* EBRD 1999.

Growth of the private sector has been rapid in the transition economies (table 2). By mid-1998 the private sector's unweighted mean share of GDP was 65 percent in Eastern and Central Europe and 47.5 percent in the former Soviet Union. While these numbers are imprecise and partly misleading (they ignore continuing state interference), they show significant variation in growth of the private sector (Frydman, Hessel, and Rapacyznski 1998). This variation can ultimately be traced to the difference in policies on subsidies and other supports to state and loss-making firms, to differences in the speed of privatization, and to the incentives facing new private sector agents.

The growth of new private firms has followed a clear pattern. At the start of transition private firms were small service firms, often operated by households and funded by informal or family finance. Depending on the tax regime and other environmental factors largely exogenous to the firm, they operated both inside and outside the tax net. Over time, new starts—and spinoffs—have grown and moved into other sectors, including manufacturing.

Evidence from Hungary and Poland demonstrates this path most clearly. While gross flows of firms are, not surprisingly, large, there is some evidence that new firms increasingly have access to bank credit—often collateralized—and hence have moved on from the small-scale, retained-finance model of the early years (Bratkowski, Grosfeld, and Rostowski 1998).[10] This has clearly not been the case farther east, where firms have been limited to small-scale operations outside for-

**Table 2. Ownership, Competition, and Transition Indicators, 1998**

| | | | Transition indicators: Privatization and competition policy | | | Cumulative change in labor productivity,[b] 1994–97 | Private sector share of GDP Mid-1998 (percent) |
|---|---|---|---|---|---|---|---|
| Country | Privatization procedures[a] Primary | Secondary | Large-scale privatization | Small-scale privatization | Competition policy | | |
| **Eastern Europe and the Baltic States** | | | | | | | |
| Albania | Buyouts | Voucher | 2 | 4 | 2 | — | 75 |
| Bulgaria | Outsider sales | Voucher | 3 | 3 | 2 | 18.7 | 50 |
| Croatia | Buyouts | Voucher | 3 | 4+ | 2 | 34.1 | 55 |
| Czech Republic | Voucher | Outsider sales | 4 | 4+ | 3 | 39.3 | 75 |
| Estonia | Outsider sales | Voucher | 4 | 4+ | 3− | 30.8 | 70 |
| Hungary | Outsider sales | Buyouts | 4 | 4+ | 3 | 49.1 | 80 |
| Latvia | Voucher | Outsider sales | 3 | 4 | 3− | 50.7 | 60 |
| Lithuania | Voucher | Outsider sales | 3 | 4 | 2+ | 11.7 | 70 |
| Macedonia, FYR | Buyouts | Outsider sales | 3 | 4 | 1 | 9.6 | 55 |
| Poland | Outsider sales | Buyouts | 3+ | 4+ | 3 | 52.6 | 65 |
| Romania | Buyouts | Outsider sales | 3− | 3+ | 2 | 49.7 | 60 |
| Slovak Republic | Outsider sales | Voucher | 4 | 4+ | 3 | 19.4 | 75 |
| Slovenia | Buyouts | Voucher | 3+ | 4+ | 2 | 34.0 | 55 |
| **Commonwealth of Independent States** | | | | | | | |
| Armenia | Voucher | Buyouts | 3 | 3 | 2 | 53.9 | 60 |
| Azerbaijan | Voucher | Outsider sales | 2 | 3 | 1 | −16.4 | 45 |
| Belarus | Buyouts | Voucher | 1 | 2 | 2 | 14.7 | 20 |
| Georgia | Voucher | Outsider sales | 3+ | 4 | 2 | — | 60 |
| Kazakhstan | Voucher | Outsider sales | 3 | 4 | 2 | 15.8 | 55 |
| Kyrgyz Republic | Voucher | Buyouts | 3 | 4 | 2 | 49.0 | 60 |
| Moldova | Voucher | Outsider sales | 3 | 3+ | 2 | — | 45 |
| Russia | Voucher | Outsider sales | 3+ | 4 | 2+ | −3.9 | 70 |
| Tajikistan | Buyouts | Voucher | 2 | 2+ | 1 | — | 30 |
| Turkmenistan | Buyouts | Outsider sales | 2− | 2 | 1 | −39.1 | 25 |
| Ukraine | Voucher | Buyouts | 2+ | 3+ | 2 | −18.0 | 55 |
| Uzbekistan | Buyouts | Outsider sales | 3− | 3 | 2 | 20.2 | 45 |

— Not available.
a. Outsider sales are direct sales to outsiders; buyouts are management and employee buyouts.
b. Labor productivity is calculated as the ratio of industrial production to industrial employment.
*Source:* EBRD 1998.

mal finance and, for the most part, outside the tax system (Kaufmann and Kaliberda 1995; Johnson, Kaufmann, and Schleifer 1997). Entry barriers have remained significant, and the incentives for remaining small and informal have been compelling. The reallocation effect has thus been significantly weaker in Eastern Europe and the former Soviet Union than in the more advanced Central European economies.

## Evidence on Ownership, Competition, and Restructuring

A considerable amount of empirical evidence has accumulated on the consequences for performance of changes in ownership and control and the choice of privatization procedure. While the findings are provisional, some patterns have emerged:

- There has been significant variation in privatization pace and procedures. Methods have ranged from management and employee buyouts to mass privatization schemes involving equity distributions to the public to direct sales to outsiders. The most common primary privatization procedures have been management and employee buyouts and voucher-based mass privatizations (see table 2). Voucher programs have been widely used in the former Soviet Union, where large concessions to insiders have generally been granted. They have also been used in the Czech Republic and the Baltic states.
- Progress in improving the policy and legal environment for governance and economic restructuring has been greatest in Central and Eastern Europe and the Baltics (figure 1 and EBRD 1998).
- Almost all countries have made rapid progress in privatizing small firms. For medium-size and large firms, however, considerably more privatization has taken place in Central Europe than in the former Soviet Union.
- Growth in labor productivity in industry—a coarse measure of restructuring—has been substantial in Central Europe. Farther east firms have adjusted employment only partially, preferring to vary working hours or to delay payments to workers. Labor hoarding has not been eliminated, a consequence of the fact that firms have generally been privatized to insiders and the state continues to interfere in decisionmaking.

**Figure 1. Regional Patterns of Enterprise Reform**

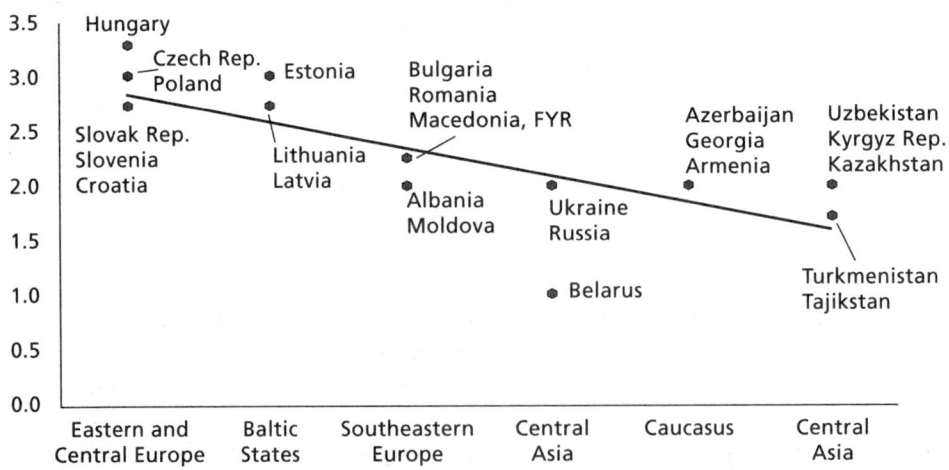

*Enterprise governance and restructuring score*

*Source:* EBRD 1999.

- The primary privatization method adopted appears to affect subsequent restructuring. During the first two years following privatization mass privatization and direct sales resulted in more than twice the productivity changes resulting from management and employee buyouts.[11]
- Regardless of the privatization methods used, incumbents, commonly comprising coalitions of workers and managers, enjoyed large gains in most countries. The gains were particularly large in the former Soviet Union.
- Insider-dominated privatizations have been associated with a wide range of distributions of control rights. In general, managers appear to have dominated. There is some weak evidence that firms privatized to managers have performed better than those privatized with dominant worker ownership (Earle and Estrin 1998).
- Predictably, insider privatizations have been associated with low investment, limited managerial change, and product innovation. Investment that has occurred has come largely from retained earnings. Resale of privatized firms—or at least realignments in equity distributions—appears to have been limited largely to other insiders. (Managers appear to have systematically acquired workers' shares, for example.)
- State involvement in enterprise decisionmaking has been considerably reduced in Central Europe. Large employment reductions have resulted, although continued overstaffing can be expected if managers continue to need the cooperation of workers to maximize their returns. In contrast, depoliticization has not occurred in much of the former Soviet Union. The result has been continued labor hoarding and provision of soft supports to firms.
- In terms of both relative cost and revenue performance, privatized firms have generally outperformed state-owned firms. The finding is far from robust, however (Earle and Estrin 1998; Frydman, Hessel, and Rapacyznski 1998; Carlin and Landesmann 1997; Commander 1998; Grosfeld and Nivet 1997; Lizal and Svejnar 1998). The lack of robustness may be attributable to lags, as well as to selection and endogeneity problems. Selection bias—possibly contingent on the privatization procedure—makes comparison difficult.
- Where controls for selection have been implemented, there is mixed evidence on the ability of the privatization procedure to sort firms by quality. The Czech Republic voucher privatizations seem to have resulted in better firms being privatized (Marcinin and van Wijnbergen 1997)—not the case in Russia (Earle and Estrin 1998).
- Firms privatized to outsiders, particularly to foreigners, have tended to perform best on measures of total factor productivity, labor productivity, or other restructuring dimensions, including investment (Claessens, Djankov and Pohl 1997; Frydman, Hessel, and Rapacyznski 1998; Carlin and Landesmann 1997). Changes in investment and technology and associated changes in management may account for the superior performance (Barberis and others 1996; Earle and Estrin 1998.

- Privatized firms tend to show a greater variance in performance than do state firms, possibly indicating greater differences in their approach to decisionmaking, including attitudes toward risk. Evidence of superior product restructuring by privatized firms may reflect both differences in the degree of risk aversion and better incentives for innovation (Frydman, Hessel, and Rapaczynski 1998).
- Capital market imperfections have remained significant, and disciplinary mechanisms exogenous to the firm, such as bankruptcy laws, have rarely been effective. There has been little protection of shareholder rights, particularly outside the more advanced Central European countries.
- Competition in product markets from both domestic and foreign competitors appears to have been important in driving restructuring in Poland and Hungary (Carlin and Landesmann 1997). Some weak evidence suggests that the extent of import competition was positively associated with product restructuring and negatively associated with industry profitability in Russia (Earle and Estrin 1998; Brown and Brown 1998). The results are derived largely from surveys of managerial perceptions, however, rather than from any robust estimation of the appropriate measure (namely, the effects of competition on productivity).
- In some countries, such as Poland, hard budget constraints have been imposed on state-run firms. More often, however, state-run firms have benefited from soft credits from the government and banks. In some cases credit has been extended to declining industries with few or no prospects. In other cases decapitalization and stealing have been prompted by uncertainty over ownership and control rights. Ownership "in limbo" has been particularly susceptible to resource diversion and subsidies, as Bulgaria's experience between 1992 and 1997 indicates.

In conclusion, where privatization has brought in outside owners—particularly foreign owners—infusions of capital and new management have promoted restructuring and resulted in large, relative productivity gains. While privatization favoring incumbents has also aligned ownership and control, lack of new investment and managerial skills has held back restructuring. In too many cases, such privatization has also facilitated looting from firms by managers, particularly when there has been continuing uncertainty over the viability of the firm and when monitoring of managers has been incomplete. In addition, mass privatizations biased toward incumbents have tended to be associated with continuing state interference in decisionmaking. Strikingly, although an important argument for the use of mass or voucher privatization has been fairness, with the important exception of the Czech Republic, countries pursuing voucher privatization have generally experienced the largest increases in income inequality.[12]

Finally, competitive pressures on firms to restructure have come through the reallocation process itself—primarily through entry, but also through trade liberalization. Given that initially most new entry was small scale and in services, import competition has been a more effective, proximate source of discipline on manufacturing firms. Levels of import penetration have risen substantially throughout, but most significantly in Central Europe and the Baltics (EBRD 1997). Some evidence points to a strong and positive effect of import penetration on total factor productivity (Falk, Raiser, and Brauer 1996).

## Restructuring and Banks

Banks should be important players in determining the scale and pace of enterprise restructuring. In addition to providing financing, banks play a critical monitoring role. They are thus an important link in enforcing hard budget constraints and improving corporate governance. When firms are unable to meet their obligations, banks can initiate bankruptcy proceedings.[13] For these mechanisms to function, however, a framework must be in place in which rules can be enforced, through contracts and other means. Insofar as financing and monitoring promote restructuring by firms, further restructuring should take place as a result of the positive impact on bank profitability. Greater profitability will attract entry of more banks, which will lower financing costs for firms, thereby facilitating additional restructuring. In short, the efficiency and stability of the banking system are likely to be vital to effective restructuring among firms.

The evidence suggests, however, that banks' ability to promote restructuring has been limited in the transition economies. Part of this failure can be attributed to the legacy of the command economy. But decisions on ownership and competition since the transition began have also played a role.

Both the scale of lending to the private sector and loan performance have varied markedly across countries (figure 2). In Croatia, the Slovak Republic, and the Czech

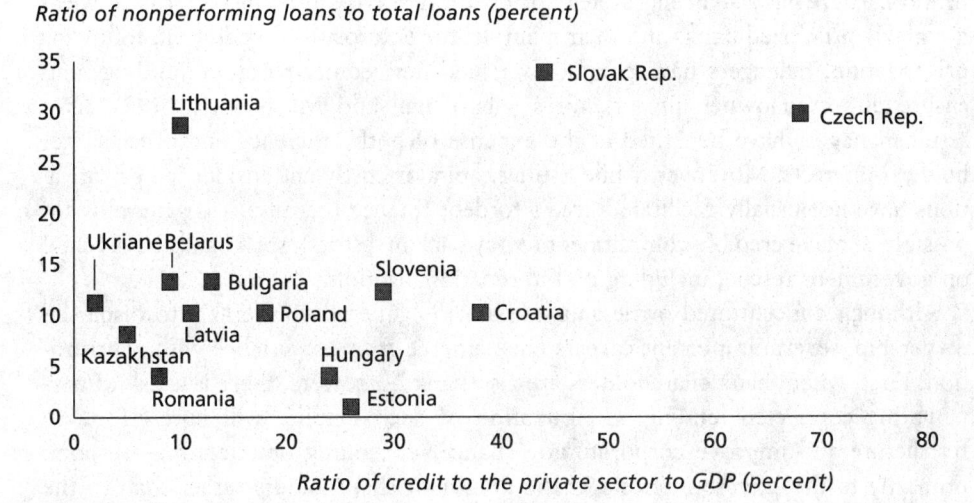

**Figure 2. Bank Lending to the Private Sector, 1997**

*Ratio of nonperforming loans to total loans (percent)*

*Ratio of credit to the private sector to GDP (percent)*

Source: EBRD 1998.

Republic the ratio of private sector credit to GDP was 40–60 percent in 1997. In contrast in Ukraine, Kazakhstan, and Romania the ratio was just 2–8 percent. Countries with the highest lending exposures have tended to have the highest rates of nonperforming loans, although several countries of the former Soviet Union have relatively high nonperforming loan rates despite the low level of lending.

OWNERSHIP OF BANKS. Privatization has proceeded more slowly for banks than for firms. It has been held back by a combination of factors, including the scale of bad debts in the portfolios of state banks, opposition by vested interests (including incumbent personnel and favored debtors), and lack of clarity regarding laws and oversight.

In the core Central European countries privatization has proceeded in a fairly orderly manner, with varying weights given to the interests of incumbents and outsiders. (Drawing in foreign strategic investment has been a major feature only in Hungary, however.) Even when privatization has gone ahead, however, governments have often retained strategic stakes in privatized banks.

The design of the privatization has mattered. In the Czech Republic, for example, investment funds' accumulation of significant holdings in privatized banks appears to have exerted little beneficial influence on governance. Dispersed ownership of the investment funds is partly to blame, leading to an incentive problem involving the behavior of managers of both funds and the banks.

Farther east privatizations have generally been led by incumbent bank managers who have successfully exploited the government's inability to organize an orderly transfer of ownership rights. A distinctive feature has been the importance of securing the participation of both insiders (bank managers and employees) and borrowers, who have historically benefited from loans granted in a regime of soft budget constraints.

Evidence from Russia shows that bank managers have been key in driving privatization. There has also been a systematic creation of cross-holding patterns between the newly privatized banks and their main debtor enterprises. In addition, following privatization, managers have commonly issued new equity to dilute holdings and ensure dispersed ownership structures (Abarbanell and Meyendorff 1997). As a result managers have benefited at the expense of both efficiency and other shareholders' interests. Moreover, while issuing capital is costly and insider-led privatizations have not usually facilitated access to debt finance (because it is generally not possible to make credible commitment to pay back investors), such banks have relied on government rescue, including partial renationalization.

Although concentrated ownership of banks is generally preferable to dispersed ownership, several important caveats have emerge from experience with privatization. First, where bank shareholders are also bank borrowers, there is a risk of perpetuating connected lending. Continuation of such lending will hurt efforts to restructure and improve corporate governance, as lending practices may respond primarily to the private interests of the dominant shareholders rather than to the interests of the bank or minority shareholders. When banks and their main shareholders form part of the same group, experience suggests that shareholders tend to be ineffectual in restraining risky investments by managers.[14]

Concentrated ownership of banks can also raise the scope for collusion, particularly where the government retains a significant ownership stake in newly privatized banks, as in Hungary. Collusion can lead to inefficient lending practices and the continuing politicization of lending decisions. In addition, there is the danger that minority shareholders will be expropriated or their interests ignored.[15]

COMPETITION AMONG BANKS. Robust competition among banks requires new entry and the expansion of more efficient institutions as well as the contraction and exit of inefficient institutions. The transition economies have continued to face major problems in imposing financial discipline and limiting the generosity of bailouts for distressed banks. Several factors have been at play:

- Bank managers have continued to pursue objectives other than strict financial discipline. Their interests have often remained more closely aligned with the interests of their employees than those of shareholders and depositors. As a result managers have tended to be very reluctant to close down projects that are no longer viable.
- Political pressures on bank managers to keep alive large state firms (as well as privatized firms in the former Soviet Union) have been significant, as governments have remained very sensitive to increases in unemployment.
- Inherited as well as subsequent accumulations of bad debt have distorted the allocation of capital, crowding out lending to the private sector and placing pressure on banks' balance sheets.
- Only limited progress has been made in implementing workable bankruptcy procedures. In most transition economies procedures have been too lenient and the courts have been too slow and too friendly to debtors.
- Strict and fair bank closure rules have rarely been enforced on the largest banks, which have been deemed "too big to fail." Regulators have generally opted for bailing out large troubled banks, as in Bulgaria in 1996 or Estonia in 1997.
- The problem of regulatory forbearance has been exacerbated by technical incapacity and lack of adequate accountability.

These constraints could be reduced through a range of measures, including capital adequacy rules, limits on explicit deposit insurance, and the breakup of banks to avoid the "too-big-to-fail" problem (EBRD 1998). However, given the importance of both stability and efficiency in the banking system, efficient exit depends critically on how entry is handled. Because of regulatory shortcomings and the importance of stability, the quality of entrants will be critical. Recent experience in the former Soviet Union demonstrates that relatively unconstrained entry leads to a proliferation of undercapitalized banks and to greater instability. Given the need to mesh superior banking technology with knowledge of local markets while reducing the risks of connected lending, foreign entry appears particularly attractive. In Central Europe, where bank concentration ratios have remained higher than in

OECD countries, a combination of breakups and increased entry would help to reduce constraints.

## Paths of Transition

This examination of ownership change and competition shows significant variation in reallocation and restructuring across the region. With some risk of simplification, two broad paths can be discerned among these variations.[16]

MAJOR REALLOCATION AND RESTRUCTURING. The first path, pursued by most of the Central European economies, has been associated with significant new entry; relatively rapid privatization, with outsiders increasingly taking major stakes; and hard budget constraints on state firms. Employment reductions and declining rent appropriation by insiders were achieved at a relatively early stage (Kollo 1998; Commander and Dhar 1998; Estrin and Svejnar 1998; Grosfeld and Nivet 1997). Increases in productivity have been translated largely into profits rather than wages. Depoliticization was achieved early in the transition, with state interference in decisionmaking in privatized firms considerably reduced, if still far from absent. Incumbents have in general been unable to lobby for significant state supports, capture other rents, or otherwise block reforms. Exit mechanisms have been developed and increasingly implemented.

Reallocation and restructuring have fuelled innovation, which has led to growth and structural change. Bank lending to the firm sector has been maintained, limiting the adverse effects of a prolonged credit squeeze. Lending decisions by banks have improved, as their capacity to screen projects has developed. Foreign direct investment has also expanded, often dramatically, as in Hungary and, more recently, in Poland. Trade data show some diminution in quality gaps in trade with the European Union (Landesmann and Burgstaller 1997). Stimulating this process has been a combination of domestic policies and competitive pressures unleashed by trade liberalization.

Entry of new firms has been accelerated both by institutional factors, which affect set-up costs, and by infrastructure. Indicators for institutional and physical infrastructure in Central Europe show significant convergence toward OECD levels. By reducing transactions costs, these infrastructure effects have put pressure on high-cost firms and stimulated product market competition (Aghion and Schankerman 1999).

New firms have attracted workers from low productivity firms, increasing the pressure to restructure. The unemployed have been provided with generous benefits—the wage replacement rate has been about 30 percent—and social assistance. Helping displaced workers has been crucial to reducing insiders' incentives to block restructuring, as the value of remaining in unrestructured firms has been relatively low and the ability to loot restricted.

LIMITED REALLOCATION AND RESTRUCTURING. The second path—pursued to varying degrees in Bulgaria, Romania, and much of the former Soviet Union—has been characterized by limited reallocation and little restructuring despite seemingly radical changes in ownership regime (Faggio and Konings 1998; Konings, Lehmann, and Schaffer 1996 ). Privatization has been conducted largely on terms that favor incumbents. Little depoliticization has taken place, and the incentive effects of privatization have been limited. Insider privatization has largely failed to improve performance or to sever the links between public resources and firms—or even to create credible conditions for severing such links. Bank credit to the private sector has declined, while connected lending and other inefficiencies in credit allocation have persisted. Permissive entry, alongside entrenched branch banking networks, has resulted in instability and rent appropriation. Foreign investment has been very restricted and volatile. Not surprisingly, the transition indicators for governance and restructuring in these countries are low relative to those for Central Europe (see figure 1).

Although significant trade liberalization has taken place, the consequences have been rather different than in Central Europe. Rather than discipline producers, trade has merely filled gaps, primarily in consumer goods markets. The growing use of barter and other nonmonetary transactions has further impeded any trade disciplining effects.

The combination of organized crime (Cohen 1995) and a predatory bureaucracy has curbed the entry of new firms. While new private firms have emerged, most have remained small and informal. Workers retain their formal sector jobs to hold on to such nonmonetary benefits as housing, while moonlighting in the informal sector (Commander and Tolstopiatenko 1998). Moonlighting has been sanctioned by formal sector firms, and firm resources are often openly used for informal sector activities.

Maintaining employment has remained a key objective of both firms and government, partly because of inadequate safety nets for the unemployed (the replacement rate for benefits has been about 10 percent; Estrin and Rosevear 1999; Earle and Estrin 1998; Commander, Dhar, and Yemtsov 1996). Restructuring seems unlikely to accelerate until measures are in place to lower setup costs and facilitate entry and also to provide compensation for those who lose out in restructuring.

As a result of these factors there has been little pull from the private sector and little push from privatized and state firms. The value of staying in formal firms has remained relatively high, not least because insiders have continued to capture large resource flows from both fiscal and quasi-fiscal institutions.

The complexity and range of actions taken to limit restructuring is reflected in the growth in bartering. A 1998 survey of Ukrainian firms found that more than 75 percent of sampled firms used some form of bartering for more than 45 percent of trades (Estrin and Rosevear 1998; Marin and Kaufman 1998). A large survey of Russian firms at the end of 1998 found that roughly two-thirds of firms had some exposure to nonmonetary transacting and that barter represented 60 percent of sales for those firms.[17] In both Ukraine and Russia bartering was prevalent across ownership forms. Indeed, in Russia privatized firms tended to barter more than other types of firms. Nonmonetary transactions by Russian and Ukrainian firms have spilled over into the markets of their trading partners, with downstream costs in other countries.

Barter and the larger problem of accumulating arrears have permitted higher output and employment levels than would have resulted from the monetary and fiscal mix notionally avowed by government. Together with the absence of an effective exit procedure, this situation has helped to perpetuate nonmonetary transactions. The distortions that have resulted have further locked firms into low restructuring equilibria and made it hard—if not impossible—to separate good from bad firms. This has impeded restructuring and exit, but at great fiscal and other cost.

Why have these survival mechanism proliferated? Why are both government and firms reluctant to sanction restructuring, including exit? An important part of the answer is the aversion to large, explicit unemployment and the associated political unrest. Yet few actions have been taken to address this constraint, whether through the financing of a workable system of fallbacks for losers in the adjustment process or through the development of institutions for delivering benefits and other supports. Instead, there has been excessive reliance—particularly in Russia and Ukraine—on wage flexibility.

## Promoting Restructuring

While countries have restructured in a variety of ways, all have encountered some common obstacles. First, capital market imperfections have remained significant, resulting in weak discipline and, in some cases, nontransparent dealing. Second, while privatization may in principle have aligned ownership and control, inadequate minority shareholder protection and other regulatory failures have limited effective discipline on managers. Third, given capital market shortcomings, competitive discipline has been largely through the product market, with external trade liberalization apparently acting as the most significant competitive impulse. Even so there is continuing evidence of significant pockets of market power, particularly in the former Soviet Union. This dominance may reflect geographic factors and the importance of regional markets, a reluctance of foreigners to enter markets, the unwillingness or inability of governments to remove remaining entry and expansion barriers, and other factors.

Given these limitations, including the importance of political economy constraints, what factors are likely to promote better corporate governance and appropriate competition for firms? How can policy be designed that facilitates entry and manages firms in distress?

### Facilitating Entry and Expansion

In the first years of transition restructuring was left largely to market forces, a "pendulum effect" reaction to direct government controls under the planned economy. Deregulation received all the attention, to the neglect of supportive regulations and institutional capacity building required to overcome market failures and ensure that restructuring decisions approximate socially desirable ones.

PROVIDING LEGAL PROTECTION FOR EXTERNAL INVESTORS. An important lesson of transition is the critical importance of legal mechanisms for protecting the rights of investors, including small investors. In addition to helping ensure broader legitimacy for the reform process and preventing managers from stripping assets, strong protection of minority shareholders and strategic investors is essential for attracting new skills, finance, and styles of corporate governance. Without safeguards for transparent secondary trading and protection of new investors, the scope for outsider participation and reallocation of control rights will be drastically diminished.

It may be necessary to impose a small number of stringent mandatory internal mechanisms of governance. These rules could include an obligation for enterprises to disclose financial statements according to minimum quality standards, ideally on the Internet; a requirement of prior shareholder approval of the purchase or disposal of substantial assets; and a clear duty for directors to act in the best interest of the company, with stricter liabilities. Where such rules are mandated, they should be publicized widely; companies that fail to comply should be sanctioned swiftly.

Other measures are also needed. Barriers on foreign participation in privatizations should be lifted. Rules for investment fund managers should be scrutinized and modified wherever possible to ensure that the rewards strongly favor both active management to promote restructuring and the sale of controlling stakes to interested strategic investors. Recent efforts by the Czech government in this area have been aimed at changing the design of funds as well as the incentives of fund managers.[18]

ESTABLISHING APPROPRIATE POLICIES ON COMPETITION. The appropriate emphasis for most transition economies differs from the traditional emphasis of antitrust on reducing price-cost margins. Competition agencies should focus more actively on eliminating barriers to the entry of new firms. They should facilitate access to essential business services, especially those that reduce economywide transactions costs, such as telecommunications and transportation (Aghion and Schankerman 1999). Competition policy should focus on supply-side stimulus and innovation.[19]

Effective competition policy in transition economies must go beyond the traditional emphasis on law enforcement against anticompetitive conduct by enterprises.[20] It requires proactive advocacy to help reduce both public and private barriers to entry. Introducing a registry of movable assets, allowing liens to be placed on motor vehicles, opening up procurement and subcontracting to large public and private enterprises, and simplifying the tax code could reduce some of these barriers. Competition agencies have an important role to play in advocating reforms in areas such as entry regulations and tax collection, where enforcement officials and individual firms come into contact. Surveys of firms have found that regulatory interference is often arbitrary and restrictive, resulting in an uneven playing field biased against startups (World Bank 1997; Frye and Zhuravskaya 1998, Dutz and

Vagliasindi 1999c). Simpler tax and other administrative rules provide less opportunity for arbitrary bureaucratic interference.

One of the most important tasks for competition agencies is to prevent other executive bodies at the state and local levels from maintaining or erecting new barriers, by restricting the flow of goods and investment between countries, regions, or even localities; by obstructing the entry of new domestic or foreign enterprises; or by granting privileges to favored existing enterprises. There is need for clear, well-publicized rules, sanctions for noncompliance, and adequate resources for enforcement that signal strong political support. Political support will in turn be strengthened by public support, which depends on education and efforts to mobilize supportive constituencies, such as small business organizations, export associations, and consumer groups.

Finally, promoting entry calls for much stronger collaboration between competition agency staff and other government officials, especially those responsible for privatization and infrastructure regulation. Competition agencies should monitor larger transactions during the privatization process. Competition is a complement to regulation; in less concentrated markets imperfect competition can often do a better job than imperfect regulation. Horizontal and vertical separation of dominant enterprises that are too large by market standards should occur before privatization. Competition agencies have an important role to play in expressing their views regarding competition-related entry and operating conditions in the provision of infrastructure services (ideally, pricing and technical regulation should be left to a specialized agency). The Polish competition agency, for example, argued vigorously over the past years for increased competition in the provision of telecommunications services.

## Managing Firms in Distress

Several complementary regulatory approaches have been used to deal with large financially distressed firms that continue to receive subsidies. The main resistance to downsizing has come from workers, often allied with managers who have also stood to lose jobs and other benefits. Their resistance has often been buttressed by local and national officials who have increasingly reflected the views of their most vocal or locally powerful constituencies. Any successful approach must directly deal with these stakeholders. The problem is so extensive in much of the former Soviet Union that targeted programs facilitating restructuring and exit will be required.

STRUCTURING TURNAROUNDS. A significant number of large firms have a core set of activities that could become profitable if the firms could shed employees and financial restructure financially. Restructuring is best undertaken by outsiders who have sufficient finance, skills, and determination, not by the state. Also needed is a supportive business environment, flexible labor regulations (with respect to layoffs and relocation), and policies to facilitate legal and organizational breakups and spinoffs of viable segments of larger enterprises.

This type of restructuring was undertaken beginning in mid-1995 by the National Investment Funds in Poland, the only transition economy that has administratively structured its investment funds in a manner conducive to active corporate governance. Fifteen funds with foreign management were each given a controlling investor position in some 35 large firms. The complexity of the scheme resulted in some delays and additional costs, but the long gestation period also permitted learning from other experiences and allowed the stock market to develop sufficiently to float the shares of firms in the portfolio. Although the program amounted to a privatization of the managerial function only, without an immediate transfer of ownership title, fund managers were given sufficient incentives to act as the main restructuring agent. While it is too early to assess fully the performance of the National Investment Funds, major restructuring has been carried out in all firms, new technology and products have been introduced by roughly 90 percent of the firms, and new private owners (mostly strategic investors) have been found for half the firms (Rapacki 1999).

RING-FENCING WITH RELATIVELY RAPID EXIT. Large firms whose asset configuration is no longer viable in the new market environment may have to be liquidated. Where the number and employment impact of such firms is relatively small, rapid exit is feasible, provided that there is sufficient new entry and growth of restructured enterprises to allow resources to be reallocated. This approach puts a premium on policies to promote entry and expansion of viable firms. Ideally, a rapid bankruptcy procedure that minimizes delays in legal procedures should complement policies promoting entry by facilitating the rapid sale of enterprise assets that can be redeployed in more efficient alternative use.

RING-FENCING WHERE RAPID EXIT IS TOO COSTLY. Where the number and employment impact of nonviable firms is large, closing firms will generally be politically infeasible unless there are sufficient reemployment opportunities. Targeted social assistance and unemployment benefits will generally be a precondition for removing barriers to reform. In much of the former Soviet Union implicit subsidies to employment need to be translated into explicit subsidies, which must decline over time. Greater emphasis needs to be placed on retraining and job placement. While some external financial assistance might be forthcoming, it is important to realize that the explicit fiscal costs of targeted supports would not necessarily exceed the current implicit and open-ended fiscal supports to failing firms.

Even with an adequate social safety net the conflicts of interest and externalities associated with restructuring large loss-makers will generally require a targeted approach. Without explicit programs it may be too difficult for the interested parties—the municipality, the firm's management, potential outsider financiers—to agree on terms of engagement. The problem stems from the inability of the parties to make credible long-term commitments in a contract that can be monitored and enforced. For the external financier the up-front costs of assessing the viability of assets and devising a feasible strategy may be prohibitive. For the municipality and entrenched managers the risks of ceding sufficient control may also be high if there is sufficient risk that the investor will renege or incompletely fulfill any up-front commitments. Introducing a workable system of benefits for displaced workers along with ancillary supports—itself a major institutional challenge in the former Soviet Union—can help by lowering associated costs on both sides.

## Conclusion

While approaches to privatization and competition have varied substantially, transition economies have generally taken one of two basic approaches. In some countries, particularly those in Central Europe, policymakers have preserved for government its proper domain while providing incentives for private agents to establish businesses, restructure, and invest. This has facilitated dynamic adjustment to earlier inadequacies in, for example, the design of privatization procedures. Growth rates have accelerated, and structural transformation has taken place, spurred by competitive discipline from the entry of new domestic firms and banks and from trade liberalization and imports.

In contrast, in Eastern Europe and the former Soviet Union excess intervention or regulation has been common, while governments have failed to perform even the minimal functions required of them. Their failures have facilitated rent-seeking and have limited restructuring and the entry of new firms. Incumbents at privatized enterprises have aligned ownership and control, but without bringing in the new finance or skills needed for restructuring. Furthermore, restructured firms have retained access to public resources, thereby limiting the incentives for restructuring and exacerbating underlying fiscal problems. The proliferation of barter and nonmonetary transacting in Russia and Ukraine reflects the lack of hard budget constraints. The weak and even perverse feedback from restructuring to reallocation has resulted in the emergence of relatively small new private sectors.

Bank lending to firms has dried up or been misallocated. The fragility of banking systems—illustrated most starkly in Russia—highlights not only the dangers of permissive entry and inadequate regulation but also the presence of continued rent-seeking and connected lending by incumbent branch banks. Unless countries encourage the entry of adequately capitalized outsiders, in part by providing access to branch networks, it is unlikely that banking systems will intermediate effectively and act as efficient financiers and monitors of firms in need of restructuring. In sum, there has been widespread failure to break the financial and other—often nontransparent—links that connect government, firms, and banks. As a result, the credibility of policies, including privatization, has been severely undermined in many cases.

Regulatory institutions remain weak in all of the transition economies. For ownership and competition to act as joint disciplinary devices on both firms and banks, simple rules must be developed and additional resources must be allocated for enforcement. Policymakers should give priority to providing external investors with greater protection and to removing entry barriers originating with government. They should also work to eliminate continuing distortions for both firms and banks.

In much of the former Soviet Union barriers to entry and the dead hand of regulation have stifled innovation and the growth of new firms while an unwillingness to accept the exit of failing firms has limited restructuring potential and contributed to the persistence of soft budget constraints. It will take better targeted programs and instruments—including explicit supports to displaced workers—to break out of this low restructuring trap.

## Notes

1. This framework is common to a range of models of transition that include; Aghion and Blanchard (1994); Blanchard (1997); Commander and Tolstopiatenko (1998); Chadha and Coricelli (1994).

2. Poland has been an outlier in terms of the slow speed at which privatization has occurred: by early 1999 more than 40 percent of nonagricultural state enterprises were still in the pipeline for privatization. The Polish economy has benefited from a large volume of new starts and expansion of existing private enterprises, however (Rapacki 1999).

3. This is another notable distinction between Central Europe and most countries of the former Soviet Union. In Central Europe a process is under way that makes it possible to introduce important policy corrections, as witnessed by recent attempts in the Czech Republic to strengthen corporate governance. In Central Europe subsequent corrections now appear even more difficult.

4. The persistence of monopoly rents, both from internally driven higher costs and prices that exceed those costs, raises the net benefit of not restructuring. For an overview of how competition can improve selection, reduce managerial slack, and spur innovation, see Armstrong, Cowan, and Vickers (1994).

5. Attempts by the state to change the conditions of sale ex post are likely to have very negative consequences for investment.

6. This section and others on this topic draw heavily on Dutz and Vagliasindi (1999a).

7. Competition tends to have a particularly strong impact on productivity growth when financial pressure is low or firms have no dominant external shareholder.

8. Czech banks, for instance, appear to have strong incentives for not dealing with problem debtors, a factor that probably accounts for the low level of bankruptcy filings in the Czech Republic (Mitchell 1998; Balcerowicz, Gray, and Hashi 1997).

9. In the analysis presented in this article the Baltic states are included in the Eastern European group rather than the former Soviet Union.

10. A feature common to developed economies (see Davis and Haltiwanger 1992). For the transition economies, see Konings, Lehmann, and Schaffer (1996); Bilsen and Konings (1998), Faggio and Konings (1998).

11. The mean labor productivity change following a management and employee buy-out was 4.1 percent. Productivity rose 8.8 percent following a Mass Privatization Program and 11.7 percent following a direct sale (Dutz and Vagliasindi 1999b).

12. Aghion and Commander (1999). Unfortunately, there is no solid evidence available on the distribution of wealth.

13. Banks can, of course, also play a governance role by holding equity. For this to be effective requires adequate supervision of banks, competition among banks, and freedom from political interference.

14. This proposition is confirmed by evidence from Japan in the 1980s (Dinc 1998) and from Russian experience with financial and industrial groups.

15. In most transition economies, minority shareholders remain poorly protected, not least by the continued absence of international accounting standards in consolidated accounts.

16. This distinction may neglect some other similarities, such as the persistence of governance problems in privatized firms, a feature as relevant in the Czech or Slovak Republics as in much of the former Soviet Union.

17. This section draws heavily on Commander and Mumssen (1999).

18. Ellerman (1998) argues that incentives originally inhibited rather than promoted restructuring. See also World Bank (1999).

19. See Romer (1994) on the larger overall welfare impact from new products arising from international trade competition and Dutz (2000) on a similar argument arising from increased competition through domestic regulatory reform.

20. Dutz and Vagliasindi (2000) define a range of competition policy implementation criteria relevant for transition and developing economies along the three main dimensions of enforcement (which includes prescriptions against anti-competitive acts of both enterprises and state executive bodies), competition advocacy and institutional effectiveness. They find a robust positive relationship between effective implementation as captured by these dimensions and expansion of more efficient private firms.

## References

Abarbanell, J.S., and J.P. Bonin. 1997. "Bank Privatization in Poland: The Case of Bank Slaski." *Journal of Comparative Economics* 25 (1): 31–61.

Abarbanell J.S., and A. Meyendorff. 1997. "Bank Privatization in Post-Communist Russia: The Case of Zhilsotsbank." *Journal of Comparative Economics* 25 (1): 62–96.

Ades, A., and R. Di Tella. 1995. "Competition and Corruption." Oxford Applied Economics Discussion Paper Series 169. Oxford University.

Aghion, Philippe, and Olivier Blanchard. 1998. "On Privatization Methods in Eastern Europe and Their Implications." *Economics of Transition* 6 (1): 87–100.

———. 1994. "On the Speed of Transition in Central Europe." *NBER Macroeconomics Annual.* Cambridge, Mass.: MIT Press.

Aghion, Philippe, and Simon Commander. 1999. "On the Dynamics of Inequality in the Transition." *Economics of Transition* 7 (2): 275–98.

Aghion, Philippe, and Mark Schankerman. 1999. "Competition, Entry and the Social Returns to Infrastructure in Transition Economies." *Economics of Transition* 7 (1): 79–101.

Aghion, Philippe, Mathias Dewatripont, and Patrick Rey. 1997. "Corporate Governance, Competition Policy and Industrial Policy." *European Economic Review* 41: 797–805.

Anderson R.W., and C. Kegels. 1998. *Transition Banking; Financial Development of Central and Eastern Europe.* Oxford: Clarendon Press.

Armstrong, Mark, Simon Cowan, and John Vickers. 1994. *Regulatory Reform: Economic Analysis and British Experience.* Cambridge, Mass.: MIT Press.

Atiyas, Izak, Mark Dutz, and Claudio Frischtak. 1992. "Fundamental Issues and Policy Approaches in Industrial Restructuring." IEN Working Paper 56. World Bank, Private Sector Development Department, Washington, D.C.

Balcerowicz, Leszek, Cheryl Gray, and Ijaz Hashi. 1997. "Exit Processes in Economies in Transition." Central European University, Budapest.

Barberis, Nicholas, M. Boycko, A. Shleifer, and N. Tsukanova. 1996. "How Does Privatization Work? Evidence from Russian Shops." *Journal of Political Economy* 104: 764–90.

Berglöf, Erik, and Gerard Roland. 1998. "Soft Budget Constraints and Banking in Transition Economies." *Journal of Comparative Economics* 26: 18–40.

Bilsen, V., and J. Konings. 1998. "Job Creation, Job Destruction and Growth of Enterprises in Transition Economies." *Journal of Comparative Economics* 26 (3): 429–45.

Blanchard, Olivier. 1997. *The Economics of Post-Communist Transition.* Oxford University Press.

Blanchard, Olivier, and Michael Kremer. 1997. "Disorganisation." *Quarterly Journal of Economics* 112 (4): 1091–1126.

Blasi, Joseph, M. Kroumova, and D. Kruse. 1997. *Kremlin Capitalism: Privatizing the Russian Economy.* Ithaca, N.Y..: Cornell University Press.

Boycko, Maxim, A. Shleifer, and R. Vishny. 1995. *Privatizing Russia.* Cambridge, Mass.: MIT Press.

Bratkowski, A., I. Grosfeld, and J. Rostowski. 1998. *Investment and Finance in de novo Private Firms: Empirical Results from the Czech Republic, Hungary and Poland.* Warsaw: CASE Foundation.

Brown, Annette, and David Brown. 1998. "Does Market Structure Matter? New Evidence from Russia." SITE Working Paper 130. Stockholm Institute of Transition Economics.

Brown, Annette, B. Icken, and Randi Ryterman. 1996. "The Myth of Monopoly." World Bank, Washington, D.C.

Carlin, Wendy. 1998. "Privatization, Enterprise Restructuring and Corporate Governance in Transition: An Update on Empirical Studies." University College, London.

Carlin, Wendy, and Michael Landesmann. 1997. "From Theory into Practice? Restructuring and Dynamism in Transition Economies." *Oxford Review of Economic Policy* 13 (2): 77–105.

Chadha, Bankim, and Fabrizio Coricelli. 1994. "Fiscal Constraints and the Speed of Transition." CEPR Discussion Paper 993. Centre for Economic Policy Research, London.

Claessens, Stijn, Simeon Djankov, and Gerhard Pohl. 1997. "Ownership and Corporate Governance: Evidence from the Czech Republic." Policy Research Working Paper 1737. World Bank, Regional Vice President, East Asia and Pacific, and Finance and Private Sector Development Division Division, Europe and Central Asia, and Middle East and North Africa Technical Department, Washington, D.C.

Cohen, Daniel. 1995. "Success and Failure in Russian Reforms." Centre d'Etudes Prospectives d'Economie Mathematique Appliquées à la Planification, Paris.

Commander, Simon, ed. 1998. *Enterprise Restructuring and Unemployment in Models of Transition.* Washington, D.C.: World Bank.

Commander, Simon, and Sumana Dhar. 1998. "Enterprises in the Polish Transition." In Simon Commander, ed., *Enterprise Restructuring and Unemployment in Models of Transition.* Washington, D.C.: World Bank.

Commander, Simon, and Christian Mumssen. 1999. "Understanding Barter in Russia." EBRD Working Paper 37. European Bank for Reconstruction and Development, London.

Commander, Simon, and Mark Schankerman. 1997. "Enterprise Restructuring and Social Benefits." *Economics of Transition* 5 (1): 1–24.

Commander, Simon, and Andrei Tolstopiatenko. 1998. " A Model of the Informal Economy." World Bank Institute, Washington, D.C.

Commander, Simon, Sumana Dhar, and Ruslan Yemtsov. 1996. "How Russian Firms Make Their Wage and Employment Decisions." In Simon Commander, Qimiao Fan, and Mark Schaffer, eds. *Enterprise Restructuring and Economic Policy in Russia.* Washington, D.C.: World Bank.

Commander, Simon, Irina Dolinskaya, and Christian Mumssen. 1999. "Non-Monetary Transactions in Russia: An Empirical Analysis." European Bank for Reconstruction and Development, London, and International Monetary Fund, Washington, D.C.

Commander, Simon, Qimiao Fan, and Mark Schaffer, eds. 1996. *Enterprise Restructuring and Economic Policy in Russia.* Washington, D.C.: World Bank.

Davis, S, and J. Haltiwanger. 1992. "Gross Job Creation, Gross Job Destruction, and Employment Reallocation." *Quarterly Journal of Economics* 107 (3): 819–63.

Dinc, I. S. 1998. "The Shareholding Structure of Japanese Banks and Their Real Estate Lending in the 1980s." Tokyo University.

Dutz, Mark. 2000. "The Role of the Regulatory Environment in Fostering Innovation and Growth." In *Privatisation, Competition, and Regulation.* Paris: Organisation for Economic Co-operation and Development.

Dutz, Mark, and Maria Vagliasindi. 1999a. "Corporate Governance and Restructuring: Policy Lessons from Transition Economies." In *Privatization and Regulation in Developing Countries and Economies in Transition.* New York: United Nations.

———. 1999b. "Insider-Outsider Ownership and Restructuring in Transition Economies: Cross-Country Evidence." European Bank for Reconstruction and Development, London.

———. 1999c. "Market Selection, Regulatory Barriers, and Competition: Evidence from Transition Economies." European Bank for Reconstruction and Development, London.

———. 2000. "Competition Policy Implementation in Transition Economies: An Empirical Assessment." *European Economic Review* 44 (4-6): 762–72.

Earle, John, and Saul Estrin. 1998. "Privatization, Competition and Budget Constraints: Disciplining Enterprises in Russia." SITE Working Paper 128. Stockholm Institute of Transition Economics and London Business School.

Earle, John, Saul Estrin, and Larisa Leshchenko. 1996. "Privatization and Corporate Governance in Russia." In Simon Commander, Qimiao Fan, and Mark Schaffer, eds., *Enterprise Restructuring and Economic Policy in Russia.* Washington, D.C.: World Bank.

Estrin, Saul, and Adam Rosevear. 1999. "Enterprise Performance and Corporate Governance in Ukraine." *Journal of Comparative Economics* 27 (3): 442–58.

Estrin, Saul, and Jan Svejnar. 1998. "The Effects of Output, Ownership, and Legal Form on Employment and Wages in Central European Firms." In Simon Commander, ed., *Enterprise Restructuring and Unemployment in Models of Transition.* Washington, D.C.: World Bank.

EBRD (European Bank for Reconstruction and Development. 1995. *Transition Report: Investment and Enterprise Development.* London.

———. 1996. *Transition Report: Infrastructure and Savings.* London.

———. 1997. *Transition Report: Enterprise Performance and Growth.* London.

———. 1998. *Transition Report: Financial Sector in Transition.* London

———. 1999. *Transition Report: Ten Years of Transition.* London.

Ellerman, David. 1998. "Voucher Privatization with Investment Funds: An Institutional Analysis." World Bank Policy Research Working Paper 1924, World Bank, Office of the senior Vice President, Development Economics, Washington, D.C.

Estrin, Saul, and Adam Rosevear. 1998. "Enterprise Performance and Corporate Governance in Ukraine." London Business School.

Faggio, Giulia, and Jozef Konings. 1998. "Gross Job Flows in Transition Countries: Results from Bulgaria, Estonia and Romania." LICOS, Catholic University of Louvain, Louvain-la-Neuve, Belgium.

Falk, M., M. Raiser, and H. Brauer. 1996. "Output Decline and Recovery in Poland: The Role of Energy Prices and Structural Adjustment." Working Paper 723. Kiel Institute of World Economics, Kiel, Germany.

Fingleton, J., E. Fox, D. Neven, and P. Seabright. 1996. "Competition Policy and the Transformation of Central Europe." Centre for Economic Policy Research, London.

Frydman, Roman, Marek Hessel, and Andrej Rapacyznski. 1998. "Why Ownership Matters? Politicization and Entrepreneurship in the Restructuring of Enterprises in Central Europe." New York University.

Frye, Timothy, and E. Zhuravskaya. 1998. "Regulation and Firms in Russia." *Russian Economic Trends.*

Grosfeld, Irena, and Jean-Francois Nivet. 1997. "'Firms' Heterogeneity in Transition: Evidence from a Polish Panel Dataset." WDI Working Paper 47. William Davidson Institute, Ann Arbor, Mich.

Jensen, Michael. 1986. "Agency Costs of Free Cash Flow, Corporate Finance, and Takeovers." *American Economic Review* 76 (2): 323–29.

Johnson, Simon, Daniel Kaufmann, and Andrei Schleifer. 1997. "The Unofficial Economy in Transition." *Brookings Papers on Economic Activity 1997 Macroeconomics 2.* Washington, D.C.: Brookings Institution.

Kaufmann, Daniel, and Aleksander Kaliberda. 1996. "Integrating the Unofficial Economy into the Dynamics of Post-Socialist Economies." World Bank, Washington, D.C.

Kollo, Janos. 1998. "Employment and Wage Setting in Three Stages of Hungary's Labour Market Transition." In Simon Commander, ed., *Enterprise Restructuring and Unemployment in Models of Transition.* Washington, D.C.: World Bank.

Konings, Josef, and Patrick Walsh. 1998. "Disorganisation in the Transition Process: Firm Level Evidence from Ukraine." LICOS, Catholic University of Louvain, Louvain-la-Neuve, Belgium.

Konings, Josef, Harmut Lehmann, and Mark Schaffer. 1996. "Job Creation and Job Destruction in a Transition Economy:Ownership, Firm Size, and Gross Job Flows in Polish Manufacturing, 1988-1991." *Journal of Labour Economics* 299–318.

Laffont, Jean-Jacques, and Tchetche N'Guessan. 1998. "Competition and Corruption in an Agency Relationship." Institut d'Economie Industrielle, Toulouse.

Landesmann, Michael, and J. Burgstaller. 1997. "Vertical Product Differentiation in EU Markets: The Relative Position of East European Producers." Research Report 234. Vienna Institute.

La Porta, R., and F. Lopez-de-Silanes. 1997a. "The Benefits of Privatization: Evidence from Mexico." NBER Working Paper 6215. National Bureau of Economic Research, Cambridge, Mass.

———. 1997b. "Legal Determinants of External Finance." *Journal of Finance* 52 (3) 1131–50.

Lehmann, Harmut, Jonathan Wadsworth, and A. Acquisti. 1998. "Grime and Punishment: Job Insecurity and Wage Arrears in the Russian Federation." WDI Working Paper 103. William Davidson Institute, Ann Arbor, Mich.

Lizal, Lubomir, and Jan Svejnar. 1998. "Investment in the Transition: Evidence from Czech Firms." William Davidson Institute, Ann Arbor, Mich., and Center for Economic Research and Graduate Education, Prague.

Marcinin, A, and Sweder van Wijnbergen. 1997. "The Impact of Czech Privatisation Methods on Enterprise Performance." CERT Discussion Paper 97/4. Heriot Watt University, Centre for Economic Research in Transition, Edinburgh.

Marin, Dalia, and Daniel Kaufmann. 1998. "Barter in Transition Economies." University of Munich and World Bank, Washington, D.C.

Megginson, William, and Jeff Netter. 1998. "From State to Market: A Survey of Empirical Studies on Privatization." Organisation for Economic Co-operation and Development, Paris.

Meyendorff A., and Snyder E. A. 1997. "Transactional Structures of Bank Privatizations in Central Europe and Russia." *Journal of Comparative Economics* 25 (1): 5–30.

Mitchell, Janet. 1998. "Bankruptcy Experience in Hungary and the Czech Republic." WDI Working Paper 211. William Davidson Institute, Ann Arbor, Mich.

Nellis, John. 1999. "Time to Rethink Privatization?" World Bank, Private Sector Development, Washington D.C.

Newbery, David, and Paul Kattuman. 1992. "Market Concentration and Competition in Eastern Europe." Cambridge University.

Nickell, Stephen. 1996. "Competition and Corporate Performance." *Journal of Political Economy* 104 (4): 724–46.

Nickell, Stephen, Daphne Nicolitsas, and Neil Dryden. 1997. "What Makes Firms Perform Well?" *European Economic Review* 41 (3-5): 783–96.

OECD (Organisation for Economic Co-operation and Development). 1997. *Economic Survey of Russian Federation.* Paris.

Perotti E., and S. Gelfer. 1998. "Investment Financing in Russian Financial-Industrial Groups." WDI Working Paper 242. William Davidson Institute, Ann Arbor, Mich.

Pinto, B, M. Belka, and others. 1993. "Transforming State Enterprises in Poland." *Brookings Papers on Economic Activity Macroeconomics 1*. Washington, D.C.: Brookings Institution.

Pohl, G, Anderson, R, S. Claessens, and S. Djankov. 1997. *Privatization and Restructuring in Central and Eastern Europe: Evidence and Policy Options.* World Bank Technical Paper 368. Washington D.C.

Rapacki, Ryszard. 1999. "Privatization in Poland: Major Issues, Trends and Policy Concerns." United Nations Department of Economic and Social Affairs, New York.

Rey, Patrick. 1998. "Competition Policy and Economic Development." World Bank, Public Sector Management Division, Poverty Reduction and Economic Management, Washington, D.C.

Romer, Paul. 1994. "New Goods, Old Theory, and the Welfare Costs of Trade Restrictions." *Journal of Development Economics* 43 (1): 5–38.

Schaffer, Mark, Alan Bevan, and Robert Mochrie. 1998. "Enterprise and Bank Restructuring: Progress, Problems and Policies." Proceedings of the United Nations Economic Commission for Europe spring seminar 20 April, Geneva.

Schmidt, K. 1997. "Managerial Incentives and Product Market Competition." *Review of Economic Studies* 64: 191–213.

Shapiro, Carl, and Robert Willig. 1990. "Economic Rationales for the Scope of Privatization." In E.N. Suleiman and J. Waterbury, eds., *The Political Economy of Public Sector Reform and Privatization.* London: Westview Press.

Shleifer, Andrei, and Robert Vishny. 1993. "Corruption." *Quarterly Journal of Economics* 108: 599–617.

———. 1994. "Politicians and Firms." *Quarterly Journal of Economics* 109: 995–1025.

———. 1997. "A Survey of Corporate Governance." *Journal of Finance* 52 (2): 737–83.

Snyder E. A., and R. C. Kormendi. 1997. "Privatization and Performance of the Czech Republic's Komercni Banka." *Journal of Comparative Economics* 25 (1): 97–128.

Steinherr, A. 1997. "Banking Reforms in Eastern European Countries." *Oxford Review of Economic Policy* 13 (2): 106–25.

Van Siclen, Sally. 1992. "A Practical Analysis of the Economics of Demonopolization." Economic Analysis Group Working Paper 92-4. U.S. Department of Justice, Washington D.C.

Vickers, John, and George Yarrow. 1988. *Privatization: An Economic Analysis.* Cambridge, Mass.: MIT Press.

Weiss A., and G. Nikitin. 1998. "Performance of Czech Companies by Ownership Structure." IED Discussion Paper 85. Boston University, Institute for Economic Development..

Willig, Robert. 1987. "Corporate Governance and Market Structure." In A. Razin and E. Sadka, eds., *Economic Policy in Theory and Practice.* London: Macmillan.

World Bank. 1999. *Czech Republic: Capital Market Review.* World Bank Country Study. Washington, D.C.

Yachestova, Irina. 1998. "The Application of Competition Laws of CIS Countries to the Actions of the Executive and Governing Bodies." Organisation for Economic Co-operation and Development, Competition Law and Policy Division, Paris.

# Comment on "Macroeconomic Lessons from Ten Years of Transition," by Charles Wyplosz, and "Restructuring in Transition Economies: Ownership, Competition, and Regulation," by Simon Commander, Mark Dutz, and Nicholas Stern

*Philippe Aghion*

The articles by Charles Wyplosz and by Simon Commander, Mark Dutz, and Nicholas Stern deal with two complementary aspects of transition—namely, macroeconomic stabilization, and privatization and restructuring. I will comment on the articles in turn.

## Wyplosz and the Role of Microeconomics

Wyplosz's article contains a lot of information about macroeconomic indicators and their evolution in transition economies. One important lesson of this survey is that the countries with the most robust GDP growth—such as Poland and Slovenia—are among those that engaged sooner in comprehensive macroeconomic stabilization. But what about countries like Russia, which embarked later on similar "shock therapy" but failed to achieve output growth? Was Russia's failure simply a matter of delay, particularly in adjusting central bank policy and cutting off subsidies to loss-making enterprises? Is it accurate to say, as Wyplosz does, that Russia essentially got it right until 1998 but then started to fail?

My view, which I believe is shared by a growing number of economists and policy advisers, is that poorly defined microeconomic reforms made Russia's stabilization of 1992–93 unsustainable. One such reform was the mass insider privatization of most state assets, including natural resources, without having implemented adequate mechanisms for taxing the newly privatized firms' revenues. Another weakness was the absence of regulatory constraints on the new banking sector, which led to pervasive connected lending.

Wyplosz is silent on a number of interesting questions about tax reform and, more generally, the interplay between the efficiency of government policy and the speed and nature of microeconomic reforms. For example, did privatizations in transition economies facilitate or hinder progress on fiscal reform and macroeconomic stabilization? In high-competition countries (those with both product market and politi-

---

Philippe Aghion is professor of economics at Harvard University and professor at University College London.

cal competition) progress on privatization is positively correlated with a higher demand for "governance of governments." The opposite correlation holds for low-competition countries (EBRD 1999).

Russia's fiscal experience raises another question: did the International Monetary Fund (IMF) set the right fiscal targets there? Or did it simply encourage the replacement of monetary subsidies with noncash subsidies—energy subsidies, tolerance of tax arrears, an illicit absorption of fiscal deficits by the banking system—by imposing overly stringent fiscal criteria with tough consolidation rules between state institutions and enterprises? Although Wyplosz provides a good overview of macroeconomic tendencies in transition economies, he remains too vague in my view on the microeconomic underpinnings of stabilization.

## Commander, Dutz, and Stern and Elements of Successful Transition

Given that I have spent the transition years at the European Bank for Reconstruction and Development, it should come as no surprise that I share most of the views offered by Commander, Dutz, and Stern. In particular, one important lesson from 10 years of enterprise reform in post-socialist countries is that successful transition requires the development of new private businesses. Success stories like Hungary, Poland, and Slovenia have created an investment climate that encourages private sector development. Crucial elements of this climate include appropriate legal and contractual frameworks, an efficient banking sector, and a stabilized economy, which in turn requires a government capable of raising taxes and enforcing the law.

Mass privatization has not been essential to successful transition, especially when it has not resulted in concentrated outsider ownership—which is required to foster product innovations and real changes in organization and management. Again, whether privatization has promoted the restructuring of state enterprises largely depends on the economic and social environment. "Reactive" restructuring has occurred only to the extent that privatization has hardened firms' budget constraints, and "structural" restructuring has occurred only to the extent that privatization has increased product market competition. Russia has not provided an environment in which privatization can benefit from (and foster) competition. The absence of a credible safety net in Russia has further impeded enterprise restructuring.

In closing, consider the Czech Republic. It undertook the right stabilization reforms early on. It also engaged in outsider privatization by combining a voucher scheme with the creation of privatization funds. And it is a small open economy with considerable product market competition. So what went wrong in this country? Why is the Czech Republic lagging behind Hungary and Poland? Is its slow progress simply the consequence of an inappropriate exchange rate policy? Or is it the result of a lack (until recently) of political competition? Or do the Czech Republic's problems derive from the fact that Czechoslovakia lived for several decades under tougher communist rule than Hungary or Poland?

## Reference

EBRD (European Bank for Reconstruction and Development). 1999. *Transition Report 1999.* London.

# The Institutional Foundations of China's Market Transition

*Yingyi Qian*

*China's transition to a market economy has taken place in two stages. In the first stage (1978–93), reformers introduced incentives, hard budget constraints, and competition by decentralizing government, allowing nonstate (mostly local government) enterprises to develop and expand, maintaining financial stability, and adopting a dual-track approach to market liberalization. In the second stage, China aimed to develop best-practice market institutions. During the first five years of reform (1994–98), it allowed convertibility of the current account, overhauled the fiscal system, reorganized the central bank, downsized the government, and began to privatize state-owned enterprises. China's experience with transition shows that significant progress can be achieved with sensible but imperfect institutions.*

In the two decades between 1978 and 1998 China transformed itself from a centrally planned economy to an emerging market economy. During this period growth averaged 10 percent a year, and per capita GDP more than quadrupled.

China's performance appears particularly impressive when compared with the average performance of the transition economies in Eastern Europe and the former Soviet Union. With only a few exceptions, by 1998 most of these countries had failed to reach their 1989 output levels, according to official statistics.

China's reform experience has always been viewed as an anomaly. Because mainstream economics has not properly accounted for that experience they have also failed to appreciate it. Many have considered that reform was easy in China because it was a poor agricultural country. China, they argue, was much less developed than Eastern Europe or the former Soviet Union at the outset of reform, and it did not face some of the problems faced in those countries, such as excess industrial capacity and comprehensive welfare coverage.

Yingyi Qian is assistant professor of economics at Stanford University. The author appreciates the comments of Masahiko Aoki, Nicholas Hope, Lawrence Lau, Boris Pleskovic, Gérard Roland, Andrew Walder, and three anonymous reviewers.

In fact, China faced many problems similar, albeit not identical, to those faced elsewhere. In addition, as a developing country, China also faced many problems that did not exist in other transition economies, such as enormous population pressure, severe shortages of human capital and natural resources, very poor industrial and infrastructure bases, and the absence of democracy.

The reasons why China's reforms are not properly understood and appreciated by mainstream economists are profound. Many economists hold strong prior beliefs about the form a transition should take—beliefs that were reinforced by the early failures of economic reform in Eastern Europe and the former Soviet Union, which did not follow that prescription. Theory and evidence together helped create conventional wisdom about a set of necessary conditions for a successful transition—conditions that included stabilization, liberalization, privatization, and democratization. The Chinese path of reform seemed to defy conventional wisdom by succeeding despite the lack of complete market liberalization, privatization and secure private property rights, or democracy.

In this article I show that for the past two decades, China has been undergoing highly dynamic and profound yet smooth internal institutional changes that have unleashed the forces of incentives, hard budget constraints, and competition for growth, but in an unconventional manner. By using the analytical tools of mainstream economics and stretching existing theories to consider the institutional features of the transition, I account for the Chinese reform experience. This approach allows me not only to explain the successful aspects of China's reform but also to pinpoint the problems it generated and thus the challenges that lie ahead. In doing so, I hope to improve our understanding of China's reform and, at the same time, to develop a new paradigm for the study of reform and institutional changes in general.

I analyze the journey of China's transition to markets as a two-stage process, using Kornai's (1992) framework for analyzing system changes in socialist countries. In the first section on the early stage of reform (1979–93), I analyze four institutional pillars—regional decentralization of government, entry and expansion of nonstate (mostly local government) enterprises, financial stability through financial dualism, and the dual-track approach to market liberalization—that played crucial roles.

I then examine the second stage of reform, which has been guided by the goal of establishing a rule-based market system, as well as privatizing and restructuring state-owned enterprises. In the five years between 1994 and 1998, China unified the foreign exchange market and made its current account convertible, overhauled the tax and fiscal systems, centralized the central bank, downsized the government bureaucracy and forced the military to give up its commercial operations, and started privatizing state-owned enterprises and laying off their workers.

China still faces many serious challenges. I highlight the three important ones: transforming the financial system, restructuring state-owned enterprises and corporate governance, and establishing the rule of law. I examine the major difficulties involved in implementing additional reforms, outline the institutional changes that are required, suggest some ways to achieve them, and propose future research topics.

In the final section I reflect on the economics of reform and institutional changes from the Chinese experience. I show how China's success in the first stage of reform allowed it to build momentum for the second stage without a political revolution. I also draw general lessons from China's reform experience.

## Reforming the System: 1979–93

The historic decision on "reform and opening up" made at the Third Plenum of the Eleventh Congress of the Chinese Communist Party in December 1978 marked the beginning of China's reform era. At the time China had a clear desire to increase productivity and raise living standards by reforming its economic system and structure. It lacked a clear notion of what the new system would be like, however, and thus proceeded with the reform as though "crossing the river by groping stones." Although China did not establish uniform rules or international best-practice institutions during its first 15 years of reform, it nevertheless underwent dynamic and fundamental institutional changes in four main areas.

### Regional Decentralization of the Government

As early as 1979 China started to devolve government authority from central to local levels, including provinces, prefectures, counties, townships, and villages. Local governments supervised about three-quarters of the state industrial firms in terms of output and also had major responsibility for fixed investments by the state. Township and village governments directly controlled township and village enterprises. Local governments were given significant regulatory authority over the local economy, issuing business licenses, coordinating business plans, resolving disputes, and attracting foreign investments. They also acquired the authority to determine the structure of local expenditure and were responsible for local public goods, such as schools, health care, utilities, price subsidies, and urban development.

Decentralization has an information advantage. Local governments are in a better position to provide local public goods than national governments because they have access to better local information and because interjurisdictional competition provides a sorting mechanism to better suit consumers' preferences. Decentralization also allows for "laboratory federalism," under which policies can be tested in certain localities before being implemented on a large scale. In China decentralization has permitted significant regional experimentation, which has minimized costs through structured learning (Qian and Xu 1993; Qian, Roland, and Xu 1999).

Decentralization also allows the problem of government incentives to be addressed (Qian and Weingast 1997). Governments in developing and transition economies have often been the chief barriers to economic development. Providing these governments with the incentives to promote markets is thus critical (Weingast 1995; Montinola, Qian, and Weingast 1995). The devolution of authority in China was accompanied by fiscal incentives, and local governments were encouraged to adopt reforms and were rewarded for promoting the development of their local economies. Beginning in 1980 the fiscal contracting system (*caizheng chengbao zhi*, known colloquially as "eating from separate kitchens," or *fenzao chifan*) replaced the system of unified revenue collection and unified spending (*tongshou tongzhi*, known colloquially as "eating from one big pot," or *chi daguofan*). Under the new fiscal system, local governments entered into long-term (usually five-year) fiscal contracts with higher-level governments. Many were allowed to retain 100 percent at the margin so that they kept any revenue above a target amount. In addition, local governments received extrabudgetary funds, which were not subject to sharing, and off-budget funds, which were not even incorporated into the budgetary process and thus were not recorded.

Using provincial panel data from 1982–92, Jin, Qian, and Weingast (1999) report three major findings about the role of decentralization and fiscal incentives in the central-provincial relationship. First, they found that the correlation between marginal budgetary revenue collection and marginal budgetary expenditure, which had average just 0.18 in the 1970s, had risen to 0.75 for the 1982–92 period. The increase suggests that China's fiscal contracting system provided local governments with much stronger fiscal incentives. Second, they found that stronger fiscal incentives, measured in terms of a higher contractual marginal revenue retention rate, were associated with faster development of nonstate enterprises and more reform in state-owned enterprises. Third, they found some evidence that horizontal distribution in per capita budgetary spending actually improved, rather than worsened, over time, with the coefficient of variation falling from 0.68 in 1982 to 0.52 in 1992. The change appears to have occurred because strong marginal incentives were provided together with the inframarginal redistribution of budgetary revenue.

Interestingly, China's regional decentralization and the fiscal contracting system have often been criticized by economists. The conventional view holds that economic reform means liberalization of markets and autonomy of enterprises and households, not decentralization within the government organization. Many Chinese economists considered regional decentralization to be the wrong direction for reform because it looked similar to "administrative decentralization" under Mao Zedong. China's fiscal decentralization was seen as highly problematic and dysfunctional by public finance experts, who believed that it distorted resource allocation, generated regional inequality, and undermined the central government's fiscal policy (Wong 1991). While some of these criticisms are valid, they fail to recognize the more significant positive contributions of regional decentralization on economic reform because they largely ignore the need for regional experimentation, and more important, the importance of the governments' incentives.

### *Entry and Expansion of Nonstate (Mostly Local Government) Firms*

Growth of the nonstate sector is the key to understanding reform in China (Qian and Xu 1993). Between 1978 and 1993 the share of nonstate enterprises increased from 22 to 57 percent. The change occurred without any privatization of state-owned enterprises and was entirely the result of fast entry and expansion of new nonstate enterprises. Most of the new Chinese firms were not private firms but local government firms; private enterprises played only a minor role, contributing less than 15 percent to national industrial output in 1993. Most of these local government firms are township and village enterprises, which numbered 1.5 million in 1993 and employed 52 million people. In 1993 such enterprises accounted for 72 percent of rural industrial output and 58 percent of rural employment (Che and Qian 1998b).

The rise of township and village enterprises has been unexpected, even by Chinese reformers.[1] Like regional decentralization, township and village enterprises and the associated "local industrialization" have been frequently criticized by economists, from both conservative and liberal camps. Conservative economists argued that the enterprises disrupted the state sector; liberal economists objected that the enterprises were subject to too much local government intervention. Economists from both sides blame township and village enterprises for being inefficiently run. But China's reform performance would look very different without township and village enterprises; it is therefore not possible to understand industrial reform in China without accounting for them (Weitzman and Xu 1994).

The central feature of township and village enterprises is township or village government control of firms. New theories have been developed to explain why such control may have been effective. These theories focus on insecure property rights, imperfect capital markets, and the particular features of China's fiscal system.

In an environment in which anti–private property ideology is strong and the rule of law is lacking, the property rights of firms owned by local government are more secure than those of privately owned firms (Chang and Wang 1994; Li 1996). Che and Qian (1998a) develop a theory of local government ownership based on incomplete contracting. They argue that the fact that community governments both provide local public goods and control township and village enterprises confers advantages given insecure property rights because community governments are more likely than private entrepreneurs to invest revenue in local public goods. Recognizing this, the central government rationally preys less on township and village enterprises than on private enterprises, and township and village enterprises are less worried about revenue confiscation. In fact, after-tax profits of township and village enterprises were used largely for reinvestment and provision of local public goods. In 1992, for example, 59 percent of the after-tax profits of township and village enterprises were reinvested and 40 percent were used for local public expenditure. Local government control over firms thus not only benefits governments but also increases efficiency by improving the degree of security of property rights and providing more local investment in public goods.

In transition and developing economies, new firms have great difficulty obtaining capital. Township and village enterprises have several advantages over private enterprises in obtaining financing. First, the community government can use its political connections with state banks to channel loans to township and village enterprises. Second, state banks are more willing to lend to township and village enterprises because discrimination against private enterprises makes lending to private firms riskier politically. Third, the community government is able to reduce the risks borne by banks by cross-subsidizing among its many diversified enterprises (Byrd 1990) or using accumulated collective assets as collateral or co-investment funds to reduce potential hazards in the lending-borrowing relationship (Che and Qian 1998b).

Insecure property rights and imperfect capital markets are also common features in other transition and developing economies, however. Why, then, have township and village enterprises or similar types of firms not developed elsewhere? China's regional decentralization appears to have played a central role. Township and village governments in China are empowered with comprehensive authority and incentives for local economic development (Byrd and Gelb 1990; Oi 1992); local governments elsewhere often do little more than collect taxes and remit them to higher levels of government.

The fact that local governments have more power in China than elsewhere may explain why they have promoted development. It does not, however, explain why township and village enterprises, but not private firms, developed. Using the incomplete contracting framework, Che and Qian (1998a) argue that ownership rights give the government control over firms' financial accounts and thus make it less costly to extract revenues from them than taxing private firms. For the same reason, local government control of firms also makes it harder for the central government to extract revenue from them; revenue is thus more likely to remain in the local areas.

Econometric studies on China's rural industry provide some evidence to support these theoretical arguments. Using panel data from 28 provinces in China between 1986 and 1993, Jin and Qian (1998) found that the share of township and village enterprises relative to private rural industrial enterprises in a province is higher when the initial collective assets under the control of community government is larger or local political strength to resist pressure from higher-level government (appropriately measured) higher. This evidence is consistent with the theory that local government ownership of firms is related to the institutional environment. Jin and Qian also examined the consequence of firm ownership for revenue distribution among the national government, community governments, and households. They found that a 1 percent increase in the share of township and village enterprises relative to private enterprises is associated with a 0.11 percent increase in the shares of revenue accrued to the national government and a 0.24 percent increase in the shares of revenue accrued to township and village governments. These results confirm that the fiscal incentives faced by local governments motivated them to develop township and village enterprises and suggest that government control of firms plays an important role in substituting for taxation institutions.

### *"Financial Dualism"*

The third institutional pillar of reform in China is "financial dualism," the fact that although government fiscal revenue declined sharply, it was accompanied—and thus partially compensated for—by an increase in "quasi-fiscal" revenue from impressive financial deepening (McKinnon 1993; Bai and others 1999). This deepening provided the basis for China's macroeconomic stability and helped it avoid a financial crisis similar to that experienced in Russia (McKinnon 1993).

As a share of GDP, China's consolidated government budgetary revenue declined from 31 percent in 1978 to 13 percent in 1993; taking into account extrabudgetary and off-budget revenues, total fiscal revenue fell from 40 percent of GDP in 1978 to about 19 percent in 1993. At the same time, however, cash in circulation rose from less than 6 percent of GDP in 1978 to 16 percent of GDP in 1993. Total household bank deposits rose from less than 6 percent of GDP in 1978 to about 50 percent in 1993 and 62 percent in 1997. The M2 to GDP ratio also climbed, rising from less than 50 percent before reform to more than 100 percent in the 1990s. This financial buildup lasted much longer than most economists expected. By one estimation, quasi-fiscal revenue collected from the banking sector averaged about 9 percent of GDP between 1986 and 1994, or more than one half of budgetary revenue (Bai and others 1999).

Bai and others (1999) study the fundamental microeconomic implications of fiscal decline and financial deepening, highlighting the coexistence of two institutional arrangements in China's financial system. The first is financial repression; that is, the combination of government control on international capital flows and restrictions on domestic interest rates and private financial activities. The second is what they call "anonymous banking," the combination of relaxed regulation on the use of cash for transactions and permission to use anonymous household savings deposits. They argue that anonymous banking together with mild financial repression implies some major advantages over direct taxation in China's institutional environment.

The conventional wisdom holds that taxation is less distortionary than revenue extraction from financial repression. This view ignores the problem of government behavior on taxation, however. In China, as in many developing and transition economies, because of the lack of rule of law, the government has difficulties committing itself to fixed let alone low tax rates. This commitment problem undermines private incentives and is often regarded as a major obstacle to economic development as well as reform (North 1997; Williamson 1995). Bai and others (1999) argue that anonymous banking provides an effective commitment device for limiting the government's predatory behavior and creating private incentives. When transactions are made with cash rather than through bank transfers, it is difficult for the government to monitor business transactions and thus to tax away the generated revenue. When bank deposits are anonymous, the government does not know the identity of depositors and is thus unable to target individuals and confiscate their financial wealth. Although the government can still (implicitly) tax financial savings through inflation or changes in interest rates, this method of revenue extraction is nondiscriminating; it entails a flat tax rate and imposes a limit. Anonymous banking thus allows the government to achieve a credible commitment for creating private incentives. Through financial repression the government can acquire some quasi-fiscal revenue.[2] Bai and others (1999) show that indirect revenue extraction through the banking system has not just prevented revenue collapses but, more important, has bound the govern-

## Market Liberalization through the Dual-Track Approach

By the mid-1990s prices of most products in China had been completely liberalized. The way the Chinese achieved this result is quite different from the way it was done in Eastern Europe. In Hungary, for example, all mandatory planning was abolished after the 1968 reform, but prices were still determined administratively by bureaucrats subject to political bargaining. There was no real market, only a simulated market (Kornai 1986). After 1990 prices were swiftly liberalized in one stroke. China took a dual-track approach to price liberalization under which the market was first liberalized at the margin. The government initially maintained (inframarginal) planned prices and quotas, phasing them out later. Under the plan track, economic agents were assigned rights to and obligations for fixed quantities of goods at fixed plan prices, as specified in the plan. Under the market track, economic agents participated in the market at free market prices, provided that they fulfilled their obligations under the plan. With this approach real market prices and markets as a resource allocation institution were created in China during the very early stages of reform. The economy was able to "grow out of the plan" (Naughton 1995).

The dual-track approach was often criticized by economists, who viewed it as a partial reform lacking the completeness of liberalization. Lau, Qian, and Roland (1997; forthcoming) argue that such a perception is incorrect. According to them, the dual-track approach to market liberalization can liberalize markets without creating losers and is thus politically appealing. It can also achieve efficiency under certain conditions. Using both partial and general equilibrium models, Lau, Qian, and Roland show that regardless of the initial supply and demand conditions (such as whether planned prices or quantities are above or below the market equilibrium), as long as the plan is enforced appropriately, the dual-track approach to market liberalization is always Pareto improving. In addition, the approach achieves efficiency under usual conditions, such as profit maximization and perfect competition, provided market resales and purchases for redelivery are allowed.

Efficiency-enhancing economic reform should allow winners to compensate losers (that is, it should be Pareto improving). In practice, however, the distortionary costs of compensation or the lack of credibility in its implementation make it very difficult to find mechanisms that make economic reform Pareto improving and even more difficult for reform to be simultaneously Pareto-improving and efficient. The dual-track approach provides one mechanism for implementing efficient Pareto-improving reform. The introduction of the market track provides the opportunity for economic agents to be better off; maintenance of the plan track provides implicit transfers to compensate potential losers from market liberalization by protecting status quo rents under the plan. Moreover, as compensatory transfers are inframarginal and thus lump sum in nature, the dual-track approach can also be efficient. While single-track (or big-bang) market liberalization will lead to efficiency under the usual conditions, Pareto improvement cannot be ensured. Furthermore, in the presence of some market imperfection (such as search frictions or imperfect competition), single-track liberalization may cause a decline in aggregate output, as shown in the models of Blanchard and Kremer (1997), Roland and Verdier (1999), and Li (1999), a problem that is avoided by the dual-track approach.

Enforcement of the plan track is clearly crucial to preserving the preexisting rents. However, sufficient state enforcement power is needed not to implement an unpopular reform but to carry out one that creates no losers, only winners. One desirable feature of the dual-track approach is that it uses the information contained in the original plan and enforces the plan through existing planning institutions. No new information and no new institutions are necessary.

## Assessing Reform

China's first 15 years of reform have been a remarkable success. GDP has grown rapidly, shortages have been eliminated, and living standards of ordinary people have improved dramatically. This experience is in sharp contrast with the frustration of Eastern European reformers in the late 1980s, when they saw their reform efforts of decades lead only to dead ends.

China was able to avoid the fate of Eastern European reform before 1990 because of its deeper institutional changes. The four pillars of institutional change contributed to China's reform success because they changed the functioning of the government, firms, the financial system, and markets to unleash the forces of positive incentives, hard budget constraints, and competition, but in novel ways. The Chinese experience has demonstrated that reforming the government and providing it with incentives is as crucial as reforming the economy, that nonprivate and nonstate ownership can be an engine of growth, that financial stability can be maintained for an extended period through quasi-fiscal revenues from the banking system, and that dual-track liberalization provides one mechanism for minimizing the number of losers from reform. Interestingly, none of these methods was recommended by economists; to the contrary, all were criticized.

Despite impressive achievements, however, many problems occurred. First, some mistakes were made. Decentralization of the banking system went too far; for example, allowing local governments to gain substantial control over the credit supply. This was a source of soft budget constraints for both local governments and state-owned enterprises, and it caused inflation as well (Qian and Roland 1998).

Second, many difficult reforms were delayed. For example, no state enterprises were privatized and almost none went bankrupt. No effort was made to establish property rights protected by the rule of law or to set up legal mechanisms for contract enforcement. Although establishing a rule-based tax system was attempted, the effort failed (Shirk 1993).

Third, and most important, the achievements up to 1993 were made through institutional innovations that either were ad hoc responses to particular constraints in the planning system or took advantages of loopholes in the system. The varieties of contracting practices between different levels of government and between government and enterprises are good examples. Although they were effective in breaking the central command, such ad hoc practices were subject to frequent renegotiation and change.

## Replacing the System: 1994–98

Since 1994 China's transition has moved into the second stage, which aims to replace the planned system with a market system.

### Evolution of the Official Goal of Reform

At the outset Chinese policymakers sought to reform the economy in order to increase productivity and improve living standards, but the leadership never thought it would move to a full market system (Perkins 1994). Establishing the goal of reform for a full market system was an evolutionary process that began in the early 1990s.

During much of the first stage of reform, official ideology supported "planning supplemented by market" and "planned commodity economy." This ideology was replaced in September 1992, when the Fourteenth Party Congress endorsed the "socialist market economy" after Deng Xiaoping's famous southern tour to mobilize local support for more radical reform.

In November 1993 the Third Plenum of the Fourteenth Party Congress approved a document that supported major advances in coordinating reform policies, establishing a rule-based system, building market-supporting institutions, and reforming property rights and ownership. Adoption of the "Decision on Issues Concerning the Establishment of a Socialist Market Economic Structure" marked the turning point on China's road to markets.

First, unlike the earlier strategy of "crossing the river by groping for stones," the new strategy emphasized the importance of coordinating various aspects of reforms. It advocated a coherent package and an appropriate sequencing of reforms, known as "combining a reform package with breakthroughs in key areas." Second, in the first stage of reform, ad hoc contracting played a dominant role. The new strategy called for a rule-based market system to create a level playing field. Third, the new strategy focused on building market-supporting institutions, such as formal fiscal federalism, a centralized monetary system, and a social safety net. Finally, the new strategy addressed enterprise reform in terms of property rights and ownership rather than, as before, "expanding enterprise autonomy." The intent was to transform state-owned enterprises into "modern enterprises" with "clarified property rights, clearly defined responsibility and authority, separation of enterprises from the government, and scientific internal management." For the first time official strategy also left the door open regarding privatization of state-owned enterprises.

Another major breakthrough occurred in September 1997, when the Fifteenth Party Congress recognized private ownership as an "important component of the economy." Although the rhetoric of public ownership was maintained, its meaning was redefined to include joint stock corporations with investment by many owners. The Fifteenth Party Congress also emphasized the rule of law, which China considers crucial for a modern market economy to work well.[3]

Private ownership and the rule of law were incorporated into the Chinese Constitution in March 1999, through an amendment that put private business on an equal footing with the public sector. Immediately after adoption of the amendment, local governments began to relax local restrictions on private enterprises.

The failure of Eastern European reform before 1990 was a persuasive argument for the necessity of having democratic reform precede economic transition (Kornai 1992). The Communist Parties in Eastern Europe were unwilling to change their ideology; their collapse soon followed. China did what had proved impossible in Eastern Europe and elsewhere: the Communist Party made the strategic shift voluntarily. China is thus the only country under Communist Party rule to embrace private ownership and the rule of law in its Constitution without a political revolution.

## Major Accomplishments in the First Five Years (1994–98)

Following the major decision of November 1993, a series of radical reforms was launched. Some of the key accomplishments of this period are outlined below.

UNIFICATION OF FOREIGN EXCHANGE RATES AND CONVERTIBILITY OF THE CURRENT ACCOUNT. Before 1994 China adopted a dual-track approach to liberalizing foreign exchange markets, a market track and a plan allocation track. As a result of the dramatic growth of the market track, by 1993 the share of plan-allocated foreign exchange had fallen to less than 20 percent of the total. On January 1, 1994, plan allocation of foreign exchange was completely abolished, and the two tracks were merged into a single market track. To compensate organizations that were accustomed to receiving cheap foreign exchange, the government provided annual lump-sum subsidies for three years. In December 1996 China went one step farther by announcing current account convertibility of its currency. It did not liberalize the capital account (this continued control helped China weather the Asian financial crisis well). Between 1994 and 1998 the exchange rate remained stable, appreciating slightly (from 8.7 yuan to 8.3 yuan per dollar). Both exports and foreign direct investment increased dramatically, and the country's foreign reserves increased from $21 billion to $145 billion.

OVERHAUL OF THE TAX AND FISCAL SYSTEMS. On January 1, 1994, China introduced major tax and fiscal reforms. A national tax bureau and local tax bureaus were established, each responsible for its own tax collection. The reform has made it very difficult for local governments to reduce national taxes, as they had in the past (Dong 1997). Reform also established fixed tax rules for the national and local governments. Under the new system, for example, the value-added tax became the major indirect tax, shared by the national and local governments at a fixed ratio of 75:25. Local governments were compensated for their revenue losses for three years.

In 1995 the new budget law took effect. The law prohibited the central government from borrowing from the central bank and from running a deficit on its current account; deficit financing of the capital account was permitted as long as it was financed with government bonds. The law also imposed more stringent restrictions on local governments, strictly controlling their bond issuance and restricting their borrowing in the financial market. An independent auditing system was also introduced.

MONETARY CENTRALIZATION AND FINANCIAL REFORM. In 1993 the central bank was centralized, and supervision of its local branches was put in the hands of the central bank headquarters. The move was intended to reduce the influence of local government over the credit policy of the central bank. In 1995 the central bank law gave exclusive responsibility for controlling monetary policy. These reforms substantially reduced local government influence over monetary policy and credit allocation decisions (Xie 1996). In 1998 the central bank replaced its 30 provincial branches with 9 cross-province regional branches, further reducing local government influence over monetary policies.

Before 1998 the state always bailed out troubled financial institutions. Since 1998 the state has demonstrated its commitment to disciplining state financial institutions, and several high-profile banks and investment companies, including Hainan Development Bank and Guangdong International Trust Investment Company, have closed or gone bankrupt.

DOWNSIZING AND REFORM OF GOVERNMENT. Despite many early reforms, the basic government bureaucratic structure in China was kept intact until early 1998, when a major streamlining of the bureaucracy took place. Most industrial ministries were abolished, replaced by much smaller bureaus that were then absorbed into the State Economic and Trade Commission. Some new ministries, such as the Ministry of Social Security, were also created. The number of ministries in the central government was trimmed from 45 to 29 (similar actions are taking place at the local level in 1999), and the number of civil servants was halved from 8 million to 4 million. Displaced civil servants were allowed to purchase apartments at discounted prices, and those who wanted to pursue undergraduate or graduate education received up to three years of tuition and stipends.

In the second half of 1998 the government severed all ties between the military, police, and judiciary branches of the government and their business enterprises. These government entities now rely solely on tax revenues to maintain their operations, not on business incomes. A major anticorruption and antismuggling campaign was also undertaken, and the reform of the judiciary system began.

PRIVATIZATION OF STATE-OWNED ENTERPRISES AND LAYOFFS OF STATE WORKERS. Large-scale privatization of state-owned enterprises and layoffs of state workers began in 1995 (Cao, Qian, and Weingast 1999).[4] Privatizations began as experiments in a few provinces, such as Shandong, Guangdong, and Sichuan. Later the central government promoted privatization with the slogan of "grasping the large and releasing the small" (*zhuada fangxiao*).

Privatization of small state-owned enterprises was very significant for China. In contrast to Eastern Europe and the Soviet Union, China's industrial state-owned enterprise sector was dominated by small and medium-size enterprises, most of them supervised by county and city governments. By the end of 1996, 70 percent of small state-owned enterprises had been privatized in pioneering provinces.

The government also reduced excess labor, laying off workers for the first time. About 10 million workers from state-owned enterprises and urban collectives were laid off by the end of 1996; an additional 11.5 million workers were laid off in 1997. Two institutions accompanied the mass layoffs. *Xiagang* ("stepping down from one's post") provides some payments to laid off workers. *Zaijiuye* ("reemployment program") helps displaced workers find new jobs. Both mechanisms helped reduce employee opposition to the reallocation of labor.

## The Political Economy of Reform and the Dynamics of Transition

Before any reform could be initiated, political opposition from the vested interests under central planning needed to be overcome. Dewatripont and Roland (1992) and Wei (1997) have shown that where a comprehensive reform package is unable to win majority support, a sequence of partial reforms may be able to do so. Some patterns of incremental and partial reform in China can be attributed to this divide and rule strategy. Creation of special economic zones and regional experimentation, for example, may have been intended to overcome ideological and political constraints. The preference for ad hoc contracting over universal rules can also be viewed as a compromise struck in order to garner support (Shirk 1993).

By the end of 1993 China's economic system was halfway between a planned and a market economy. Would incremental reform continue, or would partial reform block additional reform? In the models of Dewatripont and Roland (1992) and Wei (1997), a sequential reform strategy helps build constituencies during the interim stage of reform. According to Dewatripont and Roland (1995), in the presence of aggregate uncertainty, a sequential reform strategy can also build momentum for additional reform when those reforms complement earlier reforms, as more and more people obtain interim stakes in the reform process.

In China agricultural reform created constituencies that were interested in developing rural industrial firms and liberalizing markets. Because of the earlier massive entry of nonstate enterprises, by 1994 the state accounted for only 40 percent of national industrial output. This relatively small share of output facilitated political acceptance of the privatization of state-owned enterprises. Similar actions in 1978, when the state's share of industrial output was about 80 percent, would have had very different political consequences.

New vested interests could also have retarded reform. Hellman (1998) provides some evidence that it was the interim winners, not the losers, of partial reform who blocked additional reform in some countries in Eastern Europe. In contrast, in

China neither the old nor the new vested interests have blocked reforms in the past five years. The winners of early reforms were not necessarily the eventual losers, and these winners did not manage to "take all."

Why has China not fallen into the partial reform trap that has caught some other transition economies? Three reasons seem relevant. First, early reforms did not generate huge rents for a small number of winners or create a large number of losers. Little rent was created by the liberalization of agriculture, for example. Regional decentralization diversified rent distribution away from the central government; interregional competition among local governments, however imperfect, also limited the rent that accrued to local governments. Fast entry and expansion of nonstate firms, many of them local government firms at the township and village levels, created a competitive environment that helped eliminate rent. The lack of natural resources and the avoidance of a mass privatization program also helped reduce rent. Enforcement of the plan track under the dual-track liberalization also limited new rents because a firm that received subsidized inputs was obligated to deliver an output quota at a low price. Moreover, capital control limited the amount of rent that could be capitalized and invested abroad. As a result, the benefits of reform were relatively evenly distributed during China's first stage of reform. Not many people lost out, and a few enjoyed huge gains. Equity thus played an important political role by preventing the creation of many losers, who could have reversed initial reforms, or huge winners, who could have blocked additional reforms.

Second, the potential future gain from increased market size and the efficiency resulting from reform were large in China. The greater these gains, the less the loss of current rent matters. In 1994, for example, even local governments that had benefited tremendously from the earlier fiscal contracting system (such as Guangdong) recognized that the ad hoc nature of the contracting system created many uncertainties and that political pressures from other provinces had increased. They therefore saw the move to a rule-based tax system as in their long-term interest.

Third, both the old and the new vested interests were "bribed" when further reforms were introduced (something that was possible only because rents were low). To varying degrees, potential losers were compensated when reforms such as unification of the foreign exchange rate, tax reform, downsizing of the government bureaucracy, and layoffs of state workers were implemented.

## Completing China's Transition: Challenges Ahead and Priority Research Agenda

Much has been accomplished in China. Still more needs to be done, however, before China becomes a market economy and realizes its full potential. To achieve this goal, China needs to adopt "second-generation reform strategies" (Stiglitz 1998), especially in three important areas: the financial system, state-owned enterprises and corporate governance, and the rule of law. Major problems remain in each of these areas and deeper institutional changes are still needed.

## Transforming the Financial System

For a long time China's financial system did a good job of mobilizing financial savings and providing the government with quasi-fiscal revenue. Earlier fears of inflation and macroeconomic instability are largely gone today (in fact, policymakers are concerned now about deflation). The institutions underlying China's financial system remain primitive and weak, however. Moreover, the banking system has become more and more fragile because of the growing stock of nonperforming loans in state banks. Estimates of nonperforming loans rose from 17–25 percent of GDP in 1993 (Lau and Qian 1994) to 25–35 percent of GDP in 1997 (Lardy 1998). These numbers suggest that China's current financial system is not sustainable in the long run.

A variety of events could cause a financial crisis in China. First, a rising stock of nonperforming loans could reduce the government's ability to service its debt and increase inflationary pressure. Second, severe shocks could occur when reforms deepen in such areas as liberalizing the banking sector and loosening capital control. Third, as a result of exchange rate or political instability, depositors could lose confidence in the state banks.

Some economists have expressed the view that financial collapse similar to, or even worse than, that experienced in Asia or Russia is likely to occur in China. Most cases, however, have ignored some basic differences between China and those economies. First, banks in China are owned by the state; their bad debts thus represent government, not private, debt. By the end of 1998 explicit government debt represented about 10 percent of GDP. Assuming that half of the nonperforming loans are not recoverable, total government debt, including bad debt in state commercial banks, would still be less than 30 percent of GDP. This level of government debt compares favorably with the 70 percent in the United States, the more than 100 percent in Japan, or the 60 percent maximum to join the European Monetary Union. Even after accounting for China's weak taxation ability of about half that of industrial countries, the burden of servicing the government debt as a share of the government budgetary expenditure is comparable to that of other countries and is thus manageable. Second, China's bad debts are domestic, not foreign. As long as the state continues to control the international capital flow and restrict domestic interest rates and the entry of domestic and foreign banks, it will have the instruments of financial repression at its disposal needed to reduce the costs of financing its domestic debt. Third, neither exchange rate nor political instability seems likely in China in the immediate future.

Although a financial crisis in China is not imminent, drastic financial reform is needed, the sooner the better. Policymakers will have to deal with both the stock and the flow of bad loans. Lau and Qian (1994) argue that preventing any new bad loans from being made is more important than cleaning up bank balance sheets. The stock problem, they argue, is largely a problem of the past; the flow problem affects future expectations and behavior.

Solving the flow problem requires banking reform (and ultimately reform of state-owned enterprises, as discussed later). To address the flow problem in a fundamental way, China needs to introduce a bankruptcy procedure that clearly specifies the rights and obligations of creditors (currently mainly state banks) in the event of both liquidation- and reorganization-type bankruptcies. Banks, as major creditors, should have rights of receivership and the responsibility for reorganizing the bankrupt firms. New regulations are needed that will permit banks to temporarily hold equity during the reorganization period, something they are currently banned from doing.

To clean up bank balance sheets, Lau and Qian (1994) propose establishing a trust fund organization to serve as an intermediary to issue bonds to the state banks. They also propose recapitalizing state banks, possibly by issuing preferred stock (with no voting rights) to the public. The role of this trust fund organization would be similar to that of the Resolution Trust Corporation in cleaning up the mess that resulted from the U.S. savings and loans crisis of the 1980s. Along these lines, the Construction Bank of China, one of its four major state commercial banks, was recently selected by the central bank to experiment with ways of cleaning up its bad debts through a newly established financial assets management company. A way must be found to ensure that the cleanup does not result in moral hazard. To that end, the government must make a credible commitment not to provide bailouts in the future. Research is needed to identify methods to achieve this goal.

### Restructuring State-Owned Enterprises and Corporate Governance

The managerial contract responsibility system promoted in the 1980s had only limited success, and the performance of state-owned enterprises continued to decline in the 1990s, with more than a third of them losing money (Wu 1994). In state industrial enterprises profits and taxes per unit of net capital stock and working capital fell from 24.2 percent in 1978 to 12.4 percent in 1990 and to 6.5 percent in 1996 (*China Statistical Yearbook* 1997). Although new private firms are being formed and small state-owned enterprises are being privatized, large state-owned enterprises still constitute the backbone of the Chinese economy. Such enterprises represent the main revenue source and financial burden for the government and are ultimately responsible for the financial sector problem. Transformation of these enterprises is thus critical.

Although the excessive "social burdens" of state-owned enterprises are often blamed for their poor performance, the main problems are in fact institutional, concerning finance (the soft budget constraint problem) and personnel appointments (the party control problem). In recent years budget constraints of state-owned enterprises have been hardening. Party control over personnel has remained basically unchanged over the past 20 years, however.

The Communist Party continues to control the selection and dismissal of state enterprise managers through its organization departments at different levels. Managers of state-owned enterprises are thus political appointees. Party control over management appointments means that the process is politicized, secretive, and complicated. It also means that selection and evaluation are based on information obtained mainly through bureaucratic rather than market channels (such as the stock market, rating companies, and investment banks) and that appointments are based on both political and business criteria.[5]

Reforming state-owned enterprises without privatizing them is difficult. As Qian (1996) has noted, delegating more effective control rights to managers provides them with incentives to increase current production, but it also enables them to plunder state assets, which results in high agency costs. Maintaining party control over the selection and dismissal of managers serves to check managerial asset stripping somewhat, but it involves political interference, resulting in high political costs.

Large state-owned enterprises (including state banks) should aim to reduce both agency and political costs. This can be achieved only by simultaneously establishing corporate governance and depoliticizing these enterprises (Qian 1996). Corporatization and depoliticization are difficult tasks for China because they necessitate political reform. Future research needs to find a way to limit the party's role in the appointment and dismissal of state enterprise managers without eliminating its leadership role.

## Establishing the Rule of Law

The big challenge for China is establishment of the rule of law—a process that has already begun. The economic advantages of the rule of law over ad hoc arrangements are transparency, predictability, and uniformity. Establishment of the rule of law reduces idiosyncratic risks, rent-seeking, and corruption, which in turn reduces transactions costs. But the rule of law does more than simply put the government's words into public codes; it establishes the relationship between the government and markets that is needed to make credible commitments.

The rule of law plays two economic roles. First, when applied to the government, it commits the government to providing private incentives, the ultimate force for economic development. This role of the rule of law provides a foundation for secure private property rights against government intrusion. Second, the rule of law protects private property rights, enforces contracts, and creates a level playing field for market competition. For the rule of law to have these effects, the government must become a neutral third party, a regulator rather than a manager. The recent restructuring of the government bureaucracy reoriented agencies in just this way.

To preserve market competition, the national government needs to fight against regional protectionism. In the past, market competition in China was largely an accident of regional decentralization under Mao, combined with the more or less spontaneous emergence of small-scale industries throughout the country. To prevent local governments from erecting trade barriers, China needs to police the common market against regional protectionism and to adopt an "interstate commerce clause" similar to that in the U.S. Constitution.

Research is needed to study specific ways of implementing the rule of law. One important topic concerns how to create a substantially independent judiciary system. A completely independent judiciary seems impossible under a one-party system, but building a judicial system that is independent of the local government's influence is feasible.

## Reflections on the Economics of Reform and Institutional Change: Lessons from China

China's transition path has been so unusual that it casts doubts on some of the conventional thinking on reform and system changes (Chow 1997). Studying China's experience is thus useful for generating new theories, especially in the area of institutional change.

### The Principles of System Change

Three important conclusions can be drawn from China's reform experience. First, reforming a planned economy can be successful. China was able to do so by reforming the government, developing nonstate enterprises, deepening financial markets, and establishing markets.

Second, the system change from a planned to a market economy can occur without a political revolution. Although it is premature to predict that China will successfully complete its transition to a market system, the odds look good. If it completes its transition, China will be the first country under Communist Party rule to do so.

Third, transition to markets can be achieved in diverse ways; not all planned economies are alike or need to follow the same path to reform. Particularly where institutional changes are concerned, policymakers must accommodate country-specific conditions.

### The Process of Reform

China's experience provides several important lessons about reform in particular and institutional change in general. The general lesson is that considerable growth is possible with sensible but imperfect institutions, mainly because some transitional institutions can be more effective than best-practice institutions for a period of time. The second-best principle tells us that removing one distortion may be counterproductive in the presence of another distortion.

Transition economies lack basic market-supporting institutions (such as the rule of law) and the people and human capital to operate them (such as law enforcement officials). Both usually take years to develop. This often means that international best-practice institutions may not work well initially. It also means that some existing institutions can be useful to market-oriented reform before they eventually vanish. Fiscal contracting, township and village enterprises, and anonymous banking, for example, are all institutional innovations that worked well for a time in China.

Allocative distortions were so great and incentives so poor under central planning that all transition economies have enormous potential for improvement. Even if institutions are imperfect, impressive results are possible. Many failures in the early years of reform and the recent transition suggest that not all changes produce positive results, however. China's experience suggests three general principles regarding what works.

First, institutional changes that create incentives, impose hard budget constraints, and introduce competition should apply not only to firms but also to governments. Indeed, reforming government is an important component of economic reform.

Second, successful reform depends on political support, which in turn depends on delivering tangible benefits to a large majority of the population. Economists usually blame politics for policymakers' failure to implement well-designed reform programs. But compensating potential losers is both a political and an economic issue; a reform without many or large losers can be politically acceptable and sustainable. The dual-track approach to market liberalization, when appropriately implemented, is one example of good politics and good economics.

Third, successful institutional change requires appropriate, though not necessarily optimal, sequencing. Unlike macroeconomic stabilization policy, institutional change is an unavoidably long process. China's experience suggests that whenever politically feasible, an institutional vacuum should be avoided. Existing institutions should be dismantled only after new institutions are in place, or new institutions should be allowed to emerge from the old. China's experience also shows that what is most important is to avoid fatal mistakes rather than to fine tune solutions. Thus despite China's failure to reform its financial system and large state-owned enterprises or to establish the rule of law in the early days, reform continues.

## The Theory and Practice of Transition

The gap between conventional economic thinking and the realities of China's transition shows that our knowledge about institutional change in general and transition in particular is limited. Part of the problem is that our understanding of how a capitalist market economy works remains incomplete. As Ronald Coase has noted, "If we knew more about our own economy, we would be in a better position to advise [the transition economies]" (1992). Douglass North (1997, p. 2) agrees: "While neoclassical theory is focused on the operation of efficient factor and product markets, few Western economists understand the institutional requirements essential to the creation of such markets since they simply take them for granted. A set of political and economic institutions that provides low-cost transacting and credible commitment makes possible the efficient factor and product markets underlying economic growth." To build a market system from scratch, nothing can be taken for granted.

Our knowledge about the transition process is even more limited. There is a difference between the final destination and the process of transition; even if we have perfect knowledge about the destination, the appropriate route may still be unclear. As Robert Solow has said, "There is not some glorious theoretical synthesis of capitalism that you can write down in a book and follow. You have to grope your way" (*New York Times* 29 September 1992).

China's reform path was not designed at the outset but evolved along the way. Rather than being naive or cynical about reform, Deng Xiaoping and the Chinese reformers were pragmatic, recognizing from the beginning that they did not know what would make reform work. Studying China's experience adds a lot to economics as a social science of human beings. After all, this country houses nearly one-fifth of the world's population and sees the possibility of becoming, once again, the largest economy in the world in less than two decades (Maddison 1998).

## Notes

1. According to Deng Xiaoping, "The greatest achievement that was totally out of our expectation is that rural enterprises have developed" (*Economic Daily*, 13 June 1993).

2. As a result, financial repression in China was only "mild." During the past two decades, inflation was generally less than 10 percent. In 1988–89 and 1993–94, when inflation rose to more than 20 percent per year, the government quickly indexed time deposits (over a three-year maturity) to ensure a nonnegative real interest rate.

3. Kornai (1998) has emphasized that democracy is not a necessary basis of a market system but that a political power that is friendly to private property and the market is.

4. The Chinese do not use the term "privatization," relying instead on several other terms, such as "transformation of ownership" (*zhuanzhi*) or "restructuring of ownership" (*suoyouzhi gaizao*). Similarly, the Chinese use "nonpublic ownership" as a substitute for "private ownership."

5. It is interesting to compare state-owned enterprises with township and village enterprises in this regard. Although township and village enterprise managers are appointed by township or village governments, their appointments do not go through the higher-level party apparatus and are thus not subject to the same political process as state-owned enterprise managers. Most township and village enterprise managers are not "state cadres."

## References

Bai, Chong-En, David D. Li, Yingyi Qian, and Yijiang Wang. 1999. "Anonymous Banking and Financial Repression: How Does China's Reform Limit Government Predation without Reducing Its Revenue?" Working Paper. Department of Economics, Stanford University, Stanford, Calif.

Blanchard, Olivier, and Michael Kremer. 1997. "Disorganization." *Quarterly Journal of Economics* 112 (4): 1091–26.

Byrd, William. 1990. "Entrepreneurship, Capital, and Ownership." In William Byrd and Qingsong Lin, eds., *China's Rural Industry: Structure, Development, and Reform*. New York: Oxford University Press.

Byrd, William, and Alan Gelb. 1990. "Why Industrialize? The Incentives for Rural Community Governments." In William Byrd and Qingsong Lin, eds., *China's Rural Industry: Structure, Development, and Reform*. New York: Oxford University Press.

Cao, Yuanzheng, Yingyi Qian, and Barry R. Weingast. 1999. "From Federalism, Chinese Style, to Privatization, Chinese Style." *Economics of Transition* 7 (1): 103–31.

Chang, Chun, and Yijiang Wang. 1994. "The Nature of the Township Enterprises." *Journal of Comparative Economics* 19: 434–52.

Che, Jiahua, and Yingyi Qian. 1998a. "Insecure Property Rights and Government Ownership of Firms." *Quarterly Journal of Economics* 113 (2): 467–96.

———. 1998b. "Institutional Environment, Community Government, and Corporate Governance: Understanding China's Township-Village Enterprises." *Journal of Law, Economics, and Organization* 14 (1): 1–23.

China Statistical Yearbook. Various years. Beijing: China Statistical Publishing House.

Chow, Gregory. 1997. "Challenges of China's Economic System for Economic Theory." *American Economic Review* 87 (2): 321–27.

Coase, Ronald. 1992. "The Institutional Structure of Production." *American Economic Review* 82 (September): 713–19.

Dewatripont, Mathias, and Gérard Roland. 1992. "Economic Reform and Dynamic Political Constraints." *Review of Economic Studies* 59: 703–30.

Dewatripont, Mathias, and Gérard Roland. 1995. "The Design of Reform Packages under Uncertainty." *American Economic Review* 83 (5): 1207–23.

Dong, Furen. 1997. "The 'Budget Law' and Hardening Governments' Budget Constraints." In Tianqing Xu and Jinyan Li, eds., *China's Tax Reform*. Beijing: China Economics Publishing House.

Hellman, Joel S. 1998. "Winners Take All: The Politics of Partial Reform in Postcommunist Transitions." *World Politics* 50 (January): 203–34.

Jin, Hehui, and Yingyi Qian. 1998. "Public vs. Private Ownership of Firms: Evidence from Rural China." *Quarterly Journal of Economics* 113 (3): 773–808.

Jin, Hehui, Yingyi Qian, and Barry R. Weingast. 1999. "Regional Decentralization and Fiscal Incentives: Federalism, Chinese Style." Working Paper. Department of Economics, Stanford University, Stanford, Calif.

Kornai, Janos. 1986. "The Hungarian Reform Process: Visions, Hopes, and Reality." *Journal of Economic Literature* 24 (December): 1687–737.

———. 1992. *The Socialist System: The Political Economy of Communism*. Princeton, N.J.: Princeton University Press.

———. 1998. "From Socialism to Capitalism." Paper No.4. Center for Post-Collectivist Studies, London.

Lardy, Nicholas. 1998. *China's Unfinished Economic Revolution*. Washington, D.C.: Brookings Institution.

Lau, Lawrence, and Yingyi Qian. 1994. "Financial Reorganization of Banks and Enterprises in China: A Proposal." Paper presented at the "International Conference on China's Economic Reform: The Next Step." August 23–25, Beijing, China.

Lau, Lawrence, Yingyi Qian, and Gérard Roland. 1997. "Pareto-Improving Economic Reforms through Dual-Track Liberalization." *Economics Letters* 55 (2): 285–92.

———. Forthcoming. "Reform without Losers: An Interpretation of China's Dual-Track Approach to Transition." *Journal of Political Economy*.

Li, David D. 1996. "A Theory of Ambiguous Property Rights in Transition Economies: The Case of the Chinese Non-State Sector." *Journal of Comparative Economics* 23 (1): 1–19.

Li, Wei. 1999. "A Tale of Two Reforms." *RAND Journal of Economics* 30 (1): 120–36.

Maddison, Angus. 1998. *Chinese Economic Performance in the Long Run*. Paris: OECD Development Centre.

McKinnon, Ronald. 1993. *The Order of Economic Liberalization: Financial Control in the Transition to a Market Economy*. 2nd ed. Baltimore, Md.: Johns Hopkins University Press.

Montinola, Gabriella, Yingyi Qian, and Barry R. Weingast. 1995. "Federalism, Chinese Style: The Political Basis for Economic Success in China." *World Politics* 48 (1): 50–81.

Naughton, Barry. 1995. *Growing Out of the Plan*. Cambridge: Cambridge University Press.

North, Douglass. 1997. "The Contribution of the New Institutional Economics to an Understanding of the Transition Problem." *WIDER Annual Lectures*. Helsinki: World Institute for Development Economics Research.

Oi, Jean. 1992. "Fiscal Reform and the Economic Foundations of Local State Corporatism in China." *World Politics* 45 (1): 99–126.

Perkins, Dwight. 1994. "Completing China's Move to the Market." *Journal of Economic Perspectives* 8 (2): 23–46.

Qian, Yingyi. 1996. "Enterprise Reform in China: Agency Problems and Political Control." *Economics of Transition* 4 (2): 427–47.

Qian, Yingyi, and Gérard Roland. 1998. "Federalism and the Soft Budget Constraint." *American Economic Review* 88 (5): 1143–62.

Qian, Yingyi, and Barry R. Weingast. 1997. "Federalism as a Commitment to Preserving Market Incentives." *Journal of Economic Perspectives* 11 (4): 83–92.

Qian, Yingyi, and Chenggang Xu. 1993. "Why China's Economic Reforms Differ: The M-Form Hierarchy and Entry/Expansion of the Non-State Sector." *Economics of Transition* 1 (2): 135–70.

Qian, Yingyi, Gérard Roland, and Chenggang Xu. 1999. "Coordinating Changes in M-Form and U-Form Organizations." Working Paper. Department of Economics, Stanford University, Stanford, Calif.

Roland, Gérard, and Verdier, Thierry. 1999. "Transition and the Output Fall." *Economics of Transition* 7 (1): 1–28.

Shirk, Susan. 1993. *The Political Logic of Economic Reform in China*. Berkeley: University of California Press.

Stiglitz, Joseph. 1998. "Second-Generation Strategies for Reform for China." Address given at Beijing University, July 20.

Wei, Shang-Jin. 1997. "Gradualism versus Big Bang: Speed and Sustainability of Reforms." *Canadian Journal of Economics* 30 (4): 1234–47.

Weingast, Barry R. 1995. "The Economic Role of Political Institutions: Market-Preserving Federalism and Economic Growth." *Journal of Law, Economics, and Organization* 11 (April): 1–31.

Weitzman, Martin, and Chenggang Xu. 1994. "Chinese Township-Village Enterprises as Vaguely Defined Cooperatives." *Journal of Comparative Economics* 18 (September): 121–45.

Williamson, Oliver E. 1995. "The Institutions and Governance of Economic Development and Reform." In Michael Bruno and Boris Pleskovic, eds., *Proceedings of the World Bank Annual Conference on Development Economics 1994*. Washington, D.C.: World Bank.

Wong, Christine P.W. 1991. "Central-Local Relations in an Era of Fiscal Decline: The Paradox of Fiscal Decentralization in Post-Mao China." *China Quarterly* 128 (December): 691–715.

Wu, Jinglian. 1994. *Modern Corporation and Enterprise Reform (Xiandai gongsi yu Qiye gaige)*. Tianjin: Tianjin People's Publishing House.

Xie, Ping. 1996. *The Choice of China's Financial Systems*. Shanghai: Far East Publishing House.

# Why Has Russia's Economic Transition Been So Arduous?

*Anders Åslund*

*Russia's attempt at radical economic reform has largely failed. Why? In the early years of transition, it was because of extraordinary rent seeking by state enterprise managers through export rents, subsidized credits, import subsidies, and direct government subsidies. Managers were strong because the Soviet Union left behind large economic distortions and an essentially unconstrained economic elite. Reforms could have been more far-reaching if democratic institutions had been developed faster or if the West had provided financial support for reforms in early 1992. Although rents have dwindled in recent years, Russian institutions have been crippled by corruption. Intense competition over remaining rents contributed to the financial crash in August 1998, but the competition also limits the rents—and might ease the way for future reforms.*

Since 1989 Russia's GDP has dropped about 40 percent, and it will likely fall several percent in 1999. Russia has also seen an extraordinary increase in income differentials and poverty. Unemployment, once limited, approached 12 percent in 1998. What caused these negative developments?

Many observers have argued that Russia's reforms have been too fast and radical, criticizing "shock therapy," neoliberalism, monetarism, and privatization. But Russia's financial collapse in August 1998 made clear that reforms have not been radical or fast, but slow and partial. The state remains large and pervasive. The economy is far from liberal, and corruption thrives on excessive regulation. As Russian President Boris Yeltsin (1999) put it in his annual address to the Federal Assembly on 30 March 1999: "We have gotten stuck half-way in our transition from the planned and command economy to a normal market economy. We have created ... a hybrid of the two systems."

---

Anders Åslund is senior associate at the Carnegie Endowment for International Peace. This article draws on previous work with Peter Boone, Mikhail Dmitriev, and Simon Johnson, to whom the author is grateful. Marcus Fellman provided research assistance. The author wants to thank Leonid Grigoriev, David Lipton, Mark Gobel, Jan Svejnar, and two anonymous reviewers for comments.

*Annual World Bank Conference on Development Economics 1999*
©2000 The International Bank for Reconstruction and Development / THE WORLD BANK

Russia's main problem has been that a few people got very rich off partial reforms and have bought a large part of the country's politicians and officials. To preserve their rents, the newly rich use their power to prevent the liberal economic reforms that could boost growth and welfare. Russia's postcommunist period has been a struggle between reformers and rent seekers. For the most part the reformers have lost. Hellman (1998) summarizes this consequence of partial reforms as "winners take all." Shleifer and Vishny (1998) call these government pathologies "the grabbing hand."

Rents are usually understood to be money made on government transfers or market distortions. The rents at issue in this article are the free money made by the elite, either directly through government subsidies or indirectly through government regulations. But given the peculiarities of postcommunist transformation, this article also defines rents to include resources that are free in the sense that they are not safeguarded by the rule of law. Excluded are social transfers and government financing for genuinely social purposes, even if some of those might be considered rents as well. Rents are understood as flows. The opposite of rents is profits earned in a competitive market.

## Unwelcome Legacies of the Soviet Union

The *nomenklatura*—in which a tiny elite controlled all decisionmaking and resources—was a key feature of the Soviet system (Voslenskii 1984). In the 1980s senior bureaucrats were no longer afraid of the "supreme" leader. They implemented orders that benefited them directly and ignored commands that contradicted their interests. The demise of the Soviet system was facilitated by a division within the nomenklatura. Its economically oriented members—primarily state enterprise managers but also some officials and politicians—thrived on the inconsistencies of the collapsing socialist system. They wanted the freedom of the market for themselves but regulation for others.

These "red directors" were already well organized, primarily in the Russian Union of Industrialists and Entrepreneurs and the Russian Association of Banks. By opting out of the socialist system, the red directors left the Soviet elite split and politically vulnerable. When the Soviet Union collapsed, a country, a political system, and an economic system disintegrated, leading to general confusion. Five economic imbalances and distortions were of great importance for future attempts to move to a market economy (Åslund 1991).

First, Soviet finances collapsed in 1991, when the union republics stopped sending tax revenues to Moscow. The Soviet government faced a huge budget deficit, while international financing dried up because the country defaulted on its foreign payments. In late 1991 the central government lived on little but the emission of money.

Second, the union republics started issuing their own ruble credits without any coordination with the Soviet State Bank. The more ruble credits a republic issued, the larger the share of the common Soviet GDP it obtained. This competitive issue of one currency essentially guaranteed hyperinflation.

A third legacy was idiosyncratic price regulation that led to greatly distorted prices. External default and partial liberalization made the market exchange rate plummet in 1991, aggravating the distortion of relative prices. Commodity prices were minimal, while industrial consumer goods were overpriced. In December 1991 the state-controlled price of crude oil was 50 cents a ton—0.4 percent of the world market price (Delpla 1993).

Fourth, partial liberalization of prices and foreign trade aggravated economic distortions. The Soviet Union had a special exchange rate for every major good, and the differences between rates were large. During Soviet President Mikhail Gorbachev's gradual economic reforms a growing number of Soviet enterprises received foreign trade rights. In 1988, 213 enterprises had foreign trade rights, and in 1990 their number approached 20,000 (Åslund 1991). With the right connections, such enterprises could acquire oil or metals at low state prices, obtain export licenses and quotas, and sell the commodities abroad at high world prices.

A fifth peculiarity was the effective legalization of management theft in 1988 through the adoption of the Law on Cooperatives. That law allowed managers of state enterprises to establish private enterprises that undertook arbitrage with the state enterprises they were managing, transferring the profits of state enterprises to management-owned private enterprises. Commercial banks became the most prominent new free-wheeling cooperatives.

Russia at the end of communism is often described as an institutional vacuum, but that is not quite true. The red directors thrived on institutional anomalies and economic policies incompatible with a market economy, including monetary emission, low interest rates, distorted relative prices, multiple exchange rates, rigorous licensing of entrepreneurship, and myriad regulations. Little but banking was free. Massive rent seeking was occurring, and it would naturally lead to partial reforms.

## An Attempt at Radical Economic Reform, 1991–93

In the summer and fall of 1991 Russia was in total disarray. Monetary and fiscal discipline had disappeared, yet most prices were still regulated, leaving many shops empty. People had little or no reason to work. In this dire state, Russia started its transition to a market economy. Extraordinary rent seeking prevailed in the face of multiple shocks: external default, a collapse in state revenues, plummeting foreign trade, and a change of political regime. These shocks opened a window of opportunity for fundamental systemic change.

The first step toward profound change was the election of Yeltsin as president in June 1991. After the failed communist coup in August 1991, Yeltsin obtained actual executive power. In October Yeltsin took a second step, declaring his intention to undertake radical market-oriented economic reform in a speech to the Russian Congress of People's Deputies (*Sovetskaya Rossiya,* 29 October). A third step was that within a few days an overwhelming majority of the Congress had adopted Yeltsin's speech as a guideline for the government's economic policies. A fourth step came a week later, when Yeltsin appointed a new type of government. Almost all

Soviet branch ministries were abolished, and most new ministers were outsiders—young, liberal economists led by Deputy Prime Minister Yegor Gaidar. Yeltsin and his reform ministers declared their intention to build a normal market economy as quickly as possible.

Reformers focused on getting state finances under control and drew up a balanced budget for the first quarter of 1992. In addition, most prices and imports were liberalized, eliminating large price subsidies from the budget. Moreover, reformers slashed arms procurement by 70 percent.

Five central struggles on deregulation and macroeconomic stability occurred in this period (Åslund 1995). First, in early 1992 reformers tried to liberalize commodity prices and exports. But such liberalization was repeatedly delayed because the energy lobby resisted ferociously—and won. Managers of state oil companies, supported by communists, argued that Russia's oil industry would collapse if it faced world market prices. The energy lobby was headed by Viktor Chernomyrdin, who replaced Gaidar's liberal minister of energy in May 1992 and Gaidar himself in December 1992. In the spring of 1992 the state price of oil was still 1 percent of the world market price. Even in 1993 the average Russian oil price was only 8.3 percent of the world market price (Delpla 1993). As noted, managers of state companies producing oil and metals bought these commodities at fixed state prices, then sold them abroad at world market prices. Export rents peaked at $24 billion in 1992, or 30 percent of GDP. The resulting private revenues—benefiting a small number of state enterprise managers, government officials, politicians, and commodity traders—were accumulated abroad.

Second, a massive emission of money had started in 1991. Reformers failed to take control over the Central Bank, which issued enormous credits at subsidized rates of 10 or 25 percent a year—while inflation was 2,500 percent in 1992 (Matyukhin 1993). A credit from the Central Bank was simply a gift. In 1992 the Central Bank issued net credit equal to nearly 32 percent of GDP (Granville 1995b, p. 67). Of this, credits directed to enterprises amounted to 23 percent of GDP (IMF 1993, p. 139). While these fortunes were less concentrated than the benefits from commodity exports, they made many Russian bankers rich.

A third concern was the persistence of the ruble zone, which rendered financial stabilization impossible in the zone's member countries (Sachs and Lipton 1993; Hansson 1993). Many interests supported the ruble zone. In Russia the red directors wanted to continue "selling" unsalable goods to former Soviet republics at the expense of Russian government credits. Commodity traders exploited the differences in price regulation between former republics. The old establishment in other former republics thrived on cheap Russian credits. The cost to Russia was huge. The International Monetary Fund (IMF) calculates that in 1992 such credits cost Russia 9.3 percent of GDP in financing and 13.2 percent of GDP in implicit trade subsidies, for a total cost of 22.5 percent of GDP (IMF 1994, p. 25). Russia could hardly afford these subsidies, which exceeded the budget deficit. Strangely, the IMF supported the ruble zone. Only with the currency reform in the Kyrgyz Republic in May 1993 did the IMF take a clear stand against the ruble zone. Over the next two years financial stabilization took root in one former republic after another.

A fourth important struggle involved import subsidies. In the winter of 1991–92 there was widespread fear that Russia would suffer famine. Thus reformers had no chance of abolishing import subsidies for food. A food importer paid just 1 percent of the going exchange rate when importing essential foods, but could resell them relatively freely on the domestic market, pocketing the subsidy. These imports were paid for with Western "humanitarian" export credits, which were added to Russia's state debt. In 1992 import subsidies cost 17.5 percent of GDP (IMF 1993, pp. 133, 139). These revenues were absorbed by a limited number of Moscow traders operating through state agricultural monopolies.

A fifth battle was fought over the liberalization of entrepreneurship. In January 1992 Yeltsin issued a decree allowing anybody to trade anywhere at any time with anything at any price. This decree was modeled on Minister of Finance Leszek Balcerowicz's successful deregulation in Poland. The public response was extraordinary. In no time, tens of thousands of people took to the streets and started trading all over Russia. But established traders opposed the competition, and they solicited support from the mayors of big cities. In April 1992 Moscow Mayor Yuri Luzhkov prohibited this trade, and the police became preoccupied with chasing away street traders. Other mayors followed suit, eliminating the freedom of enterprise. In May 1993 a law was adopted imposing comprehensive licensing on nearly all economic activities.

The simple truth is that reformers dominated the Russian government only from November 1991 until June 1992. They tried to undertake radical reforms, but by June 1992 they were thoroughly beaten by large bankers and industrialists in cohort with the old parliament. By the fall, Russia was close to hyperinflation. The rent seekers were well organized, politically influential, and faced little counterweight. They amassed huge fortunes, swiftly moving Russia from an average European income distribution to one of Latin American heights (Milanovic 1998). If commodity prices, exports, and imports had been deregulated in 1992, and if market interest rates had been allowed to prevail, these fortunes would never have been generated. Then enterprises in Russia would have been forced to restructure to survive, as in Estonia and Poland.

In 1993, however, Russian reformers made amazing headway. The ruble zone was broken up, and by late 1993 every former Soviet republic had established its own currency (Granville 1995a). Subsidized credits were abolished in September 1993, and by November 1993 Russia had positive real interest rates. At the end of 1993 the exchange rate was fully unified, eliminating the last import subsidies. Privatization of small enterprises was successful, and privatization of medium-size and large enterprises was under way. By late 1993 reformers had accomplished so much that the reforms appeared irreversible.

How could these fundamental reforms be undertaken in late 1993 when they had seemed impossible in the spring of 1992? There are many explanations (Åslund, Boone, and Johnson 1996). Several rents declined for reasons beyond the control of politics. As people and enterprises learned not to hold money in any form, the velocity of money rose and monetization fell sharply, reducing the inflation tax. As a result the budget deficit could no longer be financed with the emission of credits. Similarly, an awakening market abolished extreme price distortions and the low exchange rate. As people learned what a market economy was, their tolerance of unjustified subsidies withered, aided by critical media exposing various forms of rent seeking. In 1992 state managers called for more and cheaper credits, but when subsidized credits were abolished, hardly anyone demanded their return. The same was true of import subsidies. And in an April 1993 referendum a majority of Russian voters expressed support for radical economic reforms.

Most of these changes were conditions in the first real Russian standby agreement with the IMF in the spring of 1993, and reformers used the IMF agreement to push through their demands. Moreover, the dissolution of the Congress of People's Deputies in September 1993 created a temporary political vacuum that offered both reformers and rent seekers uncommon opportunities. The abolition of subsidized credits and the unification of the exchange rate were locked-in institutional changes. But reformers suffered a setback when the December 1993 parliamentary elections forced the departure of reformist deputy prime ministers Yegor Gaidar and Boris Fedorov. Anatoly Chubais stayed as the sole reformist deputy prime minister, in charge of privatization.

## Inflation Was Defeated But Its Structural Causes Persisted, 1994–95

The exit from the government of all reformers except Chubais led to a widespread expectation that reforms would be reversed, especially since the new government was composed of industrial lobbies. But little happened to economic policy in 1994.

At the end of 1993 Prime Minister Chernomyrdin secured extraordinary monopoly rights for his creation, the mammoth natural gas company Gazprom, granting it tax exemptions worth 1–2 percent of GDP. Similarly, First Deputy Prime Minister Oleg Soskovets secured tax exemptions for the metallurgical industry worth about 2 percent of GDP. Soskovets also supported the National Sports Foundation, which got the right to import alcohol and tobacco tax free—an exemption worth as much as $10 billion, or about 3 percent of GDP (Bagrov 1999).

Although domestic commodity prices had been liberalized in 1993, commodity lobbies kept domestic prices down through quantitative export controls. The World Bank and the IMF fought hard against these controls, however. In July 1994 all export quotas apart from those for oil were abolished, and in January 1995 the oil quotas were abandoned (Bagrov 1999). Yet by rationing export volumes through the pipeline system, oil managers were able to keep the domestic oil price artificially low. Even so, by 1995 export rents had been reduced to just a few percent of GDP.

Still, the budget balance was gradually undermined, and on "Black Tuesday"—11 October 1994—the ruble's exchange rate dropped 27 percent. By that time the exchange rate had assumed a real economic meaning, and powerful economic interests had gotten used to a reasonably stable and predictable rate. Hence this mismanagement—or probably manipulation—aroused a popular outcry. The main beneficiaries of a low exchange rate, commodity traders, no longer dominated Russian business because their rents were drying up. As a result Yeltsin was able to sack leading economic policymakers—apart from Chernomyrdin—and put Chubais in charge of macroeconomic policy as first deputy prime minister.

## Stabilization

Macroeconomic stabilization was finally put on track in the spring of 1995. At that time Russia concluded its first fully fledged standby agreement with the IMF, securing more than $6 billion in financing in one year. The general government deficit was cut from 10.4 percent of GDP in 1994 to 5.7 percent in 1995, although revenues fell by 3.6 percent of GDP (table 1). The deficit was cut by trimming enterprise subsidies by 7.1 percent of GDP and regional transfers by 2.5 percent of GDP, while maintaining socially important spending. With strong IMF support, Chubais eliminated the tax exemption for the National Sports Foundation (Bagrov 1999). By the summer of 1996 financial stabilization had been attained. Inflation dropped to 22 percent in 1996 and to 11 percent in 1997.

How was it possible to achieve financial stabilization—by cutting subsidies—when the government was dominated by industrial lobbies? The answer is not obvious, and the explanations are many. First, the old rents were minimal. Subsidized credits and import subsidies were gone, and export rents were small. The sharp cut in subsidies finally made it credible that profit seeking would be more profitable than rent seeking. Second, the Russian government and Central Bank finally pursued a coordinated economic policy aimed at macroeconomic stabilization. Third, for the first time the IMF was considering substantial credits, and its standby loan in 1995 amounted to 2 percent of GDP, giving the institution

**Table 1. Key Economic Indicators for Russia, 1992–98**

| Indicator | 1992 | 1993 | 1994 | 1995 | 1996 | 1997 | 1998 |
|---|---|---|---|---|---|---|---|
| GDP (billions of U.S. dollars) | 79 | 159 | 277 | 357 | 429 | 450 | 272 |
| Change in GDP (percent) | −14.5 | −8.7 | −12.6 | −4.2 | −3.5 | 0.8 | −4.6 |
| Inflation (percent, year end) | 2,510 | 842 | 224 | 131 | 22 | 11 | 84 |
| Unemployment (percent) | 4.9 | 5.5 | 7.5 | 8.2 | 9.3 | 9.0 | 11.8 |
| *General government (percentage of GDP)* | | | | | | | |
| Revenues | 39.2 | 36.2 | 34.6 | 31.0 | 31.0 | 32.6 | 32.0 |
| Expenditures | 57.6 | 43.6 | 45.0 | 36.8 | 39.3 | 39.9 | 36.5 |
| Budget deficit | −18.4 | −7.3 | −10.4 | −5.7 | −8.4 | −7.4 | −4.5 |
| Federal revenues | 15.6 | 13.7 | 11.8 | 12.2 | 13.0 | 11.6 | 11.3 |
| Regional revenues | 13.5 | 16.7 | 18.0 | 14.2 | 14.5 | 16.1 | 14.8 |
| Transfers from the central government | 1.7 | 2.6 | 4.1 | 1.6 | 2.7 | 2.9 | 1.7 |
| Extrabudgetary revenues | 10.9 | 8.6 | 9.1 | 7.6 | 7.7 | 9.1 | — |
| Enterprise subsidies | 10.8 | 9.4 | 10.5 | 3.4 | 3.9 | 4.2 | — |

*Note:* These data are subject to continuous revision and, because they are gathered from various sources, there are minor inconsistencies between certain numbers. All, however, are based on standard IMF definitions.
*Source:* Tanzi 1999; Illarionov 1998b; World Bank 1996a; Bank of Finland 1999; Brunswick Warburg 1999.

real political weight. Fourth, the currency crisis of October 1994 greatly upset the Russian elite and created political momentum for reform. Fifth, reformers fought better than ever, hitting all the important interest groups at the same time rather than offering tradeoffs. Finally, Gaidar's party, Russia's Choice, was the largest parliamentary faction, providing reformers with a good base in the State Duma (the lower house of parliament).

These extraordinary blows to rent-seeking groups left them humbled, illustrating that the smaller their rents, the less their political power. Financial stabilization divided the Association of Russian Banks. When the interbank market dried up in the fall of 1995, financially strong banks did not call for state support but tacitly favored the bankruptcy of their competitors. At the same time, a new generation of private bankers took over from old state bankers, facilitating change (Dmitriev and others 1996). Similarly, the red directors lost ground to new businesspeople. This is how shock therapy reforms should work. By changing the paradigm and the rules of the game, it entices some businesspeople to opt for profits in competitive markets instead of rents.

Treisman (1998b) and Shleifer and Treisman (1998) offer an alternative explanation. They argue that many bankers were enticed by a new rent in the form of excessive yields on treasury bills, turning the interest of bankers from high inflation to low inflation and a reasonably stable exchange rate. Meanwhile, loss-making enterprises started living on nonpayments instead of budget subsidies. Nonpayments were in fact subsidies, but they did not boost inflation. The authors conclude that reformers used a less inflationary form of rent to lure the winners from inflationary partial reform into giving up their inflationary rents. Others have seen the loans-for-shares privatizations in late 1995 as a government payoff to new businesspeople (see below).

There are several problems with this explanation. First, it appears to be a rationalization in hindsight. In early 1995 reformers did all the right things, driving down rents and dividing the business community. Only after the December 1995 parliamentary elections did new rents mount. Second, the Shleifer-Treisman cure did not work. The yields on treasury bills were reasonable only temporarily in 1997, and they were the direct cause of the financial crash in 1998. Thus such a strategy would only have been a foolhardy postponement of a crisis. Third, successful reformers elsewhere (notably in Estonia and Poland) have beaten rent seekers by changing the rules of the game once and for all. Fourth, the purpose of reform is to defeat rent seeking and establish more productive incentives. It would be illogical and defeatist to think that people can only become honest if they are bribed. It seems more plausible that rents were driven down below a critical threshold and the reforms were rendered credible, so a sufficient share of the business community decided to opt for profits instead of rents.

Gaddy and Ickes (1998) analyze barter and offsets—when enterprises use tax debts to extract government orders instead of paying taxes (see below)—as means of hiding the economic reality, providing big enterprises with tax exemptions or subsidies. But the authors see these devices as defensive mechanisms of enterprises that resist change and argue that it is extremely difficult to change anything in the Russian economy. That explanation rings more true.

## Privatization

The other big economic event of 1994–95 was the privatization of nearly 18,000 medium-size and large enterprises. Officially, more than 70 percent of the economy—measured as a share of GDP or employment—now belongs to the nonstate sector. Many complaints have been raised about privatization. One is that the old managers acquired too much ownership. In 1996, however, only 18 percent of the shares of privatized medium-size and large enterprises belonged to the old managers (Blasi, Kroumova, and Kruse 1997, p. 193). Given that state managers essentially owned public enterprises before privatization, this implies a considerable reduction of their ownership and an extraordinary redistribution of power in Russian society.

Another concern has been that enterprise restructuring has been too limited. Yet one-third of medium-size and large enterprises changed management between 1992 and 1996, and about one-quarter underwent substantial restructuring (Blasi, Kroumova, and Kruse 1997, p. 203). Brown and Brown (1999) analyzed the Russian Enterprise Registry Longitudinal Database, covering about 30,000 medium-size and large industrial enterprises, and found that Russia's industrial structure is undergoing dramatic changes. The size distribution of enterprises is converging to that in the United States, with sizes becoming more varied. Many new small firms have entered the market, and poor enterprises risk being closed down. There is high turnover in market leadership. Competition is evident and has had positive effects. A World Bank enterprise survey found that real sales per worker increased 12 percent a year during 1995–97, though the increase was largely accomplished through labor shedding (Djankov 1999). The problem is hardly privatization but that private property rights remain limited by intrusive state regulation, as local authorities harass entrepreneurs with arbitrary taxation and numerous inspections. Moreover, land ownership remains restricted.

A third complaint is that privatization concentrated wealth. But almost all of Russia's biggest companies have been freely traded on an open stock market, and during 1996–99 total market capitalization ranged between 5 and 20 percent of GDP. That is, the market value that state enterprise managers got from the voucher privatization of their enterprises was only 1–4 percent of GDP, compared with 81 percent of GDP through export rents, subsidized credits, import subsidies, and direct subsidies in 1992. Moreover, privatization did not facilitate but complicated management theft. Thus the concentration of wealth was not caused by privatization but by other forms of rent seeking.

Popular rage was probably aroused because privatization was the only open and transparent transfer of wealth; there were other, much larger financial flows but they were covert. People tend to overestimate the value of huge industrial smokestacks. Few Russians noticed that oil managers had become tremendously wealthy before privatization (which they actually resisted) or that bankers used their wealth from subsidized credits and commodity trade to buy enterprises on which most lost money. Politically, these popular misperceptions have been extremely harmful. In addition, to facilitate privatization, reformers unwisely boosted popular expectations of privatization gains to an unrealistic level, ultimately arousing disappointment. Few Russians realized that old Soviet enterprises are of little or no value, and many suspected that somebody had taken their share.

A fourth criticism concerns the loans-for-shares scheme, which was introduced in 1995 to privatize a limited number of very large enterprises. This scheme was not formulated by the red directors, but by some new bankers—notably Vladimir Potanin of Oneximbank and Mikhail Khodarkovsky of Bank Menatep. The government's dilemma was that too many large enterprises remained state-owned even after voucher privatization was completed in the summer of 1994, and it had proven difficult to sell enterprises for cash. Stock prices were tiny relative to asset values, and large sales of additional stock would have further depressed stock prices.

Thus the idea arose to offer large blocks of state shares as collateral against bank loans in open auctions. Doing so would not depress stock prices, while the offering prices would be current market prices. But the auctions became closed, and the offering prices almost equaled the closing prices. As a result Oneximbank seized control of the huge metallurgical company Norilsk Nickel and the oil company Sidanko, Menatep took over the oil company Yukos, and Boris Berezovsky (of the car dealership Logovaz) got the oil company Sibneft at low prices.

The sales of stocks of 15 large enterprises through the loans-for-shares scheme attracted great public criticism even though not all the privatizations were profitable for the winners of the auctions. These privatizations hardly changed the system, but they transferred the benefits of management theft from some red directors to some new capitalists, and tarnished Chubais's reputation. When Oneximbank took over Sidanko, it announced that the prior management had tapped $350 million a year from the company, and these cash flows were presumably appropriated by the new owners. Still, the total cash flows that could be expropriated from these companies could hardly have been more than 0.5 percent of GDP a year. The new majority owners did not behave like owners; they just continued the ordinary management theft. After a short-lived boom, the values of these companies have fallen below the low purchasing prices. For instance, Norilsk Nickel is now worth one-third as much as Oneximbank paid for it in late 1995. The financial crash of August 1998 cut most of these tycoons down to size.

The most telling fact about privatization is that throughout the process, the most severe criticism has come from the very elite—widely perceived to have benefited from it. The reason is simple. Before privatization, state enterprise managers were quasi-owners of their enterprises—and privatization reduced their property rights. For big rent seekers the emergence of real private property rights threatens their state-oriented way of making money.

Although Chubais was the only significant reformer left in the government, reformers were publicly blamed for the continuing economic decline—while all the unabashed lobbyists in the government escaped unscathed. The parliamentary elections in December 1995 dealt another blow to reformers, with communists reemerging as a serious political threat (though mainly because reformers were split into too many parties). In January 1996 Yeltsin sacked his last reformist minister with the oft-quoted words: "Chubais is guilty of everything."

## The Stagnation of Reform, 1996–98

The December 1995 parliamentary elections cast a dark shadow as Russia entered 1996. With the June 1996 presidential elections approaching, an enormous fear of communist revenge dominated Russian politics. To counter that threat, most anticommunist forces joined hands, giving the so-called oligarchs a new position of privilege. The elections highlighted the political importance of money and owner control over media. Capitalists and media magnates Vladimir Gusinsky and Boris Berezovsky emerged as dominant political forces. The election results evidenced the political clout of Russia's new tycoons. Potanin, chairman of Oneximbank, became first deputy prime minister (if only for half a year), and Berezovsky became deputy secretary of the Security Council (for one year).

No reform occurred in 1996. The communists opposed market reforms, and the government did not contain a senior reformer. The government let the budget deficit rise from 5.7 percent of GDP in 1995 to 8.4 percent in 1996, distributing pre-election gifts. The real yields of treasury bills peaked at 150 percent a year before the presidential elections, as the government tried to sell more than the market was prepared to buy in the face of great political risks. Moreover, access to the market was informally limited to privileged Russian banks, excluding foreigners and domestic households and so making the treasury bill market a source of rent seeking. Interest payments on the federal budget jumped from 3.3 percent of GDP in 1995 to 5.7 percent in 1996 because almost 4.0 percent of GDP went to pay yields on treasury bills (Illarionov 1998b). The IMF insisted that this market be opened to foreign investors—a move that led to lower treasury bill yields but that also exposed Russia to a dangerous dependence on short-term foreign capital, attracted by high real yields. Hardly anything was done to attract household savings.

In the spring of 1996 the IMF concluded a three-year loan program with Russia, an Extended Fund Facility, though no one in the government was concerned about reform. The program called for a budget deficit of 4 percent of GDP, but this was never a serious proposition and lacked all credibility. Rather, it was a political decision made to secure Yeltsin's reelection, supported by the G–7 group of advanced industrial countries. Yeltsin was saved, but at the expense of economic policy. The Extended Fund Facility agreement set the stage for Russia's ensuing boom and bust. The soft agreement convinced foreigners and Russians alike that Russia was too big—or too nuclear—to fail, and that anything goes in Russia. The IMF delayed a tranche of the loan in September 1996, but by then it had little leverage.

The IMF agreement unleashed an extraordinary inflow of foreign portfolio investment, which rose from $8.9 billion in 1996 to $45.6 billion in 1997—or 10 percent of GDP. (Meanwhile, foreign direct investment increased from $2.5 billion in 1996 to just $6.2 billion in 1997; RECEP 1999.) Roughly half the foreign portfolio investment went into federal government bonds and half to other bonds and stocks. At the peak of the stock market in 1997, foreigners might have owned as much as 30 percent of the market capitalization of some $100 billion. In the summer of 1998 the stock of treasury bills totaled $70 billion, of which foreigners held at least $25 billion. In addition, large amounts of enterprise, regional, and municipal bonds had been issued. Thus in July 1998 accumulated foreign portfolio holdings were at least $55 billion, or 12 percent of GDP. In addition, international financial institutions had loaned the Russian government more than $20 billion, or 4.5 percent of GDP. Ironically, Russia was flooded with foreign financing—mostly private but also intergovernmental—after serious attempts at economic reform had faded.

The net result of these inflows was capital outflows of about $20 billion a year in 1996–98, whereas capital outflows had shrunk in 1994–95. Rising capital outflows are a strong indication of rising rents. Hence foreign portfolio investment contributed both to rent seeking and to the magnitude of the August 1998 financial crash. Similarly, the loans to the Russian government diminished the need for the state to collect taxes or cut subsidies. The conditionality of the loans from the IMF and the World Bank appears to have been ineffective, possibly because the large private portfolio investments were unconditional. Many Russian businesspeople made big money by grabbing the assets of minority shareholders through transfer pricing, asset seizure, or by not servicing bond debts. Thus these inflows were counterproductive to corporate governance and reform.

Although renewed attempts at reform were made in the spring of 1997 and the summer of 1998, reformers lacked the power to influence the real economy. Nonpayments, offsets, and barter increased, suggesting that enterprises' real budget constraints were getting softer, not harder. The noncash economy is growing because it is a well-entrenched system than many participants have strong incentives to maintain (Gaddy and Ickes 1998). By 1998 about half of interenterprise payments were made in barter, about one-quarter in money surrogates, and only one-quarter in money.

Barter and other noncash payments are popular because they facilitate tax avoidance and evasion. In particular, the value added tax (VAT) is based on payments, not on invoices or deliveries on an accrual basis (as in the West). Hence companies that are barely paid in money are effectively exempt from most of their potential VAT burden. Enterprises also use tax debts to extract government orders instead of paying taxes, a practice called offsets. Offsets are by their nature discretionary negotiations between big businesspeople and government officials about large amounts of money—negotiations that are naturally susceptible to corruption. Regional governments appear most corrupt, accepting 60 percent of taxes in money surrogates, compared with 43 percent for local governments and 25 percent for the federal government (OECD 1997; Illarionov 1998a).

In addition, big industrial enterprises use barter to subdue small enterprises. In 1997 some 40 percent of the barter trade was perceived as involuntary, meaning that an enterprise was compelled to accept a payment in products it did not want (Aukutsionek 1998). Barter is also an important mechanism for management theft. The essence of the post-Soviet noncash economy is large enterprises' reluctance to adjust to market conditions, at the expense of consumers, the government, and politically weaker enterprises. A monetized economy is transparent, competitive, and offers no advantages for large enterprises. A noncash economy, by contrast, makes relations with top government officials crucial for an enterprise's success—and big enterprises have more access to senior officials.

The new tycoons were no more prepared to accept free markets than the old red directors, and they demanded their due from the government in return for their support in the presidential elections. In July 1997 Berezovsky and Gusinsky turned on reformers with a vengeance because the reformers had initiated an open auction of the telecommunications holding company Svyazinvest. In October 1997, just before the Asian financial crisis started to hurt Russia, Berezovsky worked with Prime Minister Chernomyrdin and communists in the Duma to increase the budget deficit in an apparent attempt to undermine reformers. The government failed to tighten its fiscal policy until February 1998. By then annual interest rates had again risen to more than 100 percent.

In March 1998 Yeltsin sacked the passive Chernomyrdin, but the move came too late. The reformist government under Sergei Kirienko did not act fast enough, nor did it possess the political support needed to carry out reforms. As the crisis continued in 1998, Russia's financial problems became increasingly evident. For years the country had maintained an excessive budget deficit. As a result it had accumulated a fast-growing and unsustainable short-term government debt, causing creditors to withdraw. Moreover, red tape and arbitrary taxation deterred domestic and foreign investment. The Russian government and the IMF reached an agreement on budget cuts in July 1998, but four interest groups pushed their country into the abyss.

The keenest activists were Berezovsky and some oil barons, who had campaigned for devaluation—even though they knew that it would cause most banks to go bankrupt—because they held large ruble assets but hard currency liabilities. This group also suggested price controls, inflationary emission of money, and Central Bank credits and lower taxes for the oil industry (Alekperov 1998).

Second, in July 1998 the Duma refused to accept a government proposal (supported by the IMF) to move from a VAT based on payments to one based on accruals—a proposal that would have meant the taxation of barter. Nor did the Duma agree to transfer any regional revenues to the federal treasury. These two votes triggered the financial collapse.

Third, regional governors strongly resisted any transfer of their funds to the federal government. But regional revenues are almost 1.5 times as large as federal revenues, and regional governors spend more than 2 percent of GDP on enterprise subsidies, which are disbursed in a discretionary manner. Thus anyone elected governor can freely dispose of a large amount of money—a setup that entices criminals to run for regional governorships.

A fourth group, the state bureaucracy, contributed indirectly to the financial collapse. The bureaucracy has doubled since 1992, expanding by 1.2 million workers, or almost 2 percent of the labor force. Many of these new workers are inspectors. Enterprises have been subject to extraordinary bureaucratic interference, which deters investment and entrepreneurship.

The behavior of these groups was socially irresponsible, but they acted in line with their recent experiences. They had learned that the most ruthless rent seeker is the most successful. Another lesson was that the economic environment changes all the time, rendering intelligent improvisation the road to prosperity. Many games were played only once. Thus these groups instantly seized any possibility. The crash can also be seen as a result of intense competition for shrinking rents, as the rent seekers were trying to preserve their incomes.

## Russia's Main Strategic Problems

Russia suffers from three key economic problems. First, the government has continuously tried to collect more taxes than it can. The tax system is an unfortunate combination of the Soviet system, a hasty partial reform in 1992, inconsistency, and dubious legal changes often motivated by rent seeking. The system collects little revenue, but it is unjust, and the tax burden is unevenly distributed. Businesspeople with good political connections are more or less exempt from taxation, while taxation is confiscatory for others, forcing many small entrepreneurs out of business or underground.

However, Russian state revenues are not particularly small or falling sharply. Total state revenues match U.S. revenues, and in the Commonwealth of Independent States only Belarus and Ukraine have significantly higher revenues as a share of GDP. State revenues actually rose from 31 percent of GDP in 1995 to 32 percent in 1998. Even federal revenues were almost constant during 1994–98, at around 12 percent of GDP (see table 1).

Second, the government has failed to rationalize its spending, often not paying its commitments while maintaining amazingly futile public spending. Because Russian public and social spending is highly regressive, the poor are unlikely to suffer from needed budget cuts. In 1998 the Ministry of Labor and Social Affairs calculated that 70 percent of social transfers went to the richest 30 percent of households, but all attempts at reform were defeated (Dmitriev 1998). Similarly, a 1994 World Bank study found that the poorest 20 percent of Russians receive only 6 percent of social assistance (Milanovic 1998). Russian public spending has lingered around 40 percent of GDP, but almost half cannot be justified from any social point of view. Making needed cuts would increase transparency and make it easier to establish a targeted social safety net for the truly needy.

Third, markets of all kinds function badly, leading to high transaction costs and limited competition, and reflecting excess regulation and the absence of the rule of law. The liberalization of the Russian economy has been a drawn-out battle, and state intervention remains intense and arbitrary. Nearly all economic activities are subject to licensing, and multiple licenses are usually required. More than 60 state agencies inspect enterprises, and hundreds of thousands of inspectors attempt to extort bribes. As a result Russia ranks low on all liberalization indices (EBRD 1998; World Bank 1996b; De Melo, Denizer, and Gelb 1996). A natural consequence is pervasive corruption. In 1998 Transparency International ranked Russia among the most corrupt countries on its Corruption Perceptions Index, at 76th among 85 countries (Transparency International 1998). Hence prices and markups remain high, the choice and quality of goods are unimpressive, regional price differentials remain sizable, and Russia has few enterprises. The number of legally registered enterprises reached 2.7 million in 1997, which is just one enterprise per 55 Russians. A ratio of one enterprise per 10 people is normal in the West and in successful reform countries like Hungary and Poland (Åslund 1997).

Economically, the solution is obvious, and Russian reformers and international financial institutions have made reasonable proposals for years. Fundamental reform is needed to simplify the tax system, reduce the number of taxes, broaden the tax base (by abolishing exemptions), and cut top tax rates. Far-reaching deregulation is needed, and abusive government interference must be curbed. Real private property rights, including private ownership of land, are necessary. Natural monopolies require market regulation. The rule of law must be reinforced, and a firm commitment made to establishing a targeted social safety net. Hundreds of sensible laws have been drafted, but many lie waiting for consideration in the Duma.

Why have such reforms not been adopted? A Western school of political economy literature has argued that radical reforms were not democratically possible because they would have led to sharp declines in output and so would have provoked popular protests (see, for example, Przeworski 1991). But this literature suffers from two severe deficiencies. First, the assumption that radical reform would lead to a greater decline in output than would gradual reform has been disproven empirically. Moreover, the losers have suffered far worse in countries with no radical reform, because of both falling output and increasing income differentials (World Bank 1996b; Milanovic 1998). Second, these scholars assumed that workers or the public would rise in protest, but neither group has posed serious political problems. Instead the threat to reforms came from a limited number of winners who enriched themselves from extraordinary rent seeking (Hellman 1998).

The August 1998 crisis eliminated the rents from foreign financing and the excessive returns on treasury bills. The only remaining rents are enterprise subsidies and some refinancing of banks, for total rents equal to about 5 percent of GDP—down from 81 percent in 1992 and 15 percent in 1997 (figure 1). Hence the crisis seems to have cleaned out many rents and possibly laid the ground for a low-rent economy.

To keep rents low, the average tax burden should be diminished, because that reduces the value of tax exemptions—and it would be foolhardy to believe that such exemptions can be abolished in the current political climate. The dangers of large foreign portfolio investment have probably been sufficiently illustrated to foreign investors that an early repetition is unlikely. The best hope for the future seems a fierce competition over rents, which will eventually minimize them.

**Figure 1. Rent-seeking, 1991–98**

*Rents as share of GDP (%)*

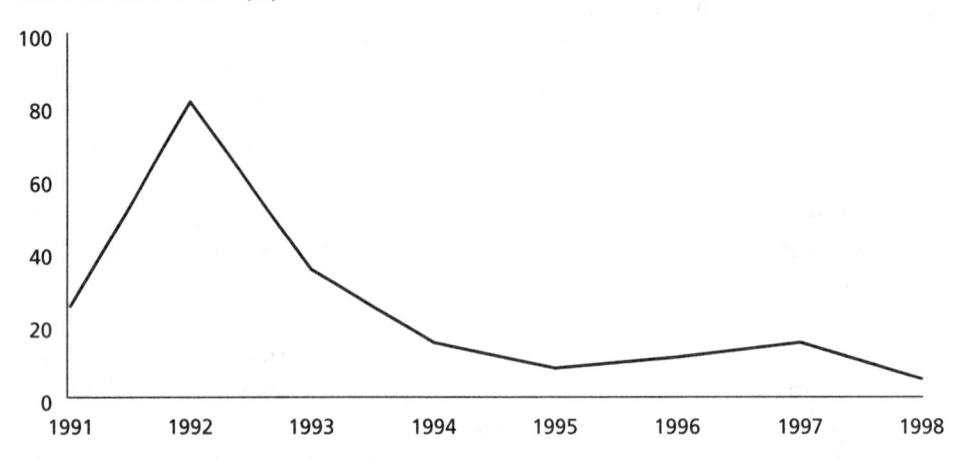

[Line chart showing rents as share of GDP from 1991 to 1998. Values start around 25% in 1991, peak at about 82% in 1992, drop to about 37% in 1993, then decline to about 17% in 1994, about 10% in 1995–96, rise slightly to about 17% in 1997, and fall to about 6% in 1998.]

*Source:* Author's calculations.

## Alternative Policies

Russia's economic policies since 1991 look like a serious failure. Yet it is still too early to judge whether the 1990s have been unproductive. During 1994–98 Poland grew by an average of 6 percent a year. But its economic success would not have been possible without a seemingly lost decade in the 1980s—a decade that changed the thinking of the people and the government, which reluctantly undertook significant reforms because of economic crisis and the absence of international financing. The reforms increasingly led young Poles from rent seeking to profit seeking, and from government service to private enterprise. Poland's real breakthrough, however, came after a second financial crisis, democratization, election victories for reformers, and a comprehensive radical reform program, supported by substantial international financing.

### Two Big Myths

Many suggestions have been made about what alternative policies would have been better for Russia. Before assessing those, however, two big myths should be debunked. First, Russia is not a neoliberal state but a crony state, with the state remaining the source of the main fortunes. Among those who promoted radical reforms, there is consensus that on the whole the reforms that were implemented were not actually radical (Dabrowski 1993; Sachs 1995; Aven 1999; Fedorov 1999). This assessment was also reflected in the World Bank's *World Development Report 1996: From Plan to Market* (World Bank 1996b). However, an extensive academic literature and broad public debate on transition in post-Soviet countries favored continued soft macroeconomic policies, including monetary emission, large budget deficits, and slow deregulation of prices and trade (Portes 1993; Nuti and Portes 1993; Vienna Institute for International Economic Comparisons 1993; Taylor 1994).

In Russia most enemies of reform argued that inflation was caused by price liberalization, while the fall in output was the result of a lack of demand stemming from overly strict monetary policy. It was argued that the problems were structural and could only be solved with government intervention—including protectionism, price and wage controls, and an industrial policy that included subsidized credits for select companies. For the most part budgetary policy was ignored. The critics argued that shock therapy had been carried out and blamed all the country's problems on it (Bogomolov 1996). Those who favored gradual reforms in Russia won the debate—and are to blame for the outcomes.

The other big myth of the Russian transition is that privatization has been the main source of ill-gotten fortunes. As noted, however, the fortunes have been made on export rents, subsidized credits, import subsidies, and other rents. Moreover, enterprise ownership is reasonably well distributed. The problem is that ownership has not become effective. In the 1998 financial crisis Russian tycoons did not behave like capitalists but like rent seekers, thinking only of the short-term cash flow.

## Other Options

From the start, Russia's market reforms were not perceived as credible. Top businesspeople knew that rent seeking was the name of the game. Given these circumstances, what could have been done to enhance the credibility of the change in economic rules? The government did liberalize most prices, abolish price subsidies, liberalize imports, and slash military procurement. And there was no going back on these radical reforms, which changed the rules for good. But the reform government failed to maintain a balanced budget beyond the first quarter of 1992, control monetary emission, unify the exchange rate, liberalize commodity prices, and deregulate exports. The shift from the old system could have been swifter, and more could have been done to build new institutions designed for democracy and a market economy.

Similarly, the reform government shrank the central Soviet government apparatus, abolishing almost all branch ministries. But the State Planning Committee, State Price Committee, agrarian organizations, and KGB survived for no good reason—and they caused considerable damage. A more forceful organizational discontinuity was feasible but was not undertaken. Because the reform did not go far enough, dozens of branch ministries soon reemerged.

Old Soviet government cadres were incredibly hostile to reforms. Staff that sabotaged government policy should have been removed, but that was never a political possibility. Still, Yeltsin could have brought in thousands of well-educated activists from the Democratic Russia movement, but he turned instead to old communist cadres. Although new cadres have since been trained, this was an enormous lost opportunity. Russia's most valuable social capital was hardly concentrated in the old state administration because of decades of negative selection (Amalrik 1980).

Yeltsin's options were always limited by intense political pressure, but he had no political or constitutional strategy. For the first year and a half of the transition, a majority of Russians supported radical economic reform. The best approach would have been to dissolve the semidemocratic parliament, hold early parliamentary elections, and form a reform party. In parallel, a new constitution could have been adopted instead of amending the dysfunctional Soviet constitution, which could be altered at any time by a qualified majority of parliament and eventually led to a violent parliamentary uprising. In addition, the ruble zone should have been abolished early on because it hindered financial stabilization and facilitated huge rent seeking. But Yeltsin failed to mobilize the reformist majority, and after his shoot out with the old parliament in October 1993 that majority no longer existed.

The West had a chance to make a big difference in early 1992. The West, and the United States in particular, enjoyed enormous goodwill in Russia and had considerable influence. All the necessary measures—liberalization of commodity prices, deregulation of exports, unification of the exchange rate, and maintenance of positive real interest rates—were standard elements of an IMF program, and they were desired by the Russian government. As never before or later, Yeltsin appealed to the West for help, but his efforts were in vain. The West was preoccupied with securing Soviet debt, and instead of providing money for reformers, it gave commodity credits to rent-seeking commodity traders.

After these opportunities passed, reforms became much more difficult. Although rent seekers were making less money, they were well entrenched, with connections in the government and parliament. The only major success was the 1995 stabilization program. Chubais scored a coup by lowering the deficit, focusing on truly indefensible spending while cutting revenue. The standby agreement in the spring of 1995 was the IMF's finest achievement in Russia. And the IMF and the World Bank were instrumental in deregulating foreign trade, which eliminated most foreign trade rents.

In contrast, the Extended Fund Facility in the spring of 1996 appears to be a great mistake by the IMF. The budget deficit was widening, and the Russian government had no credible commitment to reform. But through the facility the IMF signaled that Russia was too big to fail regardless of economic policy, which encouraged excessive foreign portfolio investment. Furthermore, the IMF responded to the high yields on treasury bills by persuading the Russian government to open the treasury bill market to foreign investors rather than pushing for a smaller budget deficit. The resulting large inflows of foreign portfolio investment increased Russia's vulnerability to contagion from the Asian financial crisis and contributed to its financial crash.

So what should have been done instead? It is often argued that reformers should have tried to compromise with the opposition. But if anything, reformers compromised far too much. The only reasonably successful compromise was the privatization scheme, which explicitly considered the interests of enterprise managers (Boycko, Shleifer, and Vishny 1995). All other attempts at compromise have been unsuccessful. When the reform government could no longer block directed government enterprise credits, it tried to steer them to "progressive" state enterprise managers whose only advantage was diplomatic skills. In the most successful reforms—in Estonia and Poland—reformers took enormous heat in the early years (Bozyk 1992). Only later did the political consensus for reform emerge (Balcerowicz 1994).

The fundamental weakness of Russia's reformers was that they never were supported by a parliamentary majority, which seems a near condition of successful reforms. Furthermore, Russian reformers compromised themselves by remaining in a government dominated by people serving the interests of rent-seeking lobbies. Although Chubais's stabilization policies succeeded in 1995, in the long term reformers might have lost public credibility for tolerating corruption by nonreformers.

Another common argument is that Russia needs a dictator like Chile's Augusto Pinochet to undertake successful reforms. But this point is usually made by people who do not want real market reforms. Moreover, the problem was not the exceedingly patient Russian people but the old Soviet establishment. Given that in the past Soviet dictators failed to control the elite, democracy, transparency, and accountability seem like better options than dictatorship (Maravall 1994). All reasonably successful reform countries in the former Soviet bloc are democracies (Åslund, Boone, and Johnson 1996)

Many observers have also highlighted the role of industrial policy. Russia's industrial lobbyists have constantly called for more active industrial policy, citing its success in Japan and the Republic of Korea. But by the standards of either country Russia has had an active industrial policy, and it has been worse than ineffective—it has been harmful. Russia's industrial policy has been a code word for subsidies, with most captured by the coal and agriculture industries and the military-industrial complex. As a result trade in their products has become criminalized, because subsidies provide a strong inducement to engage in organized crime (LaFraniere 1999). It is doubtful whether any government can manage industrial policy without sinking into the trap of corruption, but Russian industrial policy is bound to be totally corrupt.

Another common view is that it was wrong to launch reforms before adopting the necessary legislation. But in reality this is an argument against ever contemplating significant reform. A parliament that opposes reform is not going to adopt market-oriented economic legislation, as has been evident in Russia since 1992. Reformers need to thrive on momentum. Typically, they suddenly get a chance to form a reform government, often for exogenous reasons. The political situation hardly ever allows them to sit down and promulgate a couple hundred laws before they launch the reform. Only the reformers in the Czech Republic had a political mandate strong enough to do so. Most reformers must use a brief window of opportunity to change the basic rules of the game, with most reform laws adopted soon afterward. Many reform laws will never be adopted if no concrete interest has been formed that demands such laws.

A similar fallacy is that the state should simply reform or that technical assistance should teach bureaucrats to do their jobs. If bureaucrats are preoccupied with rent seeking, they are usually too corrupt to be useful. Advising a bureaucrat to reduce his power and revenues will never work. Nor is it realistic to suggest that a parliament that opposes private ownership should legislate the sanctity of private property. The impetus for reform usually comes from the outside, but little can be done if the political will is absent, and the state must be freed from the worst rent seeking before it can be reformed.

## Outstanding Policy Issues

The question remains: how could more radical reforms have been implemented? Could the reform agenda have been made more comprehensive? While more interests could have been satisfied, reformers were—and remain—extremely short on administrative capacity. Thus the focus should be on policies that cannot easily be manipulated by corrupt interests. Far too often, recommendations are offered for reforms that run counter to the key interests of major and mobilized rent seekers, yet these proposals are not accompanied by suggestions for political success. For instance, bank regulation and financial sector reform can hardly be imposed when rogue banks flourish. Social reforms require the involvement of large numbers of officials, many of whom are hostile to reform. Such officials often need to be replaced before reform can proceed.

Exchange rate policy, for example, has never been particularly successful. Initially, Russia had such small reserves that it had no choice but to float. If international support had bolstered reserves, if the ruble zone had been broken up, and if the Central Bank had pursued responsible policies, an early peg would have lowered inflation (Sachs 1995). The float did not offer much support, and the exchange rate seems to have been manipulated for rent-seeking purposes—notably in October 1994—though that facilitated the unification of the exchange rate. The financial stabilization of 1995 was achieved by establishing a currency band. But while this band facilitated stabilization, it inspired a false sense of security, encouraging excessive foreign portfolio investment. Later, when commodity prices fell, the currency band led to the overvaluation of the ruble and eventually to the financial crash. A currency board, which makes it more difficult to manipulate the exchange rate, might have been a better approach.

Similarly, orderly decentralization could have enhanced the capacity of the state and overcome corrupt bulwarks. Yet Russian thinking about the nature of the Russian Federation remains confused, and at first Westerners seemed much more interested than any leading Russians in fiscal federalism (Wallich 1994). Initially the new Russian government (understandably) thought only of the survival of the Russian Federation and tried to centralize control over monetary and fiscal policy. But the central government was overburdened and could not exert any meaningful control over the regions. There was no clear division of revenues or tasks between the three administrative levels (federal, regional, and municipal). Transfers from the federal to regional governments grew rapidly, peaking at 4.1 percent of GDP in 1994 (see table 1). The best opportunity for a clear division of responsibilities between the federal and regional governments probably came in 1995, when regional transfers were cut 60 percent.

But while everyone claims to favor fiscal reform, enormous resistance has made it politically difficult. The experiences of other countries offer some guidance (Gaidar 1998). Three other countries in the Commonwealth of Independent States (Georgia, Kazakhstan, and the Kyrgyz Republic) have managed to undertake sensible, radical tax reforms. All these reforms were preceded by a collapse in public revenues. The upshot is that Russia must opt for much lower public revenues if tax reform is to become politically possible. The logic is that lower average taxation makes tax exemptions less valuable. Russia's 1995 stabilization supports this thesis.

Similarly, in the Commonwealth of Independent States radical government and spending reform seems to be possible only with a sharp reduction in state revenues. The countries with the highest public spending (notably Belarus, Russia, and Ukraine) appear to maintain the most harmful public spending structures. None of the reform countries with sizable public spending (Moldova, Russia, Ukraine) has experienced growth, while the four Commonwealth of Independent States countries that have recorded impressive growth after hitting rock bottom (Armenia, Azerbaijan, Georgia, the Kyrgyz Republic) had unweighted average state revenues of 16.8 percent of GDP in 1997—compared with 32.6 percent in Russia (Tanzi 1999). The evidence suggests that public sectors in the region are so distorted that they must be shrunk much more than has proven necessary in Central Europe or the Baltics before they can return to performing social functions.

## Implications for International Financial Institutions

The main problem with Russia's transition to a market economy has been the lack of radical reform. In the absence of such reform, rent seeking became excessive and rent seekers became too rich and powerful. The 1998 crash minimized rents, at least temporarily. Government policy should now focus on keeping rents low and squeezing out the rent seekers. The best approach seems to be to encourage competition for rents so that it becomes more lucrative to pursue profits. To replace one rent with another is unlikely to improve the system. This reasoning leads to the following recommendations for future action by international financial institutions working in Russia:

- The overall tax rate—the share of state revenues in GDP—should be cut to 20–25 percent of GDP to reduce the value of tax exemptions. This move would reduce rent seeking and incentives to engage in barter. In addition, it would facilitate the radical tax reforms that much of the Russian and international community have long recommended. This move would require a radical change in IMF policy, which continues to call for higher state revenues. Russia undoubtedly needs a strong, well-functioning state. But the state can only grow strong and carry out its key functions if it is freed from corruption and rent seeking.
- Lower revenues would force Russia to cut public spending. Other members of the Commonwealth of Independent States have shown that when such cuts are big enough, the most harmful expenditures are eliminated. Lower

public spending should also make it easier to implement social reforms, because corrupt bureaucrats will have fewer incentives to block them.
- Lower state revenues will also facilitate substantial cuts in the public administration, as has already occurred since the 1998 crash.
- International financial institutions should remain skeptical as long as Russia does not have a government that is actively pursuing reform of its own will, supported by a reformist majority in parliament. The IMF appeared to influence Russian policy more effectively between August 1998 and July 1999, when it provided no funds, than between March 1996 and March 1998, when it gave substantial amounts.
- The IMF should not accept a large budget deficit or encourage short-term foreign borrowing by governments. Instead it should be more conservative in its demands on fiscal policy. Budget deficits of more than 3–4 percent of GDP should rule out IMF lending.
- A pegged exchange rate with insufficient reserves will likely lead to disaster. Thus the IMF should insist on a floating exchange rate—or possibly a currency board—but nothing in between.
- Russia suffers from an unresolved conflict between federalism and fiscal federalism. Thus it needs a clear division of responsibilities and taxes among the federal, regional, and municipal levels.
- A new approach to structural reform is needed. For many years the World Bank has tried to minimize the number of government authorities that are allowed to issue licenses, yet Russia now has more than 60 agencies issuing licenses or inspecting enterprises. Minimizing the number of inspectors effectively means boosting their monopoly rents. An alternative approach is to encourage competition for rents and bribes until they decline so much that corrupt bureaucrats no longer resist radical deregulation. One way of developing competition over bribes is to allow federal, regional, and municipal authorities to issue all licenses in parallel. In the Kyrgyz Republic three different authorities are competing in land registration, which has sped up land reform.
- To shield small entrepreneurs and make them part of the official economy, lump sum taxes should be introduced on a large scale. Such taxes were a major reason private enterprise succeeded in Poland under communism (Åslund 1985).
- Major indicators of success reflect structural changes in addition to macroeconomic progress. One example of a suitable microeconomic indicator is the number of legally registered enterprises. Another is a relevant liberalization index, though such indexes usually contain too many elements to be concrete objectives, and relevant weights of various elements are hard to assess.
- The World Bank should see as one of its main objectives the fight against rent seeking and corruption. Thus it should abstain from granting loans to central government authorities of notoriously corrupt industries, such as coal or agriculture.

- Russia suffers from a weak civil society. A natural task of nongovernmental organizations is to help build a social safety net. The World Bank could reach out directly to these organizations.

## References

Alekperov, Vagit. 1998. "Nuzhno ispol'zovat' opyt Yaponii [It Is Necessary to Utilize Japan's Experience]." *Kommersant Daily,* 11 November.

Amalrik, Andrei. 1980. *Will the Soviet Union Survive until 1984?* 2nd ed. Penguin.

Åslund, Anders. 1985. *Private Enterprise in Eastern Europe.* New York: St. Martin's Press.

———. 1991. *Gorbachev's Struggle for Economic Reform.* 2nd ed. Ithaca, N.Y.: Cornell University Press.

———. 1995. *How Russia Became a Market Economy.* Washington, D.C.: Brookings Institution.

———. 1997. "Observations on the Development of Small Private Enterprises in Russia." *Post-Soviet Geography and Economics* 38 (4): 191–205.

Åslund, Anders, and Mikhail Dmitriev, eds. 1996. *Sotsialnaya politika v period perekhoda k rynku: problemy i resheniya [Social Policy in the Transition to a Market Economy: Problems and Solutions].* Moscow: Carnegie Endowment for International Peace.

Åslund, Anders, Peter Boone, and Simon Johnson. 1996. "How to Stabilize: Lessons from Post-Communist Countries." *Brookings Papers on Economic Activity 1.* Washington, D.C.: Brookings Institution.

Aukutsionek, Sergei.1998. "Barter v rossiiskoi promyshlennosti [Barter in Russian Industry]." *Voprosy ekonomiki* 70 (2): 51–60.

Aven, Petr. 1994. "Problems in Foreign Trade Regulation in the Russian Economy." In Anders Åslund, ed., *Economic Transformation in Russia.* New York: St. Martin's Press.

———. 1999. "Ekonomika torga [The Economics of Negotiations]." *Kommersant Daily,* 29 January.

Bagrov, Andrei. 1999. "IMF—The Main Fighter against Corruption in Russia." *Kommersant Daily,* 4 March.

Balcerowicz, Leszek. 1994. "Understanding Postcommunist Transitions." *Journal of Democracy* 5 (4): 75–89.

Bank of Finland. 1999. *Russian Economy: The Month in Review* (3).

Blanchard, Olivier, and Michael Kremer. 1997. "Disorganization." *Quarterly Journal of Economics* 112 (4): 1,091–126.

Blasi, Joseph R., Maya Kroumova, and Douglas Kruse. 1997. *Kremlin Capitalism: Privatizing the Russian Economy.* Ithaca, N.Y.: Cornell University Press.

Bogomolov, Oleg T. 1996. *Reformy glazama amerikanskikh i rossiiskikh ychenykh [Reforms in the Eyes of American and Russian Scholars].* Moscow: Rossiisky ekonomichesky zhurnal.

Boycko, Maxim, Andrei Shleifer, and Robert V. Vishny. 1995. *Privatizing Russia.* Cambridge, Mass.: MIT Press.

Bozyk, Pawel. 1992. *Kto winien?[Who Is Guilty?].* Warsaw: PEA.

Brown, Annette N., and J. David Brown. 1999. "The Transition of Market Structure in Russia: Economic Lessons and Implications for Competition." Paper presented at the Allied Social Sciences Associations Annual Conference, January, New York.

Brunswick, Warburg. 1999. *Russian Monthly* (April). Moscow.

Dabrowski, Marek. 1993. "The First Half Year of Russian Transformation." In Anders Åslund and Richard Layard, eds., *Changing the Economic System in Russia*. New York: St. Martin's Press.

Delpla, Jacques. 1993. "Price Policy in Russia: The Case of Energy." Russia Ministry of Finance, Macroeconomic and Finance Unit, Moscow.

De Melo, Martha, Cevdet Denizer, and Alan Gelb. 1996. "From Plan to Market: Patterns of Transition." Policy Research Working Paper 1564. World Bank, Washington, D.C.

De Melo, Martha, Cevdet Denizer, Alan Gelb, and Stoyan Tenev. 1997. "Circumstance and Choice: The Role of Initial Conditions and Policies in Transition Economies." Policy Research Working Paper 1855. World Bank, Washington, D.C.

Djankov, Simeon. 1999. "Enterprise Restructuring in Russia." In Harry G. Broadman, ed., *Russian Enterprise Reform*. Washington, D.C.: World Bank.

Dmitriev, M.E. 1997. *Byudzhetnaya politika v sovremennoi Rossii [Budget Policy in Contemporary Russia]*. Moscow: Carnegie Moscow Center.

———. 1998. Personal communication. First deputy minister of labor and social affairs. Moscow.

Dmitriev, M.E., M.Yu. Matovnikov, L.V. Mikhailov, L.I. Sycheva, E.V. Timofeev, and A. Warner. 1996. *Rossiiskie banki nakanune finansovoi stabilizatsii* [Russian Banks on the Eve of Financial Stabilization]. St. Petersburg: Norma.

Ekelund, Robert B., and Robert D. Tollison. 1981. *Mercantilism As a Rent-Seeking Society*. College Station: Texas A&M University Press.

EBRD (European Bank for Reconstruction and Development). 1998. *Transition Report 1998*. London.

Fedorov, Boris G. 1999. "Vremya dlya liberalnykh reform v Rossii eshche ne prishlo [The Time for Liberal Economic Reforms in Russia Has Not Arrived As Yet]." *Kommersant Daily*, 4 February.

Gaddy, Clifford G., and Barry W. Ickes. 1998. "Russia's Virtual Economy." *Foreign Affairs* 77 (5): 53–67.

Gaidar, Yegor T. 1998. "Taktika reform i uroven gosudarstvennyoi nagruzki na ekonomiku [Tactics of Reform and the Level of State Burden on the Economy]." *Voprosy ekonomiki* 70 (4): 4–13.

Goskomstat Rossii. 1994. *Sotsial'no-ekonomicheskoi polozhenie Rossii 1993 g [The Socio-Economic Situation in Russia in 1993]*. Moscow.

———. 1997. *Rossiiskii Statisticheskii Yezhegodnik 1997 [Russian Statistical Yearbook 1997]*. Moscow.

Granville, Brigitte. 1995a. "So Farewell Then Rouble Zone." In Anders Åslund, ed., *Russian Economic Reform in Jeopardy*. New York: St. Martin's Press.

———. 1995b. *The Success of Russian Economic Reforms*. London: Royal Institute of International Affairs.

Hansson, Ardo H. 1993. "The Trouble with the Rouble: Monetary Reform in the Former Soviet Union." In Anders Åslund and Richard Layard, eds., *Changing the Economic System in Russia*. New York: St. Martin's Press. .

Hellman, Joel S. 1998. "Winners Take All: The Politics of Partial Reform in Postcommunist Transitions." *World Politics* 50 (January): 203–34.

Illarionov, Andrei N. 1998a. "Effektivnost biudzhetnoi politiki v Rossii v 1994–1997 godakh [The Efficacy of Budgetary Policy in Russia, 1994–1997]." *Voprosy ekonomiki* 70 (2): 22–36.

———. 1998b. "Kak byl organizovan rossiisky finansovy krizis [How the Russian Economic Crisis Was Organized]." *Voprosy ekonomiki* 70 (11): 20–35.

IMF (International Monetary Fund). 1993. *Economic Review: Russian Federation.* Washington, D.C.

———. 1994. *Economic Review: Financial Relations among Countries of the Former Soviet Union.* Washington, D.C.

Holmes, Kim R., Bryan T. Johnson, and Melanie Kirkpatrick. 1997. *1997 Index of Economic Freedom.* Washington, D.C.: Heritage Foundation and The Wall Street Journal.

Kornai, Janos. 1992. *The Socialist System: The Political Economy of Communism.* Princeton, N.J.: Princeton University Press.

LaFraniere, Sharon. 1999. "A Hotbed of Crime in Cold Siberia: In Gang-Run Coal Land, Authorities Take Cover." *Washington Post,* 7 January, p. A16.

Lavrov, Aleksei. 1997. *Mify i rify Rossiiskogo byudzhetnogo federalizma [Myths and Reefs of Russian Budget Federalism].* Moscow.

Maravall, Jose Maria. 1994. "The Myth of Authoritarian Advantage." *Journal of Democracy* 5 (4): 17–31.

Matyukhin, Georgy G. 1993. *Ya byl glavnym bankirom Rossii [I Was Russia's Chief Banker].* Moscow: Vysshaya shkola.

Milanovic, Branko. 1998. *Income, Inequality, and Poverty during the Transition from Planned to Market Economy. A Regional and Sectoral Study.* Washington, D.C.: World Bank.

OECD (Organisation for Economic Co-operation and Development). 1997. *Russian Federation 1997.* OECD Economic Surveys. Paris.

Nellis, John. 1999. "Time to Rethink Privatization." Paper presented at the International Monetary Fund conference on A Decade of Transition: Achievements and Challenges, 1–3 February, Washington, D.C.

Nuti, Domenico Mario, and Richard Portes. 1993. "Central Europe: The Way Forward." In Richard Portes, ed., *Economic Transformation in Central Europe: A Progress Report.* London: Center for European Policy Research.

Olson, Mancur. 1971. *The Logic of Collective Action: Public Goods and the Theory of Groups.* Cambridge, Mass: Harvard University Press.

———. 1982. *The Rise and Decline of Nations: Economic Growth, Stagflation, and Social Rigidities.* New Haven, Conn.: Yale University Press.

Portes, Richard. 1993. "From Central Planning to a Market Economy." In Shafiqul Islam and Michael Mandelbaum, eds., *Making Markets: Economic Transformation in Eastern Europe and the Post-Soviet States.* New York: Council on Foreign Relations.

Przeworski, Adam. 1991. *Democracy and the Market.* Cambridge: Cambridge University Press.

RECEP (Russian European Center for Economic Policy). 1999. "Russian Economic Trends: Monthly Update (10 February)." Moscow.

Sachs, Jeffrey D. 1995. "Why Russia Has Failed to Stabilize." In Anders Åslund, ed., *Russian Economic Reform in Jeopardy.* New York: St. Martin's Press.

Sachs, Jeffrey D., and David Lipton. 1993. "Remaining Steps to a Market-Based Monetary System." In Anders Åslund and Richard Layard, eds., *Changing the Economic System in Russia.* New York: St. Martin's Press.

Sachs, Jeffrey, and Wing Thye Woo. 1994. "Structural Factors in the Reform of China, Eastern Europe, and the Former Soviet Union." *Economic Policy* 9 (April): 101–45.

Shleifer, Andrei, and Daniel Treisman. 1998. *The Economics and Politics of Transition to an Open Market Economy: Russia.* Paris: Organisation for Economic Co-operation and Development.

Shleifer, Andrei, and Robert W. Vishny. 1993. "Corruption." *Quarterly Journal of Economics* 108 (3): 599–617.

———. 1998. *The Grabbing Hand: Government Pathologies and Their Cures.* Cambridge, Mass.: Harvard University Press.

Tanzi, Vito. 1999. "Transition and the Changing Role of Government." Paper presented at the International Monetary Fund conference on A Decade of Transition: Achievements and Challenges, 1–3 February, Washington, D.C.

Taylor, Lance. 1994. "The Market Met Its Match: Lessons for the Future from the Transition's Initial Years." *Journal of Comparative Economics* 19 (1): 64–87.

Transparency International. 1998. "The Corruption Perceptions Index." http://www.transparency.de/documents/cpi/index.html.

Treisman, Daniel S. 1996. "The Politics of Intergovernmental Transfers in Post-Soviet Russia." *British Journal of Political Science* 26 (July): 299–335.

———. 1998a. "Deciphering Russia's Federal Finance: Fiscal Appeasement in 1995 and 1996." *Europe-Asia Studies* 50 (5): 893–906.

———. 1998b. "Fighting Inflation in a Transitional Regime: Russia's Anomalous Stabilization." *World Politics* 50 (January): 235–65.

Vienna Institute for International Economic Comparisons [now Vienna Institute for International Economic Studies]. 1993. *Transition from the Command to the Market System: What Went Wrong and What to Do Now?* Vienna.

Voslenskii, Mikhail S. 1984. *Nomenklatura.* Garden City, N.Y.: Doubleday.

Wallich, Christine I., ed. 1994. *Russia and the Challenge of Fiscal Federalism.* A Regional and Sectoral Study. Washington, D.C.: World Bank.

World Bank. 1996a. *Fiscal Management in Russia.* Washington, D.C.: World Bank.

———. 1996b. *World Development Report 1996: From Plan to Market.* New York: Oxford University Press.

Yeltsin, Boris N. 1999. "Annual Address to the Federal Assembly." *Federal News Service* 30 (March).

Zavarsky, Leonid. 1999. "Imperiya Berezovskogo [Berezovsky's Empire]." *Kommersant Daily,* 7 April.

# Comment on "Why Has Russia's Economic Transition Been So Arduous?" by Anders Åslund

*Leonid Grigoriev*

At the 1991 Annual World Bank Conference on Development Economics, I commented on Anders Åslund's article on potential reforms in the Union of Socialist Soviet Republics (USSR). It seems that I was much more in agreement with him in the past about the Russian future than I am at present about the Russian past. The financial crisis that developed in August 1998 has opened a worldwide discussion on "what went wrong in Russia," "who lost Russia," and so on. It will undoubtedly take considerable time and study for economists and historians to reach closure on the complex interaction between the windows of political opportunity in Russia and the economic rationale for approaches to transition in the 1990s. To date, however, domestic and international debates on the transition and on the 1998 crash have occurred in isolation. In any case, the recent crash reflects "the failure of Russia's hopes of the transition over a short historical period from a 'medium developed planned economy' to a more efficient 'medium developed market economy' that would hold a worthy place in the modern global economic system" (Grigoriev 1999, p. 9).

Russian economists are naturally concerned about the ineffectiveness of the emerging market and the high social costs of transition in Russia. Along those lines, many questions have been posed. Why have reforms put such pressure on the very people who were supposed to benefit? What caused the rapid shift from a quasi-egalitarian to a Brazilian-type society? Why has the transition crisis been so prolonged and the economic decline so steep? What should be done with the stock of Russian human capital? Because space is too limited to cover all these points, my remarks here focus on three issues: the implications of rent seeking for reforms after 1992, the logic and outcome of privatization, and fast reforms relative to institution building. In addition, I feel obliged to present data on Russia's disappointing experience with privatization.

## Rent Seeking and Reforms after 1992

Professor Åslund makes a heroic effort to summarize in 14 pages the complicated political history of 10 years of Russian reform. His main point is that reformers were

Leonid Grigoriev is director general of the Bureau of Economic Analysis in Moscow.
*Annual World Bank Conference on Development Economics 1999*
©2000 The International Bank for Reconstruction and Development / THE WORLD BANK

in full power only in the first half of 1992, when reforms were fast and radical. Since then rent seekers have distorted reforms to serve their own interests, and reforms have been much less successful. This fatalistic assessment implies more than Åslund probably intended, specifically that:

- Reforms after 1992 were unsuccessful—though the article provides examples of some successful reforms.
- International financial institutions did not play a major role in the success or failure of Russian reforms in 1993–98.
- Nothing could possibly have been done right because rent seekers have been in control since 1992.

Åslund's article could easily be titled "Why Have the Lives of Russian Reformers Been So Arduous?" He portrays Russian reformers as faultless victims of the "bad guys" from the Soviet *nomenklatura*. Åslund's pro-reform and politically correct tone leaves readers to wonder whether reformers made any wrong moves in masterminding the 1991–92 transition or in later years. This article defines the enemies of reform—or, more precisely, of the reformers—quite consistently: the nomenklatura and other legacies of the USSR, and later some oligarchs. Åslund does not question Russia's macroeconomic policy in 1997–98. The financial crash of 1998 comes inevitably but unpredicted. And all the troubles of 1998 are caused by the "dark forces" of oil companies and antireformers. This setup does not allow the possibility that, under the circumstances, oligarchs were pursuing their rational interests.

Some legitimate questions are left unanswered—or not even asked. Why did oligarchs encounter no serious opposition? And why did they not behave like Mancur Olson's robber barons, grabbing property and then managing it well? Why was it in their rational self-interest to steal, not to earn? Were the reformers completely unprepared for the advent of rent seekers, or had they given the problem some thought? Did the Russian approach to privatization play a role in corporate governance, or was it unimportant? Who should take credit for the 1992–93 reforms, and why is it becoming increasingly difficult to find the authors of those reforms? What were the relationships between the reformers and the oligarchs? Are the oligarchs willing to assist reforms for free, or only for a price? And how high a price should reformers accept?

Just after the heroic reforms of early 1992 had ended, the International Monetary Fund (IMF) and World Bank offered ideas, conditionality, loans, and technical assistance. In my view the Russian reformers received considerable help from international financial institutions—and not everything was doomed after 1992. Grass-roots transformation has been occurring all the time. The new Civil Code, privatization, and many other important and radical steps occurred after 1992.

At almost any point during these years Russia had at least a few reformers in key government positions backed by reformers outside the government and by international financial institutions. A parliament in an emerging market is a tough place to implement fast reforms, and Russia is no exception. All the Russian budgets of these years were a result of political compromise, voted in the Duma with the communists' support, but IMF programs were also available. Thus the unfavorable political climate was an important factor for the failure of reforms. But focusing solely on the political side makes us lose sight of the substance and perspective of economic reforms, the sequencing of steps, professionalism, and the approach taken.

Åslund's claim that the unconstrained elite were the main source of difficulties contradicts Olson's theory of the stationary bandit. The bandit (who controls the state) is supposedly interested in maintaining order and, consequently, protecting his or her property rights. Even if stationary bandits (individual or collective) have a monopoly on violence, they are still constrained. So if the goal of special interest groups is to maximize rents, then robber barons acted rationally in the short term. The question that remains unanswered is why they never set up rules ensuring a stable flow of rents rather than allowing them to plummet after 1992 (according to Åslund). A case in point is Åslund's discussion of the oligarchs, who are presented as the enemies of reform in 1997 without any explanation of their origin or their relationship with the reformers during the election years of 1995–96.

Finally, the actions of robber barons were not unpredictable in 1991–92. The rent-seeking behavior of the former Soviet nomenklatura was especially easy to anticipate: "it will take time to change the mentality of rent-seekers into profit-seeking ... Uncertainty about goals and methods of privatization will affect the process for a long time. Presumably this situation is rather convenient for the old bureaucracy. It will be in charge of privatization and will try to use its control to preserve its social status and convert ulterior into legal property rights" (Grigoriev 1992, pp. 204–06).

## Logic and Outcome of Privatization

Åslund is among the few analysts who still defend voucher privatization. While it is true that the nomenklatura had controlled all state industries, not a single manager had complete control over investment or price decisions or cash flows. So while a lot of petty management corruption accompanied these arrangements—in the form of privileges, cars, and country houses. But before the 1990s managers never controlled all the cash and never owned the enterprises as private property. In 1988 Mikhail Gorbachev's co-ops punched the first big hole in state property. But only voucher privatization allowed rent seekers to retain legal and undisputed control over cash flows, resulting in capital flight. As a result, in many cases a lot of profitable property was taken almost for free by shadow figures with no accountability.

The key weakness of Russian reforms today is the poor corporate governance of privatized enterprises resulting from voucher privatization's "mass insiders" (World Bank 1996, table 3.2). Persistent nonpayment, tax evasion, and capital flight are interconnected diseases with a common cause and no remedy thus far. The Bureau of Economic Analysis has found evidence that capital flight is part of barter and tax evasion schemes. In the game they play against the state, the "New Russians" consistently keep winning.

High real interest rates reflect both the crowding out of the federal government through treasury bills (GKOs) and the limited savings by the cautious population (5.0 percent of disposable household income in 1995–97 and 1.7 percent in 1998).

Continuous economic decline has forced households to reduce savings. Capital flight has further cut national savings. Moreover, privatization proceeds were low by international standards (table 1). Foreign investors were welcomed but technically excluded from mass privatization, leaving the government with just one source of cash for stabilization: vast external borrowing. The famous loans-for-shares auctions of 1995 should be seen as a logical completion of voucher privatization—enabling major players from the previous phase to secure control of profitable resources. But endless questioning on the logic of privatization ignores one issue of tremendous importance: what should be done about the lack of corporate governance in Russia's privatized economy (Nellis 1999)?

## Fast Reforms and Institution Building

Other questions remain on Russian reforms. Institutional reforms were a failure and largely ignored in the very beginning. For a long time most international financial institutions considered institution building a separate stage to be undertaken after liberalization, privatization, and macroeconomic stabilization. The early literature on Russian privatization, in 1992–94, makes few references to corporate governance. Political windows of opportunities are generally scarce and open only briefly, and so must be used properly. Institution building is long and arduous, but it is essential to secure the market's ability to deliver the promises of privatization.

In Russia members of society who gained from early liberalization and privatization—including members of the nomenklatura and the mafia—opposed the

**Table 1. Financial Indicators of Privatization in Russia, 1992–98**

| Indicator | 1992 | 1993 | 1994 | 1995 | 1996 | 1997 | 1998 |
|---|---|---|---|---|---|---|---|
| Privatized enterprises (thousands) | 47,041 | 42,929 | 21,905 | 10,125 | 4,997 | 2,743 | 2,129 |
| Privatization proceeds (billions of 1998 rubles) | 0.16 | 0.45 | 1.07 | 3.82 | 3.23 | 26.23 | 17.54 |
| Privatization proceeds (billions of U.S. dollars) | 0.71 | 0.48 | 0.48 | 0.84 | 0.63 | 4.53 | 1.76 |
| Privatization proceeds (percentage of GDP) | 0.83 | 0.26 | 0.17 | 0.24 | 0.15 | 1.02 | 0.65 |
| Share of privatization proceeds in consolidated budget (percent) | — | 0.60 | 0.40 | 0.60 | 0.40 | 3.19 | 2.52 |
| Share of privatization proceeds in federal budget (percent) | — | 0.28 | 0.14 | 0.49 | 0.32 | 5.56 | 5.49 |
| *Distribution of privatization proceeds (percent)* | | | | | | | |
| To all budgets | — | 66.0 | 65.2 | 68.8 | 68.8 | 83.7 | 96.4 |
| Federal | — | 15.8 | 11.0 | 29.9 | 27.8 | 68.5 | 85.4 |
| To state bodies | — | 12.9 | 27.0 | 24.7 | 17.9 | 10.4 | 3.1 |
| Privatization agencies | — | 12.9 | 18.3 | 10.7 | 7.9 | 5.1 | 2.3 |
| To employees of privatized enterprises | — | 21.1 | 7.8 | 6.4 | 13.3 | 5.8 | 0.5 |

— Not available.
*Source:* BEA 1998.

introduction of reasonable market institutions and regulation so that they could preserve newly acquired rents. These groups had sufficient resources to halt the legislative process and impede law enforcement.

There is no way to build institutions before major economic reforms. But reforms that do not include adequate planning and parallel institution building may cause major economic problems, depriving the market economy of an expected efficiency. Together, lack of respect for the law, inadequate taxation, weak banking regulation, barter and money surrogates, arrears, corruption, and economic crimes show that institutions matter. But microeconomic reforms are difficult and slow. Whatever happens, however, Russia's transition is not over, and the theories we develop will have to be tested—by Russians.

## References

Åslund, Anders. 1992. "Prospects for Economic Reform in the U.S.S.R." In Lawrence H. Summers and Shekhar Shah, eds., *Proceedings of the World Bank Annual Conference on Development Economics 1991*. Washington, D.C.: World Bank.

BEA (Bureau of Economic Analysis). 1998. *Survey on Economic Policy in Russia in 1997*. Moscow.

Grigoriev, Leonid. 1992. "Ulterior Property Rights and Privatization." In Anders Åslund, ed., *The Post-Soviet Economy*. London: Pinter.

Nellis, John. 1999. "Time to Rethink Privatization in Transitional Economies." IFC Discussion Paper 38. International Finance Corporation, Washington, D.C.

World Bank. 1996. *World Development Report 1996: From Plan to Market*. New York: Oxford University Press.

# Comment on "The Institutional Foundations of China's Market Transition," by Yingyi Qian, and "Why Has Russia's Economic Transition Been So Arduous?" by Anders Åslund

*Jan Svejnar*

Yingyi Qian and Anders Åslund provide fascinating accounts of two quite different experiences with economic reform, Qian of China's successful reforms in the 1980s and 1990s, and Åslund of Russia's much less successful attempts in the 1990s. Each author draws on available data, academic and policy research, and his experience to explain country performance. Both articles provide valuable contributions to our understanding of the strikingly different performance of these two economies.

Official data may not fully capture the underlying performance of the Chinese and Russian economies. But there is no doubt that Russia's performance would still be viewed as disappointing and China's as impressive even if one could fully account for unreported economic activity in Russia and overreporting in China. Regardless of data issues, the fundamental question is what accounts for the different performance in the two economies. More broadly, the question is what accounts for the successful economic performance of China and Central European countries (especially Poland) on the one hand, and the poor record of Russia and other members of the Commonwealth of Independent States on the other.

## What Have We Learned?

Qian's basic thesis is that China's economic success can be traced to a series of carefully orchestrated reforms carried out by several layers of government, each behaving responsibly. Qian also points out that poverty, overpopulation, a paucity of natural resources, and the legacy of the cultural revolution made for difficult initial conditions in China. Indeed, few poor countries have achieved a similarly impressive long-term growth record.

The Chinese government launched reforms in 1978 by introducing incentives, imposing hard budget constraints, and unleashing competition. The primary institutional mechanism used in 1978–93 was regional decentralization of the government,

Jan Svejnar is Everett E. Berg Professor of Business Administration and professor of economics, University of Michigan, Ann Arbor.

*Annual World Bank Conference on Development Economics 1999*
©2000 The International Bank for Reconstruction and Development / THE WORLD BANK

resulting in local experiments and better provision of public goods. Decentralization stimulated the entry of new firms (township and village enterprises), ensured financial stability through dualism, and enabled a dual-track approach to market creation and liberalization.

Qian distinguishes 1978–93 from 1994–98, when the Chinese government's goal was to build a rule-based market system with international best-practice institutions—but in China's own way. Government measures during this second stage of reform included unifying multiple exchange rates, making the currency convertible on the current account, overhauling the tax and fiscal system, reorganizing the central bank, downsizing the public administration, and privatizing and restructuring state enterprises.

Qian draws the following conclusions from his examination of China's modern economic history:

- A country can achieve growth if it has sensible, albeit imperfect, institutions.
- At first it may be more effective to establish unconventional institutions than to strive for best-practice institutions.
- Incentives and hard budget constraints should be introduced not just for firms, but also for the government.
- It is possible—and politically desirable—to implement reforms without creating losers.
- Successful reforms require appropriate, though not necessarily optimal, sequencing.

Turning to Russia, Åslund explores microeconomic and macroeconomic policies in Russia during the 1990s and considers the role of domestic and external factors in explaining the failure of Russian policymakers to carry out radical economic reform. Åslund's main thesis is that rent seeking and corruption (especially in the early 1990s, then again in 1996–98) have been the main causes of this failure. Yet he argues that there were relatively few rents in Russia's privatization process and that privatization has led to enterprise restructuring. Thus Åslund provides a strong counterargument to those who see Russia's privatization as the main cause of its inferior economic performance.

According to Åslund, rent seeking and corruption have been caused by excessive government involvement in areas such as foreign trade, capital markets, and enterprise subsidies. He estimates that rents peaked at 81 percent of GDP in 1992, fell to 8 percent in 1995, and rose to 15 percent in 1997. He also points out that the availability of rents has led to the creation of a powerful group of rich people who have essentially bought politicians and public officials.

Some observers see Russia's economic decline as arising from the inability of firms to interact efficiently in the absence of central planning. Åslund, by contrast, argues that the economic decline was brought about by the collapse of the communist state. This collapse made it difficult for the central government to collect revenue (partly because individual republics were unwilling to send tax revenue to Moscow) and rationalize spending (a problem compounded by the republics' issuance of their own credit). In addition, the government failed to deregulate and create a rule of law, which led to malfunctioning markets and allowed managers to appropriate state enterprise profits and assets by establishing their own private firms. Moreover, the collapse of the state left no room for gradual reform.

Finally, Åslund notes that apart from privatization, Russia has carried out little reform, and suggests several moves that could facilitate the process. Fostering competition over rents would reduce rents and thus rent-seeking activities. The government must opt for lower public revenue if tax reform is to be feasible (because the value of tax exemptions will fall). And the willingness of Russian policymakers to carry out reforms should be made a stronger condition for international assistance.

## What Have We Not Learned?

Because Qian's and Åslund's accounts and conclusions fit with China's and Russia's policy records and performance, at one level there is little to argue with in their discussions. At another level, however, one must question how useful is the general tone of these articles for understanding the forces driving China's success and Russia's failure, and for formulating public policy in China, Russia, and elsewhere.

Starting with Qian, it is generally accepted that capable, purposeful, and socially responsible government institutions help advance a country. So is the idea that it is useful to establish incentives and hard budget constraints for firms and government, implement reforms without creating losers, and sequence reforms optimally. The problem is that propositions of this type are almost tautological if one does not identify the fundamental forces and conditions that ensure that government institutions have these properties. Moreover, Qian points to a broad interplay of factors that arguably have determined China's success, making it difficult to identify the few truly fundamental ingredients.

At one level Åslund's article is quite focused—nearly all bets are placed on rent seeking and corruption to explain Russia's failure. Yet the causes of rent seeking and corruption are explained in general terms: by excessive regulation, insufficient rule of law, the multifaceted collapse of the state and its institutions, the inability of the central government to collect revenue and rationalize spending, and so on. As with Qian's article, little attention is paid to the fundamental forces and conditions that caused the government and its institutions to have these properties. Moreover, it is not clear why the Russian government has lost the power to pursue beneficial activities (such as establishing the rule of law) but retained the power to regulate and subsidize excessively. Without understanding the forces that drive these outcomes, one cannot reliably distinguish the causes of the different performance in China and Russia.

Moreover, Qian and Åslund often attribute different outcomes to qualitatively similar factors. Regional decentralization of the government is considered beneficial in China but deleterious in Russia. In both countries local governments withhold taxes from the central government, but the problem is much more serious in Russia. In China local government officials and mayors of towns and villages support the emergence and growth of new firms (township and village enterprises), despite the fact that many of these firms compete with state enterprises. In Russia mayors of cities and towns stifle private entrepreneurs on behalf of managers of existing and former state enterprises ("red directors").

Both countries have an imperfect legal system and inadequate enforcement of laws and contracts, but the resulting problems appear much more serious in Russia. Both countries have an underdeveloped civil society, but the government is portrayed as being a strong representative of the public interest in China and a weak one in Russia. Anonymous banking is seen as beneficial in China, increasing savings and deposits, while in Russia insufficient banking regulation is viewed as one of the causes of capital flight and flows outside official channels. Finally, businesspeople and analysts report rents and corruption in both China and Russia. Yet the extent and nature of these phenomena appear much more harmful in Russia.

## Where Should We Go From Here?

Future research is needed to examine the main issues at a level where one can capture the factors behind the different performance in China and Russia. Although Qian and Åslund identify the potentially important roles of government and other institutions, we need a much better understanding of what makes institutions act in an economically enabling manner. The authors also identify potentially important associations among certain variables, but the nature and direction of causality are not always clear.

One way to proceed is to pursue the analysis at a more disaggregated level, focusing on variations in relevant variables across republics, provinces, and smaller regional units. Both countries have experienced significant regional variations in performance and in the role of local governments and institutions, and these should prove valuable in identifying the determinants of performance.

Another, complementary way to proceed is to enlarge the sample of countries. This approach offers the added advantages of increasing the number of transition strategies to be assessed and providing interesting (though obviously imperfect) control cases. Consider Poland. Like China, Poland went through a tough decade before launching its transition, had and still has a sizable agricultural sector, and has based its success during transition on stimulating the growth of small and medium-size enterprises, while delaying large-scale privatization of state enterprises. Unlike China but like its neighbors, Poland has minimized the number of losers not by pursuing a dual-track approach, but by liberalizing the economy and using social transfers to cushion shocks. More generally, by increasing the number of countries, research benefits from comparing the many ways to fail and recognizing that there is more than one way to succeed.